SAN FRANCISCO ALMANAC

Everything You Want to Know About Everyone's Favorite City

Completely Revised and Expanded

by

Gladys Hansen

CHRONICLE BOOKS
SAN FRANCISCO

Dedication

⌐◦⌐

I dedicate the third edition of the San Francisco Almanac to my son, Richard, and to my many friends who provided new and unique materials for inclusion.

Text copyright ©1995 by Gladys Hansen.
Book design and composition: Robin Whiteside.
Cover Illustration: Adam McCauley
Cover Design: Anne Marie Mililo

Photos on page 196 and 246 are reprinted with the permission of the San Francisco Public Library.

Library of Congress Cataloging-in-Publication Data available.

Printed in the United States of America.
ISBN 0-8118-0841-6

Distributed in Canada by Raincoast Books, 8680 Cambie Street, Vancouver, B.C. V6P 6M9

10 9 8 7 6 5 4 3 2 1

Chronicle Books
275 Fifth Street
San Francisco, CA 94103

Table of Contents

1 Accolades

Admirers—Past and Present

"It is not a port, but a whole pocketful of ports."

JUAN MANUEL DE AYALA,
the Spanish commander of the ship that made
first exploration of Bay of San Francisco in
1775

"There, when this bay comes into our possession, will spring up the great rival of New York."

JOHN C. CALHOUN,
Secretary of State in 1844,
indicating on a map the place where San
Francisco now stands

"San Francisco is, by her position, by her energy and wisdom, to be the Elect Lady of the Coast, and nothing but earthquakes will interfere with her growth."

REV. JOHN TODD

"San Francisco is a City of Romance and Destiny; a composite of the three P's of Progress—the Past, the Present and the Prospective. Most distinctive city of the United States, although a junior, Romance, not merely of yesterday, but of today and tomorrow, is the very kernel of the shell of it. To pass the portals of the Golden Gate is to cross the threshold of Adventure. Metropolitan as it is, San Francisco is still an outpost of the frontier line of the Grand Army of Progress, with its citizens of today as red-blooded, as full of the joy of living and the triumph of achieving as their forebears and forerunners, the Argonauts of '49."

ALLAN DUNN

"Few cities in the world can vie with San Francisco either in the beauty or in the natural advantages of her situation; indeed, there are only two places in Europe—Constantinople and Gibraltar—that combine an equally perfect landscape with what may be called an equally imperial position. The city itself is full of bold hills, rising steeply from the deep water. The air is keen and dry and bright, like the air of Greece, and the waters not less blue. Perhaps it is this light and air, recalling the cities of the Mediterranean, that makes one involuntarily look up to the tops of those hills for the feudal castle, or the ruins of the Acropolis, that must crown them."

HON. JAMES BRYCE

"San Francisco has no rival in the United States. We may contrast, but not compare it with Eastern or even European cities. London is grand but not beautiful. Paris is beautiful but not grand. Constantinople is picturesque, but has not architectural splendor. But San Francisco has all these attributes. It has been compared to Cleveland. City of beautiful avenues, Cleveland is charming; San Francisco is stupendous, romantic; Cleveland is lovely; San Francisco is grand; Cleveland is American; San Francisco is Cosmopolitan; Cleveland is a garden made by man; San Francisco looks as if it were built by the Gods."

IRA G. HOITT

"San Francisco is like Venice and Athens in having strange memories; she is unlike them in being lit from within by a large and luminous hope. Wonder and terror may pass over her spirit; still nothing changes her purpose, nothing weakens her courage."

EDWIN MARKHAM

"For this city is one of those which have souls; it is a spirit sitting on a height, taking to itself form and the offices of civilization. This is a thing that we know, because we have seen the land shake it as a terrier shakes a rat, until the form of the city was broken; it dissolved in smoke and flame. And then as a polyp of the sea draws out of the fluent water form and perpetuity for itself, we saw our city draw back its shapes of wood and stone, and statelier, more befitting a spirit that has endured so much."

MARY AUSTIN

"Even now San Francisco will impress all her visitors deeply in many ways. They will see it as very new; yet they will feel it is very old. Civilization is better organized here in some respects than in any city out of Paris; some of its streets look as if transplanted from a city of Europe; others are in the first stages of rescue from the barbaric desert. Asia, Europe and America have here met and embraced each other; yet the strong mark of America is upon and in all; an America in which the flavor of New England can be tasted above all other local elements; an America in which the flexibility, the adaptability, and the all-penetrating, all-subduing power of its own race are everywhere and in everything manifest."

SAMUEL BOWLES

"The City that knows how."

WILLIAM HOWARD TAFT,
President of the United States

"San Francisco should be called City of Flowers."

CHARLES LORING BLACK

"The City of Romance and the Gateway to Adventure."

KATHERINE AMOS TAYLOR

"San Francisco is a city where people are never more abroad than when they are at home."

BENJAMIN F. TAYLOR

"Queen of the Pacific Coast! Fair city whose changing skies for half the year shower down mist and rain, and the other half sunbeams of molten brass! Metropolis of alternate sticky mud and blinding dust! In spite of these and more thou art a city of my heart, O Ciudad de San Francisco!"

T. S. KENDERDINE

"It is impossible for one to live long in San Francisco, and become familiar with its business and business men, without becoming attached to the City and State. However much he may see to dislike, he will also find much that commands his attention and fastens on his sympathies."

JOHN S. HITTELL

"San Francisco is West as all hell."

BERNARD DE VOTO

"San Francisco is largely, more largely than many of our people are willing to confess, the child of the mines. They gave it its first start; they have generously, though not exclusively nourished it ever since. They have called into existence a very large manufacturing interest, giving employment to tens of thousands of men. They have stimulated every branch of trade and internal commerce, quickened every pulse of industrial life. Nearly all our finest buildings have been erected out of the profits of mining enterprises. Every pound of ore that is taken out of the earth, from Alaska to Arizona, pays tribute here. A man may make his fortune in the desert of Nevada or Idaho, but he is pretty sure to spend it in San Francisco."

SAMUEL WILLIAMS

"San Francisco is the most sophisticated city in the country. From prize-fights to grand opera, it is nearly always in good taste, yes, and has delicacy. A San Francisco audience is a test of a good play. As a matter of fact, a New York audience is no test at all."

KATHERINE F. GEROULD

"San Francisco—her commercial standing is in the front rank of the leading commercial cities of the world. She is even now in her infancy—in the bud—the opening of the flower and the ripening of the fruit is in reserve for her. She lies directly in the line of the great thoroughfare of swift trade and travel which girdles the earth. And when a noble group of Pacific States shall encircle her as a nucleus, all alive with a busy population, and rich in all agricultural and manufacturing wealth, she will be the New York or the London of the Occident. There is a hopeful, grand, and glorious future before San Francisco."

JOHN J. POWELL

"San Francisco holds the same relation to the State of California that Paris does to France. It forms the head and heart of, and is the miniature of, the commonwealth. The Romans had an expression which showed the importance of their city, 'urbis et orbis,' implying that the world was ruled from Rome. The same may be said of San Francisco in regard to the State of California. The city rules the state; and though topographically its site is not pleasant, the uneven surface of the country being a succession of hills and valleys, swamps and sandy plains; yet geographically the site of San Francisco is unequaled in any part of the globe."

REV. HUGH QUIGLEY

"To a traveler paying his first visit, it has the interest of a new planet. It ignores the meteorological laws which govern the rest of the world."

FITZ HUGH LUDLOW

"The port of San Francisco is a marvel of nature and may be called the port of ports."

FATHER FONT

"The bay of San Francisco has been celebrated from the time of its first discovery as one of the finest in the world. It rises into an importance far above that of a mere harbor....Its latitudinal position is that of Lisbon, its climate that of Southern

Italy, settlements attest to its healthfulness, bold shores and mountains give it grandeur, the extent and fertility of its dependent country give it great resources for agriculture, commerce and population.... To this gate I gave the name Chrysopylae or Golden Gate...."

JOHN FREMONT

"San Francisco is unique—a thing without a parallel, one that admits of no comparisons, for there is nothing like it in the histories of cities."

WILLIAM M'COLLUM, M.D.

"There is not a full grown tree of beautiful proportions near San Francisco, nor have I seen any young trees that promised fairly, except, perhaps, of certain compact clumpy forms of evergreens, wholly wanting in grace and cheerfulness. It would not be wise nor safe to undertake to form a park upon any plan which assumed as a certainty that trees which would delight the eye can be made to grow near San Francisco Bay."

FREDERICK LAW OLMSTED,
1860s

"Nobody seems to think of building a sober house. The prevailing style is what might be called the delirious Queen Anne. Of all the efflorescent, floriated bulbousness and flamboyant craziness that ever decorated a city, I think San Francisco may carry off the prize. And yet, such is the glittering and metallic brightness of the air, when it is not surcharged with fog, that I am not sure but this riotous run of architectural fancy is just what the city needs to redeem its otherwise hard nakedness."

NOAH BROOKS,
New York Times, *1883*

" ...this marvelous city, bazaar of all the nations of the globe, [compares] with the fantastic creations of 'The Thousand and One Nights.'"

EDMOND AUGER,
French gold hunter seeing
San Francisco in '49

"After some experience in many parts of the world, I freely venture the opinion, there is no sheet of water on the globe better adapted for great national and commercial purposes than the Bay of San Francisco and its vast tributaries."

COMMANDER CADWALADER RINGGOLD

"I can fancy that the Muse of Montgomery must, in some Olympian flight, have caught a glimpse of this golden land, and felt the soft influence of its evening charms, when he sang so sweetly his beautiful ode on 'Night.' Surely no person needs a talent for sleeping in San Francisco.

"San Francisco has, in its location and unrivaled harbor, elements of prosperity which cannot be overcome by any other point on the coast. It will inevitably become, on the Pacific, what New York is in the Atlantic."

E. S. CAPRON

"San Francisco is really the best city in America. There is a very free feeling in this city. People who live here have very free minds, which is very important for me to make music. I love San Francisco."

SEIJI OZAWA,
San Francisco Symphony
Conductor, 1970-76

"Nature ordained this queen of the Pacific a great metropolis—the second city on the American continent. Burned to the ground six times within eighteen months, her growth was not stopped, nor her prosperity impaired; and if a new earthquake were to shake down every building, not leaving one stone upon another, the town would soon be as large and as vigorous as ever."

ALBERT RICHARDSON

"San Francisco—no well-bred American, unless he comes from Chicago, ever says 'Frisco'—is a delicious combination of wealth and wickedness, splendor and squalor, vice, virtue, villainy, beauty, ugliness, solitude and silence, rush and row—in short San Francisco is just San Francisco, and that's all there is to it, as they say there."

GEORGE GRIFFITH

"I am a citizen of no mean city, although it is in ashes. Almighty God has fixed this as the location of a great city. The past is gone, and there is no use of lamenting or moaning over it. Let us look to the future and without regard to creed or place of birth, work together in harmony for the upbuilding of a greater San Francisco."

ARCHBISHOP P. W. RIORDAN

"Of all the marvelous phases of the Present, San Francisco will most tax the belief of the Future. Its parallel was never known, and shall never be beheld again. I speak only of what I saw with my own eyes. Like the magic seed of the Indian juggler, which grew, blossomed and bore fruit before the eyes of his spectators, San Francisco seemed to have accomplished in a day the growth of half a century."

BAYARD TAYLOR

"It is the paradise of ignorance, anarchy, and general yellowness.

"It needs another quake, another whiff of fire, and more than all else, a steady tradewind of grape-shot.

"It is a moral penal colony. It is the worst of all the Sodoms and Gomorrahs in our modern world."

LETTERS OF AMBROSE BIERCE, California Book Club, 1922

"The City of San Francisco (the metropolis of the State) considering its age, is by long odds the most wonderful city on the face of the earth."

G. W. SULLIVAN

"It [California] is the land where the fabled Aladdin's Lamp lies buried—and

she [San Francisco] is the new Aladdin who shall seize it from its obscurity and summon the genie and command him to crown her with power and greatness and bring to her feet the hoarded treasures of the earth.

"I am bidding the old city a kind, but not a sad, farewell, for I know that when I see this home again, the changes that will have been wrought upon it will suggest no sentiment of sadness; its estate will be bright, happier, and prouder a hundred-fold than it is this day. This is its destiny . . ."

MARK TWAIN, in the Alta California, upon leaving California in 1866

"People have forgotten that San Francisco is not a ranch, or rather, that it ought not properly to be a ranch. It has got all the disagreeable features of a ranch, though. Every citizen keeps from ten to five hundred chickens, and these crow and cackle all day and night; they stand watches, and the watch on duty makes a racket while the off-watch sleeps. Let a stranger get outside of Montgomery and Kearny from Pacific to 2nd, and close his eyes, and he can imagine himself on a well-stocked farm, without an effort, for his ears will be assailed by such a vile din of gobbling of turkeys, and crowing of hoarse-voiced roosters, and cackling of hens, and howling of cows, and whinnying of horses, and braying of jackasses, and yowling of cats, that he will be driven to frenzy, and may look to perform prodigies of blasphemy such as he never knew himself capable of before."

MARK TWAIN

"That City of Gold to which adventurers congregated out of all the winds of heaven. I wonder what enchantment of the 'Arabian Nights' can have equaled this evocation of a roaring city, in a few years of a man's life, from the marshes and the blowing sand."

ROBERT LOUIS STEVENSON

"It's an odd thing, but anyone who disappears is said to be seen in San Francisco. It must be a delightful city and possess all the attractions of the next world."

OSCAR WILDE

"San Francisco is a really beautiful city. China Town, peopled by Chinese labourers, is the most artistic town I have ever come across. The people—strange, melancholy Orientals, whom any people would call common, and they are certainly very poor—have determined that they will have nothing about them that is not beautiful. In the Chinese restaurant, where these navies meet to have supper in the evening, I found them drinking teas out of china cups as delicate as the petals of a rose-leaf, whereas at the gaudy hotels I was supplied with a delft cup an inch and a half thick. Then the Chinese bill was presented—it was made out on rice paper, the account being done in Indian ink as fantastically as if an artist had been etching little birds on a fan."

IBID

"You have in San Francisco this magnificent Civic Center crowned by a City Hall which I have never seen anywhere equaled."

JOSEPH STRAUSS

"Every man should be allowed to love two cities, his own and San Francisco."

GENE FOWLER

"The extreme geniality of San Francisco's economic, intellectual and political climate makes it the most varied and challenging city in the United States."

JAMES MICHENER

"San Francisco is the only populated area from the Canadian border to the Mexican border that is known as 'The City'!"

CHESTER MACPHEE

"Of all American cities of whatever size the most friendly on preliminary inspection, and on further acquaintance the most likable. The happiest-hearted, the gayest, the most care-free city on this continent."

IRWIN S. COBB

"I consider it [Coit Tower] a blemish, without the remotest artistic significance; a defacement of a natural formation that ever delighted the eye of those approaching the city by water."

H. A. HASKELL, M.D.,
1934

"San Francisco, the capital of the Gaslight Tradition."

CARL HEPP

"Every port is my oyster but San Francisco is the coo-coo clam of them all."

WILSON MIZNER

"San Francisco takes strange hold on the hearts of man. Even the most insensitive individual is conscious at times of this attraction, but it appears most importunately to young people, newspapermen, poets, and other sub-varieties of lunacy. For them (to whom Paris seems a weary bawd; and Vienna a gay girl-widow, and Chicago the 'hog butcher to the world'), San Francisco is the gray-eyed mistress of sea captains, not young, but youthful, not old, but wise, a comrade of youth, a lover of the vigorous and adventurous, always a gazer over blue water, with the salt upon her face."

GEORGE DYER

"San Francisco, the city where nobody thinks."

FRANK NORRIS

"Fancy a novel about Chicago or Buffalo, let us say, or Nashville, Tennessee. There are just three big cities in the United States that are 'story cities,' New York, of course, New Orleans, and best of the lot, San Francisco."

IBID.

"God took the beauty of the Bay of Naples, the Valley of the Nile, the Swiss Alps, the Hudson River Valley, rolled them into one and made San Francisco Bay."

FIORELLO LA GUARDIA,
Mayor of New York City

"On behalf of the city of New York, I salute the city of San Francisco, which is certainly among the best cities anywhere in the world...and I'm the ranking expert. My heart belongs to New York, so I can't leave my heart in San Francisco...but every time I visit the city by the bay, my admiration grows. The rest of the world knows San Francisco for the splendor of its scenery, the glories of its food, the world-class state-of-the-art of its arts, and its cosmopolitan atmosphere. We New Yorkers concur in these opinions. But we also see in San Francisco a kindred spirit. It is a city whose people face adversity with bravery and resilience; who can meet any challenge—including that historic earthquake—with determination and equanimity. The only problem is, you're on the wrong coast."

ED KOCH,
Mayor of New York City, 1988

"... a worldly wise yet forever juvenile hoyden swinging on her Golden Gate...the bronze buckler of the mountains at her back, the silver lance of her bay aimed at the breast of the sea."

IRVING COBB

"Los Angeles may be California's diamond stomacher, but San Francisco is the poppies in her hair."

IBID .

"San Francisco has a tradition of sin which began in the Roaring Forties, when men rooted in the earth for gold."

BENJAMIN BUFANO

"No city invites the heart to come to life as San Francisco does. Arrival in San Francisco is an experience in living..."

WILLIAM SAROYAN

"San Francisco is the genius of American cities. It is the wild-eyed, all-fired, hard-boiled, tender-hearted, white-haired boy of the American family of cities. It is the prodigal son. The city which does everything and is always forgiven, because of its great heart, its gentle smile, its roaring laughter, its mysterious and magnificent personality. It is not the easiest city in the world to like at first. It seems cold, hard, ugly, indifferent, and out of the world. It is not an easy city to know. It seems delirious with energy, incoherent because of the many things it has to say, broken-hearted with sorrowful memories. You walk through the streets of the city and feel its loneliness, and you wonder what memory is troubling its heart."

IBID.

"There are no end of ways of enduring time in San Francisco, pleasantly, beautifully, and with the romance of living in everything. Eat any kind of dish the races of the world know how to prepare. Drink any kind of wine you like. Play any game you care to play. Go to the opera. The symphony. The concert. Go to a movie or a stage play. Loaf around in the high-toned bars, or in the honky-tonks. Sail in the bay. Go down to Bay Meadows or Tanforan and bet the horses. Go to church. If you are alive, you can't be bored in San Francisco. If you're not alive, San Francisco will bring you to life. You may be a fool for a week or two, but nobody will notice that because everybody else has been a fool too, and is likely to be a fool again. San Francisco is a world to explore. It is a place where the heart can go on a delightful adventure. It is a city in which the spirit can know refreshment every day."

IBID.

"It is symbolically appropriate that we should meet at San Francisco for this purpose, for our pioneering has always been westward."

EDWARD R. STETTINIUS,
Secretary of State, when asked why
San Francisco was chosen for
the meeting of the United Nations

"San Francisco!—one of my two favorite cities. There is more grace per square foot in San Francisco than any place on earth!"

BISHOP FULTON J. SHEEN

"I love this city. If I am elected, I'll move the White House to San Francisco. Everybody's so friendly. I went down to Fisherman's Wharf and they even let me into Alioto's. It may be Baghdad-by-the-Bay to you, but to me it's Resurrection City."

ROBERT KENNEDY

"New York is getting dirtier by the minute. San Francisco is so clean. It's more beautiful than I had remembered. San Francisco people are more scrubbed than washed, but the styles sold here are no more conservative than the rest of the country."

NORMAN NORELL

"San Francisco is a city with the assets of a metropolis without the disadvantages of size and industry."

JACK KENNY

"There is a very healthy lack of cliché in San Francisco and a willingness to accept people for what they are as individuals. Nature has provided an ideal setting for a deep interaction between individuals."

WALTER LANDOR

"Frisco (as we saucy auslanders call this fair burg) is one of the few cities left in the world (and I should say the only English-speaking one) where the pleasures plainly outweigh the perfidies. I think it may be

truly said, in this century, that if you are tired of Frisco you are tired of life."

CHARLES MCCABE

"Cities, like people, have souls and that of San Francisco is beautiful."

MAYOR JOSEPH ALIOTO

"The Athens of the U.S."

MR. & MRS. HERBERT HOOVER

"San Francisco is Beautiful People wearing a bracelet of bridges."

HAL LIPSET

"San Francisco is poetry. Even the hills rhyme."

PAT MONTANDON

"It has been said that all great cities of history have been built on bodies of water—Rome on the Tiber, Paris on the Seine, London on the Thames, New York on the Hudson. If this is a criterion of a city's greatness, surely San Francisco ranks in the first magnitude among cities of the world. For never was a metropolis more dominated by any natural feature than San Francisco by its bay."

HAROLD GILLIAM

"For mercy's sake, whatever you do don't believe the stories you hear about this being a ghost town. A ghost is a departed spirit. They ain't no such thing in the City That Knows Wow. They bring in more live spirits every twenty-four hours than the feller running the hot spot we're all trying to pass up some day."

NEWSLETTER & WASP,
Oct. 21, 1938

"San Francisco is one of the most obscene cities in the United States."

O. G. ARMSTRONG

"I don't think San Francisco needs defending. I never meet anyone who doesn't love the place, Americans or others."

DORIS LESSING

"To me, San Francisco is the best city in the country."

PAUL SCHRADER

"The sea-born vapor that sweeps in from the Pacific on summer afternoons [gives] San Francisco that unique summer climate which is a wonder and envy of all the sweltering cities of the world."

ALEXANDER MCADIE

"I haven't tried any of Mayor Lindsay's methods to lure movies here, but I find no objection to turning Hollywood into a suburb of San Francisco, the most photogenic city in the world."

MAYOR JOSEPH ALIOTO, 1968

"The fact is that in many ways the city is viewed as a dying Athens overshadowed by its sprawling, brawny southern counterpart."

LOS ANGELES TIMES, 1983

Film & Theatrical Personalities

"San Francisco is very close to my heart. I first visited as a small boy, when my father appeared there with Helen Modjeska.... I played my last stage engagement in *Laugh, Clown, Laugh*. I wedged it in between screen assignments. That was in 1925. I remember many of the grand old-timers I met on other stage engagements: Frank Unger, Joe Redding, and a gentleman named Maloney, on the waterfront, who drew the finest mug of steam beer extanta—nectar fit for the gods which I have never found anywhere but in San Francisco... I remember its great artists, like William Keith, Joe Strong, McComas, who used to come up from Carmel in later years; George Sterling, the

poet, and others in the Bohemian set. I often think of them, and also, on hot days, with a little yearning, of Maloney's steam beer, which of course, I wouldn't be able to drink it now, even if it could be found."

LIONEL BARRYMORE

"I never dreamed I could like any city as well as London. San Francisco is exciting, moody, exhilarating. I even love the muted fogs."

JULIE CHRISTIE

"I like the fog that creeps over the whole city every night about five, and the warm protective feeling it gives...and lights of San Francisco at night, the fog horn, the bay at dusk and the little flower stands where spring flowers appear before anywhere else in the country...But, most of all, I like the view of the ocean from the Cliff House."

IRENE DUNNE

"San Francisco is one of the great cultural plateaus of the world...one of the really urbane communities in the United States ...one of the truly cosmopolitan places— and for many, many years, it always has had a warm welcome for human beings from all over the world."

EDWARD "DUKE" ELLINGTON

"I always see about six scuffles a night when I come to San Francisco. That's one of the town's charms."

ERROL FLYNN

"It's a marvelous city."

AVA GARDNER

"Three cities lie nearest to my affections. They are the London and Paris of before the war, and San Francisco. San Francisco, with its metropolitan air, its fine restaurants and its genial spirit, charmed me from the first. In fact, I bought my home at

Pebble Beach, where I go between pictures, largely because it is so close to San Francisco."

GREER GARSON

"I like the way the wind whips your skirts when you go by cable car up Nob Hill. I like the salt spray in your face when the surf breaks on the rocks at Fort Point. I like the white waves the ferry boats leave as they ply the bay, to the Oakland mole. I like the seals barking on the rocks at the Cliff House. I like the fog rolling over St. Francis Wood. I like the trolleys racing each other down Market Street's four tracks. I like the Irish cops and the Italian flower vendors. I just like San Francisco, I guess."

RITA HAYWORTH

"We're crazy about this city. First time we came here, we walked the streets all day—all over town—and nobody hassled us. People smiled, friendly-like, and we knew we could live here. We'd like to keep our place in Greenwich Village and have an apartment here, God and the Immigration Service willing. Los Angeles? That's just a big parking lot where you buy a hamburger for the trip to San Francisco.

"The food in this city is fantastic. Better than London. You know, more variety. And the beautiful old houses and the strange light. We've never been in a city with light like this. We sit in our hotel room for hours, watching the fog come in, the light change."

JOHN LENNON AND YOKO ONO

"Your city is so very beautiful, I think more beautiful than Naples, but not so romantic."

SOPHIA LOREN

"I don't like San Francisco, I love it!"

DOROTHY LAMOUR

"San Francisco, you know, is our favorite city on earth, due, among many things, to its beautiful grocery stores. Indeed Lynn and I would like nothing better than to settle down to live here—except, of course, that we already live in Wisconsin."

ALFRED LUNT AND LYNN FONTANNE LUNT

"I shall always feel that San Francisco is the Pacific Coast's only cosmopolitan city. It has big business, is a good show town, and if you like superb food, there is nothing to compare with it in the West."

DENNIS MORGAN

"Cities are like gentlemen, they are born, not made. You are either a city, or you are not, size has nothing to do with it. I bet San Francisco was a city from the very first time it had a dozen settlers. New York is 'Yokel,' but San Francisco is 'City at Heart.'"

WILL ROGERS

"I love San Francisco. It would be a perfect place for a honeymoon."

KIM NOVAK

"From vaudeville days to today, I've always looked forward to visits to San Francisco. It's one of the best 'show towns' in the world…It's like New York with a California climate. It's a city that's smart, without being 'upstage' as we actors call it. That's why I like to go there often."

WALTER PIDGEON

"It is beautiful, rain or no rain. My pet city, here I feel at home."

LILY PONS

"Now there's a grown-up swinging town."

FRANK SINATRA

"This is the last irreverent, impudent city in the country. There's more going on here in one day than goes on in Hollywood in a year. Don't let anybody kid you about Hollywood—it's still all plastic and tinsel."

TOM SMOTHERS

"Whenever I visit San Francisco, I can't help thinking of David Belasco, Warfield, and my dear old friend, Hobart Bosworth. San Francisco to me represents a sort of cradle of the American theater because of the San Franciscans who made fame on the stage. I love the waterfront and its interesting characters. It was on Fisherman's Wharf that I saw the character who proved so suggestive to me when I played Manuel, the fisherman, in *Captains Courageous*. And, above all, I have always loved the restaurants."

SPENCER TRACY

"This is the first place in the United States where I sang, and I like San Francisco better than any other city in the world.

"I love no city more than this one. Where else could I sing outdoors on Christmas Eve!"

LUISA TETRAZZINI

"I'm just mad for San Francisco. It looks like London and Paris all stacked on top of each other."

TWIGGY

"San Francisco audiences are like litmus paper, fast as light. Even at the matinee this afternoon they got everything. They're so intelligent and witty, and I am not being fulsome, I mean it, they encourage you, you know?"

RICHARD BURTON,
1980

Foreign Visitors

"This is such a lovely city, I think I'll retire here."

PRINCESS ALEXANDRA OF ENGLAND

"One of the most beautiful cities in the world. When we came under that beautiful bridge I felt like the Queen of Sheba before Solomon. Everyone brags about San Francisco. It seems an exaggeration till one sees it. Now I don't doubt it any more."

PRINCESS ALICE,
Countess of Athlone, of England

"San Francisco is the greatest...the hills...fabulous food...most beautiful and civilized people."

THE DUKE AND DUCHESS OF BEDFORD,
of England

"Friendly city, the city of happy memory, of beauty and hospitality."

SIR CARL BERENDSEN,
New Zealand Ambassador to U.S.

"The loveliest city in the world."

PRINCE BERTIL

"San Francisco has the quality of a fairy tale."

ELIZABETH BOWEN,
British novelist

"And if it were possible I would like to take Golden Gate Park home with me. True, we have lovely parks in Paris, but your Golden Gate has—how do you say?—extraordinary contours."

JEAN CHERIOUX

"San Francisco is so attractive that one visit is not enough. It merely makes you want to see it again."

VYACHESLAV ELUTIN,
Russia

"San Francisco continues to be a spot symbolizing our best hope of peace...the first city of the world and the promised land of world unity."

FERIDUN C. ERKIN,
Turkish Ambassador to U.S.

"City of St. Francis where the roses are always flowering and never thorned."

OSCAR GANS,
Cuban Minister of State

"I've fallen in love with San Francisco. My friends told me that this city and Rome were outstanding for their character and beauty. I heartily agree with them."

SIR ALEC GUINNESS,
England

"Everybody told me that it was the most beautiful city in the country. It is better than I expected. The people here act quickly and think quickly, and they are more cosmopolitan than in most American cities."

DR. INGEBORG HANACK,
Germany

"San Francisco is the best city in the United States. It does not need to make this claim—America accepts it.... It is blessed with beauty, an aristocrat among cities—this city of the Golden Gate and the golden heart.... San Francisco today fears nothing except another earthquake. But this is a word you must never mention, for San Francisco would be offended—and anyone who offends San Francisco is a clod."

DON IDDON,
London columnist

"To this day the city of San Francisco remains to the Chinese the Great City of the Golden Mountains."

KAI FU SHAH,
Chinese Minister to U.S.

"San Francisco is "where the earliest contacts between our two peoples took place."

JIANG ZEMIN,
Chinese President

"This is a place where people seem to be waiting for the next movie company to arrive. Almost without trying, San Francisco is a delight to the eye."

RICHARD LESTER,
British film producer

"San Francisco has only one drawback. 'Tis hard to leave."

RUDYARD KIPLING

"It is a mad city, inhabited by perfectly insane people whose women are of remarkable beauty."

IBID.

"Really I am delighted with what I've seen of San Francisco. A most picturesque city, indeed, and quite remarkable for the many opportunities for enjoyment it offers the traveler. You will excuse my preference for Madras, Bombay, and a few other cities of India, but residing there for so many years I'm rather disposed in their favor."

IBID.

"Yes there is no doubt about the greatness of this city, *en passant* as we say in Bengal, I'll freely admit that your institutions charm me. There is geniality about your policemen that appeals irresistibly to politest instincts, and I have no hesitation in stating that your Mayor is a brick, I may say a pressed brick."

IBID.

Kipling refers to the Chinatown section of San Francisco as "a ward of the city Canton set down in the most eligible business quarter of the city....

"The cable cars have for all practical purposes made San Francisco a dead level. They take no count of rise or fall, but slide equally on their appointed courses from one end to the other of a six-mile street. They turn corners almost at right angles, cross other lines and for ought I know may turn up the sides of houses. There is no visible agency of their flight, but once in a while you shall pass a five story building humming with machinery that winds everlasting wire cable and the initiated will tell you that here is the mechanism. If it pleases Providence to make a car run up and down a slit in the ground for many miles and if for two pence half penny I can ride in that car, why shall I ask the reason for the miracle."

IBID.
American Notes, 1891

"I like California, but best of all I am charmed by this beautiful City of San Francisco."

NIKITA KHRUSHCHEV,
Russian Premier

"Selection of San Francisco as the Peace Conference city was made with fitness and propriety."

MOHAMMED ZAFRULLA KHAN,
Foreign Minister of Pakistan

"It's the grandest city I saw in America. If everyone acted as the San Franciscans did, there would be hope for settlement of the world's difficulties."

FROL ZOZLOV,
First Deputy Premier of Russia

"San Francisco is a sympathetic city. It reminds me of Tangiers—but bigger."

PRINCESS LALLA OF MOROCCO

"I had heard so much about San Francisco that I was afraid I would be disappointed but it lived up to my expectations!"

PRINCESS MARGARET OF ENGLAND

"Two days in this city is worth two months in New York."

ROBERT MENZIES,
Prime Minister of New Zealand

"I have never seen such fuchsias. All of our best flower seeds come from California. And Golden Gate Park is the most beautiful I've ever visited."

MRS. TERENCE O'NEIL,
wife of Prime Minister of Northern Ireland

"San Francisco is the loveliest city in the world."

ANTOINE PINAY,
French Foreign Minister

"A very pretty place...San Francisco ...prettier than a lot of places...but not prettier than Monaco."

PRINCE RAINIER OF MONACO

"Queen of the Pacific, the city that saw the birth of the United Nations Charter and to which from now on all treaties and pacts to restore or consolidate peace will be linked."

ROBERT SCHUMAN,
French Foreign Minister

"No visit to the United States would be complete without San Francisco—this beautiful city, center of the West, very well known for its beauty and the place where the United Nations were born."

QUEEN SIRIKIT OF THAILAND

"I am deeply moved by the cordial friendship of the citizens of San Francisco."

CEVDET SUNAY,
President of Turkey

"The most beautiful city in the world. When our countries become friendlier again, what I want to be is the Soviet Consul in San Francisco."

GHERMAN TITOV,
Soviet cosmonaut

"Noel Coward told me in New York that whatever I do, I must see San Francisco. I saw San Francisco first on Saturday, a lovely spring day. This Easter day I see it in the rain. I love it both ways. The two things that have impressed me most in America are the Lincoln Memorial in Washington and San Francisco."

GODFREY WINN,
British author and lecturer

"It is a city of ever-fresh memories that will remain with me as long as I live."

SHIGERY YOSHIDA OF JAPAN

2 Arts & Entertainment

San Francisco Arts Festival

The first municipally sponsored Art Show, a project of the Art Commission, was held in the Civic Center Plaza, October 17–20, 1946. Since that date this annual festival has stimulated and promoted interest in the Fine Arts among the citizens of San Francisco.

San Francisco Ballet

The San Francisco Ballet Company, founded in 1933 by Adolph Bolm, is the oldest resident classical ballet company in America. It was originally established as an auxiliary to the Opera but is now an independent organization.

Municipal Band

Municipal music was first suggested to the Board of Supervisors in 1910 by the Musicians' Union of San Francisco, and was also a plank in the platform of the Labor Party in its campaign of 1909. Nothing was done, however, until the Rolph Board of Supervisors came into office when $10,000 of its budget for the fiscal year 1912–13 was set aside for this purpose.

The Board of Supervisors referred the matter of arrangements and organization of the municipal band to the Public Welfare Committee. That committee later recommended John A. Keogh as the director of the Municipal Band, and the appointment was finally confirmed by the Board of Supervisors on Monday, July 8, 1912.

The first concert of the San Francisco Municipal Band took place on Sunday, July 21, 1912, at Washington Square. Dr. S. A. Musante of the North Beach Promotion Association delivered a brief address of welcome, inviting those assembled to remain and enjoy the concert.

For 58 years the Municipal Band performed for visiting kings, queens, presidents, and other dignitaries, but in June 1970, it was voted out of existence by the San Francisco Art Commission, which had supervision of the band since 1932.

San Francisco's War Memorial Opera House opened with a performance of Tosca *on October 15, 1932. It was also the site of the founding of the United Nations. The San Francisco Opera recorded its first CD here on November 15, 1994, with Placido Domingo performing in Massenet's rarely performed* Herodiade.

Opera

In San Francisco operatic performances were given as early as 1850. However, the first grand opera was Bellini's *La Sonnambula* presented at the Adelphi on February 12, 1851. During the 1850s and 1860s a troupe would sometimes offer as many as thirteen seasons of opera in one year, making this city the center of opera in the West. The most important opera houses before 1906 were the Metropolitan I & II, Maguire's Opera House, Academy of Music, The Tivoli, and the Grand Opera House.

The first season of municipal opera opened on September 26, 1923, at the Civic Auditorium. Gaetano Merola directed a performance of Puccini's *La Boheme*. Opera continued to be performed at the Civic Auditorium until the Opera House was built in 1932, except in 1928 and 1929 when the company was in Dreamland Auditorium (later Winterland). The first opera presented in the new Opera House was *La Tosca*. The cast was headed by Claudia Muzio, Dono Borgioli, and Alfredo Gandolfi, and directed by Gaetano Merola.

Opera and Ballet Conductors, 1923–1995

Adler, Kurt Herbert *1943–53, 1958, 1960–61, 1973–82, 1984, 1986*
Agler, David *1983*
Arena, Maurizio *1985, 1987–1990*
Atherton, David *1978*
Barbini, Ernesto *1954–55*
Bartoletti, Bruno *1970*
Basile, Arturo *1959*
Beckman, Irving *1970*
Beecham, Sir Thomas *1943*
Bellugi, Piero *1965*
Bernardi, Mario *1967–68*
Blechschmidt, Hans *1931–32*
Bodanzky, Artur *1935*
Bohm, Karl *1976*
Bonynge, Richard *1963–64, 1966, 1971–75*
Breisach, Paul *1946–52*
Buckley, Emerson *1975*

Chilly, Riccardo *1977*
Cillario, Carlo Felice *1970–71, 1973, 1975*
Cimara, Pietro *1942–48, 1951–52*
Cimini, Pietro *1925–29, 1931–32, 1934, 1937*
Cleva, Fausto *1942–43, 1949–55*
Coppola, Anton *1969*
Curiel, Glauco *1952–58*
De Almeida, Antonio *1978*
De Fabritiis, Oliviero *1956, 1962*
Dell'Orefice, Antonio *1929–31, 1933*
DiRosa, Ottavio *1960*
Drewanz, Hans *1978*
Ehrling, Sixten *1969*
Faldi, Aldo *1968*
Ferencsik, Janos *1962–63, 1977–78*
Fournet, Jean *1958*
Gavazzeni, Gianandrea *1977*
Giovaninetti, Reynald *1972, 1974*
Gregor, Bohumil *1969–70*
Grossman, Herbert *1967*
Guadagna, Anton *1974*
Herbert, Walter *1942*
Hollreiser, Heinrich *1977*
Horenstein, Jascha *1966*
Kord, Kazimierz *1973*
Kritz, Karl *1945–46, 1949–54, 1956–58*
Kubelik, Rafael *1977*
Lawner, George *1961*
Leinsdorf, Erich *1938–41, 1948, 1951, 1955, 1957*
Leitner, Ferdinand *1964*
Leppard, Raymond *1975*
Lert, Richard *1935–36*
Levine, James *1970–71*
Lopez-Cobos, Jesus *1972, 1974*
Ludwig, Leopold *1958–65, 1967–68*
Mackerras, Charles *1969, 1971*
Martin, Wolfgang *1959*
Martinon, Jean *1965*
Marzollo, Dick *1947–48*
Mauceri, John *1976*
McArthur, Edwin *1939*
Merola, Gaetano *1923–49, 1952*
Molinari-Pradelli, Francesco *1957, 1959-66*
Montemezzi, Italo *1941–42, 1947*
Monteux, Pierre *1954*
Morel, Jean *1955*

Mueller, Leo *1954*
Murray, Earl *1959*
Papi, Gennaro *1936–41*
Patane, Giuseppe *1967–69, 1978*
Pelletier, Wilfred *1928–31, 1933, 1947*
Peloso, Paolo *1975–76, 1978*
Peress, Maurice *1972*
Perisson, Jean *1966–71, 1972–73, 1977*
Perlea, Jonel *1950*
Pretre, Georges *1963–64*
Pritchard, John *1970, 1973–74, 1976–77*
Rastrotovich, Mrs. Mstislav *1975*
Reiner, Fritz *1936–38*
Rescigno, Nicola *1950–51*
Riedel, Karl *1929–30, 1936, 1944*
Runnicles, Donald *1992–1995*
Sanzogno, Nino *1971–72*
Schaefer, Hans George *1960*
Schermerhorn, Kenneth *1975–76*
Schuller, Gunther *1967–70*
Schwieger, Hans *1956*
Sebastian, Georges *1944–46, 1958*
Serafin, Tullio *1953*
Shapirra, Elyakum *1975*
Simmons, Calvin *1978*
Solti, Georg *1953*
Stein, Horst *1965–68*
Steinberg, William *1944–49, 1956–57*
Suitner, Otmar *1969–71, 1972–74, 1976*
Szenkar, Eugen *1954*
Van Den Burg, Willem *1939*
Varviso, Jean *1976*
Varviso, Silvio *1959–61, 1971, 1973–74, 1978*
Von Dohnanyi, Christoph *1971, 1976*
Wallenstein, Alfred *1951*
Wich, Gunther *1978*
Wilson, Charles *1971*

Our Symphony Orchestra

Although the present San Francisco Symphony Orchestra is in the midst of its twenty–ninth season, its forerunners date back to 1854, when Rudolph Herold organized an orchestra and gave concerts at various times, for more than 25 years. Commencing in 1880, several seasons of concerts were given under the direction of Louis Homeier, and at the same time another organization known as the Philharmonic Orchestra was giving concerts under the direction of Gustav Hindrichs. In 1894, Fritz Scheel came to San Francisco to conduct an orchestra at the Midwinter Fair, following which he was appointed conductor of the Philharmonic Orchestra. He remained in that position until 1899 when he became conductor of the Philadelphia Orchestra. In the following years, a sporadic series was given under the direction of Henry Holmes, Paul Steindorff, Frederick Zech and Dr. J. Fred Wolle.

On December 29, 1911, the first concert of the present San Francisco Symphony Orchestra was given under the auspices of the Musical Association of San Francisco, an incorporated body, with Henry Hadley as conductor. During the following four years, the orchestra (made up of sixty–five musicians), held from ten to 20 concerts each season.

The success of the symphony concerts during the Panama-Pacific Exposition of 1915 convinced the Musical Association of the public's appreciation and prompted them to increase the personnel of the orchestra from 65 to 80, and to plan a much longer season.

Alfred Hertz, who was in San Francisco that summer to direct a series of Beethoven Festival performances, was engaged as regular conductor. As anticipated, the public responded, both in sustaining subscriptions and at the box office, to the fact that San Francisco had a symphony orchestra of high standard. Its seasons extended to seventy concerts, not only in San Francisco, but at the University of California, Stanford University, San Jose, Sacramento, Stockton, Fresno, and in fact supplied Central California with its symphonic fare.

Mr. Hertz remained as conductor for fifteen years. Following his resignation in 1929, the orchestra was under the joint direction of Basil Cameron and Issay Dobrowen for two seasons, each conducting half of the season. The following three seasons were under the direction of Issay Dobrowen, although while Mr. Dobrowen was away conducting the Philadelphia Orchestra and the New York Philharmonic-Symphony, the orchestra was conducted by Alfred Hertz and Bernardino Molinari.

Countless reasons caused the symphony structure to totter in 1934, and it was early in 1935 that facts demanded the Saving of Our Symphony. The officers of Local Six, the members of the orchestra, the Mayor and citizenry of San Francisco all answered the call. In May of 1935, a whirlwind campaign by the music lovers of San Francisco resulted in the people of San Francisco voting, by a large majority, that a half cent should be added to the tax rate for the benefit of the Symphony.

The amount derived from the city through this Charter Amendment provides the nucleus for the support of the orchestra. The rest of the money is raised by private subscription, ticket sales, and box office receipts.

For a short time the reins of the Association were in the hands of Joseph Thompson. He relinquished them in favor of Mrs. Leonora Wood Armsby, who has served as President and Managing Director ever since.

During the summer of 1935, Pierre Monteux was engaged as permanent conductor, which he still occupies, and the personnel of the orchestra was increased to eighty–six.

Pierre Monteux was born at Paris, France, April 4, 1875. He was educated at the Paris Conservatory, studying violin with Maurin and Berthelier (first prize, 1896), solfeggio and harmony with Lavignac, counterpoint and fugue with Lenepveu.

Monteux, also a master of the viola, began his public career first with the famous Colonne Orchestra of Paris, and then with the Opera Comique there. As a conductor his reputation was early achieved in Paris, at Covent Garden and Drury Lane in London, and in the opera houses of Berlin, Vienna and Budapest. He made four European tours as head of the Ballet Russe de Diaghileff, and came to America as its conductor in 1916. He conducted the French operas at the Metropolitan in New York from 1917 to 1919, and in the fall of the latter year was called to lead the Boston Symphony Orchestra, where he remained for five years.

In 1924 he became conductor of the Concertgebouw Orchestra at Amsterdam and so continued until 1934, at the same time, 1929–1936, conducting the Paris Symphony Orchestra.

In November of 1937, he conducted the first concerts of the NBC Symphony Orchestra in Radio City Music Hall, New York, pending the arrival of Arturo Toscanini, for whom the famous radio orchestra was organized.

Mr. Monteux has conducted the Philadelphia, New York and Los Angeles orchestras here in America; is the only French conductor to conduct the Berlin and Vienna Philharmonic Orchestras; and has conducted every major orchestra in Europe.

Our orchestra in its entirety during the season, and with the majority of the members during the summer season, functions as the Standard Oil Symphony Orchestra during the Standard Symphony hours on Thursday evenings. Alternate concerts with our orchestra are played by other Coast symphonies. To the San Francisco Symphony, however, will go the privilege of playing the 700th consecutive broadcast of this program on March 13.

The 700th Standard Symphony Hour was broadcast over the Mutual Pacific Coast Network, originating from KFRC in San

Francisco, on Thursday, March 13, 1941. The series of broadcasts began in October 1927.

EDDIE B. LOVE,
Secretary, A.F.M. Local 6,
from The Musical News, *March 1941*

Symphony Conductors

Henry Hadley, "Father of Municipal
   Music" *1911–1915*
Alfred Hertz *1915–1930*
Basil Cameron *1930–1931*
Issay Dobrowen *1931–1936*
Pierre Monteux *1936–1951*
Enrique Jorda *1951–1962*
Josef Krips *1962–1970*
Seiji Ozawa *1970–1976*
Edo de Waart *1977–1985*
Herbert Blomstedt *1985–1993*
Michael Tillson Thomas *1993–*

3 Bridges & Tunnels

Bridges

Golden Gate Bridge, Highway and Transportation District

The Golden Gate Bridge is world renowned. It is one of the world's greatest suspension bridges and has earned the reputation as being the most spectacular bridge in the world. Because of the excellent design and construction of the bridge, along with continuing improvements and maintenance, it is estimated that the bridge has a life of 200 years.

The Golden Gate Bridge and Highway District was incorporated as the entity to design, construct, and finance the building of the Golden Gate Bridge. Since its inception, the District has been comprised of the counties of San Francisco, Marin, Sonoma, Del Norte, Mendocino, and Napa, all located in Northern California.

Growth in traffic over the years indicated that the bridge and the Golden Gate corridor to the north would ultimately reach a saturation point. It was evident that the public needed additional means of transportation as an alternative to the automobile. In response, the California Legislature, in 1969, directed the District to develop a multimodal mass transportation program for the Golden Gate corridor.

In 1972, the District inaugurated bus service from Sonoma and Marin counties to San Francisco in addition to its ferry service between Sausalito (in southern Marin County) and San Francisco which began in 1970. In 1976, the ferry system was expanded by the addition of three vessels, and a new service was initiated between Larkspur (in central Marin county) and San Francisco. The capital cost of the bus and ferry systems was financed by a combination of federal grants from the Urban Mass Transportation Administration (now known as Federal Transportation Administration) and District reserves remaining after the bonds were paid.

By the time the bridge construction bonds were paid off in 1971, the District had approximately $22 million in reserves

Sections of the decking and roadway for the Bay Bridge were lifted into position from barges after 70,000 miles of suspension cable had been run. The San Francisco portion of the bridge consists of two suspension bridges anchored in the center to a concrete pier.

which was used to support the development of transit in the corridor. As the District does not have the authority to levy taxes, it must utilize transit fares and bridge tolls as the only available local sources to fund services for transit users and, at the same time, maintain the Golden Gate Bridge. While other Bay Area counties have a local sales tax and/or general fund property taxes in place to support transit-related projects and services, Marin and Sonoma counties do not.

Since 1971, over $260 million in bridge tolls have been used in operating Golden Gate Transit's bus and ferry system. As a result of the District's entry into the public transportation field, traffic growth on the Golden Gate Bridge has been held to levels that existed in the early 1970s. Before implementing bus and ferry services, approximately 30,000 persons in 20,000 vehicles were commuting across the Golden Gate Bridge each morning. Currently, the total number of commuters heading to San Francisco is approximately 38,000 persons, while vehicle traffic has grown to only 23,000.

The overall mission of the Golden Gate Bridge, Highway and Transportation District is to maintain and operate the Golden Gate Bridge; ensure reasonable mobility across the bridge by providing public transit services in the Golden Gate corridor insofar as resources permit; and contribute to the protection of the environment by providing efficient public transit services as an alternative to the automobile and by encouraging the use of such services.

A Race Against Time...Preparations for Earthquake Challenge

The Golden Gate Bridge is the only highway artery connecting San Francisco with the counties to its north. As such, it is a vital link in the interstate highway system. The Golden Gate Bridge was designed and built in the 1930s, prior to the advent of modern seismic engineering. While the 1989 Loma Prieta earthquake caused severe damage to many structures in the Bay Area, it caused no damage to the Golden Gate Bridge.

In 1990, a report issued by the Governor's Board of Inquiry on the Loma Prieta Earthquake recommended retrofitting all transportation structures of importance to reasonably assure that they will be seismically safe and maintain their function following a major earthquake. Prior to the findings of the Governor's Board of Inquiry, the Golden Gate Bridge, Highway and Transportation District had contracted for a state-of-the-art seismic evaluation of the Bridge to be performed by T. Y. Lin International of San Francisco in 1989–90 at a cost of $207,500. T. Y. Lin International reported that, although the Golden Gate bridge has performed well in all earthquakes since it was built, "it is vulnerableto damage in a Richter magnitude 7 or greater earthquake with epicenter near the bridge, and it could be closed for some time after such an earthquake." Accordingly, the District Engineer and consulting seismic engineers and scientists are recommending a retrofit on the bridge and its immediate approaches.

Based on the determination that retrofit measures were necessary, in 1990–91 the Bridge District contracted with T. Y. Lin International to prepare alternative design concepts for the seismic retrofit of the Golden Gate Bridge at a cost of $550,000. Following this study, T. Y. Lin International carried out the preliminary design effort along with an environmental assessment for a total cost of $1.2 million. The District funded all of these preliminary studies.

In January 1993, a $11.6 million final design phase for the seismic retrofit began. The final design is being conducted by two seismic engineering firms, T. Y. Lin International and Sverdrup Corporation, in order to speed up the overall time frame. Sverdrup Corporation, Walnut Creek, California, was awarded the contract for design of the seismic retrofit of the Fort Point arch, including pylon S1 with tie-down and pylon S2, and the south viaduct including the south anchorage. T. Y. Lin International/Imbsen & Associates, Inc., a joint venture, San Francisco, California, was awarded a contract for design of the seismic retrofit of the suspension bridge, including the Marin anchorage, pylon N1 with tiedown, pylon N2, north and south towers and piers, north viaduct, rehabilitation and strengthening of the south pier fender, and wind stabilization of the main span.

As of January 1994, the final design is fifty percent complete and is scheduled to be finished by December 1994. The final design phase is being financed in part by a $5.9 million federal funding grant through Federal Highway Administration following an express recognition by Congress of the importance and urgency of the project by the appropriation of funds in the Intermodal Surface Transportation Efficiency Act of 1991. The remaining $5.7 million was programmed into the District's Five-Year Fare and Toll Program (1991–1996) to be funded from bridge tolls in 1991–92 and 1992–93.

Following completion of the final design, the construction phase, estimated at $141.4 million (1994 dollars), will begin and take approximately three years to complete. The earthquake retrofit expense is significant, but represents only one-tenth of the replacement cost of the Golden Gate Bridge estimated to be $1.25 billion (1991 dollars).

In addition to the $5.7 million in bridge tolls set aside for final design, the District has a program in place to set aside $28.3 million from bridge toll revenue between 1993 and 1997. These funds will be set aside to go toward the $141.4 million construction phase. The $28.3 million represents a twenty percent "local match" contribution to the construction cost. Once

adequate funding is assured, the recommended retrofit for the Golden Gate Bridge can begin in about eighteen months and be completed within three years.

TIMOTHY J. MOORE
Public Information Assistant
Golden Gate Bridge,
Highway and Transportation District

Golden Gate Bridge

In 1918 the San Francisco Board of Supervisors voted for studies to determine if a span could be built across the Golden Gate.

Bridging the Golden Gate Association was formed in 1923 when Frank P. Doyle, president of the Chamber of Commerce of Santa Rosa, called and presided at a meeting of representatives from San Francisco and North Bay counties in the Chamber's Assembly Room.

A construction permit was issued by Patrick Hurley, U.S. Secretary of War, on August 11, 1930, and in November of the same year a bond issue in the amount of $35 million was approved by a vote of 107,930 for and 35,305 against. The bonds were paid off July 1, 1971.

The engineer, Joseph B. Strauss, with assistant Clifford Paine, commenced work on the bridge January 5, 1933 when steam shovels began digging the Marin anchorage.

Plaque

Bronze with cement made of materials from every county in the State, fastened to the toll plaza of the Golden Gate Bridge at a ceremony conducted by the grand officers of the Native Sons on May 27, 1937. It reads:

"Dedication by the Native Sons of the Golden West; as tribute to the engineering genius which gave to the State of California the Golden Gate Bridge—longest bridge span in the world—we, the Native Sons of the Golden West make this dedication in recognition of the beauty and utility of this great structure and the scientific achievement for which it stands. May 27, 1937."

GOLDEN GATE BRIDGE STATISTICS

STYLE . . . . suspension

LENGTH . . . . 7 miles including approaches;
6,450 ft. bridge itself

WIDTH . . . . 90 ft., center to center of cables

LONGEST SINGLE SPAN . . . . 4,200 ft.

HEIGHT OF TOWERS . . . . 746 ft. above water

HEIGHT OF SPAN OVER CENTER . . . . 220 ft. above low tide

DEEPEST PIER . . . . 100 ft. below water

LARGEST PIER . . . . 90 x 185 ft.

HEIGHT FROM BASE . . . . 144 ft.

NUMBER OF PIERS 2

CABLE WIRE:
LENGTH . . . . 80,000 miles
WEIGHT . . . . 22,000 tons
SIZE . . . . 36.5 inch diameter; 7,660 ft. long
NUMBER . . . . 27,572 strands, 0.2 inch diameter

CONCRETE . . . . 693,000 cubic yards

STEEL USED . . . . over 100,000 tons

PAINT COLOR . . . . international orange

MAN HOURS 25,000,000

FATALITIES DURING BUILDING 11

SWAY . . . . 27.7 ft.

WORK BEGUN . . . . January 5, 1933

LAST RIVET (GOLD) PLACED . . . . May 27, 1937

PEDESTRIAN DAY . . . . May 27, 1937

ANNUAL VEHICULAR TRAFFIC

1938 . . . . 3.5 million
1969 . . . . 32.0 million
1972 . . . . 34.5 million
1978 36,569,754
1980 35,908,058
1993 39,201,958
AVERAGE DAILY VEHICLES 111,974

TOTAL VEHICULAR TRAFFIC
SINCE OPENING 1,395,830,855

VALUE OF THE BRIDGE

1937 . . . . $35 million (construction cost),
to be paid through tolls
1973 . . . . $200 million (replacement cost),
paid off in 1971

OAKLAND BAY BRIDGE STATISTICS

STYLE .... 2 suspension;
                                        1 cantilever;
                                        5 truss spans;
                                        14 deck spans

LENGTH OF MAIN STRUCTURE .... 22,720 feet

LENGTH OVER WATER .... 4.5 miles

TOTAL LENGTH .... 43,500 feet or 8.5 miles

FATALITIES DURING BUILDING 24

WEST BAY CROSSING

HEIGHT OF TOWERS ABOVE WATER .... 474 and 519 ft.

DEPTH OF PIERS BELOW WATER .... 100 to 235 ft.

HEIGHT OF CENTER
ANCHORAGE ABOVE WATER .... 281 ft.

LENGTH OF CENTER SPANS .... 2,310 ft.

LENGTH OF SIDE SPANS .... 1,160 ft.

SWAY .... 27.7 ft.

EAST BAY CROSSING

LENGTH OF MAIN SPAN .... 1,400 ft.

CLEARANCE ABOVE HIGH WATER .... 185 ft.

DEPTH OF PIERS .... 50 to 235 ft.

LENGTH OF CENTER SPANS .... 2,310 ft.

Bridge dedicated: May 28, 1937 after President Roosevelt pressed a button in Washington at 12:00 noon to signal the final opening.

Golden Gate Bridge Slogan

"In order to assist as much as possible to make people enthusiastic over the building of the Golden Gate Bridge one newspaper of San Francisco has offered a substantial prize for someone to win who will suggest a suitable slogan. Judging by samples of suggestions received there are very few people who understand what a slogan really should be. In the case of this bridge the slogan should be something to be applied after the bridge spans the bay. Every slogan so far published smacks of the stupid and would in no way fit the case after the bridge is completed. The slogan should be something fit for all time and not for the moment. Recently an up country town wanted a slogan and someone most happily struck on 'The Buckle of the Prune Belt.' "

SAN FRANCISCO NEWS LETTER,
May 17, 1924

San Francisco—Oakland Bay Bridge

Senate Bill 1762 was introduced into the Senate December 15, 1927, after various plans for better and faster communication across San Francisco Bay, other than ferries, were suggested.

This bill granted to the City and County of San Francisco the right to construct a bridge across San Francisco Bay, and approaches from Rincon Hill in the City and County of San Francisco to a point near the South Mole of San Antonio Estuary, in the county of Alameda.

Construction was begun on the bridge July 9, 1933. It was completed in three years, four months, and three days, opening November 12, 1936. Cardinal Eugenio Pacelli (later Pope Pius XII) blessed the bridge at the West Tower No. 1, October 28, 1936. A portion of the upper deck col-

lapsed during the 1989 earthquake but was later repaired.

Third Street Bridge (At China Basin)

The first Third Street Bridge was a Page double-leaf bascule bridge erected in 1904 by the Atchison, Topeka, and Santa Fe Railway Co., and presented free to the City by agreement for maintenance and operation.

The contract for the new Third Street Bridge—officially the Francis "Lefty" O'Doul Bridge—was awarded on November 25, 1931, to Barrett & Hilp. The Bridge opened May 12, 1933. It is a trunnion bascule bridge.

Fourth Street Bridge (At China Basin)

This bridge dates from the same era and is named the Peter R. Mahoney bridge.

Third Street Bridge (At Islais Creek)

This bridge was redesigned and opened as a six-lane (instead of four) roller-bearing span, on March 3, 1950. Duncanson-Harrelson were awarded the $1,250,000 job of converting the bridge which opens in the center.

∽✤∾

Tunnels

Broadway Tunnel
Construction started: May 1950
Opened: Dec. 21, 1952 to vehicular and pedestrian traffic
Cost: $5,253,552
Engineer: Ralph G. Wadsworth
Width: 28.5 ft. each bore
Length: twin bores 1,616 ft., with approaches 3,300 ft., through Russian Hill from Powell Street on the east to Polk Street on the west

Duboce (or Sunset) Tunnel
Construction started: June 5, 1926
Opened: Oct. 21, 1928 to streetcars only
Length: 4,232 feet from Duboce and Noe

streets to Carl and Cole streets
Width: 25 ft.
Height: 23 ft. above invert; net clearance above rail 18 ft.
Cost: Approximately $1,651,983
Engineer: M. M. O'Shaughnessy

Fort Mason Tunnel (Belt Line Railroad)
Completed: November 1, 1914
Length: 1,537 feet Van Ness Avenue to Laguna Street
Width: 17 ft.
Cost: $273,149.30

Mile Rock Sewerage Tunnel
Contract awarded: February 11, 1914
Engineer: M. M. O'Shaughnessy
Height: 9 ft.
Width: 11 ft.
Length: 4,550 ft. (North of the Fulton Street Pumping Station, the storm water outfall extends from Cabrillo Street under the Sutro Heights to the outfall of the sea front)

San Francisco Subway (Embarcadero Tunnel)
Construction started: December 6, 1923
Opened: May 2, 1925 (to auto traffic only)
Length: 1,004 ft
Width: 23 ft.
Height: 13 ft.
Grade in approaches: 3.75%
Floor thickness: 5 ft.
Side wall thickness: 2.5 ft.
High tide level below top of subway: 6 ft.
Cost: $375,000
Filling-in operation started: April 9, 1957
Engineer: Frank G. White

Stockton Tunnel
Contract awarded: April 11, 1913
Length: 911 ft.; Stockton Street between Bush and Sacramento streets
Width: 50 ft.
Cost: In excess of $600,000
Completed: December 28, 1914 (First tunnel in San Francisco to accommodate vehicular and pedestrian traffic)

Engineer: M. M. O'Shaughnessy

We confine the following list to true tunnels, those bored through rock or earth:

Fort Point (Mountain Lake/Spring Valley Water Co.) Flume Tunnel (water):
Tunnel through bluff about 400 ft. south of the south wall of Fort Point at an elevation of about 25 ft. Work on flume from Lobos Creek to Black Point Cove began (officially) May 14, 1853, but most work took place in 1858; completed September 1858.

General Douglas MacArthur Tunnel (vehicular):
- San Francisco Presidio. State Highway 1, Funston Avenue approach to Golden Gate Bridge beneath Presidio Golf Course.
- 1,270 ft. long, 55 ft. wide, about 33 ft. tall; built 1939-40.
- Dedicated (with rest of Funston Avenue approach) April 21, 1940.
- Named/rededicated November 11 (Veterans Day), 1986.

San Francisco-Oakland Bay Bridge Tunnel (world's largest vehicular tunnel):
- Yorba Buena Island (Interstate 80).
- 540 ft. long, 65 ft. 6 in. wide, 52 ft. 8 in. tall (divided by deck 20 ft. above lower road).
- Built by Clinton Construction of San Francisco beginning May 15, 1933.
- Bridge and tunnel opened November 12, 1936.

Twin Peaks Tunnel (Municipal Railway)
- Castro and Market Street to West Portal (formerly Claremont Station).
- 2.25 miles in length, 25 feet wide, 15 feet high.
- Ground breaking: November 30, 1914; completed July 14, 1917.
- Opening celebration: July 15, 1917.
- First streetcar through tunnel: Feb. 3, 1918.
- Engineer-in-Charge: M.M.O'Shaughnessy.

Daly City Sewer:
- Ocean Beach at base of Fort Funston cliffs, east-southeast beneath Fort Funston and Olympic Club Golf Course.
- About 2,700 ft. long, 4 ft. x 7 ft.
- Built 1908.
- 4,300 ft. long under John Muir Blvd. to county line.

⚹

Open Trench-Constructed Tunnels

BART(Ferry Building to Balboa Station)
- approximately 5.4 miles total length.
- Municipal Railway above BART tracks until Van Ness. Muni-only continuing to Castro, approximately 3.4 mile.
- BART section: 17.5-foot-diameter twin tunnels.

(See transportation for additional information).

Westside Transport Sewer
- Under the Great Highway.
- 2.5 miles long, average width and depth 25 feet.
- Project approved by coastal commission: June 6, 1979.
- Project approved by Board of Supervisors: Feb. 8, 1980.
- Project completed: Feb. 5, 1987.
- Cost of tunnel-only: $92,000,000.

Northeast Transport Sewer (Marina District)
- Route: Marina Blvd., Fort Mason, Bay St., The Embarcadero, edge of Mission Creek near Highway 280 to Islais Creek Channel.
- 8 miles in length, average diameter: 12 feet.
- Part new construction (1981–1982), part enlargement and replacement of an existing sewer tunnel.
- Cost of new construction: $12,700,000.

—MICHAEL D. LAMPEN

Famed, dramatic photograph of the first traffic on the upper deck of the San Francisco-Oakland Bay Bridge, November 12, 1936.

4 Buildings

World's First Atomic Controlled Elevator

The first "atomic-controlled" elevators were installed at the Southern Pacific Hospital and at the Press Club. The controlling element is radioactive iodine, obtained by the Golden Gate Elevator Company from the Atomic Energy Commission. First commercial use of atomic energy.

HERB CAEN
SAN FRANCISCO EXAMINER,
June 5, 1952

Ferry Building and Ferry Boats Stolen

Remember the gag about selling the Ferry Building to a country cousin? Well, someone even less honest has made off with the Ferry Building, six Ferry boats and the waterfront from Mission Street to Fishermen's Wharf.

Police patrol cars today were ordered to keep an eye peeled for anyone who might have the Ferry Building sticking out of his pocket.

Thieves entered the basement of Exposition Auditorium and stole the eastern end of a huge map depicting San Francisco

in miniature. The map on which well-known buildings are recognizable, is to be the city's exhibit at the Chicago World's Fair. Rudolph Thierkauf, designer, was called to replace the stolen parts.

SAN FRANCISCO NEWS,
May 3, 1933

Tallest Flagpole

Tallest flagpole ever erected in San Francisco was outside the Oregon Building at the 1915 Panama Pacific International Fair. It was trimmed from a Douglas Fir and stood 299 feet 7 inches in height.

SAN FRANCISCO CHRONICLE,
November 22, 1982

San Francisco's Victorians

The embellished redwood legacy of nineteenth-century architecture has found recent favor with San Franciscans, who are lovingly repairing and repainting them in the city's older neighborhoods. Each decade of mass-produced housing has left its traces in a collection of fancywork homes and stores and churches. More than 1,700 architects, contractors, and builders were produc-

Ferry Building clock.

ing Victorian houses in San Francisco; many of them actually used "signature details" to identify their products, much as an artist adds his signature to a painting.

In the 1870s San Franciscans favored a tall, narrow rowhouse with vertical lines and a false front added to make the house look more imposing. These houses are now called the "Italianate" style, because some of their details are redwood replicas of early Roman classical decorations. Early in the decade the houses were flat-fronted; by the middle of the decade, the projecting slanted bay window attained enormous popularity. To see the Italianates, visit the clusters at 2115-25 Bush Street and 120-26 Guerrero Street. They were built by the Real Estate Associates, major home producers in San Francisco in that decade.

In the 1880s another version of the tall vertical rowhouse became popular. It is now called the "San Francisco Stick," to distinguish it from the much plainer Stick style developed on the East Coast. This house also has a false front, which may be further adorned with a gable or a "French" cap, the inexpensive builders' version of a Mansard roof. In the 1880s, bay window styles and the three-sided rectangle became the most popular shape. The San Francisco Stick style houses were also enlivened with exuberant redwood millwork, as if the designers could not bear to leave a bit of plain surface. The 1801 block of Laguna street, built by William Hinkel in 1889, is one of the finest clusters of these houses left in the city.

By the 1890s home design had changed radically. The style most common that decade was called the "Queen Anne." More expensive versions sported towers with conical witch-caps and jaunty finials. The more abundant builders' version had no tower, but both varieties have steep gables and horizontal bands of plaster garlands, spirals, or wreaths. Arches, spindles, and art glass windows were also associated with this house style. Visit 1701 Franklin Street to see the grand Queen Anne designed by architect W. H. Lillie in 1895.

The fire in 1906 took the grandest collection of the city's Victorian homes, those on Nob Hill and along Van Ness Avenue. However, it left the legacy of the mass builder, whose clusters of identical houses formed the Victorian neighborhoods, in a crescent around the downtown area. A 1976 inventory sponsored by the National Endowment for the Arts and executed by Judith Lynch Waldhorn found 13,487 Victorian homes left in the nine neighborhoods currently being restored: Bernal Heights, Duboce Triangle, Eureka, Glen Park, Haight-Ashbury, Mission District, Noe Valley, Potrero Hill, and the Western Addition.

Almost half of those remaining have been "disguised" as something else, a reflection of the post-1906 trend when embellishment caused embarrassment, and acres of millwork were replaced with asbestos shingles, stucco, or cultured stone.

BY JUDITH WALDHORN

TALLEST BUILDINGS IN SAN FRANCISCO

	HEIGHT IN FEET	NO. OF STORIES
TRANSAMERICA PYRAMID	853	48
BANK OF AMERICA WORLD HEADQUARTERS	779	52
345 CALIFORNIA ST.	724	42
101 CALIFORNIA ST.	600	48
FIVE FREMONT CENTER	600	43
EMBARCADERO ONE	569	45
ONE MARKET PLAZA, SPEAR ST. TOWER	565	43
FOUR EMBARCADERO	563	45
WELLS FARGO BANK BUILDING	561	43
575 MARKET, STANDARD OIL CO.	551	39
CITICORP BLDG., ONE SANSOME ST.	550	39
SHAKLEE BLDG., 444 MARKET ST.	542	38
AETNA INSURANCE BUILDING	529	38
METROPOLITAN LIFE BLDG.	524	38
PACIFIC TELESIS, KEARNY AND POST STS.	500	38
HILTON HOTEL TOWER	493	46
PG&E ANNEX, MISSION ST.	492	34
UNION BANK BLDG.	487	37
PACIFIC INSURANCE BLDG.	476	34
BECHTEL BLDG., FREMONT ST.	475	33
333 MARKET ST.	474	33
HARTFORD INSURANCE BUILDING	465	33
MUTUAL BENEFIT LIFE INSURANCE BLDG.	438	32
RUSS BUILDING	435	31
PACIFIC TELESIS HEADQUARTERS	435	26
PACIFIC GATEWAY BLDG.	416	30
EMBARCADERO THREE	412	35
EMBARCADERO TWO	412	35
595 MARKET ST. BUILDING	410	31
101 MONTGOMERY ST.	405	28
CSAA BUILDING ANNEX	399	29
ALCOA ALUMINUM BLDG.	398	27
ST. FRANCIS HOTEL TOWER	395	32
SHELL OIL CO. BLDG.	386	29
DEL MONTE BLDG	378	28
PACIFIC APPAREL MART TOWER	376	30

The tallest structure in San Francisco is Sutro Tower at 981 feet. Its base stands at elevation of 830 feet above sea level. The second tallest structure is the South Tower of the Golden Gate Bridge, rising 811 feet from the sea floor near Fort Point.

The Black Cat Cafe, 710 Montgomery, (circa 1937), a controversial "Bohemian" bar. Although a gay bar had opened its doors on the Barbary Coast as far back as 1908, the Black Cat was the first bar in the city to openly welcome the business of the city's growing gay and lesbian popluation. In 1950, the Black Cat won an landmark court case which decided for the first time that bars cannot be discriminated against soley for catering to homosexuals.

The O'Farrell grip in front of the Orpheum Theatre in 1915. The O'Farrell cablecar line was ripped out by Mayor Roger Lapham and helped spark the cable car "revolt" which saved great portions of the remaining system. Destruction of the cable car system was Lapham's sole legacy as mayor of San Francisco. The Tait-Zinkand Cafe on the left was the result of the merger of two famous San Francisco restaurants that burned during the Great Earthquake and Fire.

6 Chinese

Chinatown's Home on Dupont Street in San Francisco

San Francisco's historic Chinatown has remained in the same location for well over a hundred years despite several attempts to dislodge it and current mounting pressures from an expanding financial district for some of its valuable space.

Why and how the Chinese came to settle along Grant Avenue (originally called Dupont) and Sacramento Street has always eluded the researcher, perhaps because there is no specific answer. We do know, however, that Chinatown began at a very early date and exactly where due to the fastidious record-keeping of Hubert Howe Bancroft. In the 1880s this historian and his assistants carefully reconstructed Gold Rush San Francisco with this comment on Chinatown:

"Sacramento st(reet) was already becoming known as Little China, from the establishment of some Mongol merchants upon its north side, on either side of Dupont st...."

Sacramento was simply the most natural place in 1849 for Chinese immigrants to find lodgings and open small trading shops, for the wharf at its feet was the most prominent landing for merchandise in the city. With the exception of a few laborers, all of the earliest Chinese were merchants from the port city of Canton, China, and to remain near the wharves and water must have been a natural inclination.

Not unexpectedly too, the old traditional name still occasionally used by the Chinese for Sacramento is Tong Yan Gai or "Chinese street."

The first known Chinese person in San Francisco arrived in February 1848 under labor contract to a Charles Gillespie and shared his home on Dupont and Clay street—Clay being but one block north of Sacramento. An early hotel keeper, Charles Brown once recalled that he believed himself to be the first importer of Chinese labor to California, utilizing them in the construction of his inn at Clay and Kearny. (He was wrong; Gillespie preceded him by eight months at least.)

And one block north again of Clay, at Jackson and Kearny, the city's first Chinese restaurant opened in late 1848.

Exterior of a Chinese Joss-House in San Francisco

Here at the "Canton Restaurant" was held on December 10, 1849 the first gathering of California Chinese to discuss mutual problems and goals.

No one has yet been able to determine the first real estate purchase by Chinese and those who might have lent such invaluable aid to the founding of their first permanent settlement. The French settlers were, it seems, the most sympathetic to early Chinese housing and employment needs and when they slowly abandoned the old Gold Rush French Quarter along Dupont Street, the Chinese remained.

Ironically, although the French restaurants served some of the best food in those early years, at least part of the cooking was under the direction of Chinese chefs! Alexander Dumas, in his 1852 book *A Gil Blas In California*, expressed the Frenchman's indignation at another race tampering with French culinary art by calling it "abominable" (naturally). Other Argonauts rated Chinese cooking far ahead of the French in that period.

Early Chinatown bordered on Portsmouth Square, where San Francisco began, and as the city expanded southward and thence up Market Street, the Chinese found themselves squarely in the heart of a heated controversy. They owned some of the city's best property.

In July 1877 a horde of men attempted to burn the Chinese Quarter and failed. After the 1906 earthquake, the city supervisors discussed relocating the Chinese, and now the city's towering financial skyscrapers loom ominously over Chinatown's shops and playgrounds. Chinatown's always unsettled past appears to be fate, too, of its future.

WILLIAM F. HEINTZ

Chinese Cycle of Years

Twelve animals comprise the symbolic cycle of the Chinese lunar calendar. They are shown here, with the cycle of years of the lunar calendar, and the corresponding Western calendar year.

WESTERN CALENDAR	FORMAL CELEBRATION	SYMBOLIC ANIMAL	LUNAR CALENDAR
1984	FEB. 2	RAT	4682
1985	FEB. 20	OX	4683
1986	FEB. 9	TIGER	4684
1987	JAN. 29	HARE	4685
1988	FEB. 17	DRAGON	4686
1989	FEB. 6	SERPENT	4687
1990	JAN. 27	HORSE	4688
1991	FEB. 15	RAM	4689
1992	FEB. 4	MONKEY	4690
1993	JAN. 23	ROOSTER	4691
1994	FEB. 10	DOG	4692
1995	JAN. 31	BOAR	4693
1996	FEB. 19	RAT	4694
1997	FEB. 7	OX	4695
1998	JAN. 28	TIGER	4696
1999	FEB. 16	HARE	4697
2000	FEB. 5	DRAGON	4698

7 Chronology

1510

Ferdinand Magellan is the first navigator to cross the Pacific Ocean.

The name "California" is used for the first time in a romance called *Los Sergas de Esplandian* written by Garcia Ordonez.

1513

Vasco Nunez de Balboa, a Spanish navigator, crosses the Isthmus of Panama and discovers the Pacific Ocean.

1519

Hernando Cortes begins the conquest of Mexico.

1521

Hernando Cortes completes the conquest of Mexico and names it "New Spain."

1539

Francisco de Ulloa, a lieutenant of Cortes, explores the Gulf of California and proves that California is not an island.

1542

Juan Rodriguez Cabrillo, a Portuguese navigator, discovers the Bay of San Diego.

1543

Bartoleme Ferrelo, Juan Cabrillo's mate, passes and fails to note the Golden Gate.

1579

JUNE 17 TO JULY 23 Francis Drake, an English admiral and navigator, anchors in the bay later named after him. He was later knighted.

1595

Sebastian Rodriguez Cermeño sailing from the Philippines, takes refuge in a California bay, probably Drake's Bay.

1757

Miguel Venegas, a Mexican priest, publishes his history of California, *Noticia de la California*, in Spain. In reference to the word "California," he states that it originated from two Latin words, *calida* and *fornax*, meaning hot furnace. He also suggests that the origin might be an Indian word, *kali forno*, meaning high hill.

1769

Don Jose Galvez, the Visitador General of Mexico, orders the conquest of Upper California.

1769

San Francisco Bay is named for the first time.
Nov. 3 Bay discovered from landward near Pacifica by Sgt. Jose Ortega of the Portola-Serra expedition.

1772

Mar. 20 Capt. Pedro Fages, accompanied by Father Juan Crespi and a company of soldiers, left the Presidio of Monterey to explore the shores of San Francisco Bay by land.

1774

Juan Bautista de Anza, first non-native man over the Sierra, from near Tucson, scouts Bay Area.

1775

Aug. 5 Lt. Juan Manuel de Ayala's ship, the *San Carlos,* sails into San Francisco Bay.

1776

June 29 Father Palou celebrates Mass on the feast day of Saints Peter and Paul on the shore of La Laguna de Nuestra Señora de Los Dolores.
Sept. 17 Presidio of San Francisco founded.
Oct. 9 Mission Dolores founded.

1784

Aug. 28 Father Junipero Serra dies at age 71 at Mission San Carlos.

1791

Aug. 2 Mission Dolores dedicated.

1792

Nov. 14 Capt. George Vancouver, English explorer commanding the sloop-of-war *Discovery* sails into San Francisco Bay.

1794

Gov. Arrillaga builds El Castillo de San Joaquin at entrance to bay.

1806

Apr. 5 Nikolai Petrovich Rezanov arrives on ship *Juno* and falls in love with Concepcion Arguello, daughter of the commander of the Presidio of San Francisco.

1808

June 18 Several adobe walls were thrown down by an earthquake at the Presidio.

1811–17

Fr. Ramon Abella and Gabriel Moraga explore bay and tributaries.

1821

Don Augustin de Iturbide establishes Mexican independence and becomes Emperor Augustin I.
Oct. 18 An expedition under command of Capt. Luis Arguello left the Presidio of San Francisco on an exploration journey up the Sacramento Valley.

1824

The name Mission Dolores is used to distinguish our mission from San Francisco Solano in Sonoma.
Oct. 8 Otto von Kotzebue, commanding the Russian frigate, *Predpriatie*, anchors in bay.

1825

Capt. F. W. Beechey, R.N., maps bay. Blossom Rock named after his ship.

1826–1827
English ship *Blossom* under command of Capt. F. W. Beechey visits port.

1826
Nov. 27 Capt. Jedediah S. Smith and his party of hunters and trappers are the first Americans overland to California.

1827–1828
Nov. 6 Capt. Frederick W. Beechey, R.N., in HMS *Blossom*, anchors in bay.

1827
Frenchman Auguste Duhaut Cilly visits.

1833
Nov. 9 The Pueblo of San Francisco was duly erected and constituted a municipal corporation.

1834
Aug. 9 Mexican government secularizes California Missions bringing an end to Franciscan ownership.
Dec. 7 Elections held to elect municipal officers in the Presidio of San Francisco. Gov. Figueroa assigns boundaries to the Pueblo of San Francisco.

1835
June 25 Pueblo founded with erection of first building by Wm. Richardson. Site at 823-27 Grant Ave.
Sept. 22 The Territorial Deputation authorizes the "Ayuntamiento of San Francisco de Asis" to grant lots on which to build houses at Yerba Buena.
Dec. 13 Elections scheduled to be held in the Plaza of the Pueblo of San Francisco de Asis.
Dec. Richard Henry Dana in the brig *Pilgrim* visits.

1838
June and July Earthquake heavily damages Mission and Presidio.

1840
Monterey becomes capital of California under Gov. Alvarado.
Sept. Capt. John Sutter begins work on "Sutter's Fort."

1841
Aug. 14 Capt. Ringgold in the ship *Vincennes* arrives in port.
Nov. 4 First trans-Sierra wagon train under John Bidwell reaches Dr. John Marsh's ranch in California.

1844
Many of the Murphy-Stevens-Townsend overland party settle in Bay Area.

1845
Apr. 1 Mary Elizabeth Davis, granddaughter of George C. Yount, born. First Anglo-Saxon child born in San Francisco.

1846
May 23 War declared between Mexico and the United States.
June 14–July 9 William B. Ide serves as President of the Republic of California, as the result of the Bear Flag Rebellion.
July 1 John Fremont gave the name "Chrysoplylae" or "Golden Gate" to the entrance of San Francisco Bay.
July 7 American flag raised at Monterey by Comm. Sloat.
July 9 Capt. J. B. Montgomery, U.S.S. *Portsmouth*, raises U.S. flag over Portsmouth Square.
July 12 The first public Protestant worship was conducted by Capt. John B. Montgomery.
July 31 The ship *Brooklyn* arrives in port with 230 Mormons under the leadership of Sam Brannan.
Nov. 18 First "Thanksgiving Day" celebration observed.
John and Amanda Pelton open public school.

1847

JAN. 9 San Francisco's first newspaper, the *California Star*, publishes first issue.
JAN. 13 Mexican War in California ends.
JAN. 16 Russian brig *Constantine* from Sitka arrives in port.
JAN. 30 Yerba Buena renamed San Francisco.
APR. 18 Company F of Col. J. D. Stevenson's Regiment arrives aboard the ship *Brutus*.
APR. 19 Mail service between San Francisco and San Diego begins twice a week by two soldiers on horseback.
MAY 2 The first Protestant Episcopal service conducted by Rev. T. M. Leavenworth.

1848

JAN. 9 First Commercial bank established in San Francisco.
JAN. 24 Gold discovered in Coloma, Calif.
FEB. 2 Brig *Eagle* brings first shipload of Chinese to San Francisco.
FEB. 2 Treaty of Guadalupe Hidalgo ends the Mexican War and California is given to the United States.
MAR. 15 The *Californian* carries the news of the gold discovery at Sutter's Mill.
APR. 3 First American public school opened in San Francisco.
NOV. 9 Post Office opens at Clay and Pike streets.

1849

FEB. 18 First regular steamboat service to California inaugurated by the arrival of the Pacific Mail's *California*.
MAY 20 The First Presbyterian Church under Rev. Albert Williams organized.
JUNE 22 Stephen C. Massett performs at city's first concert in the Portsmouth Square schoolhouse.
JULY 15 230 volunteer policemen are deputized and put on patrol.
JULY 28 First clipper ship, the *Memmon*, arrives in San Francisco after 120 days from New York.

AUG. 5 The First Baptist Church of San Francisco is organized by Rev. T. Dwight Hunt.
OCT. 21 Rev. O. C. Wheeler baptizes Col. Thomas Kellam by immersion in the waters of San Francisco Bay.
OCT. 25 Meeting held in Portsmouth Square for the purpose of organizing the Democratic Party in California.
NOV. 19 Public sale of pueblo land held.
DEC. 24 Fire destroys part of the city. First book in English printed in San Francisco, *California as it is and as it May Be, or a Guide to the Gold Region*, by F. P. Wierzbicki.

1850

JAN. 3 Great sale of beach and water property.
JAN. 5 California Exchange opens.
JAN. 21 French newspaper *Le Californien* established.
JAN. 22 The *Alta California* is becomes a daily newspaper, the first in California.
JAN. 23 San Francisco's second daily journal, *The Journal of Commerce*, established by Washington Bartlett.
FEB. 18 Legislature creates bay region counties: San Francisco, Contra Costa, Marin, Santa Clara, Sonoma, Solano, and Napa.
MAR. 18 Town Council rules that all titles to land made by grants or sales in any form, by any person or persons whatever, other than the legally elected Alcalde or Town Council, are illegal.
APR. 1 San Francisco County government established.
APR. 15 City of San Francisco charter went into effect.
MAY 4 Fire destroys part of city bounded by Montgomery, Kearny, Clay, Jackson, Washington, and Dupont streets.
MAY 9 Two Boards of Aldermen met at the new City Hall, corner of Kearny and Pacific.
MAY 11 Construction begins on first brick

building (The Naglee Building) at corner of Montgomery and Merchant streets.

MAY 11 Malachi Fallon sworn in as Town Marshal.

JUNE 1 *San Francisco Daily Herald* begins publishing.

JUNE 4 Empire Engine Co. No. 1 organized.

JUNE 14 Fire destroys part of city; St. Francis Hook & Ladder Co. No. 1, Howard Engine Co. No. 3 and Sansome Hook & Ladder Co. No. 3 organized.

JULY 1 The *California Courier* established by James M. Crane and F. W. Rice.

JULY 1 At this time there are some 626 vessels lying in the Bay of San Francisco and contiguous harbors.

JULY 4 Independence Day celebrated and a flagpole, 111 ft. high, is erected on the Plaza.

AUG. 3 *Evening Picayune* established by Dr. J. H. Gihon.

SEPT. First San Francisco city directory published by Charles P. Kimball.

SEPT. 7 Bank runs occur.

SEPT. 9 California admitted to the Union.

SEPT. 12 First issue of Octavian Hoogs' paper *La Gazette Republicaine* appears.

SEPT. 17 Fire destroys part of city bounded by Dupont, Montgomery, Washington and Pacific streets.

OCT. 17 Knickerbocker Engine Co. No. 5 organized.

OCT. 29 Day devoted to celebrating the admission of California into the Union as the 31st State.

NOV. 6 Yerba Buena Island, Angel Island, and Point San Jose reserved by executive order for military purposes.

NOV. 18 Col. Chas. L. Wilson granted concession to build a plank-road from San Francisco to Mission Dolores on a toll basis.

NOV. 30 Day set apart as Thanksgiving Day for the admission of California into the Union.

DEC. 8 Newspaper *Public Balance* established by Benjamin R. Buckelew and Eugene Casserly.

1851

JAN. 31 First orphanage in California, the San Francisco Orphan Asylum, founded by the Protestants.

MAR. 14 The Foreign Miners Tax repealed.

MAR. 26 Legislature of the State of California enacts law by which the State relinquishes title to all lots below high water mark within the city limits to the City of San Francisco.

MAY 4 Fire destroys almost entire city, except for the submerged hulk of the ship *Niantic*.

MAY 6 Chamber of Commerce organized.

MAY 24 Shepard & Company commences publishing the *Morning Post*.

JUNE 9 First Committee of Vigilance organized.

JUNE 22 Fire destroys part of the city. Capital of the State moved to Vallejo.

1852

JAN. 15 Charles E. Pickett begins publishing the *Western American*, a daily newspaper.

FEB. 17 Publication of the *San Francisco Shipping List and Prices Current* begun by S. O. Johnson & Co.

APR. 8 Vigilant Engine Co. No. 9 organized.

APR. 19 California Historical Society incorporated.

MAY 20 Time ball put into operation from atop Telegraph Hill.

MAY 22 Ordinance passed by Board of Alderman for a fixed "fire district."

MAY 25 *The Evening Journal* begins publication by Pinkham Gee & Co.

JUNE 1 The French newspaper *L' Echo du Pacifique* established.

JUNE 8 The first recorded strike occurs when Chinese laborers working on the Parrott granite building strike for increase in wages.

JULY 4 The What Cheer House on Sacramento Street opens.

JULY 23 First interment in U.S. National Cemetery at Presidio.

AUG. 1 Colored Methodists organize Zion M. E. Church.

NOV. 4 Crescent Engine Co. No. 10, Columbian Engine Co. No. 11, and Pennsylvania Engine Co. No. 12 organized.

NOV. 22 Shortly before midnight, after a shock like that of an earthquake, the waters of Lake Merced sink about 30 feet.

DEC. 6 Law enacted to forbid the erection of any frame structures within densely built up portions of town.

DEC. 10 Jose Forner hangs; it is the first legal execution to take place on Russian Hill.

DEC. 19 *The Golden Era*, a literary weekly, established.

DEC. 24 San Francisco Hall, Washington between Kearny and Montgomery, opens.

1853

JAN. 2 The U.S. Land Commission begins its sittings in San Francisco to decide on the validity of claims of those holding or attempting to hold land under the old "Spanish grants."

JAN. 16 The weekly *California Farmer*, an agricultural paper, begun by J.L.L. Warren.

JAN. 27 *The Pioneer*, a monthly magazine, published by Lecount & Strong, is established.

FEB. 13 Chinese Mission House organized by Rev. William Speer.

FEB. 15 *The Curiosity Shop*, a humorous illustrated weekly, established.

MAR. 17 *The Wide West*, a Sunday literary newspaper, established by Bonestill & Williston.

APR. 4 California Academy of Sciences organized.

APR. 7 U.S. Marine Hospital established at the Presidio.

APR. 25 Fire, California Wharf, corner of Drumm Street; loss, $22,000.

APR. 28 *The Golden Hills News*, published in Chinese, established by Howard & Hudson.

MAY 1 Emma Jane Swasey crowned first Queen of May; Russ Gardens, Harrison and Sixth streets, opens.

JUNE 1 Lafayette Hook & Ladder Co. No. 2, Broadway between Dupont & Stockton, organized.

JUNE 16 Daily newspaper *Present and Future* established by Dr. E. Theller.

JULY 17 Construction starts on St. Mary's Church, California and Dupont streets.

AUG. 4 Ladies' Protection & Relief Society founded.

SEPT. 9 Pacific Engine Co. No. 8 organized.

SEPT. 16 Money appropriated for building fence around Yerba Buena Cemetery.

OCT. 1 California State Telegraph Co. line opened between San Francisco and San Jose.

OCT. 23 St. Francis Hotel, corner Dupont and Clay streets, destroyed by fire.

NOV. 17 Street signs authorized to be affixed at the various crossings.

DEC. 23 Metropolitan Theater opens, first theater to be lit by gas.

Capital of State moved to Benicia.

1854

JAN. 1 Young America Engine Co. No. 13 organized.

JAN. 21 Capt. Joshia Creesy sets sail in command of the *Flying Cloud* bound for San Francisco from New York.

FEB. 11 Principal streets lighted with coal gas for first time.

MAR. 1 California Steam Navigation Co. organized.

MAR. 30 First U.S. Mint opens on Commercial Street.

APR. 12 Walls of the U.S. Bonded Warehouse at Battery and Union collapse.

APR. 20 Capt. Creesy sets a world record by sailing from New York to San Francisco in 88 days.

MAY 6 The Catholic Church paper, the *Weekly Catholic Standard*, established.

MAY 11 The *Star of the West*, formerly the

California Temperance paper, begins publication.

MAY 19 F. A. Bonnard's *Daily Sun* appears as a weekly.

MAY 27 Marine telegraph from Fort Point to San Francisco completed.

MAY 30 Lone Mountain Cemetery dedicated.

JUNE 20 Volunteer Engine Co. No. 7 organized.

JUNE 22 San Francisco Accumulating Fund Association incorporated.

JUNE 28 First interment in Laurel Hill Cemetery.

JULY 17 Calvary Presbyterian Church organized.

SEPT. 25 The German newspaper *Abend Zeitung* established by A. J. Lafontaine.

OCT. 6 Henry Meiggs flees San Francisco to avoid charges of forging city warrants.

NOV. 2 Cobblestone paving of Washington Street between Dupont and Kearny commences.

NOV. 4 Lighthouse on Alcatraz established.

NOV. 12 William H. Mantz & Co. begin publishing *Town Talk*.

DEC. 25 Old St. Mary's Church dedicated; Capital of California moved to Sacramento.

1855

JAN. 4 *The Oriental*, a Chinese newspaper, established by Rev. William Speer.

FEB. 23 "Black Friday" Bank failures of Adams & Co., Price, Rodman, and others.

MAR. 26 Paving of Washington Street between Dupont and Kearny completed.

APR. 7 *The Fireman's Journal*, devoted to the interests of the fire department, established by C. M. Chase & Co.

APR. 7 Charley Ah You, of the Thung Shung Tung Co., and Miss Sag Sung married by Justice O. Bailey, believed to be the first civil marriage of Chinese in California.

JUNE 20 Commissioners appointed to lay

out streets and blocks west of Larkin, extending to the city charter line of 1851.

JULY 15 St. Ignatius Church, Market between 4th and 5th, dedicated.

JULY 22 French semi-weekly paper *Le Phare* established by P. Hertzberg, A. H. Rapp, and Wm. M. Hinton.

OCT. 8 *Daily Bulletin* begins publication.

OCT. 15 St. Ignatius Academy on Market Street opens to students.

DEC. 24 James P. Casey establishes the *Weekly Sunday Times*.

DEC. 25 The first German Protestant church built on the Pacific Coast, the German Evangelical Lutheran Church on Sutter, between Dupont and Stockton, dedicated.

DEC. 28 Tiger Engine Co. No. 14 organized.

1856

JAN. Coal from Coos Bay, Ore., first introduced to the San Francisco market.

JAN. 22 M. Derbec begins publication of the *Eco del Pacifico*, a daily Spanish paper.

FEB. 15 Earthquake felt at 5 a.m.

MAR. 13 Moody & Co. begin publication of the *Daily Globe*.

MAR. 26 Ladies' Seamen's Friend Society founded.

APR. 19 San Francisco city and county were consolidated.

MAY 4 Notre Dame des Victoires Church dedicated.

MAY 14 James King of William, editor of the *Daily Bulletin*, shot by Supervisor James Casey.

MAY 15 Second Vigilance Committee organized.

MAY 20 James King of William dies from gunshot wounds.

MAY 22 Lynching of James P. Casey and Charles Cora by the Vigilance Committee.

JULY 1 San Mateo County was created by legislative enactment from the southern part of San Francisco County.

Dr. W. O. Ayers lectures on the subject of "Earthquakes" at the First Congregational

Church.

Nov. 29 Maguire's Opera House opens.

Dec. 1 The *Daily Morning Call* established.

1857

Jan. 16 Concert Hall, corner Clay and Sansome, opens.

Apr. 29 Headquarters for Army's Division of the Pacific permanently established at the Presidio.

June 15 S. F. Water Works organized.

Aug. 14 Metropolitan Theater burns.

Sept. 8 Mechanics Pavilion, west side of Montgomery between Post and Sutter, opens.

1858

Jan. 1 Drs. J. B. Trask & David Wooster establish the monthly *Pacific Medical Journal.*

Jan. 2 New German Hospital opens at Steamboat Point.

Mar. 6 The *Weekly Monitor*, an organ of the Catholic Church, established by Marks Thomas & Co.

Mar. 15 French Hospital on Brannan Street opens.

June 2 Adelphi Theater burns.

Sept. 15 The first coaches of the Overland Mail left simultaneously from the eastern termini, Tipton, Missouri, and Little Rock, Arkansas, and the western terminus, San Francisco.

Sept. 16 San Francisco Water Works Company began its operation.

Oct. 1 W. H. Mantz & Co. begin publishing the *Daily Evening Telegram.*

Oct. 3 J. C. Duncan commences publication of the *Weekly California Home Journal.*

Oct. 10 First Butterfield Overland Mail arrives, having left St. Louis on Sept. 15.

Oct. 24 Clock completed on St. Mary's Cathedral tower.

Dec. 23 *The Telegraph Hill*, a weekly newspaper, begins publication.

1859

Mar. 1 Present seal of the City of San Francisco adopted.

Apr. 12 Hibernia Savings & Loan Society of San Francisco incorporated.

Sept. 13 David S. Terry shoots and wounds David C. Broderick.

Oct. 2 Cornerstone of St. Francis Church on Vallejo laid.

Dec. 19 Grading commenced for Market Street Railroad.

1860

Feb. 1 French Savings & Loan Society incorporated.

Mar. 17 Staff of Japanese Embassy arrives in San Francisco aboard the Japanese steamer *Candinmarruh.*

Mar. 24 Clipper ship *Andrew Jackson* arrives from New York in 89 days.

Apr. 14 First Pony Express rider arrives in San Francisco from St. Joseph, Missouri.

May 1 First school for the deaf founded on Tehama Street.

June 7 Workmen began laying track on Market Street Railroad.

July 1 Single track of the San Francisco and Mission Railroad completed, a distance of three miles from the foot of Market Street to the Mission.

July 4 Service commences on city's first street railway.

Aug. 16 Archbishop Alemany purchases 60 acres of Lone Mountain properties and consecrates the greater portion as Calvary Cemetery.

Sept. 3 Exempt Fire Company organized.

Oct. 4 Prince Kamehameha arrives on his private yacht.

Oct. 8 Telegraph line opened between San Francisco and Los Angeles.

Nov. 8 Calvary Cemetery dedicated.

Nov. 27 Lyceum Theater destroyed by fire.

Dec. 22 New Rincon Hill Schoolhouse dedicated; Lincoln wins state's four electoral votes by narrow 1,000 plurality.

1861

FEB. 15 Fort Point completed and garrisoned by two companies of 3rd Artillery.

APR. 4 Spring Valley Water Company celebrates the filling of the Potrero Hill reservoir.

MAY 11 Union demonstration at Market and Post streets following the news of the firing on Fort Sumter.

JUNE 1 Banking house of Donohoe, Ralston & Co. established.

JUNE 14 Howard Engine Company opens new firehouse with a banquet.

JULY 1 New public schoolhouse, corner Washington and Mason streets, opened.

JULY 3 Arrival of the Pony Express with overland letters from New York, etc.

JULY 26 Mark Twain begins his trip west.

AUG. 1 Well-attended mass meeting is held at Mechanics' Hall; the Mechanics' League is formed to carry on the fight against convict labor.

AUG. 27 The *Daily Times* suspends publication.

SEPT. 9 Military organization called the McClellan Guard organized.

SEPT. 25 Military organization called the Siegel Rifles organized.

OCT. 24 Completion of overland telegraph and end of Pony Express.

NOV. 16 Completion of the new St. Mary's Hospital on Rincon Hill.

DEC. 8 St. Joseph's Catholic Church dedicated.

DEC. 31 Incorporation of the California Powder Works with a capital of $100,000.

1862

JAN. 11 Fire destroys the boarding house known as Sarsfield Hall, Pacific and Montgomery streets.

APR. 28 Col. J. H. Carleton's California Column defeats Confederates at Pichaco Pass and invades Texas.

JUNE 18 San Francisco Savings Union incorporated.

JUNE 19 Congress passes a law outlawing slavery in the territories of the U.S.

JULY 11 Grand torchlight demonstration of firemen in honor of passage of the Pacific Railroad Bill.

SEPT. 4 North Beach & Mission Railway Co. organized.

SEPT. 6 Illumination, firing of guns, and other manifestations of joy at San Francisco in honor of supposed victory of Union forces at Manassas. Subscription started for the relief of the sick and wounded soldiers of the Union Army.

SEPT. 8 The San Francisco Stock and Exchange Board founded.

SEPT. 15 Citizens of San Francisco propose to raise a regiment of infantry for service in the East.

SEPT. 20 The sum of $100,000 sent East, as a contribution for the relief of the sick and wounded soldiers, to be disbursed by the National Sanitary Commission.

NOV. 6 Direct telegraphic communication established between New York and San Francisco.

DEC. 11 Company of cavalry, the "California Hundred," intended for service in the East, sails on the *Golden Age* for Panama.

1863

JAN. 1 The Occidental Hotel on Montgomery between Sutter and Bush opens.

JAN. 8 Gov. Stanford breaks ground at Sacramento to begin construction of Central Pacific Railroad.

JAN. 28 Society of California Pioneers incorporated.

FEB. 22 Gov. Stanford lays cornerstone for the Broderick monument in Lone Mountain Cemetery.

MAR. 15 Schooner *J. M. Chapman* seized in the bay and five men arrested as privateers.

JUNE 4 Fight at the Farallone Islands between workers of the Farallone Egg Company and a party of Italians; one killed and five wounded.

JUNE 30 St. Ignatius College conferred the

A.B. degree for the first time.

JULY 2 Water of the Spring Valley Water Works first brought to the city from Lake Honda.

SEPT. 1 Railroad and ferry connection with Oakland inaugurated.

OCT. 15 The Cliff House opens; San Francisco & San Jose Railroad formally opened.

OCT. 18 The San Francisco & San Jose Railroad begins service from San Francisco to Palo Alto.

OCT. 20 First number of *Democratic Press* issued.

OCT. 28 Telegraph cable laid from Fort Point to Lime Point.

NOV. 1 Troops begin erecting fortifications on Angel Island.

NOV. 21 Harbor Commissioners take possession of Vallejo, Jackson, Clay, Washington, and Mission wharfs.

NOV. 27 Count di Castiglione and Major Devecchi, Commissioners of Exploration, feted by the Italian merchants of the city.

DEC. 2 Irataba, Chief of the Mohave Indians, arrives in town.

1864

JAN. 5 More's Wharf caves in.

JAN. 11 Strike for higher wages by stable grooms.

JAN. 16 San Francisco & San Jose Railroad celebrates completion of their road with a grand dinner and speeches at San Jose.

FEB. 24 Meeting of German citizens regarding Holstein-Schleswig war question.

MAR. 4 Rev. Thomas Starr King dies.

APR. 2 Rincon Hose Co. No. 6 goes into service.

APR. 15 General Wright issues order forbidding vessels entering the harbor of San Francisco to pass north of Alcatraz on penalty of being fired upon.

APR. 28 Officers quarters at Black Point Battery destroyed by fire.

MAY 23 The National Freedmen's

Association organized regionally in city.

JUNE 11 300 feet of Meigg's Wharf washed away in gale.

AUG. 31 Cosmopolitan Hotel opens.

OCT. 25 Cornerstone of Temple Emanu-El on Sutter Street laid.

NOV. 14 The *Comanche*, an iron-clad monitor of the U.S. Navy, launched.

DEC. 29 Fire Department held its first annual ball.

1865

California ratified the 13th Amendment to the Constitution, abolishing slavery.

JAN. 16 First issue of *San Francisco Dramatic Chronicle* published by Charles and Michael de Young.

MAR. 1 City Hall bell removed to the Old Union Hotel building thereafter sounding the alarm in case of fire.

APR. 24 Fire alarm and police telegraph system inaugurated.

SEPT. 24 James Cooke performs ropewalking feat from the Cliff House to Seal Rocks.

SEPT. 25 Ground broken for the track of the Front Street, Mission and Ocean Railroad.

OCT. 8 Earthquake in San Francisco.

NOV. 19 Odd Fellows' Cemetery on Point Lobos Road dedicated.

DEC. 12 Hostlers strike for higher wages.

1866

MAR. 23 New Synagogue Emanu-El on Sutter Street consecrated.

APR. 16 Nitroglycerine explosion at Wells Fargo & Co. Express Office.

MAY 4 Woodward's Gardens in the Mission opened to the public.

AUG. 1 Union State Central Committee meets in San Francisco and adopts resolutions in favor of equal rights to all men, without distinction as to color.

AUG. 6 Journeymen plasterers strike and demand the 8-hour system of work.

SEPT. 20 $1,000 for the best design of a seawall awarded to Lewis & Allardt.

OCT. 13 Odd Fellows Savings Bank incorporated.

NOV. 9 Cornerstone of the new Trinity Church, at the corner of Post and Powell streets, laid with the ceremonies of the Episcopal Church.

DEC. 3 Paid Fire Department goes into active operation.

DEC. 31 China and Japan Steamship Line inaugurated with grand banquet at the Occidental Hotel.

1867

Alexis von Schmidt builds record-sized dry dock, Hunters Point.

JAN. 1 The black population throughout California celebrates the anniversary of the issuance of the Emancipation Proclamation.

FEB. 1 Bricklayers begin work under the 8-hour rule.

FEB. 3 The British ship *Schah Jehan*, outward bound, is driven on the rocks in the bay and wrecked. The crew is saved.

FEB. 12 Chinese laborers employed in excavating a lot on Townsend Street driven from their work. Their shanties and provisions destroyed by a mob of disaffected laborers who afterwards proceeded to the Potrero and drove off the Chinese employed at the rope works of Tubbs & Co., setting fire to their homes.

FEB. 20 Mass meeting held and an organization formed to establish anti-coolie clubs.

MAR. 6 A large meeting is held to discourage Chinese immigration and the employment of coolie labor.

MAR. 12 Immense Fenian meeting held. Five thousand persons attend.

MAR. 14 Important seizures of Chinese goods for violation of the U.S. Revenue Laws.

MAR. 20 The Pacific Mail steamship *Colorado* arrives in port having completed successfully her pioneer trip to Japan and China.

MAR. 29 Workingmen's Convention opens.

APR. 4 A meeting of the citizens was held for the adoption of measures for the relief of the suffering population of the Southern States. Committees were appointed, and a large amount of money was subscribed.

APR. 6 The U.S. steamship *Pensacola* arrived in the harbor.

APR. 23 Cosmopolitan Hotel fire; $150,000 damage.

MAY 13 State convention of anti-Chinese clubs meets.

MAY 20 A billiard tournament held in the city for the championship of the Pacific Coast is terminated in favor of Mr. Jamieson of Nevada.

JUNE 3 More than 2,000 men march through the streets carrying flags and banners heralding the 8-hour work day.

JUNE 27 Bank of California opens.

JULY 4 Two men belonging to the Second U.S. Artillery are killed by the discharge of a cannon at Fort Point.

JULY 14 Three noted Indian chiefs from the northern portion of the state visit in company with B. C. Whiting, Supt. of Indian Affairs for California.

JULY 15 The Merchants' Exchange opens.

JULY 21 The City Gardens on Folsom Street open for the first time.

JULY 28 The anniversary of Peruvian Independence is celebrated with much enthusiasm by the Peruvians in the city.

JULY 31 The new California Market opens.

AUG. 16 North wall of the old Chinese Hospital on Pine Street falls to the ground.

SEPT. 9 Work commenced on the first section of the seawall.

SEPT. 12 The Almshouse opens.

SEPT. 22 Trinity Church consecrated by Bishop Kip.

SEPT. 27 The *John L. Stephens*, first steamer to sail between California and Alaska, sails.

OCT. 11 *The Pacific Hygenist*, a monthly journal, issued for the first time.

NOV. 4 Blast of 90 kegs of powder exploded at Telegraph Hill to obtain rock for the seawall.

DEC. 20 Hon. Eugene Casserly of San Francisco elected U.S. Senator for California to succeed Hon. John Conness.

DEC. 22 A terrific gale rages in San Francisco, Sacramento, and other places throughout the state, doing considerable damage.

1868

JAN. 1 The bark *H. L. Rutgers* is wrecked near Point Bonita.

JAN. 12 The sloop *John Stillson* with 80 tons of wheat on board sank at San Francisco during a severe storm.

JAN. 13 The British bark, *Oliver Cutts*, is wrecked while entering the bay.

FEB. 10 German Savings and Loan Society incorporated.

FEB. 10 The first number of *Le Journal de Lundi* was issued.

FEB. 13 Cornerstone laid for the Alhambra Theater on Bush Street.

FEB. 16 The American Theater was destroyed by fire.

FEB. 22 Washington's birthday celebrated.

FEB. 21 First Labor Day.

FEB. 22 The passage of the Eight-Hour Law by the California Legislature was enthusiastically celebrated.

FEB. 28 A whale 33 feet in length captured in the bay.

MAR. 1 The *Alaska Herald* founded by A. Honcharenko.

MAR. 7 The British ship *Viscota*, bound for Liverpool with a cargo of wheat, is wrecked near Point Lobos.

MAR. 19 Two men killed and one seriously injured by the falling of a brick wall.

MAR. 28 Earthquake shock felt in San Francisco.

MAR. 31 Staff of the Chinese Embassy and suite arrive in San Francisco on the steamship *China*.

APR. 18 James Ryan killed in collapse of the Post Street sewer.

APR. 3 Cars run for the first time on the Western Pacific Railroad.

APR. 1 San Francisco Society for Prevention of Cruelty to Animals formed.

APR. 18 The cornerstone of the Young Men's Christian Association Building laid with ceremony.

APR. 27 The California Labor Exchange opens.

APR. 28 Grand banquet given at Lick House by merchants of San Francisco to the Chinese Embassy.

APR. 29 Chinese Embassy staff, in company with General Halleck, Admiral Fletcher, and others, visit fortifications in the harbor of San Francisco.

MAY 16 A charge of 7,500 pounds of powder explodes in a tunnel at Lime Point in the harbor of San Francisco tearing down a cliff to the height of 175 feet and displacing about 80,000 tons of rock.

MAY 26 Two earthquake shocks felt in San Francisco.

MAY 29 Two severe shocks of an earthquake felt throughout California and Nevada.

JUNE 17 First number of *Figaro* issued.

JUNE 19 The new Mercantile Library Building dedicated.

JUNE 20 New Olympic Theater opens.

JUNE 24 Guns were fired at the fortifications in the harbor of San Francisco in respect to the memory of the late ex-President James Buchanan.

JUNE 29 New Olympic Theater closes.

SEPT. 1 First *Morning Chronicle* issued with declarations of policy.

SEPT. 5 The first number of the *Underwriter* issued in San Francisco.

SEPT. 17 A dense smoke or fog prevails in San Francisco and other places throughout the state.

OCT. 21 Violent earthquake occurs at 7:53 a.m. Much damage done.

OCT. 24 Twelve tons of powder explodes in a tunnel at Lime Point, throwing down 70,000 tons of rock.

NOV. 3 The Presidential election on the Pacific Coast results in the success of the

Republican ticket in California and Nevada.
Nov. 13 An unusually brilliant meteoric shower occurs, lasting from 10 p.m. to 2 a.m.
Nov. 26 First baseball game played in enclosed field at 25th and Folsom streets.
Nov. 28 The schooner *Alert*, bound for San Francisco, is wrecked at Half Moon Bay.
Nov. 30 The number of cases of smallpox in San Francisco from the second of June last to this date is reported at 1,000 of which 350 proved fatal.

1869

Apr. 18 First International Cricket Match held in the city won by the Californians.
May 8 Celebration in honor of the completion of the Central Pacific Railroad across the continent, with civic and military processions.
May 10 CRRR and UPRR meet at Promontory Point, Utah. First westbound train arrives at Alameda September 6.
May 16 The new Calvary Presbyterian Church on Powell Street dedicated.
July 2 Frederick Marriott's dirigible, *Avitor Hermes, Jr.,* flies for the first time in the East Bay at Shell Mound Park. It is the first flight of a lighter than air vehicle in the Western Hemisphere.
Aug. 23 First carload of freight (boots and shoes) arrives from Boston after 16-day rail trip.
Aug. 30 First shipment of tea overland (90 baskets) sent to Williams, Butters & Co., Chicago.
Sept. 6 Steamer *Alameda* is first vessel to connect with the overland passenger train to reach San Francisco Bay.
Sept. 12 The new Italian Hospital formally opened.
Sept. 22 Red Stocking Club of Cincinnati, famous baseball club, arrives overland.
Sept. 26 Cornerstone of St. Patrick's Church laid by Archbishop Alemany.
Oct. 9 San Francisco Yacht Club formally opens new club house on Long Bridge.

Oct. 21 First shipment of fresh oysters arrives overland from Baltimore.
Nov. 4 Masonic Savings & Loan Society incorporated.
Nov. 15 Free postal delivery formally inaugurated.
Nov. 24 Humboldt Savings & Loan Society incorporated.

1870

Feb. 22 Anti-Chinese Association, the Industrial Reformers, established.
Mar. 14 Legislative act to create Golden Gate Park is approved.
Apr. 4 Golden Gate Park established by Order 800: an act to provide for the improvement of public parks in the City of San Francisco.
Apr. 8 Serious fight between rival Chinese cigar makers occurs on Battery Street.
June 1 Excursion party from Boston arrives overland.
July 25 Board of Supervisors issues order forbidding any person to hire or let rooms for sleeping purposes in which there is less than 500 cubic feet of air per person.
Aug. 8 William Hammond Hall awarded contract to make a minute topographical survey of Golden Gate Park for the sum of $4,860.
Dec. 25 Chinese Mission Institute, corner Washington and Stone streets, dedicated.

1871

Jan. 14 Aerial steamer successfully tested by an association at the City Gardens.
Jan. 25 First annual meeting of the California Woman Suffrage Society.
Jan. 31 Birds pass over western part of city in such numbers as to darken the sky.
Mar. 28 San Francisco Art Association holds opening reception in rooms at 430 Pine Street.
Apr. 10 William Hammond Hall's surveys and maps of Golden Gate Park officially adopted by the first Board of

Park Commissioners.

APR. 23 Blossom Rock, discovered and named by Capt. Beechey in 1826 in San Francisco Bay, blown up.

SEPT. 23 *The Enterprise*, a workingmen's journal, makes its first appearance.

OCT. 5 Occidental Skating Rink, Post and Stockton streets, destroyed by fire.

OCT. 11 Large and enthusiastic meeting held at the Merchants' Exchange for the relief of sufferers of the Chicago Fire; approximately $25,000 contributed on the spot.

NOV. 3 "California Rifles" mustered out of service by order of Governor Haight.

NOV. 4 First number of *The West* appears.

NOV. 11 California Olympic Club organized.

DEC. 28 First stone of the new City Hall laid with appropriate ceremonies.

1872

JAN. 20 California Stock Exchange Board organized.

JAN. 20 "Committee of One Hundred," organized to oppose give away of Goat Island to the railroad companies, holds its first meeting.

MAR. 23 The Consolidation Act of 1856 again amended to increase police force to 150 patrolmen.

APR. 20 Bar Association of San Francisco organized.

MAY 16 Lamps of the Metropolitan Gas Company lit for the first time.

MAY 17 Bohemian Club incorporated.

JUNE 18 Woman's Suffrage Convention held at Mercantile Library Hall.

JULY 2 National Guard of Virginia arrive to participate in the celebration of the Fourth of July.

AUG. 23 First Japanese commercial vessel ever in the port arrives with a cargo of tea.

NOV. 15 Telegraphic courtesies exchanged between the Mayor of San Francisco and the Mayor of Adelaide, Australia, on the completion of the telegraphic route to Australia via Europe.

NOV. 29 Hayes Park Pavilion destroyed by fire.

DEC. 21 Hercules Powder Works blows up.

1873

APR. 20 Central Presbyterian Tabernacle on Tyler Street and the Church of the Holy Cross on Eddy Street are dedicated.

MAY 8 Bodies of Capt. Thomas and Lt. Howe, killed in the Modoc War, arrive en route to the East.

MAY 9 Grand Chapter, Order of the Eastern Star, organized.

MAY 23 Postal cards sold for the first time in this city.

MAY 28 Chinese Six Companies telegraph to Hong Kong to have emigration to this port stopped.

JUNE 2 Ground broken for world's first cable street railroad on Clay Street.

JUNE 24 California Savings & Loan Society incorporated.

JUNE 29 St. Dominic's Church, Bush and Steiner streets, dedicated.

JULY 4 Aquarium in Woodward's Gardens opens.

JULY 16 Baby show at Pacific Hall.

AUG. 2 Trial run of Andrew Hallidie's cable car on Clay Street hill between Kearny and Jones, a grade of 307 feet.

NOV. 12 Bay District Race Track opens.

1874

JAN. 7 Conductors and drivers on the Bay View and Potrero Railroad strike, claiming to be overworked.

JAN. 8 Meeting of property holders to consider proposition to tunnel Russian Hill under Broadway, from Mason to Hyde.

JAN. 31 Shots exchanged between Gustavus de Young of the *Chronicle*, and F. R. Fitzgerald, of the *Sun*.

FEB. 21 Professor Allen and several citizens make ascensions in a balloon from

Woodward's Gardens.

MAR. 20 Capt. Barbiere, the aeronaut, arrives with the French Mail balloon, *Le Secours*.

MAR. 28 Capt. Barbiere makes his first ascension from Woodward's Gardens in the balloon *Le Secours*.

APR. 19 The balloon *America* ascends from Woodward's Gardens with several passengers, who in descending from an altitude of 3,000 feet, narrowly escape with their lives.

Alcatraz Island barracks destroyed by fire.

SEPT. 4 Brewer's Protective Association incorporated.

NOV. 5 The new U.S. Mint is formally transferred to Gen. O. H. La Grange, the superintendent, with befitting ceremony.

NOV. 29 King Kalakaua of Hawaii pays a visit.

1875

JAN. 7 Inauguration of the Northern Pacific Coast Railroad, from San Francisco to Tomales, via Sausalito.

FEB. 21 Immense meeting of Catholics to protest against the expulsion of Sisters of Charity from Mexico.

MAR. 2 Underwriters' Fire Patrol is organized.

MAR. 30 The painting "Elaine" by Toby Rosenthal goes on exhibit at the galleries of Snow & May.

MAY 24 Fire Insurance Patrol begins active duty.

MAY 28 Chinese purchase church north side of Washington and Stockton for mercantile and lodging use.

JUNE 5 Pacific Stock Exchange formally opens.

JUNE 19 Formal opening of the new U.S. Marine Hospital.

JULY 11 First parlor of the Native Sons of the Golden West organized.

SEPT. 9 Lotta's Fountain, located at Kearny and Market streets, dedicated; gift of Miss Lotta Crabtree to the people of

San Francisco.

SEPT. 24 James Lick presents lot on Market Street to California Academy of Sciences.

OCT. 5 Palace Hotel on Market Street opens.

OCT. 14 Grand opening of the Palace Hotel. General Phillip Sheridan is honored at a banquet lasting 3 1/2 hours.

DEC. 24 The Commercial Bank suspends business.

DEC. 26 Spanish American Church dedicated.

1876

JAN. 17 Wade's Opera House, Mission and 3rd streets, opens.

MAR. 1 A "bloody fight" occurs on Dupont Street when Chinese laborers fight the contractor to recover their deposits when two shoe factories backed out of their contract. This violent action came about when officials within the Chinese establishment could not resolve the dispute.

MAR. 6 Baldwin Hotel, Market, Ellis, and Powell streets, opens.

APR. 3 Chinese Six Companies petition Board of Supervisors for protection.

APR. 11 Senatorial Chinese Investigation Commission convened at San Francisco Benevolent and Protective Order of Elks organized.

APR. 25 Pedro II, Emperor of Brazil, arrives for visit.

MAY 2 District Judge S. B. McKee rules that ordinance imposing special tax upon Chinese laundries is unconstitutional.

JUNE 3 Ordinance providing for cutting off hair of county jail prisoners enforced by cutting off queue of Chinese convict.

JULY 4 San Francisco's first public exhibition of electric light, from roof of St. Ignatius College, Market Street between Fourth and Fifth, by Father Joseph M. Neri, S.J.

SEPT. 2 Society for the Prevention of Cruelty to Children incorporated.

Sept. 4 The first California Council of the Sovereigns of Industry established.

Sept. 5 Southern Pacific line connecting Los Angeles and San Francisco completed.

Oct. 21 Charles de Young assaulted by John Duane.

Oct. 31 Fire at the Chinese Theater on Jackson Street kills 19 people.

Nov. Diphtheria epidemic in San Francisco in the closing days of month.

Dec. 11 First asphalt paving laid in city.

1877

Apr. 17 Ariel Rowing Club organized.

June 27 The Sutter Street Railway converts from horsecar to cable operation on Sutter from Market to Larkin.

July 5 Anti-coolie convention assembled.

July 23 An estimated 8,000 people gather at open-air mass meeting called in support of the Eastern Railroad strikers.

July 24 Anti-Chinese sentiment results in first of San Francisco's "sandlot riots."

July 25 James d'Arcy speaks to jobless workers at Fifth and Mission streets.

July 25 Fire breaks out at The Pacific Mail steamship docks during anti-Chinese demonstration.

July 29 Baptist Church, Eddy near Jones, dedicated.

Aug. 3 Attempts made to burn the residence of William T. Coleman.

Sept. 16 Denis Kearney holds his first sandlots meeting.

Sept. 18 Clement Grammar School opens, named for Joseph Clement.

Sept. 24 John W. Ames appointed U.S. Surveyor General.

Oct. 5 Denis Kearney organizes his sandlot party, called the "Workingmen's Party of California."

Nov. 12 Fidelity Bank closes its doors.

1878

Jan. 1 Transportation fares are set at five cents by the State Legislature.

Jan. 3 Approximately 500 unemployed

men march to City Hall and demand that the mayor give them work.

Jan. 14 Baby contest in Platt's Hall.

Jan. 21 First state convention of the Workingmen's Party of California begins.

Mar. 26 Hastings College of Law founded by S. Clinton Hastings.

Apr. 10 Sutro Railroad opens.

Apr. 10 First day of service on the California Street Cable Railroad from Kearny to Fillmore.

Apr. 14 Convent of St. Rose dedicated.

Apr. 29 Judge Lorenzo Sawyer, of the U.S. District Court, holds that Chinese are not eligible for citizenship.

May 4 Phonograph exhibited at the Grand Opera House for first time.

June 1 San Francisco's first telephone book issued by the American Speaking Telephone Company of San Francisco and Butchertown.

July Korbel brothers' *Wasp* magazine first use of full-color cartoons.

July 1 Principal municipal offices moved into new City Hall at McAllister and Larkin.

July 8 Construction starts on the new St. Ignatius Church, Van Ness and Hayes Street.

July 26 Chen Lan Pan, Chinese Ambassador, arrives for visit.

Aug. 8 Hastings Law College inaugurated.

Sept. 12 General John C. Fremont, newly appointed Governor of Arizona, arrives for visit.

Sept. 22 Independent Order of B'nai B'rith lays cornerstone of new building on Eddy St.

Oct. 20 Cornerstone of the new St. Ignatius Church on Van Ness Ave. laid.

Nov. 10 Baseball championship won by the Athletics.

1879

Henry George writes *Progress and Poverty* in Isadore Choynski's bookstore, 34 Geary Street; Samuel Throckmorton introduces eastern striped bass into bay.

Jan. 25 Seawall between Montgomery and Sansome to Battery begun.

FEB. 10 First electric arc light used in California Theater.

FEB. 18 Ferryboats *Alameda* and *El Capitan* collide in dense fog on the bay.

MAY 24 First regatta of the Pacific Amateur Rowing Association off Long Bridge.

JUNE 3 State convention of the Workingmen's Party of California meets to nominate candidates for state, legislative, and congressional offices.

JUNE 7 Public Library opened in rented quarters on Bush Street between Kearny and Dupont.

JULY 8 Steam yacht *Jeanette* leaves on Arctic exploration voyage.

JULY 13 Dedication of new B'nai B'rith building.

AUG. 23 Charles de Young shoots and seriously wounds Rev. Isaac S. Kalloch.

OCT. 6 Golden Gate Kindergarten Association organized.

DEC. 8 Announcement made that the Atchison, Topeka and Santa Fe Company had secured the franchise of the Atlantic and Pacific for a railroad to the Pacific, on the 35th parallel.

DEC. 31 Judgment of the State Supreme Court in favor of the Trustees of the Lick Estate, settling the litigation arising from the claim of John H. Lick.

1880

JAN. 1 The New State Constitution of California goes into full effect.

JAN. 8 Water Commissioners of San Francisco pass resolution to buy Lake Merced for $1,500,000. Their act afterwards declared void by the Supreme Court; Governor George C. Perkins takes office.

JAN. 8 Emperor Norton dies.

FEB. 1 St. Ignatius Church dedicated.

FEB. 7 Crowd of 1,000 men gather on the sandlots and listen to speech by Thomas Allen.

FEB. 15 Geary Street Railroad opened.

FEB. 16 1,200 Chinese discharged by wool and jute factories in San Francisco and Oakland.

FEB. 24 Police force of San Francisco increased from 250 to 400 men; Atlantic and Pacific Railroad Company solicits terminal grounds in San Francisco.

FEB. 27 Daily parades of communists in San Francisco ceased, orderly citizens having given notice that the abuses could no longer be tolerated.

MAR. 5 The Citizens Protective Union of San Francisco organized to protect the city against communistic violence; Hurricane in the northern part of California; more destruction at Napa and Willows than elsewhere.

MAR. 11 Denis Kearney arrested on charge of using incendiary language.

MAR. 15 Local branches of the Workingmen's Party hold convention and nominate 15 freeholders for places on Board which is to draft a new city charter.

MAR. 17 Ferdinand de Lesseps, French engineer who built Suez Canal, visits.

MAR. 27 Seawall from Battery between Front and Davis begun.

APR. 17 Superior Court sustains judgment of Police Court, sentencing Denis Kearney to the House of Correction for six months.

APR. 23 Charles de Young shot and killed by Isaac Milton Kalloch, son of mayor.

MAY 8 The Narrow Gauge Railroad to Santa Cruz opened to traffic.

MAY 11 Land riot near Hanford, Tulare county. Seven persons killed.

MAY 17 H. S. Foote dies near Nashville, Tennessee.

MAY 18 Agency of the Rothschilds in San Francisco closed. At California State Convention majority of members expresses preference for Thurman.

MAY 23 Railroad accident near Santa Cruz; 14 killed and 40 wounded.

MAY 27 Paul Morrill, Surveyor of the Port, dies.

MAY 28 State Supreme Court, wrongfully converting a writ of habeas corpus into a

writ of error, releases Denis Kearney, the communist, from the House of Correction.
JUNE 1 Grand Hotel in San Francisco closes and later used as a branch of the Palace Hotel.
JUNE 15 E. L. Sullivan confirmed as Collector of San Francisco, succeeding T. B. Shannon.
JUNE 18 John A. Sutter dies in Washington.
JUNE 23 McClure Charter for San Francisco declared unconstitutional by the State Supreme Court.
JULY 19 Public Library opens to book borrowers.
AUG. 12 Seawall completed between Front and Davis on Battery.
SEPT. 4 Seamen's Protective Union formed.
SEPT. 9 President Rutherford B. Hayes visits.

1881
JAN. 10 New 75-foot flagstaff placed over Point Lobos Signal Station.
MAR. 2 Security Savings Bank incorporated.
APR. 8 Seawall completed between Montgomery and Sansome to Battery.
AUG. 1 U.S. Quarantine Station authorized for Angel Island.
SEPT. 1 Second annual convention of Woman's Temperance Union held at Young Men's Christian Association Hall.

1882
MAR. 28 Oscar Wilde visits.
APR. 12 California Safe Deposit & Trust Co. of San Francisco incorporated.
APR. 24 Trades Assembly State Convention of labor and anti-Chinese organizations meet.
MAY 9 Telegraph Hill Railroad Company organized.
JULY 4 Telegraph Hill Observatory opens.
SEPT. 1 Carpenters demand and obtain the 8-hour day for Saturday only.
NOV. 25 Fort Point renamed Fort Winfield Scott.

1883
"Black Bart" arrested; highwayman revealed as small, gray-haired bon vivant, Charles Bolton, well-known in town.
JAN. 5 Golden Gate Park Conservatory damaged by fire.
APR. 3 Palace Hotel suffers a gas explosion with casualties.
JUNE 18 Representatives of the carpenters, painters, metal roofers, bricklayers, and stair-builders meet to form Confederation of Building Trades.
AUG. 24 Laying of the cornerstone of the Garfield monument in Golden Gate Park.
SEPT. 5 Fourth annual convention of the Woman's Temperance Union held at the Y.M.C.A. Hall.
OCT. 29 Merchants' and Manufacturers' Association organized.

1884
FEB. 20 Seawall begun between Front and Davis to Drumm.
MAR. 5 First National Gold Bank of San Francisco drops the word "gold" from its title and becomes the First National Bank.
JUNE 3 Bear cub found at Pacific and Baker streets turned over to Cooper Medical College.
JUNE 12 Ocean Beach Pavilion at the terminus of the Park & Ocean Railroad opens.
SEPT. 2 Drygoods Men's Association of San Francisco organized.
OCT. 6 Golden Gate Kindergarten Association incorporated.
OCT. 19 D. F. Riehl swims from the cave on the north of the Cliff House to the central one of the Seal Rocks and back.
NOV. 27 Central Park at Market and Eighth streets opens to the public.
DEC. 18 Moulder School at the corner of Page and Gough streets dedicated.
DEC. 19 Cleveland School on Harrison between 10th and 11th streets dedicated.

1885

JAN. 6 Seawall from Drumm to Pacific begun.

FEB. 25 First Pacific Coast broadsword contest takes place on Telegraph Hill.

MAR. 13 Seawall between Front and Davis to Drumm completed.

SEPT. 5 Sutro Heights Park opened.

NOV. 13 William Sharon dies; funeral at Palace Hotel.

1886

FEB. 11 Members of the plasterers', plumbers' and gas fitters', and painters' unions, and the Laborers' Protective Benevolent Association (hodcarriers) meet and form a Building Trades Council.

APR. 3 Seawall from Drumm to Pacific completed.

MAY 11 An estimated 10,000 union members march in the largest workers' parade the city has witnessed.

AUG. 31 Crocker-Woolworth National Bank organized.

NOV. 27 California's first Arbor Day, promoted by Joaquin Miller, celebrated with ceremonies on Yerba Buena Island; Adolph Sutro plants first tree.

1887

JAN. 16 Schooner *Parallel*, carrying a cargo of powder, blows up below the Cliff House, badly damaging it.

JAN. 30 Thomas S. Baldwin makes record-breaking parachute jump from a balloon.

FEB. 5 Snow covers San Francisco.

FEB. 23 Congress grants Seal Rocks to the City and County of San Francisco.

APR. 20 Hawaiian Queen Lilioukalani visits.

MAY 12 Seawall from Pacific to Clay begun.

MAY 16 First appearance of Sarah Bernhardt in San Francisco at Baldwin Theater.

1888

E. L. Thayer, a newspaperman, publishes "Casey At the Bat."

FEB. 28 Explosion of ferry in San Pablo Bay.

MAR. 28 First day of service of Ferries & Cliff House Railway cable service on Powell Street.

JULY 2 Market Street cable road known as the Fairmont Line, via Market and Castro, opens.

AUG. 2 Incandescent lamps used for first time at the Bijou Theater, 726 Market Street.

1889

Scott and Dickie's Union Iron Works launch "new navy" ships, to include USS *Oregon* and USS *Olympia*, later famous in Spanish-American War.

FEB. 10 First Unitarian Church, at the corner of Gough and Franklin streets, dedicated.

MAR.17 Olivet Congregational Church, 17th and Noe streets, dedicated.

MAY 31 Seawall from Pacific to Clay completed.

NOV. 21 Mutual Savings Bank of San Francisco incorporated.

NOV. 23 The first jukebox was installed in the Palais Royale Saloon. Mr. Louis Glass fitted a coin slot on a wax cylinder Edison machine and provided four listening tubes for public use.

1890

Comstock silver mines close.

MAY 31 Butchertown destroyed by fire.

SEPT. 22 Construction on seawall at foot of Powell Street begun.

NOV. 27 Police Department's first signal box goes into operation.

1891

W. R. Hearst's "yellow journalism" (cartoons, contests, features, topflight reporting) causes *Alta California* to close;

Stanford University chartered.

JAN. 30 King Kalakaua of Hawaii visits.

FEB. 9 First shipment of asparagus from Sacramento arrives.

MAR. 1 Donohoe-Kelly Banking Company incorporated.

APR. 25 President Benjamin Harrison visits.

AUG. 20 The Wallace Grand Jury sworn in.

OCT. 8 Post Office site, 7th and Mission streets, selected.

DEC. 5 Salvation Army organized in San Francisco.

DEC. 10 Sequoia Chapter, D.A.R. organized.

1892

John Muir founds Sierra Club and becomes lifetime president. Isadora Duncan, 14, teaches dance. James J. Corbett dethrones John L. Sullivan in 21 rounds, New Orleans. First "Big Game," Haight Street field, Stanford 14, Cal 10.

APR. 21 First buffalo born in Golden Gate Park.

MAY 1 U.S. Quarantine Station opens on Angel Island.

DEC. 1 Army post at Alcatraz Island designated "saluting station" to return salutes of foreign vessels of war.

DEC. 1 The Japanese Baptist Church opens a night school.

1893

JAN. 18 Columbus Savings & Loan Society incorporated.

JAN. 23 Site of Fort Miley awarded to U.S. Army under condemnation proceedings.

MAY 22 Seawall from Powell to Taylor streets completed.

JULY 8 Mayor Ellert appoints Midwinter Fair Finance Committee.

AUG. 24 Groundbreaking for Midwinter Fair in Golden Gate Park.

1894

Bernard Maybeck teaches architecture at U.C.

JAN. 27 Midwinter Fair in Golden Gate Park opens.

JULY 4 Midwinter Fair closes.

DEC. 24 Cliff House, owned by Adolph Sutro, destroyed by fire.

1895

JAN. 4 Supervisors instruct Mayor to sell all contents of City Hall, Kearny, between Merchant and Washington streets; move to New City Hall.

JULY 1 Alcatraz Island designated as U.S. Disciplinary Barracks.

NOV. 2 The Chutes, Haight Street between Clayton and Cole, opens. M. H. de Young Museum opens in Midwinter Exposition building. Gelett Burgess writes "Purple Cow" jingle for first issue of his *Lark*.

1896

MAR. 14 Sutro Baths opens.

APR. 1 Building Trades Council proclaims that after this date no union member will work on jobs with men without union working cards.

MAY 27 Bay District Race Track closes.

JUNE 28 Corbett-Sharkey fight.

JULY 9 Harbor Commissioners approve use of Colusa sandstone in the construction of the new Union Ferry Depot (Ferry Building).

AUG. 30 Postal Station D moves into the new temporary post office building at the foot of Market Street.

OCT. 19 Trees planted by Daughters of the American Revolution in Golden Gate Park.

NOV. 23 The formal opening of the Velodrome, Baker at Fell streets, marks a new era in the history of athletic sport in San Francisco. It will provide a place for the holding of cycle shows, horse shows, poultry, and dog shows, football and athletic games of every description.

1897

JULY 8 The Harbor Hospital formally opened.

1898

USS *Oregon*'s 67 days around Cape Horn to join fleet off Cuba points up need for a Panama Canal.

JAN. 1 Lightship replaces whistling buoy at entrance to bay.

APR. 12 Army transfers Yerba Buena Island to Navy, retaining small plot as base port for minelayers.

MAY 3 Camp Merriman established in Presidio.

MAY 17 Camp Merritt established in Presidio.

MAY 23 First Philippine Expeditionary Troops sail from San Francisco.

MAY 25 The First California Regiment, Oregon Volunteers, and the 14th U.S. Infantry leave San Francisco for the Philippines.

MAY 26 San Francisco electorate approves new city charter, authorizing municipal acquisition and ownership of public utilities (put into effect Jan. 1, 1900).

JUNE 16 Naval authorities request the time ball atop the Ferry Building flagstaff be painted black, as the gold-painted ball cannot be seen.

JULY 13 Ferry Building opens.

AUG. 8 Adolph Sutro dies.

NOV. 23 Baldwin Hotel and Theater destroyed by fire.

1899

FEB. 18 San Francisco named as one of two ports for dispatch of Army transports.

APR. 16 Riot of 1,000 soldiers at the Presidio, 300 arrested.

JULY 1 New City Hall turned over to City after 29 years of construction.

AUG. 23 Wireless telegraph message sent from the San Francisco lightship to a station in the Cliff House restaurant building: first ship-to-shore wireless transmission to be received in the United States.

AUG. 24 First regiment, California Volunteers, returns from the Philippines.

OCT. 17 Sutro Railroad sold to Robert F. Morrow for $215,000.

NOV. 15 Bush Street Theater (formerly the Alhambra) burns.

1900

3,000 acres of bay flats filled since 1850; The Japanese Association of America founded to fight racial discrimination.

JAN. 8 Creation of City flag requested by Mayor Phelan of Board of Supervisors.

JAN. 8 "New" City Charter of 1898 takes effect.

MAR. Bubonic Plague hits San Francisco.

APR. 4 All Army installations on Angel Island redesignated Fort McDowell.

APR. 14 Veterans' Hospital established at Fort Miley.

APR. 24 Andrew Hallidie, cable car builder, dies.

APR. 30 Shag Rock in bay blown up.

SEPT. 19 Ringling Bros. Circus makes its first appearance in San Francisco at 16th and Folsom streets.

1901

Frank Norris publishes *The Octopus*, a novel damning the Southern Pacific Railroad.

JAN. 1 Department stores observe 6 p.m. closing every weekday except Saturday.

FEB. 15 Congress passes the Right of Way Act freeing San Francisco to erect a reservoir (Hetch Hetchy) if the Federal Government would grant land for that use.

FEB. 22 *The City of Rio de Janeiro* sinks outside the Golden Gate.

MAR. 31 The Southern Pacific Coast Line from San Francisco to Los Angeles opens.

APR. 19 United Railroads employees strike.

MAY 1 Recently formed Union of Cooks and Waiters calls industry-wide restaurant strike.

MAY 12 President William McKinley visits.

MAY 20 International Association of Machinists call strike.

JULY 30 Waterfront strike called.

AUG. 1 Burials within city limits prohibited.

AUG. 15 Arch Rock in the bay blown up with 30 tons of nitrogelatin.

Nov. 2 Captive balloon bursts its bonds in the block bounded by Market, Eleventh, Mission, and Twelfth Streets. It lands near Pescadero.

1902

Francis McCarty talks by wireless telephone across Stow Lake, Golden Gate Park.

JAN. 6 Derrick crashes down upon the sidewalk from the 12th story of the new Mutual Savings Bank building under construction at Geary and Market streets.

JAN. 8 Mayor Eugene Schmitz assumes office.

JAN. 28 Lumber schooner, *Mary E. Russ*, runs aground off Baker's Beach.

FEB. 10 Board of Supervisors votes down ordinance permitting racing at the Ingleside Track.

FEB. 20 Heavy waves break over Seal Rocks and damage Sutro Baths.

FEB. 22 Giant elk shot in Golden Gate Park Paddock, on orders of Park Commissioners, for presentation to San Francisco Lodge No. 2, B.P.O.E.

MAY 15 Park Emergency Hospital facing Stanyan Street opens.

JUNE 17 Police begin 8-hour work day. Chinese doctor, using the 14th amendment, sues San Francisco for admission of his children to public schools.

JULY 31 First submarine built on Pacific Coast launched today at Union Iron Works.

SEPT. Republic Theater opens.

Nov. 18 Injunction issued by Judge Carroll Cook against Gray Brothers to stop further blasting or excavation of Telegraph Hill.

Nov. 27 First religious service held in new First Presbyterian Church at Jackson and Fillmore streets.

1903

Father Richard Bell radios message from Santa Clara to San Francisco; first in State.

JAN. 6 French American Bank incorporated.

JAN. 29 Central Trust Company of California incorporated.

FEB. 7 Mission Bank, first bank in the Mission District, incorporated with James Rolph as president.

MAR. 3 Golden State Bank incorporated.

MAR. 4 Bay Counties Bank, Central Exchange Bank, Seal Rocks Bank, and United Bank & Trust Company incorporated.

MAR. 5 Standard Bank, Federal Savings Bank, Oriental Bank, State Savings & Commercial Bank, and Japanese Bank incorporated.

MAY 14 President Theodore Roosevelt visits.

JUNE 7 Republic Theater burns down.

JUNE 29 Keys to the convenience station beneath the sidewalk on the east side of Union Square presented to the city by the Merchants' Association.

JULY 4 The Pacific cable from San Francisco, by way of Hawaii and Guam to the Philippines, opened as President Theodore Roosevelt first sends a message to the Philippines, and then a message around the world in 12 minutes.

JULY 25 Castle atop Telegraph Hill destroyed by fire.

AUG. 14 Jim Jeffries defeats Jim Corbett in fight.

AUG. 18 Dirigible of Dr. August Greth makes its first flight in San Francisco.

AUG. 31 A Winton automobile completes a 63-day journey from San Francisco to New York City; first time an automobile has crossed the continent under its own power.

OCT. 26 The *Yerba Buena* is the first Key System ferry to cross bay.

Nov. 23 Tivoli Opera House closes.

DEC. 30 Seawall, foot of King to south of Berry, begun.

1904
JUNE 23 Several hundred electrical linemen strike against the Pacific States Telephone & Telegraph Company.
SEPT. 4 Odd Fellows' Conclave opens.
OCT. 17 Bank of Italy (now Bank of America) founded.
DEC. End of first bubonic plague epidemic.

1905
MAR. 18 Banquet held at St. Francis Hotel to celebrate the end of the bubonic plague.
APR. 27 Seawall, foot of King to south of Berry, completed.
MAY 7 Delegates from 67 organizations form the Asiatic Exclusion League, meet in San Francisco.
JULY 8 Secretary of War allots land on Angel Island to Dept. of Commerce and Labor for Immigration Detention Station.
AUG. Three sanitary flushing device carts are tested in city streets for cleaning purposes.
SEPT. 27 Burnham Plan for city beautification submitted to Board of Supervisors.

1906
APR. 18 Earthquake starts fire which destroys a large part of San Francisco.
APR. 19 176 prisoners moved from city jail to Alcatraz.
APR. 20 At the foot of Van Ness Avenue, 16 enlisted men and two officers from the USS *Chicago* supervise the rescue of 20,000 refugees fleeing the Great Fire. It is the largest evacuation by sea in history, and second only to the evacuation of Dunkirk in World War II.
Dr. F. Omori and Prof. T. Nakamura of the Imperial University of Tokyo arrive in San Francisco to investigate the earthquake and are attacked due to strong anti-Japanese feelings.
MAY 19 Governor Pardee asks sub-

committee of the Mayor's Committee on Reconstruction of San Francisco to write proposed legislation for special Call of the Legislature to assist San Francisco following the earthquake. Subcommittee members include Tirey Ford of United Railroads and "Boss" Ruef. Subcommittee writes Burnt Records Act, and the enabling legislation to allow the City and County of Los Angeles to acquire Owens Valley water for protection against major fires such as those that had just destroyed San Francisco.
JULY 30 United Railroads employees strike for higher wages and the 8-hour day.
AUG. 3 Stockholders of the Mission Bank organize the Mission Savings Bank.
AUG. 26 Strike of carmen.
OCT. 26 President Theodore Roosevelt sends Secretary of Commerce and Labor to San Francisco to ascertain how the rights of the Japanese could be protected.
NOV. 3 Auditorium Skating Palace, corner Fillmore and Page streets, opens.
NOV. 15 Mayor Schmitz and "Boss" Abe Ruef indicted by the Oliver Grand Jury for bribery and extortion following the "French Restaurant" scandal.
NOV. 17 The little Palace Hotel opens on Leavenworth and Post streets.
Japanese children segregated in schools; rescinded by pressure from President Theodore Roosevelt.

1907
A. P. Giannini introduces branch banking for his Bank of Italy.
Nationwide business panic; nine San Francisco banks closed between 1907 and 1909.
JAN. 17 Ruef supporters in the State Legislature introduce a Change of Venue bill to allow defendants to change the location of a trial should they be unable to get a fair hearing. Bill introduced at the specific request of Abe Ruef to derail graft trials in San Francisco.
MAR. 8 Abe Ruef disappears and is

ordered arrested. William J. Biggy is appointed an elisor of the court and he and detective William J. Burns arrest Ruef at a roadhouse in the San Francisco suburbs. Biggy holds Ruef prisoner at the St. Francis Hotel because the Chief of Police has also been indicted.

MAR. 13 The school segregation order against Japanese students rescinded by the school board.

MAR. 18 Each member of the San Francisco Board of Supervisors confesses to a grand jury that they had taken bribes from United Railroads, Pacific States Telephone Company and PG&E. All the supervisors later resign from office.

MAR. 21 Union State Bank incorporated.

APR. 1 Laundry workers strike for wage increases and the 8-hour day.

APR. 18 Fairmont Hotel reopens.

APR. 24 Denis Kearney dies at his home in Alameda.

MAY 1 Bay Area metal trades union begin their first general strike since 1901.

MAY 3 Approximately 500 women and girls of the Telephone Operators' Union begin their strike.

MAY 5 1,500 members of the Carmen's Union vote to strike for the 8-hour day.

MAY 11 The Bank of San Francisco incorporated.

MAY 15 Abe Ruef pleads guilty to extortion charge.

MAY 27 Bubonic plague reappears in San Francisco.

JUNE 13 Seawall between Brannan and Townsend to foot of King begun.

JUNE 13 Mayor Eugene E. Schmitz is convicted of bribery in the "French Restaurant" scandal. The mayor's position became immediately vacant upon conviction of Schmitz. James L. Gallagher named acting Mayor by the Board of Supervisors. Schmitz's conviction was later overturned by an appeals court.

JUNE 18 Imperial Bank incorporated.

JUNE 21 Telegraph operators in San Francisco and Oakland go on strike, paralyzing Western Union and Postal Telegraph service.

JULY 4 Pioneer Park atop Telegraph Hill has a flag-raising.

JULY 9 Mayor Eugene Schmitz sentenced to five years in San Quentin for corruption in office; Supervisor Charles Boxton is elected Mayor of San Francisco by the Board of Supervisors. He immediately leaves his swearing-in ceremony to appear before the Grand Jury. There, he confesses to his role in the "Telephone Franchise" scandal, saying, "I took bribes." He resigns one week later.

JULY 16 Edward Robeson Taylor replaces the disgraced Mayor Charles Boxton.

JULY 22 Board of Supervisors reinstates application for Hetch Hetchy project.

AUG. 21 First Federal Trust Company incorporated.

AUG. 26 Harry Houdini escapes from chains underwater at Aquatic Park in 57 seconds.

SEPT. 1 Temple Emanu-El rededicated.

SEPT. 6 Dr. Rupert Blue ordered by Federal Government to take charge of San Francisco's plague campaign.

SEPT. 7 Sutro's ornate Cliff House destroyed by fire.

SEPT. 27 Fremont Older, editor of the *Evening Bulletin*, kidnapped.

OCT. 1 Canton Bank incorporated.

OCT. 14 Demonstration against Japanese residents.

OCT. 30 California Safe Deposit & Trust Co., with four branches, forced into liquidation by bank commissioners.

NOV. 3 Banca Popolare Operaia Italiana incorporated.

DEC. 18 Citizens State Bank forced into liquidation by bank commissioners; H.C. (Bud) Fisher's "A. Mutt," first six-day comic strip in the *Chronicle*.

1908

JAN. 30 Last case of bubonic plague reported.

FEB. 21 The Market Street Bank forced into liquidation by bank commissioners.

MAR. 21 Commission men hold Fruit Banquet in Front Street to celebrate their sanitary campaign.

MAR. 24 The Thomas Flyer arrives in San Francisco, participating in the New York-to-Paris auto race.

APR. 29 Alameda home of San Francisco Supervisor James L. Gallagher dynamited.

MAY 6 Swedish-American Bank incorporated.

MAY 7 Great White Fleet arrives in bay.

MAY 23 C. A. Morrell's 450-foot, six-engine dirigible explodes over San Francisco Bay; 16 passengers fall from the airship but are not killed.

JUNE 4 Seawall between Brannan and Townsend to foot of King completed.

JULY 7 The Great White Fleet weighs anchor and departs.

AUG. 27 The Imperial Bank (Japanese) forced into liquidation by bank commissioners.

SEPT. 10 The Argonaut Hotel at 44 Fourth Street opens.

OCT. 23 Last infected rat of the bubonic plague caught.

NOV. "It is true that within the last year there has been a feeling in this community that the criminal law had broken down, and that we could not, under law, punish the offenders; and that the courts, the highest courts, abetted and aided criminals by the rankest interpretations, technical interpretations of the statutes. They refused to lean on the side of order and justice, and they have brought disgrace upon the judiciary of California, all over the world." James D. Phelan, former Mayor.

NOV. 7 Tag Day in San Francisco; 500,000 dimes wanted to benefit Children's Hospital.

NOV. 13 Francis J. Heney shot in court by Morris Haas.

"San Francisco has had many afflictions. She now has this additional affliction of the assassination of one who stood for the people's rights; of one who was fearlessly engaged in the important and priceless business of civic regeneration, and who, while in the act of performing the greatest of all duties as a citizen, (Francis J. Heney) was laid low by the bullets of an assassin." Edward Robeson Taylor, Mayor.

DEC. 11 Abe Ruef sentenced to 14 years in jail.

1909

APR. 9 Anglo-California Trust Company incorporated.

MAY 22 *David Scannell*, city's first fireboat, launched.

MAY 23 Yerba Buena School, Filbert near Fillmore street, dedicated.

JUNE 5 John Jules Jusserand, French Ambassador to Washington, presents a gold medal to San Francisco, commemorative of her rise from the ashes and ruins of the earthquake of 1906.

JUNE 15 Fireboat *Dennis T. Sullivan* launched.

JUNE 16 The sloop *Gjoa* presented to the City of San Francisco at ceremonies at the foot of Howard Street, Pier 1.

JUNE 17 Excavation work for Hall of Justice completed.

JULY 1 Golden Gate Bank closes.

JULY 5 *Gjoa* towed through the Golden Gate and beached south of Cliff House.

JULY 6 Excavation for San Francisco General Hospital completed.

JULY 17 State Savings, Commercial Bank of San Francisco, and Union State Bank of San Francisco close.

AUG. 18 Pacific Aero Club of San Francisco holds its first exhibition at Dreamland Rink.

AUG. 29 Seawall begun at point between Bryant and Brannan to foot of Main.

SEPT. 9 First annual parade of the San Francisco Work Horse Association.

OCT. 18 Japanese American Bank of San Francisco closes.

OCT. 19 Portola Festival opens to celebrate

San Francisco's recovery from the earthquake and fire.

DEC. 6 Seawall foot of Mission
Street begun.

DEC. 15 The new Palace Hotel holds a pre-
view banquet in the Great Court with 765
persons attending.

DEC. 16 Palace Hotel officially reopens.

1910

Angel Island opens the West Coast
immigration station.

JAN. 12 Cornerstone of American Music
Hall Theater, Ellis Street between Stockton
and Powell, laid.

JAN. 14 The Chutes, Fillmore and Eddy,
opens.

MAR. 10 Seawall, foot of Mission,
completed.

MAR. 22 Panama-Pacific International
Exposition Company incorporated.

MAR. 29 Seawall begun at foot of Harrison
to between Bryant and Brannan.

MAY 29–30 Aviation meet, Tanforan
Raceway.

AUG. 22 First load of passengers for the
Western Pacific was carried by the ferry
Telephone from the San Francisco Ferry
Building to the Oakland Terminal.

OCT. 9 Mount St. Joseph's Orphanage
destroyed by fire.

OCT. 31 The International Banking
Corporation purchases the Swedish-
American Bank of San Francisco.

DEC. 24 Luisa Tetrazzini sings to 250,000
at Lotta's Fountain. Progressive Party
organized.

1911

Turkey trot and bunny hug dances originated.

JAN. 5 San Francisco hosts its first
air meet.

JAN. 7 Hubert Latham pilots the French
monoplane *Antionetta* through the Golden
Gate at 2:45 p.m.

JAN. 18 Eugene Ely lands on deck of the
USS *Pennsylvania* in San Francisco Bay.

JAN. 31 Congress passes a resolution nam-
ing San Francisco the "Exposition
City" to celebrate the opening of the
Panama Canal.

FEB. 25 The International Banking
Corporation purchases the Bank of
Commerce of San Francisco.

FEB. 28 The City and County Bank
of San Francisco sold to the Western
Metropolis National Bank.

MAR. 7 Abe Ruef begins his 14-year sentence at San Quentin.

JULY 4 Hermon Lee Ensign Memorial
Fountain at Mission, Otis, and Duboce presented to city by National Humane Alliance
of New York.

SEPT. 7 Seawall completed between Bryant
and Brannan to foot of Main.

OCT. 13 President William Howard Taft
visits.

NOV. 23 Post Hospital at Presidio renamed
Letterman General Hospital in honor of
Major Jonathan Letterman.

DEC. 29 San Francisco Symphony
Orchestra formed; San Francisco inspects
and licenses prostitutes.

1912

JAN. 3 Southern Pacific Railroad Company
offers to carry the Liberty Bell across the
continent without expense to the 1915
Exposition.

JAN. 24 Bank of Daniel Meyer
incorporated.

FEB. 20 Police Dept. moves into the new
Hall of Justice.

MAR. 2 Poppies planted in the hills
surrounding Noe Valley.

MAR. 14 Fire breaks out in the Officers
Club in the Presidio; Engine 23, while
responding, overturns.

MAR. 28 Women vote for the first time in
San Francisco. Voters authorize a bond issue
at $800,000 for acquisition of Civic Center
land.

MAY 6 Bay View Police Station opens.

JUNE 15 Olympic Club's new Post Street

building opens.

DEC. 28 Mayor Rolph runs Street Car No. 1 up Geary Street to open Municipal Railway service.

1913

The California Alien Land Law is enacted. First anti-Japanese land law.

JAN. 1 Thousands take part in celebration of breaking ground for Machinery Hall at Harbor View.

JAN. 4 Seawall begun at foot of Folsom to foot of Harrison.

FEB. 22 Lowell High, Hayes and Masonic, dedicated.

MAR. 12 Tivoli Opera House opens.

APR. 5 Ground broken for new City Hall by Mayor Rolph.

JUNE John E. Raker introduces a bill that would confirm the Hetch Hetchy grant of land to San Francisco (HR 7207).

JUNE 3 Last trip of a horse-drawn streetcar, from the Ferry up to 8th Street, with Mayor Rolph at the brake.

JUNE 15 The first Loughead designed hydroplane, called Model G, is flown by Allan Loughead.

JUNE 26 North End Police Station completed.

AUG. 10 State Red Light Abatement Act becomes effective.

OCT. 22 Portola Festival begins.

OCT. 25 Cornerstone of the new City Hall laid.

OCT. 29 Three women appointed to the Police Dept. as Juvenile officers.

OCT. 31 Lincoln Highway officially dedicated.

DEC. 8 Construction begins on Palace of Fine Arts for 1915 Exposition.

DEC. 18 Dance held at Clement between 5th and 6th avenues to the music of the Muni Band.

DEC. 19 President Wilson approves the grant of Hetch Hetchy land to San Francisco.

1914

JAN. 6 Board of Supervisors passes ordinance providing for removal of all human remains in the cemeteries within the city.

JAN. 15 Travelers Aid organized.

FEB. 7 Steel work completed for the Exposition Auditorium.

FEB. 16 Silas Christofferson makes first airplane flight from San Francisco to Los Angeles.

FEB. 23 "Year Before Opening Celebration" is held on the Exposition site; 20,000 people attend.

FEB. 26 City Engineer O'Shaughnessy discusses plans for movable sidewalk on the Fillmore Street hill.

FEB. 28 Erection of the Exposition's Tower of Jewels begun.

MAY 12 Representatives from clearing houses in the 12th Federal Reserve District assemble in the rooms of the San Francisco Chamber of Commerce to discuss plans to establish the Federal Reserve Bank of San Francisco.

MAY 16 Ewing Field, off Masonic Ave., opens.

AUG. 15 The Van Ness Ave. line of the Municipal Railway system begins operation.

AUG. 29 First vessel, the steamship *Arizonan*, arrives via Panama Canal.

SEPT. 7 Potrero Ave. line of the Municipal Railroad system commences operation.

NOV. 1 Fort Mason tunnel completed, connecting the Belt Line Railroad with government transport docks.

NOV. 8 Richmond Branch Library dedicated.

NOV. 30 Ground broken for Twin Peaks Tunnel.

DEC. 11 Stockton Street Tunnel completed.

DEC. 28 Completion of the Stockton Street Tunnel celebrated.

DEC. 29 The Stockton Street line of the Municipal Railway system commences operation.

1915

JAN. 9 Masked ball celebrates dedication of the Exposition Auditorium (Civic Auditorium).

JAN. 25 First transcontinental conversation by phone; Alexander Graham Bell speaks from New York to Thomas Watson in San Francisco.

FEB. 20 Panama-Pacific International Exposition opens.

MAR. 6 The Vanderbilt Cup race run at P. P. I. E.

MAY 6 Seawall foot of Folsom to foot of Harrison completed.

AUG. 27 General Pershing's wife and three children die in Presidio home fire.

SEPT. 14 Dedication ceremonies at the western terminus of the Lincoln Highway in Lincoln Park.

SEPT. 20 Laying of the submarine cable across the Golden Gate begins.

SEPT. 26 Boulevard El Camino Del Mar opens.

DEC. 4 Panama-Pacific International Exposition closes.

DEC. 28 Dedication of City Hall by Mayor James Rolph.

1916

The Palace Hotel Company will construct a subway under Market Street. Entrances will be in the hotel lobby, on the sidewalk in front of the hotel and on the north side of Market Street at the Crocker building.

JAN. 1 The recently enacted law with regard to automobile number plates went into effect. It is ordered that the numbers be on white plates with a bear in the corner and the word "Cal" over it. The new numbers will be permanent, and not as formerly subject to annual change.

APR. The Nineteenth Avenue portion of the city boulevard system is completed and the new boulevard opened to traffic. There is now a direct route from Lincoln Way to Sloat Blvd.

APR. 18 Birthday celebration of the new San Francisco Exposition Auditorium, under the auspices of San Francisco Commercial Club.

APR. 29 Artists Ball held to raise funds to keep Palace of Fine Arts open another year.

JULY 10 The Law and Order Committee formed to bring industrial peace to the city.

JULY 22 Preparedness Day Parade and bombing.

SEPT. 22 Dedication of North American Hall, California Academy of Sciences, in Golden Gate Park.

OCT. 4 Market Street's "Path of Gold" lit for first time.

By only 4,000 California votes Woodrow Wilson is reelected President.

1917

FEB. 15 San Francisco Public Library building in the Civic Center dedicated.

APR. 8 Public dedication of the Municipal organ at Civic Auditorium.

MAY 18 San Franciscans are inducted into Army by passage of Selective Military Conscription Bill.

JUNE 26 Fort Funston named in honor of General Frederick Funston.

JULY 14 Celebration for the completion of Twin Peaks Tunnel held at the westerly portal.

AUG. 11 United Railroads employees strike against the open shop.

SEPT. 17 30,000 men called out to strike, closing shipyards, foundries, machine shops, etc.

NOV. 22 Carmen's Union votes to call off its strike.

DEC. 11 Katherine Stinson sets nonstop distance flight record of 610 miles by flying from San Diego to San Francisco in 9 hours, 10 minutes.

1918

FEB. 3 Streetcars begin to operate through Twin Peaks Tunnel.

MAR. 14 First seagoing concrete ship built by San Francisco Shipbuilding Company launched.

OCT. 26 Great flu epidemic.

DEC. 31 Ferry Building siren sounded for first time at 5 p.m.

1919

APR. 23 U.S. Army's 363rd Division known as "San Francisco's Own" returns to San Francisco from New York.

SEPT. 5 Bank of Montreal incorporated.

SEPT. 17 President Woodrow Wilson visits.

OCT. 14 Albert, King of the Belgians, visits.

NOV. 3 Crissy Field, Presidio of San Francisco airport, dedicated.

NOV. 30 James Lick Baths, at 10th and Howard, erected in 1889, closed.

DEC. 8–31 Army transcontinental group flight from New York to San Francisco and return; 10 planes complete the round-trip.

1920

APR. 20 Asia Banking Corporation incorporated.

MAY 5 Captive Army balloon sent up from Pier 32 to take aerial photographs of San Francisco and the waterfront; project sponsored by the San Francisco Chamber of Commerce, the U.S. Army, and the State Board of Harbor Commissioners.

MAY 19 Mass meeting held in the Civic Auditorium to open public fund drive for the War Memorial project.

JUNE 28 Democratic Convention begins at Civic Auditorium.

JULY 29 First transcontinental airmail flight from New York completed at San Francisco.

AUG. 1 Panama-Pacific International Exposition Corporation dissolved in Superior Court.

OCT. 26 Ocean Shore Railroad closes.

NOV. Citywide fund drive for the erection of the War Memorial buildings closed with $2,012,000 pledged. Regents of U.C. designated as Trustees for subscribers. The Alien Land Law of 1920 passed forbidding the Japanese Issei to buy land in the name of their American-born children, the Nisei.

DEC. 5 Police detectives Miles Jackson and Lester Dorman slain during an arrest.

1921

JAN. 2 De Young Museum, Golden Gate Park, opens.

JAN. 24 Asia Banking Corporation opens for business.

FEB. 22–23 Jack Knight and E. M. Allison, civilian mail pilots, fly mail from San Francisco to New York in 33 hours, 20 minutes.

JUNE 28 Joseph Strauss presents the first plan for the Golden Gate Bridge to City Engineer O'Shaughnessy.

JULY 4 Photos of Carpentier-Dempsey fight delivered by plane to San Francisco just 48 hours and 45 minutes after leaving Hoboken, New Jersey.

AUG. 8 Bank of Italy interests organize the Liberty Bank of San Francisco as a day-and-night bank on Market Street.

AUG. 19 Formal trust agreement entered into between Regents of U.C. and the group of private citizens designated as Trustees of the War Memorial.

DEC 3 Ferdinand Foch, Marshal of France, plants a sapling on the south side of the Palace of the Legion of Honor to memorialize his visit.

DEC. 31 Last fire horses leave the Fire Department's stables, and the stables are officially closed.

1922

APR. 15 The Poodle Dog Restaurant closes.

APR. 22 Radio Station KPO established.

NOV. 8 Municipal Popular Symphony Concerts begin.

DEC. 19 Excavation begun for the new Spring Valley Water Company building, Mason Street between Geary and Post.

1923

JAN. 31 Merchants National Bank of San Francisco purchased by the Sacramento -San Joaquin Bank.

JULY 29 President Warren Harding arrives.

AUG. 2 President Harding dies at the Palace Hotel.

SEPT. 17 San Francisco Fire Department responds to the Berkeley fire with four pumpers, two hose wagons, two chemical engines, and one fireboat.

SEPT. 26–OCT. 8 First season San Francisco Grand Opera, Exposition Auditorium (Civic Auditorium).

SEPT. 29 Steinhart Aquarium, Golden Gate Park, opens to the public.

DEC. 10 *The Illustrated Daily Herald* begins publication.

DEC. 30 Thousands of walnuts are cast up by waves near Fort Point, part of shipment condemned and thrown from a passing ship by Federal inspectors.

1924

APR. 15 The Huntington Apartments, Taylor and California streets, open.

JUNE 23 First "Dawn to Dusk" flight across continent, by Lt. Russell A. Maughan, successfully completed at Crissy Field.

JULY 2 First airmail plane, inaugurating the Transcontinental Air Mail Service from New York to San Francisco, lands at Crissy Field.

NOV. 11 Palace of Legion of Honor dedicated.

1925

JAN. 15 The opening of the new Southern Pacific ferry line between San Francisco and Richmond.

FEB. 22 Cornerstone of Temple Emanu-El laid, Lake and Arguello.

APR. 18 Father Peter Yorke dies.

APR. 30 Fleishhacker Playground opens.

MAY 2 Kezar Stadium in Golden Gate Park opens.

MAY 2 Embarcadero subway opens.

JULY 18 Harding Memorial Park opens.

SEPT. 6–12 Diamond Jubilee celebration (75th anniversary of California's admittance to the Union).

DEC. 26 First East-West football game played in Ewing Field to a crowd of 25,000.

1926

APR. 7 Golden Gate Ballroom, Eddy and Jones, opens.

APR. 15 Visitacion Valley branch of the San Francisco Boy's Club gymnasium dedicated.

JUNE 5 Ewing Field fire.

JULY 19 The Canton Bank closes.

1927

MAY 7 San Francisco Municipal Airport (Mills Field) dedicated.

SEPT. 17 Charles Lindbergh in San Francisco.

OCT. 4 The Model Airline between San Francisco and Los Angeles begins service.

1928

FEB. 6 The newspaper *The Telegraph Hill Alarm* publishes first issue.

APR. 14 Maddux Air Lines starts daily passenger service between Los Angeles and San Francisco.

MAY 26 Western Air Express starts daily passenger and express service between Los Angeles and San Francisco.

OCT. 21 Duboce (or Sunset) Tunnel opened.

NOV. 19 Egyptian Building of de Young Museum, Golden Gate Park, demolished by Symon Brothers Wrecking Co.

1929

JUNE 9 Seawall at Ocean Beach completed.

JULY 22 Lillie Hitchcock Coit dies at Dante Sanatorium.

AUG. 4 Police Side-Car Motorcycle Corps

officially presented to Mayor Rolph.

AUG. 15 Joseph Strauss named chief engineer of the Golden Gate Bridge.

AUG. 25 *Graf Zeppelin* airship arrives from Tokyo, Japan, sailing over San Francisco on its way to Los Angeles.

SEPT. 11 Mayor Rolph inaugurates city's new pedestrian traffic signal system.

OCT. 20 Bayshore Highway opened.

DEC. 4 Southside Playground renamed Father Crowley Playground.

DEC. 20 Mt. Davidson dedicated as a city park.

1930

Bay ferries carry 40 million passengers annually.

MAR. 3 Communist parade in downtown San Francisco.

MAR. 3 San Francisco Water Department takes over operation of system purchased from the Spring Valley Water Company.

AUG. 11 War Department establishes the minimum clear height of the future Golden Gate Bridge above mean high water at 210 feet at the piers, and 220 feet at the center of the main span.

AUG. 27 Final plans submitted for Golden Gate Bridge.

1931

FEB. 20 Congress grants the State of California the right to construct a bridge from Rincon Hill, San Francisco, to Yerba Buena Island, and then to Oakland.

FEB. 25 Celebration marks the completion of the Newark-San Lorenzo Pipe Line connection between the San Francisco Water System and that of the East Bay Municipal Utility District.

APR. 7 Seals Stadium opens.

MAY 30 Steamer *Harvard* runs aground in heavy fog at Point Arguello.

JUNE 3 Goat Island's old Spanish name

Yerba Buena ("good herb") is restored by the U.S. Geographic Board.

JUNE 17 First construction contracts for Golden Gate Bridge awarded.

NOV. 11 Cornerstones for Opera House and Veteran's Building laid.

DEC. 30 St. Ignatius Church fire, one fireman dies.

1932

JAN. 8 Ratification of present City Charter.

FEB. 10 James Lick Junior High accepted from builders by Board of Education.

MAR. 28 Golden Gate Park Police Station opens.

APR. 10 Anza Branch Library dedicated.

APR. 30 Market Street parade and gala inaugural ball in Civic Auditorium to celebrate the 200th anniversary of the birth of George Washington.

MAY 5 Police radio broadcasting begins from the Department's low-frequency station, KGPD.

JUNE 1 San Francisco Airport now under jurisdiction of the Public Utilities Commission.

JUNE 4 Dedication of Sigmund Stern Grove.

JUNE 19 First symphony concert in Stern Grove with G. Merola directing.

AUG. 22 Howard Street, from 13th to Army Street renamed Van Ness Ave., South, by resolution of the Board of Supervisors.

OCT. 15 Opera House dedicated with performance of *La Tosca*.

NOV. 8 President Herbert Hoover visits. Carlton Morse's "One Man's Family" radio soap opera, first broadcast on NBC in San Francisco; longest-running broadcast in history; ends in 1960.

1933

JAN. 5 Construction begun on Golden Gate Bridge with the digging of a pit for the Marin County anchorage.

FEB. 26 Ground-breaking ceremony at

Crissy Field for the Golden Gate Bridge.

MAR. The State (Emergency) Relief Administration of California begins operations.

APR. 27 Fremont Elementary School, McAllister near Baker, destroyed by fire.

OCT. 8 Coit Tower on Telegraph Hill dedicated.

OCT. 12 Alcatraz Island to become a Federal Prison.

DEC. 5 The 18th Amendment (prohibition) repealed.

1934

JAN. 1 U.S. officially takes over Alcatraz Island as a Federal Prison.

JAN. 10–11 Lt. Cmdr. Kneffler McGinnis leads six Consolidated flying boats on a flight from San Francisco to Pearl Harbor in 24 hours, 45 minutes, breaking three world records.

MAR. 24 Easter Cross on Mt. Davidson dedicated, lit for first time by President Roosevelt via telegraph.

MAY 9 Longshoremen strike.

MAY 25 General strike ties up city.

JUNE 30 Emperor Norton reburied in Woodlawn Cemetery by citizens of San Francisco.

JULY 1 New $850,000 jail in San Mateo County dedicated.

JULY 5 "Bloody Thursday" clash between police and strikers on waterfront; two die.

JULY 11 San Francisco relief increased from 5,100 to 15,000 persons.

JULY 12 United States Disciplinary Barracks abandoned at Alcatraz Island.

JULY 19 Longshoremen end strike.

OCT. 24 Water flows into Crystal Spring Reservoir for first time.

DEC. 14 Simson African Hall, California Academy of Sciences, opens.

1935

MAR. 14 The Folsom Street Line (36) becomes the first line in the city to use one-man trolley cars.

APR. 4 Wrecking crews begin demolishing the Odd Fellows' Cemetery Office Building, built in 1865.

APR. 16-17 Pan American Clipper flies from San Francisco to Honolulu in 18 hours, 39 minutes, for a test flight.

MAY 6 Pres. Franklin D. Roosevelt signs Executive Order No. 7034, which established the Works Progress Administration.

MAY 10 South Park is set aside by the Park Commission for "soap box speeches."

AUG. 2 First unreeling of a single wire strand across the Golden Gate closes Gate to ship traffic. First time in history Gate closed.

AUG. 6 Last SERA music program performed at Larkin Hall.

AUG. 22 Emergency Work Program (EWP) collapses.

OCT. 6 Trackless trolleys are put into service by the Market Street Railway.

OCT. 14–19 Century of Commerce celebration in Civic Auditorium.

NOV. Federal WPA Music Project begins.

NOV. 22–29 Pan American Airways starts transpacific air-mail service from San Francisco to Manila, stopping at Honolulu, Midway, Wake, and Guam.

1936

FEB. 10 Father Damien's body (famed leper priest) lies in state at St. Mary's Cathedral.

FEB. 11 Pumping begins to build Treasure Island.

FEB 29 Abe Ruef dies.

MAR. 4 George Bernard Shaw visits.

MAR. 31 Lurline Baths, Bush and Larkin streets, close.

APR. 18 The *Clipper* establishes regular passenger air service from San Francisco to Honolulu.

MAY 7 Four men atop the Golden Gate Bridge Marin Tower injured.

JUNE 30 Crissy Field abandoned as Army airport.

AUG. 21 Gov. Merriam turns earth at G.G.I.E. Fair site with a golden spade.

AUG. 23 George Washington High School dedicated.

OCT. 20 City leaders move to convert Fort Point into Museum.

OCT. 28 Cardinal Eugenio Pacelli (later Pope Pius XII) blesses the San Francisco-Oakland Bay Bridge.

OCT. 29 Waterfront strike begins.

NOV. 12 San Francisco and Oakland Bay Bridge Fiesta begins with the opening of the bridge to traffic.

NOV. 18 Main span of the Golden Gate Bridge joined.

1937

FEB. 4 Waterfront strike ends.

FEB. 17 10 men die when scaffolds fall from beneath Golden Gate Bridge.

MAR. 9 Adoption of Sect. 61.1 to the Charter by the people of San Francisco,creating a Public Welfare Dept. which shall exercise all of the functions exercised by the County Welfare Dept. and by the Citizens' Emergency Relief Committee.

APR. 3 James Rolph, Jr. and James D. Phelan bronze busts unveiled in City Hall.

MAY 27 Golden Gate Bridge dedicated.

MAY 27–JUNE 2 Golden Gate Bridge Fiesta, celebrating the opening of the world's longest single span.

JULY 1 Time ball atop the Fairmont Hotel discontinued.

AUG. 2 Furniture Mart on Market Street opens.

AUG. 5 World famous Cliff House, redecorated and refurbished, opens under ownership of George and Leo Whitney.

AUG. 26 Treasure Island pumping ends.

OCT. 17 Fishermen install La Madre del Lume Patrona di Porticello as their patron saint in ceremony at Fishermen's Wharf.

DEC. 29 Pan American begins Clipper service between San Francisco and Auckland, New Zealand, with Honolulu, Kingman Reef, and Samoa as stepping stones.

1938

JAN. 29 The President's Birthday Ball held in the Civic Auditorium for the Founding of the National Foundation for Infantile Paralysis.

FEB. 15 Frank Fuller, Jr. flies from San Francisco to Los Angeles in one hour, 7 minutes, 7 seconds.

MAY 25 Frank Fuller, Jr. flies from San Francisco to Seattle in two hours, 31 minutes, 41 seconds.

JUNE 1 Earl Ortman flies from San Francisco to San Diego in one hour, 48 minutes, one second.

JULY 5 *Chronicle* begins publishing Herb Caen column.

JULY 14 President Franklin Delano Roosevelt visits.

SEPT. 7 Mormon crickets invade all districts of San Francisco.

SEPT. 16 Spanish newspaper *Eco Hispaño* established.

OCT. 1 Horse "Blackie" swims the Golden Gate in 23.5 minutes.

NOV. 16 Cooks, Waiters and Waitresses Alliance, Local No. 31, passes resolution condemning Nazi attacks on Jewish and Catholic workers in Germany, Czechoslovakia and Austria, and urges President Roosevelt to withdraw the American ambassador to Germany in protest.

NOV. 23 1st International Goodwill bicycle race held in Golden Gate Park.

DEC. 21 Mayor Rossi hosts a Christmas party for poor children. The party is broadcast over radio station KSAN.

DEC. 28 Chamber of Commerce hosts Northern California Traveling Salesmen organization at Civic Auditorium to dispel the illusion that San Francisco is "a ghost town."

1939

The WPA is restructured and renamed the Works Projects Administration.

JAN. 7 Governor Olson pardons Tom Mooney.

JAN. 7 Governor Olson taken ill during mammoth barbecue at the State Fair Grounds during his inaugural festivities.

JAN. 22 Aquatic Park dedicated.

FEB. 14 Beginning of Fiesta Week.

FEB. 18 Golden Gate International Exposition opens on Treasure Island.

APR. 10 Dreamland Auditorium reopens under the name "Ice Palace" with a new Ice Follies show.

APR. 11 Department Store Employee's strike against Kress-Newberry Stores enters its eighth month.

APR. 14 Special shortwave program for Latin America is broadcast by KGEI from Treasure Island.

APR. 22 Musicians' Union will not allow non-member to demonstrate kazoos on the Gay Way at the World's Fair.

APR. 24 USS *Nevada* Day celebrated at Treasure Island.

APR. 27 Police Commission votes to allow cafes and nightclubs to remain open after 2 a.m., but liquor cannot be served and dancing and other forms of entertainment must also stop, according to Police Chief Quinn.

MAY 13 Southern Pacific Railroad Day is celebrated at Treasure Island.

MAY 17 Prince and Princess of Norway visit World's Fair.

MAY 17 Governor Olson speaks to mass union rally in support of propositions on the San Francisco ballot. A special election is scheduled for May 19.

MAY 20 Don Lee Cadillac Day celebrated at Treasure Island.

MAY 21 Beginning of Golden Forties Fiesta.

MAY 23 San Francisco Committee Against War Shipments to Japan urges unions to ask President Roosevelt to embargo all shipments of war materials to Japan.

MAY 27 British Empire Day celebrated at Treasure Island.

JUNE 4 Committee for Civic Progress heads conference at Knights of Columbus Hall.

JUNE 7 1894 Bell Tower in Golden Gate Park burns to the ground.

JUNE 9 Friends of the Abraham Lincoln Brigade hold meeting at Scottish Rite Auditorium.

JUNE 19 Supporters of Warren K. Billings hold meeting at Waiters' Hall to form permanent defense committee.

JUNE 21 Kay Kyser and His Kollege of Musical Knowlege open at the Golden Gate Theater.

JULY 4 Artie Shaw and His Orchestra opens an engagement at the Golden Gate Theater.

JULY 5 "Camel Caravan" radio show with Benny Goodman and His Orchestra broadcasts from Treasure Island.

JULY 12 "Orphanage Day" celebrated at Treasure Island.

JULY 22 "Salvation Army Day" celebrated at Treasure Island.

JULY 30 Municipal Railway bus No. 11 established to carry people from Union and Powell to Coit Tower.

JULY 30 "Swiss Day" celebrated at Treasure Island.

AUG. 7 *Swing Mikado* opens at the Geary Theater.

AUG. 12 "American Legion Day" celebrated at Treasure Island.

AUG. 31 Musicians' Union board of directors reprimands members of Don Kaye's orchestra for singing "Three Little Fishes" on KYA in violation of union rules.

SEPT. 4 San Francisco Labor Council President John F. Shelley and Secretary John A. O'Connell lead Labor Day celebration in Festival Hall at Treasure Island.

SEPT. 4 In a speech at Treasure Island, Mayor Rossi says, "Pray God we may remain out of war. Pray God that all Americans back our President in his struggle to keep us out of war."

SEPT. 6 Executive Board of the Musician's Union orders hazard pay for musicians playing on ships that sail from San Francisco into the Pacific war zone.

SEPT. 15 Central American Countries Day celebrated in the Open Air Theater at Treasure Island.

SEPT. 18 Striking messenger boys hold parade in San Francisco.

SEPT. 24 "Army 91st Division Day" celebrated at Treasure Island.

SEPT. 30 "San Francisco Day" celebrated at Treasure Island.

OCT. 1 "Keep America Out of War" rally held in the Temple Compound at Treasure Island.

OCT. 2 Birdbaths installed in Union Square.

OCT. 7 Union Labor Party opens convention at the Labor Temple.

OCT. 8 Community Chest holds torch lighting pageant at Civic Center as a kickoff for the annual fundraising drive.

OCT. 20 Andre Kostlanetz leads members of the San Francisco Symphony during a concert by Lily Pons at Treasure Island's Temple Compound.

OCT. 29 Closing day, Golden Gate International Exposition.

OCT. 31 Clement Street Merchants' Association holds Halloween parade.

NOV. 7 Supervisor Alfred Roncovieri runs for reelection to the board. He is the last member of the Eugene Schmitz administration in public office. He served as School Superintendent in 1906.

NOV. 21 Rally at City Hall to raise funds for opening the World's Fair in 1940.

DEC. 19 Retail Store Employees strike Kress and Newberry stores to demand an open shop.

DEC. 21 East-West football rally held at the Opera House.

DEC. 29 Annual birthday serenade to Superintendent McLaren held at Golden Gate Park.

1940

Ferry *Oakland* retired; began as *Chrysopolis*, 1860.

JAN. 9 Warren K. Billings opens a watch repair shop in Room 420 of the Grant Building, 1095 Market Street.

JAN. 16 Jan Garber, "Idol of the Airwaves," and His Orchestra open in the Mural Room of the St. Francis Hotel.

JAN. 25 The McQuaide Post of the Veterans of Foreign Wars Drum and Bugle Corps parades from Fifth and Market to the Fox Theater.

JAN. 26 The *Chronicle* sponsors "City of San Francis" radio program from the Civic Auditorium carried on the full NBC network.

JAN. 26 Fundraiser for victims of the German war against Poland and Finland held in the Roseroom Bowl of the Palace Hotel.

FEB. 16 Ray Noble and His Orchestra open at the Palace Hotel.

MAR. 8 Alec Templeton appears with the San Francisco Symphony.

MAR. 19 Guy Lombardo and His Royal Canadians open at the St. Francis Hotel.

APR. 9 Shep Fields and His Rippling Rhythm Orchestra open at the St. Francis.

APR. 16 Ferryboat *Yosemite* (now *Argentina*) sails for Montevideo.

APR. 21 $1,350,000 Funston Ave. approach and Park-Presidio Tunnel opened to Golden Gate Bridge traffic.

APR. 23 Alexander Woollcott becomes ill and *The Man Who Came to Dinner* closes at the Geary Theater.

APR. 26 Wells Fargo Bank orchestra holds annual concert for bank employees at the Veterans' Auditorium.

MAY 4 Police Chief Dullea allows nine nightclubs to offer dancing and entertainment until 4 a.m. Liquor cannot be sold after 2 a.m. The clubs are: Club Moderne, Bal Tabarin, Embassy, Lido Club, Royal Hawaiian Club, Bimbo's 365 Club on Market Street, Music Box, Fiesta and Forbidden City.

MAY 11 Herb Caen and members of the San Francisco-Oakland Newspaper Guild star in *Front Page Frolics* held at Aquatic Park Casino.

MAY 15 Ice Follies opens at Winterland,

the former Dreamland Auditorium.

MAY 18 "Golden Forties" fiesta parade held in Polk Gulch.

MAY 19 "McLaren Day" celebrated in Golden Gate Park.

MAY 19 Veterans of Foreign Wars hold rodeo at Seals Stadium.

MAY 22 Clement Street Merchants' Association sponsors Fiesta Day parade in the district.

MAY 25 Overcoming financial obstacles, the World's Fair of 1940 opens at Treasure Island.

MAY 27 Benny Goodman and His Orchestra open a two-week engagement in Peacock Court of Hotel Mark Hopkins.

JUNE 4 Harry Owens and His Royal Hawaiians open at the St. Francis Hotel.

JUNE 8 "San Francisco Conservatory of Music Day" celebrated at Treasure Island.

JULY 19 "American Antarctic Expedition Day" celebrated at Treasure Island.

JULY 26 Three-day "Negro Music Festival" begins at Treasure Island.

JULY 27 "Enlist For Defense Week" in San Francisco.

AUG. 2 "Red Cross Day" is celebrated at Treasure Island.

AUG. 4 Demonstration of an experimental radio service called "FM" (frequency modulation) is broadcast from the studios of KSFO to the National Association of Broadcasters convention meeting in the city.

AUG. 10 "Young Buddhists Day" celebrated at Treasure Island.

AUG. 11 "Junior Musicians of American Day" celebrated at Treasure Island.

AUG. 12 Fire destroys administration building on Angel Island.

AUG. 18 "Mexican Day" celebrated at Treasure Island.

AUG. 24 Fire destroys California State Bldg. at Treasure Island.

AUG. 26 City College opens.

AUG. 27 U.S. Senator Hiram Johnson, running in the California Primary, bills himself "California's Greatest Stateman."

SEPT. 9 "California Admission Day" celebrated at Treasure Island.

SEPT. 12 Artie Shaw and His Orchestra open at the Palace Hotel.

SEPT. 14 "A.F. of L. Day" celebrated at Treasure Island. San Francisco labor leader John O'Connell is the guest of honor.

SEPT. 15 "San Francisco Day" celebrated at Treasure Island.

SEPT. 17 "Women's Day" celebrated at Treasure Island.

SEPT. 20 Benefit for British War Relief held at Treasure Island.

SEPT. 22 "U.C. Day" celebrated at Treasure Island.

SEPT. 25 "Insurance Day" celebrated at Treasure Island.

SEPT. 29 211,020 people attended the last day of the 1940 World's Fair at Treasure Island.

SEPT. 29 New facade of Sts. Peter and Paul Church dedicated.

OCT. 6 Zoological Gardens, Sloat and Sunset Blvd., open.

OCT. 6 Fleishhacker Zoo dedicated.

OCT. 7 Eureka Valley Citizens Association holds annual fiesta.

OCT. 28 Post Office at Ferry Building vacated; moves to Mission and Spear streets.

OCT. 30 Wendell Wilkie is hosted at the Press Club.

NOV. 14 Ground is broken for new NBC studios at Taylor and O'Farrell streets. "Radio City" is the last Art Deco building to be constructed in San Francisco.

DEC. 1 Tait's-At-The-Beach destroyed by fire.

DEC. 6 Ernie Heckscher and His Orchestra open at the Mark Hopkins Hotel.

1941

MAR. 1 Northwestern Pacific (San Francisco to Sausalito) ferries discontinued.

MAR. 31 Ground broken for Union Square Garage.

APR. 1 Navy takes over Treasure Island.

APR. 6 Cable cars on the Fillmore and

Castro Street hills taken out of service.

JULY 24 National Unity Mass Meeting held in the Civic Auditorium, sponsored by Americans United of Northern California. Wendell L. Willkie, Douglas Miller, speakers.

AUG. 9 Civic Center Hospitality House opens.

SEPT. 3 Land's End slide wrecks home and business of the "Mayor" of Land's End, Charles L. Harris.

SEPT. 7 Bronze tablet commemorating the site of the Old Yerba Buena Cemetery unveiled by the California Genealogical Society.

OCT. 18 President Rafael Larco Herrera of Peru visits.

NOV. 15 Cow Palace opens.

DEC. 8 With declaration of war against Japan, San Francisco experiences first blackout at 6:15 p.m. Lt. Gen. J. L. De Witt, Commander of the Western Defense Commands, recommends the removal of enemy aliens from the West Coast.

1942

Federal WPA Music Project ends.

FEB. 10 President Roosevelt signs Executive Order No. 9066 and sends 110,000 people of Japanese ancestry to internment camps.

APR. 6 First San Francisco Japanese evacuation set.

AUG. 9 Adm. Daniel Callaghan wins Medal of Honor aboard USS *San Francisco* at Guadalcanal.

AUG. 20 Dimout regulations effective in San Francisco.

SEPT. 8 Wool auction held at Palace Hotel.

SEPT. 28 First scrap metal drive.

OCT. 1 Red Mass celebrated for first time by Catholics.

OCT. 4 Second scrap metal drive.

1943

JAN. 17 Tin Can Drive Day.

MAR. 5 Pepsi Cola Center, 948 Market Street, opens for servicemen.

MAR. 29 Charlotte, Grand Duchess of Luxembourg, visits.

MAY 11–30 Attu and Kiska, Aleutian Islands, retaken by military expedition from San Francisco.

JUNE 3 Fillmore Street arches removed.

AUG. 12 Free Farmer's Market opens at Market Street and Duboce.

AUG. 18 Construction begins on barracks in Civic Center for servicemen.

AUG. 30 City of Paris department store purchases its building, quarters previously rented.

OCT. 14 The Fairmont Hotel announces it will build a helicopter landing field on its rooftop.

NOV. 1 Dimout ban lifted.

1944

JULY 16 Police pistol range formally dedicated at Lake Merced.

JULY 17 An explosion at the Port Chicago munitions center breaks windows in San Francisco. More than 300 people are killed in the worst military loss of life in the U.S. during WW II. The blast was felt as far away as Nevada.

AUG. 1 City and County of San Francisco assumes management of the Farmer's Market.

AUG. 7 An emergency proclamation setting aside the Civil Service provisions of the Charter and enabling the city to employ all of the Market Street Railway operating, repair and maintenance personnel for the duration of the war was issued by Mayor Lapham.

OCT. 5 Mayfair Heights Corporation purchases the Catholic Calvary Cemetery, bounded by Geary, Turk, St. Joseph's and Masonic, for home construction.

DEC. 9 Fleet Hospital, No. 113, Crocker Amazon Playground, commissioned.

DEC. 16 Hunters Point shuttle bus begins service.

DEC. 17 The War Dept. announces the revocation of the West Coast mass exclusion order of people of Japanese descent.

DEC. 18 James Purcell wins freedom for Japanese from concentration camps.

1945

FEB. 12 San Francisco selected as site of the United Nations Conference.

MAR. 8 Bataan prisoners of war welcomed.

APR. 25 United Nations Conference begins.

JUNE 25 President Harry S. Truman visits.

JUNE 26 United Nations Conference ends.

AUG. 14 At 4 p.m. Pacific War time President Truman announces the surrender of Japan.

AUG. 15 Riot in San Francisco celebrating the end of World War II.

SEPT. 9 General Wainwright welcomed. Fort Mason war shipments totaled 1.75 million men and 24 million tons of supplies.

1946

JAN. 9 Mission Rock burned off so that the rock can become the base for extension of Pier 50.

MAY 2–4 Alcatraz Island revolt by prisoners; two guards, three prisoners die.

JUNE 30 Civic Center Hospitality House closes.

JULY 16 Attempt made to recall Mayor Lapham; first in San Francisco history.

AUG. 26 Sailors Union of the Pacific vote to strike and tie up port.

SEPT. 8 Notre Dame Hospital opens.

OCT. 17–20 First Municipal Art Exhibition by Bay Region artists held in Civic Center Plaza.

DEC. 7 Carbarn built in the 1870s at Haight and Stanyan closes.

DEC. 19 Civic Center barracks demolished.

1947

FEB. 8 Bal Tabarin nightclub on Columbus Ave. closes.

FEB. 27 The Montgomery block sold for $200,000.

APR. 3 Campaign started by Market Street Association to rid Civic Center of pigeons.

APR. 10 Galley K and the Treasure Island Mess Hall destroyed by fire.

JUNE 21 The Queen Mother of Egypt, Queen Nazli, visits.

SEPT. 1 The Humphreys' home, built in 1852, at Chestnut and Hyde, demolished.

SEPT. 2 Parking meters installed in the Polk Street District.

OCT. 10 First arrival of Pacific Area dead on the ship *Honda Knot*.

OCT. 16 O'Connor Moffat & Co., Stockton and O'Farrell, sold to Macy's.

1948

City Cemeteries removed for housing space.

FEB. 12 Second arrival of Pacific Area war dead on the U.S. Army transport *Cardinal O'Connell*.

FEB. 12 San Francisco Junior College changes name to City College of San Francisco.

MAR. 14 Freedom Train arrives in San Francisco.

MAR. 18 John D. Sullivan, Public Service Director, testifies before the Public Health and Welfare Committee of the Board of Supervisors on the removal of WW II air raid sirens.

MAR. 23 Third arrival of Pacific Area war dead on ship *Walter W. Schwenk*.

MAY 25 City gets its first telecast.

JUNE 22 City's first mailomat device goes into service.

JUNE 27 Funston Playground returned to city by Army.

JULY 2 Industrial Exposition opens in Civic Auditorium.

JULY 3 The last No. 7 streetcar to make the 65-year run along Haight Street is retired and replaced by trackless trolleys.

JULY 28 Milton Van Noland climbs up 50-foot flagpole at a used car lot on Van Ness Ave. and begins flagpole sitting.

SEPT. 28 Ground breaking for Youth

Guidance Center.

OCT. 17 Portola Festival begins.

NOV. 25 Fort Funston's 16-inch coastal guns dismantled.

DEC. 9 "Winged Victory" statue moved from Turk, Market, and Mason streets to Golden Gate Park.

1949

JAN. 22 Chinatown Telephone Exchange closes.

FEB. 12 Carbarn at beach destroyed by fire.

APR. 15 Robert L. Niles first person to make a stunt leap from the Golden Gate Bridge.

APR. 20 General Hilaro Camino Moncado of Philippines arrives.

APR. 23 Courtesy mail boxes for motorists initiated.

MAY 15 Ground breaking for U.S.F.'s Gleeson Memorial Library.

JUNE 9 Bust of Mayor Angelo J. Rossi unveiled at City Hall.

JULY 3 Old streetcars on the Nos. 5, 6, 7, and 21 lines replaced by trolley coaches.

OCT. 7 Iva Toguri D'Aquino, also known as "Tokyo Rose," sentenced in San Francisco to ten years in prison for treason.

OCT. 13 President Truman signs Fort Funston Bill; city to receive 42 acres.

NOV. 6 Sally Stanford's Pine Street residence closed.

NOV. 21 Hastings Store at 135 Post Street opens.

DEC. 11 Mohammad Reza Shah Pahlavi of Iran visits.

DEC. 20 "L" streetcar kills Burtie Lee Beal, a member of a track repair crew, in the Twin Peaks Tunnel.

1950

FEB. 15 Demolition of the Chutes-at-the-Beach commences.

AUG. 25 Hospital ship USS *Benevolence* sinks after colliding with the freighter *Luckenbach* in heavy fog off the Golden Gate.

SEPT. 20 Golden Gate Park burros replaced by ponies in the Children's area.

DEC. 3 U.S.F.'s Gleeson Memorial Library dedicated.

1951

JAN. 22 The Queen Mother of Egypt, Queen Nazli, visits.

FEB. 16 City Hall dome fire.

MAR. 11 John P. Murphy Playground, 9th Avenue and Ortega, dedicated.

APR. 18 General Douglas MacArthur visits.

MAY 27 Maritime Museum, foot of Polk Street, opens under the direction of Karl Kortum, who originated the concept of a maritime monument for the City, to include a fleet of historic ships in Aquatic Park lagoon and a Victorian Park ashore.

JUNE 10 Goat Island officially re-christened Yerba Buena Island.

JUNE 29 President Galo Plaza of Ecuador visits.

JUNE 29 Land's End scenic drive reopens after being closed for nine years due to slides.

JULY 25 California Legislature creates special commission to study Bay Area transportation problems.

SEPT. 4 Japanese peace treaty signed. First nationwide television hookup.

SEPT. 8 Prime Minister Yoshida of Japan signs treaty ending World War II at Opera House.

SEPT. 23 Josephine D. Randall Junior Museum opens.

OCT. 21 Ping Yuen, Chinatown housing project, dedicated.

DEC. 1 Golden Gate Bridge closed to traffic because of high winds.

DEC. 3 Home at 7 Castenada slides down hill to 7th Ave. A broken storm sewer and heavy rains caused foundation to crack.

1952

FEB. 1 Renaming of Union Square to United Nations Square is opposed by the

Native Sons of the Golden West.

FEB. 8 Mission Dolores designated first Minor Basilica in the West.

APR. 18 Queen Juliana of the Netherlands visits.

AUG. 24 Faisal II, King of Iraq, visits.

AUG. 26 Fluoridation of city's water begins.

SEPT. 1 Sutro Baths purchased by George Whitney.

OCT. 8 President Dwight D. Eisenhower visits.

OCT. 16 Woolworth's, corner Powell and Market, opens.

NOV. 6 Morrison Planetarium Projector in Golden Gate Park dedicated in special ceremony.

DEC. 21 Broadway Tunnel opens.

1953

FEB. 23 Downtown Theater, Mason and Ellis streets, demolished.

MAR. 26 Hastings College of Law dedication of new building, northeast corner of McAllister and Hyde.

APR. 19 Norodom Shianouk, Prince of Cambodia, visits.

APR. 30 Rent control abolished.

AUG. 26 President Elpidio Quirino of the Philippines visits.

DEC. 1 U.S. House Committee on Un-American Activities opens hearings.

1954

JAN. 15 Joe DiMaggio and Marilyn Monroe married at City Hall.

FEB. 7 Celal Bayar, President of Turkey, visits.

MAR. 24 First meeting of the Telegraph Hill Dwellers held at Schaeffer School of Design.

APR. 21 Rally on Market Street at the new Equitable Life Insurance Company building to celebrate the end of the noisy pile driver called "the monster."

JUNE 9 Miraloma Playground dedicated.

JUNE 13 Emperor Haile Selassie of Ethiopia visits.

JULY 6 Golden Pheasant Restaurant on Powell Street closes.

AUG. 7 President Syngman Rhee of Republic of Korea visits.

AUG. 29 San Francisco International Airport opens.

DEC. 17 Mohammad Reza Shah Pahlavi of Iran visits.

1955

JAN. 18 Mayor Elmer Robinson dedicates new Junipero Serra Playground on Stonecrest Drive near 19th Ave.

JAN. 27 Land's End scenic drive closed due to slide.

APR. 9 United Nations Charter hearing.

MAY 3 Sky Tram begins operation from the Cliff House Terrace to Point Lobos.

JUNE 1 President Dwight D. Eisenhower visits.

JULY 11 Four-alarm fire destroys the Italian Village nightclub.

JULY 19 The *Balclutha* ties up at Pier 43 and becomes a floating museum.

AUG. 3 Chinatown police squad disbanded.

AUG. 9 Portuguese bull fight at Cow Palace, first time held in the United States.

AUG. 27 Beniamino Bufano's 18-foot black Swedish granite statue of St. Francis set in place at the entry steps of the Church of St. Francis of Assisi.

OCT. 11 "Big Dipper" at Playland-at-the-Beach demolished.

OCT. 12 Ground broken for Town School building.

OCT. 16 Dick Pee, 9-year-old boy, swims Golden Gate.

DEC. 13 First Japanese war bride Kazue Nagai Katz, wife of M/Sgt. Frederick H. Katz, becomes a citizen in Judge Michael Roache's court.

1956

"Beatnik" phenomenon, North Beach.

MAR. 8 Giovanni Gronchi, President of Italy, visits.

APR. 12 The California Academy of Sciences unveils its new seismograph.

APR. 19 First Black and White Ball held at the Palace, St. Francis, Mark Hopkins, and Fairmont hotels.

MAY 5 William G. Irwin home (Blood Bank) at Washington and Laguna destroyed by fire.

MAY 23 World Trade Center in the Ferry Building dedicated.

JUNE 2 President Sukarno of Indonesia visits.

JUNE 4 Board of Supervisors extend 40-foot height limitation from Union Street southward to a line 120 feet from Broadway.

AUG. 1 Tommy, San Francisco's last workhorse, retired to a Los Altos ranch.

AUG. 20 Republican Convention begins at the Cow Palace.

AUG. 21 President Dwight D. Eisenhower visits.

SEPT. 2 Washington-Jackson cable line replaced by bus service.

OCT. 25 Port facility dedicated; conversion of Piers 15 and 17 into a modern terminal.

OCT. 29 San Francisco Conservatory of Music moves from 3400 block of Sacramento Street to 19th Ave. and Ortega.

NOV. 13 Martin Hanson's Twin Peaks monolith, erected in 1925, demolished in the Market Street widening project.

NOV. 19 Postmaster's Wharf in Presidio demolished.

DEC. 3 Helicopter taxi service begins from heliport at Ferry Building.

DEC. 7 Site for new Lowell High dedicated at Eucalyptus and Meadowbrook drives.

DEC. 29 Geary Street cars replaced by full-time bus service.

1957

JAN. 13 PG&E smokestack in the Marina District demolished.

JAN. 17 Nine-county Commission recommends legislation to create Bay Area Rapid Transit District.

FEB. 8 Public Library's bookmobile formally unveiled and dedicated at City Hall.

MAR. 22 Earthquake rocks San Francisco and vicinity.

APR. 7 Hyde Street cable cars run again after absence of three years.

MAY 6 Ngo Dinh Diem, President of Vietnam, visits.

JUNE 4 California Legislature approves creation of five-county Bay Area Rapid Transit District.

JUNE 5 Jackson Square celebrates its new role as San Francisco's interior design center.

JUNE 11 Governor Goodwin J. Knight signs law establishing a five-county Bay Area Rapid Transit District.

SEPT. 11 A legislative act changing the Board of State Harbor Commissioners to San Francisco Port Authority took effect today.

SEPT. 22 Rossi Swimming Pool at Arguello and Anza streets dedicated.

OCT. 1 Equitable Life Insurance Company time and temperature indicator atop the Sutter and Montgomery Street building lit for first time.

OCT. 12 Statue of Christopher Columbus by Italian sculptor Vittorio de Colbertaldo dedicated. Boeing Stratoclipper with 40 persons leaves San Francisco for Antarctica, via Hawaii and New Zealand; first commercial flight between California and Antarctica.

NOV. 11 Demolition of cable car barn at California and Hyde streets begins.

NOV. 14 BART District officially established with formal meeting of Board of Directors.

DEC. 5 Mohammed V, King of Morocco, visits.

1958

JAN. 1 Bay Area Rapid Transit District offices established in Flood Building, later moved to 814 Mission Street.

FEB. 23 City's last lighted arch (erected in 1913) over the intersection of Mission and 25th streets demolished.

MAR. 27 Mayor Christopher breaks ground for new North Beach Branch Library.

APR. 1 The responsibility of accounting for each and every criminal warrant issued by city charged to the Central Warrant Bureau.

APR. 11 Brooks Hall in Civic Center dedicated.

APR. 20 Buses replace the Key System's trains at 3:00 a.m.

MAY 8 Crystal Plunge at Lombard and Taylor streets demolished.

MAY 9 Last run of the Municipal Railway's two-man streetcars, replaced by one-man cars.

MAY 26 Union Square made an official State Historical Landmark with dedication of a plaque honoring John W. Geary, first mayor of San Francisco.

JUNE 12 President Theodore Heuss of West Germany visits.

JUNE 22 Mohammad Reza Shah Pahlavi of Iran visits.

JULY 29 Southern Pacific Bay ferries discontinued.

OCT. 21 President Dwight D. Eisenhower visits.

NOV. 24 Queen Frederika of Greece visits.

1959

MAR. 11 Peter II of Yugoslavia visits.

MAR. 23 King Hussein of Jordan visits.

MAR. 28 H.R.H. The Duke of Windsor visits.

MAY 14 Parsons-Brinckerhoff-Tudor-Bechtel retained as engineering consultants for BART's system design and construction.

MAY 21 Baudouin, King of the Belgians, visits.

MAY 31 Jefferson Elementary School, 19th Ave. and Irving Street, destroyed by fire.

JULY 10 State legislation authorizes use of Bay Bridge tolls to finance construction of Trans-Bay Rapid Transit Tube.

JULY 25 Storyland at Fleishhacker Zoo opens.

AUG. 1 Crystal Palace Market on Market Street closes.

SEPT. 21 Premier Nikita Khrushchev of U.S.S.R. visits.

NOV. 11 Seals Stadium demolished.

NOV. 29 Prince Karim, Aga Khan IV, visits.

1960

JAN. 5 Crown Zellerbach Building dedicated.

FEB. 6 Aircraft crash in Sutro Forest. Two die.

MAR. 1 Civic Center Garage opens.

APR. 27 President Charles De Gaulle of France visits.

MAY 7 Mahendra Bir Birkram Shan Deva of Nepal visits.

MAY 9 Brundage Collection of Oriental Art in Golden Gate Park opens.

MAY 13 Riot at City Hall over Red Hearing protest.

MAY 14 3,000 join in peace march.

MAY 22 President Sukarno of Indonesia visits.

JULY 1 The office of Public Administrator is created under authority of Section 5175 of the Welfare and Institutions Code.

JULY 13 King Bhumibol Adulyadez of Thailand visits.

SEPT. 12 Grace Cathedral tower lighted for first time.

OCT. 6 King Frederick of Denmark visits.

OCT. 20 President Dwight D. Eisenhower visits.

1961

JAN. 6 San Francisco and Oakland Helicopter Airlines founded.

MAR. 16 Statue of St. Francis of Assisi removed from steps of St. Francis Church and moved to Oakland.

MAY 5 Outsen Milling Company, last San Francisco grain mill, closes.

JUNE 1 Blyth-Zellerbach Committee report on Municipal Management submitted to the Mayor and Board of Supervisors.

JULY 8 Peace rally in Golden Gate Park.

JULY 20 P. & O. liner *Canberra* arrives in San Francisco on her maiden voyage.

JULY 25 Public Utilities Commission votes to purchase 12 acres of Islais Creek property for Water Department maintenance yard.

AUG. 1 New Hall of Justice opens.

SEPT. 5 Huge SP sign (installed in 1954) atop 65 Market Street removed.

SEPT. 6 New Hall of Justice dedicated.

SEPT. 14 Yerba Buena Plaza, apartment building and senior citizens recreation center, dedicated.

SEPT. 26 Royal Theater reopens.

OCT. 7 Family Rosary Rally held in Golden Gate Park.

OCT. 21 Midtown Terrace Reservoir Playground dedicated.

OCT. 28 Helen Wills Playground dedicated.

NOV. 20 Park Chung Hee, President of Korea, visits.

1962

$792 million DART bond, for first rapid transit system since Philadelphia, 1907.

MAR. 1 Alcazar Theater demolished.

MAR. 22 The Gibralter Warehouse at Sansome and Filbert destroyed by fire.

MAR. 23 President John F. Kennedy visits.

APR. 12 San Mateo County withdraws from BART district.

APR. 29 State Theater on Market Street demolished.

MAY 17 Marin County withdraws from BART district.

JUNE 11 Four men escape from Alcatraz.

JUNE 13 First police dog joins Police Department.

AUG. 30 Ground broken for Golden Gateway Project.

SEPT. 7 Fire destroys St. Mary's Cathedral on Van Ness Ave.

SEPT. 8 Statue of Father Miguel Hidalgo unveiled in Mission Park, 19th and Dolores streets.

OCT. 23 First boxing ring set up in Candlestick Park for the Gene Fulmer-Dick Tiger middleweight fight.

NOV. 6 BART's bond issue approved by a 66.9% favorable vote.

DEC. 10 Hunters Point jitney stops running after 50 years service.

DEC. 15 The Chinese nightclub, Forbidden City, closes.

DEC. 19 Street signs voted by Park Commission for Golden Gate Park.

1963

JAN. 4 Statue of St. Francis of Assisi by Bufano set in place at Beach and Taylor streets.

JAN. 31 Navy closes its San Francisco oceanographic office in the Appraisers Building.

FEB. 28 Fox Theater demolition begins.

MAR. 22 Alcatraz evacuated as a prison.

MAR. 31 Pelton Water Wheel Company at 2929 19th Street closes after being in business since 1889.

APR. 16 *Sakura Maru* arrives, first Japanese liner into the bay since World War II.

JUNE 25 San Francisco has a new day: Flower Day.

SEPT. 5 President Theater on McAllister Street, San Francisco's last burlesque house, closes.

SEPT. 13 King of Afghanistan visits.

SEPT. 27 Dedication of new Produce Terminal at Islais Creek.

OCT. 5 Hyde Street Pier reopens as a State Historical Park.

OCT. 12 Bay Bridge traffic changeover to one-way operation on each deck goes into effect at 4 a.m.

1964

Haight-Ashbury "hippie" phenomenon.

FEB. 20 Mayor's South of Market Redevelopment Committee adopts San

Francisco Redevelopment Agency proposal that the South of Market Redevelopment Area D-1 be called Yerba Buena.

MAR. 8 Band of Sioux Indians lay claim to Alcatraz Island.

APR. 27 King Hussein of Jordan visits.

MAY 23 Fire at All Hallows Church in the Bayview District kills 17.

MAY 29 Mwami Mwambusta IV, King of Burundi, visits.

JUNE 18 President Lyndon B. Johnson visits.

JUNE 19 Republican Convention begins at Cow Palace.

JULY 29 Human Rights Commission established.

OCT. 1 Cable cars declared a National Landmark.

OCT. 5 Fire Department Museum dedicated.

OCT. 11 President Diosado Macapagal of Philippines visits.

OCT. 12 President Lyndon B. Johnson visits.

1965

JAN. 27 Ground broken for "Dragon Gateway" to Grant Ave.

JAN. 27 Alcoa Building dedicated.

APR. 3 St. Nicholas Antiochian Orthodox Church on Diamond Heights dedicated.

JUNE 14 Walton Square, Golden Gateway, dedicated.

JUNE 26 President Lyndon B. Johnson visits.

AUG. 19 Crew leaves Mile Rock Lighthouse so that demolition can commence.

NOV. 4 Princess Margaret of Great Britain visits.

Examiner becomes evening paper; combines for Sunday edition with the *Chronicle*.

Bill Graham opens The Fillmore Auditorium featuring rock groups.

1966

MAR. 12 Pioneer Plaza dedicated.

JUNE 16 Allyne Park, Vallejo and Gough, opens to the public.

JUNE 26 Sutro Baths destroyed by fire.

AUG. 6 Vietnam War peace march up Market Street.

AUG. 29 Beatles concert at Candlestick Park.

SEPT. 22 President Ferdinand E. Marcos of Philippines visits.

SEPT. 26 The ship *Staten Island* is the first icebreaker to enter San Francisco Bay.

OCT. 3 Leopold Sedar Senghor of Senegal visits.

1967

JAN. 14 Human Be-In in Golden Gate Park.

JAN. 19 Autos banned from Band Concourse area in Golden Gate Park on Sundays.

FEB. 2 King Lupou of Tonga visits.

MAR. 18 Lurline Pier at Ocean Beach demolished by wrecking crews.

APR. 8 President Cevdat Sunay of Turkey visits.

APR. 15 Vietnam War peace march from 2nd and Market to Kezar Stadium.

APR. 18 Fire Dept. Headquarters at 260 Golden Gate Ave. dedicated.

JULY 1 BART construction teams begin tearing up Market Street.

JULY 4 Fireworks at Candlestick Park for first time; moved from the Marina Green because of weather.

JULY 22 President Adams of Anguilla visits.

JULY 25 Construction begins on Market Street subway.

AUG. 5 H.S.H. Rainier of Monaco visits.

AUG. 9 Peace torch arrives from Hiroshima.

AUG. 15 San Francisco Mining Exchange closes.

AUG. 15 Telenews Theater closes.

AUG. 27 Peace torch begins its journey to Washington, D.C., for a demonstration against the Vietnam War.

AUG. 28 Colonel Stewart Evans swims from the Farallone Islands to San Francisco.
SEPT. 30 Palace of Fine Arts reopens.
OCT. 5 President Diori of Niger visits.

1968

FEB. 22 President Summerskill of San Francisco State College resigns.
MAR. 22 President's daughter Lynda Johnson ordered off cable car for eating ice cream cone.
MAR. 27 Japanese Trade and Cultural Center dedicated.
APR. 18 Old Hall of Justice demolished.
APR. 27 Peace march and rally.
APR. 30 Olav V of Norway visits.
AUG. 31 President Nagush Arutyanyan of Armenia visits.
SEPT. 11 First bilingual Social Security office opens.
SEPT. 19 Baby born to Marin County couple on the Golden Gate Bridge.
OCT. 12 GIs and Vets march for peace from Golden Gate Park to Civic Center.
OCT. 19 Tolls collected southbound only on Golden Gate Bridge.
NOV. 6 First day of San Francisco State College strike.
NOV. 26 Robert R. Smith, President of San Francisco State College, resigns.
NOV. 26 S. I. Hayakawa made acting President, San Francisco State College.
DEC. 13 Playland-at-the-Beach reopens.

1969

FEB. 7 The City of San Francisco assumes complete control over the port.
MAR. 18 Bank of California Building, 400 California Street, dedicated.
MAR. 21 S.F. State College strike ends.
MAR. 28 Legislature approves half-cent district sales tax to provide $150 million needed to complete BART system.
APR. 6 Peace march.
MAY 16 Cowell Hall, California Academy of Sciences, in Golden Gate Park opens.

MAY 19 BART inspector walks under water in the tube from S.F. to Oakland.
MAY 20 Police Chief Cahill pins star on Rev. Hamilton Boswell, first chaplain on police force.
JUNE 19 Bike route, Lake Merced through Golden Gate Park, dedicated.
JULY 23 President Richard M. Nixon visits.
AUG. 21 President Richard M. Nixon visits.
NOV. 15 Thousands march for peace.
NOV. 20 Indians seize and occupy Alcatraz Island.
DEC. 15 Fire Department replaces leather helmets with plastic helmets to test their suitability.
DEC. 22 Radio Free Alcatraz broadcasts for first time on radio station KPFA.

1970

JAN. 21 Harbor Advisory Radar, a new monitoring system for ship traffic, begins operation.
FEB. 26 President Pompidou of France arrives for a visit.
FEB. 28 Bicycles permitted for first time to cross Golden Gate Bridge.
MAR. 13 4-day strike by City employees begins.
MAR. 24 The SS *Eppleton Hall*, a steam paddleboat, arrives from Newcastle-upon-Tyne, England.
MAR. 26 Golden Gate Park Conservatory made a city landmark.
MAY 15 Five-alarm fire at the Furniture Mart on Market Street.
MAY 15 Teamster strike ends.
MAY 31 Indians on Alcatraz Island celebrate "Liberation Day."
MAY 31 President Suharto of Indonesia visits.
JUNE 1 Five buildings on Alcatraz destroyed by fire.
JULY 20 Baby born to Mrs. Trudell, first baby to be born on Alcatraz.
OCT. 1 Thomas Hsieh, first Chinese appointed to Art Commission, sworn in.
OCT. 15 First mass performed in new

St. Mary's Cathedral.

Nov. 18 "Black Wednesday" protest by Police Dept.

Nov. 19 Golden Gate Park Conservatory made a California State Historical Landmark.

1971

McDonald's opens first restaurant in the city at 1201 Ocean Ave.

Jan. 14–24 Cliff House and Sutro Baths memorabilia sale.

Jan. 19 Standard Oil freighters collide beneath Golden Gate Bridge and release millions of gallons of oil into Bay.

Jan. 27 Last subway tunnel link on BART system, the Montgomery Street Station subway "holed through."

Apr. 14 Fort Point dedicated as the first National Park site in the San Francisco Bay Area.

Apr. 24 Militants cut peace rally short.

Apr. 26 San Francisco lightship replaced by automatic buoy.

May 5 Many arrested in Financial District during anti-war demonstration aimed at halting business.

June 11 United States marshals recapture Alcatraz Island from the Indians.

June 22 "Enchanted World" on Fisherman's Wharf opens.

July 1 The Golden Gate Bridge pays off its $35-million bond debt; ILWU closes all Coast ports.

July 7 New portable swimming pool set up for first time in the Chinese playground at Sacramento Street and Waverly Place.

Sept. 3 Police Chief Alfred Nelder resigns.

Sept. 13 School district begins busing students for court-ordered desegregation.

Sept. 29 H.R.H. Princess Alexandra arrives at San Francisco International Airport for the start of British Week.

Oct. 1 City of London Treasures open, City Hall.

Oct. 7 ILWU strike ends on waterfront.

Oct. 16 McLaren Park Amphitheater

dedicated.

Nov. 15 Police Bomb Squad organized.

Dec. 14 Golden Gate Bridge lights out all night due to power failure.

1972

Jan. 22 Howard-Langton mini-park, Howard between 7th and 8th streets, dedicated by Mayor Alioto.

Mar. 4 Sultan of Selangor and family visit.

Mar. 18 "Flying Scotsman," a steam train that served for 40 years on the express run between Edinburgh and London, begins weekend runs along the waterfront.

Mar. 23 The City of Paris taken over by Amfac, a Hawaiian-based corporation. To reopen June 1 as City of Paris by Liberty House.

Apr. 20 Amundsen's ship *Gjoa* removed from Ocean Beach area, and placed on ship to be returned to Oslo, Norway.

May 4 The sloop *Gjoa*, famous for its Northwest Passage, returned to Norway.

Aug. 26 Clinton's Cafeteria on Market Street closes.

Nov. 9 Golden Gate Bridge closed for two hours to install new scaffolding.

Nov. 14 Westbury Hotel, Sutter and Powell streets, opens.

Nov. 30 Five-alarm fire destroys Pier 20.

Dec. 1 Last Coast Guardsman to tend the light on the Southeast Farallon Island leaves as light is automated.

Dec. 8 Alaska Commercial Building at Sansome and California streets (6,885 square feet) sold to the Bank of Tokyo for $2,500,000; highest known price paid for land in California history.

Dec. 18 Ferry Building siren replaced by electronic Westminster type chimes.

1973

Sutro TV Tower begins operation.

Jan. 16 Hyatt Hotel on Union Square opens.

Feb. 13 Sumitomo Bank of California, celebrating its 20th anniversary, presents

50 Kanzan cherry trees to the people of San Francisco to be planted at the Palace of Fine Arts, and 50 to be planted around the Chain of Lakes in Golden Gate Park.
MAR. 21 Pier 7 destroyed by fire.
APR. 25–27 Supervisor George Chinn, first Chinese Mayor, acting in place of vacationing Joseph Alioto.
MAY 8 Hyatt Regency Hotel in Embarcadero Center opens.
AUG. 10 First train travels through transbay tube to Montgomery Street station.
SEPT. 23 A Red Cross spokesman quoted in today's newspaper says the Bay Area is better prepared for earthquakes. "If a disaster is severe enough, the federal government will gear up even before it's formally called on," says Joe Leux, Red Cross liaison to a state OES earthquake planning project. "That wasn't always the case. Red tape, which in the past delayed funds, has finally been whacked into oblivion," he said.
OCT. 26 The National Park Service begins guided tours of Alcatraz Island with ferry service departing from Pier 43.
NOV. 16 Ralph Nader visits.
NOV. 20 Abba Eban visits.

1974
MAY 1 Muni's "Fast Pass" initiated.
JUNE 20 Vice President Gerald Ford visits.
JULY 29 Vice President Gerald Ford visits.
AUG. 23 Grant School, Pacific Ave. between Broderick and Baker, demolished.
SEPT. 16 BART begins regular transbay service.
SEPT. 28 Liberty House, 120 Stockton Street at O'Farrell, opens new building to public.
NOV. 11 Olga Korbut, Russian gymnast, visits.
NOV. 18 Geary Street tunnel, 530 feet long, opens.
NOV. 20 100 Van Ness Ave., new 29-story office building, opens.
DEC. 18 Visitors Center, City Hall, opens.

1975
JAN. 9 Registration for federally funded jobs (CETA) at 45 Hyde Street begins (Comprehensive Employment Training Act).
MAR. 27 Taipei Mayor Chang Feng-shu receives two redwood trees from city in recognition of the fifth Sister City anniversary.
APR. 11 Moshe Dayan of Israel visits.
APR. 15 The Chinese American Democratic Club, Inc. announces its endorsement of State Democratic Majority Leader, George Moscone, for mayor.
JUNE 4 Labor leader James Hoffa here fighting for better working conditions.
JULY 3 Netherlands ambassador Robert Tammenoms Bakker visits.

1976
AUG. 17 Hubert Humphrey in San Francisco promoting his book.
DEC. 17 Five-alarm fire destroys China Basin warehouse.

1977
JAN. 6 The San Francisco Ballet Company debuts.
JAN. 14 Gov. Brown spends the night in the "Pink Palace," the Western Addition housing project at Turk and Steiner.
FEB. 24 The Rev. Jim Jones, pastor of People's Temple, is elected chairman of the Housing Authority.
MAR. 17 Neighborhood preferential parking plan OK'd by Supervisors for North Beach, Telegraph Hill, and Russian Hill.
MAY 31 Newly enclosed Martin Luther King Swimming Pool, 3rd Street and Carroll Ave., dedicated.
JUNE 21 Rosalynn Carter and daughter, Amy, visit.
JUNE 23 Ground breaking ceremonies at the Daniel E. Koshland Park, Page and Laguna streets.
JUNE 26 300,000 people turn out for a Gay Freedom Day Parade.

JULY 26 There are more rats than people in San Francisco, a Health Dept. report announces.

JULY 28 Mayor George R. Moscone officially renames the Margaret S. Hayward Boys Playground (Turk and Octavia streets) the James P. Lang Field.

JULY 30 Daniel E. Koshland Park dedicated.

OCT. 26 Cardinal Yee Pin of East Asia visits.

1978

APR. I The Cunard liner *Queen Elizabeth II* visits S.F.

AUG. 3 Swami Hansadutta, Secretary to God, visits.

NOV. 27 Mayor Moscone and Supervisor Harvey Milk are assassinated in their City Hall offices by former Supervisor Dan White. Board of Supervisors President Dianne Feinstein automatically becomes mayor under the City Charter; White surrenders at Northern Police Station.

1979

MAY 21 Monday night "White Night" riot and violence at City Hall after Dan White's "voluntary manslaughter" verdict for slaying of Mayor George Moscone and Supervisor Harvey Milk, Nov. 27, 1978.

JULY II Mayor Dianne Feinstein dedicates the Muni Metro Center ($17 million facility) at San Jose and Ocean avenues.

AUG. 31 BART strike begins.

OCT. 26–28 First Marijuana Reform Festival held in Brooks Hall, Civic Center.

NOV. 21 Bay Bridge is shut down by four-alarm fire at a chemical warehouse at 28 Folsom Street.

NOV. 21 The union that held up the BART labor agreement changes its mind and votes to go back to work, effectively ending BART's long labor dispute.

NOV. 22 Boater killed, second lost off Ocean Beach.

DEC. 8 Washington notifies San Francisco that the Presidio will stay open and continue to function as an active defense installation.

DEC. 19 Todd Sherratt, 17-year-old high school senior, jumps from Golden Gate Bridge, survives, and swims ashore.

1980

JAN. 7 The city marks the 100th anniversary of the death of its favorite monarch, Emperor Norton, with ceremonies at Market and Montgomery streets during the lunch hour.

JAN. 8 Dianne Feinstein sworn in as city's first elected woman mayor; Cornelius P. Murphy II sworn in as Chief of Police.

JAN. 10 Mayor Feinstein on list of worst-dressed women of 1979.

JAN. 14 Power outage traps BART riders in tube.

JAN. 20 Mayor Feinstein and Richard Blum marry in a private 20-minute Jewish Reformed wedding ceremony. A public reception follows in the rotunda of City Hall.

JAN. 22 Five-alarm Tenderloin fire hits during rush hour. Building at Ellis and Mason destroyed.

JAN. 24 Just after 11 a.m. a powerful rolling earthquake, centered 10 miles northwest of Livermore, jolts the city with a Richter magnitude of 5.8.

JAN. 26 At 6:33 p.m. an earthquake registering 5.6 on the Richter scale hits Bay Area.

FEB. 5 Eureka Valley Streetcar Station entrance of the Twin Peaks streetcar tunnel demolished.

FEB. 7 Registrar of Voters, Thomas P. Kearney, transfers to a job in city's sewer system office after Chinese citizens demanded his ouster for a racial slur.

FEB. 8 Rosalynn Carter in San Francisco for a fund-raising breakfast at the St. Francis Hotel.

FEB. 18 Muni Metro opens, providing service on the N-Judah line.

FEB. 29 Toll on Golden Gate Bridge drops to 75 cents under a program designed to refund $539,000 to commuters. The 'S' Squad (Saturation) consisting of 24 hand-picked inspectors reactivated by the Police Dept.

MAR. 6 San Francisco Mounted Police assigned to patrol Fisherman's Wharf and Union Square. First annual Bay Area Sports Hall of Fame banquet held at the St. Francis Hotel.

MAR. 8 The new $16-million, 68,000 square-foot U.C. Dental building dedicated on Parnassus Ave.

MAR. 13 Recreation and Park Commission votes unanimously to begin charging 50 cents admission to the Japanese Tea Garden July 1.

MAR. 27 Dimasalang House for elderly and handicapped opens in the Yerba Buena area.

APR. 1 Youth hostel at Fort Mason opens.

APR. 11 Senator Edward Kennedy visits San Francisco on the campaign trail.

APR. 26 Robert Carroll, Navy Seabee reservist, falls to his death from the Dutch Windmill in Golden Gate Park.

APR. 27 13 prisoners escape from city jail, seventh floor Hall of Justice.

MAY 30 Last day of home milk delivery in San Francisco.

JUNE 25 Bay Bridge closed due to a chemical spill beginning 3:55 p.m. Lanes were not reopened until Thursday morning at 1:15 a.m.

JUNE 29 Gay Freedom Day Parade.

JULY 2 Airporter Bus Terminal dedicated.

JULY 3 Willie McCovey plays his last game for the San Francisco Giants.

JULY 11 The 16th Gyalwa Karmapa, a Buddist leader, visits San Francisco as part of a seven-month tour of the U.S.

JULY 17 Hotel strike begins. The Wine Institute holds the world's largest tasting at the St. Francis Hotel. 3,000 bottles consumed during the tasting.

JULY 26 Jefferson Wilson becomes new San Francisco postmaster.

JULY 31 Golden Gate Park Senior Center, 6101 Fulton Street at 37th Ave., dedicated.

JULY 31 Acting Battalion Chief Herbert Osuna dies in a Financial District fire.

AUG. 1 Mary I. Callanan, chief accountant

at San Francisco Airport, takes over as City Treasurer upon retirement of Thomas Scanlon.

AUG. 1 Gorilla World, newest and most spectacular exhibit at the San Francisco Zoo, officially opened by Mayor Dianne Feinstein.

AUG. 27 City of Paris demolition begins with dismantling of tower.

SEPT. 3 Leak in BART tube discovered. Investigation follows; tube patching costs $55,000. Bringing China to Fort Mason, China Trade Fair opens.

SEPT. 9 Man survives 210-foot leap from Bay Bridge.

SEPT. 10 City Historical Museum proposed.

SEPT. 16 Louise M. Davies Symphony Hall inaugural benefit and gala performance.

SEPT. 19 $300,000 in silver and gold stolen at airport.

SEPT. 22 Alamo Park High School opens.

OCT. 10 Dedication of On Lok House, a congregate facility for the frail and elderly, at 1441 Powell Street.

OCT. 13 Rosalynn Carter visits.

OCT. 21 Interns and residents of San Francisco General Hospital walk out over shortages of nurses, security guards and translators.

OCT. 24 Latest 1980 census count: 674,063. San Francisco General Hospital strike ends.

NOV. 4 St. Teresa of Avila Church celebrates 100 years.

NOV. 5 District elections of supervisors defeated. Citywide election resumed; Revised Charter defeated.

NOV. 8 Large earthquake shakes north coast.

NOV. 21 Dolphin Club at Aquatic Park destroyed by fire.

1981

JUNE 16 Fire occurs on 14th floor of Tishman Bldg.

AUG. 20 Emergency 9-1-1 number activated.

SEPT. 27 Jose Napoleon Duarte,

El Salvador President, visits.
OCT. 25 Luis Herrera, Venezuela President, visits.
NOV. 1 First "Save The Cable Cars" run.
DEC. 2 Moscone Center opens.

1982
JAN. 4 First electronic mail service begins.
JAN. 4–7 Golden Gate Bridge closures due to storm.
JAN. 24 San Francisco 49ers win Super Bowl.
MAR. 19 Preservationists lose fight to save Maskey Building.
MAY 12 Nuclear attacks education launched.
JUNE 9 Self-service cable car ticket machines are put into service at Powell and Market streets.
AUG. 23 Peter Bird begins rowing from San Francisco to Australia, 9,000 miles away.
SEPT. 22 Cable cars shut down for reconstruction of track.

1983
APR. 19 City College fire; $2 million in damage.
JUNE 14 Peter Bird lands at the Great Barrier Reef in Australia after rowing from San Francisco, setting a world record.
AUG. 25 John Glenn visits.
SEPT. 6 Davies Symphony Hall opens.
OCT. 1 Mayor Feinstein proclaims "Edna Fischer Day" to honor "San Francisco's first lady of radio."
DEC. 11 First black Catholic pastor, Rev. James E. Goode, installed at St. Paul of the Shipwreck Church in the Bayview District.

1984
JAN. 13 Van Ness Ave. handicap ramp to City Hall opens.
FEB. 1 Tom Hsieh, architect, sworn in as first Asian on Police Commission.

MAY 30 Sixty-foot articulated (bend-in-the middle) diesel buses begin service.
JUNE 3 Cable cars run again.
JUNE 21 Party for returning cable car service.
JULY Muni publishes timetable booklet for first time. Consulate of Israel opens.
JULY 13 Presidential candidate Gary Hart visits.
AUG. 12 Suicide car crashes into cable car.
OCT. 2 Supervisors reject nativity scene at City Hall.
OCT. 31 Albert Samuels's jeweler's clock repaired and ticks again on Market Street.

1985
JAN. 20 San Francisco 49ers win Super Bowl.
MAY 29 Greenhouse and animal park dedicated at Laguna Honda.
JUNE 1–3 Federation of Chinese organizations holds convention at Hilton Hotel.
AUG. 26 Interior Secretary Donald Hodel visits.
OCT. 21 Dan White commits suicide.

1986
APR. 4 Huge blast and fire at Bayview Industrial Park.
MAY 30 West Sunset Soccer Fields dedicated.
JUNE 14 Ian Johnston of Australia sets sail for Kauai in a 40-foot trimaran.
JUNE 26 Ian Johnston arrives at Kauai from San Francisco, setting a world sail record.

1987
MAR. 2 San Francisco's first live-in hospice opens (Coming Home Hospice).
JULY 18 Rosie the Riveter sets a world tapdance record by leading 14 tappers through San Francisco 7.5 miles.
SEPT. 18 Pope John Paul II visits.
DEC. 28 Muni's 75th anniversary is celebrated by a parade of historic streetcars and

buses on Market Street.

1988

MAR. 28 City celebrates 100 years of Powell Street Cable Car service with a parade of cable cars.

MAY 15 More than 110,000 people take part in the *San Francisco Examiner's* Bay-to-Breakers race.

NOV. 10 Last football game played in Kezar Stadium between Sacred Heart High and Mitty High.

NOV. 24 Warren Luhrs sets out from New York in a monohull ultra-light displacement boat bound for San Francisco.

DEC. 15 The *San Francisco Progress* ceases publishing.

1989

JAN. 9 Palace Hotel closes for renovation.

JAN. 23 San Francisco 49ers win Super Bowl defeating Cincinnati Bengals.

JAN. 31 80 protesters affiliated with ACT UP (Aids Coalition to Unleash Power) close the Golden Gate Bridge to traffic.

FEB. 4 Two million telephone customers in the 415 area code must first dial "1" for calls outside their region.

FEB. 8 Liberace's clothes go on auction at Butterfield & Butterfield.

FEB. 12 Warren Luhrs arrives in San Francisco after sailing from New York, setting a world record.

FEB. 16 Duguette Pavilion of St. Francis destroyed in a five-alarm fire on Geary St

MAR. 10 Canadian George Kolesnikovs leaves New York with sails set for San Francisco in a 60-foot trimaran.

APR. 15 Bank of America begins Saturday hours.

MAY 26 George Kolesnikovs arrives by sail from New York to set a world record.

JUNE 29 French Hospital becomes part of Kaiser System (Kaiser Permanente French Campus).

JULY 21 Dedication of the H. Welton Flynn Motor Coach Division, 1940 Harrison Street, by San Francisco

Municipal Railway.

OCT. 3 BART sets an all-time record for passenger service when the A's beat the Toronto Blue Jays in the American League playoffs.

OCT. 9 Giants defeat Chicago in the National League four games to one.

OCT. 10 The Dalai Lama, the exiled leader of Tibet, meets with his followers atop Mt. Tamalpais after landing there in a helicopter.

OCT. 12 San Francisco's two teachers unions merge and become members of the American Federation of Teachers.

OCT. 14 The Oakland A's shut out the Giants in the first game of the World Series in Oakland.

OCT. 15 The A's again defeat the Giants 5–1 in the second game of the World Series.

OCT. 17 A magnitude 7.1 earthquake strikes the Bay Area just before the third game of the World Series at Candlestick Park, the worst earthquake since 1906. The tremor collapsed a portion of the San Francisco-Oakland Bay Bridge, destroyed 11 houses in San Francisco and damaged another 382. At least 134 business structures were damaged and 11 people were killed as a direct result of the earthquake. Five of the deaths occurred when the exterior of a brick building collapsed at 6th and Bluxome streets in the South of Market District. Damage was estimated at almost three billion dollars in San Francisco, which was approximately one-half of the total damage figure for the entire earthquake zone.

At least 27 fires broke out across the city, including a major blaze in the Marina District where apartment buildings sank into a lagoon filled with rubble from the 1906 earthquake in preparation for the Panama-Pacific International Exposition of 1915. Dozens of people were rescued by fire fighters from fallen buildings in the area that was imperiled by the flames. As they had done in 1906, citizens formed a bucket brigade to help firefighters in the Marina

District who were without water because of broken water mains.

The world followed the progress of the Marina District fire as it was broadcast by ABC "live" from the Goodyear blimp. San Francisco's elaborate saltwater pump stations, built after 1906 to provide fire-fighting water, were used for the first time to pump water to the Marina District once the mains were repaired. The Historic Post Office building at Seventh and Mission streets was dreadfully damaged, as it had been in 1906, and was immediately closed for reconstruction. The City Hall was also damaged, but remained in operation pending major repairs and seismic upgrading.

The earthquake also knocked out power to San Francisco, and the city was dark for the first time since the 1906 earthquake and fire. Power was fully restored by October 20. Emergency telephone service ceased because a fire broke out in the 9-1-1 telephone equipment room, and citizens had to rely on fire alarm boxes for three days for emergency protection from fire.

Sporadic but minor looting broke out in the downtown shopping district near Fifth and Market streets, the Inner Mission, and Hunters Point areas. District Attorney Arlo Smith said, "If there's anyone arrested tonight for burglary or looting, tomorrow morning we're going to go into court and demand that there be no bail. Anyone engaged in that kind of conduct can expect maximum sentences."

A performance of Mozart's "Idomeneo" at the Opera House canceled after the earthquake with no word on whether "Otello" will open the following weekend.

Municipal organ at Civic Auditorium badly damaged by the earthquake.

Oct. 18 ABC receives a strong 24.2 rating and a 35 share for its earthquake coverage in the prime 8 p.m. to 11 p.m. EDT time slot the previous night.

Vice President Dan Quayle and his wife, Marilyn, fly from San Diego to the Marina District. They leave in four hours without making contact with Mayor Agnos, who had not slept since the quake. The mayor calls the visit a "cheap publicity stunt." Quayle reacts with deep emotion when he tours the damaged Marina District. He said, "Just walking through here and seeing the loss of property, knowing of the loss of life, it hits you right here in the heart, and that's the reason I'm here."

BART is temporarily shut down after a train operator reports a leak in the Transbay Tube. It is a false alarm.

The Pacific Stock Exchange opens as dealers worked by candle and flashlight, rerouting trades by phone through Los Angeles.

A U-2 spy plane from Beale Air Force Base overflies San Francisco to record earthquake damage. The photos could be used to detect problems in structures.

The day after the San Francisco earthquake, AT&T handles 144.7 million long-distance calls, an all-time record, said spokesman Herb Linnen. On an average day, the company handles 115 million to 120 million calls.

Staff from Thornton Anderson Architects begin an evaluation of Candlestick Park during the afternoon.

Preliminary ratings for the ABC, CBS, and NBC earthquake specials Wednesday night indicated nearly half of all U.S. homes with television tuned in. According to A.C. Nielsen Co. estimates, ABC's special, "The Great Quake of '89," was the highest-rated with 13.2 percent of all households watching.

Lt. Gov. Leo McCarthy calls for an investigation about why the Bay Bridge was so badly damaged during the earthquake. McCarthy is the Acting Governor of California because Gov. Deukmejian is in Frankfurt, West Germany.

Oct. 19 The Oakland Athletics voted not to have any champagne in their clubhouse if they win the World Series. "Because of the earthquake and the feeling of the club, we didn't think it would be appropriate," A's player Dave Parker said.

Mayor's office estimates $2 billion in property losses. Most electricity restored except to the Marina District. More than 8,000 Pacific Gas & Electric customers remain without electricity, 30,000 without gas.

Repairs begin on the Bay Bridge.

Baseball commissioner Fay Vincent said tonight that the Oakland Coliseum has been certified by the city as ready to play and Candlestick Park is expected to receive official certification Monday. The third game of the World Series will be played Tuesday Oct. 24.

United Airlines, the largest carrier to San Francisco International Airport, is at 50 percent strength and expects to be about the same tomorrow, with 65 flights in and out of the airport.

Three strong aftershocks rock San Francisco. Power continues to be restored to the blacked out Financial District, although most buildings have not yet been inspected for damage. Fires start in some buildings when the electricity is turned on.

At the Pentagon, spokesman Pete Williams says 1,173 California National Guardsmen have been called to duty.

The U.S. dollar closed lower at 141.55 yen in Tokyo foreign exchange dealings because of the earthquake in San Francisco and the worsening trade deficit. A dealer at Dai-Ichi Kangyo Bank says, "Recent developments did not provide any incentive to buy dollars."

About 150 Pacific Stock Exchange traders fly to Chicago, New York and Philadelphia overnight to resume options trading because of the continuing power failure in downtown San Francisco.

AT&T still limiting some long-distance calls into the San Francisco area. Call attempts are 54 percent lower than yesterday, but still 351 percent higher than nor-mal. The previous day AT&T handled approximately 27.8 million call attempts to the San Francisco area, completing about 9.5 million.

Several Pacific Fleet warships arrive at San Francisco ready to provide electric power, fresh water, and emergency services. Members of Navy Amphibious Construction Battalion 1 convoys to the Bay Area from San Diego to join other West Coast Seabee units assigned to help restore utility services to Bay Area military bases and surrounding communities.

Oct. 20 Mayor Agnos informs enraged survivors in the Marina District that they have just 15 minutes to enter their quake damaged homes to retrieve belongings prior to demolition. Agnos did not carry the Marina District in the mayoral election.

Governor George Deukmejian tells NBC-TV: "Over the six-and-a-half, nearly seven years, that I've been Governor, I've never once been told by our people that we had any kind of a problem with respect to our freeways holding up under an earthquake situation, the severity of the one that we experienced here. So this came as a big surprise to me, a terrible disappointment."

President Bush arrives at Moffett Field Naval Air Station to tour areas damaged by earthquake. He is briefed by civic leaders, including Mayor Agnos.

Red Cross chapter in Portland ships bread and other supplies to earthquake victims in San Francisco.

Gov. Mario Cuomo of New York assists in coping with Tuesday's devastating earthquake. In a letter to Gov. George Deukmejian, Cuomo said, "New York stands ready to assist in any way we can." The New York Air National Guard has already sent crews to relieve California Air Guard members.

Cheng Hsin-Hsiung of the Kuomintang ruling party leaves Taipei for San Francisco to express the party's concerns for overseas Chinese residents and students.

Economist Frank McCormick of the Bank of America in San Francisco said earthquake damage was likely to reach $10 billion.

Oct. 22 A helicopter attempting to remove the damaged flagpole from the top of the Ferry Building drops the flagpole which crashes through the roof of the building.

More than 20,000 people gathered at the Polo Field in Golden Gate Park to hear the San Francisco Symphony and Chorus in a benefit concert of Beethoven's Ninth Symphony for earthquake survivors.

U.S. Navy helicopter carrier USS *Peleliu* housed 300 displaced earthquake victims who boarded at 1 p.m. at Pier 30-32. The *Peleliu* is homeported in San Diego and was one of three amphibious ships dispatched to assist earthquake recovery efforts.

The 49ers-Patriots game today is forced to move to Stanford Stadium because of damage to Candlestick Park.

Oct. 23 USGS has recorded 74 aftershocks of magnitude 3.0 and larger, including 17 of 4.0 and larger. The largest, measured at 5.2, occurred at 5:41 p.m., 37 minutes after the main shock on Tuesday. The second largest was 5.0 and struck at 3:14 a.m. Oct. 19. Gov. George Deukmejian will call a special session of the Legislature within two weeks to work out the state's response to the devastation. Mayor Agnos tells the Board of Supervisors that 750 to 1,000 buildings in the city need extensive repair. He estimated damage in the city at $2.2 billion to $3.2 billion. Secretary of State James A. Baker III addresses the Commonwealth Club of California. He said, "In view of the suffering, somehow it just didn't seem completely right to come here and speak to you about arms control. But you requested that I fulfill this commitment and I think that is a telling sign, if I may put it this way, of your character. It is the truly American character of facing up to disaster, taking its measure, and then going about getting on with the work. It is the truly Bay Area character, as

well, I think, of looking to the future."

Oct. 24 Bandleader Jimmy Price will introduce "The Ballad of Buck Helm" tonight at the New Orleans Room of the Fairmont Hotel and plans to record the tune. Helm was miraculously pulled from the rubble 90 hours after the Cypress Freeway collapse. "The idea came to me like a flash, I popped out of bed at 6 a.m. (Sunday) and frantically pulled out my music paper. It was like I was inspired from on high," the bandleader said.

BART placed 60 additional cars in service and scheduled trains at more frequent intervals throughout the day. As of 7 p.m., 261,903 patrons had ridden BART, an all-time record.

Enforcement of all municipal parking regulations are in effect, and street sweeping regulations related to parking will resume tomorrow, Oct. 25.

Bank of America Chairman and Chief Executive Officer A. W. Clausen is named Chairman of the American Red Cross disaster relief campaign in the San Francisco Bay Area.

Bank America Corp. shares drop $1.25 on the New York Stock Exchange on an unfounded rumor that the bank's California and Kearny streets headquarters building was damaged in last week's earthquake. A bank spokesman said that the structure was not harmed by the temblor and isn't owned by the bank.

First major convention since the earthquake opened at the Civic Auditorium. Don Dowd, spokesman for the Computer Aided Software Engineering Conference and Exposition says, "Our keynote speaker addressed a full house and our exhibits are open as scheduled, with about 1,500 delegates in attendance. No one here is talking about the earthquake—they're talking about improving their information technology systems."

Congress begins debate on an earthquake relief bill. "We were hit by ten times the amount of explosive power of World War II, including the atomic bomb," says Rep. Nancy Pelosi of San Francisco. "Please give us a chance to rebuild." A congressman from Wisconsin complained that because the median home price in San Francisco is $350,000, Californians don't need help because of their waste and affluence.

The U.S. Geological Survey today revised the magnitude of the Oct. 17 quake from 6.9 to 7.1 on the Richter scale after checking data from 18 seismic stations around the world.

BART trains carry 313,302 passengers Tuesday, 23,242 more than on Monday, and far exceeding any other weekday total. It was the first time BART patronage had climbed past the 300,000 mark.

A magnitude 4.5 aftershock jolts San Francisco, but causes no new damage.

School Superintendent Ramon Cortines announces that schools will reopen today, except Marina Middle School which is being used as a shelter.

Oct. 25 Evangelist Billy Graham tours the Marina District today. "I don't think we can say this earthquake was sent by God," says Graham. "We have to keep in mind that He is a God of love, mercy. Why this earthquake took place, I can't explain," Graham tells reporters. "I can only explain God gives grace, peace, and strength to those who trust in Him."

Mayor Agnos says engineers have determined that Candlestick Park wasn't seriously damaged by the quake and game three of the World Series can play on Friday. Rain hampered both the A's and the Giants in their attempts to practice at Candlestick. The A's go to Phoenix for workouts today and tomorrow.

Three Washington passenger ferries set sail from Port Angeles to be used for commuter service on the bay. The *Tyree*, *Skagit* and *Kalama* should reach San Francisco by Friday, barring any unexpected bad weather.

USGS scientists say there is a 50-50 chance that an earthquake big enough to cause more damage will strike during the next two months and urges officials to prepare.

BART's total ridership today reaches 324,904, a new record, and more than 100,000 over a typical pre-quake weekday of 218,000.

Pacific Union Co. says there is no evidence the earthquake will affect the real estate market. "Contrary to what the rest of the U.S. might believe, buyer interest has actually increased since last week's earthquake," said William Jansen, president of Pacific Union Residential Brokerage. "Many buyers hope to find good deals as a result of an expected seller's panic," he said.

A *San Francisco Chronicle* poll shows three out of four residents in 10 Bay Area counties admit having emotional problems since last Tuesday's major earthquake. About two-thirds say they are worried about another major tremor.

About 10,000 riders use ferryboat service across the bay, an increase of 31 percent over Tuesday's tally of 7,650. For the three days from Monday through Wednesday (Oct. 23-25), total ridership count was 24,286. Red & White Fleet said it is adding to Saturday and Sunday service between Oakland and the Ferry Building to accommodate World Series goers.

Jerusalem mayor Teddy Kolleck addresses the World Affairs Council of Northern California in the Grand Ballroom of the St. Francis Hotel.

Oct. 25 John Beckman, a survivor of the 1906 earthquake, dies in Sherman Oaks, CA. Beckman designed sets for the motion pictures *Casablanca*, *The Maltese Falcon*, and the hit TV sitcom "Designing Women." He was 91.

OCT. 26 The Emporium downtown San Francisco store will reopen Monday. The Emporium reopened its Mountain View store Tuesday but its Oakland and Alameda stores remain closed.

President Bush signs a $3.45 billion earthquake relief package for California.

Former President Reagan, in Tokyo, meets 13 Japanese college students who volunteer to help Californians clean up and rebuild their homes in the San Francisco Bay Area. "I have just met with one of the most inspiring groups of young people I have ever encountered," the former president and California governor said. "Their trip to San Francisco is a most eloquent statement about the special friendship between the people of Japan and the people of the United States," he said.

The California Grape and Tree Fruit League will deliver a truckload of fresh fruit for earthquake survivors tomorrow at Glide Memorial Church.

The *San Francisco Examiner* publishes a 16-page earthquake photo section documenting the day of the earthquake and its aftermath.

The California Office of Tourism suggests that earthquake effects are exaggerated. In a news release the organization says, "The greater San Francisco Bay Area has rebounded quickly from a major earthquake that struck the region on Oct. 17. Damage to lodging facilities, convention centers and attractions was minimal, and all major airports in the area are open and operating at full service."

OCT. 27 Officials of the International Society for Traumatic Stress Studies called off their disaster drill because of the earthquake. Yael Danieli, Israeli psychologist and president of the society, said Northern California is handling the quake in a "typically American" manner, not allowing the quake to interfere with events such as the World Series. Thousands of fans sing "San Francisco" as the third game of the World Series restarts at Candlestick Park. Oakland wins 13 to 7. Inside the park, some fans wore plastic helmets; others carried flashights and cellular telephones. Southern Pacific inaugurates round-the-bay shuttle service between Oakland and San Francisco to help in the distribution of freight while

earthquake damage to bridges and highways is repaired. Wreckage of fallen buildings in the Marina District is hauled to the Norcal Solid Waste Systems' wood reclamation facility and landfill on Zanker Rd. in San Jose. There, crews are sort and handpick personal belongings from the wreckage. Recovered items range from family photos and heirlooms, jewelry and silver to wallets, credits cards, and money.

OCT. 28 California Conservation Corps members continue to work 24-hour shifts to help Marina District residents retrieve valuables from their homes and assist with traffic control. The Corps also provides meals to earthquake victims in the Tenderloin. Part of the proceeds of the 10th annual Exotic Erotic Halloween Ball go to earthquake relief. More than 10,000 celebrants attend. The Copley News Service reports that a parakeet was recovered alive from the rubble of the fallen apartment building at Fillmore and Cervantes. The bird, the report said, was found during demolition operations. San Francisco law firm Orrick, Herrington & Sutcliffe donates an additional $100,000 to the earthquake relief effort, bringing its total donation to $150,000.

The USGS reports a 3.1 magnitude aftershock hit at 2:28 p.m. The Survey also said there had been 80 aftershocks of magnitude 3.0 or larger by 4 p.m., including 20 of magnitude 4.0 or larger.

OCT. 29 Southern Pacific officials announce new weekday rail commuter service between Sacramento, Oakland, and San Jose. Trains also will run from Sacramento to Jack London Square for connection with boats to the city.

The Japanese Red Cross Society sends 5 million yen to the American Red Cross to help victims of the earthquake in San Francisco.

OCT. 30 The Jefferson Airplane gives a concert in the Park's Polo Field.

Viacom Broadcasting Inc. agrees to buy KOFY-AM and FM in San Francisco for approximately $19.5 million.

Chinese students studying in the United States are ordered to register with the Chinese Consulate today. The order from Beijing came after two Chinese students were granted asylum in San Francisco after testifying they feared returning to China because of involvement in the Tiananmen Square demonstrations. Berkeley-San Francisco ferryboat inaugurated at 6 a.m. Service on the Oakland boat is reduced from every 20 minutes to every 30 minutes. Berkeley ferries will run from Berkeley Municipal Pier at University Ave. to the Ferry Building. BART carried almost 1.6 million passengers during the five-day work week, including nearly one million passengers through the Transbay Tube. Friday patronage—329,276—was at an all-time high for BART, and records were also set for Saturday and Sunday patronage.

The U.S. Court of Appeals and Post Office facilities at 7th and Mission streets suffered extensive damage in the recent earthquake and will remain closed until repaired.

The Bay Bridge will remain closed until at least Nov. 16 for repairs. The Embarcadero Freeway will be closed for about three months so the roadway's columns can be reinforced.

Nov. 1 BART sets a one-day record with 335,149 passengers using the system. A 4.4 Richter magnitude aftershock panics earthquake victims throughout the Bay Area. Minor damage reported in the Marina District.

Nov. 2 Proposition P, to build a new baseball stadium loses by less than 2,000 votes. Mayor Agnos says there is nothing to stop the National League champion San Francisco Giants from moving to nearby Santa Clara. Critics of the proposition claim that stadium construction would take money away from the earthquake recovery effort. Actor Paul Newman donates $250,000 and 10,000 pounds of his spaghetti sauce to victims of the earthquake.

Nov. 3 Treasure Island declared a California Historic Landmark. BART sets an all-time ridership record of 352,696. Pacific Gas and Electric Co. crews work 24-hour shifts in the Marina District to replace 10 miles of gas distribution lines at a cost of more than $10 million. Service may be restored by Christmas.

Nov. 13 BART ridership totaled 345,891, the fifth highest daily total since Oct. 23. Including Oct. 23, the first full workday since the Oct. 17 earthquake, BART patronage totaled nearly 5 million during the 15 weekdays through Friday, Nov. 10. The exact total was 4,962,181, an average of 330,812 a day. Patronage on a typical weekday prior to the earthquake was 218,000.

Nov. 14 Hurricane Hugo and the San Francisco earthquake caused enough damage to make 1989 the worst year ever for insured catastrophe losses. The private property insurance industry expects to pay a total of $6.63 billion on 31 catastrophes in 1989.

Nov. 15 The Federal Reserve Board said the strike against Boeing Co. and the earthquake pushed production at U.S. factories, mines, and utilities down a sharp 0.7 percent in October. BART carries more passengers today than on any other day in its history, a total of 355,131, surpassing the previous record of 352,696 set on Friday, Nov. 3. FEMA holds a news conference to deny charges of discrimination against low-income people affected by the Oct. 17 earthquake.

Nov. 16 The walk across the Bay Bridge costs six dollars. The event features Tony Bennett singing "I Left My Heart in San Francisco" and Carol Channing singing "San Francisco" from the 1936 movie. The party atop a new 250-ton slab of roadway marks the first time a public walk was allowed on the bridge since its inauguration 53 years ago. BART's patronage today totaled 357,135, a new record, exceeding Wednesday's figure of 355,131.

Nov. 18 The San Francisco-Oakland Bay Bridge reopens. Caltrans had hoped to open the bridge the previous day but two foggy nights created enough moisture to interrupt stripe painting on the bridge.

Nov. 20 BART patronage totaled 273,585 Monday, compared with an average of 328,549 for the three previous Mondays, down 17 percent. The drop is attributed to the reopening of the Bay Bridge.

Nov. 22 BART announces that 24-hour a day service will continue until Dec. 3.

Nov. 25 Jane Cryan, founder of the Society for the Preservation and Appreciation of San Francisco Refugee Shacks, said the 1989 earthquake "threw me for a loop. I have decided to begin life anew in my home state of Wisconsin and am returning to my ancestral town of Oshkosh."

Nov. 27 San Francisco Mayor Art Agnos and a city delegation begin a three-day junket to explain earthquake recovery plans to leaders of the tourism industry. Stops include Chicago, New York, and Washington. Tourism is down 10 to 20 percent.

Nov. 28 Crane falls from atop the Federal Home Loan Bank Building at 601 California; kills 5, injures 20.

Dec. 3 BART ends all-night "Owl" service established after the earthquake.

Dec. 15 FEMA reports 90 homeless earthquake victims are still sheltered at the old Pierce Arrow building on Polk Street.

Dec. 19 Red Cross toy distribution to children of earthquake survivors begins at the Red Cross shelter at 1550 Sutter Street.

Dec. 31 Venetian Room at Fairmont Hotel closes.

1990

Jan. 1 5K race benefits those left homeless in 1989 quake.

Jan. 23 The voters will be asked in June to approve the biggest bond issue in city history, $332.4 million, for repairing buildings and pipelines damaged by the Oct. 17 earthquake.

Mar. 23 Coast Guard Station at Fort Point closed. Relocated in Marin County.

Apr. The Grand Jury indicts five persons, including campaign consultants Jack Davis and Richard Schlachman for violating state election laws. The charge said Sacramento developer Greg Lukenbill encouraged a Marin County company to donate $12,500 to a campaign against a San Francisco ballot proposal calling for the construction of a downtown baseball-only stadium. Those indicted become known as the "Ballpark Five."

Apr. 16 Hundreds of Chinatown merchants close up shop to attend Board of Supervisors hearing on Embarcadero Freeway demolition. The merchants claim that business in Chinatown will die without the vital transportation link.

Apr. 18 Mayor Art Agnos criticizes scientists who said that odds were good for a major quake in the next 25 years: "The people who make predictions need to make their science much more precise and then, when they know exactly when it's going to happen tell us, because we want the information. I got the message. I don't need any more. Save it, and give it to those areas where they need to have that kind of alert given to them because they are not as experienced as we are." A magnitude 5.4 aftershock of the 1989 earthquake frightens younger celebrants at Lotta's Fountain as they commemorate the 1906 disaster. Survivors of the 1906 disaster shrugged off the latest tremor and headed for the Golden Hydrant at 20th and Church streets for the celebration of the Great Earthquake and Fire.

Apr. 22 Earth Day celebrated with ceremonies held in Crissy Field.

Apr. 23 A quake-weakened water main fails near Civic Center and causes a large hole in the street.

Apr. 26 San Francisco Fire Dept.'s new fireboat christened *The Guardian*.

May 10 The icebreaker *Volga*, first naval vessel from the USSR to visit since WW II, arrives.

MAY 20 70,000 run San Francisco Bay-to-Breakers race.

JUNE 4–5 Mikhail Gorbachev, Soviet president, visits.

JUNE 5–6 South Korean President Roh Tae-woo visits S.F. Meets with Soviet leader Mikhail Gorbachev.

JUNE 7 Saint Rose Academy, founded in 1862 on Brannan near 3rd Street, closes its doors due to 1989 earthquake damage.

JUNE 11 Five-alarm fire at 1370 California Street.

JUNE 15 Capt. Marsha Evans, first woman to run Treasure Island naval station, assumes command.

JUNE 19 ACT UP protestors sit in at Marriott Hotel.

JUNE 30 A mild 4.0 earthquake is felt in San Francisco at 5:36 p.m. No damage is reported. The quake was centered near San Jose on the Calaveras fault.

JULY 19 A panel of scientists say odds that a destructive earthquake will strike along one of four Bay Area fault segments at some time during the next 30 years are now 2 to 1. Scientists say they now believe the overall likelihood of an earthquake with a Richter magnitude of 7 or greater before the year 2020 is at least 67 percent.

JULY 30 An editorial on KOFY-TV criticizes Caltrans for incompetence. Station owner James Gabbert said, "This is one of the off ramps at Gough Street and Franklin. See those steel braces? They have spent millions and millions of dollars reinforcing this freeway and reinforcing 280. But you know what? They didn't check with the proper engineers and it turns out all of that work was for naught. They've got to tear everything down they did. In other words, they wasted millions and millions of dollars. We have defects. We have economic problems. Is anyone at Caltrans going to lose their job? I think the losers are you and me."

SEPT. 5 Supervisors delay their vote on Embarcadero Freeway demolition. The matter will be debated at a special hearing of the board's Economic and Social Policy Committee on Sept. 19. "It's not stalling," Supervisor Terence Hallinan said.

Supervisor Bill Maher said, "It's gotten to the point of ridiculousness. It looks like the Board of Supervisors is paralyzed and incompetent. We need to make a decision."

SEPT. 12 U.C.S.F. opens new library at Third Ave. and Parnassus.

SEPT. 15 Sears shuts Geary Street store.

SEPT. 17 Electrical fire at BART station in West Oakland, causing all trains to stop.

SEPT. 19 President Bush visits; speaks at Fairmont Hotel.

OCT. 13 Resulting from the Oct. 17, 1989 earthquake, a large fissure develops in the eastern face of Telegraph Hill. Work begins on rock removal and installation of a rock bolt system to protect against further rock droppings.

OCT. 15 The USGS says it has recorded more than 7,000 aftershocks of the 1989 quake that range in magnitude from zero to 5.4 on the Richter scale.

OCT. 17 "We will remember those we lost and celebrate the spiritual fortitude our city showed after the earthquake," said San Francisco Mayor Art Agnos. The Mayor asked churches to ring their bells at the moment the quake struck in honor of the 67 people who died one year ago. Actor Danny Glover hosted a civic ceremony at the Ferry Building where the San Francisco Symphony and San Francisco Opera performed as the waterfront building's flag was hoisted for the first time since the earth's violent shaking tilted its pole. At the same time, the Chamber of Commerce hosted a "Celebraton of Heroes" at Pier 35 for the estimated 4,000 people who helped out in the quake's aftermath.

OCT. 24 The Board of Supervisors votes 6 to 5 to demolish the Embarcadero Freeway.

OCT. 31 Televangelist Larry Lea of Texas leads 10,000 in prayer to "slay the demon" gripping San Francisco.

NOV. 15 President Chaim Herzog of Israel visits.

Nov. 26 Palace of Fine Arts lighted.

Dec. 6 The federal government will pay nearly $25 million to counties hit by the 1989 Loma Prieta earthquake to help displaced poor people. Federal Emergency Management Agency officials backed out of a similar agreement announced in February, saying it had been signed under a misunderstanding.

1991

Mar. 8 Repair schedules for two stretches of earthquake-damaged freeways fell behind one to two years, a move which Mayor Art Agnos called "ridiculous."

Mar. 23 A 4.8 magnitude earthquake rattles San Francisco at 7:44 p.m. but causes no damage. USGS scientists said the tremor was an aftershock of the 1989 earthquake.

Apr. 2 Governor Pete Wilson conducts a statewide earthquake exercise by radio. The Emergency Broadcast System tone was heard on radios in Los Angeles, San Francisco, and dozens of other cities.

Apr. 17 A survey taken shortly after the 1989 earthquake finds some people experienced a sense that their surroundings were not quite real. Some mention unusual body sensations, such as spinning or falling down a tunnel. Others said they had felt that time slowed down or that personal experiences sometimes seemed to be happening at a psychological distance, almost as if they were appearing on television. The earthquake study was released at the annual meeting of the American Psychiatric Association in New Orleans.

Apr. 18 Survivors of the 1906 earthquake gather at Lotta's Fountain for the 85th anniversary. The commemoration features Ron Fahey, winner of the "Caruso sound-alike" contest.

San Francisco Fire Chief Frederick F. Postel releases the department's official report on operations during the 1989 earthquake.

Apr. 30 The state settles a lawsuit brought by the family of a woman who drove off a collapsed section of the Bay Bridge during the earthquake. The sum was not disclosed. David Baum, attorney for the family of Anamafi Moala, said, "CHP officers and Caltrans employees were on the scene but failed to properly control traffic and a number of cars were sent toward Oakland."

June 15 Scientists close part of Washington Interstate 90 to attach 64 steel cables to a bridge and slowly pull the structure back and forth in different directions, using hydraulic jacks. The tests will last from 10 minutes to two hours to determine how to make San Francisco freeways stronger.

June 28 Demolition of the Embarcadero Freeway is only 30 percent complete one day after the original scheduled completion date. Caltrans spokesman Don Manning said demolition of the freeway will be finished by the end of September. Demolition of the upper deck of the Central Freeway will begin next week with a photo survey of the route. Demolition work on the roadway itself will begin by mid-July.

Aug. 17 A 120-year-old Spring Valley Water Company main along Valencia Street breaks and cuts off water to the Mission District during the evening. The break, between 15th and 16th streets, was two blocks from where the same main broke during the 1906 earthquake and cut the water supply to fire hydrants in downtown San Francisco. The 1906 break, between 17th and 18th streets in front of the Valencia St. Hotel, resulted in the destruction of the city by fire. Martin Lieberman, manager for city distribution for the San Francisco Water Department, conceded that the old water line might have been weakened by the 1989 earthquake.

Sept. 4 USGS research vessel S. P. Lee begins a series of tests in San Francisco Bay to determine if the region's earthquake faults are connected underwater and help predict if the Hayward Fault is ready to produce a major temblor. Compressed-air chambers will be towed underwater to allow the scientists to read acoustic energy waves bounced from the chambers to the bottom and back from earthquake faults and rock layers as deep as 15 to 20 miles. The tests were scheduled to end Sept. 19.

SEPT. 18 Scientists at UC San Diego reveal a new technology that will allow damaged double-deck freeways in San Francisco to withstand a quake as large as 1906. It features a beam supported by circular columns running along the outside of the bridge. Researchers used computer-controlled hydraulic jacks to generate a force greater than a magnitude 8.0 earthquake on the San Andreas Fault, which is considered the maximum possible for a future earthquake in San Francisco, said Frieder Seible, professor of structural engineering at the university.

SEPT. 20 A consultant's report estimates that repairing City Hall could cost more than four times the initial estimate of $23 million. Assistant City Architect Mark Primeau said the report identifies isolating the base of the building from earthquake motion as both the least expensive and most effective seismic strengthening technique. But the cost will still run between $80 million and $100 million.

OCT. 3 Part of a metal girder crashes into Geva's Restaurant on Hayes Street, forcing a slowdown in the removal of the Central Freeway. No one was in at the time of accident, but owner Opal Baker said, "My mother usually comes in early to water the garden, and I just tremble when I think that she could have been out there when this happened." The girder crushed two tables and a section of fence bordering the garden. It came to rest just 20 feet from an apartment house. No one was injured.

OCT. 12 The last span of the Embarcadero Freeway—the Broadway off ramp—is demolished. Mayor Agnos thanks those whose efforts made it possible for "return-

ing the waterfront to the people. Today we celebrate not just the end of demolition, but the beginning of renewal for a spectacular waterfront that for 32 years has been blighted by a concrete monster." About 5,500 truckloads of rubble were removed from the site. About 120,000 tons of concrete and 8,000 tons of steel were recycled.

OCT. 15 The damaged section of the Central Freeway between Lily and Turk streets is being demolished. Work is scheduled to begin in January 1992 on the repair and retrofit of Interstate Highway 280 where it crosses the filled-in Mission Bay. The project is to be completed in 1994. Caltrans says there is a possibility of limited use of the structure—one lane in each direction—sometime before 1994. The State of California lowers the official earthquake death toll from 67 to 63. A spokeswoman for the Office of Emergency Services said the change came when county coroners ruled out heart attacks as a cause of earthquake deaths. "When a person has a heart attack, for instance, that's a judgement call," said the spokeswoman.

OCT. 16 Ramon Cortines, Superintendent of Schools, and Fire Chief Fred Postel launch earthquake preparedness educational curriculum on the eve of second anniversary of the earthquake to help educators integrate information about earthquake preparedness and safety into the classroom and home.

OCT. 17 "My impression as a citizen is that the city's *joie de vivre* has recovered," said Dr. Charles Marmar, director of the Veterans Administration post-traumatic stress disorder program on the second anniversary of the earthquake.

OCT. 20 The largest urban wildland fire in the history of the United States rolls out of the Oakland-Berkeley hills. Smoke covers San Francisco, and burning debris from the conflagration falls into the city streets. Many neighborhoods in San Francisco are covered with ash. The fire is so overwhelming that the San Francisco

Fire Department sends 10 engines to Oakland and Berkeley. Battalion Chief Jim Tracey leads a strike team to Oakland and Battalion Chief Paul Tabacco leads a team to Berkeley. Chief Tabacco's strike team was responsible for saving the historic Claremont Hotel from destruction. Later, San Francisco firefighters were transported by Municipal Railway motorcoach to fight the conflagration.

Oct. 21 The 1989 earthquake apparently did not relieve the pressure on the San Andreas Fault as expected, says a scientist from the USGS. A trenching study of the fault line near Santa Cruz showed evidence of the 1906 San Francisco earthquake and a massive shaker in the 1600s, but no sign of the Oct. 17 earthquake. "The evidence from our trenching raises many questions about that segment of the San Andreas fault," said David Schwartz, a geologist from the USGS Geological Survey who took part in the study. "Because there was no surface fault-ing in 1989, strain accumulated in the shallow crust since 1906 may not have been completely relieved by the Loma Prieta earthquake."

Dec. 11 Former Police Chief Frank Jordan elected mayor in an upset victory over incumbent Art Agnos. The results were 48 percent for Agnos and 52 percent for Jordan. Jordan, a first-generation Irish American who had never sought public office, promised to restore "safe and clean streets," and his victory was seen as a triumph for conservative, middle-class activists who complained that San Francisco had become crime-ridden, dirty and a haven for the homeless. Agnos is the first incumbent to lose the mayor's race since 1943. Scientists at a San Francisco news conference reveal the existence of a deadly new earthquake fault under Hollywood. Studies by the USGS and the California Institute of Technology prompted Richard Andrews, the state's emergency services chief, to urge citizens and local officials to review and complete their plans for surviving a seismic disaster. San Francisco seemed unconcerned at this new finding. The research was announced during the American Geophysical Union's fall meeting in San Francisco.

Dec. 21 A two-alarm fire that did moderate damage to the Embassy Theater at 1125 Market Street. The theater was boarded up after the 1989 Loma Prieta earthquake. The Embassy was one of the few structures to survive the 1906 fire in the downtown area.

1992

Jan. 10 A Port Commission plan to line The Embarcadero with palm trees causes an uproar. "I think it's outrageous," said Karl Kortum, director and founder of the San Francisco Maritime National Historic Park. "They've always struck me as a kind of scrawny looking tree as seen in various chase scenes around Los Angeles on television."

Feb. 15 San Francisco firefighters evacuate 81 people from two Telegraph Hill buildings after a mudslide threatened an apartment building on the steep hillside above the Filbert Street steps. Workers in the seven-story office building at 201 Filbert Street., at the base of the hill, and one person at 22-30 Alta Street were told to leave at 2:43 p.m. Fire Chief Fred Postel says a geologist on the scene told him that the shale rock had absorbed water from the heavy rains and had "literally exploded."

Apr. 10 Golden Gate Bridge Directors announce a $10 million design contract for the seismic retrofit of the bridge. The design work for the world-famous suspension bridge is expected to be completed by mid-1994. The actual construction work, which is scheduled to be finished by mid-1997, will cost an estimated $130 million.

Apr. 30 Police crack down as looters and vandals tear through downtown San Francisco smashing windows and setting fires following the Rodney King verdict. Hundreds are arrested. Sheriff's deputies ride "shotgun" on fire apparatus responding to dozens of arson fires. Mayor Jordan goes on television to announce a state of emergency and orders a curfew. More than 1,000 people are arrested.

MAY 1 Protesters continue to skirmish with police, breaking windows and setting fires in downtown San Francisco. Conservatives and shop owners cheer Police Chief Hongisto's tough stand against looting and rioting. The curfew continues into a second day.

MAY 7 Police Chief Hongisto in a telephone call suggests to Inspector Gary Delagnes that fellow officers should clear news racks of the *Bay Times*, a gay publication that ran a cover ridiculing his crackdown on King protesters. More than 2,000 copies of the newspaper disappear.

MAY 14 Mayor Jordan ordered an investigation after hearing that Police Chief Hongisto may have been involved in the theft of thousands of copies of the *Bay Times*. The newspaper's headline read: "Dick's Cool New Tool: Martial Law." The composite cover photograph showed the chief lewdly fondling a police nightstick.

MAY 15 Police Chief Hongisto is fired after an eight-hour hearing. Police Commission President Harry Low said Hongisto "exercised poor judgement and abused his power in this incident." At a 3 a.m. news conference Low says Hongisto's "explanation of this incident is difficult for this commission to accept in light of the evidence." Deputy Chief Thomas Murphy was named Acting Police Chief.

MAY 20 Ex-Police Chief Hongisto demands his job back at a raucous meeting of the Police Commission, but his demand is rebuffed. Liberals were outraged at the thefts. "It's unbelievable. It's so depressing," says Supervisor Terence

Hallinan. "How can our city survive this?"

MAY 30 Chamber of Commerce solicits businesses for donations to help disguise damage at City Hall suffered in the 1989 quake.

JULY 27 The chairman of Lloyd's of London, David Coleridge, announces he will step down at the end of 1992 because of heavy losses suffered by the famed insurer. He attributes the losses to such natural disasters as Hurricane Hugo and the 1989 San Francisco earthquake. But investors, such as Claud Gurney, said Lloyd's had been conducting its business "like a game of poker in a Lebanese casino."

SEPT. 6 Carter Hawley Hale Stores, Inc., owner of the historic Emporium, reported a $6 million loss, equaling 22 cents a share, because of damage to company properties by the 1989 earthquake.

OCT. 24–25 First International Accordions Festival held in city.

1993

APR. 23 Cesar Chavez dies. In 1988 he led a march in San Francisco to win rights for farm workers.

MAY 6 Former police officer Tom Gerard arrested on charges of stealing classified government documents.

MAY 27 U.S. government announces that San Francisco is the top ranked metropolitan area in nation for per capita personal income.

AUG. 4 Catholic Archdiocese considers closing five churches.

OCT. 15 Golden Gate Bridge begins a lead clean-up.

OCT. 26 Michael Marcum, ex-convict, appointed as San Francisco's assistant sheriff.

OCT. 27 A key Board of Supervisors committee approves a far reaching ban on smoking in the workplace, restaurants, and at Candlestick Park.

NOV. 15 Board of Supervisors votes 9-0 for a ban on smoking in the workplace.

1994

JAN. 1 A New Year's Day earthquake measuring 2.7 rattles the western portion of San Francisco but does no damage. Father Alfred Boeddeker, founder of St. Anthony Dining Room, dies at age 90.

JAN. 14 Mayor Jordan's office confirms that the City has entered into talks with Walt Disney Co. about eventually converting Treasure Island Naval base into an amusement park. The base is slated for closure in 1997.

JAN. 17 Southern California is shaken by a major earthquake. San Francisco firefighters are dispatched to the Northridge area to help with the disaster.

8 Churches & Cemeteries

Cemeteries

On March 26, 1900, the Board of Supervisors passed Bill No. 54, Ordinance No. 25, "Prohibiting the Burial of the Dead Within the City and County of San Francisco from and after the First days of August, 1901." It was approved by Mayor James D. Phelan, on March 30, 1900.

In 1914 the Board of Health sent out notices to all persons owning or claiming lots in Calvary, Masonic, Odd Fellows, and Laurel Hill cemeteries to remove within 14 months from January 17, 1914, all bodies as they had been declared to be "a public nuisance and a menace and detriment to the public health and welfare."

Today, there remain within the city limits two cemeteries. They are:

Mission Dolores Cemetery

Located alongside Mission Dolores Church, Dolores Street, between 16th and 17th streets. First burial in Mission Dolores Cemetery took place on December 21, 1776.

National Cemetery

Presidio of San Francisco. 25 acres. First interment was on July 23, 1852. It became a National Cemetery in 1884.

Early Burial Grounds

North Beach 50-vara lot on corner of Powell and Lombard. (Vara = 137.5 sq. ft.)
Telegraph Hill Southerly slope.
Russian Hill Summit.
Calvary Cemetery (Catholic) 48 acres bounded by Geary, Turk, St. Josephs, and Masonic Avenue. Cemetery dedicated November 8, 1860. Bodies moved to Holy Cross Cemetery, San Mateo County.
Chinese Cemetery Located at rear of Laurel Hill Cemetery from Parker Avenue west. Later moved to Golden Gate Cemetery.
Gibbath Olom Cemetery (Hills of Eternity, Jewish) Located at Dolores and Church, and 19th and 20th streets. Opened February 26, 1861; closed December 31, 1888.
Golden Gate Cemetery (Clement Street Cemetery and City Cemetery) Roughly 200 acres of land purchased by the city in

1868 for cemetery purposes. Located at Clement Street and 33rd Avenue. In 1909 the supervisors secured consent of the various cemetery organizations for the use of the land as a park. Today many bodies remain buried beneath the turf of Lincoln Park Golf Course.

Greek Cemetery Located on ground purchased from Archbishop Alemany, south of Odd Fellows Cemetery on a sand hill (Stanyan and Golden Gate Avenue). Access was through Odd Fellows Cemetery. Cemetery later moved to Golden Gate Cemetery.

Hebrew Cemetery Two 50-vara lots located at Broadway and Vallejo, Franklin and Gough. Cemetery used for the period 1850–1860.

Laurel Hill Cemetery See Lone Mountain.

Lone Mountain Cemetery Bounded by California, Geary, Parker, and Presidio. Cemetery dedicated May 30, 1854. Renamed Laurel Hill Cemetery in 1867. Bodies moved to Cypress Lawn Cemetery, San Mateo County. Tombstones used on seawall.

Masonic Cemetery Masonic Cemetery Association organized January 26, 1864, on 30 acres bounded by Turk and Fulton, Parker and Masonic Avenue.

Nevai Shalome Cemetery (Home of Peace, Jewish) Located at Dolores and Church and 18th and 19th streets. Opened July 25, 1860; closed December 31, 1888.

Odd Fellows Cemetery Cemetery dedicated November 19, 1865. Located at Geary and Turk, Parker and Arguello. Bodies moved to Greenlawn Cemetery in Colma. Stonework from cemetery used on seawall at Aquatic Park.

Yerba Buena Cemetery 10 acres bounded by Market, Larkin, and McAllister streets. Burials made 1850-1861. Bodies exhumed and moved to Golden Gate Cemetery in 1870.

Birth and Death Records Available for San Francisco

Births. All local records prior to April 18, 1906 were destroyed, with the exception of July 1, 1905 to March 31, 1906. These are on file with the State Registrar of Vital Statistics, Sacramento, California.

Deaths. Only the following death records are available. Most were destroyed in the 1906 earthquake and fire.

Book 1 Nov. 8, 1865 to Sept. 30, 1869
Book 2 Oct. 1, 1869 to April 30, 1873
Book 3 April 1, 1882 to June 30, 1889 (Coroner's cases only)
Book M August 1, 1894 to June 30, 1896
Book O July 1, 1898 to March 16, 1900
Book P March 17, 1900 to Oct. 22, 1901
Book Q Oct. 23, 1901 to June 30, 1903
Book R July 1, 1903 to June 30, 1904

July 1, 1904 to January 31, 1905: Index and Records intact to December 1, 1904. Records for Dec. 1904 and January 1905 are missing.

Churches

(Limited to those of historical or architectural interest)

Chapel of Our Lady Presidio of San Francisco

The original adobe chapel put up in 1776 collapsed in the 1812 earthquake. The second chapel built on the same spot burned in 1846 and was replaced in 1873 by a New England styled chapel, which served as a house of worship for both Catholic and Protestant military men until 1931. The present remodeled chapel is used for Catholic services only.

First Baptist Church of San Francisco Market and Octavia streets

The first church building was erected on Washington, near Stockton, in 1849. It was followed by a new church located on Eddy, between Jones and Leavenworth, which was dedicated July 29, 1877. After the destruction of their church in the 1906 earthquake and fire, the congregation sought out a new location and purchased property at Octavia and Market streets. Ground was broken on August 30, 1909 and today's church, of classic design, was dedicated on September 14, 1910.

First Unitarian Church
1187 Franklin Street

First located at Stockton near Sacramento in a building dedicated July 17, 1853; later moved to Geary Street near Stockton in 1864. Today's stone church located at 1187 Franklin Street was dedicated February 9, 1889. Damage to the amount of $16,300 was suffered in 1906 when a portion of the bell tower crashed through the roof, but the church reopened September 16, 1906. Thomas Starr King, the church's most famous clergyman, is buried beneath a small marble sarcophagus in front of the church.

Grace Cathedral
California and Taylor streets

The third Episcopal church to be known as Grace was constructed in 1860 at California and Stockton streets. From the time Bishop William I. Kip placed his Bishop's Chair in the new church in 1861 it was known as Grace Cathedral, until destroyed by the earthquake and fire of 1906.

The new Grace Cathedral, built on land donated by the Crocker family (California, Sacramento, Jones, Taylor), had its cornerstone laid by Bishop William Ford Nichols on January 24, 1910, but construction was not begun until 1928. Lewis P. Hobart, the architect, described the Gothic-spired church as "a truly American Cathedral." The third largest Episcopal Cathedral in the United States was consecrated on Friday, November 20, 1964 and Sunday, November 22, 1964.

Holy Trinity Russian (Eastern) Orthodox Cathedral
1520 Green Street

Built in 1868 at 1715 Powell Street, the Holy Trinity Russian Orthodox Cathedral was the first Russian cathedral built in the United States.

The Cathedral was completely destroyed in the earthquake and fire of 1906, but its seven bells were saved and installed in the new $10,000 church relocated at 1520 Green Street in 1909.

Mission San Francisco de Assisi – Mission Dolores
Dolores and Sixteenth streets

Fray Francisco Palou established the first Mission Dolores, a brush shelter, at about 18th and Church streets in June 1776. This site served until the present adobe mission was completed in 1791.

The Church, built completely by Native Americans, is 114 feet long, 22 feet wide, with adobe walls four feet thick.

On April 4, 1952, Mission Dolores was designated a Minor Basilica by Pope Pius XII. It was the fourth such designation in the United States and the first west of the Mississippi.

Notre Dame des Victoires
566 Bush Street

The exterior of today's church, built in 1913, is copied from Notre Dame de Fourvieres, in Lyon, France. The first church building located on the same site was consecrated by Archbishop Alemany on May 4, 1856 and destroyed in 1906.

Old First Presbyterian
Van Ness Avenue and Sacramento Street

The first church building was shipped around the Horn and erected at Stockton, between Broadway and Pacific. Dedication services were held January 19, 1851. It was destroyed by fire in less than six months and a new church was dedicated October 12,

1851. Another dedication took place May 13, 1858 when an ornate brick building began service as the new church.

The final move in 1882 brought the church to the corner of Van Ness Avenue and Sacramento Street where it was destroyed by fire in 1906. It was rebuilt in 1911 and is said to be "the finest piece of Byzantine architecture on the West Coast."

Old St. Patrick's
820–22 Eddy Street
(next to Holy Cross Church)

The oldest frame church building in San Francisco began as St. Patrick's Church built in 1851 on the site where the Palace Hotel now stands. The parish limits were bounded by Pine, Ninth, Mission Creek, and the Bay. It was moved in 1873 to Eddy, between Octavia and Laguna, and called St. John the Baptist Church. In 1891 it moved again to its present location where it served as Holy Cross Church until the new church was completed in 1899. It now serves as Holy Cross Parish Hall.

Russian Holy Virgin Cathedral of the Church in Exile
6210 Geary Boulevard

The cornerstone of the new Russian Orthodox Cathedral at Geary, between 26th and 27th avenues, was laid June 25, 1961. Oleg N. Ivanitsky, the architect, noted "the cathedral will be built to the highest standards of Russian ecclesiastical architecture," and "will be the largest and most beautiful on the Pacific Coast." Previously the Holy Virgin Cathedral was located at Fulton near Fillmore, where the church building was originally built as an Episcopal church called St. Stephen's in 1880.

St. Boniface Church
133 Golden Gate Avenue

The first St. Boniface Church at Sutter, between Montgomery and Kearny streets, was dedicated April 15, 1860.

Three churches have been dedicated on the Golden Gate Avenue site. The first on June 5, 1870; the second on October 23, 1887; and the present church, in Rhineland Romanesque style of pressed stone, on November 1, 1908.

St. Dominic's Church
Bush and Steiner streets

The Dominican Fathers opened a small wooden church at Bush and Steiner streets in 1873. In 1886 a large brick church was dedicated and used until destroyed in 1906 by the earthquake. The present eight-spired Gothic church has been in use since 1928. Flying buttress added after 1989 earthquake.

St. Francis of Assisi
610 Vallejo Street

The first parish church built within the limits of Yerba Buena was dedicated June 17, 1849. In 1972, after 123 years of continuous service, a bronze plaque was unveiled proclaiming the church as Registered Landmark No. 5. The white, twin-towered Gothic church withstood the 1906 earthquake and fire. Closed 1992.

St. Ignatius Church
Fulton Street and Parker Avenue

A parish church on Market Street until made a college church in October, 1863. The new relocated St. Ignatius was constructed at Van Ness and Hayes and dedicated on February 1, 1880. Destroyed in 1906, the grey brick church was rebuilt at Fulton and Parker Avenue at a cost of $300,000 and dedicated in 1914.

St. John's Presbyterian
1–25 Lake Street

Since 1905, the site of this Gothic shingle church has been the southwest corner of Arguello and Lake. First located at Post and Mason streets in 1870, it was relocated at California and Octavia in 1889. Damaged in

1906 by the earthquake, it was formally dedicated April 28, 1907.

St. Luke's Episcopal Church
Van Ness Avenue at Clay Street

Founded in 1868 on Pacific between Polk and Van Ness, it moved to its present site in 1884. The new church, which opened in 1900, was destroyed in 1906, but four years later the present stone church was dedicated.

St. Mark's Evangelical Lutheran Church
1111–1135 O'Farrell Street

In 1866 three Lutheran congregations united, taking the name St. Mark's Evangelical Lutheran Church. The present site was purchased in 1893 and the Gothic-designed church at Van Ness Avenue and O'Farrell Street was dedicated in 1895.

St. Mary's Cathedral
Geary and Gough streets

The Catholic cathedral has been located in four different locations since 1849. The first cathedral of San Francisco was the little frame shanty built as St. Francis' Church by Father Langlois in 1849.

From 1853 to 1891 the present Old St. Mary's Church, at California and Grant Avenue, served as the cathedral. On January 11, 1891 the new cathedral at Van Ness Avenue and O'Farrell Street was dedicated. It was used for 71 years until destroyed by fire September 7, 1962.

The present cathedral, located atop Cathedral Hill, at Geary and Gough streets, was dedicated May 5, 1971. The architects were Angus McSweeney, Paul Ryan, and Jack Lee. The $7-million building unites the Nave, Sanctuary, Trancept, Baptistry, and Narthex in one space, crowned by a colorful skylight shaped in the form of a cross. The windows represent the four elements: the blue north window, water; the light-colored south window, the sun; the red west window, fire; the green east window, earth. The cathedral seats 2,400 people.

St. Patrick's
756 Mission Street

The present church properties were purchased in 1862 and the church was dedicated by Archbishop Alemany on March 17, 1872. Destroyed in 1906, the church was rebuilt using many of the original bricks. Fire scars are still apparent on the original walls of this Victorian Gothic structure.

St. Paulus Evangelical Lutheran Church
999 Eddy Street

This Gothic church, dedicated in 1894, was saved from the 1906 fire but was nearly destroyed by fire in 1940. St. Paulus is a wooden reproduction of the Cathedral at Chartres.

Sts. Peter and Paul Church
666 Filbert Street

Designed by Charles Fantoni after the earthquake and fire, this church is sometimes called "The Italian Cathedral." The Romanesque designed church was dedicated March 30, 1924. Previously, when founded in 1884, it had been located at Grant Avenue and Filbert Street.

Swedenborgian Church
2107 Lyon Street

A. Page Brown was the architect of this rustic little church which seats only 80 people. It was built in 1894 with emphasis on natural objects, many with religious symbolism. William Keith paintings grace the north wall. The church was first established in 1849 and by 1865 was housed in a small, wooden building on O'Farrell, between Taylor and Mason streets. Thirty years later funds were raised for the new building.

Temple Emanu-El
Arguello Boulevard and Lake Street

Built in 1925 at a cost of $3,000,000 to replace the earlier Temple at Sutter and Powell streets destroyed in 1906. The architects for this Byzantine stucco building were Schnaittacher, Bakewell, and Brown. The building was completed in 1927.

Temple Sherith Israel
(Loyal Remnant of Israel)
California and Webster streets

Albert Pissis served as the architect of this brownstone domed Temple whose cornerstone was laid February 22, 1904. The synagogue was consecrated on September 24, 1905 on which occasion the principal address was delivered by Jacob Voorsanger.

Suffering only $1,000 damage to the roof during the 1906 earthquake, this building received public attention when it served as the courthouse for the Ruef-Schmitz trials.

Trinity Episcopal Church
1668 Bush Street

In 1849 located at the southwest corner of Powell and Jackson, later moved to Pine near Montgomery. By 1867 this building was felt to be too small, so a new church rose at Post and Powell. Since 1892 the sandstone Norman styled church has stood at Bush and Gough streets.

Grace Cathedral, atop Nob Hill.

9 City Department Heads

Alcaldes

Alcalde is derived from the Turkish term *cadi*. In Spain and Portugal, an alcalde was a sheriff, or justice of the peace; in early California, however, his functions were often broader, including that of mayor and judge.

Mexican Alcaldes
Francisco de Haro, *1834*
Jose Joaquin Estudillo, *1835*
Francisco Guerrero, *1836*
Ignacio Martinez, *1837*
Francisco de Haro, *1838–39*
Francisco Guerrero, *1839–41*
Francisco Sanchez, *1842–43*
William Hinckley, *1844*
Juan N. Padilla, *1845*
Jose de la Cruz Sanchez, *1845*
Jose de Jesus Noe, *1846*

American Alcaldes
Lt. Washington Allon Bartlett, *July 1846–Feb. 1847*
Edwin Bryant, *Feb. 22, 1847–June 1847*
George Hyde, *June 1, 1847–April 1848*

Dr. John Townsend, *April 1848–Sept. 1848*
Thaddeus M. Leavenworth, *Sept. 1848–Aug. 1849*

Francisco de Haro
Accompanied the San Blas Infantry to California after the Hippolyte Bouchard attack on Monterey in 1818. He served twice as alcalde, living and maintaining his office at Mission Dolores. He died January 1, 1849.

Jose Joaquin Estudillo
Born in Monterey in 1798. On January 1, 1836 he took office as alcalde with Gregario Briones and Jose C. Sanchez as regidores. He died in 1852.

Francisco Guerrero
Mexican by birth, came to California from Tepic in 1834 as a member of the Hijar-Padres colonizing venture. He was a justice of the peace at Mission Dolores where he lived with his family and had his office. He died in 1851.

James "Sunny Jim" Rolph, Jr., 27th Mayor of San Francisco. He served from January 1912 until he was inaugurated Governor in 1931.

Ignacio Martinez

Born in Mexico City. He entered military service at an early age, retiring in 1831 as a Lieutenant, after 41 years of service. In 1837 he was appointed alcalde. He was the owner of Rancho Pinole in Contra Costa County where he lived until his death in the early 1850s.

Francisco Sanchez

First municipal elector to choose members to the Departmental Assembly at Monterey in 1836. In 1835 and 1836 he was secretary to the *Ayuntamiento*. From 1837 to 1840, military commandant at the Presidio, and justice of the peace for the years 1842–43. His office was at Mission Dolores.

William Sturges Hinckley

Born in Hington, Massachusetts, about 1807. He became a prominent merchant in Honolulu before coming to California in 1829. In the early 1840s he became a naturalized Mexican citizen and settled in Yerba Buena. Hinckley was elected alcalde January 9, 1844, and died in June 1846.

Juan Nepomuceno Padilla

A barber and saloon keeper, elected alcalde December 22, 1844. He resigned from office March 15, 1845 but was persuaded to continue as alcalde until replaced by Jose de la Cruz Sanchez. He later commanded a party of Californians against the Bear Flaggers.

Jose de la Cruz Sanchez

Second alcalde elected in 1845. He had his office at Mission Dolores, afterwards moving to his farm in the country. He died in 1878.

Jose de Jesus Noe

Arrived in California as a member of the Hijar-Padres colony. He served as the last Mexican alcalde from the back of his office on Dupont Street.

Lt. Washington Allon Bartlett

Appointed Chief Magistrate, or alcalde, by Capt. John B. Montgomery, commander of the U.S. sloop-of-war *Portsmouth*, who formally took possession of Yerba Buena on July 8, 1846. This appointment was subsequently ratified by a formal election by citizens. He held the office until February 1847.

Edwin Bryant

Native of Massachusetts, came to Yerba Buena after leaving Fremont's battalion. He served as alcalde from February 22 to June 1847. He left San Francisco June 2, 1847 for the East and returned in 1849. He died in Louisville, Kentucky, in 1869.

George Hyde

Born in Pennsylvania on August 22, 1819. He was educated at Mount St. Mary's College in Maryland, studied law in Philadelphia, and was admitted to the bar in June 1842. He arrived in Yerba Buena August 10, 1846 on the U.S. frigate *Congress* having served as clerk to Commodore Stockton. He was appointed alcalde June 1, 1847, and served until April 1, 1848. He died August 16, 1890.

Dr. John Townsend

Born in Fayette County, Pennsylvania, in the early nineteenth century. He received his medical degree from Lexington Medical College and headed West, arriving in California with the Stevens-Murphy overland party in 1844. He settled in Yerba Buena in 1845. In April 1848, he was appointed alcalde, serving until September 1848. He died of cholera in December 1850.

Thaddeus M. Leavenworth

Born in Connecticut and educated in medicine and theology. He came to California with Stevenson's Regiment as chaplain, and in September 1848 became the alcalde, serving until August 1849. In 1850 he went to Sonoma County where he was claimant for part of Agua Caliente rancho. He died in Santa Rosa, January 30, 1893.

Alcaldes and Mayors

Before May 1, 1850, the title of the Chief Executive Officer was Alcalde; from that day until July 1, 1856, Mayor; then for six years, President of the Board of Supervisors; and beginning July 1, 1862, Mayor.

Mayor

The Mayor is the chief executive of San Francisco in both name and power. The Mayor is elected directly by the people for a term of four years and has the general duty of enforcing all of the laws of the city. The Mayor appoints numerous city officers, commission members, and board members; prepares the annual budget for submission to the Board of Supervisors, and is responsible for the administration of all city departments that have been placed under his control by the charter. The Mayor has the power to veto any ordinance passed by the Board of Supervisors, and may compel the Board to reconsider rejected measures.

The Mayor is elected for a four-year term, and has extensive appointive and budgetary powers.

Mayors, Date of Inauguration

John White Geary, *May 1, 1850*
Charles James Brenham, *May 5, 1851*
Stephen Randall Harris, *Jan. 1, 1852*
Cornelius K. Garrison, *Oct. 3, 1853*
Stephen Palfrey Webb, *Oct. 2, 1854*
James Van Ness, *July 1, 1855*
George J. Whelan, *July 8, 1856*
Ephriam Willard Burr, *Nov. 15, 1856*
Henry F. Teschemacher, *Oct. 3, 1859*
Henry Perrin Coon, *July 1, 1863*
Frank McCoppin, *Dec. 2, 1867*
Thomas Henry Selby, *Dec. 6, 1869*

William Alvord, *Dec. 4, 1871*
James Otis*, *Dec. 1, 1873*
George Hewston**, *Nov. 4, 1875*
Andrew Jackson Bryant, *Dec. 6, 1875*
Isaac Smith Kalloch, *Dec. 1, 1879*
Maurice Carey Blake, *Dec. 5, 1881*
Washington Bartlett, *Jan. 8, 1883*
Edward B. Pond, *Jan. 3, 1887*
George Henry Sanderson, *Jan. 5, 1891*
Levi Richard Ellert, *Jan. 3, 1893*
Adolph H. J. Sutro, *Jan. 7, 1895*
James Duval Phelan, *Jan. 4, 1897*
Eugene E. Schmitz+, *Jan. 8, 1902*
Charles Boxton**+, *July 9, 1907*
Edward Robeson Taylor**, *July 16, 1907*
Patrick Henry McCarthy, *Jan. 8, 1910*
James Rolph, Jr. +, *Jan. 8, 1912*
Angelo Joseph Rossi**, *Jan. 7, 1931*
Roger Dearborn Lapham, *Jan. 8, 1944*
Elmer Edwin Robinson, *Jan. 8, 1948*
George Christopher, *Jan. 8, 1956*
John Francis Shelley, *Jan. 8, 1964*
Joseph Lawrence Alioto, *Jan. 8, 1968*
George Richard Moscone*, *Jan. 8, 1976*
Dianne Feinstein***, *Dec. 4, 1978*
Art Agnos, *Jan. 8, 1988*
Frank Jordan, *Jan. 8, 1992*

+Resigned
*Died in office
**Appointed to fill term
***Elected by Board of Supervisors

Mayors

John White Geary (1819–1873)

Born December 20, 1819 in a loghouse, situated near Mount Pleasant, Westmoreland County, Pennsylvania. On January 22, 1849, President Polk appointed him Postmaster of San Francisco, with powers to create post-offices, appoint postmasters, establish mail routes, and make contracts for carrying the mails throughout California. Geary was elected alcalde in August 1849 and became the city's first mayor on May 1, 1850. He returned to Pennsylvania in 1852 where he served as Governor from 1867 to 1873.

He died February 8, 1873, in Harrisburg, Pennsylvania.

Charles James Brenham (1817–1875)

Born in Frankfort, Kentucky, November 6, 1817. He was well-known on the Mississippi as a steamboat captain. He arrived in San Francisco August 18, 1849 and took command of the steamer *McKim*, which ran between San Francisco and Sacramento. In 1850 he received the unsolicited nomination of the Whig Party for the mayoralty, but the nomination went to Geary. He was elected mayor in 1851 and again in 1852, serving unconnected terms. He was the second and fourth mayors of San Francisco. In 1852 President Fillmore appointed him Treasurer of the Mint and Assistant Treasurer of the United States but Brenham declined the appointments. He later served as agent for the California, Oregon and Mexico Steamship Company. He died in San Francisco, May 10, 1875.

Stephen Randall Harris (1802–1879)

Born in Poughkeepsie, New York, in 1802. He was a graduate of the College of Physicians and Surgeons, Columbia University, New York, and for six consecutive years a New York health commissioner. He arrived in San Francisco in June 1849, and founded the city's first real drug store at the corner of Clay and Montgomery streets. He became mayor in 1852, but continued to carry on his practice. From September 19, 1864 to December 2, 1967 he served as coroner of San Francisco. He died at Napa, California, April 27, 1879.

Cornelius Kingland Garrison (1809–1855)

Also known as Commodore Garrison because of the large shipping interests he controlled. He was born March 1, 1809 at Fort Montgomery, New York. He began his career in Canada, and afterward engaged in various enterprises on the lower Mississippi, near New Orleans. The discovery of gold in California led to his acceptance of the San Francisco agency of the Nicaragua Steamship Line. Within six months of his arrival in 1853 he was elected mayor. He returned to New York in 1859. During the Civil War he rendered great assistance to the government and received formal acknowledgment from President Lincoln. At a time when the U.S. merchant marine had almost entirely disappeared from the high seas he founded the only mail steamship line carrying the American flag on the Atlantic Ocean. He died in New York City, May 1, 1855.

Stephen Palfrey Webb (1804–1879)

Born in Salem, Mass., on March 20, 1804. He graduated from Harvard in 1824 after which he studied law with the Honorable John Glen King and was admitted to the Essex Bar. He practiced law in Salem, served as Representative and Senator in the Massachusetts State Legislature, and was elected mayor of Salem in 1842, serving three years. He was also treasurer of the Essex Railroad Company in the late forties. About 1853 Webb arrived in San Francisco and served as mayor from 1854 to 1855. He returned to Massachusetts and was again elected mayor of Salem for the period 1860-1862, later becoming city clerk for the years 1863-1870. He died there on September 29, 1879.

James Van Ness (1808–1872)

Born in Burlington, Vermont, in 1808. He arrived in San Francisco in 1851 and served as alderman for many years before being elected mayor in 1855. He moved to San Luis Obispo in later years and became a farmer. He was elected Joint-Senator from San Luis Obispo and Santa Barbara counties in 1871. He died at San Luis Obispo, California, December 28, 1872.

George J. Whelan

On Tuesday, November 12, 1974, the Board of Supervisors adopted Resolution No. 882-74, declaring official recognition of the Honorable George J. Whelan as the seventh mayor of the City of San Francisco. Up to this time Whelan had never been officially credited for such service, undoubtedly because he was not an elected official. However, city records clearly show that he was installed as the legally appointed President of the Board of Supervisors on July 8, 1856, and that he served until November 15, 1856. Whelan had come into office under the new city charter which was known as the Consolidation Act. This act empowered four sitting Justices of the Peace to serve as the Supervisory Board and to appoint an interim president to govern San Francisco.

This temporary government met much opposition in the papers and they were asked to resign. When they did not, newspapers continued to report in detail each week the meeting of the Board and its president. The San Francisco *Daily Evening Bulletin* for July 1, 1856 stated: "God help the City of San Francisco. She has in time past, been the worst governed and best plundered city that it was ever our fortune to live in. We have had one charter a year for several years past; and this last and crowning act of absurdity, the famous Consolidation Act, is the capstone. It is said it will go into operation today, but its provisions are so covered up in mystery and contradiction, that neither Judge, Jury, its framers nor the people are able to discern its objects, or declare its legality."

Little is known of Whelan's background. His name first appears in the 1861 city directory as an attorney. The last listing is 1861. Wherever he came from, and wherever he went is unknown at this time.

Ephraim Willard Burr (1809–1894)

Born in Rhode Island, March 7, 1809. He came to California in 1850 to secure crews for whaling ships; however, realizing he could no longer provide men to man the ships, he turned his attention to new business enterprises. He became a commission merchant in partnership with J. Mattoon and later established the San Francisco Accumulating Fund, later called the Savings and Loan Society, but more popularly known as the Clay Street Bank. This was the first savings bank on the Pacific Coast. The People's Party elected him mayor in 1856 and he officially took office Nov. 15th. After his three-year term as mayor he returned to the Clay Street Bank as its president and remained there until forced to resign in 1878 because of charges that he had accepted a five percent commission for granting loans on Navy Paymaster's Certificates. He died in San Francisco, on July 20, 1894.

Henry Fredrick Teschemacher (?–1904)

Arrived in California in 1842 representing the Boston firm of Wm. Appleton & Co., hide and fur traders. He settled in San Francisco after 1849 and was elected mayor in 1859. He died November 29, 1904, at Territet, Switzerland.

Henry Perrin Coon (1822–1884)

Born in Columbia County, New York, September 30, 1822. He received his degree in medicine, and established himself as a physician upon his arrival in San Francisco in 1853. He purchased a drug business and in February 1854 founded the San Francisco Chemical Company. He was elected Police Judge November 15, 1856 and served two terms. On July 1, 1863 he took over the office of mayor after being elected by the People's Party. He was re-elected May 16, 1865. He was an elder, trustee, and one of the founders of Calvary Presbyterian Church. After leaving the office of mayor he was engaged in the real estate and life insurance business until 1870. He died in San Francisco, at the Palace Hotel, December 4, 1884.

Frank McCoppin (1834–1897)

Born in the city of Longford, Ireland, on July 4, 1834. He arrived in San Francisco in 1858 and was engaged as superintendent of construction of the Market Street City Railroad. He was elected Supervisor for four terms commencing in 1860, and was elected mayor in 1867. He became a naturalized citizen of the United States on December 12, 1864. He was elected to the State Senate from the 13th Senatorial District in 1875. He died in San Francisco, May 26, 1897.

Thomas Henry Selby (1820–1875)

Born in New York City, May 14, 1820. He landed in San Francisco in August 1849. In the summer of 1850 he erected a brick building at California and Montgomery streets in which he established the business of Thomas H. Selby & Co., and commenced the importation of metals and merchandise. In April 1851, he was elected Assistant Alderman of the fifth ward and reelected in 1852. He took the office of mayor on December 6, 1869, and served the city free, donating the salary of his office to various charitable institutions. He declined to accept renomination. He served as President of the Merchant's Exchange and as the first President of the Industrial School Association, President of the Board of Trustees of Calvary Church and of City College, and as a life director of the Mercantile Library Association. He died in San Francisco, June 9, 1875.

William Alvord (1833–1904)

Born in Albany, New York, on January 3, 1833 and educated at the Albany Academy. He arrived in California in 1853, settled at Marysville and established the hardware store of Alvord & Haviland. After two years of successful business at Marysville he came to San Francisco and opened the large wholesale and importing house of William Alvord & Co. In 1871 he was nominated and elected Mayor of San Francisco. He later served as Police Commissioner, Park Commissioner, President of the San Francisco Art Association and President of the California Academy of Sciences. He also served as president of: the Alaska-Treadwell Gold Mining Company, the San Francisco Clearing House, the Spring Valley Water Company, the Pacific Club, the Loring Club, and the Astronomical Society of the Pacific; also as director of the Selby Smelting & Lead Works, the United Railroads of San Francisco, Spreckels and Western Sugar Refining Companies, the Security Savings Bank and the California Title Insurance Company. He died in San Francisco on December 21, 1904.

James Otis (1826–1875)

Born August 11, 1826 in Boston. In 1849, at the age of 23, he sailed for San Francisco by way of the Isthmus. He worked three years as a partner in Macondray & Co., before returning to Boston. After a year's absence he returned to California and reentered the firm, which he headed for many years prior to his death. He took a prominent part in all civic work, and also in politics. He was twice President of the Chamber of Commerce, twice President of the Mercantile Library Association, and twice elected to the Board of Supervisors. During the Civil War he was chosen Secretary of the Pacific Branch of the United States Sanitary Commission. He was also delegated to cast the electoral votes of California for Abraham Lincoln and General Grant. He became mayor in 1873 and died in office on October 30, 1875, of diptheria.

George Hewston (1826–1891)

Born in Philadelphia, Pennsylvania, on September 11, 1826. He graduated from the Philadelphia College of Medicine in 1850, receiving his degree as Doctor of Medicine. In 1851 he commenced his private practice, continuing until coming to California in 1861. He was for seven years Surgeon on the Staff of Major General Allen, commanding the State Militia from 1863 to 1870. Dr. Hewston was elected to the Board of Supervisors in 1873 and in 1875 was chosen by the Board to fill the unexpired term of Mayor Otis, the first mayor of San Francisco to die in office. George Hewston died September 4, 1891 in San Francisco.

Andrew Jackson Bryant (1831–1888)

Born in Ettingham, Carroll County, New Hampshire, in 1831. In April 1850 he arrived in California after coming around the Horn on the brig *Ark*. He went directly to the northern mines but soon found he was better suited to business and established himself in Benicia, where he was twice elected City Marshal. He later moved to Sacramento and engaged in merchandising liquor, afterwards moving to San Francisco. In 1866 he was appointed Naval Officer by President Andrew Johnson and held the office until 1870 when he was made general agent on the Pacific Coast for the Brooklyn Life Insurance Company. He later became manager of the State Investment and Insurance Company. He served two terms as mayor, from 1875 to 1879. From 1882 until his death he served as president of the California Light Company. On May 11, 1888, he fell from the ferry *Encinal* on San Francisco Bay and was drowned.

Isaac Smith Kalloch (1832–1887)

Nicknamed "Golden Voice." He was born in East Thomaston (now Rockland), Maine, on July 10, 1832. He attended Colby College, Maine, a Baptist institution, from which he was expelled in his freshman year. Because he was a brilliant pulpit and platform orator, he was later awarded an honorary Master of Arts degree from Colby and Colgate universities and became the Rev. Dr. Kalloch. In 1875 he left Leavenworth, Kansas, for San Francisco, giving as his reason: "There are more wicked people of both sexes in San Francisco and I feel compelled of God to go and convert them." He built the Metropolitan Temple at the corner of Fifth and Jessie streets, and it was in front of this temple on August 23, 1879 that he was shot twice by the *Chronicle*'s Charles de Young. From these wounds, and with the help of the Workingman's Party, he gained the office of mayor. "I am not going to steal any money from the city, get drunk, or do any other dishonorable act," he stated before he took office. During his administration (1879–1881), he was continually opposed by the Board of Supervisors and in 1880 an attempt was made to impeach him. He resigned as pastor of the Metropolitan Temple in July 1883, and moved to Whatcom (Bellingham), Washington, where he died on December 9, 1887.

Maurice Carey Blake (1815–1897)

Born in Otisfield, Maine, on October 20, 1815. He graduated from Bowdoin College in 1838. He was admitted to the bar and began the practice of law in Camden, Maine. He was a Whig in politics and in 1846 was elected his party's representative to the Legislature. Under President Taylor's administration he was appointed Collector of the Belfast Customs District, an office he held for four years. He arrived in San Francisco in 1853 and continued to practice law. He was a member of the Vigilance Committee and in 1857 was elected a member of the Legislature from San Francisco. The following year he was elected Judge of San Francisco County by the People's Party, subsequently serving as Probate Judge and Judge of the Municipal Criminal Court. In 1881 Judge Blake was elected mayor. Following his one-year term of office he returned to his legal practice and in 1884 was a delegate to the Republican Convention. He died in San Francisco on September 26, 1897.

Washington Bartlett (1824–1887)

Born at Savannah, Georgia, February 29, 1824. He sailed around Cape Horn from Charleston, South Carolina, in January 1849, arriving in San Francisco in November. Being a trained printer he soon opened a printing shop and was responsible for printing the first English-language book in California: *California as it is and as it May Be, or a Guide to the Gold Region.* He was appointed deputy county clerk for San Francisco County in 1857. In 1859 he won election as County Clerk, a position he was reelected to in 1867. He was admitted to the bar in 1863. Governor Haight appointed him State Harbor Commissioner in 1870 and in 1873 he was nominated by the Citizen's Independent Party, and the People's Union Party, as one of the State Senators from San Francisco. He was elected Mayor of San Francisco in 1882 and reelected in 1884. In 1886 he won the gubernatorial election, and was inaugurated on January 8, 1887. Governor Bartlett died September 12, 1887, in Oakland, California.

Edward B. Pond (1833–1910)

Born December 7, 1833 at Bellville, New York. He crossed the plains and settled in Chico, California, in 1855. After many years in Chico he moved to San Francisco where he was the head of the wholesale house of Pond & Reynolds. He was elected to the Board of Supervisors in 1882 and served two terms. He assumed the office of mayor beginning January 3, 1887, and was reelected in 1888. Following his second term of office he returned to private business. He

was director of the San Francisco Savings Union for 19 years, vice-president for five years, and president for 11 years, retiring in 1909. He died in San Francisco at the Granada Hotel on April 22, 1910.

George Henry Sanderson (1824–1893)

Born in Boston, Massachusetts, in 1824. He came to California during the height of the gold fever in 1849. In 1865 he moved to San Francisco where he was employed by the grocery firms of Weaver, Wooster & Co. and Jones & Co. In 1878 he became a member of the wholesale grocery firm known as Root & Sanderson. He served two terms as president of the Board of Trade and was mayor from January 5, 1891 to January 3, 1893. He died very suddenly of acute pneumonia on February 1, 1893 in San Francisco, just one month after retiring from office.

Levi Richard Ellert (1857–1901)

San Francisco's first native-son mayor, born in the city on October 20, 1857. He established the druggist firm, L. R. Ellert & Co., at the corner of California and Kearny in 1883. His first venture into the political field was an unsuccessful attempt for election as School Director. In 1888 he was elected Supervisor on the Republican ticket and reelected in 1890. He was elected mayor in 1892 on the Non-Partisan ticket. During his incumbency he appeared before the Supreme Court, passed the bar examination, and was admitted to the bar. He served as director of the California Title Insurance & Trust Company, and the Continental Salt & Chemical Company, and as president and general manager of the Sanitary Reduction Works, a position he held until October 1899. Ellert died July 21, 1901, in San Francisco.

Adolph Heinrich Joseph Sutro (1830–1898)

Born in Aachen (Aix-la-Chapelle), Prussia, on April 29, 1830. He was well-educated in the field of mining engineering. He arrived in San Francisco aboard the steamship *California* on November 21, 1850, and immediately engaged in trade, first in San Francisco and later in Stockton. In 1859, when the Comstock Lode made headlines, he was again attracted to mining. He established a small mill, called the Sutro Metallurgical Works, in East Dayton, Nevada, for the reduction of ores by an improved process of amalgamation and was responsible for the planning and building of the Sutro Tunnel. This tunnel made it possible to drain and ventilate the many mines in the Comstock Lode and permit the miners to bring out the rich silver ore. In 1879 Sutro sold his tunnel to the McCalmont Brothers and countless lesser investors, and returned to San Francisco. In 1894 he ran for mayor on the Populist ticket and served one term. At one time he owned one-twelfth of the acreage in San Francisco. He purchased the Cliff House in the early eighties and a thousand acres of land facing the ocean, now called Sutro Heights. He built the Sutro saltwater baths and planted Sutro Forest. He owned the finest private library in America, most of which was destroyed in the 1906 earthquake and fire. Sutro died in San Francisco on August 8, 1898.

James Duval Phelan (1861–1930)

Born in San Francisco, April 20, 1861. He was educated at Saint Ignatius High School and graduated with an A.B. degree from the University of San Francisco in 1881, followed by a degree in law from the University of California. However, he did not pursue a law career but became a partner in the banking firm of Phelan & Son, assuming responsibility for the First National Bank, the Mutual Savings, and the Bank of Santa Cruz County upon the death of his father in 1892. Without any previous political experience Phelan was elected mayor for three terms beginning in 1897.

Following the earthquake of 1906, Phelan became President of the Relief & Red Cross Funds, and was designated by President Theodore Roosevelt as custodian of the Relief Funds, amounting to $9,000,000. He was elected United States Senator in 1913 and served six years. Senator Phelan died at his country estate Villa Montalvo, Montalvo, California, August 7, 1930.

Eugene E. Schmitz (1864–1928)

Born in San Francisco on August 22, 1864. A musician and occasional orchestra conductor, he rose to the presidency of the Musicians' Union, a position giving him entry into society along with nominal membership in the labor movement. Perhaps it was because of this unique position that "Handsome Gene" came under the appraising eye of Abraham "Boss" Ruef, who, with minimal delay, installed the handsome and popular Schmitz as his newly-formed Union Labor Party's mayoral candidate. To the considerable surprise of all concerned, 1901 saw him elected Mayor of San Francisco, the first Union Labor mayor in United States history. 1906 brought San Francisco two shocks: (1) the Earthquake and Fire, and (2) the arrest of Mayor Schmitz on 27 counts of graft and bribery. Convicted and given the maximum penalty, he appealed and the conviction was reversed by both the Appelate Court and the State Supreme Court. Freed of this legal stigma Schmitz returned to politics and, after an unsuccessful bid for the mayor's chair in 1915, was elected to the Board of Supervisors where he remained until 1925 (running again for mayor in 1919). He was engaged in private business until he died in San Francisco on November 20, 1928.

Charles Boxton (1860–1927)

Born in Shasta County, California, on April 24, 1860. He studied dentistry and reportedly left a flourishing practice to join the California Volunteers on their way to participate in the quelling of the Philippine Insurrection. He returned from the wars covered with glory and decided to enter politics, winning election to the Board of Supervisors in 1899. Along with his rising political career, his professional status increased and he became the Dean of the Dental Department of the College of Physicians and Surgeons. Although involved in considerable scandal generated by the Schmitz-Ruef trials, the Board of Supervisors selected him to fulfill the remainder of the term of the convicted mayor. The new chief executive was not terribly pleased with their choice and stated upon his appointment, "It is with great feeling of sadness that I take this office." He did not suffer too long, however. He resigned and was replaced upon the seventh day of his administration after testifying about receiving graft payments. He returned to the practice of dentistry and died in San Mateo on August 29, 1927.

Edward Robeson Taylor (1838–1923)

Born in Springfield, Illinois, September 24, 1838. He arrived in California on February 4, 1862. He received the degree of Doctor of Medicine from the Toland Medical College in San Francisco in 1865. While acting as private secretary to Governor Haight of California (1867–71) he studied law and was admitted to the Bar of the Supreme Court in January, 1872. Seven years later he was admitted to practice in the Supreme Court of the United States. He also served as a Public Library and Law Library trustee, vice-president of Cooper Medical College, president of the San Francisco Bar Association, president of the Bohemian Club, and dean of Hastings College of Law. He was appointed mayor by the Board of Supervisors to replace Charles Boxton on July 16, 1907. His position had to be officially confirmed by the State Supreme Court on August 19, because the convicted Eugene Schmitz claimed to hold the

mayor's office. In November of the same year he was elected by the people as their Democratic Mayor for a two-year term. He was also the author of numerous volumes of verse which won him worldwide acclaim. His "To Arms" written in 1920 following World War I, was responsible for his decoration with the cross of the Legion of Honor from the French government. He died in San Francisco on July 5, 1923.

Patrick Henry McCarthy (1863–1933)

Born in County Limerick, Ireland, on March 17, 1863. He came to America in 1880 and to San Franciso in 1886. He became president of the San Francisco Building Trades Council in 1894, and served as its head for 29 years, also serving 22 years as president of the State Building Trades Council. He was responsible for the eight-hour law for city labor, and the $2 minimum wage clause in the charter. He served as civil service commissioner for four years under Mayor Phelan. He was defeated in his first campaign for mayor by Edward Robeson Taylor. His second attempt was more successful; he was elected on November 2, 1909, carrying almost the entire Union Labor ticket into office with him, and for one term, was the last symbol of Union Labor's complete control of San Francisco government. In 1915 he served as a director of the Panama-Pacific International Exposition. Upon retiring from active participation in the Building Trades Council in 1923, he engaged in the investment banking business. He died in San Francisco on July 1, 1933.

James Rolph, Jr. (1869–1934)

Born August 23, 1869 in San Francisco. He was educated in Mission District schools and began his business career as an office boy in the commission house of Kittle & Co. In 1900 he formed a partnership with George Hind and engaged in the shipping and commission business. In 1903 he helped found the Mission Bank, of which he became president, also serving as president of the Mission Savings Bank. He founded the Rolph Navigation & Coal Company, the Rolph Shipbuilding Company, and the James Rolph Company. He was asked to run for mayor in June 1909, but declined, choosing to run in the 1911 election. For the next 19 years Rolph was "Sunny Jim" to San Franciscans with "There Are Smiles That Make You Happy" as his theme song. Along with his job as mayor, and his private shipping interests, he also served as director of the Ship Owners & Merchants Tugboat Company, the San Francisco Chamber of Commerce, president of the Merchants Exchange, and vice president of the 1915 Panama-Pacific International Exposition. In November 1930, James Rolph Jr. won the California gubernatorial election. He resigned as mayor effective simultaneously with his inauguration as governor, on Tuesday, January 6, 1931. On November 9, 1933, Brooke Hart, son of a wealthy San Jose merchant, was kidnapped. The two men responsible were caught, later forcibly removed from jail in San Jose and hanged by a vigilante committee. Governor Rolph, by condoning the lynching, was given the name "Governor Lynch" and received extremely bad publicity across the nation. Following this episode he suffered several heart attacks and died at Riverside Farm, Santa Clara County, on June 2, 1934.

Angelo Joseph Rossi (1878–1948)

Born January 22, 1878 in Volcano, Amador County, California. In 1890 his family moved to San Francisco where he attended the North Cosmopolitan School. He began work as an errand boy for the florist firm of Carbone & Manti, eventually heading the firm as president and manager. He served as director of the Downtown Association of San Francisco for many years, and as its president during 1920 and

1921. Mayor James Rolph, Jr. appointed him a member of the playground commission, and he served on this board from 1914 to 1921. He was elected to the Board of Supervisors in 1925 and again in 1929. Upon the election of Mayor James Rolph, Jr. as Governor of California, Rossi was elected mayor by the Board of Supervisors on January 7, 1931. He was reelected by the people in 1935 and 1939. He died in San Francisco on April 5, 1948.

Roger Dearborn Lapham (1883–1966)

Born in New York City on December 6, 1883. He attended Harvard University, then entered his family-founded American Hawaiian Steamship Company as a clerk, and rose to its presidency in 1925. He was appointed a member of the National Defense Mediation Board in 1941 by President Franklin Roosevelt. Returning to San Francisco in 1943 he ran for mayor as an independent candidate, pledging he would accept the office for one term only. "I know nothing about city administration but I think I can learn," were his campaigning words. He later survived a recall movement in 1946 opposing his consolidation of the private Market Street Railway with the Municipal Railway. After leaving office in 1948 Lapham headed the U. S. Economic Cooperation Administration's mission to China, and in 1950-1951 headed the E.C.A.'s mission to Greece. He died in San Francisco on April 16, 1966.

Elmer Edwin Robinson (1894–1982)

Born in San Francisco on October 3, 1894. After graduating from night law school, he was admitted to the California Bar in 1915. As a young lawyer, he worked as a deputy in the District Attorney's office from 1915 to 1921, then branched out on his own. After 15 years before the bench, he was appointed Municipal Judge in January 1935, and Superior Judge nine months later. He was elected to a six-year Superior Court term in 1936 and reelected in 1942. In 1933, under appointment by Franklin Roosevelt, at the request of the Disabled American Veterans, he directed adjustment of compensation claims for veterans of World War I. During World War II, Judge Robinson served as State Chairman of a national salvage committee. He resigned his seat on the Superior Court Bench in 1947 to run for the office of mayor, winning this election and the following one in 1951. Upon his retirement from office in January 1956 he returned to his law practice and to the position of president and general manager of Woodlawn Memorial Park. He died in San Francisco on June 9, 1982.

George Christopher (Christopheles) (1907–)

Born in Arcadia, Greece, December 8, 1907. He was brought to San Francisco at the age of two and educated in the public schools, later graduating with a degree in accounting from the Golden Gate Night College. In 1930, after becoming a citizen of the United States, he changed his name to Christopher. The Excelsior Dairy made him an official in 1937, followed by a partnership in the Meadow Glen Dairy, which eventually became the Christopher Dairy. In 1945 he began his political career by election to the Board of Supervisors, with reelection in 1949 when he served as President of the Board. He was elected mayor in 1955 and served two terms. In the 1966 primary election George Christopher ran against Ronald Reagan for the office of governor but was defeated.

John Francis Shelley (1905–1974)

Born September 3, 1905 in San Francisco. He graduated from the University of San Francisco Law School in 1932, and was elected president of the San Francisco Labor Council in 1937. From 1948 to his election to Congress in 1949, he was secretary-treasurer of the Council and from 1947 to

1950 was also president of the California State Federation of Labor. He was elected in 1938 to the State Senate, and in 1949 began the first of his eight terms in Congress. Jack Shelley was elected mayor on November 5, 1963, defeating Supervisor Harold Dobbs by 120,560 votes to 92,627. Because of ill health he declined to run for a second term, saying, "The job of Mayor is an endless, impossible and exhausting drain, trying not only to keep a City intact, but on the right track." Shelley served as San Francisco's lobbyist in Sacramento until his death September 1, 1974.

Joseph Lawrence Alioto (1916–)

Born in San Francisco on February 12, 1916. He is a graduate of St. Mary's College, and the Catholic University of America Law School in Washington, D.C. He has also received Honorary Doctor of Law degrees from St. Mary's College, Santa Clara University and the Catholic University of America. From law school, Alioto joined the Department of Justice where he worked five years in the anti-trust division under Judge Thurman Arnold and Justice Tom Clark. In the 1950s he served as president of the Board of Education and was then appointed to the Redevelopment Agency. In 1959, Alioto became general manager and president of the Rice Growers Association and rapidly expanded its annual sales from $25 to $70 million. He revolutionized production methods and pioneered the use of ships as seagoing silos for the transportation of edible bulk rice. He was elected mayor on November 7, 1967, defeating Harold Dobbs, and was reelected to a second term in 1971.

George Richard Moscone (1929–1978)

Born in San Francisco on November 24, 1929, he attended St. Brigid Elementary School and St. Ignatius High School. He went to the College of Pacific on an athletic scholarship, and then won an academic scholarship to the Hastings College of the Law. After serving in the Navy, he began practice of law in San Francisco in 1956. In 1963 he was elected to the Board of Supervisors, and three years later was elected to the State Senate. In 1975, in a runoff election, he defeated Supervisor John Barbagelata for the office of mayor. Monday, November 27, 1978, ex-Supervisor Dan White shot and killed Mayor Moscone in his City Hall office. He was buried in Holy Cross Cemetery on November 30, 1978, after lying in state at City Hall and at St. Mary's Cathedral.

Dianne Goldman Feinstein (1933–)

Born in San Francisco on June 22, 1933, Dianne Feinstein received her primary education in public shools and her secondary education at the Convent of the Sacred Heart. She graduated from Stanford University in 1955 with a degree in history and political science. In 1970 she was elected to the Board of Supervisors, becoming its first woman president. As Board President, she automatically became mayor upon the death of George Moscone. She was elected mayor December 4, 1978, by a six-to-two vote by the Board of Supervisors to fill out the remaining thirteen months of Moscone's term. She is the first woman mayor in San Francisco's history and the city's second Jewish mayor. After 10 years in office, she ran against Pete Wilson for governor but lost the election. Later, she ran for the U.S. Senate seat of retiring Alan Cranston. She won the election, receiving more than 80 percent of the vote in San Francisco. In the Senate, she was appointed to several key committees and became a confidante of President Clinton.

Art Agnos (1938–)

Born September 1, 1938 in Springfield, Mass., the son of Greek immigrant parents. He holds a bachelor's degree from Bates College in Lewiston, Maine, and a Masters of Social Work from Florida State University.

He came to San Francisco in 1966 and worked as Assistant Director of Human Relations for the San Francisco Housing Authority before joining the staff of then-Assemblyman Leo McCarthy. He was elected to the California State Assembly in 1976 serving six terms.

Art Agnos was elected mayor on December 8, 1987 with 70 percent of the vote, the largest vote for any non-incumbent in this century, but was defeated for reelection.

Frank M. Jordan (1935–)

Born in San Francisco on February 20, 1935. He attended Sacred Heart High School and the University of San Francisco. He began his service to the City as a police officer who worked his way up through the ranks. He was appointed Chief of Police by Mayor Feinstein in 1986 and retained the chief's position during the early years of the Agnos administration. He retired from the Police Department in 1990 to run against Mayor Agnos. Jordan said he decided to challenge the Mayor "out of love for San Francisco and a belief that the city had got ten off track, and that city government was neither accessible nor responsive to the city's neighborhoods."

Mayor Jordan took office on January 8, 1992, after beating Mayor Agnos in a runoff election. During his administration he created the Mayor's Office of Economic Planning and Development to ensure that city government can accurately forecast economic performance and take a proactive approach to business development. He said the top priorities for his administration were public safety, homelessness, children's services, and cleaning up the City.

Mayor Jordan married Wendy Paskin, a Vice President of Wells Fargo Bank, while in office.

Chief Administrator

Alfred J. Cleary, January 8, 1932 – February 16, 1941

Thomas A. Brooks, February 20, 1941 – July 1, 1958

Chester MacPhee, July 1, 1958 – January 31, 1959

Sherman P. Duckel, January 31, 1959 – September 1, 1964

Thomas Mellon, September 1, 1964 – September 1, 1976

Roger Boas, January 3, 1977 – December 26, 1986

Rudy Nothenberg, January 5, 1987 –

City Assessor

The Assessor, with a four-year term, appraises all property subject to taxation, prepares the assessment roll, and collects certain personal property taxes.

Charles R. Bond, 1856 – 1861

Christopher C. Webb, 1862 – 1863

William Wheaton, 1863 – 1867

Ben Harris, 1868 – 1869

Levi Rosener, 1870 – 1875

Alexander Bedlam, 1875 – 1882

Louis Holtz, 1883 – 1886

James C. Nealon, 1887 – 1890

John D. Siebe, 1891 – 1898

Washington Dodge, 1889 – 1912

John Ginty, 1912 – 1925

Russell L. Wolden, Sr., 1926 – 1938

Russell L. Wolden, Jr., 1938 – 1966

Joseph Tinney, 1966 – 1979

Sam Duca, 1979 – 1991

Richard Hongisto, 1991 – 1992

Doris Ward, 1992 –

City Attorney

The City Attorney, who serves for four years, represents San Francisco in all civil legal actions and serves as legal advisor to all departments and the Board of Supervisors. The City Attorney also prepares or approves as to form all ordinances and other legal documents.

Thomas H. Holt, 1850

Frank M. Pixley, 1851

Charles McC. Delany, 1852

John K. Hackett, 1852

Solomon A. Sharpe, 1853

Lewis Sawyer, 1854

Balie Peyton, 1855 – 1856

Frederick P. Tracy, 1857 – 1859

Samuel W. Holladay, 1860 – 1861

John H. Saunders, 1861 – 1866

Horace M. Hastings, 1866 – 1868

Joseph M. Nougues, 1869 – 1870

Wellington C. Burnett, 1871 – 1879

John L. Murphy, 1880 – 1881

Jabez F. Cowdery, 1872

William Craig, 1883 – 1884

John L. Love, 1885 – 1886

George Flournoy, Jr., 1887 – 1890

John H. Durst, 1890 – 1891

Harry T. Creswell, 1893 – 1898

Franklin K. Lane, 1899 – 1900

Percy V. Long, 1904 – 1905

William G. Burke, 1906 – 1907

Percy V. Long, 1908 – 1916

George Lull, 1917 – 1925

John J. O'Toole, 1926 – 1948

Dion R. Holm, 1949 – 1961

Thomas M. O'Connor, 1962 – 1977

George Agnost, 1977 – 1986 (Died in office)

Philip Ward, August 4 – 24, 1986

Louise Renne, August 26, 1986 –

Coroner

Edward Gallagher, 1850

Nathaniel Gray, 1851 – 1852

J. W. Whaling, 1853 – 1854

John H. Kent, 1855 – 1856

James M. McNulty, 1857 – 1861

Benjamin A. Sheldon, 1862 – 1864

Steven R. Harris, 1864 – 1867

Jonathan M. Letterman, 1868 – 1871

Jacob D. Stillman, 1872 – 1873

John R. Rice, 1874

Benjamin R. Swan, 1874 – 1877

Levi L. Dorr, 1878 – 1881

Freeman L. Weeks, 1882

Marc Levingston, 1883 – 1884

Charles C. O'Donnell, 1885 – 1886
James I. Stanton, 1887 – 1888
William E. Taylor, 1889 – 1890
William T. Garwood, 1891 – 1892
Jerome A. Hughes, 1893 – 1894
William J. Hawkins, 1895 – 1898
Edward E. Hill, 1899 – 1900
R. Beverly Cole, 1900 – 1901
Thomas B. Leland, 1901 – 1905
William J. Walsh, 1906 – 1907
Thomas B. Leland, 1908 – 1909
William J. Walsh, 1910 – 1911
J. Michael Toner, 1911 – 1912
Thomas B. Leland, 1912 – 1940
John J. Kingston, 1941 – 1952
Henry J. Turkel, 1952 – 1971
Ervin Jindrich, 1971 – 1972
Boyd G. Stephens, 1972 –

District Attorney

The District Attorney is elected for a four-year term. His duties include preparing and prosecuting all criminal cases; legal advising for the Grand Jury; and working in cooperation with the police, welfare, and probation departments.

Henry H. Byrne, 1856
William K. Osborn, 1857
Harvey S. Brown, 1858 – 1860
Nathan Porter, 1861 – 1867
Herry H. Byrne, 1868 – 1871
Daniel J. Murphy, 1872 – 1873
Thomas P. Ryan, 1874 – 1875
Daniel J. Murphy, 1876 – 1879
David L. Smoot, 1880 – 1881
Leonidas E. Pratt, 1882
Jeremiah D. Sullivan, 1883 – 1884
John N. Wison, 1885 – 1886
Edward B. Stonehill, 1887 – 1888
James D. Page, 1889 – 1890
William S. Barnes, 1891 – 1898
Daniel J. Murphy, 1899 – 1900
Lewis F. Byington, 1900 – 1905
William H. Langdon, 1906 – 1910
Charles M. Fickert, 1910 – 1919
Matthew Brady, 1920 – 1943
Edmund G. Brown, 1944 – 1950

Thomas C. Lynch, 1951 – 1964
John J. Ferdon, 1964 – 1975
Joseph Freitas, 1976 – 1979
Arlo Smith, 1980 –

Librarian
Albert Hart, 1878 – 1879
C. H. Robinson, 1879 – 1880
Fred B. Perkins, 1880 – 1888
John V. Cheney, 1888 – 1895
George T. Clark, 1895 – 1907
William R. Watson, 1907 – 1912
Robert Rea, 1913 – 1945
Laurence J. Clarke, 1946 – 1960
Frank Clarvoe, 1960
William R. Holman, 1960 – 1967
Harold D. Martelle, Jr., 1967 – 1968
John F. Anderson, 1968 – 1973
Kevin Starr, 1973 – 1976
Vivian Goodwin, 1976
William Ramirez, 1976
Edwin Castagna, 1976 – 1977
John C. Frantz, 1977 – 1987
Karen Scannell, 1987
Kenneth Dowlin, 1987 –

Park Department
Superintendent of Parks: Golden Gate Park
William Hammond Hall, 1871   1876
William Bond Pritchard, 1876 – 1881
Francis P. Hennessy, 1881 – 1882
John J. McEwen, 1882 – 1886
John McLaren, 1887 – 1943
Julius Girod, 1943 – 1957
Bart Rolph, 1958 – 1964
Frank Foehr, 1964 – 1970
Emmett O'Donnell, 1970 – 1974
John J. Spring, 1974 – 1975
Carl Poch, 1975 – 1977
Aldo C. Cima, 1977 – 1978
Bernard Barron, 1978 – 1991
Ron De Leon, 1991 –

Recreation and Park Department
General Manager
Harvey E. Teller, 1950 – 1951
David E. Lewis, 1951 – 1954

Max Funke, 1954 – 1958
Raymond S. Kimbell, 1958 – 1963
James P. Lang, 1963 – 1969
Edward McDevitt, 1968 – 1969
(Acting General Manager during illness
of James Lang)
Joseph M. Caverly, 1969 – 1975
John J. Spring, 1975 – 1980
Thomas Malloy, 1980 – 1984
Bernard Barron, 1984–1985
(Acting General Manager)
Mary E. Burns, 1985–

The Park Department was merged with the Recreation Department by initiative in November 1949.

Public Defender

The Public Defender, with a four-year term, provides free legal counsel and service to those who cannot afford to hire an attorney.
Frank Egan, 1921 – 1932
Gerald J. Kenny, 1934 – 1953
Edward T. Mancuso, 1954 – 1974
Robert Nicco, 1974 – 1985
Jeff Brown, 1985 –

Public Guardian

(Created by State Legislature, Section 5175, Welfare and Institutions Code, July 1, 1960)
Con Shea, 1960 – 1978
James Scannell, 1978 – 1988
Frank Weiner, 1989
Ricardo Hernandez, 1989 –

Public Utilities Commission
General Manager

Edward G. Cahill, 1932 – 1945
James H. Turner, 1945 – 1956
T. N. Bland, 1956 – 1958
Robert C. Kirkwood, 1959 – 1964
James K. Carr, 1964 – 1970
John D. Crowley, 1970 – 1976
John B. Wentz, 1977 – 1979
Richard Sklar, 1979 – 1984
Rudolf Nothenberg, 1983 – 1987

Donald Birrer, 1987 – 1988
Dean Coffey, 1988 – 1989
Thomas J. Elzey, 1989 –

Registrar of Voters

The office of Registrar of Voters was created by an amendment to the Consolidation Act of 1856.
Louis Kaplan, 1978 – 1980
Joseph L. Tharp, 1981 – 1982
James A. Johnson, 1983 – 1984
Patrick F. Walsh, 1985 – 1987
Benjamin A. Prindle, 1988
Thomas J. Smiley, 1989 – 1990
William A. Brown, 1991 – 1992
Alfred J. Evans, 1993 – 1994
William M. Hinton, 1995 – 1997
William J. Biggy, 1998 – 1999
Thomas J. Welsh, 1900 – 1903
George P. Adams, 1904 – 1907
Joshua H. Zemansky, 1908 – 1910
Edward C. Harrington, 1910 – 1911
Joshua H. Zemansky, 1912 – 1929
Charles J. Collins, 1929 – 1941
Cameron H. King, 1941 – 1947
Thomas A. Toomey, 1947 – 1960
Charles A. Rogers, 1960 – 1967
Basil Healy, 1967 – 1969
Virgil Elliott, 1969
Emmery Mihaly, 1969 – 1974
Frank R. Quinn, 1974
Gilbert Borman, 1974 – 1975
Lawrence LeGuennec, 1975
Frank R. Quinn, 1975
Hugh Maguire, 1975 – 1976
Jay Patterson, 1976
Thomas Kearney, 1976 – 1980
Jay Patterson, 1980 – 1988
Michele Corwin, 1988
Germaine Wong, 1988 –

San Francisco Water Department
General Managers

Nelson A. Eckart, 1930 – 1948
George W. Pracy, 1949 – 1957
James H. Turner, 1957 – 1963
Oral L. Moore, 1963 – 1965 (co-manager)

H. Christopher Medbery, 1963 – 1965
(co-manager)
Arthur H. Fry, Jr., 1965 – 1976
Kenneth R. Boyd, 1976 – 1978
Eugene J. Kelleher, 1978 – 1984
Arthur Jensen, 1984 – 1985 (acting)
Dean W. Coffey, 1985 – 1986
James Cooney, July 1986 – June 1989
Arthur Jensen, 1989 – 1990 (temporary
appointment)
John Mullane, 1990 –

Salaries, Department Heads

POSITION	ANNUAL SALARY
Executive Director, S.F. General Hospital	$144,456
Mayor	122,356
Chief Administrative Officer	121,212
General Manager, Public Utilities Commission	118,326
Director, Public Works	118,326
Director, Health	118,326
Controller	114,790
Director and Curator, Museums	109,954
City Attorney	109,174
District Attorney	109,174
Airports Director	108,888
Executive Director, Port of San Francisco	108,852 *
Deputy Director for Operations, Health	108,264
Director, Systems and Data Processing	108,264
Chief of Police	107,676 *
Chief of Fire Department	107,676 *
General Manager, Municipal Railway	106,756
General Manager, Social Services	106,132
Chief Medical Examiner	105,742
Director of Planning	104,156
Deputy Director, Mental Health	104,156
Deputy Director, Community Health	104,156
Administrator, Laguna Honda Hospital	103,714

POSITION	ANNUAL SALARY
Chief Assistant City Attorney	103,714
Deputy City Attorney	103,714
Airports General Counsel	103,714
Assistant Deputy City Attorney	103,714
Public Utilities General Counsel	103,714
Chief Assistant District Attorney	103,714
Manager, Utilities Engineering Bureau	103,558
Public Defender	102,882
General Manager, Retirement System	101,660
Programs Chief, Community Health	101,660
Chief Assistant Controller	101,088
General Manager, Water Department	101,088
Deputy Director for Institutions, Health	100,126

* Salary estimate

SAN FRANCISCO EXAMINER,
April 3, 1989

Sheriff

The Sheriff is the keeper of the county jail, transports prisoners to and from court, and delivers them to the state prison and other institutions. It is also his duty to carry out all lawful orders and serve all legal notices of the court. The Sheriff's duty of executing condemned criminals ceased in 1891 when the State of California assumed that task.

John C. Hays, 1850–1851
Thomas P. Johnson, 1851–1852
William R. Gorham, 1853–1854
David Scannell, 1855–1856
Charles Doane, 1857–1861
John S. Ellis, 1862–1864
Henry L. Davis, 1864–1867
P. J. White, 1868–1871
James Adams, 1872–1873
William McKibbin, 1874–1875
Matthew Nunan, 1876–1879
Thomas Desmond, 1880–1881
John Sedgwick, 1882

Patrick Connolly, 1883–1884
Peter Hopkins, 1885–1886
William McMann, 1887–1888
Charles S. Laumeister, 1889–1892
John J. McDade, 1893–1894
Richard I. Whelan, 1895–1898
Henry S. Martin, 1899
John Lachmann, 1900–1904
Peter J. Curtis, 1904–1906
Thomas F. O'Neil, 1906–1908
Lawrence J. Dolan, 1908–1910
Thomas F. Finn, 1910–1911
William J. Fitzgerald, 1928–1935
Daniel C. Murphy, 1936–1952
Dan Gallagher, 1952–1956
Matthew C. Carberry, 1956–1971
Richard D. Hongisto, 19712–1978
Eugene A. Brown, 1978–1979
Michael Hennessey, 1980–

Treasurer

The Treasurer, with a four-year term, receives, pays out, and keeps records of money belonging to the City and County. With the Controller has joint custody of all public funds.

County Treasurer

George W. Endicott, 1850
Joseph Shannon, 1851–1852
George W. Green, 1853–1854
R. E. Wood, 1855–1856

City Treasurer

Charles G. Scott, 1850–1851
Richard H. Sinton, 1851–1852
Smyth Clark, 1852
Hamilton Bowie, 1852–1854
David S. Turner, 1854–1855
William McKibbin, 1855–1856
William Hooper, 1856

William H. Tillinghast, 1857–1861
Joseph S. Paxson, 1862–1867
Otto Kloppenburg, 1868–1871
John A. Bauer, 1872–1873
Charles Hubert, 1874–1879
William R. Shaber, 1880–1881
Christian Reis, 1883–1884
John A. Bauer, 1885–1886
Christan Reis, 1887–1889
James H. Widber, 1891–1897
Christian Reis, 1898–1899
Irwin J. Truman, 1899–1900
Sam H. Brooks, 1900–1902
John E. McDougald, 1902–1905
Charles A. Bantel, 1906–1907
John E. McDougald, 1907–1925
John H. Thieler, 1926–1929
Duncan Matheson, 1929–1942
Thomas K. McCarthy, 1942–1947
John J. Goodwin, 1947–1971
Thomas Scanlon, 1971–1980
Mary Callanan, 1980–

Zoo Director

George M. Bistany, 1932–1935
Edmund Heller, 1935–1939
Carey Baldwin, 1941–1967
Ronald T. Reuther, 1967–1973
Jack Spring, 1973–1975
Saul Kitchener, 1975–1989
David E. Anderson, 1990–

San Francisco City Hall, Van Ness Avenue entrance. The Board of Supervisors' chambers are behind the columns above the entrance. Their offices extend along the second floor to the right. This city hall replaced the structure wrecked during the Great Earthquake and burned in the following fire. Ground was broken for this City Hall on April 5, 1913, by Mayor Rolph. The cornerstone was laid Oct. 25, 1913 "Sunny Jim" Rolphopen dedicated the new structure Dec. 28, 1915. It suffered significant damage during the 1989 earthquake and was evacuated in 1995 for repairs scheduled for completion sometime during the early part of the 21st century.

10 City General

363d Infantry ("San Francisco's Own")

The 363d Infantry was formed at Camp Lewis, Washington, on September 5, 1917, as a part of the 91st Division, one of the sixteen "National Army Divisions created by General Order No. 101, August 3, 1917." The original enlisted personnel of the Regiment was comprised of men inducted into the service from Central and Northern California counties, and a majority of these came from San Francisco, which caused the Regiment to be named: "San Francisco's Own."

The Regiment returned to San Francisco April 22, 1919, at which time Mayor James Rolph, Jr. said: "Some of those to whom we bade good-bye in 1917 from the steps of our City Hall lie today beneath the fields of France and Belgium and we will see them no more. Gold Star mothers and wives and sisters there are who will watch your triumphant homecoming with tear-dimmed eyes, weeping for their own boys whom you left sleeping 'over there.' To these we extend our boundless sympathy. To these we

do honor, as do you, who know better than any others the noble manner in which the flower of our man-hood laid down their lives. Again boys of the 363d, boys of the Glorious West, we say to you: 'Welcome, a hundred times. Welcome Home.' We love you. We admire you. You are our own."

The Regiment was later mustered out at a ceremony at the Palace of Fine Arts.

The 363d Infantry was later brought back to active duty and made part of the 30th Infantry. Authorized by an act of Congress dated February 2, 1901, it was organized and equipped at the Presidio of San Francisco where it early embarked for service in the Philippines.

Again from 1909 to 1912, and for a short period before World War I, the 30th called the Presidio home. The ensuing years took the Regiment to Alaska, New York, and then to San Antonio.

On April 1, 1918, the 30th sailed for service with the American Expeditionary Force in France. It returned to the Presidio on August 26, 1922, where it remained until

World War II. Sometime between 1922 and 1931, Mayor James Rolph, Jr. presented the Regiment with a flag bearing the city's seal and designating it "San Francisco's Own."

Since World War II the Regiment has been assigned to the 3d Infantry Division stationed in Schweinfurt, Germany.

City Colors

On February 13, 1979, black and gold were officially recognized as city colors by passage of resolution 94–79 by the San Francisco Board of Supervisors.

City Flower

The dahlia, long regarded as the city flower, was officially designated as such on October 4, 1926.

The Board of Supervisors in resolution No. 26244 said, "The dahlia partakes essentially of the character of our beloved city, in birth, breeding and habit, for it was originally Mexican, carried thence to Spain, to France and England in turn, being changed in the process from a simple daisylike wild flower to a cosmopolitan beauty."

City Halls

1. Northwest corner of Kearny and Pacific streets (ex-Graham House), May 1850–June 1851.
2. California Exchange, northeast corner of Kearny and Clay streets, March 1852–Feb. 1853.
3. Jenny Lind Theater, Kearny between Clay and Sacramento streets, 1853–1878. Referred to as "Old City Hall" 1878–1895.
4. "New" City Hall, southeast corner of McAllister and Larkin streets, 1895–1906.
5. Temporary City Hall, 1231 Market Street, 1912–1915. Building used later as the Whitcomb Hotel; presently Ramada Inn hotel.
6. City Hall, Polk, Van Ness, Grove and McAllister streets, 1915–

City Hall occupies two square blocks on the west side of the Civic Center, the main entrance facing the central plaza, the rear entrance facing Van Ness Avenue.

Ground was broken April 5, 1913; dedication ceremonies were held December 28, 1915; cost of the structure was $3,996,163.

City Hall is considered one of the finest examples of French Renaissance architecture in America. The design and details of both interior and exterior were executed by master architects of national reputation.

The exterior is of Raymond granite from the foothills of the High Sierra and forms the main portion of the building, with a 390 foot frontage and a depth of 273 feet, 3 inches.

The distinctive feature is a large dome which is expressed in both plan and facade. In plan, this dome extends through the various floors as a rotunda forming the center of circulation on each floor.

The lofty dome rises 301 feet, 5 1/2 inches from the curb on Polk Street, 39 feet, 6 1/2 inches higher than the Capitol in Washington, D.C.

The central rotunda rises through all four stories to the inner vaulting dome which springs from a ring of Corinthian columns and terminates in an open lantern through which may be seen a boldly carved cartouche at the apex of the inner dome.

The dome rests upon four 50-ton and four 20-ton girders, 9 feet deep and 60 feet long, which are supported by four groups of five columns each, latticed together from the second story to the top. Diameter of the dome at spring-line, 191 feet above ground, is 86 feet. Wind load of 50 pounds per square foot was used in calculations.

Approximate weight of the structure is 90,000 tons, of which 7,900 tons is structural steel.

City Hall suffered interior damage during the 1989 earthquake and extensive repair and seismic retrofitting of the structure began in the 1990s.

City Tree

The official city tree is a 100-foot Monterey Cypress located in front of McLaren Lodge at Kennedy Drive, near Fell Street in Golden Gate Park.

Final Honors

Citizens Who Have Lain in State in the City Hall before Burial.

Frederick Funston, General, U.S.A.
February 23–24, 1917

Timothy J. Collins, SFFD
October 8, 1917

Joseph A. Allen, SFFD
October 8, 1917

Steven D. Russell, SFFD
October 8, 1917

John Joseph Conlon, SFFD
March 3–4, 1919

Miles Jackson, SFPD
December 8–9, 1920

Lester H. Dorman, SFPD
December 8–9, 1920

Edward I. Wolfe, Supervisor
January 27, 1922

Joseph Brady, SFPD October 7, 1924

George Campbell, SFPD
April 12–13, 1925

John B. Badaracco, Supervisor
February 28, 1928

James D. Phelan, Mayor and U.S. Senator August 11, 1930

James Rolph, Jr., Mayor and Governor
June 4, 1934

Winifred Black Bonfils (Annie Laurie)
May 27, 1936

Leonard S. Leavy, Controller June 14, 1937

John McLaren, Supt. Golden Gate Park
January 14, 1943

Hiram Johnson, U.S. Senator and Governor
August 13, 1945

Charles P. Lynch, SFFD August 1, 1946
John Borman, SFFD August 1, 1946
Albert Hudson, SFFD August 1, 1946
Walter Elvitsky, SFFD August 1, 1946
Angelo J. Rossi, Mayor April 7, 1948

Dan Gallagher, Sheriff May 8, 1956
Francis J. Ahern, SFPD
September 2, 1958
Thomas A. Brooks, Chief Administrator
September 24, 1959
George Moscone, Mayor
November 29, 1978
Harvey Milk, Supervisor
November 29, 1978
Zeno Contreras, SFFD July 18, 1979
Ella Hill Hutch, Supervisor
March 1, 1981
Phillip Burton, US Congressman
April 13, 1983
George Agnost, City Attorney
August 6, 1986
Sala Burton, US Congresswoman
February 5, 1987
Tom Waddell, Chief Physician, Central Emergency Hospital July 18, 1987
Terry A. Francois, Supervisor
June 14, 1989

First Public Building

The first public building for the use of the City Government was the hulk of the brig *Euphemia*, anchored in the Bay, at the crossing of Jackson and Battery streets. It was used as a prison.

Key to San Francisco

Twenty-eight men served as the mayor of San Francisco before one chose to use a key as a symbol of welcome to distinguished visitors. That mayor was James Rolph, Jr. who was in office for 19 years.

Proud of the city he was born and raised in and with the theme song "There Are Smiles That Make You Happy," he was just the man to begin a tradition of welcoming special visitors with a large hollow metal gold key.

When Mayor Rolph left office to become Governor of California in 1931, the now-established key ceremony was taken up by Mayor Angelo J. Rossi and was continued through his 13 years in office.

When the supply of metal keys ran out, redwood gavels were made the official souvenir gift. However, at a cost of $20 each the redwood gavels had a short life and were soon replaced with a cardboard key which cost about $1. These cardboard keys were designed by Mayor Christopher and Darrell Pischoff. The first of the cardboard keys was presented to Mayor Christopher and the second key went to Benny Bufano.

By 1964 when the cardboard keys were costing the city $2.25 each, Mayor John Shelley considered replacing them with another metal key. Ideas rolled in from everywhere, but soon a sketch submitted by Schlage Lock Co. was adopted. The new and present key is modeled after an old Mission Dolores key.

Municipal Work Force

Here is how San Francisco ranked nationally in city workers per 1,000 residents:

San Francisco	34.1
Baltimore	25.6
Denver	21.7
Seattle	21.5
Richmond, Va.	21.2
New York	20.8

SAN FRANCISCO EXAMINER
Dec. 3, 1990

Mysterious San Francisco

San Francisco's rich and colorful past is full of obscure and mysterious events. Psychic phenomena, including apparitions and poltergeist activity, have been documented in San Francisco since the 1860s when Mark Twain described poltergeist activity in a Kearny Street house. The Manrow home (which stood at Larkin and Chestnut streets) experienced extensive ghost, voice, and poltergeist activity at about the same time, apparently connected with the owner's 14-year-old niece. The apparition of an 1876 debutante, Flora Summerton, who spurned her beau and fled to Montana, has been seen occasionally on California Street, Nob Hill. A 1930s "phantom hitchhiker" account tells of a secretary who hitched a ride from 5th and Mission streets to her Twin Peaks home, but disappeared before arriving, having died a few years earlier in an auto accident. More than a dozen haunted buildings survive in San Francisco. Among the best known are the San Francisco Art Institute (tower) and the Atherton Mansion.

Flying saucers and "air ships" have buzzed San Francisco skies for more than a century. The famous and unresolved "air ship" mystery of late 1876 featured nocturnal visits by dirigible-like "air ships" that beamed bright lights on parts of the city. Mayor Adolph Sutro had a sighting as did other prominent citizens. In 1897 the phenomenon became nationwide. More recent unidentified flying object "waves" occurred in 1973 and 1981–82. An outer Richmond District resident claimed a small saucer-shaped craft landed in her back yard in early 1981.

San Francisco Bay has also hosted some strange visitors. A large unidentified creature was seen near Yerba Buena Island in 1934. In 1985 a 60-foot multi-humped creature was seen off the Marina District shore, and similar "sea serpents" have been seen over the years in Bolinas and Monterey bays.

A variety of other San Francisco mysteries have included a phantom ship seen near the Farallons, a mystery kangaroo in Golden Gate Park (1980), the veiled woman of Fillmore Street (1930s), a deep nocturnal hum that disturbed northern city residents (1980s) and the elusive Zodiac killer (1966–69) who was never caught.

MICHAEL D. LAMPEN

San Franciscans' Fear

San Franciscans' most common fear is Gephydrophobia, the fear of crossing bridges.

DR. GERRIT BLAUVELT
San Francisco psychiatrist

Seal of San Francisco

There have been two city seals in the history of San Francisco. The first was the Seal of the City of San Francisco. The second is the Seal of the City and County of San Francisco.

The Seal of the City of San Francisco was adopted on November 4, 1852 and was quite similar to the Seal of the State of California. It showed the Golden Gate and the hills on each side, and ships sailing around the harbor. At the bottom was a Phoenix, the legendary Greek bird arising from burning fire. Around the margin of the seal were the words "Seal of the City of San Francisco."

The Board of Supervisors on March 1, 1859, adopted a new seal for the City and County. In this seal, the main figures, a miner and a sailor, stand on either side of a shield on which is depicted a steamer entering the Golden Gate. At the bottom is a scroll with the words, "Oro en Paz, Fierro en Guerra." At the top of the shield is the Phoenix. At the bottom also are the symbols of commerce, navigation, and mining. Around the outside circle are the words "Seal of the City and County of San Francisco."

On March 26, 1900 the Board of Supervisors passed Ordinance No. 39 which states:

> That a corporate seal of the City and County of San Francisco bearing upon its face: A shield supported by a miner on the left and a sailor on the right, with a device of a steamship passing the Golden Gate. At the foot of the supporters emblems of commerce, navigation and mining. Crest, Phoenix issuing from flames. Motto, "Oro en Paz, Fierro en Guerra" (Gold in Peace, Iron in War). Around the margin the words, "Seal of the City and County of San Francisco."

Violence or Threats to City Officials

August 23, 1879 Isaac Smith Kalloch shot by Charles de Young in left thigh. Later Kalloch was elected mayor in sympathy election.

April 23, 1880 Charles de Young murdered by Milton Kalloch, son of Mayor Kalloch. He was later acquitted.

April 29, 1908 Alameda home of James L. Gallagher, President of the San Francisco Board of Supervisors, is dynamited.

July 29, 1970 Mayor Alioto received a series of threats.

January 12, 1976 Quentin Kopp and John Barbagelata receive candy box bombs.

June 24, 1976 Mayor Alioto's home bombed.

December 14, 1976 Supervisor Dianne Feinstein receives a flower box bomb.

February 4, 1977 Car of District Attorney Joseph Freitas, Jr., is bombed.

March 16, 1977 Shots fired at Dianne Feinstein's beach house in Watsonville.

March 22, 1977 Supervisor John Barbagelata's life threatened. Bomb explodes close to his home.

March 31, 1977 Gunman gained access to Mayor Moscone's office.

November 27, 1978 Mayor Moscone shot and killed by former Supervisor Dan White.

November 27, 1978 Harvey Milk, Supervisor, shot and killed by former Supervisor Dan White.

June 25, 1981 A letter containing a threat against the City of San Francisco was delivered to Mayor Dianne Feinstein. The letter stated that a nuclear device would be detonated in San Francisco on July 15, 1981 if the City refused the demand for $100 million in industrial diamonds. A U.S. sailor stationed at Mare Island was arrested on July 23rd for writing the extortion demand.

October 2, 1990 Lynn Falske arrested after making death threats against six members of the Board of Supervisors who voted to tear down the quake-damaged Embarcadero Freeway.

11 City Government

City Charter

"On April 15th, 1850, San Francisco was incorporated as a City, by act of the Legislature. By that act it became the legal successor of the Pueblo of San Francisco, vested with all its property, and that same statute took away all the power of the Prefect. The title to the Pueblo Lands was therefore vested in the City of San Francisco. This charter was subsequently repealed by the Charter of 1851, which, in its turn was repealed by that of 1854; but the charter of 1850 authorized the city to 'hold, lease, sell and dispose of property for the benefit of the city.' The charter of 1851 empowered the city to purchase, receive, and hold property, real and personal, and sell or otherwise dispose of the same for their common benefit; the charter of 1855 continued the power in the city to 'purchase, receive, hold and enjoy real and personal property, and sell, convey, mortgage and dispose of the same for the common benefit.'"

John W. Dwinelle
The Colonial History of
the City of San Francisco, *1866*

"The 1856 Charter was not efficient; it was said that nobody knew what it meant except the city clerk and one or two lawyers. The California Constitution of 1879 provided for the city to pass a freeholder's charter, but attempts to do so were defeated four times until, finally in 1900, a strong-mayor-council type was adopted. However, under the 1900 Charter, the Mayor was not so strong as was expected and his executive powers were weakened by boards and commissions which chose their own executives."

Martin W. Judnich
San Francisco Government, *1967*

The city's present Charter was ratified by vote of the people on March 26, 1931; ratified by the Legislature of the State April 13, 1931: in effect January 8, 1932. It has been amended nearly 400 times since its adoption in 1931.

The San Francisco Citizens Charter Revision Committee was appointed by the Mayor in February 1968 pursuant to a resolution of the Board of Supervisors unanimously adopted in October 1967. The Committee consisted of 21 members selected to be broadly representative of the citizenry of San Francisco.

In the November 4, 1969 election, the voters were asked to revise their Charter for the first time since 1931. Sixty-three percent of the voters rejected Proposition E.

Later the Committee decided to restructure, but not change, the present Charter and received voter approval of Proposition R on November 2, 1971.

On November 7, 1978, the voters approved Proposition X which authorized a complete rewriting of the Charter to bring it up to date. The proposition won by a vote of 99,076 to 77,381. The 15 members of the new Charter Commission were inducted January 15, 1979, in ceremonies in the Board of Supervisors Chambers. The commissioners had two years to rewrite the document.

In the election of Tuesday, November 4, 1980, the proposal for a new city Charter was defeated by the voters with a vote of "Yes," 91,961 and "No," 106,541.

City Name 1847

Alcalde Bartlett, on January 23, 1847, issued the following order: "Whereas the local name of Yerba Buena as applied to the settlement or town of San Francisco is unknown beyond the immediate district and has been applied from the local name of the cove in which the town is built—therefore, to prevent confusion and mistakes in the public documents, and that the town may have the advantage of the name given on the published maps, it is hereby ordered that the name San Francisco shall hereafter be used in all official communications and public documents or records appertaining to the town."

City Planning

Early city planning was rudimentary, stemming from the rectilinear block plan laid out by the early surveyors. Capt. Jean Jacques Vioget, a Swiss sailor and surveyor, made the first survey and plan of Yerba Buena in 1839. His survey was bounded by Pacific, Montgomery, Sacramento and Dupont streets. Later surveys, each more extended than its predecessor, were made officially by Jasper O'Farrell in 1847 and William Eddy in 1849.

In 1904, Chicago architect Daniel Burnham, working with the Association for the Improvement and Adornment of San Francisco, laid out a plan for the city's improvement and beautification. This plan was completed and published just before the earthquake and fire of 1906, but San Franciscans, in their haste to rebuild, ignored the plan. Later, some of the Burnham proposals were initiated, specifically the Great Highway development, the Yacht Harbor, Aquatic Park, the Civic Center location, John McLaren Park, and the Telegraph Hill Park.

After the 1906 catastrophe, San Francisco began developing new areas further to the west. Mayor Edward R. Taylor was fearful that the city might be broken up into boroughs and said, "I don't believe San Francisco will ever consent to have her body carved up into boroughs. I don't believe that San Francisco or San Franciscans will ever consent to put aside all of her great traditions, all of her great glories, all of her great deeds, all of her sorrows, all of her triumphs, and be known no more—as she would be known no more. Would San Francisco be 'San Francisco' if you have a Western Addition Borough, if you have a Mission Borough, if you have a Telegraph Hill Borough? San Francisco would not be San Francisco anymore. Of course it would not be. You would have greater San Francisco, but that greater San Francisco would be made up of innumerable boroughs, and not one of those boroughs would be San Francisco. I for one should never consent to any such project."

On December 28, 1917 Mayor James Rolph appointed the members of the first City Planning Commission. However, it wasn't until 1929 that the City Planning Commission became a separate agency of local government, charged with the responsibility under the Charter to make, adopt, and maintain a Master Plan for the physical development of the city.

The 1948 Progress Report issued by the City Planning Commission stated: "San Franciscans, in the process of developing a Master Plan, have been comparing the city that exists with the city that could be—a city with a smooth-functioning circulation system, healthful housing, neighborhoods with adequate parks, playgrounds, schools, social halls, branch libraries, and public health offices, efficiently organized business and industrial areas, and outstanding cultural and recreation facilities. They have discovered excellent features of the city of today that can be integrated into the city of tomorrow. But they have learned that much must be replaced, and the task, viewed in its entirety, poses problems that might be discouraging to the fainthearted.

"A matured metropolitan city like San Francisco that has used all the available land within its boundaries for housing, business, industry, parks and open areas, must develop planning areas for study purposes to determine its ultimate capacity for growth without losing the established and recognized characteristics.

"Boundaries of these planning areas are definite and seldom change as depicted on the area map."

Consolidation Act

Between the years 1856 and 1900, while the City and County was operating under the "Consolidation Act," all legislative acts were designated "Orders." Since 1900, under the provisions of the Charter, all legislative acts are designated "Ordinances." Since the earthquake and fire of April 18, 1906, the term "Ordinance" (new series) has been used.

Recall Elections

Year	Public Official	Results of Election
1913	Police Judge Charles Weller	Approved
1914	State Senator Edwin E. Grant	Approved
1921	Police Judge John J. Sullivan	Approved
1921	Police Judge Morris Oppenheim	Approved
1946	Mayor Roger Lapham	Failed
1983	Mayor Dianne Feinstein	Failed

Dramatic view of the Board of Supervisors' chambers at San Francisco City Hall. This room was the site of the infamous House Committee on Un-American Activities meeting in 1960 where protestors were washed down the rotunda steps with fire hoses. It has also been a set for several movies. Ex-supervisor Dan White shot Harvey Milk in a small office behind the chambers.

12 Communications

Air Warning System

The San Francisco Air Raid Warning System was installed immediately after the Japanese attack at Pearl Harbor on December 7, 1941.

With the end of the Cold War in the 1990s, the system was redesignated the Air Warning System and is to be used for such emergencies as tsunami wave warnings or hazardous materials spill evacuation notification.

Sirens are tested each Tuesday precisely at noon and are controlled from the Central Fire Alarm Station at 1003 Turk Street.

Fifty-five sirens were originally installed, but only 48 remain. Most are installed at schools, fire stations, or major downtown buildings. A number of them are also installed on telephone-style poles in various districts of San Francisco.

Siren Locations

- 8th Avenue and Ortega Street
- 18th Avenue and Judah Street
- 24th Avenue and Rivera Street at Lincoln High School
- 26th Avenue and El Camino Del Mar
- 32nd Avenue and Anza Street at George Washington School
- 41st Avenue and Vicente Street at Ulloa School
- 43rd Avenue and Kirkham at Francis Scott Key School
- 47th Avenue and Pacheco Street
- 3rd Street and 22nd Street
- 3rd Street and Bryant Street at the Schwabacher Building
- 22nd Street and Bartlett Street at the Douglass School
- 30th Street and Noe Street at the Kennedy School
- Alemany Blvd. and Naglee Street
- Alvarado and Douglass streets at the Alvarado School
- Army Street and South Van Ness Avenue
- 1000 Brannan Street atop the Hiram Walker Building
- 235 Buckingham Way atop the apartment building
- California Street and Funston Avenue
- California and Quincy streets
- Chestnut and Fillmore streets at the Marina Junior High School

San Francisco's tallest structure is Sutro Tower that transmits television and FM signals throughout the Bay Area. It was constructed in the early 1970s on the site of the Sutro Mansion in Sutro Forest.

- Euclid Avenue and Cook Street
- Excelsior Avenue and London Street at the Excelsior School
- Federal Appraisers' Building at 630 Sansome Street
- Federal Office Building at Fulton and Leavenworth streets
- Ferry Building Tower at The Embarcadero
- Fire Dept. Ashbury Tank at Clayton and Carmel streets
- Fire Station No. 5 at Webster and Turk streets
- Fire Station No. 6 at 135 Sanchez Street
- Fire Station No. 15 at Ocean Avenue and Phelan Street
- Fire Station No. 34 at Point Lobos Avenue and Geary Blvd.
- Foerster Street and Flood Avenue at the Sunnyside School
- 100 Font Blvd. at Chumasero Drive in Park Merced Apartment complex
- Frederick Street and Arguello Blvd.
- Fremont and Folsom streets
- Haight Street and Masonic Avenue at Stone School
- Jamestown Avenue and Ingalls Street
- Jerrold Avenue and Quint Street at the DPW Plant
- Lafayette Square at Laguna and Clay streets
- McLaren Park and Sunnydale Avenue
- Mission and Plum streets
- Palou Avenue and Hawes Street
- Post and Leavenworth streets
- Taraval Street and Claremont Blvd.
- Union Square at Geary and Powell streets
- Upland Drive and Aptos Avenue at Aptos School
- Visitacion and Schwerin streets at Visitacion School
- Wayland and University streets
- Youth Guidance Center at Portola Drive and Woodside Avenue

Radio and Television in San Francisco

San Francisco's first radio station, KPO, began broadcasting in 1922, but as early as 1909 Charles "Doc" Herrold had broadcast from his San Jose engineering college. His station (later KQW) is today's KCBS-AM, San Francisco. Other San Francisco stations of note are KALW-FM, oldest American noncommercial station, the former KMPX-FM which pioneered free-form rock programming, and KSAN-FM which began the progressive rock format.

In 1925 KPO transmitted the first pictures by radio using the "radiovision" process of Francis Jenkins. Philo T. Farnsworth, working in his 202 Green Street laboratory, was a noted television pioneer. His invention of the image dissection tube (1927, patented 1930) enabled him to produce the first all-electronic television image (1927). San Francisco's first regular television station, KGO-TV, Channel 7, began broadcasting in 1948.

This chronology lists national network radio and television series made, or set, in San Francisco. In some cases only the opening sequence (television) was made in San Francisco.

Radio
Al Pearce and His Gang
Comedy and music, 1933–1947
One Man's Family
Barbour family soap opera set in Sea Cliff—longest-running American serial, 1932–1960 (see television list)
Hawthorne House
Mother Sherwood and family struggle through hard times, 1935–1942
Sam Spade
Dashiell Hammett's San Francisco detective, 1946
Johnny Modero—Pier 23
Detective on the docks, 1947

Television
One Man's Family
Television version of popular radio series, 1949–1955
The Lineup
Two SFPD detectives on the beat, 1954–1959 (called *San Francisco Beat* in reruns)

Have Gun, Will Travel
Hired gun in 19th-century San Francisco, 1957–1963
Sam Benedict
Based on files of attorney Jake Ehrlich, 1962–1963
Ironside
Raymond Burr as disabled attorney, 1967–1975
The Doris Day Show
Widowed journalist raising two sons, 1968–1972
San Francisco International Airport
Drama at SFO, 1970–1971
McMillan and Wife
Police commissioner's wife draws him into investigations, 1971–1977
Streets of San Francisco
Popular updated version of *The Lineup*, 1972–1977
Me and Ducky
Teenage girls at San Francisco High School (pilot), 1979
Trapper John, M.D.
Hospital drama, 1979–1986
Too Close for Comfort
Misadventures of father and daughters, 1980–1983. Spawned pilot *Family Business*, 1983
Hotel
Soap Drama set at the Saint Gregory (Fairmont) Hotel, 1983–1988
Partners in Crime
Female version of *Streets of San Francisco*, 1984
Crazy Like a Fox
Offbeat detective drama, 1984–1986
Me and Mom
Woman detective drama, 1985
Hooperman
Cuddly detective show, 1987–1989
Full House
Domestic comedy of widower and children, 1987
Wolf
Rebel detective show, 1989
Midnight Caller
Controversial radio call-in drama, 1989–91

Over My Dead Body
Private investigator and sidekick, 1990
Walter and Emily
Battling grandparents raise grandson, 1991
MICHAEL D. LAMPEN

San Francisco Telephone Prefixes

San Francisco's first telephone directory, issued in 1878, linked 173 businesses in a local network. Before 1895 various exchanges were in local use (central, private, special, temporary, public). Prefixes were introduced in 1895. The first transcontinental telephone call was made by Alexander Graham Bell, from New York to San Francisco, on January 25, 1915. Bell's words to his associate, Thomas A. Watson, were "Hoy, hoy, Mr Watson! Are you there? Can you hear me?" The number of local prefixes was expanded in 1928 with the introduction of dial phones. In 1948, San Francisco had more telephones per capita than any other city on Earth (47.7 per 100 persons). Named prefixes were phased out by 1966.

1895–1928

(Several prefixes continued in use after 1928.)

Black, Blue, Brown, Bush, Butchertown, Capp, China, Church, Clay, Davis, Douglass, Drumm, East, Fell, Folsom, Franklin, Front, Geary, Grant, Green, Grove, Howard, James, Jessie, John, Main, Market, Mint, Mission, Montgomery, Ohio, Pacific, Page, Park, Red, Scott, South, Sutter, Texas, Waller, West

1928–1966 (GRaystone was the first of the dial telephone prefix)

ATwater, BAyview, DAvenport, DElaware, EVergreen, EXbrook, FIllmore, GArfield, GRaystone, HEmlock, JOrdan, JUniper, KEarny, KLondike, LOmbard, MOntrose, ORdway, OVerland, PLaza, PRospect, RAndolph, SEabright, SKyline, TUxedo, UNderhill, VAlencia, WAlnut, YUkon

MICHAEL D. LAMPEN

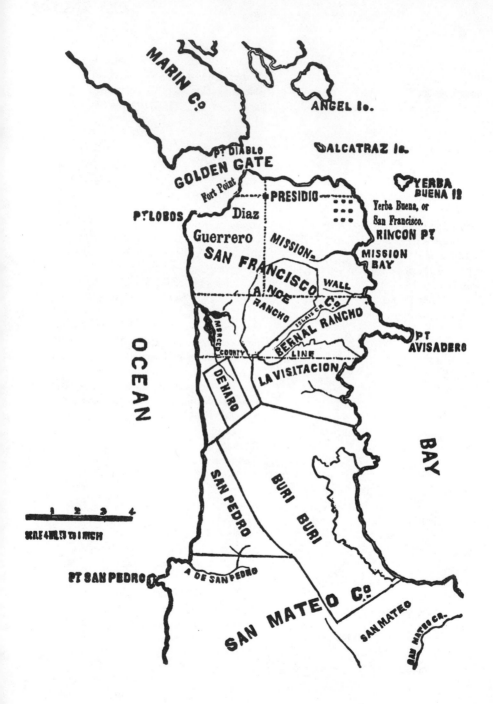

13 Counties

Nine Bay Area Counties

Alameda   San Mateo
Contra Costa   Santa Clara
Marin   Solano
Napa   Sonoma
San Francisco

San Francisco County

San Francisco County is California's smallest at 128.76 square miles. Its ocean, land, and bay portions make up 17, 36, and 47 percent respectively of its total area. The total county area is similar to the city area of Montgomery, Alabama (128 sq. mi.). The land area of San Francisco is 46.38 square miles, similar to the city area of Boston (46 sq. mi.) and the land area of St. Helena Island (site of Napolean's exile in the South Atlantic Ocean, 47 sq. mi.) San Francisco shares a short common land border with Alameda County, the result of filling a portion of the bay within the city limits to create the southwest corner of the Alameda Naval Air Station. The geographical center (land only) is between Alvarado and 23rd streets on the east side of Grandview Avenue (latitude N 37°45'10", longitude W 122°26'27").

References: San Francisco Almanac *(1980),* and World Almanac and Book of Facts *(1994)*

Unseen San Francisco County

Some two-thirds of San Francisco County's solid surface lies hidden beneath the waters of the Pacific Ocean and San Francisco Bay. Swept by tides which change direction four times a day, the ocean and bay floors display a wide variety of sediments and topography. The ocean portion of the county has an irregular sandy floor which rises northeastward from a depth of 70 ft. A large underwater sand bar, the San Francisco Bar (dangerously shallow in its northern stretch) curves from off Golden Gate Park to the west, then north and east to Pt. Bonita. Behind the Bar, the Golden Gate floor deepens across tide-swept terraces and sand dunes to a 340-foot-deep bedrock basin extending beneath the Golden Gate Bridge (deepest spot, 351 ft.). Rocky ridges rise at the eastern edge of the basin.

The moderately deep central bay floor (mostly exceeding 60 ft. in depth) has a varied topography, including deep tidal holes south of Angel and Alcatraz islands, and west of Yerba Buena Island. Rocky hills, a danger to ships before removal lie northwest of Alcatraz Island, and a large field of sand dunes, 3–16 ft. tall, lies between Alcatraz and the Presidio. Shallow mud plains lie east and north of Treasure Island, with the deeper sandy main channel to the west.

In the southeast part of the bay lying within San Francisco County, the main channel extends south next to the city shore, past Hunters Point, while shallow mud flats lie to the east.

MICHAEL D. LAMPEN

14 Court of Historical Review

Court of Historical Review and Appeals

San Francisco's famed Court of Historical Review and Appeals began in 1975 when City Archivist Gladys Hansen asked civic leader Bernard Averbuch to help publicize a police exhibit in the History Room at the Main Library.

Averbuch chose the case of Police Chief George Wittman who was fired in 1905 for "failure to control gambling in Chinatown." He asked Judge Harry W. Low to conduct a noon hearing to exonerate Chief Wittman. Judge Low did so. The hearing attracted a good deal of publicity, and it was decided to continue the unique hearings.

The "mock court" has an authentic judge, and noted attorneys defend and prosecute while civic leaders act as witnesses. The judge gives his ruling at the conclusion. The cases are held several months apart, and the variety has expanded over the years.

Judge Low ruled on the real author of "Casey at the Bat" (Ernest Thayer of San Francisco) and that Mark Twain never made the remark "The coldest winter I ever spent was a summer in San Francisco." He also ruled that Enrico Caruso did not panic in the 1906 earthquake, as legend holds, but was indeed a hero.

Judge Michael Hanlon took over the court next, and one of his classic rulings was that the Martini cocktail originated in San Francisco, and not in New York.

Judge Roy Wonder presided next and ruled that Abner Doubleday did not invent baseball and that the San Francisco bagel tasted better than those from New York, flown in for evidence. Judge Wonder also ruled that the City should honor General Douglas MacArthur, and as a result the tunnel leading to the Golden Gate Bridge was renamed in MacArthur's honor.

15 Culture

Post-War Countercultural San Francisco

In an expression of rebellion against the perceived spiritual emptiness and complacency of post-World War II America, bohemian communities blossomed in New York's Greenwich Village, Los Angeles's Venice, and San Francisco's North Beach in the mid-1950s. Strongly literary and individualistic in tone, San Francisco's beatnik movement centered around novelist Jack Kerouac (*On the Road*, 1957), poet Allen Ginsberg (*Howl*, 1956), and poet-publisher Lawrence Ferlinghetti, owner of the City Lights Bookstore (founded 1953). Noted younger poets included Gary Snyder, Michael McClure, and Philip Whalen. Popular North Beach hangouts included the Coexistence Bagel Shop, The Place, Vesuvio's, and the taverns and cafes along upper Grant Avenue. Popular clubs included The Cellar, the Purple Onion, and the hungry i. *Chronicle* columnist Herb Caen coined the word "beatnik" from "beat" (Kerouac—"short for beatitude") and the Yiddish "nudnik" (a boring, bothersome person). Beatnik code words included "hepcat," "square," "groovy," and the suffix ". . . ville."

The hippie movement, the idealistic drug-discovering rock-music-voiced child of the beat generation, burst upon the San Francisco scene in 1965 with the visit of the Beatles, the drug advocacy of novelist Ken Kesey, and the rise of the Jefferson Airplane rock band. Western Haight Street, near Golden Gate Park, became the hippie mecca in 1966, and San Francisco hippiedom climaxed in the 1967 "Summer of Love." Hippie hangouts on Haight included the Drogstore Cafe, the Psychedelic Shop, and the Pall Mall Lounge, as well as the Panhandle and Hippie Hill in nearby Golden Gate Park. Popular rock auditoria were Fillmore West, the Avalon Ballroom, and the People's Ballroom. The word "hippie," derived from "hip" (meaning "aware and part of the current scene"), was coined by *Examiner* writer Michael Fallon. Hippie code words included "cool," "acid," "trip," and "bummer."

MICHAEL D. LAMPEN

Midwinter Fair of 1894 Fine Arts Building, later called de Young Museum was torn down in 1927. Today the site of the original entrance is marked by two stone Sphinxes.

16 ℰarthquakes

San Francisco Fire Department Operations during the October 17, 1989, Earthquake

The Loma Prieta earthquake struck at 5:04:15 p.m., Pacific Daylight Time. The epicenter of the earthquake was a remote area of the Santa Cruz Mountains, about ten miles northeast of Santa Cruz and 56 miles south-southeast of San Francisco. The principal regions of destruction were in the Santa Cruz Mountains, coastal communities in Santa Cruz and Monterey counties, and in San Benito County. Parts of San Francisco and Alameda counties were also hard hit.

Of both immediate and long-range concern to the San Francisco Fire Department was the excessive damage from earth shaking in the Marina District, South of Market area, and portions of the Inner Mission District where, in places, severe liquefaction occurred which damaged water mains and structures. There was also liquefaction on Treasure Island which is, technically speaking, within the city limits of San Francisco. Further, in addition to the collapse of two decks of the San Francisco-Oakland Bay Bridge, there was near-failure of a westerly portion of the structure which also lies within the jurisdiction of the San Francisco Fire Department.

The U.S. Geological Survey's (USGS) initial report on the earthquake said, "The major damage in the Marina District was caused by locally amplified shaking and permanent deformation of the ground due to liquefaction of the sand and debris used to fill the former lagoon for the 1915 Panama-Pacific International Exposition. During the 1906 earthquake, locally violent ground shaking was experienced along the margins of the lagoon."

In "Lessons Learned from the Loma Prieta, California, Earthquake of October 17, 1989," the USGS also wrote, "Areas underlain by thick deposits of water-saturated unconsolidated sand and mud were not only strongly shaken but were also affected by compaction and loss of strength in sediment that liquefied during the shaking; many of these same areas experienced similar processes in the 1906 earthquake."

San Francisco's City Hall shortly after the Great Earthquake and Fire. The great building was unfortunately built in part of the Mission Bay swamp and collapsed immediately during the earthquake. City Hall had been under construction 27 years and cost $7,000,000 in 1906 dollars.

The USGS, in another report titled "The Loma Prieta Earthquake of October 17, 1989," wrote that, "Events of magnitude 7 or larger, each with a probability of 20 to 30 percent...are expected...at three locations in Northern California." The locations in Northern California are the San Francisco segment of the San Andreas fault and the northern and southern segments of the Hayward fault in the East Bay.

"A magnitude of 7 shock on any one of these fault segments will probably cause considerably more damage than the recent Loma Prieta event because of their proximity to larger population centers," the report said.

On July 20, 1990, the U.S. Geological Survey revised upward the probability factor for a Richter-magnitude 7 event to 67 percent by the year 2020. This latest revision makes another major earthquake an inevitability as far as Fire Department planning is concerned.

Another significant concern to the San Francisco Fire Department is the large number of freeway viaducts that transverse the City, and which were damaged during the earthquake. A report titled "Competing Against Time, Report to Governor from the Governor's Board of Inquiry on the 1989 Loma Prieta Earthquake" said, "The Loma Prieta earthquake was, for the San Francisco Freeway Viaducts, a minor to moderate earthquake. These viaducts (Embarcadero Viaduct, [Transbay] Terminal Separation Viaduct, Central Viaduct, China Basin Viaduct, Southern Freeway Viaduct, and Alemany Viaduct) in San Francisco were all built with the same technology used for the Cypress Viaduct and are the only structures in the State of this design. All of the freeway structures, with the exception of the Alemany Viaduct, were damaged during the earthquake and subsequently closed to traffic." The report also said, "Many of the crack patterns are similar to those observed in the collapsed and damaged portions of the Cypress Viaduct." Most of the damaged

San Francisco viaduct system had not been repaired by October 1990, but had been seismically stabilized with combustible wood bracing.

The earthquake shook for 15 seconds and resulted in at least 67 deaths from direct earthquake causes, 3,757 injuries, more than 12,000 left homeless, and property damage in excess of $10 billion throughout the affected zone, according to the California Office of Emergency Services.

In San Francisco, 11 people died as a direct result of the earthquake and hundreds were injured. Thirty buildings either collapsed or were immediately demolished, and 91 others were condemned, and were either extensively rebuilt before being reoccupied, or were demolished.

From 5:04 p.m. October 17 to midnight October 19, 36 fires involving structures were reported to the San Francisco Fire Department. Of these, 34 fires were directly or indirectly attributable to the earthquake and subsequent aftershocks.

When the earthquake struck, the electric supply was lost to most of San Francisco. Initially, failure of electric service may have been beneficial in reducing the number of potential fires because of the loss of an ignition source for hundreds of PG&E gas leaks. As anticipated, natural gas was responsible for some of the fires following this earthquake.

An estimated 500 dispatches were transmitted by midnight of October 17, of which 80 percent were investigations of natural gas odors.

Damage to private and public property in San Francisco was in excess of $3.2 billion. Fire losses from causes due to earthquake are in excess of $10 million.

The Fire Department suffered $327,000 damage to facilities and $80,000 to equipment that was either damaged or lost during the earthquake emergency. Almost $1 million was expended for earthquake-related labor and overtime. Costs of repairing the

Auxiliary Water Supply System (AWSS) were in excess of $200,000.

The Initial Response

The Communications Center dispatched Engine Co. 8, Co. 29, and Co. 37, Truck Co. 8 and Co. 3, and Battalion No. 2 and No. 3 to Box 2241 at Fifth and Bluxome streets for a reported building collapse at 665 Sixth Street.

The building on the southeast corner of Sixth and Bluxome streets was a four-story structure. The fourth floor wall peeled away from the building during the earthquake and showered the street below with tons of bricks. Five people were killed, crushed in their automobiles or while walking on the sidewalk.

Responding Fire Department companies, with the help of police officers and many brave citizen volunteers, used pry bars and power cutting tools, as well as bare hands to free victims trapped in crushed automobiles, in the hope that survivors might be found. To speed this rescue effort, members of the San Francisco Fire Department operated a PG&E backloader that was parked near the scene to move heavy debris.

Firefighters, police officers, and citizen volunteers worked to remove the fallen bricks for more than two hours as several aftershocks rocked the tottering walls of the remaining lower three stories of the severely damaged structure. Five bodies were recovered.

Six minutes after the earthquake, the Communications Center dispatched Engine No. 19 to Box 8436 on a report of fire in the basement at 354 Byxbee Street. Lieutenant Richard A. Robinson of Engine Co. 19 saw smoke as his company responded, and he spotted the engine at the intersection, connected to the hydrant at Holloway and Byxbee streets, and made a supply line lead to the fire. A citizen volunteer with a garden hose in front of the house attempted to hold back the fire that was rolling from the garage. The crew of Engine Co. 19 lead a ready-line to the garage entrance in an attempt to knock down the fire and prevent its spread.

Battalion Chief George L. Politis of Battalion No. 9 heard the alarm on the Department radio and also responded. At 5:14 p.m., as he arrived, Box 6913 for San Francisco International Airport special-call was broadcast. This box called for the response of Battalion No. 9. However, because of the conflagration risk from this fire, Battalion Chief Politis placed himself out-of-service at the Byxbee Street fire and requested additional companies. Because of the immediate and massive drain on the resources of the Department, the Communications Center advised Battalion Chief Politis that the only available unit in that district was a truck company, and Truck Co. 19 was dispatched to the fire at 5:18 p.m.

At 5:09 p.m., Engine Co. 15 had been dispatched to 105 Lee Street for a reported natural gas leak. There was no leak, and Lieutenant Harry L. Conry of Engine Co. 15 saw the smoke rising from the fire on Byxbee Street. Upon arrival, Engine Co. 15 led a supply line from Byxbee and Garfield streets to the fire. Now, with the aid of Truck Co. 19 and Engine Co. 15, the fire, which would have been a normal second alarm assignment, was knocked down, but not before 354 Byxbee Street and the exposure building at 350 Byxbee Street were lost.

The majority of the Fire Department's post-earthquake calls were for PG&E gas leaks. At 6:45 p.m., the Communications Center dispatched Engine Co. 20 and Truck Co. 12 to 69 Castenada Avenue for a reported gas explosion. Lieutenant Gary A. May of Engine Co. 40 heard the call on the Department radio and also responded. Arriving companies found that a natural gas explosion at 69 Castenada Avenue had blown the house from its foundation and started a small fire. The companies quickly extinguished this fire and reported the incident under control at 7:04 p.m.

The San Francisco Fire Department also provides fire protection to San Francisco International Airport located in San Mateo County, south of the City and County of San Francisco. At the time of the earthquake, there were 14 firefighters and three officers on duty. The Division of Airports is composed of eight pieces of apparatus, with several other reserve engines, vans, first-aid units, light units, and small boats also available.

When the earthquake struck, all apparatus was removed from quarters and the buildings inspected for damage. The two fire stations were not damaged and units began to respond to calls at various parts of the airport. The first major rescue operation was at Gate 78 of the North Terminal where passengers were trapped and buried under fallen debris. Additional fire units responded to other airport terminals and the crews began to search for and treat victims injured generally by fallen ceiling materials.

At 5:13 p.m., Lt. Dan Dobbins ordered the recall of all off-duty airport fire personnel. Sixty seconds later, he sent a special-call request to Central Fire Alarm Station, and Battalion No. 10, Engine Co. 44, and Truck Co. 15 were dispatched from San Francisco to the airport.

Upon arrival, Truck Co. 15 was immediately detailed to assist in treating injured passengers who were milling about outside the terminal buildings. Engine Co. 44 was staged at Airport Fire Station No. 1 to await dispatch for any possible structure fires. However, Lt. Dobbins, the senior officer on duty at the time of the earthquake, saw television coverage of the Marina District fire and ordered the special-call companies to return to San Francisco for duty.

Because of conditions in communities surrounding the airport, no mutual aid forces were available and all subsequent calls at San Francisco International Airport were handled by recalled personnel.

While the rescue operation continued at Gate 78 and other terminals, additional units were dispatched on numerous PG&E gas leaks and water line breaks. Natural gas service was shut down at the Chevron Hanger and TWA cargo area because of the danger of aftershocks and fires.

Recalled personnel began to arrive at Airport Stations No. 1 and No. 2 by 6 p.m., just a few minutes before a fire was reported at the United Airlines maintenance building. Upon arrival at the maintenance building's dock area at 6:05 p.m., the firefighters found that the foam deluge and sprinkler systems had been activated by the earthquake, and foam had risen to a height of more than six feet. Firefighters worked their way through the foam and darkness to find the seat of the fire which appeared to be on the second floor of the maintenance structure. There was also a significant amount of nonstructural damage in the building, and the firefighters climbed over and around fallen lockers, cabinets, and miscellaneous equipment in the darkness, foam, and smoke to reach the second floor.

The fire was found and extinguished with a hose attached to a wet standpipe. This fire occurred because flammables, including paper, fell upon a floor heater in the electrical room during the earthquake and ignited. The blaze was extremely smoky, but the heat did set off a sprinkler which partially controlled the spread of the fire, but the flow was not sufficient to reach the seat of the fire under the fallen debris.

By midnight, 26 officers and firefighters had returned to duty, which more than doubled the normal staffing level. It should be noted that one firefighter on sick leave and two on disability leave reported for duty at the airport. One officer and two firefighters while responding to the recall signal heard that freeway access to the airport had been closed and so reported for duty at the Marina District fire.

Recalled personnel were assigned

throughout the night to continue to shut down damaged gas and water service to various structures and to inspect major facilities including the fuel tank farm and sewage treatment plant which were not damaged. They also readied the rescue boat to pump water from San Francisco Bay should the domestic water supply to the airport fail. Later, personnel provided a fire watch detail at the damaged North Terminal because the water supply had been cut by a broken main.

The Division of Airports responded to more than 26 alarms in 15 hours and resumed normal staffing on Thursday, October 19.

DAVID FOWLER

Fighting the 1989 Marina District Fire

(Compiled and Edited from San Francisco Fire Department Reports)

Two off-duty San Francisco police officers reported collapsed buildings on Divisadero Street with people trapped inside to Captain Robert Jabs of Truck Co. 16. Captain Jabs then ordered the truck company to respond to Divisadero and Beach streets.

Upon arrival, the crew of Truck Co. 16 found two fully collapsed four-story apartment buildings. The apartment building at the northwest corner, 3701 Divisadero Street, and the building at the northeast corner, 2090 Beach Street, had both fallen as the ground beneath them liquefied during the severe shaking. Both apartment buildings were precariously pitched over Beach Street and threatened to further collapse from numerous earthquake aftershocks.

Captain Jabs notified the Communications Center that he had ten or twelve buildings fully or partially collapsed with trapped victims, and one of the buildings was on fire. He requested immediate assistance.

The crew of Truck Co. 16 found trapped victims in the wreckage of 2090 Beach

Street and Capt. Jabs ordered Firefighters Howard W. Cross, Jr. and Wayne A. Martin to begin rescue operations in the building. He then, along with Firefighters Thomas R. Bailon and John H. Reed and citizen volunteers, entered 3701 Divisadero Street to begin search and rescue operations.

There were many citizen volunteers and they, in fact, were the first on the scene and had heard voices calling for help. Captain Jabs, with citizen volunteers, attempted to reach victims through the exterior side wall of the building, but the attempt was proving difficult, when Firefighter Bailon inside the structure called out, "I've found them!" Captain Jabs, with four or five citizen volunteers, entered the building. Firefighters Bailon and Reed had cut open the floor and found a man and woman trapped below.

Then, a strong Richter-magnitude 5 aftershock rocked the fallen structure, followed by a loud explosion. Smoke began to fill the wreckage and Capt. Jabs saw flames rolling from the front of the building. However, the firefighters continued to work to save the trapped victims.

Captain Jabs ordered power saws and jacks brought into the burning building. The crew of Truck Co. 16 worked on as the fire rapidly spread. The crew heard voices calling from the outside, "The building is going to collapse!" Captain Jabs looked through the window and saw the top floor fully involved in fire. The trapped man was able to crawl from the hole cut through the floor by the firefighters. Captain Jabs, with the aid of a citizen volunteer, carried him across a partially collapsed roof to safety. The crew of Truck Co. 16 continued this effort to rescue the trapped woman until extreme heat and dense smoke drove them from the building.

At 5:34 p.m., the Communications Center dispatched Engine Co. 41 and Truck Co. 9 to the Marina District. Engine Co. 41 had just come in-service from a dispatch at Howard and New Montgomery streets in the downtown area, several miles from the Marina District. Truck Co. 9 also responded from several miles away.

At 5:39 p.m., the Communications Center also dispatched Truck Co. 10 , which had just gone in-service from Box 3162 at O'Farrell Street and Van Ness Avenue near Civic Center, to Divisadero and Beach streets. Upon arrival, Captain Robert G. Boudoures of Truck Co. 10 radioed the Communications Center that…"we have a lot of smoke and a building collapse. We're going to need assistance." He found Truck Co. 16 on the scene, but no engines. Heavy smoke was coming from 3701 Divisadero Street. Citizens also told him there were trapped people in other collapsed buildings.

Captain Boudoures sent Firefighters Joseph R. Conway and John R. Porter to assist Truck Co. 16 in the wrecked building at 3701 Divisadero Street. Then, Capt. Boudoures, along with Firefighters James W. Jenkins and John J. Carvajal, attempted to find a woman trapped in the building at 2090 Beach Street. However, they were soon forced to leave the building because of a severe natural gas leak from a PG&E main. They closed the PG&E gas valve and again entered the building to begin the rescue attempt. They were soon joined by Firefighter Porter.

But again, the crew of Truck Co. 16 was forced to retreat from the building because the fire from 3701 Divisadero Street was radiating such intense heat that it caused the building at 2090 Beach Street to catch fire.

A rescue attempt was under way at Fillmore Street and Cervantes Boulevard as Battalion Chief Shannon saw the smoke column rising from the fire. He heard Capt. Boudoures of Truck Co. 10 asking the Communications Center for assistance, and he ordered Engine Co. 41, which had just arrived at Cervantes Boulevard, to respond to the column of smoke.

Engine Co. 16, Rescue No. 2, and Truck Co. 5 were engaged in the continuing rescue at Cervantes Boulevard and Fillmore Street, so Battalion Chief Shannon ordered members of Engine Co. 38 and Chief's Aide David W. Jackson, along with the driver of Engine Co. 6, to take Engine Co. 16's apparatus to the fire.

When the successful rescue operation ended at 2 Cervantes Boulevard, Battalion Chief Shannon ordered Truck Co. 5 and the crew of Engine Co. 16 to the fire. He also ordered the driver of Engine Co. 38 with his apparatus to stay in place because the PG&E main was still spewing gas and there was a serious and continuing threat of fire in the vicinity. Battalion Chief Shannon then responded to the fire along with Truck Co. 9 which had also just arrived at Cervantes Boulevard.

Engine Co. 41, commanded by Lt. Peter M. Cornyn, was the first San Francisco engine company to arrive at Divisadero and Beach streets. "Upon arrival," wrote Lt. Cornyn in his report, "the scene was as follows: The four-story building at the northeast corner of Divisadero and Beach had collapsed onto Beach Street, covering the low pressure hydrant, with approximately a floor and a half [of the building] still standing. The four-story building at the northwest corner had collapsed onto the sidewalk on Beach Street with approximately two stories still upright [but] at a 75-degree angle. This building was on fire in the northeast corner. The fire at this time was not of great magnitude. In front of this building was a High Pressure hydrant about two feet from the building, with the top of the building hovering over the High Pressure hydrant. On the southwest corner was a four-story building with the first floor buckled about three feet and the building was leaning toward Beach Street."

The driver of Engine Co. 41 positioned the apparatus along Beach Street next to the fire building at 3701 Divisadero Street to utilize the engine's pre-connected master-stream nozzle. The engine was connected through a Gleeson Pressure Reducing valve to the High Pressure hydrant on the northwest corner of Beach and Divisadero streets, but there was little water. Later, the burning structure collapsed upon the hydrant.

With the aid of the firefighters already on the scene, off-duty police officers and many citizen volunteers, Engine Co. 41 led three lines to the fire building. All lines, as well as the pre-connected master-stream nozzle on Engine Co. 41, were charged, but there wasn't sufficient pressure to simultaneously operate them. All but two lines were shut down. However, the pressure was still too low and the hose stream could not reach the fire.

The extreme heat from the fire forced the crew to reposition Engine Co. 41 to another location on Divisadero Street. Citizen volunteers dragged a supply line to a low pressure hydrant at Divisadero and Bay streets, but there was also insufficient pressure. Engine Co. 16 was then connected to the High Pressure hydrant on the northwest corner of Beach and Scott streets and, again with the aid of citizen volunteers, the crew dragged two supply lines to Engine Co. 41, but there was still too little pressure. Firefighters and citizen volunteers fought the fire and attempted to keep it from spreading with use of the limited water supply from Engine Co. 41.

The collapsed building at 2090 Beach Street ultimately ignited, and firefighters attempting to rescue the trapped woman were driven from the building by flame and heavy smoke. A line from Engine Co. 41 was used to put out this exposure fire and cool the firefighters so the rescue effort could proceed. A bucket brigade composed of citizen volunteers also attempted to put out this exposure fire with the use of water leaking from hose connectors.

While the crew of Engine Co. 41 was scrambling on the south side of the fire, Engine Co. 2 of the Presidio of San Francisco Fire Department responded to the north side of the fire from Marina Boulevard, but found no water in the city's domestic low pressure hydrant because the main had been broken by either the earthquake shock or by lateral earth spread caused by liquefaction.

These firefighters repositioned the Presidio Fire Department apparatus on Divisadero Street north of the fire building and then led a small line into the structure. This small line was charged from Presidio Fire Department Engine Co. 2's water tank and provided protection for the San Francisco firefighters inside 3701 Divisadero Street until those rescuers were driven away by spreading fire and dense smoke. The Presidio Fire Department crew continued this operation until the engine's water tank was exhausted. The Presidio Fire Department crew then repositioned the apparatus on Jefferson Street to the north.

Truck Co. 9, along with Battalion Chief Shannon, arrived from rescuing victims in a building on Cervantes Boulevard. Battalion Chief Shannon found Engine Co. 41 connected to the High Pressure hydrant at Beach and Divisadero streets as the south side of the fire building was becoming fully involved. Members of the crew of Truck Co. 9 assisted the crew of Engine Co. 41 in this attempt to get an adequate water supply to the fire. Battalion Chief Shannon established his command post at Beach and Divisadero streets.

Lieutenant Vincent J. Nolan of Truck Co. 9 saw that shoring was needed to keep the tottering facade of 2090 Beach Street from fully collapsing and trapping the firefighters within the structure. He asked citizen volunteers in the area to pull shoring materials from the rubble of other wrecked structures to halt any further collapse. This use of shoring materials, known as scantling, by citizen volunteers stabilized the structure and allowed search and rescue operations to continue during numerous aftershocks.

Firefighter Gerald R. Shannon of Truck Co. 9 entered 2090 Beach Street where other firefighters were searching for victims. He returned to the street to get assistance because another victim was found buried more deeply in the rubble. He then went around the building to the Divisadero Street side where the fire was extending, and entered with Captain Boudoures of Truck Co. 10.

Firefighter Shannon found a woman trapped in the wreckage. For almost two hours Firefighter Shannon, Captain Boudoures, Firefighter Jerome M. (Duke) Polizzi of Truck Co. 2, and others struggled to rescue her while the fire across the street threatened to extend into the wreckage of the fallen structure.

Several times during the rescue, fire ignited the building and firefighters used what water they had to extinguish exposure fires, along with a bucket brigade spontaneously formed by citizen volunteers.

Lieutenant Nolan wrote, "There were exposure fires igniting on the side of the collapsed building, caused by the radiant heat from the fully involved building across the street. We grabbed a ready-line [a pre-connected one-and-one-half-inch diameter hose, 150 feet in length] and began hitting the exposure fires, trying to also keep [Firefighter] Jerry Shannon and [Captain] Bob Boudoures cool. The heat was so extreme that we couldn't turn our faces toward the building for more than a moment. We stayed on the line until it felt as though our pants were on fire and then were forced to retreat. We started to attack in teams of two, hitting the fires as long as we could and then calling for relief to cool off. While this was going on, the building across the street was exploding from pockets of gas and collapsing."

After finding the trapped woman, Firefighter Shannon prepared to return to the street for more rescue tools. But the woman pleaded for him not to leave. Firefighter Shannon stayed with the woman and comforted her as other firefighters passed rescue tools into him. He said, "... after I saw her, I just couldn't leave..." After several hours of struggle, as repeated aftershocks threatened to collapse the remaining portions of the structure, Firefighter Shannon was able to free her from the wreckage.

Battalion Chief Shannon found that the low pressure hydrant system was dry shortly after he arrived on the scene. He also found that, although there was some water in the High Pressure system, the supply was inadequate to stop the spread of the fire. The Auxiliary Water Supply System (AWSS) was being bled dry by five breaks in the South of Market Street area where a combination of lateral earth spread and severe liquefaction caused some portions of the gridded main system to fail during the earthquake. The 750,000-gallon AWSS tank at Clay and Jones streets, which supplies the High Pressure hydrants in the lower zone, emptied within 40 minutes.

Because the AWSS supplies water by gravity to the High Pressure hydrants from sea level to 150 feet in elevation, these breaks were responsible for the loss of water in the Marina District High Pressure hydrants. There were no breaks in the High Pressure system in the Marina District.

At 6:16 p.m., one hour and twelve minutes after the initial earthquake shock, and after water from the High Pressure system had been fully expended, Battalion Chief Shannon special-called the fireboat *Phoenix* from Pier 22 1/2 to provide saltwater to companies fighting the Marina District fire.

Off-duty Battalion Chief Greg W. Abell, responding to the Emergency Duty Recall Signal, drove his car directly to the Marina District fire and reported to Battalion Chief Shannon. At 6:17 p.m., Battalion Chief Abell ordered the Communications Center to dispatch a hose tender with five-inch hose and the associated valve system to the Marina District. The Communications

Center dispatched Engine Co. 22 with Hose Tender No. 22 and advised the units to take a lead from the fireboat *Phoenix* as soon as it berthed in the Marina Yacht Harbor.

Engine Co. 10 commanded by Lt. William P. Shore was in the Marina District, south of the fire zone, manually closing numerous PG&E street valves to stop gas leaks, and at 6:13 p.m. responded to the Marina District fire. Lieutenant Shore found the southern approach blocked by automobiles, so he circumvented the congestion and approached the fire by driving east on Beach from Baker Street.

Lieutenant Shore found that Truck Co. 10 was the only unit on that exposure of the fire. The crew of Engine Co. 10 then tested and found water in the High Pressure hydrant on the northeast corner of Beach and Broderick streets. Two lines were led from the hydrant to Engine Co. 10 positioned on Beach Street just west of the fire.

Truck Co. 5 also responded to the fire from the collapsed building at Cervantes Boulevard and Fillmore Street. Lieutenant John R. Donham, Jr., and members of his company operated one of the large lines that was supplied by Engine Co. 10 on Beach Street.

At this time, 2101 Beach Street, the buckled four-story structure on the southwest corner at Divisadero Street, caught fire on the third floor. Hose streams were used to extinguish the incipient fire and to cool the front of the building. This action prevented the fire from jumping Beach Street to the south.

Operating in this area was extremely dangerous for both firefighters and citizen volunteers. The building at 2101 Beach Street threatened to collapse during frequent aftershocks. If the fire were to jump Beach Street it would spread into another block of severely damaged combustible wood-frame structures. The stand made here by firefighters, with this limited water supply and citizen volunteers operating hose lines and a bucket brigade, was responsible for stopping the spread of the Marina District fire from the block of origin.

Chief John J. Hickey of Battalion No. 2 was in the area of City Hall shortly after the earthquake and, after handling two calls, responded toward the Marina District. He had noticed that smoke from the fire was now being pushed along by a light westerly wind that had risen, and there was a commensurate increase in the size of the fire. He ordered Engine Co. 36 by department radio to check High Pressure hydrants along Chestnut near Divisadero Street for water, but the pressure in each hydrant was too low for suppression operations. Chief Hickey then ordered the task force to respond to the Palace of Fine Arts.

At 6:12 p.m., Engine Co. 21 had cleared the scene of a reported natural gas leak at 700 Grove Street in the Western Addition, and was directed by department radio to the Marina District fire several miles distant. Upon arrival, Capt. Guido J. Costella of Engine Co. 21 was ordered by Battalion Chief Shannon to attack the fire from the west along Beach Street. While responding, Capt. Costella tested the low pressure system at Divisadero and Bay streets and found no water, so he planned to use the High Pressure hydrant at the northeast corner of Beach and Broderick streets. This hydrant was already in operation and was providing some limited water to Engine Co. 10. However, the hose line was soft, which indicated that the hydrant capacity had been exceeded.

Captain Costella ordered his company to Beach and Baker streets, one block to the west. There, the crew of Engine Co. 21 tested the High Pressure hydrant at the southeast corner and found it was apparently capable of supplying sufficient pressure. The crew of Engine Co. 21 led two supply lines to Beach and Broderick streets. It was Capt. Costella's intent to have his apparatus act as a manifold. However, when the two supply lines were charged, the flow ceased.

At this point, Engine Co. 14 arrived at Beach and Broderick streets, and members of Engine Co. 21 then broke their lines and connected them to Engine Co. 14. Captain Costella planned to have Engine Co. 21 supply water by draft from the lagoon of the Palace of Fine Arts but found all access blocked by automobiles. Finally working through the congestion, the crew of Engine Co. 21 began to draft from the lagoon and supplied two lines to Engine Co. 14.

Upon arrival at the lagoon of the Palace of Fine Arts, the task force and Battalion Chief Hickey found that Engine Co. 21 was just being positioned to begin drafting operations. He said, "I told the officer of Engine Co. 3 to bring [large line] leads from the fire to Engine Co. 21. After they finished, they [members of the task force] could meet me at the fire corner." Engine Co. 3 led a third line from Engine Co. 21 to the fire.

Engine Co. 21 supplied Engine Co. 14 which in turn relayed water to Engine Co. 10. Engine Co. 3 was directly supplied from Engine Co. 21. This water supplied by Engine Co. 21 was instrumental in preventing the fire from further extending westward along Beach Street.

Battalion Chief Hickey and Chief's Aide Joseph D. Driscoll left their buggy, a chief's command vehicle, at the lagoon of the Palace of Fine Arts because of severe traffic congestion and then ran to the fire, but were driven away by the extreme radiant heat and earthquake aftershocks.

The situation at the Marina District fire as understood at the Communications Center was not clear because of the grossly overtaxed radio communications system. However, commercial television stations had begun to broadcast live reports from the fire scene and Deputy Chief Farrell was better able to understand conditions on the fire ground as seen from a live picture transmitted by the Goodyear Tire & Rubber Co. airship, *Columbia*, that had been hovering near Candlestick Park to televise the third game of the World Series.

He ordered Assistant Chief Harry F. Brophy of Division No. 2 to the Marina District fire to assume Incident Command. At 6:29 p.m., Assistant Chief Brophy, upon arrival at the Marina District fire, radioed to the Communications Center, "Send PG&E out here to the area of Cervantes and Fillmore. You've got major gas in the area— major gas leak." Moments later, Battalion Chief Abell radioed, "Our fire here is still out of control. We've got a lot of companies, but we're having trouble with water."

Battalion Chief Shannon had earlier attempted to have engines draft saltwater directly from the bay, but this was unsuccessful because of low-tide conditions.

At 6:40 p.m., Assistant Chief Brophy ordered the Communications Center to dispatch all available hose tenders with five-inch-diameter hose and associated valves to the Marina Yacht Harbor at the foot of Divisadero Street. He reported to the Communications Center, "We have three blocks that are going to be involved. We'll have to give away some houses to make a stop, but we need hose. We have the [staffing] to pull it; we've got a lot of volunteers, but get [the hose] here!"

At 6:45 p.m., Battalion Chief Abell reported the fire was moving west, and at 6:49 p.m., Assistant Chief Brophy radioed that there was difficulty positioning the fireboat *Phoenix* in the Marina Yacht Harbor because of low-tide conditions, and there was the possibility of insufficient draft to berth the vessel.

At 6:59 p.m., Assistant Chief Brophy reported that water from the three-engine relay had reached the fire, and firefighters and citizen volunteers were attempting to make a stop. Chief Brophy also reported the fire was spreading north, halfway along the block toward Jefferson Street, and citizen volunteers and firefighters were attempting to keep the blaze from consuming the block.

At 7 p.m., the fireboat *Phoenix* had been maneuvered into position despite the low-tide conditions. "I reported to Chief Brophy," said Battalion Chief Hickey, "and told him, 'If we could get some lines from the [fire] boat, we could make the stop right here.'" Assistant Chief Brophy responded, "Okay, let's give it a try."

By this time the crew of Engine Co. 2 had completed laying the hose which came from Engine Co. 31 at the Marina dock. Members of Truck Co. 2, using water relayed by Engine Co. 2 from Engine Co. 31, began to attack the fire on the north from Jefferson and Divisadero streets. The truck company aerial was used as a water tower and thousands of gallons of saltwater were used to help stop the northerly progress of the Marina District fire.

It was Battalion Chief Hickey's understanding that victims were still trapped within the fallen four-story apartment building at the southwest corner of Divisadero and Jefferson streets, and it was therefore necessary to stop the northerly swing of the Marina District fire to protect these possible victims.

Members of Engine Co. 3, 5, and 36; Truck Co. 3 and 5 and Rescue No. 1; two off-duty firefighters from Tiburon, Michael J. and John A. Hickey—both sons of Battalion Chief Hickey; as well as off-duty firefighter Philip A. Tripp of the Novato Fire Department reported to the scene with protective clothing provided by the Presidio of San Francisco Fire Department and were immediately put to work.

Aftershocks continued to shake damaged structures within the Marina District as this pickup company broke down the door of 3745 Divisadero Street to gain entry to the roof. Battalion Chief Hickey was concerned about the stability of the structure because of recurring aftershocks and said, "I ordered Lt. Jack Conway to bring two large lines into the first floor of the structure and then up to the roof, and then I ordered one [large line] to be brought over the fire escape to act

as a supply line and as a possible escape route. We could feel the building shaking."

Members of Engine Co. 36 then breached the wall of the third floor of 3745 Divisadero Street and pulled the large lines across rooftops to the wood-frame building immediately adjacent to the fire. These large lines were led in anticipation of saltwater being supplied by the fireboat *Phoenix* which had just completed the extraordinarily hazardous docking at the Marina Yacht Harbor.

Lieutenant John T. Conway, who was on the rooftop, became concerned with fire conditions and advised Chief Hickey that the situation was rapidly deteriorating, and that the company could not stay there much longer without water. Chief Hickey advised Lt. Conway to stay as long as possible, because water from the fireboat would soon be available.

Seven buildings were on fire at Beach and Divisadero streets as firefighters and citizen volunteers led lines from the boat to the fire. The crew of Hose Tender No. 22, with civilian volunteers, under the direction of members of the Department, also dragged a five-inch line to the front of 3745 Divisadero Street, and with two of the associated valves, provided saltwater to the pickup company within and atop the structures for the frontal attack on the fire. An endless supply of saltwater from San Francisco Bay, pumped by the fireboat, allowed fire companies and citizen volunteers to move in for the attack.

At 7:27 p.m., Battalion Chief Abell notified the Communications Center that one half block was still fully involved in fire, but the exposure buildings were covered. Water from Capt. Costella's three-engine relay from the lagoon of the Palace of Fine Arts was, at the time, protecting the western flank, as well as exposures on the south and east of the Marina District fire.

The northerly front of the fire began to develop its own wind, and intense heat caused the tar upon rooftops to bubble, and the boots of these firefighters began to stick to the roofing materials. Steam and smoke were also seen rising from their turnout coats.

At about 8 p.m., inspection of the High Pressure system by San Francisco Fire Department Bureau of Water Supply personnel was completed, and Pump Stations No. 1 and No. 2 were brought on line. This supply of 10,000-gpm saltwater, along with saltwater supplied by the *Phoenix*, allowed fire companies to begin to bring the Marina District fire under control.

Battalion Chief Hickey's pickup company fought the fire for more than two hours, stopping the northerly spread of the fire within the wood-frame structure, two buildings to the south of 3745 Divisadero Street.

DAVID FOWLER

Initial Response to the Cypress Freeway Disaster

(Compiled from Oakland Department of Fire Services Reports and Radio Transcripts)

Oakland Fire Dept. Lt. William R. Jarrett first knew of the disaster at the Cypress Freeway a few moments after the earthquake when he and the crew of Fire Engine No. 5 saw large columns of dust and smoke rising from the area of 32nd Street at the Cypress Freeway. Lt. Jarrett immediately responded with his engine and crew and, upon arrival, saw people scrambling along the upper deck screaming for help.

To Firefighter Gary Klinger who was on Engine No. 5, "It looked like an atom bomb had just gone off. People were running around in all directions screaming for help here, there, and everywhere," and indeed, the collapsed freeway appeared to have been shelled by heavy artillery.

Lt. Jarrett tried to radio a report of the disaster to fire alarm, but could not get through because of other frantic radio traffic overloading the Fire Department communications system.

Citizens who lived in a nearby housing project ran to the wrecked freeway moments after the earthquake. Dozens of extraordinarily brave citizens climbed shattered support columns and—holding on to curled steel reinforcement rods that had been bent and exposed by the fearsome collapse—made their way along the top deck.

Dust and smoke rose straight up into the warm afternoon air. These brave people covered their faces with handkerchiefs and rags for protection from cement dust and the acrid smoke of many burning automobiles, and went from car to car to search for survivors. Strong earthquake aftershocks rocked the teetering, insecure freeway. One of these citizen rescuers began to yell, "I need something to pry the door open! He's alive...alive...he heard me!" as the first Oakland firefighters arrived.

Dr. Steve Mahin, Professor of Civil Engineering and Chairman of the Structural Engineering Department at UC Berkeley was on the seventh floor of the Engineering building and also saw what Lt. Jarrett did: "I have the fortune or misfortune of having an office on the Berkeley Campus which has a panoramic view of Oakland and portions of San Francisco," the professor said, "and during the earthquake I was in my office and looking out the window as soon as the earthquake occurred; I could note very clearly the collapse of the 880 structure and almost immediately subsequent fires that erupted."

There were several expert eyewitnesses on the Cypress Freeway at the time of the earthquake, and Dr. David Rogers, who testified before the California Senate Transportation Committee, said some of them were civil engineers "...and they described driving over the waves and decided to get off while other people decided to stop, and that they believe the failure [of the Cypress Freeway] emanated from the north end...and came back towards the south." The California Highway Patrol's report on the collapse confirmed that the various sections collapsed from north to south.

The first telephone call reporting the Cypress collapse didn't get through to the overwhelmed Oakland Fire Dispatch Center until 5:10 p.m., six minutes after the freeway had fallen.

Oakland Engine Co. 1 had been dispatched to Fourth Street and Martin Luther King Jr. Way for a reported collapsed building. When Lt. Mark Hoffman found nothing he suggested the Fire Dispatch Center cancel the call and assign responding units to other emergencies. The Fire Dispatch Center then radioed, "Engine No. 1, 880 and Cypress, the freeway is down. We need you." Lt. Hoffman calmly acknowledged the call and the dispatch center then ordered Engine Co. 2 to also respond.

Meanwhile, Assistant Chief John Baker attempted to organize the limited resources of the Oakland Department of Fire Services after riding out the massive earthquake while standing in the doorway of the Dispatch Center. Hundreds of calls for assistance swamped the fire dispatchers, and he called Chief Reginald (Reggie) Garcia at Battalion 3 by telephone and ordered him to headquarters to assist with operations.

Battalion Chief Garcia was quartered at Station 20, about fifteen minutes away by automobile from the Fire Dispatch Center at headquarters.

Battalion Chief Garcia drove away from Station 20 at 5:10 p.m. While driving to headquarters, he could hear sketchy radio reports from various units around the city, and he heard the dispatch of Engine Co. 1 to a reported freeway collapse near I-880 and Cypress Street. Later, as he approached headquarters, he began to hear other scratchy, fragmentary, and garbled radio transmissions from various fire companies just arriving at the Cypress collapse. However, it was still not possible to tell from these sketchy radio transmissions just how extensive this collapse might be.

From what he could see of conditions in the east end of Oakland and hear from the few intelligible radio transmissions, it was clear that most of the earthquake damage was in the central and west parts of the city.

Radio reports from units in the field were either still too fragmented or simply too sketchy to tell of the true conditions at the Cypress collapse, but what could be heard alarmed Assistant Chief Baker who then tried to borrow the Oakland Police Department's helicopter for an aerial survey of the city. It was out of service for maintenance.

All along the one-and-a-quarter-mile stretch of the Cypress collapse, the first arriving fire companies immediately began to try to free survivors wherever they found a need, and that seemed to be everywhere. At any point along the broken structure, trapped and injured victims awaited first-aid treatment or assistance.

These chronically understaffed fire companies—victims of years of budget reductions—had to split into squads to begin rescue attempts and to treat dazed and injured survivors along and atop this unstable structure.

Lt. Hoffman, of Engine Co. 1, at first used the Tele-squirt (a telescoping ladder boom that extends 45 feet with a nozzle at the top) engine to reach the collapsed upper deck on the west side of the freeway at Cypress and 18th streets. The crew then brought an extension ladder up the Tele-squirt and raised it from the collapsed section to the elevated section of the freeway which miraculously remained standing.

Engineer Jerry Prola stayed with the engine and helped survivors down the Tele-squirt boom and handled their immediate first-aid needs. Firefighter Charles Gerow and a group of citizen volunteers raised other ladders to rescue more survivors who had begun to slowly crawl from the smoking freeway wreckage.

Lt. Hoffman and Firefighter Ken Costa

were soon joined by two off-duty members of the U.S. Marine Corps stationed at the Alameda Naval Air Station. One of these Marines, Guillermo R. Guillen, began to interpret for injured Spanish-speaking victims. Another volunteer was an off-duty employee of Alameda County who was not identified in Oakland fire reports. This combined Fire Fighter and volunteer crew crawled along the sandwiched lower deck peering between the decks for more trapped victims and noting the location of the fatalities.

While Lt. Hoffman led this group in this search, the crew of Engine Co. 8 raised ground ladders on the opposite side of the freeway to extricate more victims trapped on the east side of the lower deck.

Engineer Prola went to the assistance of Engine Co. 8's crew in this rescue effort and moved the Tele-squirt to the east side of the freeway, then raised the boom to a point where entry could be made.

The crew of Engine Co. 1 then worked with Engine Co. 8 and Ladder Truck Co. 20 on the extrication of the Beruman children that would last through the night.

At about 5:25 p.m., Ladder Truck Co. 1 arrived at 32nd and Cypress streets to assist Engine Co. 1. John D. Thomas, captain of this ladder truck, wrote that upon arrival, "we found large amounts of rubble in the street," at 32nd and Cypress streets and he could see "directly at the intersection a semitrailer truck crushed between the two decks and was burning. Vehicles at street level were crushed by falling concrete and steel or appeared to have fallen from the upper deck of the freeway." The rescue work of the ladder truck company was further complicated because "travel along Cypress Street was blocked by fallen rubble," he said.

Capt. Thomas also split his understaffed ladder truck crew into two teams. Part of his crew began to work with Engine Co. 5 on the upper deck as other crew members grabbed ladders from the truck and raised them to get to the freeway deck. The truck fire between the decks was put out single-handedly by Firefighter Robert Sibley who led a hoseline from a nearby hydrant and attached it directly to the ladder truck aerial nozzle, then squirted the water between decks without benefit of a pump—a highly irregular but effective maneuver.

This blockage of Cypress Street by wrecked automobiles and thousands of tons of rubble was of grave and immediate concern because it severely hampered the initial rescue and fire fighting efforts.

The City of Oakland was again remarkably lucky because 60 Department of Public Works employees were attending driving school at the public works yard and, when alerted to the Cypress collapse, went immediately to the scene. On arrival, they began the extraordinary task of removing the debris with heavy moving equipment so rescue workers could get more ladders to the freeway deck and more ambulances to triage areas set up to treat the wounded.

These public works crews found hundreds of citizen volunteers frantically pushing and shoving huge chunks of concrete and debris by hand to clear the street.

At the Fire Dispatch Center troubling reports of the disaster filtered in. An alarmed Assistant Chief Baker sent Battalion Chief Garcia to the Cypress Freeway collapse to begin command operations and to assess the need for additional assistance. Battalion Chief Garcia drove to the southern end of the freeway because most of the fragmentary reports concerning the collapse had come from fire companies near 18th Street.

In this first hour, staff at the Fire Dispatch Center relied to a great degree on commercial television for coverage of earthquake damage. Some of the early information about the collapse came from pictures transmitted by a KGO-TV news helicopter. Dispatcher Williams wrote, "I remember getting a call reporting the Bay Bridge had collapsed. I envisioned the whole bridge, cars and all, in the Bay. When the call came regarding the Cypress Freeway structure collapsing, I never realized it was as devastating as it was until we could see the report on the TV news."

The KGO-TV helicopter was transmitting live pictures of the disaster, and Assistant Chief Baker and the dispatchers at the fire alarm office could see the rippled upper roadway and smoke billowing from between sandwiched decks on the small television set. It was clear this horrific collapse extended from 18th Street to 34th Street.

Even so, Lt. Hoffman of Engine Co. 1 had difficulty putting the disaster into context when he radioed, "We are at 880 along Cypress and we have complete structural collapse of the entire freeway between the streets of 17th as far as I can see going toward 32nd, so we are going to need some trucks down here as soon as you can get them!"

Battalion Chief Garcia arrived and gasped at what he saw. He later wrote of his first view of the collapse, "As I approached the Cypress Freeway, I could see the top deck collapsed down onto the lower level. I parked my car at the intersection of 18th and Cypress. Looking north along Cypress Street, I could see a complete collapse of the upper deck as far as I could see. The scene was unreal, almost beyond comprehension. There was total chaos with people scrambling through the rubble attempting to assist those who were trapped."

He remained in the area of 18th and Cypress streets and established a South Division command post responsible for the rescue operations between West Grand Avenue and 17th Street.

It was his view that the collapse was so huge that it required the division of the rescue operation into areas which could be more easily managed, and at about 5:50

p.m. Battalion Chief Manuel Navarro arrived at the Command Post and began to coordinate rescue operations north of West Grand Avenue.

By 6 p.m., fifty-four minutes after the earthquake, Cypress operations had been organized into two major divisions: North, commanded by Battalion Chief Navarro, and South, commanded by Battalion Chief Garcia. Overall Incident Command was led by Assistant Chief Al Sigwart from the West Grand Avenue Command Post.

Dr. Mahin arrived at the Cypress Freeway at 6:20 p.m. "Following a very quick evaluation of some buildings on the Berkeley Campus," he said, "I made my way down to the 880 structure within about an hour and fifteen minutes of the earthquake..." to begin the scientific study to find out why there had been such a catastrophic collapse.

The only clear picture of conditions at this time was that most of the available on-duty and recalled fire force had been depleted, and there were no more fire companies available for response anywhere in Oakland. Emergency supplies on the engines and ladder trucks were also running dangerously low. Lt. Hoffman appealed to Battalion Chief Garcia by radio: "If you could round up any extra medical equipment, we need some inhalators and other first-aid equipment to assist us here. All our engine companies are stripped and we need more medical assistance."

A task force of two Oakland engines and a ladder truck company, along with an ambulance and paramedic units, operated on the west side of the collapse led by Capt. Frank Baleria of Fire Engine Co. 2. On the east side of this same area, Engine Co. 1, Engine Co. 8, and Ladder Truck Co. 20 began the very long, difficult, and horrific rescue of two young children, Julio and Cathy Berumen.

Engine Co. 5 was positioned on the west side of the Cypress Freeway near a burning automobile, and with the aid of citizens, a small fire hose was used to put out this blaze. Jeff A. Hillstrom, a hoseman on Engine Co. 5, wrote, "I jumped off the rig, grabbed a New York hook and proceeded to free a male trapped in a Blazer on the street below the collapsed freeway. Lt. Jarrett, Hoseman Klinger, and Engineer Thompson threw a ladder to the superstructure and went to the west side of the Cypress to put out a car [fire]."

The engine crew was then able to climb to the top of the freeway. They found a van with six people inside; two were injured and four were dead, and there were several other injured people lying about on the pavement. Lt. Jarrett left his crew with these victims and worked his way along the Cypress structure toward 26th Street. There he found more dazed and injured people who were walking around, and others who were still trapped in the wreckage.

Ladder Truck Co. 1 had arrived and the crew brought up a hydraulic rescue tool. Eight badly injured victims were placed atop a shipping container that had been raised to the freeway deck by a forklift operator.

Lt. Jarrett went to the command post after finishing the rescue operation at 32nd and Cypress streets and was told to report to Battalion Chief Navarro at Peralta and Cypress streets. Engine Co. 5 and two other engine companies were directed to make a sweep of the structure back toward 32nd Street. As the crew of Engine Co. 5 drove along Cypress Street, they came upon more citizens on the freeway yelling that a man was trapped in a vehicle in the center of the structure opposite 26th Street.

Other citizens from the West Oakland housing projects, nearby machine shops, and warehouses carried a fire extinguisher up a ladder and told the firefighters that gasoline was running through the area where the man was trapped. Lt. Jarrett, along with Firefighters Hillstrom and Klinger, climbed the freeway to rescue the

victim. They found him in an automobile that had been crushed to a height of two feet and gasoline was running over him. Lt. Jarrett called for a small fire hose line to be brought up to the wreckage to protect the trapped victim from fire.

At the same time, workers from a private roofing company raised a conveyor belt up to the firefighters to allow rescue equipment to be quickly moved to the lower deck. An Alameda County mutual aid engine crew arrived and brought the hose line up to the freeway then helped lead it through the collapsed upper deck to the center of the roadway and to the crushed automobile.

All the equipment that might be needed for the rescue—hydraulic power tools, cutters, and jacks—were brought up by conveyor belt. Unfortunately, the only equipment that would fit in that confined space were hacksaw blades and small tools. Firefighter Hillstrom, two paramedics identified only as Marty and Bruce, as well as several citizen volunteers worked feverishly with these tools in that narrow area to cut away the steering wheel and brake pedal and give the victim medical care and lifesaving oxygen.

As this desperate rescue attempt continued, fire broke out above them on the upper deck. The hose was swung around and brought up to the fire and it was put out. As the victim was finally freed from the crushed vehicle, a Castro Valley Fire Department aerial ladder truck was raised and a stretcher was brought up to them. Because of limited space, the stretcher containing the victim was dragged across the pavement toward the aerial ladder truck where it was tied with rope and lowered to the street and waiting paramedics.

U.S. Army Capt. Stephen M. Park of Letterman Army Medical Center was on the Cypress Freeway and stopped his car when the shaking began. He was later given the Army's Commendation Medal for "heroic efforts on the collapsed Cypress Street overpass.... With total disregard for his personal safety, Capt. Parks initiated immediate life-saving actions for four critically injured motorists and evacuated a dozen or more from the disaster area. Throughout the evening, he continued to provide medical assistance to the Oakland Fire Department, working under perilous conditions between the collapsed smoke-filled sections of the roadway."

Capt. Park was an Army lawyer assigned to Letterman Army Medical Center and had worked his way through college and law school as an EMT. With his automobile still on the freeway, Army Capt. Park was given a ride home by Capt. Gerald Flom of the Oakland department at about midnight.

Navy Hospital Corpsman Bill Wicker was approaching the Cypress structure in his ambulance when the quake hit. The 21-year-old Wicker, a trained emergency medical technician at the Naval Hospital in Oakland, climbed to the top deck and went from car to car administering first aid. "Even though he was drenched in gasoline from ruptured fuel tanks, and risked certain death should a fire break out, Wicker continued to help victims. Using makeshift stretchers and braces, he loaded his ambulance with some of the most seriously injured," said a Navy report.

Corpsman Wicker became a victim himself. Nurses and doctors at the hospital had to almost physically restrain him to keep the corpsman from going back to the fallen freeway. He was admitted to the hospital suffering from smoke inhalation.

San Francisco Firefighter Michael R. Bryant of Engine Co. 25 was off duty at the time of the earthquake and was also on the freeway. He scrambled to assist victims and organize rescue parties. He was later awarded a meritorious citation for his bravery by the California Highway Patrol which read, "He personally rendered aid, organized volunteers, and searched for survivors at great risk to his own life."

Lt. Steve August of Ladder Truck Co. 15 and his crew were also dispatched to the Cypress Freeway but, as he wrote, "Heading north between 14th and 15th streets, we found Willow Street was obstructed by debris from a three-story brick warehouse whose roof and third floor had collapsed. In questioning a worker of the building, we determined all employees were accounted for and were out of the building."

The officer also found a major natural gas leak and radioed to the Dispatch Center. "We got civilians cordoning off the area and there is no one trapped. But, if possible, we need PG&E to trace out a major gas leak in this whole block area.... We're going to head over [where] the freeway collapsed and see if we can lend assistance there."

"Upon arrival at Cypress and 32nd Street," Lt. August wrote, "we encountered mass confusion and destruction. We were informed by several civilians at the scene that there were mass casualties on both decks of the freeway, so we moved 15 Truck up the off-ramp on the west side of I-880, just north of 32nd Street," near where the crew of Ladder Truck No. 1 were involved in a rescue operation.

He wrote, "The crew then threw a 38-foot ladder to the upper deck about 100 feet north of where the aerial ladder truck was placed. The upper deck looked like a war zone. There were approximately four CHP officers and half a dozen civilians assisting casualties from all the wrecked autos."

Lt. August was surprised by rotor noise from a helicopter that was about to land on the tottering, shifting freeway. "I was informed by the CHP that the chopper had been summoned for casualty evacuation. Given the condition of the freeway and the potential for collapse, I waved the chopper off just prior to its touchdown. I felt we could handle the evacuation of these casualties and the helicopter would only compound the hazards."

Then, wrote the lieutenant, ". . . civilians

informed us that there were still people trapped between the two decks of the freeway in the same area. We repositioned the aerial [ladder truck] further down the off-ramp in order to gain access to the lower deck. We scanned the entire area and found only empty cars or vehicles that were so badly crushed that survival of the occupants was impossible. But, a few minutes later, Capt. Flom, who had returned to duty after the earthquake, came upon Firefighters [Christopher] McCotter and [Gary] Schroeder who showed me a victim in a white Blazer between decks. The top of the victim's head was visible from the passenger side."

The ladder truck company was again moved to about 300 feet south of 32nd Street, and Lt. August and his crew began to raise ladders to the lower deck of the freeway. The lieutenant wrote, "Capt. Flom then crawled between the decks to a small pickup truck [the Blazer] in order to determine if the occupant was still alive. He was able to partially open the driver's door and he confirmed that the victim was still breathing, but was pinned in the driver's seat. We started to move a backboard and the jaws [Hurst tool also known as the 'Jaws of Life'] between the decks when additional movement of the entire structure caused us to evacuate to the aerial [ladder truck]."

Aftershocks continued to roll through the vast, unstable structure and, as Capt. Flom wrote, "In the process of moving equipment and people to the first level, a distinct shock was felt and the deck dropped a short distance. I ordered everyone to the ground and reevaluated the situation with Lt. [Brian] Lawrence."

"I went to the ground to assess the stability of the freeway," wrote Lt. Steve August, "and found that even the support structure for the lower deck was fractured and was continuing to move. I called everyone off of the structure and I called for Caltrans and the Army Corps of Engineers to advise me as to the stability of the lower deck.

Understanding that time was critical for the victim, Capt. Flom and I dismissed the idea of shoring and elected to make this a two-man rescue operation in order to minimize the chance of further casualties."

Lt. August continued: "With the assistance of Lt. Lawrence we set up the [Hurst tool] power unit on the lower deck and Capt. Flom crawled between the decks with the spreader to extricate the victim. Capt. Flom then came out to discuss a plan for evacuation of the victim. Capt. Flom and I crawled back in between the decks with a backboard while Lt. Lawrence stayed just outside and manned a 'lifeline' that was attached to the backboard."

"I went in and opened the driver door with the Hurst [tool] spreader," wrote Capt. Flom. "The victim was pinned from the waist up. He moved his legs, indicating he was not completely unconscious."

"Once the victim was pulled out from between the decks," wrote Lt. August, "the rest of the crew assisted in lowering the unidentified man down the aerial to the waiting paramedics.

"I think it appropriate," Lt. August suggested, "that the Oakland Fire Department consider Capt. Gerald Flom to be honored with a Medal of Valor award. His action and disregard for his own safety went well beyond what we consider normal, everyday heroics."

It was certainly clear to Assistant Chief Baker at the Fire Dispatch Center that the department had no fire apparatus in service for dispatch and that the City of Oakland was in extreme danger. The fire communications center was gridlocked because hundreds of emergency calls were being received, but there were no fire engines or trucks to send.

Lt. Charles E. Nelson of the Oakland Police Department Communications Division complained after the earthquake, "[The Oakland Department of Fire Services] was overwhelmed and would not take information on, or respond to, gas leaks or lines down. We [the Oakland Police] could not get through to PG&E with these calls because of phone congestion."

In the city of Fremont, about 20 miles south of the Cypress collapse, Fire Chief Dan Lyden had begun to set up the Emergency Operations Center with the help of the mayor and the city manager a few minutes after the earthquake. Mayor Gus Morrison was listening to a portable radio when he suddenly whirled and said to the chief, "I just heard that the Bay Bridge has collapsed!"

"I said 'My God!' when I heard that," said Chief Lyden, "I then checked and found that our city was not in serious trouble and I immediately went to the telephone to call Oakland Fire Alarm, and they answered right away." Chief Lyden knew that a portion of the Bay Bridge was within the city limits of Oakland, and he also knew that years of budget cutbacks had left the Oakland Fire Department with just seven understaffed ladder truck companies. His 25 years of experience in the fire service also told him all of those truck companies would be needed for potential heavy rescue operations on the Bay Bridge. He was not yet aware, however, of the disastrous collapse of the Cypress Freeway.

When the call miraculously got through the overtaxed commercial telephone system at 5:25 p.m., Assistant Chief Baker was still not fully aware of the extreme magnitude of the Cypress Freeway collapse himself, but had full knowledge that virtually all of Oakland's fire companies had either already begun rescue operations at many places along the freeway or were out of service on other major emergencies. There were no fire engines left.

Assistant Chief Baker quickly came to the telephone and said, "Danny, you're the first outside person I've talked to since this thing hit. Every company is committed and we need ladder companies quickly...the Cypress is down!"

"I've known John for 30 years," said Chief Lyden, "and I could tell by the fright in his voice that his department was in trouble, and I asked him if he was requesting mutual aid. 'Danny, call it what you want,' Chief Baker said, 'just send me ladder companies! We can't reach the [upper deck of the Cypress Freeway], the ground ladders won't get to it!' "

Fremont Mayor Morrison and City Manager Kent McClain gave instant approval to send a ladder truck company to help Oakland. Chief Lyden also called other fire departments in southern Alameda County to see if truck companies were available. There were none. Assistant Chief Baker also asked Chief Lyden to contact the Contra Costa County Consolidated Fire District and request ladder truck companies from them.

Oakland was quite fortunate that the city of Fremont was in a unique position to help and had a mayor, city manager, and a progressive fire chief who were more than willing to send immediate help. First, there was little major damage in Fremont and, second, there was an outpouring of off-duty fire department personnel who quickly returned to the fire stations and, fortunately, the regular day staff was still at work when the earthquake struck.

"We had two 100-foot, brand-new, tillered aerials [ladder trucks] that had just been delivered and we were just in the final stages of mounting [rescue] equipment on them. Ironically, our people had been trained by the San Francisco Fire Department, because this was a new piece of equipment to us. So, we recognized that we had enough people to staff the department and still send ladder companies to Oakland," said Chief Lyden.

Fremont is also the only city in Alameda County that provides advanced life support on fire engines, so Chief Lyden also sent six paramedic firefighters to Oakland to assist at the Cypress disaster.

Under normal conditions Assistant Chief Baker's call for additional fire equipment to Oakland, instead of going directly to Chief Lyden, should have been handed off to what is known as a county mutual aid coordinator. This coordinator, as the title implies, coordinates assistance to local fire departments within Alameda County. However, Chief John Sharry of the Lawrence Livermore Laboratory Fire Department, who held the position of coordinator at the time of the earthquake, apparently did not seem to grasp the magnitude of this disaster. He also seemed not to anticipate the severe demand upon mutual aid resources, even though he was aware of major damage in the western part of Alameda County because his operations log notes that he heard such reports on KCBS-AM, the news-radio station in San Francisco.

Despite having a direct hotline system known as the TAC telephone to these fire departments in full operation after the earthquake, Chief Sharry did not, if his log is correct, react to the disaster for at least 34 minutes, some ten minutes after Chief Lyden had dispatched a ladder truck company and paramedics to the Cypress collapse. By this time the situation in Oakland had deteriorated to an alarming degree with major rescues, gas leaks, building collapses and, of course, the ghastly freeway collapse. So Chief Lyden's spontaneous telephone call offering immediate assistance was a godsend to Oakland.

Chief Sharry played this extraordinary and horrific disaster rigidly and strictly by the rules and, as he wrote in his report, "At approx. 1740 hrs. [5:40 p.m.] we received a TAC phone request from Fremont Fire . . . asking for truck companies to go to Oakland. Upon questioning the caller he stated that Oakland had contacted them and that they needed truck companies at the Cypress St. Rt. 880 overpass. The overpass had collapsed. I asked if this was a relay

from Oakland to the County Coordinator for County Mutual Aid. The person stated that he did not know—that he was just trying to help Oakland. He stated that Fremont had dispatched some truck companies to their assistance."

But by 5:40 p.m., Oakland was stripped of fire engines and trucks by the enormous number of emergency calls—there were no fire resources left. On the northern border of Oakland, the Berkeley Fire Department was fighting a major earthquake-caused blaze that required the use of all engines and trucks in that city, and it could not send apparatus. The smaller Emeryville and Albany fire departments were also committed to various emergencies, which included mutual aid to Berkeley, and could not be counted on for assistance.

For all practical purposes this major American city was without organized fire protection when at 5:48 p.m.—45 minutes after the earthquake—Chief Sharry placed his first call to the Oakland Fire Department.

"I contacted Oakland Fire Dispatch," he wrote, "via TAC phone to determine their needs. Oakland requested that we send them anything we could spare. I informed them that I could not deal with that kind of request. They needed to give me their needs in numbers. After some discussion, Oakland requested two Engine Strike Teams and two Truck Strike Teams. I informed Oakland that Truck Companies were at a premium, but I would organize the best available resources." Each strike team was to be made up of five fire engines or five ladder trucks.

"I contacted Contra Costa County [Consolidated Fire District which adjoins Alameda County to the east] to ask for an Immediate Response Strike Team to Oakland. Contra Costa County informed me that they had already dispatched several Truck companies to Oakland. They would try to put together an Engine Company

Strike Team and would get back to me." These were the ladder truck companies that had been earlier requested by Chief Lyden of Fremont. Chief Sharry then dispatched Alameda County Task Force 14 to Oakland, made up of apparatus from Lawrence Livermore Laboratory Fire Department, Livermore City Fire Department, as well as units from Pleasanton and the small community of Dougherty.

This task force was certainly of assistance, but given the magnitude of the disaster, fell far short of the resources needed to sustain major rescue operations at the Cypress Freeway. Assistant Chief Baker did, in fact, need "everything you can spare," and much more, in a rescue operation that would ultimately require resources from the United States Army, Navy, Marine Corps, Air Force, and fire departments as far away as Los Angeles.

At 6 p.m., Battalion Chief Walden of the Walnut Creek Fire Department was told by Chief Sharry to lead a Heavy Rescue Strike Team made up of San Ramon Ladder Truck No. 34 and Consolidated Fire District Ladder Truck No. 1 to Oakland. His strike team was dispatched to 16th Street and Martin Luther King Jr. Way for a reported building collapse.

When Battalion Chief Walden's strike team stopped at a roadblock at San Pablo Avenue and Martin Luther King Jr. Way, it was mistakenly directed by the Oakland Police Department to the Cypress Command Post at West Grand Avenue and Cypress Street.

Oakland Engine Co. 4 was sent to the Cypress collapse and when it arrived, Firefighter Victor M. Cuevas wrote, "Words can't describe the feeling that came over me as the structure came closer in sight. It was very confusing. The engine stopped at about 2600 block of Cypress [at Peralta Street], where we were directed to the west side of the structure."

A California Highway Patrol officer told the crew that a man was trapped alive in an automobile on the lower deck. They grabbed all the tools from Engine Co. 4, then commandeered a forklift to raise them to the lower deck. Firefighter Cuevas began to check the seriousness of the injuries as Firefighter Andrew Papp began to pry and pull at the wreckage. Firefighter Cuevas continued, "During my patient assessment, I established his identity, which was Tim Peterson, a Treasure Island firefighter and son of an Oakland fireman, Dave Peterson."

As this rescue went on, this section of collapsed freeway began to shift and settle, and as Firefighter Cuevas wrote, "CHP officer Tim Goodman informed us that the structure had moved one-and-one-half inches since he had arrived 20 minutes before. This made Andy and me very nervous."

Lumber and jacks were needed to support the tottering structure, and Firefighter Cuevas yelled down to citizen volunteers below for assistance. Within a few minutes the necessary equipment was hauled to the lower deck to shore this unstable section of freeway—to protect the victim as well as those people involved in the rescue effort. "Andy's experience in extrication became evident as he pried and pulled, sometimes with his bare hands," observed the firefighter, and soon Tim Peterson was being dragged from the wreckage inch-by-inch.

A few minutes later, Fremont Truck Co. 1, the first unit dispatched by Chief Lyden, arrived with the Hurst tool needed to finally pry the Treasure Island firefighter from the wreckage. Firefighter Cuevas wrote, "We all gave a sigh of relief and hurried to get our butts off the collapsing structure."

Chief Sharry's report on the Cypress Freeway operations concluded stiffly: "Representatives of the Alameda County EOC requested several resources via nonauthorized means. Not being able to verify the requester for these resources, the requests were not honored. In order to gain control of the Fire and Rescue Resources only requests from Fire and Rescue Agencies were honored, unless I could verify the source of the requests. This action seemed to work well and enabled me to properly control Fire and Rescue Resources."

In the first seven hours of intensive search and rescue operations, 18 of 21 Oakland Fire Department companies, assisted by 15 more mutual aid companies—and dozens of ambulance and paramedic units—performed dozens of heroic rescues. More than 200 firefighters worked at the Cypress collapse during the first night of operations, and each of these firefighters was given a critical incident stress debriefing after they were relieved of duty at the scene.

Despite Chief Sharry's initial failure to poll fire departments within his mutual aid zone, and Chief Lyden's necessary intervention to provide Oakland with badly needed truck companies, Sharry wrote, "Overall the County Mutual Aid System and the OES Mutual Aid System worked well after the initial confusion and the failure of Oakland to properly utilize the Mutual Aid System."

On Friday, October 20, 1989, Chief Sharry called a meeting of the chiefs of fire departments in Alameda County to chastise the Oakland department for not following the proper protocols and procedures when requesting mutual aid. Oakland Fire Department Assistant Chief Andrew Stark had to leave the continuing rescue efforts at the Cypress Freeway to explain Oakland's actions to Chief Sharry.

What caused the collapse is still not thoroughly understood. Dr. Mahin, in his testimony to the state Senate's Kopp Committee said, "At this stage, we sent out teams after the earthquake and asked people what they saw, and there seems to be some disagreement amongst the people. And so at this stage I don't have a feeling for it. I suspect there was some domino effect where the cable restrainers did do their job, and as the one section came down, it also contributed to pulling it down until you got to the por-

tions where we have a freeway on-ramp, and the more firm ground and the additional columns on one end and the curved portion of the viaduct on the other side which tend to be a little stiffer, and then at those locations the cable restrainers did fail and the remaining portions of the structure did stand up."

The Cypress Freeway rescue efforts continued for several more days. To allow rescuers to continue to safely punch through the rubble of the unstable wreck, the U.S. Geological Survey installed a special alarm attached to a seismograph near the epicenter of the earthquake. If an aftershock greater than Richter magnitude 4.5 occurred, a signal would be transmitted to an alarm to rescuers. The alarm operated on the principal that the warning signal traveled at the speed of light along the wire to the freeway, but the earthquake waves traveled only at about the speed of sound. This would give rescuers at least 15 to 20 seconds advance warning to get off the tottering structure.

Forty-two people died in the collapse. Afterward, many of the rescuers were treated as heroes and many given awards by the State of California, the California Highway Patrol, and other agencies and groups. However, the Oakland Department of Fire Services did not issue any awards for heroism or valor to its firefighters who responded to the collapse and rescued so many victims.

DAVID FOWLER

Official USGS Magnitude Readings

The U.S. Geological Survey initially recorded the earthquake of October 1989 as measuring 6.9 on the Richter scale. After further study it was upgraded to 7.1. This is the official bulletin on the earthquake issued shortly after the disaster:

"The following is a release by the United States Geological Survey, National Earthquake Information Center: A strong earthquake occurred in the Santa Cruz area of California at 6:04 p.m. MDT today, Oct. 17, 1989. The magnitude was computed at 6.9 on the Richter scale. The quake was recorded by the U.S. Geological Survey at Golden, Colorado. Damage and casualties have occurred in the San Francisco Bay Area. The quake was felt as far away as western Nevada."

From the Weekly Earthquake Report for the San Francisco Bay Area Following the 1989 Earthquake

"People must not be lulled into believing that because we have had one large earthquake, we are now safe for a while. Quite the contrary is true—if anything, Loma Prieta increased the likelihood of another large earthquake in the Bay Area in the years ahead.

"Furthermore, in 1865 there was a M6.5 earthquake on the same segment of the San Andreas that produced the recent Loma Prieta event—it was followed three years later by a M7 earthquake on the Hayward fault.

"We have no way of knowing if that scenario will be repeated this time, but the people of the Bay Area must realize that such a possibility exists, and that it is up to them, and their elected officials, to take steps now to reduce the loss of life, and economic disruption, when (not if) another large earthquake strikes the Bay Area.

"Even worse, because such an event would be much closer to the major metropolitan areas, it will result in much greater levels of damage, and many more casualties, than Loma Prieta did."

DR. ALLAN LINDH,
USGS Seismologist

Great Earthquake and Fire of April 18, 1906

- Time: 5:12:06 a.m.
- Magnitude: 8.25 Richter scale
(A new analysis of seismic data by Hiroo Kanamori, of the California Institute of Technology, rates the 1906 earthquake at 7.9)

- Duration: 48 seconds
- Fire temperature: 2,700 degrees. Fifty-two original fires were officially reported, more than 300 water main breaks and over 23,000 service pipes broken
- Buildings destroyed by fire: 28,000
- Area of destruction: 4.05 square miles or 2,593 acres
- Gas and electric arc street lamps destroyed: 2,465 gas; 180 electric arc
- Cost of destruction: $1,000,000,000 in 1906 dollars, according to fire insurance estimates
- Amount of rubble: 10 to 11 million cubic yards were removed before reconstruction began
- Air temperature: 8:00 a.m., 51.5 degrees F; 8:00 p.m., 61.8 degrees F
- Deaths:
City officials took an extremely conservative view when counting casualties. The standard applied called for counting only those victims whose bodies were recovered within the city. Not counted were those who died in other cities or, in some cases, other states nor where deaths were caused by indirect effects of the earthquake.
- The official 1906 toll:
Killed outright. 315
Shot for crime 6
Shot by mistake 1
Missing 352
Total 674

Gladys Hansen, as Archivist for the City and county of San Francisco, found that earthquake injuries and deaths resulting from causes other than "killed outright" or "shot" were not counted. In 1987, Donald Cheu, M.D., F.A.C.S., a member of the Governor's Earthquake Task Force, developed a new standard for defining earthquake deaths. Dr. Cheu's definition included direct casualties caused by falling structures or other objects, burns, and explosions within one year of the event. His indirect casualty definition included suicides, injuries caused by other than falling objects, and unsanitary conditions caused by the earthquake.

The death toll using this new definition is more than 3,000 dead.

The 1994 Northridge earthquake in Southern California highlights the confusion on death statistics. The official death toll, tallied by the Governor's Office of Emergency Services, stood at 58 as of July 1994. However, the state paid out funeral benefits for at least 117 additional deaths certified by physicians as earthquake related. Causes included Valley Fever, heart attacks, and suicides. With these additional certified deaths, Northridge earthquake fatalities would rise to 175, or approximately two-thirds higher than the official death toll.

It should be noted that the additional 117 counts only those victims whose families asked for state assistance for burial expenses and, therefore, would not be statistically conclusive.

California Earthquakes —The Big Picture

California is earthquake country because of large-scale geologic activity along the edge of the North American continent. Because of convection and ocean-floor spreading, almost the entire Pacific Ocean floor is moving slowly northwest. A small spreading zone formed beneath the edge of North America has broken Baja California away from the continent, creating the Gulf of California. Further north, the San Andreas Fault forms the boundary between the continent and a northwest-moving sliver of coastal California.

The periodic release of continually building stress along the fault system causes earthquakes. In the San Francisco Bay Area, a series of active faults fan out from the San Andreas Fault, and cause additional earthquakes. Further north, off Oregon and Washington, a local spreading center has created the local coast range and the inland row of Cascade Range volcanoes.

MICHAEL D. LAMPEN

Earthquake Saint

"Soon after the earthquake of 1868, the feast-day of St. Emidius (August 9) was set apart as a day of prayers for protection against Earthquakes by Pope Pius IX on the request of the Archbishop of California."

ARCHBISHOP ALEMANY

March 22, 1957, Earthquake

The strongest shock since the 1906 earthquake was experienced by San Francisco and the Bay Area at 11:45:20 on the morning of Friday, March 22, 1957. It registered 5.3 on the Richter scale and, for a whole new generation of the local population, it was the greatest earthquake they had ever experienced. Earlier in the day two other quakes had been felt. The first, at 8:38 a.m., was 3 on the Richter scale, and the second, at 10:48 a.m., registered 3.75.

No lives were lost, there were no serious injuries, and structural damage to homes was slight, although a large number of homes in the Westlake-Palisades-Daly City area suffered more or less superficial damage, generally confined to exterior plaster. Damage to buildings in San Francisco was noted throughout the city, but was most extensive in the western portions.

Mercalli Earthquake Intensity Scale

This scale from 1 to 12 can be used in populated areas to judge the strength of earthquakes before the official Richter reading is given.

1. Not felt except by a very few under especially favorable conditions.

2. Felt only by those at rest on upper floors. Delicately suspended objects may swing.

3. Noticeably felt indoors on upper floors. Automobiles may rock slightly. Vibration like passing of truck.

4. Felt indoors by many, few outdoors. Dishes, windows, doors disturbed; walls make creaking sound. Standing motorcars rocked noticeably.

5. Felt by nearly everyone. Some windows,

dishes broken; a few instances of cracked plaster. Pendulum clocks may stop.

6. Felt by all. Heavy furniture may move; a few instances of fallen plaster or damaged chimneys. Damage slight.

7. Everybody runs outdoors. Damage negligible in buildings of good design and construction; slight to moderate in well-built ordinary structures; considerable in poorly built or badly designed structures; some chimneys broken. Felt by those in automobiles.

8. Damage slight in specially designed structures; considerable in ordinary buildings, with partial collapse; great in poorly built structures. Panel walls thrown out of frame structures. Fall of chimneys, factory stacks, columns, monuments, walls. Heavy furniture overturned. Sand and mud ejected in small amounts. Changes in well water. Persons driving automobiles disturbed.

9. Damage considerable in specially designed structures; well-designed frame structures thrown out of plumb; great in substantial buildings, with partial collapse. Buildings shifted off foundations. Ground cracked conspicuously. Underground pipes broken

10. Some well-built wooden structures destroyed; most masonry and frame structures destroyed with foundations; ground badly cracked. Rails bent. Landslides considerable from river banks and steep slopes. Shifted sand and mud. Water splashed over banks.

11. Few, if any, masonry structures remain standing. Bridges destroyed. Broad fissures in ground. Underground pipelines completely out of service. Earth slumps and land slips in soft ground. Rails bent greatly.

12. Damage total. Waves seen on ground surfaces. Lines of sight and level distorted. Objects thrown upward into air.

October 21, 1868, Earthquake

"The Results and Lessons of the Earthquake" October 21, 1868, 7:53 a.m.

"The State was visited yesterday by an earthquake, and the shock in San Francisco was the most severe felt here since the foundation of the Mission, ninety-two years ago, with perhaps one exception, in 1808, when several adobe walls were thrown down, but of that shock we know so little that it is impossible to make any satisfactory comparison with it.

"Amidst the multitude of slight movements of the earth's surface observed here since 1848, the only one which did any damage before that of yesterday occurred on the 8th of October, 1865, when several cornices and parts of green brick walls were thrown down. In that shock the motion was mainly perpendicular, and perhaps it was for that reason that the amount of glass broken was far greater in 1865 than in the horizontal movement of 1868. On the other hand, more cornices were thrown down yesterday.

"The main facts of the earthquake as felt in this city, are that four persons were killed by the falling of cornices and chimneys, that a dozen brick buildings on made ground are shattered so that they are untenantable; that the cornices of two buildings have been thrown down, and many walls cracked, much plastering loosened and many window panes broken.

"On the other hand, no person was seriously injured in a house, and the great majority of the buildings on the natural upland show no signs of having been damaged in the least.

"The spires of the churches, towers of the Masonic Temple, Merchants Exchange and Synagogue Emanuel, the four and five story buildings on Montgomery and Kearny Streets, are uninjured.

"The foundation of buildings should, on the made ground, be as solid as possible; and high chimneys should be secured by iron bars, fastened on with bands and running down below to top of wall. Brick buildings should be tied together by strong iron rods, their walls should be thick, the best best mortar should be used and the height should not exceed three stories."

DAILY ALTA CALIFORNIA,
October 22, 1868

Post Office Quakeproofing

The San Francisco Post Office and Courthouse is the largest and heaviest building in the United States ever equipped with an earthquake isolation system.

The 60,000-ton building was lifted from its foundation by hydraulic jacks and 256 steel columns were cut. Engineers then installed a friction pendulum system with a shallow metal bowl attached upside down to each column. A metal bearing or ball was then placed on a portion of the column extending from the foundation, and the building was lowered.

Scientists expect the building will move back and forth, like a pendulum, on these metal bearings during an earthquake rather than shake itself to pieces.

The building was seriously damaged in the 1906 and 1989 earthquakes.

DAVID FOWLER

RICHTER SCALE

Magnitude	Equivalent TNT Energy
1.0	.6 pounds
1.5	.2 pounds
2.0	13 pounds
2.5	.63 pounds
3.0	397 pounds
3.5	1,990 pounds
4.0	.6 tons
4.5	.32 tons
5.0	199 tons
5.5	1,000 tons
6.0	6,270 tons
6.5	31,550 tons
7.0	199,000 tons
7.5	1,000,000 tons
8.0	6,270,000 tons
8.5	31,550,000 tons
9.0	199,000,000 tons

BASED ON CALIFORNIA DIVISION OF MINES AND GEOLOGY DATA

TEN LARGEST EARTHQUAKES IN THE CONTIGUOUS UNITED STATES

MAGNITUDE	DATE	LOCATION
8.25	April 18, 1906	SAN FRANCISCO, CALIFORNIA
8.2	Feb. 7, 1812	NEW MADRID, MISSOURI
8.0	Dec. 16, 1811	NEW MADRID, MISSOURI
7.9	Jan. 9, 1857	FORT TEJON, CALIFORNIA
7.8	Jan. 23, 1812	NEW MADRID, MISSOURI
7.8	Mar. 26, 1872	OWENS VALLEY, CALIFORNIA
7.8	Oct. 3, 1915	PLEASANT VALLEY, NEVADA
7.8	July 21, 1952	KERN COUNTY, CALIFORNIA
7.7	Aug. 31, 1886	CHARLESTON, SOUTH CAROLINA
7.6	Dec. 16, 1811	NEW MADRID, MISSOURI

TEN LARGEST EARTHQUAKES IN THE UNITED STATES

MAGNITUDE	DATE	LOCATION
9.2	March 28, 1964	PRINCE WILLIAM SOUND, ALASKA
8.6	Sept. 10, 1899	YAKUTAT BAY, ALASKA
8.3	Sept. 4, 1899	YAKUTAT BAY, ALASKA
8.3	Oct. 9, 1900	CAPE YAKATAGA, ALASKA
8.3	June 2, 1903	CAPE PROVIDENCE, ALASKA
8.3	Nov. 10, 1938	EAST OF SHUMAGIN ISLANDS, ALASKA
8.25	April 18, 1906	SAN FRANCISCO, CALIFORNIA
8.2	Feb. 7, 1812	NEW MADRID, MISSOURI
8.1	Mar. 9, 1957	ANDREANOF ISLANDS, ALASKA
8.0	Dec. 16, 1811	NEW MADRID, MISSOURI

SOURCE: U.S. GEOLOGICAL SURVEY

17 Fairs/1894—1940

California Midwinter International Exposition
January 27–July 4, 1894
Admission: 50 cents adults,
25 cents children (ages 6–12)

While in Chicago as National Commissioner at large to the Columbian Exposition of 1893, Michael H. de Young conceived the idea of a similar exposition for San Francisco. It was San Francisco's first World Fair.

During the month of June citizen meetings were held, presided over by the Mayor. The State Board of Trade took favorable action, committees were appointed, and a plan of organization adopted. M. H. de Young was created President and Director General; Irwin C. Stump, Vice President; and R. Cornely, Associate Director-General in charge of Foreign Affairs. On July 10, Concert Valley, in the heart of Golden Gate Park, was selected as the site of the California Midwinter International Exposition. Ground was broken on August 24, 1893, at the spot where the bronze statue "Roman Gladiator" now stands in front of the de Young Museum. After the task of grading and leveling had been completed, the erection of the five large buildings was commenced. They were situated on the four sides of a quadrangle, called the Grand Court, in the center of which was the Electric Tower, which rose 266 feet into the air. Within the quadrangle the grounds were laid out in terraces, and planted with palms and other semitropical plants. Outside the exhibition buildings were located the various concessions and county buildings.

The following foreign nations participated in the exposition which opened January 27, 1894: Brazil, France, Ottoman Empire, Oriental Countries, Serbia, Montenegro and Roumania, Canada, Austro-Hungary, Great Britain, Italy, Russia, Portugal, Siam, Spain, Switzerland, Belgium, Hawaii, and Japan.

Besides the California counties which displayed, there were four states which added colorful exhibits to this first fair. They were: Nevada, Utah, Montana, and Arizona.

Filled-in for fun. What is now the Marina District was tidal lands until construction of the Panama-Pacific International Exposition of 1915. The Tower of Jewels dominates this picture taken during construction in early 1915. The two light-colored domes immediately to its right mark the site of some of the worst damage during the 1989 earthquake. The amusement center in the foreground was known as "The Zone" and was most popular.

Music of the Midwinter Fair, 1894

"Our International Expositions, A Bit of Reminiscence and Brief Resume"

[Editor's Note: With the Golden Gate International Exposition in full swing, it occurred to us that stories of our international expositions, past and present, by our own historian, Caesar Brand, would provide interesting reading material and striking comparisons. We approached Caesar and found him in a most receptive mood. With ye scribe of the Old Guard, writing in his most masterful manner, and so willing to open up his storehouse of memories, facts, fancies and familiar names and faces of the past and present, we present with pride and pleasure this series of articles in which the reader may sit back and, in his mind's eye, see the musical history of San Francisco's fairs pass by on parade.]

The Midwinter Fair of 1894

This enterprise was a private one, conceived by M. H. de Young of the *Chronicle* and others. The thought of it undoubtedly emanated from the Chicago Exposition in 1893. It was a very interesting fair, not as vast as later ones, of course, but there was a lot going on nevertheless. Some of the buildings remained and only very recently the Tower burned down. If I remember correctly the Japanese Tea Garden and also the older Museum hail from the Midwinter Fair.

It was opened on January 27, 1894, the original date having been set for New Year's Day of that year, the inclement weather doubtlessly having delayed the opening.

From the standpoint of music, the record of the Midwinter Fair was most creditable. The General Music Director was Dr. H. J. Stewart, a very good musician, an eminent

Captive balloon photograph of the 1894 Midwinter Fair held in Golden Gate Park. The Horticultural and Agricultural Building is at the right, where the Asian Art Museum now stands. The Mechanical Arts Building on the left is the site of the California Academy of Sciences. The Grand Concourse was dominated by the electric tower and cafe.

organist, and a man not confined, as to his efforts musically, merely in one sphere, for Dr. Stewart's standing was high as regards to religious music. He was organist at Trinity Church and perhaps other churches of the city, was composer of masses and music of like character, but he also composed several meritorious melodic comic operas, two of these being written for the annual production of the San Francisco Art Association. These were "Bluff King Hal" and "His Majesty." In 1899 he wrote "The Conspirators," which was also produced in San Francisco.

The standing Midwinter Fair Exposition Band was under the direction of Charles H. Cassasa, who is still with us, and composed of the best men available then. Soloists were Hugo Schmidt (cornet, later with Victor Herbert), J. Morrelli, John A. Keogh (clarinet). The latter is also among those present as is Louis Klotz (euphonium). Then there was F. K. Tobin (trombone). This is merely mentioning a few.

The prominent visiting bands were the Iowa State Band, with Fred Phinney, bandmaster, and Sousa's Band, with the popular John Philip at its head. Probably the musical factor that contributed the most toward the development of music in this region was the body of some fifty men brought to the Vienna Prater under Fritz Scheel. This was a first-class organization, being both an orchestra of symphony proportions as well as a concert band, for most of the string players doubled in reed or brass. It may be truthfully stated that Fritz Scheel, who stayed here for several years, was certainly a developing figure, musically speaking. Quite a few of his men also located here and contributed their share as to activities. There was John Marquardt (violinist and concertmaster), his wife Mme. Breitschuck Marquardt (harp), Franz Hell (Fluegel horn), Grienauer (cello), Lehnert (trumpet), Bates (cornet), Adelman and Overbeck (percussion). All of these located here.

Others who made temporary stays were Bernard Mollenhauer (violin), Schuy (viola), Reiter (horn). I do not remember whether Fritsche (clarinet), remained for any length of time after the Fair, but Rodemann (flute) did locate also.

Fritz Scheel was a fine musician. He had come to this country with Carl Ziehrer's Viennese Orchestra to the Chicago Exposition of 1893 as assistant director, I believe. He had been concertmaster for Hans Von Buelow in Europe and could handle and direct every variety of music. His programs at the Vienna Prater, and later at his popular concerts at the Alhambra, Eddy and Jones streets, likewise his symphonic efforts, were first class in every respect.

From here Scheel went to Philadelphia where he lifted the Philadelphia Symphony Orchestra out of a rut, and he was on the verge to crash into New York when he died. His flutist, August Rodemann, was his assistant in the East, I believe, and also handled the orchestra for a short period. I spoke to Rodemann in New York in 1930. He was then a member of Goldman's Band, probably just for the annual summer season.

Besides these major musical attractions there were men employed at the Royal Roumanian Pavilion, at Boone's Wild Animal Arena, in the Forty-nine Camp and others. Besides, there was a very popular resort just outside the Fair Grounds, Papa Seidl's, where a small but excellent group played. At Boone's show "Bill" Belard played. It may be also stated that Florenz Ziegfeld practically made his start at this Fair through his handling of Sandow, the strong man.

Some of our members played there in the orchestra, among them, Max Nelson, and when Ziegfeld took Sandow East, Genaro Saldierna and Charley Prince were among those who went along. Prince stayed many years, but Saldierna returned after some eight years and continued his activities mostly here. He passed away in 1920 and

Prince died a year or so ago. He also spent his last years here.

The Midwinter Exposition, or, as we called it, the Midwinter Fair, has pleasant recollections for all those who attended it, because it was an entertaining affair, and musically, it can hold up its head with any like function at any time for it certainly contributed its share toward the city's development in the music line.

CAESAR BRAND

From *The Musical News*, Official Journal of the Musicians' Union, Local Six, A. F. of M. 1938.

～～～

Panama-Pacific International Exposition
February 20, 1915–December 4, 1915
Admission: 50 cents adults,
        25 cents children (ages 5–12)

On December 29, 1909 President William Howard Taft said, "San Francisco has shown such a spirit that if the exposition is held there it will be a great success." Within five years, lacking three days, San Francisco the stricken city of 1906, had, Phoenix-like, risen from her ashes and been officially chosen as the place in which to hold an Exposition to commemorate the completion of the Panama Canal.

The location was the "Harbor View" site, now the Marina District. It was a natural amphitheater with a floor about three miles long and from a third to a half-mile wide, backed by the hills of Pacific Heights, and flanked at each end by government reservations. The grounds comprised 635 acres, divided into three sections. In the center were grouped the 11 great exhibit palaces and Festival Hall. To the west, spreading fan-shaped along the bay, were located the pavilions of foreign nations and the buildings of the States, while still beyond these were the livestock exhibit buildings and racetrack, covering 65 acres, the aviation field, and the drill field. To the east of the exhibit palaces were the amusement concessions known as "The Zone." The Exposition established a record in the history of world expositions by being structurally complete three months beforehand, and completely ready on the opening day, February 20, 1915.

The following foreign nations participated in the Exposition:

Argentina, Australia, Austria, Bolivia, Brazil, Bulgaria, Canada, China, Cuba, Denmark, Germany, Great Britain, Holland, India, Italy, Japan, New Zealand, Norway, Panama, Persia, Portugal, Siam, Spain, and Sweden.

There were 43 states and territories counted as participants. Among these were:

Alabama, Arizona, Arkansas, California, Colorado, Delaware, Florida, Georgia, Hawaii, Idaho, Illinois, Indiana, Iowa, Kansas, Kentucky, Louisiana, Maryland, Massachusetts, Michigan, Mississippi, Missouri, Montana, Nebraska, Nevada, New Jersey, New York, North Carolina, North Dakota, Ohio, Oklahoma, Oregon, Pennsylvania, Philippines, Rhode Island, South Carolina, Tennessee, Texas, and Utah.

The Exposition had attracted 18,876,438 persons when it closed December 4, 1915, with a reading of a toast from President Woodrow Wilson:

"The Panama-Pacific International Exposition:

"Which in its conception and successful accomplishment gave striking evidence of the practical genius and artistic taste of America;

"Which in its unusual and interesting exhibits afforded impressive illustration of the development of the arts of peace; and

"Which in its motive and object was eloquent of the new spirit which is to unite East and West and make all the world partners in the common enterprises of progress and humanity."

What Was Said About the 1915 Exposition

"They who built this Panama-Pacific Exposition were so wise in adopting all the good features and avoiding those which marred the preceding ones that to me it seems as near perfection as the mind and hand of man have ever wrought. This is the university of the world. It has a chair fully endowed to meet the wants and needs of each. The eye, the ear, the mind, the heart, the soul, each may have its horizon here enlarged."

VICE-PRESIDENT THOMAS R. MARSHALL

"I am really sorry that the English language is so mean in superlatives that I cannot tell you thoroughly what I think of your Exposition. You have an Exposition which, more than any other Exposition we have had in all these years, is conceived in a spirit of the finest art, and executed with the highest degree of intelligence."

WILLIAM G. MCADOO
Secretary of the Treasury

"It is the greatest revelation of beauty that has ever been seen on earth."

EDWIN MARKHAM

"It is indescribably beautiful. It is so beautiful that it gives you a choky feeling in your throat as you look at it."

NEW YORK WORLD

Golden Gate International Exposition
February 18, 1939–October 6, 1939
Reopened May 25–September 29, 1940
Admission: 50 cents adults,
25 cents children under 12

President Franklin D. Roosevelt said in his 1938 visit to Treasure Island, "I think you people out here on the Pacific Coast, when you start to do something, do it better than anyone else in the United States."

He was speaking of the nearly completed Golden Gate International Exposition which was to commemorate the completion of the Golden Gate and San Francisco Bay bridges and to be held on a man-made island dredged out of San Francisco Bay.

Mayor Angelo J. Rossi in his opening day greeting to Exposition visitors on February 18, 1939, said, in part:

"To us is given the honor and responsibility of staging the Golden Gate International Exposition and acting as host city in welcoming the world to participate in a celebration dedicated to the future of the Pacific empire.

"In the spirit of western hospitality we invite the world to share the beauty and grandeur of Treasure Island in 1939.

"As chief executive of the host city, it affords me genuine pleasure to assure visitors that a heartfelt welcome awaits their coming to the Exposition. Speaking for the citizenry of San Francisco, we look forward to upholding western tradition of cordiality and friendship. We know that the journey will be worth while, that the visit will be replete with interest and entertainment, and that memories will be stored with treasures of the Golden Gate International Exposition and the attractions of California and the west's vacationlands."

The Exposition closed October 6, 1939, and reopened May 25, 1940, as a new "streamlined" exposition. The 1940 Fair was a new venture in the old buildings on the old site. A new plan of operations had to be created; new attractions had to be secured; old structures had to be given new beauty and color. The 1940 management had four months to conceive and build an entirely new and different show. When the Exposition closed on September 29, 1940, more than 17 million visitors had been attracted to the Treasure Island fairs.

1939 State and Territorial Participation

Arizona	Nevada
California	New Mexico
Colorado	Oregon
Idaho	Territory of Hawaii
Illinois	Utah
Missouri	Washington
Montana	Wyoming

1939 Foreign Participation

Argentina	Japan
Australia	Johore
Brazil	Mexico
British Columbia	Netherlands
Chile	Netherlands East
Colombia	Indies
Czechoslovakia	New Zealand
Denmark	Norway
Ecuador	Panama
El Salvador	Peru
France	Philippines
French Indochina	Portugal
Guatemala	Sweden
Italy	

1940 State and Territorial Participation

Arizona	Territory of Alaska
California	Territory of Hawaii
Illinois	Utah
Missouri	Washington
Nevada	
Oregon	

1940 Foreign Participation

Belgium	Malaysia
Brazil	Mexico
British India	Norway
British West Indies	Netherlands
Colombia	Netherlands East
Czechoslovakia	Indies
Denmark	Persia
Ecuador	Peru
France	Philippines
French Indochina	Portugal
Great Britain	Russia
Hungary	Switzerland
Italy	Turkey
Japan	

"The Golden Gate International Exposition was the dream of many states and cities and counties, and boys and girls and men and women. Lights are made by men in beauty and last for just a little while. Memories come from God and live forever. So will our memories of this beauty live until Time's End!"

LELAND W. CUTLER,
President, 1939 Exposition

"Yesterday's bright version of Treasure Island today becomes an enduring memory. To have added another chapter to San Francisco's prismatic history is something in which we can all take pride. 'A thing of beauty is a joy forever: Its loveliness increases; it will never Pass into nothingness' ...The feast is over and the lamps expire!"

MARSHALL DILL,
President, 1940 Exposition

18 Films

Films of San Francisco

Films photographed entirely or partly in, or about, San Francisco. Most films made before 1931 about San Francisco were B-grade films.

1914 — *Money*
Pageant of San Francisco
1915 — *A Jitney Elopement*
Fatty and Mabel at the Fair
In the Park
Madame Butterfly
Rose of the Misty Pool
Salvation Nell
The Tramp
1916 — *City of Dim Faces*
The Aryan
1917 — *The Narrow Trail*
1918 — *Amarilly of Clothesline Alley*
Finger of Justice
1919 — *Rough Riding Romance*
The Petal on the Current
1920 — *Always Audacious*
Cradle of Courage
Dinty
The Money Changers
The Testing Block

White Hands
1921 — *Big Town Roundup*
Bits of Life
Blind Hearts
Cappy Ricks
Don't Neglect Your Wife
Guile of Women
Heart of the North
Life's Greatest Questions
Men-Women-Marriage
Outside the Law
Partners of the Tide
Prisoners of Love
Shame
Tale of Two Worlds
The First Born
The Heart Line
The Night Rose
The Sea Lion
The Silent Call
Where Lights Are Low
1922 — *East Is West*
In the Name of the Law
Island Wives
Moran of the Lady Letty
Pawned

Overleaf: Clark Gable's Blackie Norton makes sweet talk with Jeanette McDonald's Mary Black at the Paradise Cafe in MGM's 1936 musical **San Francisco.**

The Ballad of Fisher's
   Boarding House
The Broadway Madonna
The Gray Dawn
The Prisoner of Zenda
The Woman He Loved

1923 — Greed
Her Accidental Husband
Man of Action
Plum Center (series)
Purple Dawn
Stepping Fast
The Abysmal Brute
The Drivin' Fool
The Flying Dutchman
The Fog
The Man Alone
The Shock
The Ten Commandments

1924 — Chalk Marks
Dorothy Vernon of Hadden Hall
Girl on the Stairs
Half a Dollar Bill
Hello Frisco
Little Robinson Crusoe
Never Say Die
Paying to the Limit
Poison
Stop at Nothing
The Man Who Never Came Back
The Roughneck
Three Days to Live
Through the Dark
Waterfront Wolves

1925 — Beauty and the Bad Man
Camille of the Barbary Coast
Easy-Going Gordon
Everlasting Whisper
Excuse Me
Going the Limit
Her Market Value
If I Marry Again
Let Women Alone
Never the Twain Shall Meet
Paths of Paradise
Pride of the Force
Proud Flesh
Ridin' Pretty

Soft Shoes
Speed Wild
The Flower of Night
The Last Edition
The Wise Virgin
Too Much Youth
Wandering Footsteps
Wedding Song

1926 — Arizona Sweepstakes
Everybody's Acting
Lawless Trails
Miss Nobody
More Pay, Less Work
Non-Stop Flight
Shadow of the Law
The Awful Truth
The Boaster
The Border Sheriff
The Buckaroo Kid
The Little Irish Girl
The Sea Wolf
Trip to Chinatown

1927 — Blood Ship
Frisco Sally Levy
Hello Frisco
Little Journey
Shanghaied
The Chinese Parrot
The Jazz Singer
Three Hours

1928 — After the Storm
Burning Daylight
Docks of New York
Hellship Bronson
In Old San Francisco
Old San Francisco
Sal of Singapore
San Francisco Nights
The Fleet's In
The Hawk's Nest
The Secret Hour
Waterfront

1929 — Behind that Curtain
Flight of the Southern Cross
Lucky Boy
Midnight on the Barbary Coast
Shanghai Rose
Smiling Guns

The Duke Steps Out
The Painted Angel
Trail of '98
Welcome Danger
Wild Orchids
1930— Just Imagine
Madonna of the Streets
Safety in Numbers
Song of the West
Son of the Gods
1931— Never the Twain Shall Meet
The Maltese Falcon
1932— Docks of San Francisco
One-Way Passage
The Hatchet Man
The Son-Daughter
1933— Frisco Jenny
King of the Jungle
Wells Fargo
1934— Fog Over Frisco
1935— Barbary Coast
Chinatown Squad
Frisco Kid
Frisco Waterfront
In Person
Mister Dynamite
Stranded
1936— After the Thin Man
China Clipper
Follow the Fleet
Klondike Annie
Night Waitress
San Francisco
1937— Alcatraz Island
San Quentin
Song of the City
The Go-Getter
The Man Who Could Work Miracles
1938— Alexander's Ragtime Band
King of Alcatraz
Mr. Wong, Detective
The Sisters
1939— Charlie Chan at Treasure Island
Fisherman's Wharf
Mr. Moto Takes a Vacation
Mr. Wong in Chinatown
The Mystery of Mr. Wong

1940— House Across the Bay
They Knew What They Wanted
They Drive By Night
1941— Golden Gate Girl
San Francisco Docks
Shadow of the Thin Man
The Maltese Falcon
The Sea Wolf
1942— Frisco Lil
Gentleman Jim
The Fleet's In
The Mad Doctor of Market Street
The Mad Martindales
This Gun for Hire
1943— Air Force
Hello Frisco, Hello
Jack London
Seven Miles from Alcatraz
Silver Queen
1944— Adventures of Mark Twain
Barbary Coast Gent
Desk Talk
Girl Rush
I Love a Soldier
Man from Frisco
The Impatient Years
Thirty Seconds Over Tokyo
Up in Arms
Waterfront
Winged Victory
1945— Adventure
Flame of the Barbary Coast
Frisco Sal
Nob Hill
Salome, Where She Danced
The Falcon in San Francisco
1946— San Quentin
Shadows over Chinatown
The Well-Groomed Bride
1947— Dark Passage
My Favorite Brunette
Night Song
Out of the Past
T-Men
1948— April Showers
Every Girl Should Be Married
I Remember Mama

Lady from Shanghai
Race Street
Raw Deal
The Time of Your Life
1949— I Married a Communist (Woman
    on Pier 13)
Impact
Thieves' Highway
Treasure of Monte Cristo
1950— All About Eve
Chinatown at Midnight
D.O.A.
Key to the City
Woman on the Run
1951— Inside Straight
The Golden Girl
The House on Telegraph Hill
The Raging Tide
1952— San Francisco Story
Sudden Fear
The Sniper
The World in His Arms
1954— Cry Vengeance
Duffy of San Quentin
Fireman, Save My Child
The Caine Mutiny
The Glenn Miller Story
The High and the Mighty
The Steel Cage
20,000 Leagues Under the Sea
1955— Battle Cry
Cell 2455, Death Row
Hell on Frisco Bay
Hit the Deck
I'll Cry Tomorrow
It Came from Beneath the Sea
1956— Around the World in Eighty Days
Revolt of Mamie Stover
The Rack
1957— Escape from San Quentin
Kiss Them for Me
Pal Joey
The Midnight Story
The Unholy Wife
1958— In Love and War
I Want to Live
The Lineup

Vertigo
1959— Night of the Quarter Moon (Flesh
    & Flame)
On the Beach
The Beat Generation (This Rebel
    Age)
The Five Pennies
1960— Pollyanna
Portrait in Black
The Subterraneans
1961— Flower Drum Song
The Pleasure of His Company
1962— Days of Wine and Roses
Experiment in Terror
Lover Come Back
How the West Was Won
The Birdman of Alcatraz
1963— Take Her, She's Mine
The Birds
1964— Good Neighbor Sam
Man's Favorite Sport
The Disorderly Orderly
Where Love Has Gone
1965— Dark Intruder
Once a Thief
1966— Crazy Quilt
Ground Zero
1967— Guess Who's Coming to Dinner
Point Blank
The Graduate
1968— Bullitt
Finian's Rainbow
Petulia
Psych-Out
The Boston Strangler
They Came to Rob Las Vegas
Yours, Mine, Ours
1969— Daddy's Gone a Hunting
Eye of the Cat
Flower Thief
Picasso Summer
Revolution
Skidoo
Take the Money and Run
The Love Bug
1970— Fools
Gimmie Shelter

The Owl and the Pussycat
They Call Me Mister Tibbs
Zabriskie Point
1971— Dirty Harry
Face of Fear
Incident in San Francisco
The Organization
THX-1138
1972— Butterflies Are Free
Dealing
Fillmore
Harold and Maude
One Is a Lonely Number
One on Top of the Other
Pete 'n' Tillie
Play It Again, Sam
Poor Devil
Steelyard Blues
That Certain Summer
The Candidate
What's Up, Doc?
1973— American Graffiti
Magnum Force
The Counselor
The Nack
1974— Freebie and the Bean
Girl on the Late, Late Show
Herbie Rides Again
Lennie
The Conversation
The Front Page
The Laughing Policeman
Towering Inferno
1975— Mr. Ricco
The Black Bird
The Killer Elite
1976— Enforcer
Family Plot
Nightmare in Blood
Street People
1977— Heroes
High Anxiety
Mr. Billion
Spectre
Telefon
The Chinatown Kid

The Domino Principle
1978— A Night Full of Rain (The End of
the World in Our Usual Bed in
a Night Full of Rain)
California Suite
Foul Play
Invasion of the Body
Snatchers
Olly Olly Oxen Free (The Great
Balloon Adventure)
Superman
The Cheap Detective
The Manitou
Who'll Stop the Rain
1979— Apocalypse Now
Chinatown Kid
Escape from Alcatraz
Hardcore
More American Graffiti
Star Trek—The Motion Picture
The Frisco Kid
The Promise
1980— Alcatraz—The Whole Shocking
Story
Baby Comes Home
Can't Stop the Music
Cardiac Arrest
Die Laughing
Heart Beat
Inside Moves
Nine to Five
Serial
Tell Me a Riddle
The Competition
Time After Time
1981— Charlie Chan and the Curse
of the Dragon Queen
Chu Chu and the Phillie Flash
Eye for an Eye
Slaughter in San Francisco
Street Music
Ticket to Heaven
1982— Brain Waves
Chan Is Missing
Cujo
Forty Eight Hours (48 HRS)

Petaluma Pride
Shoot the Moon
Star Trek II - The Wrath of Khan
Twice Upon a Time
Yes, Giorgio

1983— Hammett (recut of 1971 release)
Signal Seven
Sudden Impact
The Black Stallion Returns
The Right Stuff
Trench Coat

1984— Crackers
Dim Sum
Electric Dreams
Hard to Hold
Indiana Jones and the Temple
of Doom
No Small Affair
The Killing Fields
The Times of Harvey Milk
The Woman in Red
Thief of Hearts

1985— A View to a Kill
Brewster's Millions
Creator
Maxie
On the Edge
The Jagged Edge

1986 — Big Trouble in Little China
Flight of the Navigator
Howard the Duck
Monster in the Closet
Peggy Sue Got Married
Quicksilver
Star Trek IV—The Voyage Home
The Great Wall is a Great Wall

1987— Burglar
Innerspace
Leonard Part VI
Patty Hearst
Telephone
The Wash
Weeds

1988— Beaches
'68
The Dead Pool

The Presidio
True Believer
Tucker

1989— Eat a Bowl of Tea
Fat Man, Little Boy
Kinjite
The Virgin Machine

1990— Another 48 Hours
Flashback
Life is Cheap
Pacific Heights

1991— Class Action
Dogfight
Dying Young
The Doctor
The Doors
The Marrying Man
Split
Until the End of the World

1992— Basic Instinct
Final Analysis
Joy Ride
Kuffs
Made in America
Memoirs of an Invisible Man
Raising Cain
Sister Act
Sneakers
So I Married An Axe Murderer
Stealing America

1993— And the Band Played On
Fearless
Hearts and Souls
Homeward Bound
Mrs. Doubtfire
Robo-Cop III
Sister Act II
The Joy Luck Club

1994— (expected releases)
Being Human
Chalk
Getting Even with Dad
Golden Gate
Significant Other
Tales of the City
Unforgiven

MICHAEL D. LAMPEN

San Francisco Television Movies
(selected list)

1967— "Ironside" (pilot)
1969— "Picasso Summer"
1970— "Incident in San Francisco"
"San Francisco International"
1971— "The Cable Car Murders"
"Face of Fear"
1972— "That Certain Summer"
"Poor Devil"
"Streets of San Francisco" (pilot)
1974— "Girl on the Late, Late Show"
1975— "Barbary Coast"
1977— "Spectre"
1979— "And Baby Makes Six"
"The Golden Gate Murders"
1980— "Alcatraz—The Whole Shocking Story"
"Baby Comes Home"
"Christmas Without Snow"
1981— "Bitter Harvest"
"Fallen Angel"
"Golden Gate"
1987— "Love Among Thieves"
1991— "Streets of San Francisco"
1992— "In Love With an Older Woman"
1994— "Tales of the City"

MICHAEL D. LAMPEN

San Francisco International Film Festival

The Film Festival is a civic, nonprofit corporation, sponsored by the San Francisco Art Commission. It is the only film festival in North America that is sanctioned by the International Federation of Film Producers Associations, and has been held yearly since 1957. In the past, films have been shown at the Metro Theater, Coronet Theater, and Masonic Auditorium, the Palace of Fine Arts, and currently at the Kabuki Theater.

19 Fire Department

Volunteer Fire Department

The Volunteer Fire Department of San Francisco, which will pass out of existence as an active organization on the first of December, deserves more than a passing notice as a tribute to its worth. A city of tents and rough wooden structures, crowded together on the shores of the bay, the first large conflagration, which took place in December 1849, called the attention of citizens to the great insecurity of property from the ravages of fire. Although it was then in the height of the rainy season, the fire, which commenced in the Dennison Exchange, situated where the present City Hall stands, swept over the larger portion of the square bounded by Kearny, Washington, Montgomery and Clay streets before it was checked. It made plain to the dullest comprehension that a fire happening in the upper part of town, with the usual summer wind blowing, would consume all before it until the water's edge was reached, possibly burning shipping as well, destroying millions of property and ruining hundreds of men if not thousands. The danger was so imminent that steps were soon taken to organize a Fire Department, the germ of which was formed by the loan of several small hand engines of a now obsolete pattern, which some of the merchants had received on consignment from the Atlantic States.

DAILY ALTA CALIFORNIA,
November 16, 1866

San Francisco Fire Department

Soon after the December 24, 1849 fire, some six volunteer fire companies were organized by the citizenry of San Francisco. Many of these men had been active firemen in New York, Boston, Philadelphia, and other eastern cities before coming to this gold rush city.

The city was constructed, at this time, mostly of combustible materials in the form of wood, cloth, and canvas, which accounted for the large amount of property destroyed by the following fires:

Dec. 24, 1849	$1,000,000
May 4, 1850	$3,500,000

June 14, 1850 $3,000,000
Sept. 17, 1850 $450,000
May 3, 1851 $12,000,000
June 22, 1851 $3,000,000

The first election for Chief Engineer (Fire Chief) took place on October 19, 1850, when Frederick D. Kohler was elected to that office.

The Paid Fire Department (148 members) went into active operation on December 3, 1866. It stemmed from legislation approved by the State Legislature on March 2, 1866.

Fire Chiefs

Frederick D. Kohler,
Jan. 28, 1850–Nov. 3, 1851
Franklin E. R. Whitney,
Nov. 3, 1851; resigned Nov. 17, 1851
George H. Hossefross,
Dec. 6, 1851; resigned Oct. 1, 1853
Charles P. Duane,
Acting Chief, Oct. 1, 1853,
Chief, Dec. 5, 1853–Dec. 3, 1855
James E. Nuttman,
Dec. 3, 1855–Dec. 1, 1856
Franklin E. R. Whitney,
Dec. 1, 1856–Dec. 3, 1860
David Scannell,
Dec. 3, 1860–Dec. 3, 1866
Franklin E. R. Whitney,
Dec. 3, 1866–July 20, 1870
Charles H. Ackerson,
July 20, 1870–April 4, 1871
David Scannell,
April 4, 1871–April 22, 1873
Franklin E. R. Whitney,
April 22, 1873–Dec. 1, 1873
David Scannell,
Dec. 1, 1873–March 30, 1893
Dennis T. Sullivan,
April 4, 1893–April 22, 1906
John Dougherty*,
Acting Chief, April 18–June 15, 1906
Patrick H. Shaughnessy,
June 15, 1906–March 16, 1910
Thomas R. Murphy,
March 16, 1910–May 1929

Charles J. Brennan,**
Acting Chief, July 2, 1929,
Chief, Nov. 11, 1929–March 16, 1943
Albert J. Sullivan,
March 17, 1943–Jan. 21, 1948
Edward P. Walsh,
Jan. 21, 1948–Aug. 20, 1953
Frank P. Kelly,
Aug. 21, 1953–Nov. 13, 1956
William F. Murray*,**
Acting Chief, Nov. 13, 1956,
Chief, Dec. 16, 1956–Jan. 4, 1971
Keith Calden,
Jan. 4, 1971–March 8, 1976
Andrew C. Casper,
March 8, 1976–Aug. 1, 1982
Emmet D. Condon,
Acting Chief, Aug. 1, 1982,
Chief, Aug. 11, 1982–Jan. 8, 1987
Edward J. Phipps,
Jan. 8, 1987–Jan. 30, 1988
Michael T. Farrell,
Acting Chief, Jan. 30, 1988,
Reverted to Deputy Chief, April 14, 1988
Frederick F. Postel,
April 14, 1988–July 21, 1992
Joseph A. Medina, July 21, 1992–

First Assistant Chief Engineer Dougherty was appointed "Acting Chief Engineer" on the morning of April 18, 1906, by Mayor Schmitz after Chief Sullivan was mortally wounded during the earthquake.

**When ill health forced Chief Brennan's retirement he was appointed "Fire Chief Emeritus"—the first award of its kind in United States fire fighting circles—receiving a gold badge and scroll and title of "Chief Emeritus"*

***Fire Chief Emeritus.*

First Fire Engine

The first apparatus used to extinguish fires in San Francisco was an old engine imported in 1848 from Honolulu by the firm of Starkey, Janion & Co. This engine was named the "Oahu," and was loaned to Howard Company, No. 3. The first fire which occurred in San Francisco took place

Lillie Hitchcock Coit loved to chase fires, the bane of early redwood-built San Francisco. A wealthy socialite, this lady made it her cause to aid and supply the firefighters, many of whom were volunteers. After her death, her fortune built Coit Tower and a bronze statue in Washington Square Park to memorialize the courageous fire fighters.

SAN FRANCISCO'S VINTAGE FIREHOUSES

ADDRESS	DATE COMPANY ORGANIZED OR BUILDING WENT INTO SERVICE
1458 Valencia St.	Engine 13. 1884 (oldest standing)
52 Waller St.	Corporation Yard-Storehouse 1886
	Engine 19. 1893
1152 Oak St.	Engine 21 & Truck 6. 1893
3022 Washington St.	Engine 23. 1894
1757 Waller St.	Engine 30, later Chemical
	Engine 5 & Truck 12. 1895
117 Broad St.	Engine 33. 1896
1348 10th Ave.	Chemical Engine 2,
	later Engine 22 1899
3160 16th St.	Engine 7. 1908
147 Natoma St.	Underwriter's Fire Patrol 1908
460 Bush St.	Engine 2. 1908
1088 Green St.	Engine 3. 1908
3816 22nd St.	Chemical Engine 44 1909
451 Pacific Ave.	Engine 1. 1909
1249 Clayton St.	Engine 40. 1909
724 Brazil St.	Engine 43. 1911
1298 Girard St.	Engine 44, now Station 44 . . . . 1913 (oldest active)
100 Hoffman Ave.	Engine 24, now Station 24 1914
798 Wisconsin St.	Engine 48, now Station 37 1914
2501 25th St.	Engine 37. 1917
870 Bush St.	Chief's Residence 1922
909 Tennessee St.	Former Engine 16 1926

in June 1849 at North Beach, in the vicinity of the present County Hospital. The damage was small, it being confined to the structure in which the fire commenced.

DAILY ALTA CALIFORNIA,
November 16, 1866

Fire Department's "Tom Sawyer"

The original Tom Sawyer was born in New York City on January 1, 1832. He arrived in San Francisco in February 1850, and assisted in organizing Liberty Hose Company, No. 2. Tom Sawyer was an associate of Mark Twain (Samuel Clemens) in the 1860s. Mark Twain dedicated his first book to this old-time friend, who had been the inspiration for his best work. Tom Sawyer was hit by a hook and ladder truck and seriously injured on April 23, 1869.

San Francisco Firefighter's Helmets

San Francisco firefighters wear the traditional Cairns and Bro. "New Yorker" helmet, which has been modified to meet modern health and safety requirements. For a period in the 1980s the San Francisco Fire Department switched to a dark plastic "Darth Vader" helmet unfavorably reminiscent of those worn by the German Army in WW II. They were not popular and some of the helmets actually melted in fires. In the late 1980s the Department switched back to the traditional Cairns leather helmet.

This 1930 *New Yorker* magazine article explains the history of the San Francisco firefighter's helmet.

"The Eagle on the Helmet"

In our simple, childish way, we always believed that the eagle adorning a fireman's helmet meant something special—the spirit of American enterprise, maybe, or onward to victory. We were wrong. The eagle, it seems, just happened, and has no particular significance at all. Long, long, ago, around 1825 to be exact, an unknown sculptor did a commemorative figure for the grave of a volunteer fireman. You can see it in Trinity Churchyard today; it shows the hero issuing from the flames, his trumpet in one hand, a sleeping babe in the other, and, on his hat, an eagle. Now, nobody was wearing eagles at the time; it was a flight of pure fancy on the sculptor's part, but as soon as the firemen saw it they thought it was a splendid idea, and since every fire company in those days designed its own uniforms, it was widely adopted at once. It has remained on firemen's hats ever since, in spite of the fact that it has proved, frequently and conclusively, to be a dangerous and expensive ornament indeed. It sticks up in the air. It catches its beak in window sashes, on telephone wires. It is always getting dented, bent and knocked off. Every so often, some realist points out how much safer and cheaper it would be to do away with the eagle, but the firemen always refuse.

We learned all this about firemen's hats in the course of a little talk we had the other day with Mr. John Arthur Olson, of 183 Grand Street. Mr. Olson's father started making hats for firemen in 1867, and Mr. Olson himself has been at it all his life. Recently, he amalgamated with his only rivals, Cairns & Brothers, a few doors down the street; they comprise now the only firm in America in the business. Foreign firemen wear a metal helmet which weighs five pounds, but our fire laddies' hats weigh only thirty ounces. Despite this they give even better protection against falling bricks than the European ones do. They are made of stout tanned Western cowhide, a quarter of an inch thick, hand-sewed, reinforced with leather strips which rise like Gothic arches inside the crown, padded with felt. The long duckbill, or beavertail, effect which sticks out at the rear is to keep water from running down firemen's necks. Hats for battalion chiefs and higher officers, are white, everyone else's black. Hook-and-ladder companies have red leather shields (attached just under the eagle), engine companies black with white numerals, the rescue squad blue.

According to Mr. Olson, there isn't much money in making firemen's hats. They sell for eight dollars and seventy-five cents, and as it is all handwork the profit is small. Besides, they last so long—about ten years, on the average. Matter of fact, the only thing that keeps the shop busy is the business of repairing the eagles, which are always coming in for regilding, refurbishing. For fixing eagles, the standard rate is one dollar, and has been for generations.

THE NEW YORKER,
June 14, 1930

SFFD Rank and Helmet Colors

White: Chief Officer (In addition to the white helmet, chief officers wear a white turnout coat.)
White and Black: Chief's Aide (black and white on crown)
Red and White: Truck Company members (red and white on crown)
Black: Engine Company members
Light Blue: Fire Investigators
Red: Members of the Fire Commission

Resolution Establishing the Scannell Medal Fund

WHEREAS, the Board of Fire Commissioners, composed of the following gentlemen, to wit, Colin M. Boyd, John W. McDonald, Joseph Marshall, Frank T. Edwards and George T. Bohen, at a meeting of said Commissioners held on the 15th day of December, 1898, received a communication from the Chief Engineer of the Fire Department, D. T. Sullivan, calling the attention of the Commissioners to the fact that no record is kept by the Trustees of the "Scannell Medal Fund," of which he is a member, of the names of the recipients of the Scannell Medal, nor is any record made or kept of the names of other members of the Fire Department who may perform acts of bravery while in the discharge of their duty, and therein suggesting and recom-

mending that a Roll of Honor should be established for the inscription of the names of the recipients of the Scannell, or other special medal for bravery, and of others who may perform acts of valor deserving public recognition whose names may be ordered inscribed thereon by the Board of Fire Commissioners, and

WHEREAS, the secretary was at said meeting instructed to have prepared a suitable Roll of Honor in accordance therewith, therefore, be it

Resolved, that the names of each member of the Fire Department who has already been awarded a Scannell medal, and also the date of presentation, and a short synopsis of the act performed by each be, and they are hereby ordered, inscribed thereon. Be it further

Resolved, that upon the order of the Board of Fire Commissioners the name of each member of the Fire Department who may hereafter be awarded the Scannell medal, or other special medal for valor, or who may at great risk of his own life, or of great risk of serious personal injury to himself save human life, shall have their names, together with such information as may be deemed necessary inscribed thereon.

Provided, however, that a member of the Department who may save or assist in the saving of human life in the ordinary course of his duty and when no great risk of serious personal injury to himself has been taken shall not be deemed eligible to have his name inscribed thereon. Be it further

Resolved, that each person whose name is placed upon the Roll of Honor of the Fire Department shall be furnished with a suitable certificate setting forth the same, signed by the President and Secretary of the Board of Fire Commissioners, and Chief Engineer of the Department.

COLIN M. BOYD
President, Board of Fire Commissioners

Chief David Scannell died on duty of natural causes on March 30, 1893. According to a 1900 history of the Department, "By his will he left a sum of $2,000, the annual interest of which is to be applied to the purchase of suitable medals to reward firemen who have performed any meritorious service, at personal risk of their own lives, whilst in the discharge of their duty. The Chief Engineer of the fire department and the Mayor of the city are custodians of the fund. Since Chief Scannell's death, this medal has been awarded four times."

The four, as of 1900, were:

Battalion Chief John Wills,
August 20, 1896
Battalion Chief M. J. Dolan,
September 11, 1897
Firefighter James Cuminsky,
February 22, 1899
Assistant Foreman Fred Says,
February 22, 1899

The latter two awards were for actions performed at the Baldwin Hotel fire on November 23, 1898. Battalion Chiefs Wills and Dolan would later be responsible for executing the fire defense plan that saved the Mission District during the Great Earthquake and Fire of 1906.

"Every year there is a gold medal, most exquisitely designed and executed by the firm of Hammersmith & Field, that is awarded by the Commissioners to the fireman that has rescued a human life at the peril of his own. The late Chief David Scannell, at his death, bequeathed his fortune of a few thousand dollars to the Department for this purpose, and the interest on the money is used to buy the medal."

HISTORY OF THE EXEMPT FIRE DEPARTMENT,
1900

Scannell Medal Award

The following members of the San Francisco Fire Department have been awarded the Scannell Medal since 1964:

Captain Andrew K. Benton,
September 1, 1964
Firefighter William J. Azich,
September 17, 1966
Lieutenant Joseph Baggetta,
August 2, 1970
Lieutenant Sylvester J. Cotter,
April 15, 1972
Firefighter Terry Millard,
August 15, 1973
Firefighter Gerald R. Shannon,
October 17, 1989

Captain Benton was posthumously awarded the Scannell Medal for heroic actions which cost him his life in the line of duty.

The Trustees of the Scannell Medal Fund awarded the medal to Firefighter Gerald R. Shannon of Truck Co. 9 for his heroic actions following the earthquake of October 17, 1989.

In his official report, Lieutenant Vincent J. Nolan wrote, "Firefighter Shannon's heroic disregard for his own well-being in order to courageously save another's life was well above and beyond the call of duty. These actions are truly worthy of merit in the highest tradition of the City of San Francisco and the San Francisco Fire Department."

Sullivan Medal Award

This award was established December 10, 1908, with a donation from Raphael Weill, founder of the White House department store, in memory of Dennis T. Sullivan, Chief Engineer of the San Francisco Fire Department.

Chief Sullivan died as a result of injuries sustained on April 18, 1906, when the chimney of an adjoining structure fell upon the fire station on Bush near Kearny Street.

This award is for the bravest act performed by a member of the Department in the saving of human life, at the risk of his or her own life, while engaged in the performance of his or her duty as a firefighter.

The following members of the San Francisco Fire Department have been awarded the Sullivan Medal Award since 1964:

Lieutenant Joseph A. Sullivan,
January 10, 1965
Battalion Chief Herbert M. Osuna,
July 31, 1980
Firefighter Daniel R. Salazar,
February 23, 1983
Captain Robert G. Boudoures,
October 17, 1989

Battalion Chief Osuna was posthumously awarded the Sullivan Medal for heroic actions which cost him his life in the line of duty.

The Trustees of The Sullivan Medal Fund awarded this medal to Captain Robert G. Boudoures of Truck Co. 10 for his heroic actions during rescue operations in the Marina District following the earthquake of October 17, 1989. Captain Boudoures performed these rescue operations with total disregard for his personal safety and in the best tradition of the San Francico Fire Department.

FREDERICK F. POSTEL,
Chief of Department
1988–1992

Awards for Meritorious Conduct During the Earthquake and Fire, October 17, 1989

SULLIVAN MEDAL
Captain Robert G. Boudoures,
Truck No. 10

SCANNELL MEDAL
Firefighter Gerald R. Shannon,
Truck No. 9

Both firefighters did outstanding work in the rescue of a woman trapped in a collapsed structure. The building was once a four-story apartment complex that had col-

lapsed to a height of one story. While the rescue continued, the building across the street caught fire and the heat was so intense that hose lines were used to cool down the two rescuers. For their extraordinary bravery Captain Boudoures was awarded the Sullivan Medal and Firefighter Shannon was awarded the Scannell Medal.

Class A Meritorious Awards

To entitle a member of the Department to an award in this class the act must have been voluntary in relation to the saving of human life under the most adverse conditions and at extreme personal risk.

Captain Robert G. Boudoures
Captain Robert C. Jabs
Lieutenant Richard P. Allen
Firefighter Thomas R. Bailon
Firefighter Jerome M. Polizzi
Firefighter John H. Reed
Firefighter Gerald R. Shannon

Class B Meritorious Awards

To entitle a member of the Department to an award in this class the act must have been voluntary in relation to the saving of human life under the most adverse conditions and at great personal risk.

Lieutenant Jimmie T. Braden
Firefighter John J. Carvajal
Firefighter Rudolph J. Castellanos
Firefighter Howard W. Cross, Jr.
Firefighter James W. Jenkins
Firefighter Ronald R. Lewin
Firefighter Wayne A. Martin
Firefighter Siulagi L. Sala

Certificates of Commendation

Battalion Chief Gregory W. Abell
Captain Guido J. Costella
Lieutenant Gerald J. Kilroy
Lieutenant Vincent J. Nolan
Firefighter James J. Crabtree
Firefighter Eugene E. Eden
Firefighter Mark J. Johnson
Firefighter William E. Kneis

Firefighter David W. Lee
Firefighter Thomas W. Posey
Firefighter Gerald Sullivan
Firefighter James R. Vargas

Unit Citations

Lieutenant Federico J. Sanchez,
Rescue Squad No. 1
Firefighter Anthony P. Soule,
Rescue Squad No. 1
Firefighter Marty A. Ross,
Rescue Squad No. 1
Firefigher Gerald K. Scullion,
Rescue Squad No. 1

These firefighters constantly risked their lives under the worst possible fire conditions to rescue an elderly woman and to extinguish the Marina District fire in disregard for their personal safety.

Lieutenant John M. Payne,
Engine No. 3
Firefighter Andrew J. Assereto,
Engine No. 3
Firefighter Francis D. Kelly,
Engine No. 3
Firefighter Charles L. Schafer,
Engine No. 3
Lieutenant Gerald J. Kilroy,
Truck No. 3
Firefighter Ernest C. Aitken,
Truck No. 3
Firefighter Daniel R. Salazar,
Truck No. 3
Firefighter John R. Sanchez,
Truck No. 3
Firefighter Charles H. White,
Truck No. 3

These companies arrived at the Marina District fire and found collapsed structures and leaking natural gas. The officers and firefighters of Engine No. 3 and Truck No. 3 led hand lines into fallen structures and rescued trapped occupants. They were also instrumental in stopping the spread of the fire. They performed these duties in disregard for their personal safety.

Assistant Chief Harry F. Brophy,
Division No. 2
Chief's Aide Charles L. Terry, Jr.,
Division No. 2
Lieutenant John T. Conway,
Engine No. 5
Firefighter Daniel P. Aronson,
Engine No. 5
Firefighter James Hentz,
Engine No. 5
Firefighter William B. Koehler,
Engine No. 5
Lieutenant John R. Donham, Jr.,
Truck No. 5
Firefighter Thomas M. Gallegos,
Truck No. 5
Firefighter Richard I. Johnson,
Truck No. 5
Firefighter Richard W. May,
Truck No. 5
Firefighter Matthew J. McNaughton,
Truck No. 5

Under the command of Assistant Chief Brophy, these companies worked to rescue victims from fallen buildings in the Marina District that were fully charged with natural gas. These officers and firefighters risked their lives performing rescue operations while advancing hand held lines into many burning structures.

Chief's Aide Dennis W. Carroll,
Battalion No. 3
Lieutenant Joel H. Pera,
Engine No. 8
Firefighter James J. Crabtree,
Engine No. 8
Firefighter Gary E. Dolan,
Engine No. 8
Firefighter Gerald Sullivan,
Engine No. 8
Lieutenant Gerald F. Doherty,
Truck No. 8
Firefighter James L. Favero,
Truck No. 8
Firefighter Jack Fitzpatrick,
Truck No. 8

Firefighter Steven H. Hill,
Truck No. 8
Firefighter William E. Kneis,
Truck No. 8
Firefighter Derek O'Leary,
Truck No. 8

Members of Fire Station No. 8 responded to a partially collapsed five-story brick structure at Sixth and Bluxome streets. For more than an hour these firefighters worked to free victims from the rubble as aftershocks rocked the tottering structure. Their actions at this disaster exemplify teamwork and dedication to duty under the most hazardous of conditions.

Captain Robert G. Boudoures,
Truck No. 10
Firefighter John J. Carvajal,
Truck No. 10
Firefighter Joseph R. Conway,
Truck No. 10
Firefighter James W. Jenkins,
Truck No. 10
Firefighter John R. Porter,
Truck No. 10

These firefighters rescued several people from collapsed buildings and assisted Captain Boudoures and Firefighter Shannon during their lengthy rescue operations.

Lieutenant Jimmie T. Braden,
Engine No. 16
Firefighter Rudolph J. Castellanos,
Engine No. 16
Firefighter Eugene E. Eden,
Engine No. 16
Firefighter Siulagi L. Sala,
Engine No. 16

These firefighters entered many collapsed buildings, the first of which was at 2 Cervantes Boulevard, to rescue many people. Many of the structures were fully charged with natural gas and they performed these rescue operations in disregard for their personal safety.

Captain Robert C. Jabs,
Truck No. 16
Firefighter Thomas R. Bailon,
Truck No. 16
Firefighter Howard W. Cross, Jr.,
Truck No. 16
Firefighter Wayne A. Martin,
Truck No. 16
Firefighter John H. Reed,
Truck No. 16

These firefighters repeatedly entered a partially collapsed building that was ablaze on Divisadero Street and rescued several trapped victims in disregard for their personal safety. These rescues were accomplished while the crew of Truck No. 16 was surrounded by natural gas leaks and during numerous earthquake aftershocks.

Captain Guido J. Costella,
Engine No. 21
Firefighter Mario S. Ballard,
Engine No. 21
Firefighter James E. Mellberg,
Engine No. 21
Firefighter Bruce A. Navarret,
Engine No. 21

These members of Engine No. 21 provided the water from the lagoon of the Palace of Fine Arts which kept the fire from progressing along Beach Street. This action saved a great portion of the Marina District from fire.

Lieutenant King A. Strong,
Engine No. 29
Firefighter Jerry E. Butler,
Engine No. 29
Firefighter Frank J. Flores,
Engine No. 29
Firefighter Dennis M. O'Leary,
Engine No. 29

Members of Engine No. 29 responded to a partially collapsed, five-story brick structure at Sixth and Bluxome streets. For more than an hour these firefighters worked to free victims from the rubble as aftershocks rocked the tottering structure. Their actions at this disaster exemplify teamwork and dedication to duty under the most hazardous of conditions.

Lieutenant Mark S. Kearney,
Engine No. 31
Firefighter Harry M. Payne,
Engine No. 31
Firefighter George A. Saribalis,
Engine No. 31
Firefighter Richard E. Wagner,
Engine No. 31

Members of Engine No. 31 assisted the fireboat *Phoenix* as it attempted a hazardous docking at the Marina Yacht Harbor during extreme low tide. Further, this company sought out a water supply that was utilized to save several buildings in the Marina District from fire.

SAN FRANCISCO FIRE DEPARTMENT

Home of San Francisco Fire Chiefs: Dennis Sullivan Memorial

Some time after Chief Dennis T. Sullivan's death on April 22, 1906, a fund of more than $15,000 was raised by subscription to build a memorial to his memory. Building of the home was delayed until 1922 owing to differences of opinion as to a location, and the great advance in the cost of building materials. The home is situated on the north side of Bush Street near Taylor.

There is a bronze tablet on the front of the building with a picture of Chief Sullivan and the following words by famed San Francisco poet George Sterling:

"By fire shall heroes be proven
Lest virtue's gold grow dim.
And his by fire was tested,
In life's ordeal of him,
Now California renders
The laurels that he won—
Dead on the field of honor,
Her hero and her son."

Response of the San Francisco Fire Department to the Berkeley Conflagration of September 17, 1923

Extracted from the Report on the Berkeley, California, Conflagration of September 17, 1923, issued by the National Board of Fire Underwriters' Committee on Fire Prevention and Engineering Standards.

The Berkeley fire began in Wildcat Canyon around noon, and by 2:20 p.m.—spread by fierce "Santa Ana" winds—had rolled into the city limits. At 2:30 p.m., aid was requested from Oakland, Alameda, Emeryville, Piedmont, Richmond, and Hayward. The Oakland Fire Department had 13 fires burning at the time of the call and was not immediately able to provide assistance.

At 3:30 p.m., the Oakland Fire Department had not responded to the aid request, and Berkeley Chief of Department G. Sydney Rose then ". . . ordered the fire alarm operator to call assistance from San Francisco: due to congestion of the lines this call had to be put through at the Berkeley exchange under the personal supervision of Manager Glover of the Pacific Telephone and Telegraph Company," said the Underwriters' report.

"San Francisco responded to the call for aid with four engines, two hose wagons, two chemicals and one fire boat. Engines are 750-gallon pumpers, each having hose body and chemical tank: hose wagons each carried 2,000 feet of hose: chemicals having double 100-gallon tanks. Engine companies consist of 6 men each; chemical companies, 2 men each; fire boat crew, 7 men. The fire boat left the San Francisco water front at 4:15 p.m., proceeded to the Berkeley wharf and reported to Chief Rose at about 5:00 p.m. Later, after collecting a wagon load of hose, the crew of the fire boat worked a line from Engine 5 of the Oakland department west along Ridge Road to Euclid Avenue.

"Engine Companies 5 and 9, and Chemical Company 3 left the city on the 4:20 Southern Pacific Ferry, landed at the Oakland mole and reported to Chief Rose shortly after 5:00 p.m.

"Engine Company 9 was assigned to the hydrant at Vine and Oxford streets where, with the assistance of the hose company from Richmond, two 1,000-foot lines were worked along Vine and Spruce streets to Cedar Street and along Vine to Arch Street, checking the fire at both locations.

"Engine Company 5 was sent to Euclid Avenue and Ridge Road, but finding no water at that location helped control a fire at the municipal dumps at the foot of Cedar Street, following which the company was sent to the Durant Avenue fire station, working later in the evening along the east side of the burning district.

"Chemical Company 3 was sent to the Durant Avenue fire station, working later on the dump fire and the east side of the burned area.

"The remaining San Francisco companies left 20 minutes later. Engine 12 worked two 1,000-foot lines from Shattuck and University avenues until 10:00 p.m. Engine Company 2 was sent to the Durant Avenue fire station, worked at the municipal dump fire and later worked at the south-eastern corner of the burned area. Chemical Company 4, after extinguishing several roof fires, was stationed at the Regent Street fire station."

In 1991, Captain Frank Trainor of the fireboat said the company journal for September 17, 1923, as entered by Relief Pilot Flanison, reported that the fireboat departed San Francisco at 4:15 p.m. and tied up at the West Berkeley Pier at 4:45 p.m. A further notation from the relief pilot indicated that the fireboat was "ordered to go home" at 9:15 p.m., which gave the fireboat company five hours of land firefighting duty in Berkeley.

1991 Oakland-Berkeley Fire

The San Francisco Fire Department's involvement began at 12:29 p.m., Sunday, October 20, 1991, with a telephone call from Oakland Fire Alarm which requested the dispatch of two strike teams to Hiller Dr. and Tunnel Rd. in Oakland because of the conflagration then burning through the Oakland hills.

At the time of the Oakland battalion chief's order, the conflagration had jumped state Highway 24, and Oakland fire engines were believed lost or trapped within the conflagration zone. Oakland firefighters were trapped within the fire zone in the 7000 block of Marlborough Terrace, and Oakland Battalion Chief James Riley had been killed.

Fire was rolling out of the hills in some places, according to eyewitnesses. Oakland Police Sergeant Paul S. Brock said that around 11:45 a.m., ". . . Hiller Dr. just exploded—it was all over. Hiller Dr. instantly vaporized, and a big sheet of fire rolled over the area like a wave."

When the telephone call for assistance came, the S.F. Department had 41 engines, 18 trucks, two rescue squads, and a fireboat in service, with a staff of 296 on duty. Two of those truck companies were out of service on calls.

Lieutenant John F. McGreevy, watch commander at the Communications Center, was requested to send two strike teams to Oakland. Moments later, Lt. McGreevy notified Frederick F. Postel, the Chief of Department, who gave immediate approval for the response.

The initial assignment for Strike Team 1 called for San Francisco Engine Companies 1, 3, 8, 29, 36, and Battalion 3. Strike Team 2 was comprised of Engine Companies 6, 7, 13, 17, 25, and Battalion 9. The strike teams rendezvoused at Fifth and Bryant streets near an on-ramp to the San Francisco-Oakland Bay Bridge. The northbound lanes of the Golden Gate Bridge were closed for a few minutes at 5:30 p.m. to allow mutual aid companies from the north to transit the bridge and proceed through the City to the San Francisco-Oakland Bay Bridge.

Shortly after 6 p.m., Mayor Agnos asked the news media to alert people in San Francisco to watch for fires in their neighborhoods because of the increased smoke and heavy ashfall.

"I was a member of the first strike team," said Lt. King A. Strong, "and we reported with Engine 29 to the Oakland command post on Highway 24."

He and the crew of San Francisco Engine 29 were initially assigned to the heart of the conflagration zone in the area of Eustice and Golden Gate, near Broadway Terrace. The crew then led lines and put the Multiversal [water cannon] to work to fight the conflagration.

"We were sent to an intersection about a block to the west of Golden Gate. Battalion Chief Jim Tracey was there. An Oakland officer—on Battalion Chief Tracey's orders—then told us to go to Golden Gate. When we got there, we backed into the intersection and put our Multiversal to work

with water pumped from Oakland Engine 18. We also made a couple of large-line leads to houses in the area," he said.

"The fire just kept on coming, and we were losing water pressure. So, we shut down our Multiversal to keep the large lines pressurized. However, the fire jumped the street—it was on both sides of us—and it grew dark because the smoke was so intense it blocked out the sun. It felt like we were in the dead of night."

The conflagration in this area appeared to assume the characteristics of a firestorm.

"I saw embers flying; I actually saw little balls of fire flying all around in the air. You'd see fire flying everywhere; the intensity of it was incredible. I'd heard of firestorms, but this was the first time I was ever in one.

"Because of the smoke and firebrands, our efforts seemed ineffective, so I spoke with the officer of Oakland Engine 18. We decided to pull out. He wanted to drop the hose and get out, but I wanted to save our hose because we were useless without it. We picked up and drove forward through a tunnel of smoke to the light at the end. It had gotten so hot there that the fire had singed my

1991 OAKLAND-BERKELEY CONFLAGRATION STATISTICS

Deaths	25
Injuries	150
Single Family Dwellings Destroyed	2,843
Single Family Dwellings Damaged	193
Apartment Units Destroyed	433
Total Living Units Damaged or Destroyed	3,469
Total Acreage Burned by the Fire	1,520
Fire Perimeter	5.25 miles
Estimated Dollar Fire Loss	$1,537,000,000

SOURCE: OAKLAND FIRE DEPARTMENT

hair. I left Edward Ghilardi, the driver, and Firefighter Robert Muniz with the rig until the Oakland officer decided what to do with it."

The engine was backed down to a low-pressure red-top hydrant in the area of Brookside and Buena Vista after Lt. Strong and Firefighter Michael S. Estebez had left, and a one-block lead was extended to an Oakland engine, and then on to San Francisco Engine 8.

"Firefighter Estebez and I found Lt. Kearney of [San Francisco] Engine 8 working along Brookside, and we helped him make leads. We made some ready-line leads off the engine in an attempt to save some houses," said Lt. Strong. "A lot of citizens were helping us here. They were pulling lines and would hold them while we broke windows of burning structures, trying to vent them and stop the fire. We stayed for a while, but eventually left so that we could regroup with our original company."

Lieutenant Strong, an 18-year veteran of the Department, said, "It was amazing to me. It made me think of the movie *Apocalypse Now*, because of the fire burning all over the place. It was all around you—above you and below you—it is hard to describe until you see it. I'd never experienced anything so terrible. The 1989 earthquake was difficult because I had dealt with crushed bodies at the Bluxome St. collapse, but this fire was an ongoing, uncontrolled catastrophe.

"We found our engine down the hill at Brookside and Buena Vista. There was only one house on the corner that was not on fire. We took small line off the engine and stopped the fire in the garage next door. We stopped it at that one house. A citizen came up to me and said: 'It's nice that you saved that house, but the woman who lived there died last spring.'

"We left the engine and Firefighter Muniz at the corner while firefighters Estebez, Ghilardi, and I went with Engine 1 up to Margarido where they were getting ready to lay the five-inch line. We went with Engine 1 as the apparatus was backed down to find a hydrant, and we took all the line off and dragged it up to several houses. We were going from one house to another, stopping the fire whenever we could. We then lost pressure on the Oakland domestic water system, and the fire got so hot we had to back out. It was another firestorm situation. At 3:45 p.m., we began to help Hose Tender 8 lay the five-inch line and put out the portable hydrants. We then connected Engine 1 to one of the portable hydrants and led lines, and again tried to make another stand.

"At about this time, Ed Ghilardi, my driver with Engine 29, which was at Buena Vista and Brookside, called on the Department radio to find out where we were. He managed to locate us, and brought the rig up to Engine 1's location. The beacon on the engine was melted, and there were streak marks on the front from where he drove the apparatus through downed wires. To get the engine to us, he actually had to cut his way out of downed wires at one point. He backed Engine 29 down the street and gave us more hose, and then went to replace Engine 8 at the hydrant. We stayed with Engine Companies 1 and 36 for the rest of the day. We were just making leads and trying to stop the fire and make as many saves as we could.

"Someone from the Oakland department, or from the California Department of Forestry, then got the idea of going through the buildings and pulling the drapes and blinds off to keep them from catching fire from radiated heat. We also shut off the gas valves to structures that had already burned.

"When it got dark, the Red Cross came by with sandwiches and cartons of sodas for the crew. For the rest of the night, it was in and out, and from that time on it didn't seem as dangerous since the winds had finally died down. We were relieved at about 9 p.m., and were sent home at 4 a.m. because our engine would not shut down when the 'kill' switch was pulled."

Operations to Save the City of Berkeley and the Claremont Hotel

San Francisco Strike Team 2 under the direction of Battalion 9 Chief Paul J. Tabacco responded to the Claremont Hotel at Ashby and Domingo avenues.

There was extreme concern about the Claremont Hotel. If the structure caught fire it would become a conflagration-breeder and spread firebrands ahead of the main body of the firefront. Those firebrands would then spread the conflagration to downtown Berkeley.

There was historical precedent for this concern. During the Great Earthquake and Fire of 1906, the Palace Hotel at Market and New Montgomery streets became a conflagration-breeder when it burned. This was partially responsible for the destruction of much of downtown San Francisco. The Palace Hotel had an independent water supply, and its pumps and reservoirs supplied water to hydrants along Market Street used by San Francisco and Oakland engines in the attempt to stop the conflagration then burning several blocks away through the Financial District. Loss of the Palace Hotel and its water supply caused the loss of water to engines in the Financial District, and the area was then lost to conflagration.

The Claremont Hotel is said to be the second-largest wood-frame structure in the United States and had its own water supply. Evacuation of the hotel complex was begun at 11:30 a.m. by Dennis M. Tucker, a member of the Claremont's engineering staff.

Upon arrival at the hotel complex, Strike Team 2 reported to Oakland Capt. Donald R. Parker who was designated Division C commander, and had already established a staging and operations base in the hotel's parking lot. Captain Parker briefed the San Francisco officers and firefighters, and told them to establish a water curtain around the

hotel utilizing San Francisco Fire Department Multiversals, Gorter pipes [water cannons], and Oakland Truck 18's aerial water tower.

Engine crews connected to the hotel's low-pressure hydrants and then extended leads with master streams to wet thick foliage and blue gum eucalyptus trees between the hotel and the firefront.

Captain Parker felt that the unchecked firefront would soon sweep down from the canyon above the hotel and ordered Oakland Truck 18, equipped with an aerial water tower, to be placed in the mid-level parking lot to take the conflagration head-on. If this strategy failed, Battalion Chief Tabacco and Capt. Parker considered drafting from the hotel's pools to protect the structure.

"Battalion Chief Tabacco had companies in the second strike team set up a perimeter on the back side of the hotel," said Chief's Aide Michael R. Bryant, "and he told me to place one company in the employee's parking lot, and the other one on the access road next to the eucalyptus trees. He wanted the companies to basically stop the fire there if it came down that far. He also wanted the units to face away from the fire and to drive out if the fire rolled down upon them. He told them, 'Just be prepared to leave.'"

After placing apparatus in position around the hotel, Battalion Chief Tabacco climbed the steep hill and put his companies to work. He also found Hayward Battalion Chief Dennis O'Sullivan and firefighters from that department also at work along Alvarado Rd.

Battalion Chief Tabacco's strategy was to stop the northwest front of the conflagration before it attacked the hotel. He felt this strategy would also save downtown Berkeley from destruction.

Upon climbing to the first level of Alvarado Rd., Battalion Chief Tabacco saw that many of the homes there were already fully involved in fire, and some had burned to the foundations. At 1:54 p.m., Oakland

Captain Parker radioed to Oakland Fire Alarm, "This is Division Commander C. I have a report from Berkeley Fire that on Alvarado we have approximately 50 houses on fire. They're asking for evacuation." Captain Thomas F. Underwood's crew from San Francisco Engine 25, operating on foot, first attacked the fire along the 100 block of Alvarado Rd. with water pumped by his apparatus 500 feet uphill from the Claremont Hotel.

Lieutenant Roland D. Lee, the officer of San Francisco Engine 7, was first assigned to the San Francisco command post at the Claremont Hotel, and his apparatus replaced Piedmont Engine 2 which was moved up to Alvarado Rd. His crew led two lines which belonged to the Piedmont Fire Department to the Oakland aerial water tower. He then ordered the extension of almost 600 feet of line, gathered from various apparatus at the command post, up the steep hillside behind the hotel to the firefront along the 100 block of Alvarado Rd.

Downed power lines, utility poles, and firebrands—as well as the fierce lateral and downward sweep of the firefront—made movement of fire engines impossible, and hose leads were advanced with extreme difficulty in the steep and heavily wooded terrain. The heavy fire volume driven by erratic winds up to 65 mph made these excessively long leads a necessity.

At 3 p.m. Chief's Aide Bryant relayed to Central Fire Alarm Station a request from the Claremont command post for more firefighters from San Francisco. Four minutes later, he notified Battalion Chief Tabacco by Department radio that the conflagration was sweeping over the hill and was two blocks away from the Claremont Hotel. He said: "There's a heavily wooded area between us and the fire and it's roaring."

Assistant Chief John Hickey and Battalion Chief Richard Seyler arrived at about this time at the San Francisco command post. Chief Postel ordered Temporary

Battalion Chief Peter Roybal to lead an additional force of 20 recalled firefighters along with Attack Hose Tender 7 to the Claremont Hotel because of these Department radio reports of fearsome fire conditions within the conflagration zone.

Chief's Aide Bryant further advised Battalion Chief Tabacco by Department radio at 3:28 p.m. that citizen volunteers were en route from the Claremont Hotel to assist him with suppression operations along Alvarado Rd.

"They started showing up at the command post and asking, 'What can I do?' I told them to stand by for a minute, and I talked by Department radio to Battalion Chief Tabacco, and he said: 'Have them start carrying equipment up to assist units up here.' I then led them up the trail to where the chief was along Alvarado," said Chief's Aide Bryant.

These volunteers included 15 students from the University of California at Berkeley who had equipped themselves with shovels, and told hotel officials they wanted to "assist the hotel any way they could," according to Sharon Kaitner of the hotel's staff. Several of the UC students assisted in spraying the eucalyptus grove behind the building with water from the building's hose line. One student brought a cellular telephone for emergency use by firefighters. Other citizens, or "convergent volunteers," also flocked to the hotel, eager to assist in the firefighting efforts. Battalion Chief Tabacco teamed these volunteers with individual company officers.

Earlier, at 3:15 p.m., Strike Team 12 of the South Alameda County task force had taken a position at Alvarado Rd. and Alvarado Pl. Fremont Engine 1053 took the hydrant there and supplied Union City Fire Department Engine 1 and San Leandro firefighters with a line. Castro Valley Engine 5 was also part of this task force.

Captain Richard B. Dickinson of the Fremont Fire Department, commander of

Engine 1053, said, "All the lines were extended from Strike Team 12. The San Leandro engine backed into Alvarado Pl., then the Union City rig backed in, then we backed in too and took the hydrant. The fire was coming over the hill and had crested about two blocks above us."

The crew of Castro Valley Engine 5 extended lines to homes in the 100 block, and as it extinguished the fire at 111 Alvarado Rd., "We heard a woman screaming for help behind a fence so we knocked a hole in the fence and found [that] she was cornered in another yard by the fire," wrote Castro Valley Capt. Richard Brown in his report. "We knocked the fence down of the yard where she was trapped...and told her to retreat from the area. She was a photographer who was taking pictures of the oncoming fire when she got trapped. We were the strike team at Hiller Highlands," said Fremont Capt. Dickinson, "and found all the bodies, so we knew how fast this thing could move. From that point we figured it would hit us pretty quick. Over to the north of us was the stairway [Eucalyptus Path]," he said, "and my thoughts were that there were strike teams above us, but there weren't. We did a reconnaissance mission and met firefighters who were pulling lines they had taken from our rig" down the path.

San Francisco Engine 7's crew, now composed of two firefighters and two citizen volunteers, with the assistance of firefighters from Engine 13, made an initial attack upon the fires burning 633 Alvarado Rd. and the neighboring home at 637 with a line supplied by Hayward Engine 2.

This lead was pulled uphill to the rear yard of 633, but the fire volume on either side of the structure was so great that Lt. Lee extended the lead into the burning house. The crew of Engine 7 put out the fire in this building then pulled the lead out the front door to the street. The lead was about one-and-a-half blocks long. Lieutenant Lee's crew advanced the line across the street to 624 where he, Firefighter James R. Kircher, and two citizen volunteers dragged the charged line up the stairway to the porch of the burning structure. Fire had weakened the porch supports and the two firefighters fell as it collapsed. "As soon as I made some headway," said Lt. Lee, "I told them to pass the line up. Then, I went through the porch. I suffered a hip injury, and Kircher went off [injured] also with a hip injury."

Nick Bamont of Oakland, one of those citizen volunteers, grabbed Lt. Lee and Firefighter Kircher and kept them from falling farther into the opening, which saved the pair from serious injury or possible death.

Mr. Bamont said, "We threw bricks through the living room windows so we could spray in the interior of the house. Then we pulled more hose and went up on the front porch. I was helping Lt. Lee when Jim [Kircher] came up behind us. That's when the porch collapsed and Roland and the firefighter fell in the hole. There was fire under them when I pulled them out."

Fierce winds in excess of 70 mph began to push the firefront with greater speed in a northwesterly direction toward their location in the 600 block of Alvarado Rd. It swept from Gravatt Dr. above them, and in rapid succession burned homes along Grand View Dr. and Vicente Rd. to Alvarado Rd.

Battalion Chief Tabacco ordered lines extended farther up the steep hillside from 688 Alvarado Rd. in the direction of Gravatt Dr. Firefighters and citizen volunteers who pulled those lines were met with tremendous fire volume and excessively hot and dry fire-generated winds which pushed the firefront directly down upon them.

Fremont Engine 1053 had earlier been assigned to the hydrant at 115 Alvarado Rd. at the foot of Eucalyptus Path to supply lead to Union City Engine 1 and the lead to San Leandro firefighters. This three-inch lead was further extended up the hill by engine relay at about 4 p.m. Eucalyptus Path is a 1,000-foot stairway in excess of 40 percent grade which cuts across the uphill switch-back from the 100 to the 600 block of Alvarado Rd.

Pleasanton Captain Paul B. Molkenburhr with a crew of ten hiked from the 100 block of Alvarado Rd. to the top of Eucalyptus Path, leaving the apparatus at Alvarado Rd. and Bridge Rd. "We had been ordered to lay three-inch lines taken from a Castro Valley engine and extend a previously laid line farther up Eucalyptus Path."

A five-inch hoselay supervised by Hayward Battalion Chief O'Sullivan began at the foot of Eucalyptus Path and paralleled an existing three-inch line. Leads were pulled by firefighters and citizen volunteers from each end by hand and were joined along Eucalyptus Path. This effort took more than one hour and the total length of this hoselay was in excess of 2,500 feet at greater than 45 percent grade.

The air temperature recorded at the Oakland Museum was 87° F at 5 p.m.—a record—with wind speeds at the Mount Diablo reporting station in excess of 40 mph, according to Norman Hui, public service forecaster for the National Weather Service.

Chief officers O'Sullivan of Hayward and Tabacco met with Assistant Chief Hickey. They felt that a secure water supply was absolutely necessary to hold the fire-front which was then roughly 2,000 airline-feet from the Claremont Hotel. They decided that the five-inch supply line should be extended to the upper elevation of Alvarado Rd., more than one-half mile uphill from the hotel at grades sometimes in excess of 45 percent.

"I got up at the top of Alvarado Rd.," said Assistant Chief Hickey, "and there was a building fully involved. I said to myself, 'If this were in the City, I would pull a second or third [alarm].' Then I looked down the street and there were 7 or 8 other buildings in the same condition. We had lines there, but the fire jumped the street and got into

the trees and we knocked that down. Then I saw that there was a fire up to the north of us that was heading for the eucalyptus grove behind the Claremont Hotel."

An air tanker and two water-bearing helicopters were dropping strikes about one-half mile or so north of the officers.

Assistant Chief Hickey contacted the Claremont command post on the Department radio to order air strikes at their location to slow the firefront while the five-inch hose lead was extended.

Gary L. Cates, Chief of Department of Berkeley, arrived at the hotel and conferred with Oakland Capt. Parker and San Francisco Assistant Chief John Hickey about felling the two large eucalyptus groves which stood between the hotel and the head of the conflagration. They were not cut because falling trees would destroy power lines that supplied electricity to the Claremont Hotel and would have meant loss of the pumps which supplied water to wet foliage around the building.

Fifteen minutes after the call for air support, one air tanker chemical retardant drop and two helicopter water strikes hit the firefront near Alvarado Rd. and Gravatt Dr. This slowed the advancing firefront long enough to allow crews to finish the hoselay, and allow for the positioning of companies along the fire line.

Homes and structures along both sides of Alvarado Rd. between Claremont Ave. and Siler Pl. were fully involved in fire, and other homes and structures along the north-east side of the street between Siler Pl. and Gravatt Dr. were also consumed.

Lieutenant Gerald K. Scullion and his crew from San Francisco Engine 6, operating on foot, found fire wildly skipping from house to house in the area and made leads to knock down this fire.

"It was getting dark from the smoke," said Chief's Aide Bryant, "and we were advancing lines up the hillsides to try to keep the fire from coming down to the roadway. It was steep and got pretty muddy because of all the water we were pumping, and that made the hill hard to climb. The fire was high in the trees, and houses down from us were fully involved. I saw a few trees just explode; it gets your attention when they go, and you know it's not a dream—this is for real. I didn't hear them make a noise when they went, I just saw them blow up and I watched in amazement."

The conflagration swept across Alvarado Rd. from the northeast to the southwest, and it was decided by the chief officers to take a stand here and attack the firefront. This strategy was developed to keep the fire from swinging across, then running down the southwest side of the hill along Alvarado Rd. from Siler Pl. to the Claremont Hotel and then on to the city of Berkeley.

Battalion Chief Frank Cercos III had been assigned to relieve Battalion Chief Tabacco at 8 p.m. "There was enough fire for everyone," Battalion Chief Cercos said, and Battalion Chief Tabacco remained on the fire line until midnight.

Lieutenant Lee of Engine 7, operating on foot, said, "We took a lead from the fire back down to the supply provided by the Pleasanton engine," and then began to move on the firefront. This lead of three-inch hose, according to Capt. Brown of Castro Valley Engine 5, was in excess of 1,000 feet. The length of this combined five- and three-inch hoselay then was in excess of 3,500 feet at 30 to 45 percent grade.

On the orders of Hayward Battalion Chief O'Sullivan, Berkeley Lt. Richard J. Schmidt and a lieutenant from the Lawrence Berkeley Laboratory Fire Department began to move the Berkeley relief engine up Alvarado Rd. "The streets were congested with electric wires, fire equipment, firemen, and telephone poles; we knew that we would have to run out if we couldn't stop it," Lt. Schmidt wrote.

The Berkeley relief apparatus was staged at 845 Alvarado Rd. where a portable hydrant from the Hayward apparatus was dropped.

The relay engines in order were: Fremont Engine 1053 at the hydrant at the foot of Eucalyptus Path, Union City Engine 1, Pleasanton Engine 61, Hayward Engine 2, and Berkeley Relief Engine 14.

At 9:18 p.m., Battalion Chief Tabacco reported by Department radio that the conflagration jumped Alvarado Rd. Rising and erratic fire-driven winds in excess of 65 mph preheated structures and foliage, and temperatures approached 2,000° F. Large homes and large trees exploded in flame, and they would then generate firebrands which were picked up by the fierce, hot winds which, in turn, ignited other structures and trees, and soon they too would explode.

In some places aluminum engine blocks and parts of burning automobiles melted and ran into the gutter. Battalion Chief Cercos said, "The trees would simply explode. I'd never seen anything like that before." Some officers reported seeing fire devils and devilkins in the area. Pleasanton Capt. Molkenburhr saw an automobile explode from radiant heat while working in the Alvarado Rd. area.

Sometime around 10 p.m., three leads were led from the Hayward street manifold and extended farther up the hill to about 901 Alvarado Rd. near Robinson Dr. "Initially," said Battalion Chief Cercos, "there were heavy fire conditions with two homes involved in the 900 block—it was above Gravatt Dr.—and there we met personnel from Fremont, Hayward, and Novato."

Battalion Chief Cercos also said at times the conflagration's firefront almost overran firefighters along Alvarado Rd. Seven hose lines were also extended from the Berkeley engine to stop the fire in the 700 and 800 blocks of Alvarado Rd.

The battalion chief officers began to establish a fire defense perimeter along

Alvarado Rd. They deployed personnel from the various departments and citizen volunteers, and prepared to cut a fuelbreak.

Lines from the portable hydrant were swung around and attached to two Gorter pipes that Battalion Chief Tabacco special-called from the San Francisco command post. Master streams from these pipes helped knock down the fire in the 900 block.

The fire attempted to sweep up from the canyon floor. Firefighters from San Francisco, Hayward, Union City, San Leandro, Pleasanton, Fremont, Castro Valley, Novato, Berkeley, the California department of Forestry, and citizen volunteers—about 100 in all—took a stand and fought the conflagration in these extreme conditions in a successful suppression effort which lasted more than two hours.

The attack line held, and the upward sweep of the conflagration was stopped before it could destroy those homes and those left on both sides of the 600 block, as well as the remaining structures in the 700 and 800 blocks of Alvarado Rd.

Total Department equipment sent to Oakland was 11 engine companies, one truck company, two hose tenders, one attack hose tender, one mini-pumper, four chief's buggies, three vans, and one motor coach from the Municipal Railway. Fifty-four on-duty officers and firefighters—about 20 percent of the on-duty staffing—were sent to Oakland in addition to 90 officers and firefighters who were recalled to duty.

Mutual aid expenses incurred by the Department in response to the fire from October 20 to 28 included about $154,000 for the salaries of on-duty and recalled personnel, approximately $31,000 for 92 lost work days because of injuries to nine firefighters, and about $23,000 for lost, damaged, or consumed equipment. Total reimbursable cost to the Department was $225,305.92.

DAVID FOWLER

Old fire station.

20 Flags

Flags that Flew Over California

Spanish Royal Standard, 1542–1822
Cross of St. George, 1579 (Sir Francis Drake)
Spanish National Flag, 1769–1821 (Portola)
France, 1786 (10 days)
Russian American Company, 1812–1841
Argentina, 1818 (16 Days, Hupolite Bouchard)
Mexico, 1822–1846
Bear Flag, June 14–July 9, 1846
Republic of Rough and Ready, 1849 (3 months, mining town secession)
Pacific Republic, May 4, 1861 (El Monte, Confederate sympathizers)
Stars and Stripes, July 7, 1846, raised by Commodore Sloat

Municipal Flag and Motto

Mayor James Phelan, in his message to the Supervisors on January 8, 1900, recommended the Board adopt a flag for the City of San Francisco and appointed a committee to request designs.

Over 100 drawings were submitted, and on April 14, 1900, the design of John M. Gamble was adopted. The Phoenix, the crest of the city, taken from its seal, is used to symbolize the municipality. It is shown arising from the ashes of the old Consolidation Act to renewed power under the New Charter, and may be taken as an emblem of the era of prosperity in store for the city under improved conditions. This was the designer's idea, but now it is generally interpreted as meaning the rebirth after the fire of 1906.

A white flag is bordered in gold with the crest of a Phoenix bird arising from a ring of fire, and the motto, "Oro en Paz, Fierro en Guerra" (Gold in Peace, Iron in War), is written in gold on a black banner with "San Francisco" printed in blue across the lower portion of the white body of the flag.

In 1952 the original flag of handwoven heavy silk with gold filigree edges was located in the Hall of Justice. It had been entrusted to Police Chief William P. Sullivan in a May 1, 1900, ceremony. The flag was carried to safety in 1906.

Overleaf: "Gold in Peace, Iron in War" is the motto of the official flag of San Francisco.

Mayor Elmer Robinson presented the flag to the Society of California Pioneers "in order that historical value of the flag be preserved and it be displayed for the benefit of the people of San Francisco and of California."

Pavilion of American Flags

San Francisco's charming Civic Center (James Rolph, Jr. Civic Center, official name since 1941) is graced with a Pavilion of American Flags. These flags, eighteen in number, form an imposing historical corridor leading to and from the City Hall.

The flags, on their eighteen white staffs, were first flown in 1964. They are:

1 Bennington Flag. (First Stars and Stripes of the United States)
2 Betsy Ross Flag. June 14, 1777
3 Grand Union Flag. Jan. 2, 1776
4 Pine Tree Flag. 1775
5 Gadsen Flag. Dec. 3, 1776
6 Moultrie Flag. Dec. 3, 1775
7 Liberty Tree Flag. 1775
8 Continental Flag. June 17, 1775
9 Taunton Flag. 1774
10 15 Stars and Stripes. May 1, 1795
11 Lake Erie Flag. Sept. 10, 1813
12 First Official United States Flag (Old Glory). July 4, 1818
13 Lone Star Flag. Jan. 25, 1839
14 California State Flag. June 14, 1846
15 Civil War Flag. July 4, 1861
16 California 100. 1861
17 48 Stars, Flag of United States. July 4, 1912
18 50 Stars, Flag of United States. July 4, 1960

21 Gay and Lesbian

Introduction to Gay and Lesbian History

As a cosmopolitan port city, San Francisco certainly entertained its share of same-sex activities, but it was not particularly noted as a homosexual center until World War II when it served as a major port of embarkation for the Pacific theater of war. From 1941 to 1945 millions of service men and women came through the active port. Attracted by San Francisco's charm and physical beauty, many stayed after demobilization or returned later. Unpredictable anti-homosexual purges from the armed forces also deposited dishonorably discharged lesbians and gay men in San Francisco.

In addition, by the '50s, California was the one state whose courts upheld the right of homosexuals to congregate in bars and other public establishments, giving homosexuals a modicum of security, despite the continual police harassment. By the late '50s, although there were approximately thirty gay male and lesbian bars, police raids, entrapment, and blatant discrimination were taken for granted.

In the mid-'50s, the bohemian literary scene in North Beach began attracting national attention. Many of the central figures of San Francisco's beat subculture were gay men: Robert Duncan, Paul Mariah, James Broughton, and Allen Ginsberg. The hippies flocking to the Haight-Ashbury district in the summer of 1967 also no doubt contributed to the development of the San Francisco lesbian and gay subculture.

In late June 1969, the attention of the mainstream media was caught by several nights of gays retaliating against police harassment at the Stonewall Inn in New York. In the wake of the Civil Rights and anti-Vietnam War movements, the Stonewall Rebellion came to represent a national watershed which can also be used to define historical periods in San Francisco. The annual San Francisco Lesbian and Gay Pride Parade and Celebration, held the last Sunday of June to commemorate Stonewall, is now the most attended event in the city.

By the mid-'70s San Francisco had become a mecca for lesbians and gay men,

Harvey Milk in Supervisors' Chambers, San Francisco, August 1978.

either as tourists or residents. Polk Street gulch was eventually surpassed by the Castro district as the center of gay life, while Folsom Street attracted those interested in the leather and/or S&M subculture. Upper Market, Noe Valley, and the Mission remain popular residential neighborhoods for lesbians.

The AIDS crisis began striking the gay men of San Francisco in 1981. Lesbians and gay men formed many medical, educational, and fundraising organizations to combat the epidemic, some of which have served as models for other parts of the country, including the San Francisco AIDS Foundation, Mobilization Against AIDS, the AIDS Health Project, and Shanti.

Over the years, San Francisco has been home to many nationally renowned lesbian and gay figures in the arts, literature, education, politics, medicine, and other disciplines. They have all contributed to making San Francisco the "gay capital" of the world.

This brief chronology of some of the significant events in San Francisco's lesbian and gay history, while in no way comprehensive, nevertheless illuminates the development of one of the city's diverse populations.

JIM VAN BUSKIRK
Director, Gay and Lesbian Center,
San Francisco Public Library

Gay and Lesbian Chronology

APRIL 30, 1877 Alice B. Toklas born in San Francisco; later becomes Gertrude Stein's "companion" (cook, secretary, manager, nurse, and lover). Toklas and Stein are buried head-to-head at Père Lachaise cemetery in Paris.

1879 Laura deForce Gordon pencils a note stating that she is a "lover of her own sex" on a copy of her *The Great Geysers of California and How to Reach Them*, later found in the Cogswell time capsule in Washington Square Park in 1979.

MARCH 27, 1882 Oscar Wilde visits San Francisco.

1896 Robert Allan Nicol writes to Edward Carpenter, the British reformer who championed homosexual rights, "really you have quite a following in San Francisco alone."

1903 Charles Warren Stoddard writes *For the Pleasure of His Company: An Affair of the Misty City*, an early gay autobiographical novel, in San Francisco.

1908 The Dash, San Francisco's first gay bar, opens at Pacific and Kearny in the Barbary Coast.

1908 Edward Stevenson privately publishes *Intersexes: A History of Similisexualism as a Problem in Social Life*, in which he refers to incidents of soldier prostitution at the Presidio, "a garrison noted for its homosexual contingent...especially during the time of the sudden Spanish American War excitement."

JUNE 1915 Alexander Berkman, an anarchist associate of Emma Goldman, gives a public speech in San Francisco, "Homosexuality and Sex Life in Prison," attended by large crowd.

1918 Dr. Albert Abrams's "Homosexuality A Military Menace," one of the earliest medical articles on how to recognize homosexuals in the United States armed forces, is published in San Francisco.

JANUARY 11, 1919 Frederik Hammerich, 51, who had emigrated from Denmark at age 25 because of his involvement in a homosexual "scandal," commits suicide in San Francisco.

1929 Finocchio's, a speakeasy featuring entertainment by female impersonators, opens in the Barbary Coast.

1933 The Black Cat, controversial "bohemian" bar, opens at 710 Montgomery Street.

1936 Mona's, San Francisco's first lesbian bar, opens at Broadway and Columbus Avenue in North Beach.

1930S Jack's Turkish Baths and the Third Street Baths, first San Francisco homosexual bathhouses, open.

AUGUST 1944 San Francisco poet Robert Duncan acknowledges his own homosexuality and defends the humanity of homosexuals in "The Homosexual in Society," one of the first public defenses of homosexuality to appear in the United States.

1950 Sol Stuman's challenge to the State Alcoholic Beverage Control Commission's attempts to close his bar, the Black Cat, is taken to the California Supreme Court, which decided for the first time that bars cannot be discriminated against solely for catering to homosexuals.

1953 Dr. Karl M. Bowman and Bernice Engle, of the Langley Porter Clinic in San Francisco, publish "The Problem of Homosexuality," one of a number of reports during the '50s and '60s discussing the effects of castration, lobotomy, and electroshock treatment on homosexuals.

OCTOBER 19, 1955 The Daughters of Bilitis (DOB), the first lesbian organization in North America, is founded by four lesbian couples including Del Martin and Phyllis Lyon.

OCTOBER 1956 *The Ladder*, the monthly magazine of the DOB, begins publication.

1957 The Mattachine society, the early homophile organization, moves its headquarters from Los Angeles to San Francisco.

SEPTEMBER 6, 1957 Allen Ginsberg, author of *Howl*, and Lawrence Ferlinghetti, owner of City Lights Bookstore, tried on charges of selling obscene literature because of the poem's descriptions of male homosexuality.

1959 George Christopher, the incumbent mayor, and his chief of police accused by Russ Wolden during mayoral campaign of allowing San Francisco to become "the national headquarters of organized homosexuals in the United States."

MAY 1960 First national DOB convention, the first national lesbian conference, takes place in San Francisco.

MAY 3, 1960 State Alcoholic Beverage Control official caught taking a bribe from the Castaway, a Market Street gay bar, launching the controversial "gayola" scandal; officer acquitted.

1961 Guy Strait starts League for Civil Education (LCE) to organize a "gay vote" in San Francisco. Begins publishing *LCE News*, the first gay newspaper, and distributing it free in bars.

1961 José Sarria, a drag queen known as the Dowager Widow of the Emperor Norton, Empress of San Francisco, and Protectress of Mexico, kicks off his campaign for San Francisco Supervisor, receives 6500 votes, and becomes the first openly gay man to run for public office.

1961 Police arrest 81 men and 14 women at the Tay-Bush gay bar in the largest vice raid in San Francisco history.

OCTOBER 1961 First annual Beaux Arts Ball launches years of popular drag balls.

1962 Tavern Guild, the first gay business association, formed by proprietors and employees of several gay bars.

SEPTEMBER 1964 Society For Individual Rights (SIR), the largest homophile organization in the country, is formed.

DECEMBER 1964 Council on Religion and the Homosexual, the first gay religious organization, founded by the Reverend Ted McIlvenna.

JANUARY 1, 1965 New Year's Eve costume ball at California Hall to raise funds for the Council on Religion and the Homosexual is harassed by police, becoming a turning point in the San Francisco gay rights movement. ACLU takes the case, which is dismissed.

1965 Citizens Alert, a 24-hour hotline to respond to incidents of antigay police brutality, established.

1966 Several nights of window breaking and demonstrations by drag queens, gay hustlers, and others fighting for the right to be served at Compton's Cafeteria at Turk and Taylor streets.

1966 Rikki Streicher opens Maud's Study,

the world's longest surviving lesbian bar, in the Haight.

APRIL 1966 First gay community center in America, sponsored by SIR, opens on 6th Street.

MAY 21, 1966 (Armed Forces Day) "Rally to Protest Exclusion of Homosexuals from the Armed Forces" on the steps of the Federal Building.

AUGUST 22, 1966 The burgeoning National Planning Conference of Homophile Organizations, the first national convention of gay and lesbian groups, meets in San Francisco, before changing its name to North American Conference of Homophile Organizations (NACHO).

APRIL 1969 Firing of States Line Steamship company employee, Gale Whittington, because of his homosexuality, instigates formation of one of the West Coast's earliest gay liberation groups, the Commitee for Homosexual Freedom.

1970 Sally Gearhart and Rick Stokes, first open homosexuals hired by City of San Francisco, serve on Family Services Agency.

JUNE 27, 1970 Commemoration of Stonewall riots with small parade from Aquatic Park down Polk Street to City Hall.

JUNE 28, 1970 Commemoration of Stonewall riots with "gay-in" in Golden Gate Park.

APRIL 1971 *Bay Area Reporter* (BAR), the longest continuous San Francisco gay publication and one of the oldest gay newspapers in the country, is published by Bob Ross.

MAY 19, 1971 Dianne Feinstein, President of the San Francisco Board of Supervisors, speaks at SIR meeting, becoming the first city official to speak before a gay group.

FEBRUARY 8, 1972 Alice B. Toklas Democratic Club, the first gay Democratic club in California, formed from SIR political committee by Jim Foster.

APRIL 3, 1972 Board of Supervisors bans gay discrimination in municipal employment.

JUNE 25, 1972 San Francisco's first official Gay Day Parade from Kearny and Sutter to City Hall attracts thousands.

JULY 1972 The speech on behalf of gay rights given by Jim Foster, one of two San Francisco delegates to the Democratic National Convention in Miami, is nationally televised.

1974 Golden Gate Business Association, a gay and lesbian business organization, formed.

SEPTEMBER 1974 First issue of the *Journal of Homosexuality* edited by John De Cecco, who also establishes a center for the study of sexuality at San Francisco State University.

1975 The Brown Bill, AB 489, a limited gay rights bill, is passed.

1975 Billy Sipple saves President Gerald Ford during assassination attempt but loses effort to keep the press from revealing his homosexuality.

JULY 1975 First gay American Indian liberation organization, Gay American Indians, founded in San Francisco by Randy Burns and Barbara Cameron.

MAY 25, 1976 Armistead Maupin's "Tales of the City" first appears in the *San Francisco Chronicle*, becoming national bestseller when published as a book in 1978.

JANUARY 1, 1977 Theatre Rhinoceros, one of the best known and most successful gay theater companies, is founded by Alan Estes and Lanny Banquiet.

FEBRUARY 9, 1977 First Gay Film Festival of Super-8 Films, which became the San Francisco International Lesbian and Gay Film Festival, the oldest continuing lesbian and gay film festival in the world.

MAY 25, 1977 San Francisco School Board votes 7–0 to include materials on homosexuality and gay lifestyles in public school curriculum.

JUNE 21, 1977 Robert Hillsborough is murdered in the Mission District by four youths screaming, "Faggot, faggot, faggot." Mayor

Moscone orders flags flown at half-mast.

JULY 1977 Bay Area Physicians for Human Rights formed by gay doctors wanting to improve medical care for gay people.

NOVEMBER 8, 1977 Harvey Milk's election to San Francisco Board of Supervisors, reported by the national press, indicates the impact of the gay vote originally envisioned in 1961.

DECEMBER 1, 1977 *Word is Out: Stories of Some of Our Lives*, the pioneering documentary by Peter Adair and Mariposa Film Group premieres at Castro Theater.

1978 National Gay Rights Advocates, a public-interest law firm, created in San Francisco to expand and defend gay civil rights.

1978 Gilbert Baker designs the first rainbow flag, which becomes an international symbol of lesbian and gay pride.

MARCH 20, 1978 San Francisco Board of Supervisors passes "most stringent gay rights law in country." Dan White is the only supervisor to vote against.

JUNE 1978 Jon Reed Sims founds San Francisco Gay Freedom Day Marching Band & Twirling Corps, the first lesbian and gay musical organization in the world.

NOVEMBER 1978 Allen Bennett becomes the first openly gay rabbi when he is outed, with his permission, by the *San Francisco Examiner*.

NOVEMBER 7, 1978 Defeat of Proposition 6, the "Briggs Initiative," an antigay initiative sponsored by State Senator John Briggs to expel from the school system gay and lesbian teachers as well as those who present homosexuality positively.

NOVEMBER 13, 1978 San Francisco Police Department becomes first city in the United States to induct openly gay officers.

NOVEMBER 27, 1978 Mayor George Moscone and Supervisor Harvey Milk assassinated by Dan White; 20,000 hold candlelight march to City Hall.

1979 San Francisco Gay Men's Chorus, first gay chorus in America, founded.

JANUARY 8, 1979 Acting Mayor Dianne Feinstein names openly gay Harry Britt to fill Harvey Milk's seat on the San Francisco Board of Supervisors.

MARCH 31, 1979 Peg's Place, a lesbian bar on Geary Street, harassed by a group of men, including off-duty policemen.

APRIL 14, 1979 (Holy Saturday) Sisters of Perpetual Indulgence forms as a nonprofit group of social activists/philanthropists/spiritualists/drag artists.

MAY 21, 1979 "White Night" riots follow announcement of voluntary manslaughter rather than murder verdict in Dan White trial; later, as gays and police confront each other on Castro Street, police rampage erupts at Elephant Walk bar.

1980 Bay Area Career Women, largest lesbian organization in the United States, founded by Nicole Shapiro.

1980 Black and White Men Together (BWMT) founded in San Francisco.

APRIL 26, 1980 "Gay Power, Gay Politics" airs on CBS, purportedly documenting the emergence of gay political clout in San Francisco; San Francisco Board of Supervisors sends letter to CBS protesting sensationalism and poor journalistic standards.

1981 First cases of "gay cancer," called "Gay-Related Immune Deficiency" (GRID), later AIDS and HIV-disease, reported in San Francisco.

AUGUST 26, 1981 Mary Morgan is appointed by Governor Brown to San Francisco Municipal Court, becoming the first openly lesbian judge.

NOVEMBER 1981 Atlas Savings and Loan, the nation's first gay-owned bank, opens at Market and Duboce streets.

DECEMBER 10, 1981 Bobbi Campbell, registered nurse and the sixteenth San Franciscan to be diagnosed with Kaposi's sarcoma, is the first person with AIDS to go public when he proclaims himself the "KS Poster Boy" in the *San Francisco Sentinel*.

1982 Randy Shilts, reporter for the *San*

Francisco Chronicle, publishes *The Mayor of Castro Street: The Life & Times of Harvey Milk.*

AUGUST 28, 1982 First annual Gay Olympics (later called Gay Games, after a successful lawsuit by the US Olympic Committee), founded by Dr. Tom Waddell, is held at Kezar Stadium with 1,300 male and female athletes participating in 16 sports.

1983 The Bay Area Non-Partisan Alliance, largest lesbian and gay political action committee in California, founded.

JULY 15, 1984 National March for Lesbian and Gay Rights moves from Castro and Market to Moscone Center the day before the Democratic National Convention begins in San Francisco.

MARCH 15, 1985 San Francisco Bay Area Gay and Lesbian Historical Society, later the Gay and Lesbian Historical Society of Northern California, founded.

MARCH 25, 1985 *The Times of Harvey Milk*, directed by Rob Epstein, wins Academy Award for best feature documentary; producer Richard Schmiechen thanks the title character "for his courage, for his pride in being gay, and for his hope that one day we will all live together in a world of mutual respect."

1986 The Names Project AIDS Memorial Quilt founded by Cleve Jones as he creates the first panel commemorating his best friend, Mark Feldman.

JULY 21, 1986 Frances FitzGerald's two-part article on the Castro district appears in the *New Yorker*, later published in *Cities on a Hill: a Journey through Contemporary American Cultures.*

SEPTEMBER 9, 1987 James Short is awarded more than $2 million by a San Francisco jury after he broke up with his lover of 19 years, in what is considered the first gay palimony case.

JANUARY 1988 Gay Asian Pacific Alliance formed, dedicated to furthering the interest of gay and bisexual Asian/Pacific Islanders.

SPRING 1988 *OutLook*, national lesbian and gay quarterly, begins publishing.

JUNE 1989 "Gay in America," a 16-part special report, appears in *San Francisco Examiner.*

1990 Donna Hitchens becomes the first openly lesbian elected judge as well as the highest ranking openly gay elected official in California.

MARCH 1990 OutWrite '90, first national convention of lesbian and gay writers, held at Cathedral Hill Hotel.

NOVEMBER 5, 1990 "The Lavender Sweep": open lesbians Carole Migden and Roberta Achtenberg elected to San Francisco Board of Supervisors; openly gay Tom Ammiano elected to San Francisco School Board.

FEBRUARY 14, 1991 Over 275 lesbian and gay couples register at City Hall as Domestic Partners referendum goes into effect.

MAY 1991 World Premiere of *Millennium Approaches*, first part of Tony Kushner's epic, two-part play *Angels in America: A Gay Fantasia on National Themes,* commissioned by Eureka Theater, which, with *Perestroika,* wins a Pulitzer Prize.

MAY 1991 *Deneuve*, highest circulation lesbian periodical, publishes first issue.

SEPTEMBER 29, 1991 Governor Pete Wilson vetoes Senate Bill AB101, a law banning employment discrimination on the basis of sexual orientation, sparking demonstration.

OCTOBER 10, 1991 Mayor Art Agnos announces the Gay and Lesbian Center, the world's first research center devoted specifically to the documentation and study of lesbian and gay history and culture to be part of a public library, scheduled to open in new main San Francisco Public Library in early 1996.

MARCH 30, 1992 Debra Chasnoff, San Francisco filmmaker, wins an Oscar for her documentary short film *Deadly Deception: General Electric, Nuclear Weapons and*

Our Environment, becoming the first lesbian to acknowledge her partner, Kim Klausner, in her acceptance speech.

JUNE 25, 1992 First annual conference of the National Association of Gay Journalists attracts more than 200 journalists.

JUNE 3, 1993 Former San Francisco Supervisor Roberta Achtenberg sworn in as Assistant Secretary for Fair Housing and Equal Opportunity, becoming the highest-ranking open lesbian to serve in the federal government.

FEBRUARY 17, 1994 Randy Shilts, author of *The Mayor of Castro Street: The Life and Times of Harvey Milk* and *And the Band Played On*, dies of AIDS.

JIM VAN BUSKIRK

22 Geography

San Francisco Bay

- Once covered 780 sq. miles; today 540 sq. miles
- Shoreline of bay 276 miles
- Length of bay 50 miles
- San Francisco Bay is, in fact, an estuary, a mix of salt and fresh water. Sixteen rivers empty into it.
- Bays: San Pablo, Honker, Richardson, San Rafael, San Leandro, Grizzly, Suisun
- 295 Navigational aids (lights, buoys, beacons)
- Bay jurisdiction: Some nine counties and 36 cities have jurisdiction over the bay to some degree, as well as state, federal, and regional agencies, working on such issues as spills, pollution, sewage, development, parks, etc.

SUNSET MAGAZINE
Oct. 1980

San Francisco Boundaries

1834 Boundaries set down by M. G. Vallejo in 1834:

". . . commencing at the little cove at E. of the Fortaleza, following the line traced by you as far as the shore leaving the north of the Casamata and the Fortaleza; thence following the border of the said shore to the Point of Lobos on its southern side; thence following a straight line as far as the peak of the Devisadero (Lookout) continuing to the said line towards the E. as far as the Point of Rincon, embracing the Canutales and the Gentil. Said line shall terminate within the bay of the Mission Dolores, whose estuary shall serve for a natural boundary between the municipal jurisdiction of that Pueblo and the aforesaid Mission de Dolores."

1844 Boundaries related to Henry L. Ford by Captain Hinckley, Alcalde of San Francisco:

"Pueblo line commenced at a point of rocks on the coast, beyond the Presidio, and ran over in a direct line, crossing Mission Creek near its mouth, to a point of rocks or boulders, at a place known at that time, as the 'Potrero.' "

Aerial view of Ayala, or Hospital, Cove at Angel Island.

1849 Boundaries of San Francisco as related to Julius K. Rose, attorney, by Francisco Guerrero:

"The northern line of Buriburi, and the lines of Rancho de la Merced, Mr. Noe's rancho, which, I think, was called 'San Miguel'; Mr. Ridley's rancho, which I think, is called 'Visitacion,' and a rancho belonging to a Spanish woman, called I think, 'The Widow Bernal,' and the rancho known as 'the Potrero.' He described the boundaries as commencing just at the entrance of the bay at the Golden Gate, running from that point, to a hill about half a mile distant from that point; to the hill on which we stood, (Devisadero) and which is a very high, round hill, from that place to the southern extremity of Rincon Point, where it runs into Mission Bay, and from that point by the line of the bay to the Golden Gate, at the place of beginning."

(Documents, Depositions and Brief of Law Points Raised Thereon on Behalf of the United States, in Case Number 28, Before the U.S. Board of Land Commissioners. San Francisco. 1854)

1850 In the year 1850 the State Legislature defined the limits of San Francisco as follows:

"The southern boundary shall be a line two miles distant in a southerly direction from the center of Portsmouth Square, and which line shall be a parallel to the street known as Clay Street. The western boundary shall be a line one and a half miles distant in a westerly direction from the center of Portsmouth Square, and which line shall be parallel to the street known as Kearny Street. The northern and eastern shall be the same as the County of San Francisco."

1851 Boundaries of the City under act to reincorporate, passed April 18, 1851:

"On the south by a line parallel with Clay Street, two and one-half miles distant, in a southerly direction from the centre of Portsmouth Square; on the west by a line parallel with Kearny Street, two miles dis-

tant, in a westerly direction from the centre of Portsmouth Square. Its northern and eastern boundaries shall be coincident with those of the county of San Francisco."

1856 "The boundaries of the City and county of San Francisco shall be as follows: Beginning in the Pacific Ocean, three miles from the shore, and on the line (extended) of the United States Survey, separating townships two and three, south (Mount Diablo meridian) and thence running northerly and parallel with the shore so as to be three miles there from opposite Seal Rocks; thence in the same general direction to a point three miles from the shore, and on the northerly side of the entrance to the bay of San Francisco, thence to low-water mark on the northerly side of said entrance, at a point opposite Fort Point; thence following said low-water mark to a point due north-west to Golden Rock; thence due south-east to a point within three miles of the natural high water mark on the eastern shore of the bay of San Francisco; thence in a southerly direction to a point three miles from said eastern shore, and on the line first named (considered as extending across said bay), and thence along said first named line to the place of beginning. The islands in said bay, known as Alcatraces and Yerba Buena, and the island in said ocean, known as the Farallones, shall be attached to and form a part of said City and County."

(SECTION 1 - CONSOLIDATION ACT)

(Prior to the consolidation of the governments of the City and County of San Francisco, July 1, 1856, the present County of San Mateo, containing an area of 154,981 acres, formed the southerly portion of San Francisco. The County of San Mateo is bounded on the south by Santa Clara and Santa Cruz.)

1971 "Begining at the southwest corner, being the northwest corner of San Mateo, in the Pacific Ocean, on the extension of northern line of T. 3S., of Mount Diablo base; thence northerly along the Pacific Coast, to its point of intersection with the westerly extension of the low-water line on the northern side of the entrance to San Francisco Bay, being the southwest corner of Marin and northwest corner of San Francisco; thence easterly, through Point Bonita and Point Cavallo, to the most southeastern point of Angel Island, all on the line of Marin; thence northerly, along the easterly lein of Marin to the northwest point of Golden Rock (also known as Red Rock), being a common corner of Marin, Contra Costa, and San Francisco; thence due southeast four and one-half statute miles to a point established as the corner common to Contra Costa, Alameda, and San Francisco; thence southeasterly, on the western line of Alameda County to a point on the north line of T. 3S., R. 4W., M. D. B. & M.; thence westerly on the township lines and an extension thereof to the place of beginning. The islands known as the Farrallones (Farallons) are a part of said city and County."

Boundaries of San Francisco County (excluding the Farallones)

Northeast boundary line extends due southeast from Red Rock to a point three miles from the (19th century) east bay shore, due south of the western point of Brooks Island.

East central boundary line extends southward from the above point to a point 2,500 feet due east of the summit of Yerba Buena Island.

Southeast boundary line extends from the above point southeastward to a mid-bay point at 37°42'30" North Latitude, the boundary line paralleling a line linking Points Potrero and Avisadero (Hunters Point) (19th century points). The boundary line crosses a corner of the Alameda Naval Air Station on Alameda Island.

South boundary line extends from the above point due west along 37°42'30"North Latitude to a point three miles west of the ocean shore of San Francisco.

West boundary line extends northward at a distance of three miles from shore, and three miles west of a line linking Points Lobos and Bonita, to a point three miles due west of the south shore of Point Bonita, at 37°48'54" North Latitude.

Northwest boundary line extends due east along 37°48'54" to the south shore of Point Bonita, then east along the mean low water line of the Marin headlands shore to Point Cavallo. (Horseshoe Cove piers are within San Francisco County.)

North central boundary line extends northeastward from Point Cavallo to the south shore of Point Blunt, Angel Island.

North/east-side boundary line extends northward from Point Blunt, Angel Island, to Quarry Point, Angel Island, then from Quarry Point to Red Rock.

MICHAEL D. LAMPEN

A Great City

On the west coast of a large continent is a big peninsula. Built on hills at the end of a peninsula is a major port city that was once destroyed by a great earthquake and fire. A graceful twin-towered suspension bridge links the city with its suburbs across the bay. In the ocean to the west are islets called the Farrallones. The city is at 38° north latitude. its mild climate brings summer temperatures in the mid 60s and winter temperatures in the low 50s. The city is called Lisbon.

MICHAEL D. LAMPEN

Elevation of San Francisco

"In San Francisco most elevation figures refer to 'City Base,' a point established in 1850 as a point 6.7 feet above mean high tide. The Coast Survey datum was mean low water, and City Base is 11.67 feet above this point. The modern U.S. Geological

Survey datum, for the familiar quadrangle sheets, is mean sea level; San Francisco base is 8.6 feet above this datum plane. It is easy to overlook the fact that an elevation given in one place may refer to a different base than a second elevation with which it is being compared."

OFFICIAL GRADES OF THE
PUBLIC STREETS OF THE
CITY AND COUNTY OF SAN FRANCISCO,
1909

Heartburn Cities

Warner-Lambert, the manufacturer of Rolaids, provided the results of its survey seeking the heartburn capital of the United States.

10 WORST	10 BEST
(in descending order)	(in descending order)
Eureka	El Paso
San Francisco	Fort Smith, Ark.
Chico	Ada, Okla.
Santa Barbara	Colorado Springs, Col.
Sacramento	Columbia, Mo.
Boise, Idaho	St. Joseph, Mo.
Reno, Nev.	Lubbock, Texas
Fresno	Panama City, Fla.
Bakersfield	Springfield, Mo.
Seattle	Albany, Ga.

SAN FRANCISCO CHRONICLE,
June 14, 1990

Land Use in San Francisco

The topographic and climatic diversity of San Francisco is matched by a diversity of land use, which ranges from downtown skyscrapers to ocean beaches, from light industrial areas to large urban parks.

- residential
- commercial and maritime
- business and financial (largely skyscrapers)
- commercial (downtown area, tall buildings)
- hotels (near downtown) and condominium clusters (areas of tall buildings)
- government and cultural (tall buildings)
- institutional (school grounds, university campuses, hospital grounds)
- light industrial and maritime industrial with some scattered residential (includes

former Hunters Point Naval Shipyard)
- undeveloped open space in light industrial areas (largely filled land)
- military reservations
- Mission Bay complex (future residential/ commercial/business development)
- Presidio (U.S. Army reserve to become part of Golden Gate National Recreation Area parkland in 1995
- open space: public (parks, playgrounds, golf courses, lakes, beaches)
- open space: private or restricted

MICHAEL D. LAMPEN

San Francisco's Shoreline

The following lists give the current ownership and original state of San Francisco's 29.5-mile-long shoreline. Piers and inlets are not included. Islands and the Marin–Golden Gate shoreline of San Francisco County are not included. The current length of the shoreline is approximately the same as the original length, despite extensive reconfiguration.

CURRENT OWNERSHIP:
Federal, 44% (GGNRA, 40%; Army, 4%)
State, 13% (Candlestick Point State Recreation Area)
City, (Port of San Francisco, 36%; former Navy, Hunters Point Shipyard, 7%)
Private, 2% (Sea Cliff)
CURRENT STATE OF SHORELINE:
filled, 65% (port facilities, 24%; other 41%)
natural, 35% (unaltered, 22%; slightly altered, 13%)
ORIGINAL STATE OF SHORELINE:
muddy beach/mudflat, 41%
clean sand beach, 31%
rocky shore of cliff, 21%
marsh, 7%

Smallest U.S. Major City

Geographically, is San Francisco the smallest of U.S. major cities? No—Buffalo, New York—42 square miles.

MICHAEL D. LAMPEN

DISTANCE FROM SAN FRANCISCO TO MAJOR FOREIGN CITIES

CITY	MILES	KILOMETERS	CITY	MILES	KILOMETERS
Accra	5,137	8,267	Mogadishu	9,570	15,401
Addis Ababa	8,976	14,445	Monaco	5,983	9,632
Algiers	6,212	9,997	Monrovia	7,100	11,426
Amman	7,416	11,934	Montevideo	6,568	10,570
Amsterdam	5,449	8,769	Montreal	2,434	4,078
Ankara	6,840	11,008	Moscow	5,866	9,440
Asuncion	6,014	9,679	Munich	5,859	9,429
Athens	6,770	10,895	Nairobi	9,585	15,426
Baghdad	7,446	11,983	Naples	6,351	10,221
Bangkok	7,915	12,738	Nassau	2,767	4,453
Beijing	5,899	9,494	Niagara Falls	2,282	3,673
Beirut	7,283	11,721	Nicosia	7,159	11,521
Belgrade	6,275	10,099	Osaka	5,368	8,639
Berlin	5,653	9,098	Oslo	5,178	8,333
Bethlehem	7,419	11,940	Ottawa	2,433	3,915
Bogota	3,750	6,035	Palermo	6,481	10,430
Brasilia	6,067	9,764	Panama City	3,324	5,349
Brazzaville	8,899	14,322	Paris	5,558	8,945
Brussels	5,514	8,874	Perth	9,154	14,732
Bucharest	6,423	10,337	Phnom Penh	7,850	12,633
Budapest	6,080	9,785	Port-au-Prince	3,279	5,277
Buenos Aires	6,461	10,398	Port Moresby	6,639	10,684
Cairo	7,446	11,983	Port Sudan	8,247	13,272
Canberra	7,571	12,184	Prague	5,818	9,363
Caracas	3,897	6,272	Pretoria	10,524	16,937
Casablanca	5,964	9,598	Pyongyang	5,589	8,995
Colombo	9,025	14,524	Quebec	2,638	4,245
Copenhagen	5,456	8,781	Quito	3,829	6,162
Dacca	7,681	12,361	Rio de Janeiro	6,613	10,643
Damascus	7,321	11,782	Rome	6,240	10,042
Dar es Salaam	10,005	16,101	Rotterdam	5,460	8,787
Delhi	7,672	12,347	Saint Petersburg	5,507	8,862
Dublin	5,078	8,172	San Salvador	2,630	4,233
Geneva	5,813	9,355	Santiago	5,936	9,553
Glasgow	5,019	8,077	Santo Domingo	3,409	5,486
Guatemala City	2,519	4,054	Sarajevo	6,283	10,112
Hanoi	7,301	11,750	Seoul	5,609	9,027
Havana	2,563	4,125	Shanghai	6,145	9,889
Helsinki	5,420	8,723	Singapore	8,436	13,576
Hiroshima	5,516	8,877	Sofia	6,472	10,416
Ho Chi Minh City	7,814	12,575	Stockholm	5,354	8,616
Islamabad	7,395	11,901	Stuttgart	5,759	9,268
Jakarta	8,658	13,934	Sydney	7,421	11,943
Jerusalem	7,414	11,932	Taipei	6,430	10,348
Johannesburg	10,531	16,948	Tangier	5,931	9,545
Kabul	7,382	11,880	Tegucigalpa	2,702	4,348
Kathmandu	7,564	12,173	Tehran	7,342	11,816
Kingston	3,063	4,929	Tel Aviv	7,386	11,887
Kowloon	6,889	11,087	The Hague	5,444	8,761
Kuala Lumpur	8,438	13,580	Thule	3,121	5,023
Kuwait City	7,754	12,479	Timbuktu	6,989	11,248
Kiev	6,121	9,851	Tokyo	5,134	8,262
La Paz	5,137	8,267	Trieste	6,058	9,749
Lima	4,522	7,277	Tripoli, Lebanon	7,250	11,668
Lisbon	5,660	9,109	Tripoli, Libya	6,778	10,908
Liverpool	5,174	8,327	Tunis	6,457	10,392
London	5,350	8,610	Ulan-Bator	5,783	9,307
Luxembourg	5,630	9,061	Vancouver	796	1,281
Madrid	5,785	9,310	Venice	6,033	9,709
Managua	2,842	4,574	Vienna	5,974	9,614
Mandalay	7,607	12,242	Vientiane	7,595	12,223
Manila	6,962	11,204	Vilnius	5,764	9,276
Marrakech	6,044	9,727	Vladivostok	5,159	8,303
Mazatlan	1,380	2,221	Warsaw	5,835	9,391
Mecca	8,180	13,164	Wellington	6,740	10,847
Melbourne	7,857	12,645	Yokohama	5,147	8,283
Mexico City	1,885	3,034	Zagreb	6,107	9,828
Milan	5,943	9,564	Zanzibar	9,962	16,032
			Zurich	5,818	9,363

23 Geology

Geology of San Francisco

The varied bedrock geology of San Francisco is the product of subduction, the slow descent of the ocean floor crust beneath the edge of the North American continent. During this process, detached slices of the ocean floor, ocean floor surface sediments, volcanic island chains, and debris from the adjacent continent were wedged against the edge of the continent. Tens of millions of years of folding, faulting, and uplift followed. The wedges of rock, differing widely in origin, age, and composition, are called terranes. Most of the San Francisco Bay Area, and the coast ranges of central and northern California, are composed of a collection of terranes called the Franciscan Complex, which is Jurassic and Cretaceous in age (200-60 million years old).

Four terranes make up the bedrock of San Francisco. The varied topography of the city is partly an expression of the varied resistance to erosion of the different terrane rock types.

Marin Headlands terrane (200–90 million years old, Lower Jurassic to Upper Cretaceous). Volcanic pillow lava (brown to green called greenstone) erupted onto the deep ocean floor, bedded chert (thin brick-red layers) between thin shale layers (chert is made of billions of silica shells of oceanic protozoa called radiolaria), and coarse sandstone (greywacke). These hard rocks resist erosion and form the central and southeastern hills of San Francisco and the adjacent Marin Headlands.

Central terrane (165–130 million years old, Upper Jurassic to Lower Cretaceous). Sandstone and shale containing pulverized fragments of other terranes, probably deposited in the offshore subduction trench and subducted between terranes. Extensive intrusion of serpentinite (mint green) from beneath the ocean crust is seen in the eastern CT zone (the Presidio, Mint Hill, Potrero Hill, Hunters Point). Areas of the western CT zone — a narrow strip from Fort Miley to Visitacion Valley — show indications of related sub-ocean crust rocks.

Alcatraz terrane (135–130 million years old, Lower Cretaceous). Coarse sandstone (greywacke) and shale were deposited as submarine deltas (fans) on the seafloor adjacent to the continent (Alcatraz and Yerba Buena Islands, Nob, Russian, and Telegraph hills).

San Bruno Mountain terrane (age unknown, perhaps Late Cretaceous or Tertiary). Greywacke and shale of similar origin to the Alcatraz terrane (Sutro and Merced heights).

Merced formation (3–0.4 million years old, Pliocene to Recent). Not a terrane, but very recent gently folded sands and silts deposited on and near a shifting shoreline (offshore, beach, lagoon, and dune deposits; Fort Funston and cliffs). The block on which the material was deposited has subsided between the San Andreas Fault and San Bruno Fault.

Most of the terranes dip northeast and probably narrow with depth. Columbus Avenue follows the axis of a downfold (syncline in the Alcatraz terrane, with Russian, Nob and Telegraph Hills being the eroded edges of the fold. An upward fold (anticline) is exposed in the northern part of the central hills (Mt. Sutro, etc.). Two erosion-resistant chert caps have formed the famous Twin Peaks profile.

Artificial Fill Filled shoreline areas include the Marina (Harbor Cove), North Beach (Bilgewater Bay), downtown (Yerba Buena Cove), South Beach, Mission Bay, the northeast part of the Mission district (Dolores Lagoon), flat areas south of Potrero Hill (Islais Cove and marsh) and east of Potrero Hill (Irish Hill area), and much of South Basin (flat areas of Hunters Point, Candlestick Park).

MICHAEL D. LAMPEN

Ice Age San Francisco

During the ice age, actually the ice ages, beginning half a million years ago, sea levels dropped up to 300 feet as ice accumulated in polar regions. The California coastline, in the vicinity of San Francisco, was some 25 miles west of its present location, and the Farallon Islands formed a coastal ridge. For much of this time, San Francisco Bay was a cool grassy valley, populated by herds of horse, camel, bison, and mammoth. During the four to seven intervening warmer periods, the bay filled to form estuaries of varying size. San Francisco was a taller, more rugged hill area to the west, partly forested with juniper and Douglas fir. The remains of a giant sloth (excavated at Broadway and Kearny Street) show that these strange creatures grazed on local vegetation.

Several interesting topographic features of the time were later buried under younger sands and clays. For example, an apparent buried sea cliff stands beneath the outer Sunset district. The later, large, east-draining Islais Creek was but a small stream, and what later became its upper course drained in the opposite direction southwest into a deep canyon south of Merced Heights. Dolores Creek and its tributaries drained into a deep gulch which curved around the western and northern sides of Rincon Hill, avoiding the later creek route via Mission Creek and Bay. Another deep canyon cut into the eastern side of the present Marina district. The canyon of the Golden Gate is probably not much more than 20,000 years old. In earlier times, the estuary probably emptied through the Merced lowland, south and west of Mount San Bruno.

MICHAEL D. LAMPEN

SAN FRANCISCO COUNTY MINERALS

Apophyllite	Hydromagnesite
Aragonite	Jasper (var.
Barite	Kinvadite)
Brucite	Magnesite
Calcite	Mercury
Chalcedony	Pectolite
Chromite	Prehnite
Cinnabar	Pryolusite
Curtisite	Psilomelane
Datolite	Quartz
Diallage	Sphene
Diopside (lilac)	Wollastonite
Enstatite	Xonotlite
Gyrolite	

Some of these minerals were found many years ago, in mines now long abandoned; others are of rare or single occurrence; still others are so unusual for the area in which they are reported to occur that they need verification.

San Francisco's Land Surveys

MAY 1835
William Antonio Richardson drew unofficial plan of the pueblo Yerba Buena for Mexican Governor Figueroa.

OCT. 1835
William Antonio Richardson drew first official plan of the pueblo Yerba Buena.

1839
Jean Jacques Vioget surveyed area bounded by Montgomery, Pacific, Sacramento, and Dupont streets.

1847
Jasper O'Farrell surveyed area included between Vallejo, Powell, and Sutter streets. Later surveyed the district bounded by Post, Leavenworth, and Francisco streets and the waterfront.

1849
William Eddy began his survey with Front Street and extended westward to Larkin and 8th streets.

1852
Clement Humphreys surveyed the northern portion of San Francisco County.

1868
George F. Allardt surveyed the Salt Marsh and Tide Lands by order of the Tide Lands Commissioners.

1868
James Stratton surveyed Tide and Pueblo Lands. Survey approved by the U.S. Surveyor General on August 13, 1868.

1883
Ferdinand Von Leicht resurveyed the Pueblo Lands, completed.

JAN. 17, 1884
Brought the southern boundary of the Pueblo about 980 feet further north and excluded from the Pueblo boundaries a strip of land about 980 feet wide by two miles long, bounded by the Pacific Ocean on the west, the San Miguel Ranch on the east, the Patent Line on the north, and Stratton's Four League Line and the Merced Ranch on the south.

1905
Daniel H. Burnham surveyed and laid out a plan for the improvement and adornment of San Francisco.

24 *Hills*

We frequently hear the phrase San Francisco and Her Seven Hills, but the city by the Golden Gate is not really limited to that number. Her topography is such that as many as 43 hills of varying heights have been counted. But the seven, doubtless suggested by the number of hills that form the city of Rome, has struck popular fancy, and visitors to the city often make inquiries concerning them. The so-called seven hills are: Telegraph Hill, named for the signal station erected on its summit during the early days that informed the citizenry of the arrival of ships; Nob Hill, where the mining and railroad millionaires built their palatial mansions (the name is derived from nabob, an Indian prince); Rincon Hill, close to the southern portion of the Embarcadero, or waterfront, now cut down to act as anchorage for the Bay Bridge (*rincon* is Spanish for "corner"); the Twin Peaks, forming the background at the western end of Market Street; Russian Hill, named in honor of the early Russian colony and burial ground on its slopes; Lone Mountain, around which the early cemeteries of San Francisco were laid out; and the highest hill, Mt. Davidson, where Easter morning services are held annually.

At left: Panorama of San Francisco and the Bay as seen from Twin Peaks.

SAN FRANCISCO'S 43 NAMED HILLS

ALAMO HEIGHTS	225'	LONE MOUNTAIN	448'
ANZA HILL	260'	McLAREN RIDGE	515'
BERNAL HEIGHTS	325'	MERCED HEIGHTS	500'
BUENA VISTA HEIGHTS	569'	MT. DAVIDSON	938'*
CANDLESTICK POINT	500'	MT. OLYMPUS	570'
CASTRO HILL	407'	MT. ST. JOSEPH	250'
CATHEDRAL HILL	206'	MT. SUTRO	918'
CITY COLLEGE HILL	350'	NOB HILL	376'
COLLEGE HILL	200'	PACIFIC HEIGHTS	370'
CORONA HEIGHTS	510'	PARNASSUS HEIGHTS	400'
DOLORES HEIGHTS	360'	POTRERO HILL	300'
EDGEHILL HEIGHTS	600'	PRESIDIO HEIGHTS	370'
EXCELSIOR HEIGHTS	315'	RED ROCK HILL	689'
FOREST HILL	700'	RINCON HILL	120'
GOLD MINE HILL	679'	RUSSIAN HILL	294'
HOLLY HILL	274'	STRAWBERRY HILL	412'
HUNTERS POINT RIDGE	275'	SUTRO HEIGHTS	200'
IRISH HILL (NOW 50')	250'	TELEGRAPH HILL	284'
LAFAYETTE HEIGHTS	378'	TWIN PEAKS (NORTH)	903' 8"
LARSEN PEAK	725'	(SOUTH)	910' 5"
LAUREL HILL	264'	UNIVERSITY MOUND	265'
LINCOLN HEIGHTS	380'	WASHINGTON HEIGHTS	260'

HIGHEST

25 Islands

Alcatraz

The 22.5-acre Isla de Alcatraces (Spanish for Pelican Island) was named in August 1775 by Lt. Juan Manuel de Ayala, Spanish commander of the survey vessel *San Carlos*, the first ship to enter San Francisco Bay.

Alcatraz was granted by Governor Manuel Micheltorena in 1843 to Jose Yves Limantour, and later claimed by Julian Workman and John Fremont.

The Alcatraz lighthouse, built in 1854, was the first on San Francisco Bay. The station switched to remote control on November 4, 1963.

In 1859 Fort Alcatraz was established and occupied by troops. The island was held by the Army until January 1, 1934, when it became a Federal penitentiary. The prison closed July 1, 1963, after housing such notorious criminals as Al Capone, Mickey Cohen, George "Machine Gun" Kelly, Joseph "Dutch" Critzer, and Robert Stroud, better known as the "Bird Man of Alcatraz."

On January 10, 1963, Congressman John F. Shelley introduced the bill to establish a Federal Commission on the disposition of Alcatraz. However, Bay Area residents were far from unanimous on the question of Alcatraz. There was talk of making it a park, erecting a peace monument, opening a revolving restaurant, a hotel, etc.

In the 1870s Indians from the Arizona Territory and some participants from the Modoc War were held as federal prisoners for disciplinary purposes. Almost 200 years later, on March 8, 1964, five Sioux Indians staked claim to the island. They acted on an 1868 treaty with the Sioux Nation that allowed Indians off the reservation to claim "unoccupied government land." On November 9, 1969, Indian leader Richard Oakes and four others landed on the island but were talked off the next day by Thomas Hannon, regional director of the General Services Administration. However, on November 20, about 80 college-aged Indians again took possession of the island and held it until removed by U.S. marshals on June 11, 1971.

The island is approximately 1.5 miles from the mainland and is entirely without resources within itself. The soil is scarcely perceptible, the island being rocky and precipitous on all sides. The purple

growth visible at certain times of the year is mesembryanthemum, more popularly known as ice plant.

Alcatraz Island is now a part of the 24,000-acre, $119-million park plan called the Golden Gate National Recreation Area approved by President Nixon in 1972.

Angel Island

Angel Island is the largest island in the bay (640.2 acres), and is located seven miles northeast of San Francisco.

One acre of Point Blunt—the southern point—and 13.2 acres of Quarry Point (the east-central point at East Garrison–Fort McDowell) lie within San Francisco.

Visited and named Nuestra Señora de Los Angeles by Lt. Juan Manuel de Ayala in 1775, the island later served early whalers as an anchorage for replenishing supplies of wood and water. In 1839 Governor Alvarado granted Antonio Osio the entire island to breed horses and mules, but the grant was later voided by the U.S. Supreme Court.

President Fillmore reserved the island for military purposes on November 6, 1850, and on September 12, 1863, Camp Reynolds was established. The name of the military reservation was changed to Fort McDowell by War Department Order on April 4, 1900. The Army remained on the island until September 20, 1946, when the War Department officially declared the island and its installations "surplus." The remains of 131 soldiers and civilians buried on the island were removed to Golden Gate National Cemetery in 1947. Some of the civilian dead were victims of the 1906 earthquake and fire.

The U.S. Quarantine Station was established on 28.6 acres of land December 22, 1888. It was followed in 1909 by the Immigrant Station, which later served as a temporary detention area for enemy aliens during World War I. The station closed Nov. 5, 1940.

Today Angel Island is a part of the new Golden Gate National Park System providing hiking, fishing, and picnicking areas. Transportation to the island is provided from the following points: San Francisco (Fisherman's Wharf), Sausalito, and Tiburon.

The Farallones

The Farallon (or Farallone) Islands, 32 miles west of the Golden Gate, are a group of seven islands visible to San Franciscans on a clear day. They are within the city limits.

The islands were sighted by Cabrillo on November 16, 1542, followed by Francis Drake in 1579. Drake was the first to land on the islands and named them "The Islands of St. James."

Sebastian Vizcaino in 1603 called the islands "Los Frailes," and Juan Francisco Bodega y Quadra in 1775 gave them the name "Los Farallones de los Frayles." (Los Farallones comes from the Spanish word meaning "cliff or small pointed island in the sea.")

The gathering of murre eggs for table consumption brought early Russian settlers to the islands during the years 1812–1841. Later the Americans, too, consumed large quantities of eggs taken from the islands until the government banned all egg gathering in 1897. The Farallones became a Federal Bird Reserve February 27, 1907, by Theodore Roosevelt's Executive Order No. 1043.

The U.S. Light Station established in 1855 is now automated and radio-controlled. The station is located atop Beacon Rock, 350 feet above mean sea level and the highest peak.

The island's only humans now are the biologists and volunteers of the Point Reyes

During the years in which the island of Alcatraz served as a high security prision, kids in the City would gaze out along the Bay thinking about Capone, gangsters, and G-men. If the wind was right, prisoners inside Alcatraz could hear the sounds of the city. Former prisoners recall the cheers of kids playing, people having New Year's Eve boat parties, and big bands playing on Fisherman's Wharf. That they should be so near such a beautiful life and city, yet so far was for many prisoners the most difficult aspect of Alcatraz. 241

Bird Observatory, who founded a Farallones field research station in an abandoned Coast Guard barracks in 1968.

Treasure Island

On February 11, 1936, construction of the 400-acre (5,520 feet long, 3,400 feet wide) Treasure Island was begun as the site of the 1939 Golden Gate International Exposition. The man-made island would lie on shoals adjacent to Yerba Buena's northern shore, and the reclamation work would be under command of Lt. Col. Janus A. Dorst, Army Engineers Corps. Dredging was completed August 26, 1937. Later, in 1943, an additional 6.7 acres were added.

The secondary task was the creation of a rock seawall over three miles in length and 13 feet above mean low water level. This seawall contains 287,000 tons of quarried rock.

Funds for the seawall and fill were provided through a $3,043,000 federal WPA grant. The roadways, causeway, trestles, landscaping, and drainage of water systems were provided through an additional WPA grant of $1,306,000.

Water for the island is pumped to a 3-million-gallon reservoir on Treasure Island through a 10-inch steel pipeline 10,000 feet in length, supported under the upper deck of the San Francisco-Oakland Bay Bridge.

On February 28, 1941, after the Golden Gate International Exposition, the island was leased from the City and County of San Francisco by the U.S. Government. The U.S. Navy moved in on July 1, 1941, and still maintains the island as headquarters of the 12th Naval District.

Yerba Buena

Jose de Canizares in 1776 gave Yerba Buena the name "Isla del Carmen." Later, Californians referred to it as Wood Island and Bird Island. Today the island is best known as the connecting link between the San Francisco and Oakland Bay Bridge.

The 198-acre island was granted by Juan B. Alvarado to Jose Castro in 1838 and in 1843 claimed by Jose Y. Limantour.

The first legislature on February 18, 1850, passed an act establishing the limits of San Francisco County and gave the island the name of Yerba Buena. This name was changed in 1895 by the U.S. Geographic Board to Goat Island. It remained Goat Island until June 3, 1931, when the name Yerba Buena was reinstated by the U.S. Geographic Board.

The military history of the island begins with the Army, which established a post on December 19, 1866, consisting of one sergeant, 10 privates, and a commissioned officer; the Coast Guard, responsible for the lighthouse; and the Navy, which opened a Naval Training Station on April 12, 1898.

The tunnel linking the bridges was built by the Clinton Construction Company of San Francisco with work commencing May 15, 1933.

A 900-foot-long causeway links Yerba Buena Island to Treasure Island.

Red Rock

This five-acre island lies at the northern edge of San Francisco Bay, near the Richmond-San Rafael Bridge. Its 170-foot summit is the northernmost point of San Francisco County. Formerly called Isla de Carmen (Crimson Island for its red chert rock), Isla de Oro, Treasure Island, and Golden Island, the privately owned island is a haven for sea birds and harbor seals. Selim Woodworth lived on the waterless island for five years in the 1850s.

26 Lakes and Streams

Present Day Lakes

Golden Gate Park Lakes

North Lake, Middle Lake, and South Lake, also known as the Chain of Lakes in the west end of the park, are the only lakes in the park not man-made. The following lakes are man-made:

Alvord Lake
Elk Glen Lake
Lloyd Lake
Mallard Lake
Metson Lake
Quarry Lake (also known as Lily Pond, Duck Pond, and Hobo Lake)
Spreckles Lake
Stow Lake

Lake Merced

(Spanish, Laguna de Nuestra Señora de la Merced)

The Lake of Our Lady of Mercy is situated in the southwest corner of the City and County of San Francisco, crossing the boundary line into San Mateo County. The lake has a water surface of 336 acres with a total lakeshore of about 38,000 feet. It is 30 feet deep and fed by innumerable springs in the bottom and around the shores. The lake was divided into two lakes when the central peninsula was extended to the west shore in 1925.

Mountain Lake

(Spanish, La Laguna de Las Presidio de San Francisco)

It was here March 27, 1776, that Juan Bautista de Anza camped. In Spanish times it was known as Laguna de Loma Alta (Lake of the High Hill), referring to the 400-foot elevation of the Presidio.

Pine Lake

Once called Laguna Puerca (Dirty Lake) and Lake Lilenthal, it is bordered by Crestlake and Wawona streets.

Laguna Honda

Located at 7th and Clarendon avenues between Golden Gate Heights and Mt. Sutro, Laguna Honda (Deep Lake) was converted to a municipal water supply for the San Francisco Fire Department.

Islais Creek (north fork)

The north fork of former Islais Creek survives in Glen Canyon Park between Mt. Davidson and Diamond Heights.

Lobos Creek

Flowing from near Mountain Lake to Baker Beach, this stream was San Francisco's first water supply. It forms the west half of the Presidio's southern border and is the last free-flowing coastal stream in San Francisco.

Former Lakes and Creeks

Dolores Creek

18th Street to Mission Street (from Eureka Valley to Dolores Lagoon).

Dolores Lagoon

Northeast quadrant of the Mission district—main area: 14th to 18th streets and Shotwell to Harrison streets, with arms west to 18th and Mission streets and south to Harrison and 20th streets.

Islais Creek

Approximately Cayuga Avenue and 280 Freeway northwest, then winding (slough) along Industrial and Selby streets, Kirkwood Avenue, Toland Street, McKinnon Avenue, north at Upton Street and McKinnon, merging eastward into Napoleon Street—principal north branch of Glen Canyon (Islais Creek was the largest creek in San Francisco).

Lake Merced Creeks

Six feeder creeks flowed into Lake Merced from the east side of Brotherhood Way, marking the route of the largest feeder—a creek flowed from the north end of Lake Merced northwest to the ocean (lake in zoo is a remnant).

Mission Creek

Division Street (from Dolores Lagoon to Mission Bay).

Precita Creek

Approximately 24th Street east to Church Street, south on Church to Army Street, east on Army to Evans Street (from Noe Valley to Islais Creek Slough).

Presidio Creek

North of El Polin Spring on McArthur Avenue, continuing north to and along Halleck Street (to slough on site of Crissy Field).

Presidio Slough

East behind Crissy Field sand spit to Chestnut and Divisadero streets (to Harbor Cove). Palace of Fine Arts Lagoon is an altered remnant.

Trocadero Creek

West on Ulloa Street and West Portal Avenue into Stern Grove and Pine Lake Park to Pine Lake.

Washerwoman's Lagoon

Gough and Greenwich streets

Fishing at Lake Merced.

27 Legends

While most of these tales are versions of local Native American Creation myths, others, such as the Legend of the Queen of Tamalpais, are fanciful tales of non-Native origin.

Legend of Alcatraz and Yerba Buena

There was a time when the waters rose over the earth. Clouds were rent asunder and out of them poured torrents which overflowed the rivers and they in turn the lakes until but the peak of Mount Tamalpais was above the flood. Upon this peak were gathered the Tamal Indians, the sole survivors in all the world. They prayed to the Great Spirit to send them aid. From above the storm clouds in the sky came a voice that all could hear: "Tamals, I have heard your prayers and your wishes shall be granted. I am sending you the Albatross and Beaver and on their backs you will ride in safety till the ending of the flood." And so the Albatross and Beaver came to the aid of the Indians.

They came from afar off beyond the edge of the world. The nearer they came the larger they grew and when they reached the mountain they were large enough to carry all the people on their broad backs. For many moons the Indians rode over the face of the waters on the backs of these two great animals. At last the waters began to subside and the Indians were brought back to their beloved Tamalpais. Then they gathered together and thanked the Great Spirit for His help, and again a voice from above answered them: "I will leave with you the Albatross and Beaver. They shall be islands that you may see for all time, that you may remember me in the ages to come. They are a token that never more shall the waters rise, even over the backs of the Albatross and Beaver."

The two islands still rest on the waters of San Francisco Bay. White man calls them Alcatraz and Yerba Buena.

H. B. HOYT
for the SAN FRANCISCO EXAMINER

The legendary Emperor Norton.

Legend of the Name San Francisco

San Francisco. — This is a derivative word, from sand and Francisco. In the early settlement of the country, it was the custom of an old monk of the interior, by the name of Jeremiah Francisco, to perform a pilgrimage to this place every month, to visit the tomb of a brother of the order whose remains he had here interred. The wind "blew like mad" here, and upon his return he was usually so covered with the dust and sand, that his neighbors were unable to recognize him; hence, they soon began to call him sand Francisco. On one of his pilgrimages, he happened, by mistake, to die here, and the place ever after was called by his name. From the difficulty of enunciating the "d," it was usually called San Francisco, and has so continued to this day.

CALIFORNIA WEEKLY COURIER,
August 1, 1850

Legend of the Farallones

So long ago that man cannot count the time, an enemy from across the sea came to conquer the Red Men who lived on the shores of San Francisco Bay. Eagle, who was on a trip, saw them coming from afar out at sea, and rushed homeward to warn the people. The warriors gathered their weapons and went to the edge of the Bitter Waters to meet the invaders. The foe came in large canoes such as the Indian had never before seen. These canoes had broad white pinions and skimmed over the surface of the waters at a great pace, and many strange men rode on their backs. So great were their numbers that the Indians were overcome and taken prisoners. Great was the slaughter amongst them and but one escaped. This was Tanya, little daughter of the chief, who had been playing in a wooded valley. The strangers bound the Indians with strong grasses, took them upon the canoes and sailed away. Tanya, returning home and seeing all her people carried away, called to friend, Coyote, and gave him a message.

Coyote ran swiftly to the place where Eagle was perched in a tree.

Eagle took the message and, soaring high into the Heavens, gave it to the Great Spirit. Great Spirit heard, and seeing the great wrong that had been done His people changed the canoes of the foe into giant rocks, upon which the Indians climbed in safety. The foe He changed into sea birds, which laid many eggs. These eggs were food for the Red Men. Tanya and Coyote and Eagle gathered reeds and grasses and made a mighty raft with which they brought their people back to their own shores. The rocks stand to this day as a warning to the stranger that he must not take the Red Man from his land. The White Man names these rocks the Farallones.

H. B. HOYT
for the SAN FRANCISCO EXAMINER

Legend of the Queen of Tamalpais

There was a time when Mount Diablo was the southern, and Mount Saint Helena the northern end of a continuous mountain chain. Where the Golden Gate now is was a rocky wall of which Mount Tamalpais was a link, and which extended far to the north and south. Between these two ranges lay a beautiful lake. On the slopes of Tamalpais lived the Tribe of Tamal, a gentle folk who hunted and fished and kept within their own borders. On Mount Diablo, across the lake, lived a warlike tribe. Fierce men, they were cruel. They would often stand on top of their barren mountain and look with longing eyes at the forest covered country of the Tamals. They decided to take this country for their own. Many moons they worked making boats of reed and tule. When all was ready they set forth and so great was their number that they resembled a great black cloud upon the waters. The Queen of the Tamals saw the foe from her mountain home. Quickly the warning was spread and the Indians fled to the shelter of the wooded valleys. The Devil Men were soon across the waters and in pursuit of the fleeing Tamals. The Queen saw that her beloved people would stand no chance against the invaders and raising her face to Heaven prayed to the Great Spirit to send aid, even offering herself as a token if He would save her tribe. The Great Spirit was pleased with her prayer and rent the ground asunder between the Tamals and their enemies and the devils from across the waters plunged into the chasm and were swallowed up. The earth closed upon them, leaving not a sign, and the Tribe of Tamals were saved. They stopped in their flight to give thanks to the Great Spirit for their deliverance, and as they raised their eyes to Heaven they saw a wonderful change in the contour of their mountain. Where before had been but jagged rocks, now rested the form of a beautiful maiden, even the form of their beloved Queen, forever carved on the face of the mountain as a sign to the Tamals that the enemy was destroyed and that nevermore would the warrior from afar intrude upon their boundaries. And to this day the Queen of the Tamals sleeps, her face raised toward Heaven, her feet bathed in the cool waters of San Francisco Bay, as token to all people that peace reigns in the Land of the Tamal.

H. B. HOYT
for the SAN FRANCISCO EXAMINER

Legend of the Sequoias

This is the legend of the Sequoias as retold by Chief Strongbow and which has been handed down by Indian women to their children from time immemorial.

Thousands of moons ago when the earth first arose from the ocean this part (California) was a flat waste of sand, constantly changing its shape from the action of the mighty waves. A wolf, fox and an eagle were the only living creatures. And they had only a small expanse of sand to rest on, they were constantly being washed out of the holes they had dug to rest in. So they took council together. Said the eagle, "I am of the air, and although I must come to earth to rest, I cannot help you to build a secure place, but I can watch the waves and give you warning of the high waters while you work." So it was agreed that the wolf and the fox build a mound to rest on while the eagle kept watch. The two worked hard digging in the sand and throwing it up in a great heap, and when the eagle gave them warning of high water they had raised a large mound where the waves could not reach them. For two days they rested in safety, but still they greatly lacked shade which try as they would, they could not discover.

Gitchie Manitou, the Great Spirit, looked down in pity on them, and as a reward for their cunning, cast a handful of small twigs to earth. Wherever they fell sprang the giant Sequoias, the oldest living thing today on the face of the earth. Most of the twigs fell in the hollows that the animals had dug, and that is why the biggest trees are found in the valleys. Gitchie Manitou caused the sand heaps to turn to mountains so that the animals might sleep in holes in their sides, and be sheltered from the sun and rain under the foliage of the Sequoias, while the eagle perched contentedly in the topmost branches.

DOROTHY HOSFORD

Legend of the Wind and Fog

One night, away back in the early time, the Wind and the Fog had been playing monte at Los Angeles. The Devil, who lived there, had been dealing the game.

The night was warm and sultry, the game was dull by reason of a fandango in another part of the town, and the Devil said to his two friends, "Let's stroll along the ocean beach; I have friends at Buenaventura, Barbara, and Monterey."

So the three, after filling their pockets with fruit from the orange groves, went sauntering along the shore, the Devil stopping now and then to make little inlets in which the waves might play.

249

At San Luis Obispo he picked up a coni-cal stone from the hills, and placing it in the ocean sat down upon it and bathed his feet, while the Wind and Fog went inland for a frolic over the hills.

The Rock is the Moro, and may be seen today.

"How is it," said the Wind to the Devil, "that all the most beautiful places along this shore are named after saints?"

The Devil smiled, and with an artful wink, replied:

"Strategy. I sent the Jesuits before I came with instructions to take all the best places, and as I would have the people the saints might have the names, and so I have lived in friendly intercourse with the church ever since."

At the point now known as Pinos, the Sun came up, and the Devil raised a grove of pines and Cypress to walk in its shade. Thus, in friendly chat, the trio sauntered along the shore till they came to the Golden Gate. Here the fresh sweet waters of the valleys and the hills brought cool snow-flakes from the Sierra.

"Snow is a luxury to me," remarked the Devil, "and if there is one thing that more delights me than another it is a good swim in a water bath."

The Wind was tired, and went to sleep among the sand dunes. The Fog was weary, and laid himself down beside the sea. The Devil, taking off his horns, and hoofs, and tail, laid them upon the Seal Rock, and plunged into the ocean for a swim. A Walrus passing by seized the Devil's horns for tusks, and swam away northward to a region so cold that the Devil could not pursue him. From off an island in the bay there came a cunning animal, and stole his hoofs—Goat Island they call it now. Down from Tamalpais came a mountain spirit, and whisked up the Devil's tail—it may be seen now along the mountain-side, looking like a scar among the rocks and chaparral.

And so when the Devil had had his swim, and came back to dress himself, he asked the Wind and Fog for his clothes. They had been asleep, and were innocent of any collu-sion with their loss. But the Devil, ever sus-picious, even of his best friends exacted of them a solemn oath that they should never go away till he should find the Walrus, and the Goat, and get from the mountain geni his forked tail, so indispensable to his appearance in good society.

The Devil still swims in the waters of our bay, and lurks around our Golden Gate. The Wind and Fog keep him company. The Fog drifting now inland and now far out to sea. The Wind sporting on the waves or sweep-ing over the land. The Fog lifts himself to the heights of Tamalpais, and clouds his summit that the Devil may crawl in naked-ness up its sides to secure his tail. Fog and Wind sweep in upon our harbor, but the cunning Goat sleeps with his hoofs on, lest he should be caught napping. The sly old Walrus stays in his icy northern home, and the poor Devil has nothing but his seductive cunning, and his scandalous tongue, with which to do harm. With these he lures sui-cides to their watery graves, induces bankers, stock brokers, business men, and politicians to peril their souls. He aids them to escape with Fog and Wind, or drowns them in the bay, and drifts their bodies out to sea.

This true and faithful narrative accounts for the drifting Fog of our peninsula, the dismal Wind, that sweeps our city, and the Devil that lurks around to tempt and destroy us.

SAN FRANCISCO ARGONAUT,
Nov. 10, 1877

Legend of Twin Peaks

On the site where San Francisco now stands was once a forest of mighty Redwoods and amongst them roamed the Red Man. Here the Tamal hunted, fished and built his tepee. There was but one thing that caused these Red Men trouble. That was a tribe of warriors that came out of the Northland each year and had battle with them. For many years this had come to pass and each year the strangers from the North were stronger and came in greater numbers. The Indians knew that it was but a short time before they would be overcome and defeated by their enemies. The time was approaching for the coming of the Northmen and the chiefs lit the council fire and gathered together. While they were still in council there came into the tent two daughters of the chief; twins they were, and of great beauty. They told the chieftains that a spirit had appeared to them, and given warning that the foe was even then approaching, but that they would do the Indians no harm if they, the twins, would do as the spirit bade. After delivering the message the maidens ran to a hilltop as the Spirit had said and there plucked a flower, each petal of which meant a wish fulfilled. Then from the sea came the foe. Hundreds of canoes raced for the openings in the coast line and for landings on the shore. One maiden looked to Heaven, plucked a petal from the flower and prayed: "Oh, Great Spirit, send the fog banks that the Northmen may not enter." The Spirit answered and such fog as was never seen in all time rolled along the shore. The Northmen dashed blindly against the rocks, their canoes were shattered and many were lost in the waters. Then the other maiden took a petal of the flower and, sending it wafting on the wind to Heaven, spoke: "Oh, Great Spirit, change this foe into sea creatures that they may no more attack us and our tribe may rest in peace." Immediately the foe were changed to great black creatures, with flappers and a long tail, and with a voice like the barking of dogs. Into the water they scrambled, snarling and fighting, and to this day they may be seen lying on the rocks, off the Cliff House, in the sunshine. One more petal remained on the flower and together the maidens plucked it and threw it to the wind

and to the Great Spirit they whispered: "Great Spirit, we pray thee that forevermore we may guard the welfare of our people." The Great Spirit was pleased with the prayer and granted their wish. They were changed into Twin Peaks and to this day they overlook all the land, ever watching and guarding those who sleep at their feet.

H. B. HOYT
for the SAN FRANCISCO EXAMINER

28 Maritime

Foghorns

These foghorns are located in, or audible from, San Francisco County. Foghorns outside county boundaries are marked with asterisks. Horns are listed roughly from west to southeast. Key: SB = seconds of blast, SS = seconds of silence. Thus "2SB, 28SS" means the foghorn sounds for 2 seconds, followed by 28 seconds of silence, before the cycle is repeated. Individual horns can be recognized by their distinctive signature patterns. Musical notes are given in parentheses after the blast pattern for some often-heard horns.

SAN FRANCISCO APPROACH BUOY
(8.6 miles west of Pacheco St. and Great Highway) 3SB, 27SS (continuous)

POINT BONITA *
(northwest entrance of Golden Gate) 2SB, 2SS, 2SB, 24SS (C)

MILE ROCK
(.33 mile northwest of Land's End) 2SB, 28SS (C)

POINT DIABLO *
(mid-north shore of Golden Gate) 2SB, 13SS (D sharp)

GOLDEN GATE BRIDGE
midspan (diaphone) 1SB, 2SS, 1SB, 36SS (low G sharp)

GOLDEN GATE BRIDGE
base of south tower (2 simultaneous horns) 2SB, 18SS (A below low A)

LIME ROCK *
(northeast entrance to Golden Gate) 2SB, 2SS, 2SB, 24SS

ALCATRAZ ISLAND
northwest point 2SB, 2SS, 2SB, 24SS

ALCATRAZ ISLAND
southeast point 3SB, 27SS

POINT BLUNT *
(south point of Angel Island) 2SB, 13SS

NORTH CHANNEL BUOY #4
(1 mile east of Point Blunt) 1SB, 9SS (continuous)

PIER 52
(Santa Fe Ferry Slip) 3SB, 3SS, 3SB, 21SS

Above left: Crowds at the Ocean Beach as the Norwegian sloop GJOA is brought ashore to be permanently displayed at the western end of Golden Gate Park. Norwegian explorer Roald Amundsen (1872–1928) was the first to navigate a vessel, the GJOA, through the Northwest Passage between 1903 and 1906. He later, in 1911, was the first person to reach the South Pole. The GJOA was the gift to San Francisco from the Norwegian community, and was returned to Norway in 1972. Lower left: Crew of the GJOA. Captain Roald Amundsen at lower left.

SAN FRANCISCO-OAKLAND BAY BRIDGE

- West Crossing, base of tower A (western-most tower, Pier 24) 1SB, 29SS
- West Crossing, base of tower B (second tower from west) 1SB, 1.5SS, 1SB, 26.5SS
- West Crossing, base of tower D (third tower from west) 1SB, 1.5SS, 1SB, 1.5SS, 1SB, 24SS
- West Crossing, base of tower E (fourth tower from west) 2SB, 1.5SS, 1SB, 25.5SS
- East Crossing, base of tower G (western-most tower, on Yerba Buena Island) 1SB, 19SS
- East Crossing, base of tower H (second tower from west) 1SB, 1.5SS, 3SB, 14.5SS

YERBA BUENA ISLAND

south point 3SB, 27SS

MICHAEL D. LAMPEN

Maritime History

"Daniel Webster declared in Congress that San Francisco Bay was 20 times more valuable to the U.S.A. than was Texas. Accordingly, President Jackson offered $3.5 million for the San Francisco Bay area during the Texas boundary negotiations. Governor Santa Anna refused the bid."

THE NAUTICAL MAGAZINE
Glasgow, October 1978

Pre–Gold Rush

From April 1, 1847, to the same date in 1848, two ships, one bark and one brig, arrived in San Francisco with cargo from Atlantic ports: a total of four vessels.

Gold Rush

In December of 1848, President Polk announced that gold had been discovered in California: "the abundance of gold in that territory would scarcely command belief." As a result, in 1849, 777 vessels set out from the East Coast for San Francisco. This flotilla consisted of 242 full-rigged ships,

218 barks, 170 brigs, 132 schooners, and 15 steamers. The historian J. D. B. Stillman declared: "Never since the Crusades was such a movement known."

The Grain Fleet

Some 30 years later, an even larger fleet of sailing ships, in point of tonnage, gathered in San Francisco Bay. The San Joaquin Valley had become a bread basket for northern Europe, and in 1881, no fewer than 559 sailing ships assembled at San Francisco to load a season's grain harvest. The average size of the square riggers in the grain trade in 1879 was 1,249 tons (in contrast, the average tonnage of the Gold Rush vessels in the bay in 1850 was 274 tons). Nearly two-thirds of these square riggers were British ships built of iron or steel. The steel-hulled *Balclutha*, now moored on San Francisco's north waterfront, is a typical British deep-waterman of the 1880s.

Clipper Ships

Small in number, but gripping the public imagination then and now, were the clipper ships. They followed on the hastily assembled fleet that had departed the East Coast for San Francisco in 1849—mostly tubby, small vessels, nearly one in ten of which was an ex-whaler. The Annals of San Francisco (1855) described the clippers as "virtually the creation of San Francisco." The next sentence described why they were created: "The necessity of bearing merchandise as speedily as possible to so distant a market, one too which was liable to be suddenly overstocked by goods, early forced merchants and shipbuilders interested in the California trade to invent new and superior models of vessels."

The great size, sharp lines, enormous sail plans, and redoubtable seamanship aboard the clippers and their romantic names caught the attention of the nation. Editorials appeared in the New York papers when the *Flying Cloud* raced around the Horn to San

Francisco in only 89 days. (In contrast, the average passage to San Francisco from the East Coast in 1849 is estimated at 182 days.)

Clippers were never numerous. In the 12 years between 1843 and 1855, 2,656 merchantmen were built in American yards, and of them no more than 256 were "clipper-built."

The "Under 100-day Club"

Dr. John Lyman, the maritime historian, estimated that 10,000 sailing ship voyages were made around Cape Horn to San Francisco. Of these, only 26 passages were made in less than 100 days. A list is given in Basil Lubbock's book *The Last of the Windjammers*.

DATE	SHIP	POINT OF EMBARKATION	DAYS OUT
1850	Sea Witch	New York	97
1851	Flying Cloud	New York	89
1851	Surprise	New York	96
1852	Swordfish	New York	90
1852	Flying Fish	Boston	98
1853	Contest	New York	97
1853	Flying Fish	New York	92
1853	John Gilpin	New York	93
1854	Flying Cloud	New York	89
1854	David Brown	New York	98
1854	Hurricane	New York	99
1854	Romance of the Seas	Boston	96
1854	Witchcraft	New York	97
1855	Herald of the Morning	New York	99
1856	Antelope	New York	97
1856	Sweepstakes	New York	94
1857	Sierra Nevada	New York	97
1859	Flying Dragon	New York	97
1860	Andrew Jackson	New York	89
1863	Great Republic	New York	94
1866	Seminole	New York	96
1872	Young America	Liverpool	96
1874	Glory of the Seas	Liverpool	94
1889	Senator	Cardiff	90
1894	Eudora	Lundy	99
1897	Merioneth	Cardiff	96

Seven out of the 26 passages were made by vessels built by master clipper ship builder Donald McKay of Boston. The *Flying Cloud*, his most famous clipper, twice made it to San Francisco in 89 days. The last three passages in the list were made by British iron ships in the grain trade.

Down-Easters

The down-Easters were the barks and full-rigged ships constructed in New England yards beginning after the Civil War and continuing until the end of wooden square-rigged shipbuilding in this country in the early 1890s. They followed the short-lived clipper ship era, and their owners frequently advertised them as clippers. However, the down-Easters had fuller lines than the clipper ships and carried smaller crews, although they were maintained with all the "Yankee smartness" that had come to be associated with their predecessors.

The most impressive fleet of wooden, deepwater, square-rigged sailing vessels that the nation had ever known, home port San Francisco, was assembled by W. E. Mighell in 1899. It comprised 11 down-Easters of which Mighell was already managing owner: *Carrollton, Charmer, Elwell, General Fairchild, Jabez Howes, J. B. Brown, James Nesmith, Oregon, Rufus E. Wood, Sea King*, and *Wachusett*, and ten other vessels (including three of Chapman & Flint's "Saints") mostly purchased from Flint & Co.: *Henry B. Hyde, S.D. Carleton, Pactolus, John McDonald, R.D. Rice, St. Frances, A.J. Fuller, St. James, St. David*, and the iron-hulled *May Flint*, a former steamer.

These vessels under Mighell's management flew the house flag of the California Shipping Co. Subsequently the company acquired the *Reuce, Abner Coburn, Henry Failing, Governor Robie, Florence, Alexander Gibson, James Drummond, John Currier, Joseph B. Thomas, Mary L. Cushing*, and *William H. Smith*.

These wooden down-Easters, the cream of the American flag square-rigger fleet, had many years of life left in them, but in the eighties they were forced from the grain trade by Lloyd's discriminatory insurance rates favoring iron-hulled ships. At the turn of the century they lost the general cargo trade, New York to San Francisco, to the big new steamers of the American Hawaiian Steamship Co., which used the Strait of Magellan instead of taking the windjammer path around Cape Horn. During the early years of the century Mighell and his California Shipping Co., involving many shareholders on the street of the same name, its vessels mostly engaged in the export lumber and coal trade, was rated as the most extensive owner of sailing ships in the world.

Some 975 down-Easters were launched in all. The inspiration for the building of the larger down-Easters once again came from California—this time it was the grain trade.

By the turn of the century, almost all of the Cape Horners in the down-Easter fleet ceased to hail from New York and New England; their new home port was San Francisco. They were used in the Pacific to carry coal to fuelless San Francisco (from Vancouver Island and Australia) as well as for the offshore lumber trade and as salmon packets.

A few down-Easters were still sailing out of San Francisco in the Alaska salmon trade in the early 1920s. Several of these vessels eventually went to Southern California to play the role of clipper ships in various movies (with their double topsails stitched together to make a single topsail of the old style) and also to be elaborately converted to replicate *Old Ironsides*, Lord Nelson's *Victory*, and other historic ships.

Two-Masted Schooners

Turning to less lordly vessels, the type of craft most frequently built in San Francisco Bay shipyards (and indeed on the whole Pacific Coast) was the two-masted schooner. In 1876 there were 462 two-masted schooners and 11 three-masters owned in San Francisco.

Many of the two-masters were "scow schooners," a type used on the bay and rivers, with a square transom at both bow and stern. But great numbers of conventional, sharp-ended two-masters put to sea from San Francisco: a sailor called "Flatfoot" Hansen recalled that one day in the 1880s he counted over 50 outbound schooners becalmed in the lee of Point Reyes.

The two-masted coastal schooner is extinct—no specimen survives. However, a typical three-masted schooner, the *C. A. Thayer*, and a scow schooner, the *Alma*, are moored at Hyde Street Pier as part of the National Maritime Museum, San Francisco.

River Steamers

The first river steamer in California was the tiny *Sitka*, purchased in Alaska by merchant William Leidesdorff and brought here in the hold of the Russian bark Naslednich. The *Sitka*, 37 feet long, departed San Francisco for the Sacramento River on November 29, 1847, but she made only one trip—an ox team was said to have made better time. The *Sitka*'s steam engine was removed and used to power a coffee grinder; the hull was made into a schooner. Although the community treated the *Sitka* as a joke, three years later steam-boating had come to stay. Twenty-eight assorted paddle-wheelers plied the Sacramento and Feather rivers alone; the Gold Rush had changed everything. Like the *Sitka*, a number of the early river steamers of small size had come around Cape Horn, knocked down, as cargo in a sailing ship.

In 1854 the California Steam Navigation Company was formed by a number of independent owner-captains and was long a dominant riverboat company. Commercial navigation prospered. Sixty "inland steamers," including eight or ten ferryboats, were at work on San Francisco Bay and its tributaries in December of 1866. Most of these were sidewheel paddle steamers to be found at work on the Sacramento, San Joaquin, Feather, American, Mokelumne, Napa, and Petaluma rivers, but the figure also includes a few propeller-driven tugs on the bay. All the river boat traffic had its connection with San Francisco, as a source of supplies and as a destination for cargoes of farm produce brought down the rivers.

Sidewheelers for the passenger trade like the *Capital* (the largest riverboat of her day at 1,625 tons), the *Chrysopolis*, and the *Yosemite*, all built in the early 1860s, had interior opulence to match the finest Mississippi river packet. The *Chrysopolis*, launched at Steamboat Point in San Francisco by John G. North, holds the record between Sacramento and San Francisco of five hours, nineteen minutes.

The last great passenger sternwheelers were the *Delta King* and the *Delta Queen*, their steel hulls and machinery built in Scotland and reassembled at Stockton in 1926. The *Delta Queen* runs today as a passenger steamer on the Mississippi River.

Early Passenger Liners

The ocean-going steam passenger fleet plying in and out of San Francisco in 1875 numbered 50 vessels. These steamers regularly ran to China; Panama; Australia; Mexico; Victoria and Puget Sound ports; Portland, Oregon; Humboldt Bay; the southern ports of California; and lesser harbors up and down the Pacific coast. At this date, about half of these steamers were still paddlewheelers. Passengers travelled by sea in those days; roads were poor and railroads almost nonexistent.

The vessels in this fleet were larger than the river steamers, of course. In fact, the trans-Pacific side-wheelers *Alaska*, *China*, *Japan*, and *Great Republic* of the Pacific Mail Steamship Company were the largest ocean-going wooden steamers ever con-

structed. The *Alaska* grossed 4,011 tons. Unlike the river boats, few of these coastal and offshore liners were built in San Francisco Bay. Most of the wooden sidewheelers came from the New York area, but an increasing number of the propeller-driven steamers like the long-lived *City of Peking* were built of iron on the Delaware River.

Wooden-Ship Builders

Many capable wooden-ship builders had yards, large and small, on the shores of San Francisco Bay. In the early days there were Domingo Marcucci, George Middlemas, John G. North, William I. Stone, Patrick Tiernan, and others. Later came Matthew Turner; the Dickie brothers (John, James, George, and their father, William); (Alexander) Hay & Wright; (George) Boole & Beaton; William A. Boole; Charles G. White; William I. Stone's son, William F.; and his son, Lester. (In 1970, Lester Stone finally ended his family's 117-year dynasty of fast vessels and good craftsmanship.)

Of the wooden-ship builders, Matthew Turner was the most prolific. He was noted around the entire Pacific Basin for his hand some brigantines and for his more than 60 two-masted schooners. Many of these were for the South Seas trade and for owners in these islands. Turner began building his fast vessels in San Francisco in the early 1870s. He later moved to Benicia where the relatively dry climate enabled him to produce vessels built of Douglas fir that could withstand the tropical sun better than could vessels built in the shipyards of the Pacific Northwest. As a result, it is believed that Turner built more wooden vessels for foreign owners than any other man in the U.S. His total output of 228 vessels has probably not been equalled by any other individual shipbuilder in North America.

In all, 113 three-masted schooners, 142 four-masted schooners, 21 five-masted schooners, and 87 barkentines were built on the Pacific Coast.

Steam Schooners

The builder of the first steam schooner—the type of vessel that eventually replaced the sailing schooner in the coastal trade—was Charles G. White, who launched half a dozen steam schooners between 1884 and 1887 at his shipyard in North Beach at the shore end of Meiggs Wharf. In 1887, 12 more steam schooners took the water, most of them products of the shipyards of Alexander Hay and Boole & Beaton on Channel Creek at Sixth Street.

The steam schooners could enter the outside ports of Sonoma and Mendocino counties—the so-called "dog-holes"—more safely and frequently than the sailing schooners. Like the sailing schooners, they loaded their redwood cargoes, sling by sling, from a trolley on an overhead wire to the cliffs (a "wire chute") or board by board, or tie by tie, down a wooden "apron chute."

A total of 225 steam schooners were built in all. They were called "the workhorses of the Pacific," or alternately, "Russian-Finn men-of-war" for the prevailing nationality of their crews.

Steel Shipbuilding

The Union Iron Works was established by Irving Scott in 1883 for the building of steel steamships and men-of-war. A cadre of "fine old Scottish mechanics from the Clyde" created the Union Iron Works' massive machinery-beam benders, vertical boiler rolls, a 600-ton hydraulic flange press, and a 30-foot boring mill. (Potrero Hill, where these men had their homes, was for many years known as "Scotch Hill.") Eighty-six vessels were built by the Union Iron Works between 1884 and 1906, among them the battleship Oregon and Admiral Dewey's flagship—the cruiser Olympia—which is still afloat and on display in Philadelphia.

The Union Iron Works was for many years the foremost industrial plant in the western United States. It dominated life and employment "south of the slot" (Market Street) for two generations, hiring at times as many as 10,000 workmen. The plant survives, on a reduced scale, as a Bethlehem Steel Corporation shipyard.

Other early builders of engines, steel hulls, or both were Fulton Iron Works, Risdon Iron Works, and Main Street Iron Works.

Whaling Capital of the World

It is little realized that for more than a quarter century—from 1882 to 1908—San Francisco was the whaling capital of the world, sending out more whalers each year than the traditional New England whaling port of New Bedford. Legendary old blubber hunters like the *Charles W. Morgan* (which still survives, restored, at Mystic, Conn.) and the bark *Wandered*, among dozens of others, made San Francisco their home port. Dickie Brothers built a series of successful whaling barks with a steam engine as auxiliary power for use in the Arctic Ocean. The venerable builder of whaleboats, J.C. Beetle, shifted his boat-building shop from New Bedford to Alameda during these years.

The reason for San Francisco's prominence was proximity to the Arctic Ocean and its bowhead whales. The bowhead, in addition to oil, provided a springy substance, found in the whale's mouth, called "whalebone." In the Victorian era, whalebone was the source of the nation's hoop skirts, buggy whips, corset stays, fishing rods, etc. Whale oil began to lose its importance with the invention of kerosene in 1857; whalebone, which sustained the fleet of old whaling barks into the twentieth century, was superceded by the invention of a light spring steel and the passing of the fashionable "wasp waist."

The ancient barks John & Winthrop and

Gay Head made the last old-fashioned whaling voyages out of San Francisco in 1912 and 1914 respectively.

The Panama Route

William H. Aspinwall, a New York merchant trading to Panama, gambled when he took over the rights to run a steamship line from the Isthmus to Oregon in 1848. The venture was a daring one even with the aid of a $200,000 government subsidy to carry the mails. The fuel bill would exceed that figure, coal being as high as $50 a ton. There were no drydocking or machine-shop facilities on the West Coast. The slim passenger and cargo business to the Pacific Northwest could hardly be expected to make the enterprise profitable.

Nevertheless, Aspinwall ordered three wooden, side-wheel steamers as per the terms of the subsidy contract. It was a time —the first China clippers were being built—when adventure was part of commerce. The keels of the *California* and *Panama* were laid at the yard of the well-known New York shipbuilder William Webb, while Smith & Dimon started construction on the *Oregon*. And three months after the subsidy contract was signed, gold was discovered where the steamers were to ply—California.

Aspinwall was in luck. When his steamers arrived in the Pacific, they were overwhelmed with Argonauts willing to pay anything to get to the gold fields. The steamers then carried the gold from San Francisco back to Panama. Other steamers connected the Atlantic side of the Isthmus with New Orleans, New York, and other cities on the East Coast. The Panama Route soon replaced Cape Horn as the favored way for passengers to travel to (and from) the diggings (although cargo continued to come by way of Cape Horn).

To share in the lucrative trade, Commodore Cornelius Vanderbilt organized an opposition line, using Nicaragua as a crossing. One of Vanderbilts' Nicaragua Steamship Company's first vessels was the *Orizaba*, built by Jacob A. Westervelt in New York in 1854 and entering service in the Pacific in 1856.

By 1869, when completion of the transcontinental railway across the United States ended the near monopolies of the Panama and Nicaragua routes, the *Orizaba* had already entered coastal service. This durable wooden steamer ran from San Francisco to San Diego (after 1875 for Goodall, Nelson & Perkins) from 1865 until she was beached near the Union Iron Works in 1887 and her engine and boilers removed.

The Last of the Square-Riggers

In 1893 Henry Fortmann merged a number of competing salmon cannery companies into the Alaska Packers Association. At the turn of the century, the Packers acquired the Belfast-built medium clippers *Star of France*, *Star of Italy*, *Star of Russia*, and *Star of Bengal*. Thereafter as they bought other iron- or steel-hulled ships, they changed the name to the "Star" appellation. There were 19 *Stars* in all.

The last voyages to Alaska under sail were made in 1929. Two *Stars* survive—the *Balclutha*, ex-*Star of Alaska*, and *The Star of India*, ex-*Euterpe*, at San Diego.

The Alaska Packers fleet was at one time the largest sailing ship fleet under the American flag. The second largest fleet belonged to Mayor James ("Sunny Jim") Rolph of San Francisco, who told his son in 1918: "Sonny, as long as there's wind, there will be sail."

Although few were keeping the sea, in 1928 there were 76 square-riggers under the American flag, and 52 of them were registered in San Francisco. Of those 76, 31 were barkentines and, of these, 20 were registered in San Francisco.

Founders of Steamship Companies

Captain Charles Goodall came from

Wales in 1859 at the age of 26. With Christian Nelson he spent many years carrying fresh water from Sausalito to San Francisco in the *Rincoln*. When the pioneer Pacific Mail Steamship Company decided to go out of the coasting trade, Goodall, Nelson, and Perkins (a new partner, who later became governor) purchased its fleet of steamers and created a transportation network called the Pacific Coast Steamship Co., which linked Pacific ports from San Diego to Victoria.

Charles Nelson, a Danish boy of twenty, arrived in San Francisco the same year as Goodall. He soon purchased some small schooners on the Sacramento River and later bought shares in the barkentine *Monitor*, owned by John Kentfield & Co., a firm with sailing vessels and sawmills. Captain Nelson began his own business in 1879, and by 1904 he owned several sawmills, four steamers, twelve schooners (one named for his wife of forty years, Metha Nelson), one bark, and six barkentines. Under the management of Captain Nelsons' nephew, James Tyson, the Charles Nelson Company became the largest lumber shipper in the world and at one point owned nearly thirty steamers.

In 1867, Captain William Matson came to San Francisco around Cape Horn as a young sailor on the ship *Bridgewater*. He was born in Sweden in 1849. Young Matson was soon in command of scow schooners carrying coal from Mt. Diablo mines to the Spreckels sugar refinery in San Francisco. He next had command of a larger schooner carrying sugar from the Hawaiian Islands. He then built a brigantine, *Lurline*, and soon bought other sailing vessels; the seven stars on the present-day Matson flag represent these early vessels, including the *Falls of Clyde*, now preserved in Honolulu. In the early 1900s, Matson bought out a competing line of sailing ships, Welch & Co., and thereafter turned increasingly to the building of steamships for the Hawaiian route. The

Matson Navigation Company owned 42 steamers in 1939 and was renowned for introducing luxury liners into the Pacific trade—the *Malolo*, the third *Lurline*, the *Monterey*, and the *Mariposa*.

In 1849, Captain William Talbot departed East Machias, Maine, with a steam sawmill in the hold of the *Oriental*, a tiny brig of 140 tons. He joined his future brother-in-law Andrew Pope, already in California, and the longest lived lumber/shipping dynasty of all was established. By 1875 Pope & Talbot were the "lumber kings of the Pacific Coast." They ordered down-Easters from Maine to carry their lumber and later had barkentines and schooners built on this coast. Pope & Talbot steamers were in the intercoastal trade as late as 1963.

Robert Dollar and Charles McCormick were lumbermen who left the dwindling pine forests of the Middle West for the redwoods of California and the Douglas fir of the Pacific Northwest. Dollar, born in Scotland, had started as a $10-a-month chore boy in a Canadian sawmill. Both men created lumber and shipping empires on the West Coast. Dollar became the nation's largest shipowner; he instituted around-the-world service in the early 1920s. McCormick built an outstanding fleet of steam schooners, carrying passengers as well as lumber. One of his fleet, the *Wapama*, dating from 1915, survives today at the National Maritime Museum, Hyde Street Pier. Steel freighters were later purchased, and in the early 1930s more McCormick ships passed through the Golden Gate than did ships of any other line.

Old Shipping Firms

There were other venerable San Francisco firms in the first few decades of this century, most with offices in what they called "The Street" (California Street): Eschen & Minor; George Billings; C. A. Hooper; A. P. Lorentzen; Beadle Bros.; Barneson & Hibberd; Sanders and Kirchmann; Oliver J. Olson; Sudden &

Christenson; E. K. Wood Lumber Co.; J. R. Hanify; Fred Linderman; Byxbee & Clark; B. H. Tietjen; W. G. Tibbitts; Olson & Mahony; Hobbs, Wall; Hartwood Lumber Co.; Alexander Woodside; Thomas Crowley; Hammond Lumber Co.; Swayne & Hoyt. Several of these shipping companies began in the era of sail, then owned wooden steam schooners, and finally operated steel steamships.

Going back into the 1890s, '80s, and '70s, the prominent firms were: William E. Mighell (California Shipping Co.), George E. Plummer, Jacob Jensen, Joseph Knowland, J. S. Kimball, Lorenzo E. White, George Howes & Co., Capt. Asa M. Simpson, Samuel Blair, G. A. Meigs, John Rosenfeld, Nicholas Bichard, J. D. Spreckles & Bros. In the South Seas trade in those early days were Andrew Crawford, Turner (the wooden shipbuilder) & Chapman, and John Wightman (Robert Louis Stevenson traveled in his schooner *Equator*). In whaling were the Pacific Steam Whaling Co. (Capt. Josiah Knowles and Millen Griffith), Wright & Bowne, and Capt. James McKenna. In whaling and the fur trade were the Alaska Commercial Co. (Capt. Gustave Niebaum) and H. Llebes.

Going back to Civil War times, in whaling were J. C. Merrill, D. C. McRuer, A. T. Lawton, and R. B. Swain. In the 1850s, with San Francisco whaling just beginning, the prominent firms were Todd & Co., Tubbs & Co. (for whom Capt. C. M. Scammon, discoverer of Scammon's Lagoon in Mexico, sailed), G. B. Post & Co., and Moore & Folger. Well-known contemporaries of the famous Scammon were Captains Jared Poole and F. S. Redfield.

Pioneers in the Bering Sea Codfishing industry (again following the ubiquitous Matthew Turner, who began fishing for cod in 1863 in the Gulf of Tartary) were Nicholas Bichard and Israel Kashow, Thomas W. McCollam, and Lynde & Hough. The latter two firms formed the Union Fish Co. in 1898 and built a plant on Belvedere Island. They sent their last cod-fishing schooner (a dory fisherman) north in 1937. She was the *Louise*, a near sister of the *C. A. Thayer*, which is preserved in the National Maritime Museum at Hyde Street Pier. (They were both originally lumber schooners, part of a long series built by H. D. Bendixsen of Eureka for San Francisco owners.) In 1902 Edward Pond took a plunge into codfishing but his schooners were driven from the Okhotsk sea by a Russian gunboat and Pond went broke.

In competition with the Alaska Packers, Frank B. Peterson operated the Naknek Packing Co. and the Red Salmon Canning Co. in Alaska. As late as 1924 he sent a few old down-Easters north—the *Pactolus*, *Hecla*, *St. Katherine*, and *Emily F. Whitney*. His former partner, L. A. ("Hungry") Pedersen, was also active during these years with a large cannery on Bristol Bay and several vessels, among them the Newburyport-built bark *McLaurin*, which he last sent to Alaska in 1923.

The First Sailors' Union

The first American seamen to be effectively organized into a labor union manned lumber schooners on the West Coast—the fleet that came in time to be known as "The Scandinavian Navy." A good proportion of the officers of this fleet had come to San Francisco as sailors in Cape Horn square-riggers and had then jumped ship. Finns, Danes, Swedes, Norwegians, and Germans, they joined coastwise vessels here, then worked their way up, starting as winch drivers or quartermasters. An egalitarianism was found on the Pacific Coast which was largely missing from East Coast seafaring.

This fact abetted "solidarity," always valuable to the labor movement. The Coast Seamen's Union was organized by Sigismund Danielwicz among the lumber piles of the Folsom Street wharf in 1885. In its first few shaky years the organization (soon to be called the Sailors' Union of the Pacific) was fortunate to find a remarkable leader in an ascetic, craggy Norwegian sailor and fisherman named Andrew Furuseth. Furuseth was elected secretary in 1887 and yielded the seat to another stubborn Norwegian sailor, Harry Lundeberg, in 1934.

To drug, intoxicate, or make insensible a man in order to put him aboard a ship was called "shanghaiing." The word originated on the San Francisco waterfront in the 1850s; the shanghaiing of sailors or landsmen to fill out a crew was a not infrequent feature of the boardinghouse business. For a half century the boardinghouse keepers, or "masters" as they called themselves (another word was "crimps"), plied their trade. They lured sailors off incoming sailing ships and, after a brief stay in the boardinghouse, put them on an outward-bounder, charging the captain a premium called "blood money." With 559 sailing ships requiring crews at the height of the grain trade in 1881, this was a profitable business. In 1891 a committee of the San Francisco Chamber of Commerce found that blood money in the amount of $120,000 (at $40 a head) had been paid in one year in San Francisco. In addition, the boardinghouse masters would only release a sailor after he had signed over his advance—his first three months' pay once he put to sea.

Furuseth set himself against all this and against the Shipowners' Association and its periodic attempts to lower wages and hire nonunion crews. Throughout the nineties and into the new century the City Front was wracked with pitched battles when a sailing ship or steamer tried to sail without a union crew. In 1901 a major strike occurred and in 1902 the Sailors' Union won full recognition from the shipowners. The situation retrogressed, however, when the union lost a strike in 1921, leading, in due course, to the most violent strike of all in 1934.

Furuseth had begun in the1890s to direct

part of his efforts to Washington, D.C. His first legislative victories were the Macguire and White Acts, which came after public opinion was aroused by a listing of brutalities aboard the down-Easters in the Cape Horn trade. These brutalities—unpunished by the courts—were published in "The Red Record" in the union paper, the Coast Seaman's Journal, beginning in 1895. As a seaman of the time ruefully put it: "On board those 'down-easters' and 'blue nose' (Nova Scotia) craft, where discipline is enforced by a plentyful use of belaying pin, knuckle duster, and boot, the work done is stupendous, and the ship is certainly kept in a wonderfully trim state."

Furuseth had another success when, in 1907, Senator Alger of Michigan introduced a bill that became law: "An Act to Prohibit Shanghaiing in the United States." In 1915 Furuseth won his greatest victory with the Seaman's Act sponsored by Sen. Robert M. LaFollette of Wisconsin; this act, a breakthrough for American maritime labor, abolished corporal punishment and imprisonment for desertion and established a hiring system that did away once and for all with crimping.

KARL KORTUM
Chief Curator
National Maritime Museum at San Francisco

Port Mileage, Port of San Francisco

The Port's 7 1/2 miles of waterfront stretch from Aquatic Park to the South Container Terminal at India Basin, Piers 94–96.

Ferryboats

The small steamer *Kangaroo* began the first ferry service of record in 1850, making two trips weekly from San Francisco to a landing in San Antonio Creek (later Oakland Estuary) on Oakland's southern shore.

Ferry service to Marin County began in 1868 when a land promotion company began running the steamer *Princess* from Sausalito to Meiggs Wharf near the foot of

Powell Street.

The first ferry connecting with a rail system was announced in the September 1, 1863, issue of the *Alta California*: "Oakland Ferry-Railroad Line, being now completed from Oakland . . . cars will begin running in connection with the steamer *Contra Costa* on Wednesday, Sept. 2 . . . every facility which could be wished is afforded for the safe and speedy transportation of passengers and freight; also every accommodation for the loading of horses and vehicles with safety and convenience."

Combination rail and ferry service to Alameda started August 25, 1864, when the San Francisco & Alameda Railroad Company (later absorbed, like many others, by the Southern Pacific Company) placed the former riverboat *Sophie MacLane* on the run from Alameda Point (then the western-most point of the island) to San Francisco.

In 1863, a 6,900-foot pier with a single ferry slip at the end was built in Oakland as an extension of Seventh Street. In 1869 this pier was extended by the Central Pacific Railroad (later to become the Southern Pacific Railroad) to serve as the terminus for their transcontinental trains. It was subsequently enlarged and opened January 22, 1882, as the famous Oakland Mole.

By the 1870s most of the ferries were owned by railroad companies and the ferries served as continuations of the rail lines.

In 1902 the Key System was organized, combining a number of small independent rail traction companies. On October 26, 1903, it started connecting ferry service from a terminal at the end of a San Francisco pier to a location a half mile west of the present Bay Bridge toll plaza. The Key System terminated commuter service January 14, 1939, but their ferries found brief employment carrying visitors to San Francisco's World Fair of 1939–40.

The two longest ferry routes were the Monticello Steamship Company's hour-and-forty-five-minute run to Vallejo, and the San

Francisco & North Pacific Railway's route to Donahue Landing on Petaluma Creek. Begun in 1870, the latter company extended the connecting rail lines to Tiburon, and in 1884 the terminal was relocated on San Francisco Bay.

Early ferries were designed to carry foot passengers with lower deck space for teams of horses, drays, and baggage carts. In recognition of the arrival of the "horseless carriage," the Southern Pacific Company in 1908 built an auto ferry, the *Melrose*, the first of more than thirty auto ferries that were to come. Automobile ferries began operation from Oakland Pier in 1923 and from Alameda Pier in 1926. By 1930, when Bay ferry business reached its peak, Southern Pacific and affiliated companies, including Northwestern Pacific, had 43 ferries on bay waters—the largest ferry fleet in the world. In that year 40,211,535 passengers and 6,117,186 vehicles were carried.

All commuter ferry service to the East Bay ended January 14, 1939, when Key System electric trains began service over the lower deck of the new Oakland-San Francisco Bay Bridge. Ferries continued to meet the transcontinental trains at the Oakland Mole until July 29, 1958, when that service, too, ceased.

The Golden Gate Bridge opened in May 1937, immediately diverting Marin County passengers from the Hyde Street and Ferry Building ferry routes. The last regular ferry run across the Golden Gate was made on February 28, 1941. (A survivor of this fleet, the Northwestern Pacific ferry *Eureka*, is preserved by the National Park Service at the Hyde Street Pier.)

The Richmond-San Rafael ferry service began in 1915 with the sidewheeler *Ellen* and ended in September 1956 when the new north bay bridge was opened for traffic. Except for the short crossing from Martinez to Benicia (since replaced by a bridge), this was the last auto ferry in the Bay area.

From the beginning in 1850 to the end in

1958 there were over 20 ferry routes and some 30 operating companies.

In 1967 a citizen group led by Maritime Museum curator Harlan Soeten, attorney Stephen Leonoudakis, and businessman Oris Willard commenced a drive to return ferry service to Marin County as an alternative to building a second automobile deck on Golden Gate Bridge—an action then being urged by the State Highway Department. This drive generated wide public support and in 1970 led to the Golden Gate Bridge District establishing a one-vessel ferry system from the Ferry Building to Sausalito with the converted sight-seeing boat, *Golden Gate*.

In 1976 the service was expanded by the addition of three 750-person capacity jet propelled ferries providing service to Larkspur in central Marin. Today's ferry commuter is provided with service from the following terminals: Pier 41 (Alcatraz Ferry Service); Pier 43½ (Angel Island Ferry Service and Tiburon Ferry Service); Ferry Building (Golden Gate Ferry Service).

USS *Carl Vinson*—"San Francisco's Own"

Mayor Dianne Feinstein on March 2, 1984, issued a proclamation declaring the USS *Carl Vinson* "San Francisco's Own" and named a 32-member Mayor's Vinson Committee to express the city's goodwill to the giant carrier's crew. The *Carl Vinson* was commissioned in 1982 and can carry almost 90 aircraft.

USS San Francisco

The first USS *San Francisco* was a cruiser built at the Union Iron Works of San Francisco. The ship was commissioned in 1890 and later converted into a mine layer called the *Yosemite*.

The new heavy cruiser USS *San Francisco* was launched at Mare Island March 9, 1933, the first warship to be commissioned during the administration of President Franklin D. Roosevelt. Captain Royal E. Ingersoll was the first commanding officer.

On December 7, 1941, the *San Francisco* was alongside the dock at the Navy Yard, Pearl Harbor, when Japanese planes attacked. The ship was not directly attacked, but the dock was strafed.

Under command of Rear Admiral Daniel J. Callaghan, she was the flagship of his fleet of four other cruisers and eight destroyers. The vessel participated in an engagement off Guadalcanal in the Solomons against a Japanese fleet of two battleships, a cruiser, and force of destroyers in an action that was fought at point-blank range. The *San Francisco* in leading the attack received 45 hits and 25 fires were started aboard her. Her death toll included Admiral Callaghan; the commanding officer of his flagship, Captain Cassin Young; and 98 crew members.

The *San Francisco*'s survivors, under command of Lt. Comdr. Herbert E. Schonland, saved their ship to fight again in the Aleutians; at Wake; in the Gilbert, Marshall, Caroline, and Palou islands; off New Guinea; and the Marianas. Later she joined forces supporting the amphibious landings in the Philippine Islands, on Iwo Jima and Okinawa, and in Korea and China. The *San Francisco* was deactivated at the Philadelphia Navy Yard, January 19, 1946.

The USS *San Francisco* won the Presidential Unit Citation, the Nation's highest tribute to a ship and all her company.

The Memorial to the USS *San Francisco* (actual bridge structure, riddled with shells, together with the ship's mast upon which is mounted the ship's bell) is emplaced 200 feet above the shoreline of the Pacific Ocean on the edge of a natural esplanade on Lands End.

The third United States Navy ship to bear the name USS *San Francisco* is the nuclear-powered attack submarine, SSN-711, commissioned in 1980.

USS *Coral Sea*

In a letter written to Mayor John F. Shelley, in July 1967, Captain William Shawcross, of the USS *Coral Sea*, asked the City of San Francisco to "adopt" his ship, as his men had always considered San Francisco their home port. Shelley agreed to the adoption and presented the matter to the Board of Supervisors who formalized the agreement with Resolution No. 417-67.

On July 24, 1967, in ceremonies in the City Hall rotunda, Captain Shawcross accepted the 96-piece set of wardroom silverware, which had originally been presented to the old cruiser *San Francisco* in 1890, and then to the new cruiser *San Francisco* in 1934. The ship was also presented two 40-by-6-foot banners inscribed "San Francisco's Own" to be flown port and starboard on the island of the ship as she enters and leaves port.

The USS *Coral Sea*, under command of Captain L. E. Allen, Jr., was decommissioned in Norfolk, Virginia, April 30, 1990.

Wharves and Docks 1847–1870

Note: Wharves extend out into the water; docks are built alongside the water. Not all piers and docks existed at the same time. Most were built in the late 1850s and 1860s. Described locations, not always clear, relate to expansion of San Francisco into Yerba Buena Cove after 1849.

ABERNETHY'S
(from Steuart, northeast between Market and Mission)
ALAMEDA FERRY
(from Davis, east between Pacific and Broadway)
BEALE STREET
(foot of Beale)
BLACK DIAMOND/BELLINGHAM BAY
(foot of Steuart, formerly Rincon Dock)
BROADWAY
(east, from between Battery and Front)

BUCKELEW'S
(Green, east from Battery)
BURR'S
(north just west of Bay and Montgomery)
CALIFORNIA/OREGON AND MEXICAN STEAMSHIP CO.
(see Folsom)
CALIFORNIA STREET
(also see Market) (east, from between Montgomery and Sansome, then northeast along Market)
CARR'S
(see Meiggs')
CENTRAL
(called "Long & Commercial"; Commercial Street, east from Montgomery)
CLARK'S
(see Broadway—first wharf in San Francisco, 1847)
CLAY STREET
(east, from between Montgomery and Sansome)
COWELL'S
(from Battery, east between Union and Filbert)
COUSIN'S DRY DOCK
(see Merchant's Dry Dock Co.)
CUNNINGHAM'S
(from Battery, east between Green and Vallejo)
DEWEY'S
(foot of Third)
DOCKMAN'S
(Steuart)
HUNTERS POINT DRY DOCK CO.
(Hunters Point)
EAST STREET
(the Embarcadero extended northwest and south from Market)
FILLMORE STREET
(north, from Chestnut)
FLINT'S
(north, from end of Battery)
FOLSOM
(northeast, from foot of Folsom)
FRONT STREET
(north on Front at Vallejo)

GREENWICH DOCK
(north end of Battery)
GRIFFING'S
(Battery, from Filbert to Greenwich)
HAM AND HATHAWAY'S
(Spear, southeast at Harrison)
HOBB'S
(east, off Long Bridge at 3rd near Alameda)
HOWARD STREET
(northeast, from Steuart)
HOWISON'S
(Sacramento, east from Leidesdorff)
INDIA DOCK
(between Battery and Front, Filbert to
Greenwich)
JACKSON STREET
(east, from Montgomery)
LARUE'S
(northeast, from East near Market)
LAW'S
(east, from Battery between Union and
Green)
LOMBARD DOCK
(Lombard, east from Sansome)
LONG
(see Central)
MAIN STREET
(southeast, from foot of Main)
MARKET
(see California Street)
MASTICK'S
(east, from Steuart between Mission and
Howard)
MEIGGS'
(north, from Francisco between Mason and
Powell)
MERCHANTS DRY DOCK COMPANY
(Kearny and Bay)
MISSION STREET
(northeast, from Steuart)
MONTGOMERY AND FRANCISCO STREETS
(east, from foot of Francisco)
MOORE AND COMPANY DOCK
(east at Potrero Point)
NELSON'S
(east, between Market and Commercial)
NORTH AMERICAN STEAMSHIP LINE

(foot of Mission)
**NORTH PACIFIC TRANSPORTATION
COMPANY**
(foot of Folsom)
NORTH POINT DOCK
(Sansome, north from Lombard to
Chestnut)
OAKLAND FERRY (TWO)
(Pacific, east of Davis; foot of Second)
PACIFIC STREET
(east, from Montgomery and Sansome)
PACIFIC MAIL STEAMSHIP COMPANY
(foot of Folsom; later, southeast, on First at
Brannan)
PACIFIC ROLLING MILLS
(Potrero Point)
RAND'S
(east, between Clay and Commercial)
RINCON DOCK
(Rincon Point Dock; south, from foot of Steuart)
ROBINSON'S
(between Jackson and Pacific, part of East
Street Wharf)
ROUSSET
(northeast on Howard from Steuart)
RYAN AND DUFF'S
(northeast on Mission from Steuart)
SACRAMENTO STREET
(see Howison's)
SHAW'S
(see Cowell's)
SMITH'S
(southeast on Steuart at Howard)
THIRD STREET
(southeast, from foot of Third)
UNION STREET
(east, from Battery; first Fisherman's Wharf)
VALLEJO STREET
(east, from Battery)
WASHINGTON STREET
(east, from between Montgomery and
Sansome)

Unnamed Wharves

Eight small wharves existed along the
eastern shoreline of North Beach (near Bay
and Francisco streets) in the 1850s. Five

small wharves stood along the South Beach shoreline (east of Rincon Hill) at the same time.

Shipwrecks of San Francisco County

The following is a list of shipwrecks that occurred, or ended up, in San Francisco County. It does not include many small vessels wrecked in and near the Golden Gate, or intentional scuttlings (Gold Rush ships, etc.). Most wrecks were caused by inaccurate navigation through thick sea-level fog, most common in winter, when bay (tule) fog mingles with ocean fog. Remains of several ships are visible at Point Lobos/Lands End at low tide—the *Coos Bay*, *Frank H. Buck*, *Lyman Stewart*, and *Ohioan*.

(Please see next page for a full accounting of shipwrecks.)

San Francisco has a long history as major sea port. The original Union Ferry Building at the foot of Market Street before construction of a new edifice in 1896. This earlier version was built in 1877 by the Central Pacific Railway.

San Francisco Shipwrecks

NAME	TYPE	YEAR	PLACE	FATALITIES
ABERDEEN	SHIP	1852/53	FORT POINT	0
ABERDEEN	STEAM SCHOONER	1916	ENTRANCE OF GOLDEN GATE	SEVERAL
AIMER	SCHOONER	1871	OCEAN BEACH, FOOT OF VICENTE	0
AMERICAN BOY	SCHOONER	1890	WEST OF NORTH FARALLON ISLAND	0
ANN PARRY	BARK	1865	OCEAN BEACH, NEAR FOOT OF BALBOA	4
ANNIE SISIE	SHIP	1871	MAINTOP ISLAND, FARALLON ISLANDS	0
ATLANTIC	BARK	1886	OCEAN BEACH, FOOT OF QUINTARA	32
BENEVOLENCE	C-4 FREIGHTER	1950	WEST OF GOLDEN GATE	18
BESSIE EVERDING	SCHOONER	1888	OCEAN BEACH, FOOT OF LAWTON	0
BREMEN	SHIP	1882	WEST OF MAINTOP ISLAND, FARALLONS	0
BRIGNARDELLO	BARK	1868	KELLY'S COVE, OCEAN BEACH	0
CAROLINE AMELIA	BARK	1850	MILE ROCK	0
"CAYUCO" OF SAN CARLOS	ROWBOAT	1775	KELLY'S COVE	UNKNOWN
CHAMPLAIN	SHIP	1875	NORTHWEST OF NORTH FARALLON ISLAND	2
CHATEAU PALMER	SHIP	1856	FORT POINT	0
CITY OF CHESTER	STEAMER	1888	NEAR FORT POINT (COLLISION)	16
CITY OF NEW YORK	STEAMER	1893	POINT BONITA	0
CITY OF RIO DE JANEIRO	STEAMER	1901	NEAR FORT POINT	128
COOS BAY	FREIGHTER	1927	DEADMAN'S POINT, LANDS END	0
C. W. LAWRENCE	REV. CUTTER	1851	OCEAN BEACH, NEAR ZOO SITE	0
DAISY ROWE	SCHOONER	1900	NEAR POINT DIABLO	0
DUBLIN	BARK	1882	OCEAN BEACH, FOOT OF RIVERA	0
ELIZA	SLOOP	1871	POINT LOBOS	0
ELKO	SCOW SCHOONER	1881	PYRAMID ROCK, LANDS END	0
EUTERPE	SHIP	1860	FORT POINT BEACH (SALVAGED)	0
FRANCONIA	SHIP	1881	MAINTOP ISLAND, FARALLON ISLANDS	0
FRANK H. BUCK	TANKER	1937	GOLDEN GATE (COLLISION)	0
FRANK JONES	SHIP	1877	FORT POINT ROCK	0
F. W. BAILEY	SHIP	1863	OCEAN BEACH, FOOT OF TARAVAL	0
GENERAL CUSHING	SHIP	1858	NEAR FORT POINT ROCK	0
GEORGE LOUIS	SCHOONER	1882	NEAR LANDS END	0
GOLDEN FLEECE	CLIPPER	1854	FORT POINT	0
GRANADA	STEAMER	1860	FORT POINT BEACH	0
HENRY BERG	EC-2 FREIGHTER	1944	SOUTH FARALLON ISLAND	0
H.J. CORCORAN	STEAMER	1912/13	SOUTH OF ANGEL ISLAND (COLLISION, SALVAGED)	0

San Francisco Shipwrecks

NAME	TYPE	YEAR	PLACE	FATALITIES
ISAAC JEANNES	BARK	1876	FORT POINT BEACH	0
JENNY LIND	SHIP	1853	BONITA COVE (SALVAGED)	0
JOSEPHINE WILCOTT	SCHOONER	1872	NORTH OF POINT LOBOS	0
JULIA CASTNER	BARK	1859	OCEAN BEACH FOOT OF SOUTH DRIVE	0
KATH. DONOVAN	STEAMER	1941	SEAL ROCKS (SALVAGED)	0
KING PHILIP	BARK	1878	OCEAN BEACH, NEAR FOOT OF NORIEGA	0
LAWRENCE	CUTTER	1851	OCEAN BEACH, NEAR ZOO SITE?	0
LOUIS HARKER	SCHOONER	1907	SOUTH FARALLON ISLAND	0
LOUIS HARKER	SCHOONER	1864	CLAY ST. WHARF	0
LUCAS	SHIP	1858	SEAL ROCK, SOUTH FARALLON IS.	15-30
LYMAN A. STEWART	TANKER	1922	NEAR HERMIT ROCK, LANDS END	0
MERSEY	BARK	1850	BONITA COVE	0
MIDNIGHT CITY	SLOOP	1853	NEAR PT. BONITA	8
MORNING LIGHT	SCHOONER	1868	EAST OF SOUTH FARALLON ISLAND	0
NAVY BOAT	BOAT	1945	SOUTH OF YERBA BUENA ISLAND	11
NEPTUNE	SCHOONER	1900	OCEAN BEACH, MID- FORT FUNSTON	0
NOONDAY	CLIPPER	1863	NOONDAY ROCK, FARALLON ISLANDS	0
OHIOAN	FREIGHTER	1936	POINT LOBOS	0
PARALLEL	SCHOONER	1887	POINT LOBOS	0
PATHFINDER	PILOT SCHOONER	1914	POINT DIABLO	0
PET	SCHOONER	1888	POINT BONITA	0
POINT LOBOS	FREIGHTER	1939	KIRBY COVE (SALVAGED)	0
REPORTER	SCHOONER	1902	OCEAN BEACH, FOOT OF MORAGA	0
ROBERT HENDERSON	BARK	1850	OCEAN BEACH, FOOT OF LINCOLN	0
SAGAMORE	SHIP	1850	EMBARCADERO, (EXPLODED)	30 TO 40
SAN CARLOS	GALLEON	1797	WEST OF CRISSY FIELD BEACH	UNKNOWN
SAN FRANCISCO	CLIPPER	1853	POINT BONITA	0
SAN RAFAEL	FERRY	1901	EAST OF ALCATRAZ (COLLISION)	3
SCHAN JEHAN	SHIP	1867	NORTH OF POINT LOBOS	0
SEMINOLE	FERRY		(SEE H.J. CORCORAN, SALVAGED)	
TONQUIN	SHIP	1849	TONQUIN SHOAL, NORTH BEACH	UNKNOWN
VISCATA	SHIP	1868	NORTH END BAKERS BEACH	0
WM. FREDERICK	SCHOONER	1887	OCEAN BEACH, MID–FORT FUNSTON	2
WM. L. BEEBE	SCHOONER	1894	OCEAN BEACH, FOOT OF SLOAT	0
YOSEMITE	STEAM SCHOONER	1926	OCEAN BEACH, FOOT OF FULTON	0
ZENOBIA	SHIP	1858	POINT BONITA	0

MICHAEL D. LAMPEN

29 Native Americans

Native Americans of San Francisco

The first people to inhabit western North America were nomadic hunter-gatherer groups who were present more than 15,000 years ago (perhaps as much as 40,000 years ago). The earliest human remains uncovered to date in San Francisco were the bones of a young woman found in 1970 during the construction of the Civic Center BART subway station. The remains date to 3,100 BC (plus or minus 250 years). By 2,500 BC a Bay Area variation of the so-called Early Horizon culture of central California can be recognized. It is thought that the people of this culture spoke Hokan, a language stock then common throughout central California.

Cultural change beginning about 1,000 BC probably represents the spread of different, Penutian-speaking people through the Bay Area and Great Valley, displacing the Hokan speakers. With the new people came technical advances such as the bow and arrow (replacing the earlier spear-thrower) and more sophisticated craft tech-

niques. The language group of the Penutian-speaking people of the central and southern Bay Area (and Santa Cruz/Monterey areas) was called Costanoan by early anthropologists although an Indian tribelet name, Ohlone, has gained considerable popularity as a name for both the language group and people. The tribelets of the San Francisco peninsula spoke the Ramaytush language. Perhaps 500 people lived within the present county boundaries of San Francisco at the time of the Spanish Conquest.

Ohlone village sites are recognized by large shell/debris mounds of which over two dozen have been identified in San Francisco. Most known sites cluster along the south-facing bay shores of Bayview Heights and Hunters Point, with other grouped sites along Islais Creek (where it entered its marsh) and Black Point (the Fort Mason headland). Several South-of-Market marsh-side sites have been uncovered, as well as sites in North Beach, the Presidio (near the former marsh), Sutro Heights, and

The Ohlone Indians, the first San Franciscans.

near Lake Merced. Several other sites were destroyed, and others remain to be discovered. Several village names were recorded by the Spanish.

The Ohlone way of life was closely linked to, and respectful of, nature—the source of food and raw materials, and the repository of spiritual powers. The rhythms of the seasons were reflected in the many ceremonies and rituals that provided a spiritual bond between the Ohlone and their world. A rich variety of foods was available, gathered from bay, ocean, marsh, or grassland, while other foods and raw materials (e.g., pine nuts, obsidian) were obtained by trade. Like most central California peoples, the Ohlone were known for their superb woven baskets, used for everything from carrying to cooking. Men usually went naked and women wore rush/tule and deerskin skirts. Villages consisted of a cluster of tule or bark huts, a semisubterranean dance house and/or sweathouse, racks for drying food, sunshades for working areas, and small granaries for acorns (where available).

Villages were not permanent, and tribelets moved with seasonal changes in food supply. Communities consisted of several extended families gathered in a clan. A chief (man or woman) and council were in charge, and a village shaman saw to the spiritual and medical needs of the community. The creation myth envisioned a primeval flood, followed by the creation of humans by Coyote, assisted by Eagle and Hummingbird. Dance ceremonies marked puberty, spring fertility, bear and other cults, ghosts, and death. Recreation included ball games and gambling. Warfare, usually territorial, was ritualized and involved reparations for casualties.

The arrival of the Spanish brought the Ohlone people and their culture to a swift and tragic end. The hard mission regimen of work and punishment, combined with culture shock and the spread of European diseases, killed most of the Ohlone people in the space of two or three generations.

MICHAEL D. LAMPEN

San Francisco Wildlife in the Ohlone Indian Economy

Remains of the following invertebrates, fish, birds, and mammals were identified from three Ohlone Indian sites at Fort Mason, San Francisco, in 1981. The list features local wildlife important for the food and material needs of the first San Franciscans, the Ohlone Indians. Animal populations have been severely depleted over the last century by habitat destruction, water pollution, and freshwater diversion. No large native mammals survive in San Francisco.

INVERTEBRATES

Mussel	(Mytilus sp.)
Oyster	(Ostrea lurida)
Basket Cockle	(Clinocardium nuttalli)
Bent-Nosed Clam	(Macoma nasuta)
Clam	(Cryptomya californica)
Littleneck Clam	(Protothaca staminea)
Checkered Periwinkle	(Littorina scutulata)
Dog Whelk	(Nucella lamellosa)
California Horned Snail	(Cerithidea californica)
Barnacles	(Balanus cariosus, Balanus sp.)
Crabs	(Cancer sp., Cancridae)

FISH

Soupfin Shark	(Galeorhinus galeus)
Leopard Shark	(Triakis semifasciata)
Brown Smoothhound	(Mustelus henlei)
Bat Ray	(Myliobatis californica)
Ray	(Raja sp.)
Sturgeon	(Acipenser sp.)
Pacific Herring	(Clupea pallasi)
Pacific Sardine	(Sardinops sagax)

King Salmon (*Oncorhynchus tshawytscha*)
Plainfin Midshipman (*Porichthys notatus*)
Topsmelt (*Atherinops affinis*)
Jacksmelt (*Atherinopsis californiensis*)
Brown Rockfish (*Sebastes auriculatus*)
China Rockfish (*Sebastes nebulosus*)
Grass Rockfish (*Sebastes rastrelliger*)
Kelp Greenling (*Hexagrammos decagrammos*)
Rock Greenling (*Hexagrammos lagocephalus*)
Buffalo Sculpin (*Enophrys bison*)
Bull Sculpin (*Enophrys taurina*)
Cabezon (*Scorpaenichthys marmoratus*)
Barred Surfperch (*Amphistichus argenteus*)
Calico Surfperch (*Amphistichus koelzi*)
Redtail Surfperch (*Amphistichus rhodoterus*)
Black Surfperch (*Embiotoca jacksoni*)
Striped Surfperch (*Embiotoca lateralis*)
Walleye Surfperch (*Hyperprosopon argenteum*)
Rainbow Surfperch (*Hypsurus caryi*)
White Surfperch (*Phanerodon furcatus*)
Rubberlip Surfperch (*Rachochilus toxotes*)
Monkeyface
Prickleback (*Cebidichthys violaceus*)
Sand Sole (*Psettichthys melanostictus*)

BIRDS

Common Loon (*Gavia immer*)
Western Grebe (*Aechmorphus occidentalis*)
Eared Grebe (*Podiceps nigricollis*)
Brown Pelican (*Pelecanus occidentalis*)
Brandt's Cormorant (*Phalacrocorax penicillatus*)
Double-Crested Cormorant (*Phalacrocorax auritus*)
Pelagic Cormorant (*Phalacrocorax pelagicus*)

Diving Ducks (*Aythya sp.*)
Cinnamon Teal (*Anas cyanoptera*)
Geese (*Branta sp., Chen sp., Anser sp.*)
Surf Scoter (*Melanitta perspicillata*)
Sharp-Shinned Hawk (*Accipiter striatus*)
Red-Tailed Hawk (*Buteo jamaicensis*)
American Coot (*Fulica americana*)
Sandpiper (*Calidris sp.*)
Red Phalarope (*Phalaropus fulicarius*)
Western Gull (*Laurus occidentalis*)
Common Murre (*Uria aalge*)
Great Horned Owl (*Bubo virginianus*)
Common Crow (*Corvus brachyrhynchos*)
Raven (*Corvus corvax*)

MAMMALS

Brush Rabbit (*Sylvilagus bachmani*)
Beechey Ground Squirrel (*Spermophilus beecheyi*)
Valley Pocket Gopher (*Thomomys bottae*)
Mouse (*Peromyscus sp.*)
Dusky-Footed Wood Rat (*Neotoma fuscipes*)
California Meadow Vole (*Microtus californicus*)
Dog (*Canis sp.*)
(possibly Gray Wolf)
Grizzly Bear (*Ursus arctos*)
Raccoon (*Procyon lotor*)
Sea Otter (*Enhydra lutris*)
Bobcat (*Lynx rufus*)
California Sea Lion (*Zalophus californianus*)
Harbor Seal (*Phoca vitulina*)
Tule Elk (*Cervus elaphus nannodes*)
Mule Deer (*Odocoileus hemionus*)
Harbor Porpoise (*Phocoena phocoena*)
Cow (*Bos taurus*)
Domestic Goat (*Capra hircus*)

WILLIAM N. ESCHMEYER
JACQUELINE SCHONEWALD
California Academy of Sciences

30 *Natural History*

Biotic Communities of Natural San Francisco

The following abbreviated lists give some of the plants and animals commonly found in the ten diverse biotic communities that once occupied the site of San Francisco and the adjacent bay and ocean. Geologic, climatic, marine/estuarine, and human factors, which influenced these communities in various ways, are not considered here. The biota listed were not rigidly confined to their respective communites but were most often found in or near them. Animals marked with an asterisk have been identified from faunal remains in prehistoric/early historic Indian sites at present-day Fort Mason (William Eschmeyer and Jacqueline Schonewald, California Academy of Sciences, 1981). The faunal section of the Bay/Ocean community list is enlarged to contain all the bird and fish remains found at Fort Mason. "Sp" after a name means the species is not given, or was not identifiable from remains.

BAY/OCEAN

Flora—bull kelp, giant bladder kelp
Fauna—California grey whale, harbor porpoise*, grebes (western, eared)*, brown pelican*, cormorants (Brandt's, double-crested, pelagic)*, diving duck sp.*, cinnamon teal*, surf scoter*, knot*, red phalarope*, western gull*, common murre*, sharks (soupfin, leopard)*, brown smoothhound*, bat ray*, skate sp.*, sturgeon sp.*, Pacific herring*, Pacific sardine*, king salmon*, plainfin midshipman*, jacksmelt*, rockfish (brown, china, grass)*, greeling (kelp, rock)*, buffalo sculpin*, cabezon*, surfperch (barred, calico, redtail, black, striped, walleye, rainbow, white, rubberlip)*, monkeyface prickleback*, sand sole*

INTERTIDAL

(ocean and near-ocean nonmarsh bay)
Flora—rock weed, eel grass, oar weed
Fauna—Steller sea lion, California sea lion*, harbor seal*, sea otter*, western gull,

Conservatory of Flowers following a rare snowstorm on Feb. 5, 1887. The official record shows that 3.7 inches of snow fell during the storm, with up to 7 inches at the highest elevations of Twin Peaks. The next substantial snowstorm in the City occurred on February 5 also, but the year was 1977.

275

sanderling, line shore crab, beach hopper sp., abalone, bent-nosed clam, sand dollar sp.

COASTAL BLUFFS

Flora—seaside daisy, golden aster, bluff chickweed, common stone crop, lupine sp., coyote mint, coast strawberry
Fauna—California gull, California ground squirrel*, common checkerspot butterfly

COASTAL STRAND

(sand dunes, with coastal scrub cover inland)
Flora—beach lupine, coyote brush, dune sagebrush, common yarrow, dune bluegrass, beach primrose, arroyo willow (in wet spots), lotus sp., dune tasy, yellow sand verbena, coast fiddleneck
Fauna—Xerces blue butterfly, sand wasp sp., sand treader cricket sp. (see Coastal Scrub)

COASTAL SCRUB

(also found in scattered locations in grassland)
Flora—coast barberry, poison oak, coffee berry, bush monkeyflower, California sagebrush, islay cherry, coyote brush, blue blossom ceanothus, toyon, bush lupine, huckleberry, yerba buena
Fauna—grizzly bear*, mule deer*, mountain lion, bobcat*, grey fox*, brush rabbit*, dusky-footed wood rat*, white-footed mouse sp.*, great hornel owl, chickadee, California quail, western rattlesnake

GRASSLAND

(coastal prairie grading toward interior, valley, grassland)
Flora—red fescue, purple needlegrass, California oatgrass, junegrass, big squirreltail, pearly everlasting, footsteps of spring, bitter cress, shooting star, owl's clover, gold fields, California poppy
Fauna—tule elk*, badger, coyote, California ground squirrel*, California pocket gopher*, California vole*, California

condor, common crow, western meadowlark, gopher snake, field cricket, Mission blue butterfly

RIPARIAN

(streamside, also springs and seeps)
Flora—arroyo willow, common horsetail, adder's tongue, western lady fern, buckbean, yellow-eyed grass, rush sp., sedge sp.
Fauna—tule elk*, grizzly bear*, raccoon*, striped skunk, California vole*, common crow, downy woodpecker, yellow warbler, California newt, mourning cloak butterfly

FRESHWATER MARSH

(including lakes/lagoons)
Flora—California wax myrtle, arroyo willow, cattail sp., California tule, cotton grass, walking sedge, hornwort, duckweed sp.
Fauna—raccoon*, California vole*, vagrant shrew, western pond turtle, western toad, red-winged blackbird, American coot, mallard duck

COASTAL SALT MARSH

(grading in places to freshwater marsh)
Flora—saltgrass, pickleweed, cord grass, sea-blite, sea lavender, salt marsh dodder
Fauna—tule elk*, saltmarsh harvest mouse, snow goose, blue heron, clapper rail, northern harrier, knot*, California horned snail

MIXED EVERGREEN FOREST

Flora—Coast live oak, California buckeye, California bay, poison oak
Fauna—grizzly bear*, mule deer*, bobcat*, grey fox*, raccoon*, great horned owl, common raven, long-eared bat, California slender salamander

Earlier Biotic Communities of San Francisco

Ice Age (Pleistocene) San Francisco was a cooler, moister place with California juniper, Monterey pine, and Douglas fir on the uplands, and rich grassland in the lowlands—the future San Francisco Bay site.

Grazing mammals included mammoth, musk ox, bison, camel, horse, giant ground sloth, elk, deer, pronghorn, and peccary. Carnivores included sabre-tooth cat, dire wolf, and coyote. Walrus gathered on off-shore rocks.

In warmer pre–Ice Age (Pliocene) times, the local presence of mastodon, rhinoceros, hyena, giant tortoise, and flamingo suggests a mild savannalike climate. Tropical conditions prevailed in earlier (Eocene-Oligocene) times, and the site of San Francisco probably lay beneath a shallow sea.

A few scattered fossils have been found in the tropical marine rocks of Jurassic and Cretaceous age that make up the bedrock of San Francisco. These include primitive clams, oysters, sea urchins, ammonites, and more than 15 species of radiolaria (microorganisms with star- and cone-shaped shells) in the chert bedrock.

Michael D. Lampen

Farming, Forestry, and Fishing in San Francisco

During the Spanish-Mexican period, San Francisco's principal farming activity was the care and grazing of cattle and horses. The fertile land between Mission Dolores and Dolores Lagoon was used for vegetable farming and orchards with limited success. After the American conquest, vegetable and grain farms spread throughout the Mission District, and were established in the Marina (Cow Hollow) District. Dairy farming was also a major activity in the Marina District (and briefly in North Beach), as it was later in Glen Canyon.

After World War I, vegetable farms were created in the Lakeshore-Parkmerced, Sunnyside-Cayuga, western Portola, Silver Terrace, Sunnydale and Little Hollywood districts. Excepting Little Hollywood and Lakeshore-Parkmerced, these districts had extensive greenhouse complexes, growing vegetables and flowers. Only a few green-

houses survive today.

In the 1880s, future mayor Adolph Sutro planted pine, cypress, and eucalyptus trees on the western part of the city's central hills (western half of the former Rancho San Miguel) with the idea of future timber profits. The Greene family did the same in the Trocadero Creek-Parkside District to the west. Sutro Forest, Mt. Davidson Park, and Stern Grove are surviving remnants.

Early members of San Francisco's Chinese community set up fishing camps at China Beach and Rincon Point. They later had four shrimping camps on outer Hunters Point. A Danish crab-netting center was located in Harbor Cove. San Francisco's Italian-run fishing fleet was located at Union Street pier until it moved to today's Fisherman's Wharf in 1900.

Michael D. Lampen

Flora

Before construction began in San Francisco, the local plant communities reflected the mild local (Mediterranean) climate, with its coastal winds, and dry but unusually cool (foggy) summers. Two other important factors shaping the local flora were the varied soils and topography. All three factors had changed over geologic time, further diversifying the flora.

In the floral region between central Marin and central San Mateo counties, an area often called the Franciscan flora, the plants were, and are, characteristically tolerant of winds, drought, and poor soils. The Franciscan flora were in many ways transitional between the moisture-dependent northern coastal flora and the drought-tolerant southern coastal flora.

The unusually high diversity of local plant species, a Mediterranean characteristic, resulted in several (probably evolutionarily older) endemic species unique to the area. (See Unique and Extinct Plant and Butterfly Species of San Francisco.)

Shrubs and herbaceous plants dominated

the coastal scrub community, and grasses made up the more interior coastal prairie community. Trees were small and confined to rare permanent stream banks, usually on north-facing slopes. Hardy, long-rooted plants grew in sheltered swales among the sand dunes with scrub on the interior dunes. Brackish to freshwater plant communities grew in the bayside marshes. Specialized floral communities grew on the extensive local serpentine outcrops, toxic to many species, and around the occasional vernal pools (springtime marshes).

MICHAEL D. LAMPEN

Fossils (selected list of nonmicroscopic fossils)

The following fossil remains have been found in San Francisco:

PLANTS

Juniperus california (California juniper) — Russian Hill. 30,000 years old.

Pinus radiata (Monterey pine)—Ocean Beach/Fort Funston. Less than 1 million years old.

ANIMALS

Ammonites *Douvilleiceras* cf. D. *mammilatum* (flattened coiled shell of primitive squid)—cliff west of China Beach, Lands End. 98–118 million years old.

Echinoids *Anorthoscutum interlineatum* (sand dollar)—Ocean Beach/Fort Funston. .5 to 3 million years old.

Mollusks *Inoceramus ellioti* (large primitive oyster)—Alcatraz Island. 135–140 million years old.

Lucina alcatrazis (small clam)—Alcatraz Island. 135–140 million years old.

Mammals *Bison latifrons* (large "buffalo" with 6-foot horn spread)—North Beach. 25,000 years old.

Glossotherium harlani (cattle-sized herbivorous ground sloth)—Eureka Valley (Castro). 250–300 thousand years old.

Homo sapiens (human female)—Civic Center (BART station site). 7,000 years old (oldest human remains found to date in San Francisco).

Mammuthuss columbi (large shaggy mammoth with very long tusks)—North Beach. 25,000 years old.

MICHAEL D. LAMPEN

Landscape of San Francisco

Before the arrival of the Spanish in 1769, San Francisco had a varied landscape of much complexity. Hills and flats, lagoons and creeks, dunes and grassland, scrublands and coastal cliffs, sloughs and marshes, coves and beaches offered a wide variety of habitats for plants and animals. Vegetation patterns reflected the cool, dry summer climate, windy or sheltered locations, and varied soil conditions.

Active sand dunes extended inland over much of the Richmond and Sunset districts and the site of Golden Gate Park, although small ponds commonly formed little oases in the interdune swales. A small, active dune also extended from near Lobos Creek over Presidio Hill, and another spread eastward from Harbor Cove (the present Marina District) behind Black Point (Fort Mason) to Tonquin Point, now the site of the Cannery.

Further inland, a broad band of less active dunes, partly stabilized by coastal scrub, extended eastward from between Mountain Lake and Mount Sutro to Yerba Buena Cove and the Mission Bay marshes. Some swales supported grassland.

Marshlands drained by meandering sloughs bordered most bayside coves. Presidio Slough flowed east to Harbor Cove. Mission Bay was bordered by marshes interspersed with active sand dune "peninsulas." The southwest part of the marshes merged into Dolores Lagoon in the northeast Mission District. Islais Creek Marsh, drained by its large slough, extended east from the eastern base of Bernal Heights. Yosemite Creek marsh occupied the central Bayview District south of Silver Terrace.

Most streams flowed into marsh sloughs and a few disappeared into the dunes or formed small lakes behind them, such as Laguna Honda, Pine Lake, and Washerwoman's Lagoon. Lake Merced occupies branches of a drowned creek gulch.

Stretching across most of central, southern, and southeastern San Francisco was a rolling landscape of bunchgrass, interspersed with scrub. Coastal scrub thickly covered the hill slopes that faced west. A remnant survives above Laguna Honda. Coastal scrub and grasses also extended eastward from the Sutro Heights–Land's End area to the Presidio. Scrub oak grew on sheltered Presidio slopes that faced north. Grassland occupied much of the Presidio extending eastward through the Cow Hollow–Golden Gate Valley area. The grasslands reappeared near North Beach and Telegraph Hill. Scrub covered much of Pacific Heights as well as Russian and Nob hills.

Shorelines were varied. Sandy cliffs and beaches of the Pacific shore gave way northward to ocean cliffs and small pockets of beaches. On the bay shore, sand spits, low cliffs, and gravel beaches alternated with, or backed, marshlands or mudflats.

Extensive grazing during the Spanish and Mexican periods may have aided somewhat in the eastward spread of the open sand dunes (western San Francisco) and reduced coastal scrub in favor of grassland in the central and eastern hills. Some deforestation of north-facing slopes also occurred.

MICHAEL D. LAMPEN

Flora and Fauna

The information contained herein on the flora and fauna of San Francisco was obtained from and compiled by the following staff members of the California Academy of Sciences: Dr. Robert T. Orr, Dr. Elizabeth McClintock, Dr. Laurence C. Binford, Mr. Thomas Davies, and Mr. Kenneth Lucas.

The 49 square miles occupied by the City of San Francisco are almost completely urbanized and industrialized. The hills, dunes, and marshes once so conspicuous have all but disappeared, and along with these features the native plants have also gone. Of the hills, Mt. Sutro and Mt. Davidson are covered now with a man-made forest and residences; only on Twin Peaks, in a few places, are still to be found remnants of natural areas with grassland and rocky outcroppings and some native plants. Almost nothing of the sand dunes remains except along the ocean as in the Fort Funston area, and of the marshes probably nothing at all remains.

San Francisco even before its urbanization was a region with few trees. California buckeye (*Aesculus californica*) and California laurel (*Umbellularia californica*) here once in reduced numbers are long since gone. Only the California live oak (*Quercus agrifolia*), the arroyo and yellow willows (*Salix lasiolepis and Salix lasiandra*) and probably the California wax-myrtle (*Myricaca californica*) can still be seen in a few places. The planted trees making up the man-made woodland of Mt. Sutro, Mt. Davidson, the Presidio and Golden Gate Park are mostly two conifers, Monterey pine (*Pinus radiata*) and Monterey cypress (*Cupresus macrocarpa*), and the blue gum from Australia (*Eucalyptus globulus*). Introduced at the end of the last century, these (particularly the blue gum) are becoming naturalized and dense enough to resemble a woodland.

As urbanization progressed and the native plants disappeared, another group of plants appeared on bits and pieces of disturbed and vacant ground. These spontaneously appearing plants are called weeds. These newcomers to our scene were brought by man either directly or indirectly. Some were brought intentionally, being either edible or ornamental, while others were carried unintentionally and serve no useful purpose to man—at times they may even become a nuisance.

Another group of plants which we often call ornamentals has appeared along with urbanization. These are always carried about intentionally and are always planted. They are made available by the nursery industry to gardeners, home owners, and landscape architects. These are the plants seen most frequently in San Francisco, in gardens, along the streets, and in the parks. Like weeds, they are mostly not native to San Francisco, or even to California, but have been brought here for their esthetic value from other parts of the world where climates are similar to ours. They beautify the city and make it an attractive, pleasant, and enjoyable place to live.

The plants listed here belong to the first two categories, those native to San Francisco and the nonnative naturalized weeds. No ornamentals are listed; however, a few of the weeds were once ornamentals which have "escaped" from cultivation and are now naturalized. A few localities are listed, such as Twin Peaks and the Presidio, where still may be seen some of the native plants which once covered the northern San Francisco Peninsula.

(Reference: *A Flora of San Francisco, California* by John Thomas Howell, Peter Raven and Peter Rubtzoff. Since this was published in 1958, certain areas which had been undisturbed are now urbanized and their plants have disappeared.)

ELIZABETH MCCLINTOCK
California Academy of Sciences

Selected Plants of San Francisco

(N = natives; W = weeds)

Polypodiaceae (Fern Family)

Athyrium filix-femina. Western Lady-Fern. (N) Wet or marshy areas in gullies and canyons. Lobos Creek, Lake Merced.

Pityrogramma triangularis. Goldback Fern. (N) Rocky and brushy slopes. Presidio, Lake Merced, Bayview Hills.

Polypodium californicum. California Polypody. (N) Rocky slopes of hills. Above Baker Beach, Lands End, Lake Merced, Twin Peaks, Russian Hill.

Polypodium scouleri. Leather Fern. (N) Crevices and surfaces of exposed rocks. Twin Peaks, Bayview Park, McLaren Park.

Polystichum munitum. Western Sword Fern. (N) Widespread on brushy or rocky slopes and canyon bottoms. Point Lobos, Golden Gate Park, Lake Merced, Twin Peaks, Bayview Hills.

Pteridium aquilinum. Bracken Fern. (N) Widespread on dune hills, grassland and brushy slopes. Presidio, Golden Gate Park, Sunset Heights, Lake Merced, Bayview Hills.

Woodwardia fimbriata. Western Chain Fern. (N) In moist places. West end of Lake Merced.

Equisetaceae (Horsetail Family)

Equisetum telmateia. Giant Horsetail. (N) On the edge of marshes and along streams and seepages on coastal bluffs and hills. Laguna Honda, Lake Merced, Bayview Hills.

Pinaceae (Pine Family)

Pinus radiata. Monterey Pine. (W) Commonly cultivated in parks and gardens. Presidio, Golden Gate Park, Laguna Honda, McLaren Park.

Cupressaceae (Cypress Family)

Cupressus macrocarpa. Monterey Cypress. (W) A commonly cultivated tree. Presidio, Golden Gate Park, Laguna Honda, Pine Lake, Lake Merced, Bayview Hills.

Typhaceae (Cat-Tail Family)

Typha domingenis. Cat-tail. (N) Wet and marshy places. Bayview Hills.

Typha latifolia. Soft-flag. (N) Ponds and marshes. Bayview Hills.

Gramineae (Grass Family)

Agropyron repens. Quackgrass. (W) Often a weed in gardens. Sutro Heights, Golden Gate Park.

Agrostis semiverticillata. (W) Common in moist waste places. Fort Point, Golden Gate Park, Laguna Honda, Lake Merced, San Miguel Hills, McLaren Park.

Aira caryophyllea. Silvery Hair-grass. (W) Grassy or brushy slopes. Presidio, Point Lobos, Golden Gate Park, Lake Merced, Mt. Davidson, Twin Peaks, San Miguel Hills, McLaren Park, Bayview Hills.

Ammophila arenaria. Beachgrass. (W) Common on dunes along the coast. Presidio, Lake Merced.

Avena fatua. Wild Oat. (W) On grassy hillsides. Golden Gate Park, Lake Merced, Twin Peaks, Bayview Hills.

Briza maxima. Rattlesnake Grass. (W) In waste places. Golden Gate Park.

Briza minor. Little Quaking Grass. (W) On grassy slopes. Golden Gate Park, Lake Merced, Bayview Hills.

Bromus marginatus. (N) Shallow soil on sunny slopes. Presidio, Bernal Heights, Bayview Hills.

Bromus mollis. Soft Chess. (W) Abundant in grassland. Presidio, Lake Merced, Twin Peaks, Bayview Hills.

Cynodon dactylon. Bermuda Grass. (W) Common in waste places and about the margins of lawns and sidewalks. Seacliff district, Lake Merced, Golden Gate Park.

Dactylis glomerata. Orchard Grass. (W) Common in lawns. Presidio, Golden Gate Park, Lake Merced.

Danthonia californica. (N) Grassy or brushy hillsides. Presidio, San Miguel Hills, McLaren Park, north slope of Bayview Hills.

Elymus glaucus. Blue Wild-Rye. (N) In grassland and on brushy slopes. Presidio, Lands End, Golden Gate Park, Pine Lake, Lake Merced, Laguna Honda, Mt. Davidson, San Miguel Hills, McLaren Park.

Festuca dertonensis. (W) Grassy and brushy slopes. Presidio, Golden Gate Park, Twin Peaks, San Miguel Hills, Bayview Hills.

Festuca megalura. (N) On grassy slopes, flats, and dunes. Near Baker Beach, Presidio, Golden Gate Park, Lake Merced, Twin Peaks, Mt. Davidson, San Miguel Hills, McLaren Park, Bayview Hills.

Holcus lanatus. Velvet Grass. (W) Moist places and about the margins of lawns. Presidio, Golden Gate Park, Lake Merced, Mt. Davidson, San Miguel Hills.

Hordeum brachyantherum. Meadow Barley. (N) On grassy or brushy slopes and flats. Presidio, Point Lobos, Laguna Honda, Mt. Davidson, San Miguel Hills, McLaren Park, Bayview Hills.

Hordeum leporinum. Farmer's Foxtail. (W) Widespread and often abundant on grassy slopes and flats. Presidio, Golden Gate Park, Lake Merced, Mt. Davidson, San Miguel Hills, Bayview Hills.

Lagurus ovatus. Hare's-Tail Grass. (W) Occasional dense colonies on sandy slopes. Point Lobos, Golden Gate Park.

Lolium multiflorum. Italian Ryegrass. (W) On grassy slopes. Presidio, Lands End, Golden Gate Park, Lake Merced, Laguna Honda, Mt. Davidson, San Miguel Hills, Bayview Hills.

Lolium perenne. Perennial Ryegrass. (W) In lawns and commonly naturalized in waste places and in moist ground. Golden Gate Park, Lake Merced, San Miguel Hills, Bayview Hills.

Melica californica. (N) Fairly common in rocky grassland. Corona Heights, Twin Peaks, Mt. Davidson, San Miguel Hills, Bernal Heights, Bayview Hills.

Phalaris canariensis. Canarygrass. (W) Widespread in waste ground. Golden Gate Park, Lake Merced, near Russian Hill, Bayview Hills.

Poa annua. Annual Bluegrass. (W) Abundant about gardens, especially where the soil is moist. Presidio, Golden Gate Park, Lake Merced, Mt. Davidson, Twin Peak, San Miguel Hills, Bayview Hills.

Poa pratensis. Kentucky Bluegrass. (N) Common in lawns, also on brushy canyon slopes. Presidio, Golden Gate Park, Lake Merced.

Poa unilateralis. (N) On rocky open slopes. Presidio, Lake Merced, Corona Heights, Mt. Davidson, Twin Peaks, San Miguel Hills, Bernal Heights, McLaren Park, Bayview Hills.

Polypogon monspeliensis. Rabbitfoot Grass. (W) Common in wet areas or in areas which have been moist. Presidio, Point Lobos, Golden Gate Park, Lake Merced, Laguna Honda, Mt. Davidson, San Miguel Hills, Bayview Hills.

Stipa pulchra. (N) Common in rocky grassland. Presidio, Golden Gate Park, Lake Merced, Corona Heights, Laguna Honda, Mt. Davidson, Twin Peaks, San Miguel Hills, Bernal Heights, Bayview Hills.

Cyperaceae (Sedge Family)

Carex barbarae. (N) Open grassy or brushy slopes that are wet in the spring. Lake Merced, Mt. Davidson, San Miguel Hills, Bayview Hills.

Carex brevicaulis. (N) Forming turfy patches on open exposed slopes, frequently in shallow soil. Presidio, Lone Mountain, Lake Merced, Twin Peaks, McLaren Park, Bayview Hills.

Carex densa. (N) Moist soil of flats and hillside seepages. Presidio, San Miguel Hills, McLaren Park, Bayview Hills.

Carex harfordii. (N) Wet places on open or brushy hills. Mountain Lake, Lone Mountain, Golden Gate Park, Sutro Forest, Laguna Honda, Bayview Hills.

Carex subbracteata. (N) In moist grassland, brush, or woods. Presidio, Lone Mountain, Golden Gate Park, Sutro Forest, Lake Merced, between Mt. Sutro and Twin Peaks, Mt. Davidson, San Miguel Hills, Bayview Hills.

Cyperus eragrostis. (W) Common in wet places in wild and cultivated areas. Presidio, Golden Gate Park, Lake Merced, San Miguel Hills, McLaren Park, Bayview Hills.

Cyperus esculentus. Nut-Grass. (W) Often seen as a garden weed. Golden Gate Park, Lake Merced.

Scirpus californicus. California Tule. (N) In shallow water of lakes and ponds or in wet ground in marshes. Mountain Lake, Golden Gate Park, Pine Lake, Lake Merced.

Scirpus cernuus. (N) Wet soil of marshes, strands and seepages. Fort Point, Lands End, Golden Gate Park, Pine Lake, Lake Merced, San Miguel Hills, marsh north of McLaren Park, Bayview Hills.

Scirpus microcarpus. (N) Common in wet and marshy places. Mountain Lake, Lobos Creek, Golden Gate Park, Lake Merced, San Miguel Hills.

Araceae (Calla Family)

Zantedeschia aethiopica. Common Calla. (W) In wet or marshy ground. Lobos Creek, Sutro Heights above Point Lobos, Chain of Lakes and Stow Lake, Golden Gate Park.

Juncus bufonius. Toad Rush. (N) Common and widespread in moist or wet soil, both in wild and disturbed places. Mountain Lake, Point Lobos, Golden Gate Park, Lake Merced, San Miguel Hills, Bayview Hills.

Juncus effusus. Bog Rush. (N) In wet ground of marshes and about seepages. Presidio, Point Lobos, Golden Gate Park, Laguna Honda, Twin Peaks, San Miguel Hills, Bayview Hills.

Juncus leseurii. Salt Rush. (N) On wet slopes and flats, frequently in sandy soil, sometimes bordering salt marshes. Presidio, Point Lobos, Lake Merced, Golden Gate Park, Twin Peaks, Mt. Davidson, San Miguel Hills, Bayview Hills.

Juncus occidentalis. Western Rush. (N) Open slopes and flats that are moist in the spring. Presidio, Mt. Davidson, San Miguel Hills, McLaren Park, Bayview Hills.

Juncus patens. (N) Sandy soil that is wet in the spring. Presidio, Pacific Heights, Twin Peaks, Golden Gate Park, Laguna

Honda, San Miguel Hills, Bayview Hills.

Juncus phaeocephalus. (N) Wet soil of sandy flats or marshy places. Presidio, Lake Merced, San Miguel Hills, Bayview Hills.

Luzula multiflora. Wood Rush. (N) Grassland and borders of brush in shallow soil. Lands End, Presidio, east of Lake Merced, Twin Peaks, San Miguel Hills, Bayview Hills.

Liliacecae (Lily Family)

Allium dichlamydeum. Coastal Onion. (N) Open rocky slopes, in shallow soil. Presidio, often on serpentine, McLaren Park, Bayview Hills.

Brodiaea Laxa. Grass-Nut. (N) Open grassy places in sandy or rocky soil. Presidio, McLaren Park, Bayview Hills.

Brodiaea pulchella. Blue Dicks. (N) Common in grassy or brushy places. Presidio, Twin Peaks, Mt. Davidson, Lake Merced, Corona Heights, McLaren Park, Bayview Hills.

Brodiaea terrestris. (N) Open grassy slopes in shallow sandy or rocky soil. San Francisco is the type locality. McLaren Park, Bayview Hills.

Calochortus luteus. Yellow Mariposa. (N) Rocky soil of open flats and slopes. Serpentine hills near Hunters Point.

Chlorogalum pomeridianum. Soap Plant. (N) Rocky or shallow soil of open slopes. Presidio, Lake Merced, Twin Peaks, Bayview Hills.

Fritillaria lanceolata. Mission Bells. (N) In brushy or grassy places. Presidio, Twin Peaks, and the gully east of Lake Merced.

Iridaceae (Iris Family)

Iris douglasiana. Douglas Iris. (N) Open grassland and brushy slopes. Presidio, the gully east of Lake Merced, Twin Peaks, near McLaren Park.

Iris longipetala. Field Iris. (N) Open grassy slopes. Presidio, Laguna Honda, McLaren Park, Bayview Hills.

Sisyrinchium bellum. Blue-Eyed-Grass. (N) Widespread in open grassland and on brushy slopes. Presidio, Golden Gate Park, gully east of Lake Merced, Bayview Hills.

Orchidaceae (Orchid Family)

Habenaria greenei. Rein-orchis. (N) In grassland or on brushy slopes. Presidio, Point Lobos, Laguna Honda, Pine Lake, Mt. Davidson.

Salicaceae (Willow Family)

Salix lasiandra. Yellow Willow. (N) Along the edge of creeks and lakes. Mountain Lake, Lake Merced, Bayview Hills.

Salix lasiolepis. Arroyo Willow. (N) In marshes, and along streams, or on slopes that are wet in the spring and dry in the summer. Golden Gate Park, Lake Merced, McLaren Park, Bayview Hills.

Corylaceae (Hazel Family)

Corylus californica. California Hazel. (N) On brushy slopes. On the gully east of Lake Merced, Strawberry Hill in Golden Gate Park.

Fagaceae (Oak Family)

Quercus agrifolia. Coast Live Oak. (N) Shrubs or low trees on brushy slopes, canyon sides, and dune hills. Golden Gate Park, Lake Merced, McLaren Park, Bayview Hills.

Myricaceae (Bayberry Family)

Myrica californica. California Wax Myrtle. (N) In wet and marshy places in gullies and on dunes. Moist gullies east of Lake Merced.

Urticaceae (Nettle Family)

Urtica holosericea. Nettle. (N) Brushy place in wet or dry soil. Presidio, above Baker Beach, Mountain Lake, Golden Gate Park, Lake Merced.

Aristolochiaceae (Birthwort Family)

Asarum caudatum. (N) Naturalized in moist shaded places in Golden Gate Park.

Polygonaceae (Buckwheat Family)

Eriogonum latifolium. (N) In sandy soil or on rocky slopes. Presidio, Twin Peaks, Bayview Hills.

Polygonum aviculare. Dooryard Knotweed. (W) Along sidewalks and in gardens. One of the commonest plants in San Francisco. Presidio, Golden Gate Park, Laguna Honda, Lake Merced, Hunters Point, Bayview Hills.

Rumex acetosella. Sheep Sorrel. (W) Widespread in wild grassland and in gardens. Presidio, Golden Gate Park, Lake Merced, San Miguel Hills, Nob Hill, Bayview Hills.

Rumex cripus. Curly Dock. (W) Common in low weedy places and about marshes. Mountain Lake, Golden Gate Park, Lake Merced, Bayview Hills.

Chenopodiaceae (Goosefoot Family)

Chenopodium allbum. Pigweed. (W) Rather common in weedy places. Presidio, Golden Gate Park.

Chenopodium ambrosioides. Mexican Tea. (W) In low ground or in weedy places. Presidio, Golden Gate Park, Lake Merced.

Chenopodium multifidum. Cutleaf Goosefoot. (W) A common weed. Presidio, Point Lobos, Golden Gate Park, Lake Merced, Twin Peaks, Russian Hill, Bayview Hills.

Chenopodium murale. Nettle-Leaf Goosefoot. (W) Widespread in waste and cultivated ground, also occasional in undisturbed areas. Presidio, Golden Gate Park, San Miguel Hills, Nob Hill, Embarcadero, Bayview Hills.

Amaranthaceae (Amaranth Family)

Amaranthus powellii. (W) A weed of cultivated or waste ground. Golden Gate Park, near San Francisco State College, southeastern San Francisco.

Nyctaginaceae (Four-O'Clock Family)

Abronia latifolia. Yellow Sand-Verbena. (N) Dune hills and sandy flats. Baker Beach, Pine Lake, coastal dunes south of Fort Funston.

Aizoaceae (Carpetweed Family)

Mesembryanthemum chilense. (N) Sandy slopes and flats near the ocean. Above Baker Beach, Point Lobos.

Mesembryanthemum elude. Hottentot-Fig. (W) Extensively planted to prevent erosion. Presidio, Golden Gate Park, Twin Peaks, Bayview Hills.

Tetragonia tetragonioides. New Zealand Spinach. (W) A weed in sandy places. Presidio, Lands End, Golden Gate Park, Lake Merced, Bayview Hills.

Portulacaceae (Purslane Family)

Calandrinia ciliata. Red Maids. (N) Open places in sandy or rocky soil. East of Lake Merced, Bayview Hills.

Montia perfoliata. Miner's Lettuce. (N) Common in grassland or brush. Presidio, Golden Gate Park, Lake Merced, Bayview Hills.

Portulaca oleracea. Common Purslane. (W) A common weed. Golden Gate Park, Embarcadero, near Mission Rock Terminal.

Caryophyllaceae (Pink Family)

Silene gallica. Windmill Pink. (W) Common and widespread in wild areas. Presidio, Golden Gate Park, Sunset Heights, Lake Merced, Twin Peaks, Bayview Hills.

Silene verecunda. (N) Forming colonies on sandy or rocky slopes. Above Baker Beach, Lake Merced.

Spergularia macrotheca. (N) Common on ocean bluffs, also in salt marshes, and occasionally on open grassy hillsides. Presidio, Point Lobos, Lake Merced, Hunters Point.

Spergularia rubra. Sand-Spurrey. (W) In hard ground of roads or paths. Golden Gate

Park, Twin Peaks, San Miguel Hills, Bayview Hills.

Stellaria media. Chickweed. (W) Common and widespread in gardens and on moist brushy or grassy slopes. Presidio, Golden Gate Park, Lake Merced, Mt. Davidson, San Miguel Hills, Pacific Heights, Russian Hill, Bayview Hills.

Ranunculaceae (Buttercup Family)

Ranunculus californicus. California Buttercup. (N) Ocean bluffs, grassy hills, dunes, and wooded slopes. Presidio, Golden Gate Park, Lake Merced, Laguna Honda, Twin Peaks, McLaren Park, Hunters Point, Bayview Hills.

Ranunculus repens. Creeping Buttercup. (W) Common in lawns. Golden Gate Park, Pacific Heights, Fort Mason.

Berberidaceae (Barberry Family)

Berberis pinnata. Coast Barberry. (N) Rocky slopes and summits of hills. Lake Merced, Twin Peaks, Mt. Davidson, San Miguel Hills, McLaren Park, Bayview Hills.

Papaveraceae (Poppy Family)

Eschscholzia californica. California Poppy. (N) Coastal bluffs, grassy hills, and rocky ridges. Presidio, Lands End, Golden Gate Park, Lake Merced, Corona Heights, McLaren Park, Bayview Hills.

Platystemon californicus. Cream Cups. (N) Sandy soil of open or brushy hills and dunes. Lake Merced, Twin Peaks.

Cruciferae (Mustard Family)

Arabis blepharophylla. Coast Rock-Cress. (N) Ocean bluffs and rocky outcrops in the hills. Above Baker Beach, Twin Peaks, McLaren Park, Bayview Hills.

Arabis glabra. Tower Mustard. (N) Grassy and brushy slopes. Above Baker Beach, Lands End, Laguna Honda, Twin Peaks, Bayview Hills.

Barbarea verna. Winter-Cress. (W) Coastal slopes, grassland, and cultivated

ground. Lands End, Golden Gate Park, Mt. Davidson, Lake Merced, Laguna Honda, San Miguel Hills, McLaren Park, Bayview Hills.

Brassica campestris. Field Mustard. (W) Common on grassy hills. Presidio, Golden Gate Park, Nob Hill, Bayview Hills.

Cakile maritima. (W) On beaches and dunes. Presidio, Lands End, Stow Lake, Golden Gate Park, beach west of Lake Merced.

Cardamine obligosperma. Bitter-Cress. (N) Moist wild and cultivated places. Presidio, Golden Gate Park, gully east of Lake Merced.

Dentaria integrifolia. Toothwort. (N) Open or brushy slopes. Lands End, Laguna Honda, Twin Peaks, McLaren Park, Bayview Hills.

Erysimum franciscanum. Franciscan Wallflower. (N) Grassy or brushy slopes, dune hills and ocean bluffs in the western part of the city. Above Baker Beach, Point Lobos, Laguna Honda, Lake Merced.

Lepidium nitidum. Shining Pepper-Grass. (N) Rather common on rocky slopes and in grassland in the central and eastern part of the city. Corona Heights, McLaren Park.

Lobularia maritima. Sweet Alyssum. (N) Commonly naturalized on coastal slopes and dunes. Lands End, Twin Peaks, Bayview Hills.

Raphanus saticus. Radish. (N) On the edge of wild areas. Presidio, Golden Gate Park, Lake Merced, Bayview Hills.

Crassulaceae (Stone Crop Family)

Echeveria farinosa. Bluff Lettuce. (N) Coastal bluffs and rocky outcrops in the hills. Lands End, Golden Gate Park, Twin Peaks, McLaren Park, Bayview Hills.

Saxifragaceae (Saxifrage Family)

Lithophragma affine. Woodland Star. (N) Moist shaded slopes in brush or grassland. East of Lake Merced, Bayview Hills.

Ribes sanguineum. Flowering Currant.

(N) Moist slopes. Between Baker Beach and Fort Point, Lands End, Golden Gate Park.

Rosaceae (Rose Family)

Fragaria californica. California Strawberry. (N) Grassy and brushy slopes. Twin Peaks, Bayview Hills.

Fragaria chiloensis. Beach Strawberry. (N) Coastal slopes and dunes or in grassland in shallow rocky soil. Lands End, above Baker Beach, Golden Gate Park, Lake Merced, Fort Funston, Twin Peaks, San Miguel Hills.

Holodiscus discolor. Ocean Spray. (N) Brushy slopes. Gully east of Lake Merced, Twin Peaks, McLaren Park, Bayview Hills.

Osmaronia cerasiformis. Oso Berry. (N) Moist brushy slopes, along the coast and inland. Laguna Honda, gully east of Lake Merced, McLaren Park, Bayview Hills.

Photinia arbutifolia. Christmas Berry. (N) On brushy hills. Golden Gate Park, Laguna Honda, Lake Merced.

Potentilla egedii. Cinquefoil. (N) In marshy places. Golden Gate Park, Pine Lake, Lake Merced, Twin Peaks.

Potentilla glandulosa. Stickly Cinquefoil. (N) Grassy and brushy slopes that are dry in the summer. Presidio, Laguna Honda, gully east of Lake Merced, Twin Peaks, Corona Heights, Bayview Hills.

Prunus demissa. Western Choke-Cherry. (N) On brushy or rocky slopes. San Miguel Hills, Bayview Hills.

Prunus ilicifolia. Holly-Leaved Cherry. (N) Rocky summit ridge of Bayview Hills.

Rosa californica. California Wild Rose. (N) In brushy places. Presidio, gully east of Lake Merced, north base of Bayview Hills.

Rubus ursinus. California Blackberry. (N) On coastal bluffs, in brushy thickets, among oaks and willows, and on open rocky ridges. Above Baker Beach, Lobos Creek, Golden Gate Park, Lake Merced, Laguna Honda, Twin Peaks, San Miguel Hills, McLaren Park, Bayview Hills.

Leguminosae (Pea Family)

Albizzia lophantha. Stink Bean. (W) Near Baker Beach, Lake Merced, Bayview Hills.

Astragalus nuttallii. (N) Brushy places, usually in sandy soil. Lake Merced.

Cytisus monspessulanus. French Broom. (W) Weedy in neglected gardens as well as in natural areas. Lands End, Golden Gate Park, Lake Merced, Twin Peaks, Bayview Hills.

Cytisus scoparius. Scotch Broom. (W) Becoming a bad weed. Presidio, Golden Gate Park, Laguna Honda, Corona Heights.

Lathyrus vestitus. Pacific Pea. (N) On grassy and brushy slopes. Near Baker Beach, Laguna Honda, Twin Peaks, Lake Merced, McLaren Park, Bayview Hills.

Lotus corniculatus. Bird's Foot Trefoil. (W) Occasional in waste ground and lawns. Golden Gate Park, Lake Merced, Bayview Hills.

Lotus scoparius. Deerweed. (N) Sandy flats and brushy hills. Presidio, Golden Gate Park, Lake Merced, Bayview Hills.

Lotus subpinnatus. (N) Open and brushy slopes in sandy or rocky soil. Presidio, Twin Peaks, Hunters Point, McLaren Park, Bayview Hills.

Lupinus albifrons. Silver Bush Lupine. (N) Open rocky ridges. Twin Peaks, Bayview Hills.

Lupinus arboreus. Yellow Beach Lupine. (N) Common and widespread in sandy soil, frequently growing in disturbed places. Presidio, Lone Mountain, Golden Gate Park, Lake Merced, Bayview Hills.

Lupinus bicolor. (N) Widespread in sandy or rocky soil, our commonest annual lupine. Above Baker Beach, Point Lobos, Lone Mountain, Lake Merced, Twin Peaks, McLaren Park, Bayview Hills.

Lupinus chamissonis. Blue Beach Lupine. (N) Sandy soil of dune hills and flats. Above Baker Beach, Golden Gate Park, Lake Merced.

Lupinus nanus. Sky Lupine. (N) Hillsides in sandy soil. Lake Merced, Presidio, Twin Peaks, McLaren Park, Bayview Hills.

Trifolium amplectens. Sack Clover. (N) Grassy slopes, generally in clay soils. Presidio, Golden Gate Park, Corona Heights, Bayview Hills.

Ulex europaeus. Gorse. (W) Escaping from cultivation and becoming rampantly weedy. Pine Lake, southeastern San Francisco.

Vicia americana. (N) Open grassland or brushy slopes. Presidio, Laguna Honda, Twin Peaks, gully east of Lake Merced, Bayview Hills.

Geraniaceae (Geranium Family)

Erodium botrys. Broad-Leaf Filaree. (W) Grassland. Golden Gate Park, Lake Merced, Bayview Hills.

Erodium cicutarium. Red-Stem Filaree. (W) Common on grassy hills. Twin Peaks, San Miguel Hills, Bayview Hills.

Erodium moschatum. White-Stem Filaree. (W) Open hillsides and cultivated areas, particularly lawns. Golden Gate Park, Bayview Hills.

Geranium dissectum. Cut-Leaved Geranium. (N) Widespread and rather common in natural areas or cultivated ground. Lobos Creek, Point Lobos, Lone Mountain, Golden Gate Park, Mt. Davidson, Twin Peaks, Fort Mason, Bayview Hills.

Oxalidaceae (Oxalis Family)

Oxalis pes-caprae. Bermuda Buttercup. (W) An attractive but difficult weed in cultivated ground. Point Lobos, Lone Mountain, Presidio, Golden Gate Park, Pine Lake, Lake Merced, Mt. Davidson, San Miguel Hills, Telegraph Hill.

Tropaeolaceae (Tropaeolum Family)

Tropaeolum majus. Garden Nasturtium. (W) Widely cultivated and becoming established in moist places. Lobos Creek, Golden Gate Park, Telelgraph Hill.

Euphorbiaceae (Spurge Family)

Rhus diversiloba. Poison Oak. (N)

Common on brushy slopes, rocky ridges, and sandy flats. Presidio, Lands End, McLaren Park, Bayview Hills.

Rhamnaceae (Buckthorn Family)

Ceanothus thyrsiflorus. Blue Blossom. (N) Forming mats and thickets on coastal bluffs and on brushy slopes. Near Baker Beach, between Lands End and Golden Gate Bridge, Lake Merced.

Rhamnus californica. Coffee Berry. (N) Hills and bluffs, forming thickets or mats. Presidio, east of Lake Merced, Laguna Honda, Bayview Hills.

Malvaceae (Mallow Family)

Lavatera arborea. Tree Mallow. (W) In natural areas, a fugitive from cultivation. Presidio, Golden Gate Park, Lands End, Fort Funston.

Sidalcea malvaeflora. Wild Hollyhock. (N) Open grassy slopes. Lake Merced, Presidio, Laguna Honda, Twin Peaks, McLaren Park, Bayview Hills.

Violaceae (Violet Family)

Viola adunca. Blue Violet. (N) Forming colonies on open grassy hills. Baker Beach, Twin Peaks.

Viola pedunculata. Yellow Violet. (N) Open grassy hills. East of Lake Merced, McLaren Park, Bayview Hills.

Lythraceae (Loose-Strife Family)

Lythrum hyssopifolia. (W) Moist or wet places, or in dry places that are wet in the spring. Mountain Lake, Lake Merced, San Miguel Hills, Bayview Hills.

Myrtaceae (Myrtle Family)

Eucalyptus globulus. Blue Gum. (W) Often weedy in the vicinity of planted trees. Presidio, Golden Gate Park, Sigmund Stern Grove, Lake Merced, Bayview Hills.

Onagraceae (Evening Primrose Family)

Clarkia rubicunda. (N) On grassy or

brushy slopes and coastal bluffs. Lands End, Lake Merced, Twin Peaks, Bayview Hills.

Epilobium watwonii. San Francisco Willow-Herb. (N) Very common in wet places, often weedy in gardens. Presidio, Lands End, Golden Gate Park, Lake Merced, Laguna Honda, Twin Peaks, Bayview Hills.

Epilobium paniculatum. Willow-Herb. (N) On flats and slopes both in sandy and clay soils. Presidio, Lake Merced, Point Lobos.

Oenothera cheiranthifolia. Beach Primrose. (N) Sandy slopes and flats. Above Baker Beach, Lands End, Golden Gate Park, Lake Merced.

Oenothera ovata. Sun-Cups. (N) On grassy slopes and flats. Presidio, Golden Gate Park, Lake Merced, Twin Peaks, Bayview Hills.

Araliaceae (Aralia Family)

Hedera helix. English Ivy. (W) Widely cultivated in San Francisco. Presidio, Golden Gate Park.

Umbelliferae (Parsley Family)

Angelica hendersonii. (N) On brushy hills. Point Lobos, Lake Merced, Bayview Hills.

Conium maculatum. Poison Hemlock. (W) A common weed of fertile soil, and along streams. Golden Gate Park, Lake Merced, Twin Peaks, Bayview Hills.

Foeniculum vulgare. Sweet Fennel. (W) Common in vacant lots. Point Lobos, Laguna Honda, Corona Heights, Mt. Davidson, Russian Hill, Bayview Hills.

Heracleum maximum. Cow-Parsnip. (N) Moist slopes, along streams and on coastal bluffs. Lobos Creek, above Baker Beach, Lands End, Laguna Honda.

Lomatium caruifolium. Alkali Parsnip. (N) Open rocky grassland, on serpentine. Presidio, Corona Heights, Laguna Honda, Twin Peaks, McLaren Park, Bayview Hills.

Lomatium dasycarpum. Lace Parsnip. (N) Open rocky grassland. Presidio, Mt.

Davidson, Bayview Hills.

Oenanthe sarmentosa. (N) Common in wet places. Mountain Lake, Lobos Creek, Lands End, Golden Gate Park, Lake Merced, Mt. Davidson, San Miguel Hills, swamp north of McLaren Park.

Perideridia kelloggii. (N) Open grassy hillsides. Coastal bluffs between Lobos Creek and Fort Point, Laguna Honda, Mt. Davidson, Twin Peaks, San Miguel Hills, Bayview Hills.

Sanicula arctopoides. Footsteps-of-Spring. (N) In open rocky grassland. Above Baker Beach, Presidio, dunes south of Golden Gate Park, Lake Merced, Laguna Honda, Corona Heights, Mt. Davidson, Twin Peaks, Bayview Hills.

Sanicula bipinnatifida. Purple Sanicle. (N) Open rocky grassland. Presidio, Lake Merced, Corona Heights, Laguna Honda, Twin Peaks, Mt. Davidson, McLaren Park, Bayview Hills.

Sanicula crassicaulis. Pacific Sanicle. (N) Open or shaded places, often under brush. Golden Gate Park, Lake Merced, Laguna Honda, Twin Peaks, Mt. Davidson, Bayview Hills.

Ericaceae (Heather Family)

Arctostaphylos franciscana. Franciscan manzanita. (N) Forming colonies on open rocky slopes on serpentine, known only from San Francisco. North of Baker Beach, Mt. Davidson.

Gaultheria shallon. Salal. (N) Around rocks or in brush of rock-strewn hilltops. Mt. Davidson, San Miguel Hills.

Vaccinium ovatum. Huckleberry. (N) Moist brushy slopes. Mt. Davidson.

Primulaceae (Primrose Family)

Anagallis arvensis. Scarlet Pimpernel. (W) In gardens and natural areas. Presidio, Point Lobos, Lone Mountain, Golden Gate Park, Lake Merced, Laguna Honda, Mt. Davidson, San Miguel Hills, Russian Hill, McLaren Park, Bayview Hills.

Dodecatheon clevelandii. Shooting Stars. (N) Open grassy hilltops. Point Lobos, Bernal Heights, McLaren Park.

Dodecatheon hendersonii. Shooting Stars. (N) Shaded brushy slopes. Summit of Mt. Davidson.

Plumbaginaceae (Thrift Family)

Armeria maritima. Sea-Pink. (N) Coastal bluffs, dunes, and hills. Point Lobos, Lake Merced.

Vinca major. Periwinkle. (W) Commonly cultivated and becoming an aggressive weed in shaded places. Above Baker Beach, Golden Gate Park, Laguna Honda, Mt. Davidson, McLaren Park.

Convolculaceae (Morning-Glory Family)

Convolvulus arvensis. Orchard Morning-Glory. (W) A weed often seen in gardens. Point Lobos, Golden Gate Park, Lake Merced, San Miguel Hills, Russian Hill, Bayview Hills.

Convolvulus occidentalis. (N) Moist brushy slopes and coastal bluffs, sometimes on open rocky slopes. Presidio, Point Lobos to Fort Point, Lands End, Lake Merced, Laguna Honda, Twin Peaks, San Miguel Hills, Mt. Davidson.

Polemoniaceae (Phlox Family)

Gilia capitata. (N) On dunes and sandy flats. Presidio, near Baker Beach, Lake Merced.

Linanthus androsaceus. (N) Forming colonies in grassland in sandy soil. Lake Merced.

Navarretia squarrosa. Skunkweed. (N) Sandy moist depression. Lobos Creek to Fort Point, Presidio, Golden Gate Park, Laguna Honda, San Miguel Hills.

Hydrophyllaceae (Waterleaf Family)

Nemophila menziesii. Baby-Blue-Eyes. (N) Moist open grassland. Presidio, Point Lobos, Lake Merced, Twin Peaks, Mt. Davidson, San Miguel Hills, Bayview Hills.

Nemophila pedunculata. (N) Open grassland or underbrush. Lake Merced, Point Lobos, McLaren Park.

Phacelia californica. (N) In rocky or sandy soil on open or brushy slopes. Lake Merced, Laguna Honda, San Miguel Hills, Corona Heights, Mt. Davidson, McLaren Park, Bayview Hills.

Phacelia distans. Wild Heliotrope. (N) Rocky or brushy slopes. Point Lobos, Golden Gate Park, Lake Merced, Laguna Honda, Mt. Davison, Bayview Hills.

Phacelia malvaefolia. Stinging Phacelia. (N) Shaded brushy slopes. Lobos Creek, Point Lobos, Golden Gate Park, Lake Merced, Mt. Davidson, San Miguel Hills, Bayview Hills.

Boraginaceae (Borage Family)

Allocarya chorisiana. (N) Common in moist places. Near Lobos Creek, Golden Gate Park, Twin Peaks.

Amsinckia intermedia. Common Fiddle-Neck. (N) On grassy slopes. Golden Gate Park, Lake Merced, San Miguel Hills, McLaren Park.

Amsinckia latifolia. Coast Fiddle-Neck. (N) On dunes and on sandy and grassy flats. Above Baker Beach, Mountain Lake, Point Lobos, Golden Gate Park, Pine Lake, Lake Merced.

Myosotis sulvatica. Forget-Me-Not. (W) Shaded places near cultivation. Presidio, Golden Gate Park, Mt. Davidson, San Miguel Hills, Russian Hill.

Labiatae (Mint Family)

Monardella villosa. Coyote-Mint. (N) On brushy or open rocky slopes. Twin Peaks, San Miguel Hills, Bayview Hills.

Satureja donglasii. Yerba Buena. (N) Brushy slopes. Near mouth of Lobos Creek, Laguna Honda, Twin Peaks, Pine Lake, Lake Merced.

Stachys chamissonis. Coast Hedge Nettle. (N) Marshy places. Golden Gate Park.

Stachys rigida. Hedge Nettle. (N) Open

grassy slopes and brushy hillsides. Lands End, Golden Gate Park, Lake Merced, Laguna Honda, Corona Heights, Mt. Davidson, Twin Peaks, San Miguel Hills, McLaren Park, Bayview Hills.

Solanaceae (Nightshade Family)

Nicotiana glauca. Tree Tobacco. (W) Established in moist places. Golden Gate Park.

Solanum umbelliferum. Blue Witch. (N) Brushy slopes. Baker Beach, Lobos Creek.

Scrophulariaceae (Figwort Family)

Castilleja latifolia. Seaside Paint-Brush. (N) Slopes in coastal brush and grassland. Above Baker Beach, Lobos Creek to Fort Point, Point Lobos, Lake Merced.

Collinsia multicolor. Franciscan Blue-Eyed Mary. (N) Forming colonies in openings in woodland and brush. Bayview Hills.

Mimulus aurantiacus. Sticky Monkey-Flower. (N) Brushy slopes. Fort Point, above Baker Beach, Golden Gate Park, Lake Merced, Laguna Honda, Mt. Davidson, Twin Peaks, San Miguel Hills, Bayview Hills.

Orthocarpus densiflorus. Owl's Clover. (N) In shallow soil on open slopes. Presidio, Golden Gate Park, Corona Heights, Mt. Davidson, Twin Peaks, San Miguel Hills, McLaren Park.

Orthocarpus erianthus. Popcorn Beauty. (N) In low fields, on sandy flats, and on bluffs. Presidio, Lake Merced, McLaren Park.

Orthocarpus floribundus. (N) Colonies on coastal bluffs. Above Fort Point, near Baker Beach, Presidio.

Orthocarpus pusillus. (N) On grassy flats and slopes, often in shallow soil. Presidio, near Baker Beach, Lone Mountain, Golden Gate Park, Lake Merced, Corona Heights, Twin Peaks, Mt. Davidson, San Miguel Hills, Bayview Hills.

Scrophulari californica. California Bee-Plant. (N) Brushy slopes and in wooded areas. Lobos Creek, above Baker Beach, Lands End, Lone Mountain, Golden Gate Park, Pine Lake, Lake Merced, Laguna Honda, Mt. Davidson, Twin Peaks, San Miguel Hills, Bayview Hills.

Veronica americana. American Brookline. (N) Marshy places. Lobos Creek, Mountain Lake, Sigmund Stern Grove, Lake Merced, Laguna Honda, Mt. Davidson, San Miguel Hills.

Plantaginaceae (Plantain Family)

Plantago erecta. (N) On open grassy slopes and dune flats, often in shallow soil. Near Fort Point, above Baker Beach, Presidio, Golden Gate Park, Pine Lake, Corona Heights, Laguna Honda, Mt. Davidson, Twin Peaks, San Miguel Hills, Bernal Heights, McLaren Park, Bayview Hills.

Plantago lanceolata. Ribwort. (W) Cultivated ground and in wild areas. Above Baker Beach, Presidio, Lands End, Golden Gate Park, Lake Merced, Laguna Honda, Mt. Davidson, Twin Peaks, San Miguel Hills, Bayview Hills.

Plantago major. Common Plantain. (W) Common in wild areas. Mountain Lake, Golden Gate Park, Laguna Honda, Pine Lake, Lake Merced, Mt. Davidson, San Miguel Hills, McLaren Park.

Caprifoliaceae (Honeysuckle Family)

Lonicera involucrata. Twinberry. (N) Wet soil near streams and marshes. Between Baker Beach and Fort Point, Lobos Creek, Mountain Lake, Golden Gate Park, Lake Merced, Laguna Honda.

Sambucus callicarpa. Red Elderberry. (N) Moist brushy slopes. Golden Gate Park, Laguna Honda, Mt. Davidson, Twin Peaks.

Sambucus coerulea. Blue Elderberry. (N) On brushy slopes, near streams, and about the margins of swamps. Golden Gate Park, San Miguel Hills, swamp north of McLaren Park.

Symphoricarpos rivularis. Snowberry. (N) Partially shaded brushy slopes. Golden

Gate Park, Sunset Heights, Lake Merced, Laguna Honda.

Valerianacene (Valerian Family)

Centranthus ruber. Jupiter's Beard. (W) On rocky slopes, and about gardens. Presidio, Golden Gate Park, Lake Merced, Telegraph Hill, McLaren Park, San Miguel Hills, Russian Hill.

Cucurbitaceae (Gourd Family)

Marah fabaceus. Manroot. (N) On dunes and on grassy or brushy slopes. Lands End, Fort Point, near Lobos Creek, above Baker Beach, Golden Gate Park, Laguna Honda, Twin Peaks, Mt. Davidson, San Miguel Hills, Bayview Hills.

Compositae (Sunflower Family)

Achillea borealis. Yarrow. (N) Widespread in sandy soil in natural areas. Lands End, Presidio, Golden Gate Park, Pine Lake, Lake Merced, Laguna Honda, Twin Peaks, Mt. Davidson, San Miguel Hills, Bayview Hills.

Agoseris apargioides. Coast Dandelion. (N) Dunes, grassy hills, and rocky slopes. Presidio, Point Lobos, Lake Merced, Twin Peaks, San Miguel Hills, Mt. Davidson, Bayview Hills.

Agoseris grandiflora. California Dandelion. (N) Open or brushy slopes. Mt. Davidson, San Miguel Hills, Bayview Hills.

Anaphalis margaritacea. Pearly Everlasting. (N) Open or brushy slopes. Presidio, Point Lobos, Golden Gate Park, Lake Merced, Laguna Honda, Twin Peaks, San Miguel Hills, McLaren Park, Bayview Hills.

Artemisia californica. California Sagebrush. (N) Brushy and open hillsides. Point Lobos, Laguna Honda, Twin Peaks, San Miguel Hills, McLaren Park, Bayview Hills.

Artemisia pycnocephala. (N) Dunes and sandy flats. Lobos Creek, Baker Beach, Lake Merced.

Aster chilensis. (N) Rocky slopes in natural areas, occasionally cultivated ground. Lands End, Golden Gate Park, Lake Merced, Laguna Honda, Twin Peaks, San Miguel Hills, Bayview Hills.

Aster subspicatus. (N) Brushy slopes. Sutro Heights above Point Lobos, Laguna Honda, Pine Lake, San Miguel Hills.

Baccharis douglasii. (N) Moist soil or in places that are wet in the spring. Sigmund Stern Grove, San Miguel Hills.

Baccharis pilularis. Fuzzy-Wuzzy. (N) Open hillsides. Presidio, Point Lobos, Lake Merced, Twin Peaks, Potrero Hill.

Baccharis pilularis var. *consanguinea.* Coyote-Brush. (N) Brushy hillsides, invading grassland, and disturbed ground. Golden Gate Park, Laguna Honda, Corona Heights, Twin Peaks, San Miguel Hills, Bayview Hills.

Baeria chrysostoma. Gold Fields. (N) Open grassy slopes. Presidio, McLaren Park, Bayview Hills.

Bellis perennis. English Daisy. (W) Moist grassy places, common in lawns. Presidio, Golden Gate Park, Pine Lake, San Miguel Hills, Pacific Heights, Russian Hill, Fort Mason.

Chrysanthemum coronarium. Crown Chrysanthemum. (W) Common in cultivated areas. Pine Lake, Lake Merced, San Miguel Hills, McLaren Park.

Cirsium occidentale. Western Thistle. (N) On sandy slopes. Above Baker Beach, Golden Gate Park, Lake Merced, Twin Peaks, Mt. Davidson, San Miguel Hills.

Cirsium quercetorum. Brownie Thistle. (N) Open slopes in grassland. Presidio, Twin Peaks, Mt. Davidson, San Miguel Hills, McLaren Park, Bayview Hills.

Cotula coronopifolia. Brass Buttons. (W) Wet or marshy flats or slopes. Presidio, Golden Gate Park, Pine Lake, Lake Merced, Laguna Honda, San Miguel Hills, Bayview Hills.

Erigeron glaucus. Seaside Daisy. (N) Coastal bluffs and rocky hills. Presidio, Point Lobos, west of Lake Merced, Mt.

Davidson, San Miguel Hills.

Eriophyllum confertiflorum. Yellow Yarrow. (N) Brushy and open rocky slopes. Corona Heights, San Miguel Hills.

Eriophyllum staechadifolium. Lizard Tail. (N) Bluffs and brushy hills on or near the coast. Fort Point, Point Lobos, Golden Gate Park, Lake Merced, Twin Peaks, Mt. Davidson, Laguna Honda.

Franseria chamissonis. Beach Bar. (N) Sandy flats, occasionally near the shore. Presidio, Golden Gate Park, Lake Merced.

Grindelia maritima. (N) Coastal bluffs, and open or brushy slopes. Presidio, Point Lobos, Lake Merced, Laguna Honda, Twin Peaks.

Haplopappus ericoides. (N) Common low shrub of dunes and sandy hills. Presidio, Golden Gate Park, Lake Merced, Laguna Honda.

Helenium puberulum. Sneezeweed. (N) Wet ground of marshes, and hillside seepages. Fort Point, Laguna Honda, Lake Merced, San Miguel Hills.

Hypochoeris glabra. Smooth Cat's-Ear. (W) On grassy or brushy slopes. Presidio, Golden Gate Park, Lake Merced, Twin Peaks, Mt. Davidson, Bernal Heights, McLaren Park, Bayview Hills.

Hypochoeris radicata. Hairy Cat's-Ear. (W) Grassy places in cultivated ground. Presidio, Lake Merced, San Miguel Hills, McLaren Park, Bayview Hills.

Layia platyglossa. Tidy-Tips. (N) Common in grassy places in sandy soil. Presidio, Point Lobos, Lake Merced, Twin Peaks, San Miguel Hills.

Madia gracilis. Slender Tarweed. (N) Grassy or brushy slopes. Lake Merced, San Miguel Hills, Bayview Hills.

Madia sativa. Common Tarweed. (N) Grassy or brushy places. Presidio, Point Lobos, Golden Gate Park, Lake Merced, Laguna Honda, Twin Peaks, San Miguel Hills.

Matricaria matricarioides. Pineapple Weed. (W) In natural and cultivated areas.

Mountain Lake, Presidio, Golden Gate Park, Lake Merced, Mt. Davidson, San Miguel Hills, Bayview Hills.

Senecio aronicoides. Butterweed. (N) Grassy or brushy slopes, generally in partial shade. Above Baker Beach, Presidio, Lake Merced, Twin Peaks, Mt. Davidson, Bayview Hills.

Senecio mikanioides. German Ivy. (W) Forming dense tangles in shrubs and trees in moist places. Presidio, Point Lobos, Golden Gate Park, Lake Merced, Twin Peaks, Mt. Davidson, San Miguel Hills.

Senecio vulgaris. Common Groundsel. (W) A common weed. Presidio, Golden Gate Park, Lake Merced, Mt. Davidson, San Miguel Hills, Bayview Hills.

Solidago spathulata. Dune Goldenrod. (N) Open slopes and flats in rocky or sandy soil. Lone Mountain, Pine Lake, Lake Merced, Mt. Davidson, San Miguel Hills.

Sonchus oleraceus. Sow-Thistle. (W) One of the most common weeds in San Francisco. Presidio, Lands End, Golden Gate Park, Sigmund Stern Grove, Lake Merced, Mt. Davidson, San Miguel Hills.

Taraxacum officinale. Dandelion. (W) Common and widespread in wild or cultivated places. Presidio, Golden Gate Park, Twin Peaks, San Miguel Hills.

Wyethia angustifolia. Mule Ears. (N) Grassy or open brushy hills. Presidio, Twin Peaks, Mt. Davidson, Corona Heights, San Miguel Hills, McLaren Park, Bayview Hills.

Xanthium spinosum. Spiny Clotbur. (W) A weed of cultivated areas. Golden Gate Park, Lake Merced, San Miguel Hills, Bayview Hills.

Reptiles and Amphibians of San Francisco

Taricha torosa. California Newt. Ponds, lakes, and reservoirs. Golden Gate Park, Presidio, Lands End.

Aneides lugubris. Arboreal Salamander. Under moist logs, boards, and rocks. Lands End, Presidio, Golden Gate Park, Sutro

Forest, Bayview Park, Mt. Davidson.

Batrachoseps attenuatus. California Slender Salamander. Under moist logs, boards, and rocks. Lands End, Presidio, Golden Gate Park, Sutro Forest, Mt. Davidson, Bayview Park.

Ensatina eschscholtzi. Ensatina. Moist bark, logs, and deep leaf litter. Golden Gate Park.

Bufo boreas. Western Toad. Grasslands and woodlands. Presidio, Golden Gate Park.

Hyla regilla. Pacific Treefrog. Ponds and under moist logs. Presidio, Golden Gate Park, Fleishhacker Zoo, Lake Merced.

Rana aurora. Red-legged Frog. Wooded lakes and ponds. Lakes of Golden Gate Park, Presidio, Lake Merced, Lands End.

Clemmys marmorata. Western Pond Turtle. Ponds, lakes, and reservoirs. Stow Lake, Elk Glen Lake.

Gerrhonotus coeruleus. Norther Alligator Lizard. Under rocks, boards, and logs. Sutro Forest, Lake Merced, Golden Gate Park, Lands End.

Eumeces skiltonianus. Western Skink. Under rocks, logs, and leaf litter. Presidio, Bayview Park.

Sceloporus occidentalis. Western Fence Lizard. Woodlands and grasslands. Golden Gate Park, Presidio, Lake Merced, Lands End.

Charina bottae. Rubber Boa. Moist woodlands. Lake Merced, Presidio.

Coluber constrictor. Racer. Grasslands and broken woodlands. Golden Gate Park, Lake Merced.

Pituophis catenifer. Gopher Snake. Grasslands and woodlands. McLaren Park.

Lampropeltis getulus. Common Kingsnake. Grasslands, open forest, and woodlands. Presidio.

Thamnophis elegans. Western Garter Snake. Meadows. Golden Gate Park, Lands End, Lake Merced, Mt. Davidson, Presidio, Fort Point, Sutro Forest.

Butterflies of San Francisco

Coenonympha california. California Ringlet. Feeds on grasses. Mt. Davidson, Forest Hills.

Cercyonis sthenele. Sthenele Satyr. Once common on sand dunes in Sunset District. Man's destruction of the dunes pushed this butterfly to extinction.

Danaus plexippus. Monarch. Feeds on milkweeds. Golden Gate Park.

Euphydryas chalcedona. Common Checkerspot. Feeds on plants of the figwort family. Golden Gate Park.

Euphydryas editha bayensis. Editha Bay-Region Checkerspot. Feeds on plants growing on serpentine hills. Twin Peaks.

Phyciodes campestris. Field Crescent. Larva feed on wild asters. Golden Gate Park.

Phyciodes mylitta. Mylitta Crescent. Feeds on various thistles. Forest Hills.

Polygonia satyrus. Satyr Anglewing. Feeds on nettles. Fairly common in vacant lots of the city.

Numphalis californica. California Tortoiseshell. Feeds on wild lilac, buck brush, and other species of Ceanothus. Golden Gate Park.

Nymphalis antiopa. Mourning Cloak. Feeds on cottonwoods and willows. Mt. Davidson, West Portal District, Golden Gate Park.

Vanessa atalanta. Red Admiral. Feeds on nettles. West Portal District, Golden Gate Park.

Vanessa cardui. Painted Lady. Feeds on thistles and nettles. Golden Gate Park.

Vanessa virginiensis. American Painted Lady. Feeds on members of the Compositae. Golden Gate Park.

Vanessa carye. West Coast Lady. Feeds principally on mallow. Golden Gate Park.

Junonia coenia. Buckeye. Feeds on several plants, including snapdragon, plantain, and Gerardia. Forest Hills, Golden Gate Park.

Limenitis lorquini. Lorquin's Admiral. Feeds on cherry, willow, cottonwood, and poplar. Golden Gate Park.

Limenitis bredowii californica. California Sister. Larva feeds on Coast Live Oak. Golden Gate Park.

Strymon melinus pudica. Common Hairstreak. Vacant lots and open grasslands. Feeds on numerous native plants.

Incisalia iroides. Western Brown Elfin. Feeds on various species of Ceanothus. Golden Gate Park.

Incisalia eryphon. Western Banded Elfin. Feeds on various species of pine. Presidio.

Callophrys dumetorum. Bramble Hairstreak. Feeds on buckwheat and lotus. Seen along sand dunes near Forest Hills.

Callophrys viridis. Green Hairstreak. A butterfly with a limited habitat. Lives along the rocky hills of San Francisco.

Plebejus icarioides missionensis. Mission Blue. Feeds on various species of lupines. Twin Peaks.

Plebejus icarioides pheres. Pheres Blue. Once fed commonly on lupines growing on sand dunes of the Sunset District. Now dunes and Pheres Blue are gone.

Plebejus acmon. Acmon Blue. Feeds on many species of legumes. Golden Gate Park.

Glaucopsyche lugdamus behrii. Behr's Silver Blue. Feeds on various leguminous plants. Grasslands and open woodlands.

Glaucopsyche xerces. Xerces Blue. Now extinct, this butterfly once occurred in sand dunes throughout the city.

Colias eurytheme. Common Sulphur. Feeds on various leguminous plants. Vacant lots.

Pieris rapae. Cabbage Butterfly. Feeds on various vegetables. Golden Gate Park.

Battus philenor hirsuta. Hairy Pipe-vine Swallowtail. Lives near its favorite food plant, Dutchman's Pipe (Aristolochia).

Papilio zelicaon. Anise Swallowtail. Feeds on anise and parsley plants. Mt. Davidson.

Papilio rutulus. Western Tiger Swallowtail. Feeds on willow, poplar, and hops. Mt. Davidson, Golden Gate Park.

Pyrgus communis. Common Checkered Skipper. Feeds on members of the mallow family. Golden Gate Park.

Erynnis propertius. Propertius Duskywing. Feeds on the Coast Live Oak. Grassland and broken forests.

Hylephila phyleus. Fiery Skipper. Various species of grasses are preferred by this butterfly. Vacant lots and marshes.

Atalopedes campestris. Field Skipper. Feeds on various grasses. Golden Gate Park.

Paratrytone melane. Umber Skipper. Feeds on grasses. Golden Gate Park.

Mammals of San Francisco

Didelphis marsupialis. Opossum. Golden Gate Park.

Scapanus latimanus. Broad-footed Mole. Golden Gate Park.

Neurotrichus gibbsi. Shrew-mole. Moist, broken forests.

Sorex trowbridgei. Trowbridge Shrew. Grass-covered hills.

Sorex vagrans. Vagrant Shrew. Humid grasslands.

Myotis lucifugus. Little Brown Bat. Golden Gate Park.

Lasiurus cinereus. Hoary Bat. Golden Gate Park.

Lasiurus borealis. Red Bat. Deciduous forests.

Tadarida mexicana. Mexican Free-tailed Bat. Often roosts in buildings.

Procyon lotor. Raccoon. Golden Gate Park, Sutro Forest, Presidio.

Mustela frenata. Long-tailed Weasel. Golden Gate Park.

Mephitis mephitis. Striped Skunk. Golden Gate Park, Presidio.

Taxidea taxus. Badger. Golden Gate Park.

Urocyon cinereoargenteus. Gray Fox. Golden Gate Park, Presidio, Lands End.

Zalophus californianus. California Sea Lion. Seal Rocks.

Eumetopias jubata. Steller Sea Lion. Seal Rocks.

Citellus beecheyi. California Ground Squirrel. Lands End, Twin Peaks.

Sciurus carolinesis. Eastern Gray Squirrel. Golden Gate Park.

Sciurus niger. Fox Squirrel. Golden Gate Park.

Thomomys bottae. Botta Pocket Gopher. Golden Gate Park.

Reithrodontomys megalotis. Western Harvest Mouse. Open grassland.

Peromyscus maniculatus. Deer Mouse. Golden Gate Park.

Rattus norvegicus. Norway Rat. Golden Gate Park.

Rattus rattus. Black Rat. Golden Gate Park.

Mus musculus. House Mouse. Golden Gate Park.

Sylvilagus bachmani. Brush Rabbit. Golden Gate Park, Presidio.

Birds of San Francisco

The following list includes all species of birds ever noted within the city limits of San Francisco. Some species have been noted only once or just a few times.

The localities are presented as a general aid to visitors and are not intended to be complete. A species should be sought whenever suitable habitat is present. The habitats listed are those in which a species is most likely to be found within the city.

Gabiidae. Loons

Gavia immer. Common Loon. Lakes and Bay. Stow Lake (Golden Gate Park), Lake Merced.

Gavia arctica. Arctic Loon. Bay and ocean. Ocean Beach.

Gavia stellata. Red-throated Loon. Lakes and Bay. Golden Gate Park, Lake Merced.

Podicipedidae. Grebes

Podiceps grisegena. Red-necked Grebe. Lakes, Bay, and ocean. Presidio, Stow Lake (Golden Gate Park), Lake Merced.

Podiceps auritus. Horned Grebe. Lakes, Bay, and ocean. Golden Gate Park, Lake Merced.

Podiceps caspicus. Eared Grebe. Lakes, Bay, and ocean. Golden Gate Park, Lake Merced.

Podilymbus podiceps. Pied-billed Grebe. Lakes and marshes. Golden Gate Park, Lake Merced.

Procellariidae. Fulmar and Shearwaters

Puffinus creatopus. Pink-footed Shearwater. Ocean. Ocean Beach.

Puffinus griseus. Sooty Shearwater. Bay mouth and ocean. Ocean Beach, mouth of San Francisco Bay.

Hydrobatidae. Storm Petrels

Oceanodroma homochroa. Ashy Petrel. Nests on offshore islands; feeds over the open ocean. Ocean Beach (rare).

Pelecanidae. Pelicans

Pelecanus erythrorhynchos. White Pelican. Lakes and Bay. San Francisco Bay.

Pelecanus occidentalis. Brown Pelican. Bay, ocean, and occasionally lakes. Ocean Beach, Golden Gate Park.

Phalacrocoracidae. Cormorants

Phalacrocorax auritus. Double-crested Cormorant. Lakes and Bay. Cliff House, Lake Merced.

Phalacrocorax penicillatus. Brandt's Cormorant. Bay and ocean. Ocean Beach; nests on Seal Rocks off the Cliff House.

Phalacrocorax pelagicus. Pelagic Cormorant. Bay and ocean. Ocean Beach.

Ardeidae. Herons and Bitterns

Ardea herodias. Great Blue Heron. Marshes, ponds, and lakes. Lake Merced.

Butorides virescens. Green Heron. Marshes, streams, ponds, and lakes. Golden Gate Park, Lake Merced.

Nycticorax nucticoras. Black-crowned Night Heron. Marshes, ponds, and lakes. Golden Gate Park, Lake Merced.

Ixobrychus exilis. Least Bittern. Marshes. Golden Gate Park.

Botaurus lentiginosus. American Bittern. Marshes. Golden Gate Park, Lake Merced.

Anatidae. Swans, Ducks, and Geese

Olor columbianus. Whistling Swan. Lakes and Bay. Lake Merced.

Branta canadensis. Canada Goose. Marshes, lakes, and Bay. Golden Gate Park.

Branta nigricans. Black Brant. Ocean and Bay. Golden Gate Park.

Anser albifrons. White-fronted Goose. Marshes, lakes, and Bay. Golden Gate Park.

Chen hyperborea. Snow Goose. Marshes, lakes, and Bay. Golden Gate Park.

Anas platyrhynchos. Mallard. Marshes, ponds, and lakes. Golden Gate Park, Lake Merced.

Anas strepera. Gaswall. Marshes, ponds, and lakes. Golden Gate Park.

Anas acuta. Pintail. Marshes, ponds, and lakes. Golden Gate Park.

Anas carolinensis. Green-winged Teal. Marshes, ponds, and lakes. Golden Gate Park.

Anas cyanoptera. Cinnamon Teal. Marshes, ponds, and lakes. Golden Gate Park, Lake Merced.

Mareca penelope. European Widgeon. Marshes, ponds, and lakes. Stow Lake (Golden Gate Park).

Spatula clypeata. Shoveler. Marshes, ponds, and lakes. Golden Gate Park.

Aix sponsa. Wood Duck. Wooded ponds and lakes. Golden Gate Park.

Aythya americana. Redhead. Lakes and Bay. Golden Gate Park.

Aythya collaris. Ring-necked Duck. Marshes, ponds, and lakes. Golden Gate Park, Lake Merced.

Aythya valisineria. Canvasback. Lakes and Bay. Golden Gate Park, Lake Merced.

Aythya marila. Greater Scaup. Lakes and Bay. Golden Gate Park.

Anythya affinis. Lesser Scaup. Marshes, lakes, and Bay. Stow Lake (Golden Gate Park), Lake Merced.

Aythya fuligula. Tufted Duck. Lakes. Golden Gate Park (on record).

Bucephala clangula. Common Goldeneye. Lakes and Bay. Golden Gate Park.

Bucephala albeola. Bufflehead. Ponds, lakes, and Bay. Golden Gate Park, Lake Merced.

Melanitta deglandi. White-winged Scoter. Lakes, Bay, and ocean. Ocean Beach, Golden Gate Park, Lake Merced.

Melanitta perspicillata. Surf Scoter. Bay and ocean. Ocean Beach.

Oidemia nigra. Common Scoter. Bay and ocean. Ocean Beach.

Oxyura jamaicensis. Ruddy Duck. Marshes, ponds, lakes, and Bay. Golden Gate Park, Lake Merced.

Lophodutes cucullatus. Hooded Merganser. Wooded ponds and lakes. Golden Gate Park.

Mergus serrator. Red-breasted Merganser. Lakes and Bay. Lake Merced.

Cathartidae. Condors and Vultures

Cathartes aura. Turkey Vulture. Soars over fields and wooded hills. Often flies over Golden Gate Park.

Accipitridae. Kites, Hawks, and Eagles

Elanus leucurus. White-tailed Kite. Marshes and meadows. Lake Merced.

Accipiter striatus. Sharp-shinned Hawk. Woodlands. Sutro Forest, Golden Gate Park.

Accipiter cooperii. Cooper's Hawk. Woodlands. Twin Peaks, Golden Gate Park.

Buteo jamiacensis. Red-tailed Hawk. Meadows and open woodlands. Sutro Forest, Twin Peaks, Golden Gate Park.

Buteo lineatus. Red-shouldered Hawk. Woodlands. Golden Gate Park.

Buteo platypterus. Broad-winged Hawk. Woodlands. Moraga Hill (rare).

Aquila chrysaetos. Golden Eagle. Flying overhead. Twin Peaks.

Circus cyaneus. Marsh Hawk. Marshes and fields. Golden Gate Park, Lake Merced.

Panionidae. Ospreys

*Pandion haliaetu*s. Osprey. Lakes and the coastline. Sutro Forest, Lake Merced.

Falconidae. Falcons and Caracaras

Falco sparverius. Sparrow Hawk. Open areas. Golden Gate Park.

Phasianidae. Quail and Pheasants

Lophortyx californicus. California Quail. Scrub and open woodlands. Golden Gate Park.

Alectoris graeca. Chukar. Grass and brush-covered hills. Golden Gate Park (rare).

Rallidae. Rails

Rallus limicola. Virginia Rail. Marshes. Golden Gate Park, Lake Merced.

Porzana carolina. Sora. Marshes. Lake Merced.

Gallinula chloropus. Common Gallinule. Marshes. Golden Gate Park, Lake Merced.

Fulica americana. American Coot. Marshes, ponds, lakes, and golf courses. Golden Gate Park, Lake Merced.

Charadriidae. Plovers

Charadrius semipalmatus. Semipalmated Plover. Sandy beaches and mud flats. Presidio of San Francisco.

Charadrius alexandrinus. Snowy Plover. Sandy beaches and mud flats. Presidio of San Francisco.

Charadrius vociferus. Killdeer. Shorelines, fields, and tops of buildings. Golden Gate Park.

Squatarola squatarola. Black-bellied Plover. Sandy beaches and mud flats. Ocean Beach, Cliff House.

Scolopacidae. Snipe and Sandpipers

Aphriza virgata. Surfbird. Rocky shorelines of ocean and Bay. Ocean Beach, Cliff House.

Arenaria melanocephala. Black Turnstore. Rocky shorelines of ocean and Bay. Ocean Beach.

Capella gallinago. Common Snipe. Marshes and lake margins. Lake Merced.

Numenius phaeopus. Whimbrel. Sandy beaches, mud flats, and rocky shorelines. Presidio of San Francisco.

Actitis macularia. Spotted Sandpiper. Lake margins. Lake Merced.

Heteroscelus incanus. Wandering Tattler. Rocky shoreline. Ocean Beach.

Catoptrophorus semipalmatus. Willet. Sandy beaches, mud flats, and rocky shorelines. Presidio, Ocean Beach, Lake Merced.

Erolia ptilocnemis. Rock Sandpiper. Rocky shorelines along ocean. Cliff House (rare).

Erolia minutilla. Least Sandpiper. Mud flats and lake margins. Ocean Beach.

Ereunetes mauri. Western Sandpiper. Mud flats. Ocean Beach.

Limosa fedoa. Marbled Godwit. Mud flats. Ocean Beach.

Crocethia alba. Sanderling. Sandy beaches, mud flats, and rocky shorelines. Ocean Beach.

Phalaropodidae. Phalaropes

Lobipes lobatus. Northern Phalarope. Lakes, Bay, and ocean. Golden Gate Park, Lake Merced.

Laridae. Gulls and Terns

Larus hyperboreus. Glaucous Gull. Lakes and coastal waterfront. Ocean Beach, Golden Gate Park (rare).

Larus glaucescens. Glaucous-winged Gull. Lakes and coastal waterfront. Ocean Beach, Golden Gate Park.

Larus occidentalis. Western Gull. Lakes and coastal waterfront. Ocean Beach, Golden Gate Park, Lake Merced.

Larus argentatus. Herring Gull. Lakes and coastal waterfront. Ocean Beach, Golden Gate Park, Lake Merced.

Larus californicus. California Gull. Lakes and coastal waterfront. Ocean Beach, Golden Gate Park, Lake Merced,

Larus delawarensis. Ring-billed Gull. Lakes and coastal waterfront. Ocean Beach, Golden Gate Park, Lake Merced.

Larus canus. Mew Gull. Lakes and coastal waterfront. Ocean Beach, Golden Gate Park, Lake Merced.

Larus philadelphia. Bonaparte's Gull. Lakes and coastal waterfront. Golden Gate Park, Lake Merced.

Larus heermanni. Heermann's Gull. Lakes and coastal waterfront. Ocean Beach, Golden Gate Park.

Xema sabini. Sabine's Gull. Ocean and sandy beaches. Ocean Beach.

Sterna hirundo. Common Tern. Lakes, Bay, and ocean. Presidio.

Thalasseus elegans. Elegant Tern. Bay and ocean. Fort Point.

Hydroprogne caspia. Caspian Tern. Lakes and Bay. Golden Gate Park, Lake Merced.

Alcidae. Auks and Murres

Uria aalge. Common Murre. Ocean and Bay mouth. Ocean Beach.

Cepphus columba. Pigeon Guillemot. Ocean and Bay mouth. Cliff House.

Brachyramphus marmoratum. Marbled Murrelet. Ocean. Ocean Beach (rare).

Columbidae. Pigeons and Doves

Columba fasciata. Band-tailed Pigeon. Woodlands. Golden Gate Park.

Columba licia. Rock Dove (Domestic Pigeon). Settled areas. Ubiquitous.

Zenaidura macroura. Mourning Dove. Vacant lots, gardens, and open woodlands. Golden Gate Park.

Cuculidae. Cuckoos and Roadrunners

Geococcyx californianus. Roadrunner. Open areas. Lake Merced (one record).

Tytonidae. Barn Owls

Tyto alba. Barn Owl. Residential areas, open woodlands, and fields. Golden Gate Park.

Strigidae. Owls

Otus asio. Screech Owl. Woodlands. Golden Gate Park.

Bubo virginianus. Great Horned Owl. Woodlands. Sutro Forest, Sigmund Stern Grove.

Speotyto cunicularia. Burrowing Owl. Open hills. Golden Gate Park, Lake Merced.

Asio otus. Long-eared Owl. Woodlands. Ingleside District.

Asio flammeus. Short-eared Owl. Marshes and fields. Sunset District.

Aegolius acadicus. Saw-whet Owl. Woodlands. Golden Gate Park.

Apodidae. Swifts

Cypseloides niger. Black Swift. Flying overhead, especially along coast. Golden Gate Park.

Chaetura vauxi. Vaux's Swift. Flying overhead. Golden Gate Park.

Aeronautes saxatalis. White-throated Swift. Flying overhead, especially along coast. Golden Gate Park, Candlestick Park.

Trochilidae. Hummingbirds

Calypte anna. Anna's Hummingbird. Scrub, woodlands, and gardens. Golden Gate Park.

Selasphorus rufus. Rufous Hummingbird. Scrub, woodlands, and gardens.

Selasphorus sasin. Allen's Hummingbird. Scrub, woodlands, and gardens. Golden Gate Park.

Alcedinidae. Kingfishers

Megaceryle alcyon. Belted Kingfisher. Streams, ponds, and lakes. Golden Gate Park, Lake Merced.

Picidae. Woodpeckers

Colaptes auratus. Yellow-shafter Flicker. Woodlands. Golden Gate Park.

Colaptes cafer. Red-shafted Flicker. Woodlands and gardens. Golden Gate Park.

Melanerpes formicivorus. Acorn

Woodpecker. Woodlands, especially oaks. Golden Gate Park.

Asyndesmus lewis. Lewis's Woodpecker. Woodlands. Golden Gate Park.

Sphyrapicus varius. Yellow-bellied Sapsucker. Woodlands. Golden Gate Park.

Dendrocopos pubescens. Downy Woodpecker. Woodlands. Golden Gate Park.

Tyrannidae. Tyrant Flycatchers

Myiarchus cinerascens. Ash-throated Flycatchers. Open woodlands. Golden Gate Park.

Sayornis phoebe. Eastern Phoebe. Margins of fresh water. Golden Gate Park.

Sayornis nigricans. Black Phoebe. Open areas, usually near water. Golden Gate Park, Lake Merced.

Sayornis saya. Say's Phoebe. Grassy areas. Twin Peaks.

Empidonax traillii. Traill's Flycatchers. Scrub and open woodlands, often near water. Golden Gate Park.

Empidonax difficilis. Western Flycatcher. Woodlands. Golden Gate Park.

Nuttallornis borealis. Olive-sided Flycatcher. Woodlands. Sutro Forest, Twin Peaks, Golden Gate Park.

Alaudidae. Larks

Eremophila alpestris. Horned Lark. Fields and sand dunes. Presidio, Twin Peaks.

Hirundinidae. Swallows

Tachycineta thalassina. Violet-green Swallow. Open areas. Golden Gate Park, Lake Merced.

Riparia riparia. Bank Swallow. Open areas. Ocean Beach, Lake Merced.

Stelgidopteryx ruficollis. Rough-winged Swallow. Open areas. Ocean Beach, Lake Merced.

Hirundo rustica. Barn Swallow. Open areas. Golden Gate Park, Lake Merced.

Petrochelidon pyrrhonota. Cliff Swallow. Open areas. Lake Merced.

Progne subis. Purple Martin. Open areas. Lake Merced.

Corvidae. Jays, Magpies, and Crows

Cyanocitta stelleri. Steller's Jay. Coniferous forests. Golden Gate Park.

Aphelocoma coerulescens. Scrub Jay. Woodlands. Golden Gate Park.

Corvis corax. Common Raven. Coastal cliffs. Golden Gate Park, Lake Merced.

Corvis brachyrhynchos. Common Crow. Woodlands and open areas. Presidio, Golden Gate Park.

Nucifraga columbiana. Clark's Nutcracker. Woodlands. Presidio, Twin Peaks (rare).

Paridae. Chickadees and Bushtits

Parus rufescens. Chestnut-backed Chickadee. Coniferous forests. Golden Gate Park.

Psaltriparus minimus. Common Bushtit. Woodlands and scrub. Golden Gate Park.

Sittidae. Nuthatches

Sitta carolinensis. White-breasted Nuthatch. Oak woodland. Golden Gate Park.

Sitta canadensis. Red-breasted Nuthatch. Woodlands. Twin Peaks, Golden Gate Park.

Sitta pygmaea. Pygmy Nuthatch. Pine woodlands. Golden Gate Park.

Certhiidae. Creepers

Certhia familiaris. Brown Creeper. Forests. Golden Gate Park.

Chamaeidae. Wrentit

Chamaea fasciata. Wrentit. Scrub. Golden Gate Park.

Troglodytidae. Wrens

Troglodytes aedon. House Wren. Scrub and woodland undergrowth. Golden Gate Park.

Troglodytes troglodytes. Winter Wren. Woodland undergrowth. Twin Peaks, Golden Gate Park.

Thryomanes bewickii. Bewick's Wren. Scrub and woodland undergrowth. Golden Gate Park.

Telmatodytes palustris. Long-billed Marsh Wren. Marshes. Lake Merced.

Mimidae. Mockingbirds and Thrashers

Mimus polyglottos. Mockingbird. Residential areas. Presidio.

Turdidae. Thrushes

Turdus migratorius. Robin. Meadows, gardens, and woodlands. Golden Gate Park.

Ixoreus naevius. Varied Thrush. Forest undergrowth. Golden Gate Park.

Hylocichla guttata. Hermit Thrush. Woodland undergrowth. Golden Gate Park.

Sialia mexicana. Western Bluebird. Meadows and other open areas. Golden Gate Park.

Myadestes townsendi. Townsend's Solitaire. Woodlands. Golden Gate Park (rare).

Sylviidae. Old World Warblers and Kinglets

Regulus satrapa. Golden-crowned Kinglet. Woodlands, especially coniferous forests. Golden Gate Park, Lake Merced.

Regulus calendula. Ruby-crowned Kinglet. Woodlands. Golden Gate Park, Lake Merced.

Motacillidae. Pipits

Anthus spinoletta. Water Pipit. Fields and margins of fresh water. Golden Gate Park.

Bombycillidae. Waxwings

Bombycilla cedrorum. Cedar Waxwing. Woodlands, residential areas. Golden Gate Park.

Laniidae. Shrikes

Lanius ludovicianus. Loggerhead Shrike. Fields. Twin Peaks.

Sturnidae. Starlings

Sturnus vulgaris. Starling. Open fields and city parks. Golden Gate Park.

Vireonidae. Vireos

Vireo huttoni. Hutton's Vireo. Woodlands. Golden Gate Park, Lake Merced.

Vireo solitarius. Solitary Vireo. Woodlands. Golden Gate Park.

Vireo gilvus. Warbling Vireo. Woodlands. Twin Peaks, Golden Gate Park.

Parulidae. Wood Warblers

Protonotaria citrea. Prothonotary Warbler. Margins of wooded lakes. Lincoln Park (one record).

Vermivora pinus. Blue-winged Warbler. Woodlands. San Francisco (one record).

Vermivora peregrina. Tennessee Warbler. Woodlands. Lake Merced (rare).

Vermivora celata. Orange-crowned Warbler. Scrub and woodlands. Twin Peaks, Golden Gate Park.

Dendroica petechia. Yellow Warbler. Woodlands. Golden Gate Park.

Dendroica caerulescens. Black-throated Blue Warbler. Woodlands. Lake Merced (rare).

Dendroica coronata. Myrthle Warbler. Woodlands. Lake Merced.

Dendroica auduboni. Audubon's Warbler. Woodlands. Golden Gate Park, Lake Merced.

Dendroica nigrescens. Black-throated Gray Warbler. Woodlands. Golden Gate Park.

Dendroica townsendi. Townsend's Warbler. Woodlands, especially coniferous forests. Golden Gate Park.

Dendroica occidentalis. Hermit Warbler. Woodlands, especially coniferous forests. Twin Peaks.

Seiurus noveboracensis. Northern Waterthrush. Margins of wooded lakes and streams. Golden Gate Park (rare).

Oporornis tolmiei. MacGillivray's Warbler. Scrub and woodland undergrowth. Lincoln Park.

Geothlypis trichas. Yellowthroat. Marshes and lake edges. Golden Gate Park.

Icteria virens. Yellow-breasted Chat. Scrub and open woodland undergrowth. Lake Merced.

Wilsonia pusilla. Wilson's Warbler. Woodlands. Golden Gate Park.

Ploceidae. Weaverbirds

Passer domesticus. House Sparrow. Ubiquitous. Gardens, parks, and vacant lots.

Icteridae. Orioles, Meadowlarks, and Blackbirds

Sturnella neglecta. Western Meadowlark. Grassy areas. Golden Gate Park, Lake Merced.

Xanthocephalus xanthocephalus. Yellow-headed Blackbird. Marshes. Golden Gate Park.

Agelaius phoeniceus. Red-winged Blackbird. Marshes, lake margins, and parks. Golden Gate Park.

Agelaius tricolor. Tricolored Blackbird. Marshes and fields. Presidio.

Icterus cucullatus. Hooded Oriole. Woodlands and residential areas. San Francisco gardens.

Icterus bullockii. Bullock's Oriole. Woodlands and residential areas. Golden Gate Park.

Euphagus cyanocephalus. Brewer's Blackbird. Open areas. Golden Gate Park, Lake Merced.

Molothrus ater. Brown-headed Cowbird. Woodlands and open areas. Lake Merced.

Thraupidae. Tanagers

Piranga liboviciana. Western Tanager. Woodlands. Twin Peaks, Golden Gate Park.

Fringillidae. Sparrows, Buntings, and Finches

Pheucticus ludovicianus. Rose-breasted Grosbeak. Woodlands. Golden Gate Park.

Pheucticus melanocephalus. Black-headed Grosbeak. Woodlands. Golden Gate Park.

Passerina amoena. Lazuli Bunting.

Scrub. Golden Gate Park.

Carpodacus purpureus. Purple Finch. Woodlands. Sutro Forest, Golden Gate Park.

Carpodacus mexicanus. House Finch. Woodlands, residential areas, and open areas. Ubiquitous.

Spinus pinus. Pine Siskin. Woodlands. Golden Gate Park.

Spinus tristis. American Goldfinch. Fields and scrub. Lake Merced.

Spinus psaltria. Lesser Goldfinch. Fields and scrub. Glen Park.

Spinus lawrencei. Lawrence's Goldfinch. Fields and scrub. Golden Gate Park.

Loxia curvirostra. Red Crossbill. Coniferous woodlands. Golden Gate Park.

Piplo erythrophthalmus. Rufous-sided Towhee. Scrub and woodland undergrowth. Golden Gate Park.

Pipilo fuscus. Brown Towhee. Scrub and gardens. Twin Peaks.

Passerbulus sandwichensis. Savannah Sparrow. Marshes and fields. Presidio, Twin Peaks, Lake Merced.

Junco oreganus. Oregon Junco. Woodlands. Twin Peaks, Golden Gate Park.

Spizella passerina. Chipping Sparrow. Open woodlands. Twin Peaks.

Zonotrichia leucophrys. White-crowned Sparrow. Scrub and gardens. Golden Gate Park.

Zonotrichia albicollis. White-throated Sparrow. Woodland undergrowth. Golden Gate Park.

Zonotrichia atricapilla. Golden-crowned Sparrow. Scrub and gardens. Golden Gate Park.

Passerella iliaca. Fox Sparrow. Scrub and woodland undergrowth. Golden Gate Park, Lake Merced.

Melospiza melodia. Song Sparrow. Marshes and scrub. Golden Gate Park.

Plant Type Locality

In the 18th and 19th centuries, several plants new to botanical science were first identified within the present boundaries of

San Francisco. In 1792 botanist Archibald Menzies, with the Vancouver expedition, collected samples from formerly unknown tree species along the north shore of San Francisco—California Bay (or Laurel) (*Unbellaria californica*) and California Buckeye (*Aesculus californica*). Several species new to science were collected in and near the Presidio in 1816 by Adelbert von Chamisso, naturalist with the Kotzebue expedition. These included the California Poppy (*Eschscholzia californica*), California Wild Rose (*Rosa californica*), Francican Wallflower (*Erysimum franciscanum*), Yerba Buena (*Satureja douglasii*), and two trees, California Hazel (*Corylis cornuta*) and California Wax Myrtle (*Myrica californica*). Johann Friedrich Eschscholtz, naturalist with the second Kotzebue expedition in 1824, collected several additional plants in the same area, including Blue Blossom (*Ceanothus thyrsifloris*), California Coffee Berry (*Rhamnus californica*), Chaparral Currant (*Ribesmalvacetum*), Yellow Sand Verbena (*Abronia latifolia*), Skunkweed *(Navarretia squarrosa)*, and Blue Witch (*Solanum umbelliferum*).

Some 37 additional plant species were first identified in San Francisco in later years, notably "Presidio Evening Primrose" (*Clarkia franciscana*), "Presidio manzanita" (*Arctostaphylos franciscana*), California Mugwort (*Artemisia douglasii*), Leather Fern (*Polypodium scouleri*), Blue Wild Rye (*Elymus glaucus*), Willowleaf Dock (*Rumex salicifolius*), Coast Rock-Cress (*Arabis blepharophylla*), California Blackberry (*Rubus ursinus*), Common Fiddle-Neck (*Amsinckia intermedia*), and Thimble Berry (*Rubus parviflorus* var. *velutinus*).

MICHAEL D. LAMPEN

Unique and Extinct Plants and Butterflies of San Francisco

The rapid development of San Francisco has resulted in the extinction of several unique plant and butterfly species. Remaining rare species are increasingly endangered as development of the last fragments of undisturbed habitat proceeds. Most of the rare butterflies depend on specific species of native plants as a food source, and the fates of several rare butterflies and plants are closely linked. Some butterflies once common in the natural landscape of San Francisco now make their last stand on Mount San Bruno, just south of the San Francisco County line, in San Mateo County.

Two endangered plant species are unique (endemic) to San Francisco. *Clarkia franciscana* (Lewis and Raven, 1949) is an annual wildflower of the Evening Primrose family found on serpentine slopes in the Presidio. *Arctostaphylos franciscana* (Eastwood, 1895) is a manzanita unique to the serpentine bluffs of the Presidio. Only a single plant survived until recent artificial propogation on nearby slopes. *Grindella maritima* (Greene, Steyermark) is a gumweed of open brush-covered slopes and sandy flats of the Presidio and Lands End. It is a hybrid of *G. hirsutula* and *G. humilis* of Marin, San Francisco, and San Mateo counties. *Lessingia germanorum* (Chamisso), of the *Compositae* or sunflower family, is found only in the Presidio and on Mount San Bruno.

Extinct butterfly species endemic to San Francisco were *Glaucopsyche xerces*—the Xerces Blue—a small lilac-blue butterfly of the sand dunes, and *Icaricia icarioides pheres*—the Pheres Blue—a small gray-blue sand dune butterfly. *Ceryonis sthenele sthenele*—the Sthenele Satyr—a gray grassland butterfly with a dark hind wing band, ranged into San Mateo County. Endangered butterflies now largely confined to Mount San Bruno include *Speyeria callipe callipe*, a local subspecies of the multicolored

San Francisco Silverspot, and *Icaricia icarioides missionensis*—the iridescent blue-winged Mission Blue—of which a few also survive on Twin Peaks and southern Marin County. All three butterflies are grassland species. (*Glaucopsyche* and *Icaricia* are of the family Lycaenidae. Ceryonis is of the family Satyridae, and Speyeria is of the family Nymphidae.)

MICHAEL D. LAMPEN

31 Panoramic Views

Panoramic Views of San Francisco

San Francisco is renowned for its superb views. The following selected list covers the ten best publicly accessible, ground-level panoramic viewpoints within, and of, San Francisco. Suggested times of day for visits are given in parentheses. Several formerly popular viewpoints are now obscured by trees or buildings.

1. Twin Peaks (north peak):
A sweeping panorama of the northern and eastern parts of the city, plus portions of southern and western districts. (afternoon)

2. Bernal Heights (slopes adjacent to summit):
A walk around the summit reveals most of eastern and southeastern San Francisco. (morning)

3. Golden Gate Heights (north summit, Grand View Park):
A broad northern view from the Sunset district to downtown, plus southwest views behind the trees. (midday)

4. Mount Davidson (northeast ridge):
A distant but vast view of eastern and southern San Francisco. (afternoon)

5. Fort Funston (eastern slopes):
A little-known panorama of southwest and central San Francisco.

6. Pacific Heights (Alta Plaza Park, top of south steps):
A broad view of north central and eastern San Francisco. (afternoon)

7. Bayview Heights (upper northwest slope):
A wide view of southern and eastern San Francisco. (morning)

8. Merced Heights (west summit, slopes of Brooks Park):
A little-known western panorama from the county line to Sutro Heights. (morning)

9. Sutro Heights (south side of Sutro Heights Park):
A broad view of western San Francisco and the Pacific Ocean. (afternoon)

10. Telegraph Hill (parking lot-park):
A wide panorama of northeast San Francisco and the bay (morning) plus downtown area from park. (afternoon)

MICHAEL D. LAMPEN

A tugboat passes through the Golden Gate bound for the pacific. Point Bonita Lighthouse is perched on the edge of the Marin Headlands in the distance.

32 Golden Gate Park

Golden Gate Park is San Francisco's largest park, comprising 1,013 acres. It is a narrow parallelogram approximately 3 miles long by 1/2-mile wide, extending from its eastern boundary at Stanyan Street, between Fulton Street on the north and Lincoln Way on the south, to the Great Highway on the west.

The park was an outgrowth of the city's legal fight to establish its title to the four square leagues (17,000 acres) originally granted it under Mexican law, called the Outside Lands, and settled by squatters.

Shortly before 1866 a clamor for a large public park started and the city authorities directed their efforts to obtaining the land. A compromise settlement (Order #800) between the city and squatters and other so-called land owners was approved by the Mayor and the Board of Supervisors on January 14, 1868 and approved by the Legislature March 27, 1868.

The first Park Commissioners (S. F. Butterworth, D. W. Connely, and Charles F. MacDermott) appointed William Hammond Hall to survey and make maps of the park area on August 8, 1870. He was later elected the first Superintendent of Golden Gate Park on August 14, 1871. He was succeeded by the following superintendents:

William Bond Pritchard, *1876–1881*
Francis P. Hennessey, *1881–1882*
John J. McEwen, *1882–1886*
William Hammond Hall, *1886–1889*
John McLaren, *1890–1943*
Julius Girod, *1943–1957*
Bart Rolph, *1958–1964*
Frank Foehr, *1964–1970*
Emmett O'Donnell, *1970–1974*
John J. Spring, *1974–1975*
Carl Poch, *1975–1977*
Aldo C. Cima, *1977–1978*
Bernard Barron, *1978–*

First meeting of Commission
May 3, 1870.
First money received by Commission from Sale of Bonds
August 1, 1870.

Post-World War II photograph of the Wishing Bridge at the Japanese Tea Garden in San Francisco's Golden Gate Park. The studios of famed San Francisco photographer Gabriel Moulin are credited with this photograph.

First Permanent Employee
Patrick J. Owens, "Keeper of the Grounds," hired November 17, 1870.
First Contract for Work on Panhandle
Awarded to B. Kenny on May 12, 1871.
First Restaurant
"Casino," built in 1881 by Jake and Rheinhart Daemon.
First Park Lodge:
A-frame Victorian structure built in 1874. Second lodge built in 1895.
First Life Saving Station
Established in 1879. Station discontinued in 1950.
First Transportation to Park
"Geary, Park, & Ocean Railroad" 1881 (Steam Dummy).
First Buffalo Purchased
February 26, 1891.
First Windmill Built
"The Dutch Mill" in 1902. It was designed by Alpheus Bull, and had a capacity to pump 30,000 gallons per hour.
Oldest Building in Park
Conservatory, erected 1879. Designated as California Historical Landmark No. 841 on November 19, 1970.
Oldest Monument
Garfield, erected 1884. Music Stands: First, built in 1881; second, built in 1886; third, built in 1900.
Japanese Tea Garden
Built in 1894 by G. T. Marsh for the Midwinter Fair.
De Young Museum
Established in 1895 from Midwinter Fair. New building opened Jan. 2, 1921.
Brundage Collection of Oriental Art:
Opened May 9, 1960.

California Academy of Sciences:
North American Hall
dedicated Sept. 22, 1916.
Steinhart Aquarium
opened Sept. 29, 1923.
Simson African Hall
dedicated Dec. 14, 1934.

Morrison Planetarium
opened Nov. 6, 1952.
Cowell Hall
opened May 16, 1969.

John McLaren

The famed superintendent of Golden Gate Park came to the United States from his native Scotland in the late 1860s. "I learned my trade in Scotch gardens around Edinburgh," he said, "and had gotten as far as Gosford House, seat of the Earl of Wemyss.... Right after that I went to do some real studying at Edinburgh's Botanical Gardens."

In 1870, as Bismarck was deliberately goading the French government into attacking Prussia, John McLaren left New York by ship for Panama where he crossed the isthmus by train, and then came by ship to San Francisco about the time Napoleon III was captured at Sedan.

He was appointed Assistant Superintendent of the Park in 1887, and was appointed Superintendent in 1890. In the early 1890s he oversaw the construction of the Midwinter Fair that was scheduled to occupy just five acres of land in the center of the Park.

John McLaren once said, "Always work with Nature, never against it. Never interfere with the beauty the Creator has given us," and his stewardship of the Park proved this point of natural law.

The Park Commission decided in 1909 that McLaren needed an automobile, and authorized the purchase of a Chalmers-Detroit car. However, he could not drive and so the Commission authorized the employment of a chauffeur. Later the Commission removed the chauffeur's position, and John McLaren had to learn how to operate the vehicle. Unfortunately on his first solo outing he drove the expensive automobile into Spreckels Lake. The Commission rehired the chauffeur for the superintendent to avoid future accidents.

He reached the mandatory retirement age of 70 in 1916, but the citizens of San Francisco petitioned the Board of Supervisors for a waiver of that rule, and he continued as the superintendent until his death in 1943 at McLaren Lodge, located at the entrance to the Park.

Among other honors, McLaren was elected to the Royal Horticultural Society of England in 1930.

John McLaren, who helped wrest Golden Gate Park from one thousand acres of sand, died in January 1943. His body lay in state in the rotunda of San Francisco's City Hall, and then the funeral cortege drove through Golden Gate Park as a final tribute to the man known as "the man who lived to plant a million trees."

William Hammond Hall

William Hammond Hall was the designer and first Superintendent of Golden Gate Park. He held that position from 1871–1876. Hall was responsible for surveying the Park, building roads, planting trees, and designing the Children's Playground.

Mr. Hall said, "Destroy a public building and it can be rebuilt in a year; destroy a city woodland park and all the people living at the time will have passed away before its restoration can be effected."

Reclamation of the Sand Dunes

Reclamation attempts in the area of what was to become Golden Gate Park began after the American Civil War. In the 1860s, the U.S. Army Corps of Engineers built fortifications along Ocean Beach to protect San Francisco because the U.S. War Department suspected England might attack and invade California to gain control of the state's gold fields. The results of these early reclamation attempts by the Corps of Engineers were mixed.

Many great ideas are the result of accidents, and the best system for reclamation of the sand dunes is no exception. In the early 1870s a saddle horse spilled its nosebag of barley upon one of the sand dunes.

Hall later went by the spot and found green sprouts of barley holding the sand.

He later combined the barley with slow-growing lupine, and spread the seeds in areas to be reclaimed. The barley growth generally lasted a few months, sufficient time to allow the lupine to grow and properly root. Beach grass was utilized in place of barley and lupine in areas where sand was freshly washed up from the sea. Almost all the sandy areas of the Park were reclaimed by this method.

In 1886 Mr. Hall became the consulting engineer to the Park, by order of California Governor George Stoneman. The Park was in frightful condition, according to Mr. Hall, who found thousands of trees planted too close together, and many of them were dead or dying because the groves had not been thinned or trimmed in 15 years. He began to clean up the Park and improved the horticultural techniques of the Park's staff.

The governor of California appointed the Golden Gate Park commissioners and top staff in the late 1800s because the Park was technically not in the city limits of San Francisco. The City of San Francisco did not attain the power to appoint park commissioners until 1900.

Mr. Hall ended his association with the Park in 1886, when a new governor took office and appointed a lobbyist for the powerful Southern Pacific Railroad to the Commission. However, before Mr. Hall left, he appointed a young Scotsman named John McLaren to be the Assistant Superintendent, and put him to work landscaping the Children's Playground that was then under construction.

The legacy of Mr. Hall can still be seen and felt in Golden Gate Park because he deliberately designed roads and pathways with curves and bends to discourage fast drivers in horse and buggies, and to shelter visitors from the wind. Walkways were kept away from roads, and low spots, known as dells, were planted with shrubbery and plants to attract birds and small wildlife for the visitors' pleasure.

ICE SKATING RINK AT S___
SAN FRANCISCO

76

33 Place-Names

The Term "Frisco"

The ladies of the Outdoor Art League have formed an Anti-Frisco Committee, for the purpose of discouraging the use of the term "Frisco." They are especially incensed at the poets who sing of the glories of "Frisco." The committee declares that any person possessed of the poor taste to use this obnoxious term would wear diamonds to breakfast.

SAN FRANCISCO NEWSLETTER,
Christmas, 1907

Do Call It Frisco.

The University of Michigan Database shows these communities and areas sharing the name "Frisco." There is no "Frisco" in California.

FRISCO
Coffee County, Alabama
Longitude: 31° 35' 43" N
Latitude 85° 51' 56" W

FRISCO
Benton County, Arkansas
Longitude: 36° 15' 23" N
Latitude: 94° 04' 41" W

FRISCO
Summit County, Colorado
Longitude: 39° 34' 28" N
Latitude: 106° 05' 49" W

FRISCO
Shoshone County, Idaho
Longitude: 47° 30' 44" N
Latitude: 115° 51' 30" W

FRISCO
Franklin County, Illinois
Longitude: 38° 06' 48" N
Latitude: 88° 46' 42" W

FRISCO
Pointe Coupee Parish, Louisiana
Longitude: 30° 35' 08" N
Latitude: 91° 31' 32" W

FRISCO
Stoddard County, Missouri
Longitude: 36° 45' 32" N
Latitude: 89° 51' 44" W

FRISCO
Dare County, North Carolina
Longitude: 35° 14' 06" N
Latitude: 75° 37' 44" W

Above left: 1950s interior of Sutro Baths after it has been converted to an ice skating rink. Sutro Baths burned to the ground during a spectacular fire in 1966. Lower left: The famous "Chutes" amusement park at 10th and Fulton featured a roller coaster purported to be the most thrilling on the West Coast.

FRISCO
Pontotoc County, Oklahoma
Longitude: 34° 38' 52" N
Latitude: 96° 34' 43" W

FRISCO
Beaver County, Pennsylvania
Longitude: 40° 50' 52" N
Latitude: 80° 16' 05" W

FRISCO
Collin County, Texas
Longitude: 33° 09' 02" N
Latitude: 96° 49' 24" W

FRISCO
Beaver County, Utah
Longitude: 38° 27' 23" N
Latitude: 113° 15' 29" W

FRISCO
Scott County, Virginia
Longitude: 36° 35' 38" N
Latitude: 82° 37' 57" W

Communities Sharing Name of San Francisco

The Geographic Name Server of the University of Michigan contains the names of these communities sharing the name San Francisco. In addition to San Francisco, California, there is:

San Francisco
Socorro County, New Mexico
Longitude: 34° 23' 45" N
Latitude: 106° 50' 19" W

San Francisco
Brewster County, Texas
Longitude: 29° 53' 36" N
Latitude: 102° 24' 13" W

San Francisco
Arecibo County, Puerto Rico
Longitude: 18° 27' 02" N
Latitude: 66° 42' 51" W

Other San Franciscos

Although San Francisco, California is the best known, there are several other San Franciscos in Central and South America, and in the Philippines. San Francisco, Argentina, is a large town, and there are San Francisco villages in Colombia, Panama, and Costa Rica. The Philippines has two villages named San Francisco. There are another sixteen towns and villages named *San Francisco de* or *del*, plus a place-name (e.g., San Francisco de Rincon, Mexico). Eight of these towns or villages are in Mexico; the rest in Argentina and the Dominican Republic.

The 1,200-mile-long San Francisco River is the main river of eastern Brazil. The 300-mile-long San Francisco River is in the Andean foothills of Argentina. The 100-mile-long San Francisco River in Arizona/New Mexico is a tributary of the Gila River. Its upper reaches are bordered by the San Francisco Mountains.

Towns named Frisco, in probable reference to San Francisco, California, are found in Texas and Pennsylvania, and formerly existed in Colorado, Missouri, and North Carolina.

BRITANNICA ATLAS,
Encyclopedia Britannica, *Chicago, 1986*

San Francisco Place-Names

This is a selected list of present and past place-names used in the City and County of San Francisco. Current or last-used place-names are featured, followed by earlier names, listed from earliest to latest. Current street names are used to define boundaries, and boundaries are described in clockwise fashion (north, east, south, west). District and neighborhood boundaries are not always clear and may vary or overlap. Space limitations prevent the listing of many small tracts and farms.

A-1 PROJECT 1956 city redevelopment project in north-central Western Addition. Bounded by Post, Franklin, Eddy, Broderick. See Fillmore Center and Geary Corridor.

A-2 PROJECT 1964 city redevelopment project surrounding A-1 Project. Includes 1971 Friendship Village. Approximate boundaries: Post, Franklin, Fulton, Steiner, Golden Gate, Broderick.

ACADEMY HOMESTEAD ca. 1876 tract in Islais Creek valley bounded by San Jose, Mission, Tingley, Alemany.

ALAMEDA ISLAND The filled western tip of the island, part of the Alameda Naval Air Station, lies within San Francisco County. The 1794 name "alameda" is Spanish for "poplar or cottonwood grove."

ALAMO SQUARE Hill, neighborhood, and historic district in Western Addition. Name is Spanish for "poplar or cottonwood" and was given to the hilltop park in the 1860s. Approximate historic district boundaries are Golden Gate, Steiner, Fulton, Webster, Grove, Steiner, Fell, Scott.

ALCATRAZ ISLAND Island in San Francisco Bay, one mile north of Fisherman's Wharf. Former fort and prison, now part of Golden Gate National Recreation Area. 1775 Spanish name (of Ayala) was "Isla de Alcatraces," "Pelican Island," for nesting White and Brown Pelicans, *Pelecanus erythrorhynchos* and *Pelecanus occidentalis*. Later names included White Island (for bird droppings), Bird Island or Rock, the Rock (1860s Army fort name also used in prison days), Devil's Island (for the French South American prison island), and Hellcatraz (romanticized prison name). Local features include Alcatraz Beach at Pirate's Cove (romanticized 1860s name) on the southwest shore, and Alcatraz or Seal Rock, (for Harbor Seals, *Phoca vitulina*) off the northwestern point. See also Arch Rock, Shag Rock.

ALCATRAZ SHOAL Underwater shoal curving southwest from Alcatraz Island. 19th-century name.

ALEMANY GAP Pass between Merced Heights and Mount San Bruno through which summer ocean fog penetrates. Named in 1950s for principal boulevard through gap.

ALEMANY MAZE Complex intersection of Highway 101 and 280 freeways. 1950s drivers' name.

ALMS HOUSE TRACT ca. 1876 tract on present site of Laguna Honda grounds. Named for earlier city alms house on site.

ALTA PLAZA Ridgetop park and neighborhood in central western Pacific Heights. 1870s name from Spanish "high square." Neighborhood surrounds park along Jackson, Steiner, Clay, Scott.

ALVORD LAKE Artificial lake at east end of Golden Gate Park. Named in 1881 for former park commission president and mayor William Alvord (who wanted to call it The Lakelet). Near Haight and Stanyan.

AMUTAJA OR AMUCTAC Former Indian village in or near Visitacion Valley. 18th-century Ohlone dialect name meaning unclear (suffix "tac" means "place of").

ANGEL ISLAND Named Isla de los Angeles by the Spanish in 1775.

ANITA ROCK Hazardous submerged rock north of Crissy Field Beach. Called Anita Rocks in 1850s. Name origin unclear, possibly a ship name.

ANZA VISTA Hill and neighborhood east of Lone Mountain. Site of 19th-century cemetery. 1948 promotional name by Mayfair Heights Corp. is Spanish for "Anza View" and recalls the 1776 exploration of San Francisco by Col. Anza. Neighborhood boundaries are Geary, Baker, St. Josephs, Turk, Masonic.

APPAREL CITY 1949 garment industry project by Ward and Bolles east of Bernal Heights. Bounded by Palou, Industrial, Barneveld (see Islais Creek).

AQUATIC PARK ca. 1939 name for cove, artificial beach, and park east of Black Point/Fort Mason.

ARCH ROCK Former hazardous rock 3/4 mile west of Alcatraz Rock in San Francisco Bay. May have had a small natural arch. Also called Bird Rock (see Alcatraz). Blown up in 1901 (see Shag Rocks, Harding Rock).

ASHBURY HEIGHTS 1911 tract and neighborhood on Mount Olympus and its north slope. Named for principal street.

1890s name was Ashbury Park. Also called Upper Ashbury or Upper Haight. Ashbury Terrace was a 1909 development along Piedmont and Ashbury Terrace. Bounded by Frederick, Masonic, Roosevelt, 17th, Clayton.

AUTO ROW Former automobile showroom strip (1920s to 1970s) of which fragments remain. Van Ness from Clay to Eddy.

AWASTE Former Indian village near former bay shore of Visitacion Valley. 18th-century Ohlone name may mean "salt place" or "north place."

AZALEA HILL Low hill east of Concert Valley in Golden Gate Park, south of Rhododendron Dell. Named in 1940s for massed plantings.

BABY PARK Informal name for McKinley Square, popular with mothers and infants. At 20th and Vermont.

BACCHIAN WAY The early 20th-century downtown San Francisco bar-crawl route. Also called the Trail of Bacchus, Cocktail Route, or Whiskey Belt. Named for Bacchus, Roman god of wine.

BAKER BEACH OR BAKER'S BEACH Beach along southern half of the western shore of the Presidio, facing South Bay of the Golden Gate. Named in 1860s for local landowner and U.S. Senator Col. Edward D. Baker. Name originally confined to China Beach and portion of Baker Beach west of Lobos Creek, adjacent to Baker ranch (on present site of Sea Cliff). After 1910 name was shifted east and north to present site.

BALBOA TERRACE Developed neighborhood south of Saint Francis Wood. Created in 1910s by Joseph Leonart of Urban Realty Co. Named for Spanish explorer who first saw Pacific Ocean, visible from area. Bounded by Monterey, San Benito, Ocean, Junipera Serra.

BALDWIN PARK 1880s development in western Pacific Heights. Named for developer A. S. Baldwin. Bounded by Greenwich, Scott, Vallejo, Broderick.

BARBARY COAST Former district at the south base of Telegraph Hill, notorious from the 1860s to the 1910s for its saloons, bordellos, and crime. Named in mid-1860s for the then infamous pirate coast of Algeria/Tunisia ("Barbary" being the "land of the Berbers"). Heart of the district was Pacific from Grant to Montgomery and adjacent alleys (Devil's Acre or Terrific Street, the latter a 1910 name of sportswriter Bill McGeehan). Battle Row, named for brawls, was Kearny from Pacific to Broadway; Murderer's Corner was Kearny and Jackson; and Deadman's Alley was nearby. Approximate boundaries were north side of Broadway, Embarcadero, Washington, Grant.

BATTERY POINT Former east shore point of Telegraph Hill. Named for 1847 U.S. battery (Fort).

BAY PARK HOMESTEAD 1890s development north of Bayview Heights. Included present Double Rock and Candlestick Heights neighborhoods. Bounded by Gillman, Griffith, Jamestown, Third.

BAYSIDE VILLAGE 1980s development in South Beach district. Bounded by Bryant, Second, Embarcadero.

BAYVIEW District in southeast San Francisco adjacent to and often linked with Hunters Point district. Name derived from 1864 racetrack near South Basin (Bay View Track). Approximate boundaries: Selby, Evans, Third, Palou, Mendel, Newcomb, Keith, Palou line to S. F. Bay, north slope of Bayview Heights, Highway 101, Phelps, Williams, extension of Newhall, extension of Quesada. See Bret Harte, Candlestick Heights, Double Rock.

BAYVIEW HEIGHTS Prominent hill at southeast corner of San Francisco, west of Candlestick Park, the eastern end of the Black Hills. Former name was Visitacion Knob for Visitacion Valley adjacent to west. See Candlestick Heights, Candlestick Point.

BAYVIEW HOMESTEAD See Bret Harte.

BAYVIEW-HUNTERS POINT MODEL NEIGHBORHOOD 1966 housing redevelopment in northern Bayview and adjacent Hunters Point districts.

BEER TOWN Informal 1890s neighborhood in Richmond district, built to serve patrons of the nearby 1894 Midwinter Fair in Golden Gate Park, and revived by 1906 earthquake and fire refugees. Also called the New Barbary Coast. Centered at 10th and Fulton.

BEIDEMAN TRACT Neighborhood in Western Addition developed in 1870s by Jacob C. Beideman. Bounded by Geary, Pierce, Turk, Divisadero.

BELLE ROCHE CITY OR BELLEROCHE CITY 1870s development northeast of City College Hill. French name means "beautiful hill or rock" but may be a personal name. Bounded by Circular, San Jose, Havelock.

BERMUDA TRIANGLE Area of bars and restaurants in Cow Hollow frequented by young urbanites. Satirical 1980s name refers to area of Atlantic Ocean where ships and planes have disappeared.

BERNAL 1890s tract west of St. Mary's Park. Named for local Mexican landowner Jose Bernal, whose ranch house stood nearby. Bounded by San Jose, St Mary, Mission, Highway 280.

BERNAL HEIGHTS Prominent hill and neighborhood south of the Mission district. The Spanish Potrero Viejo ("old pasture") and the northern part of the Mexican rancho of Jose Bernal. A later name was Nanny Goat Hill (for local goat farms). (See Billy Goat Hill, Dolores Heights, Potrero Hill.) Northeast developed ridge is Peralta Heights, named for a principal street; the southern upland extension (Crescent neighborhood) is sometimes considered part of the hill. Approximate boundaries are Precita, Highway 280, Courtland, Mission.

BERNAL HOMESTEAD 19th-century development in western Crocker-Amazon district. Bounded by Rolph, Curtis, Morse, Mission.

BILGE-WATER BAY Former cove between Tonquin Point and North Point, now filled as Fisherman's Wharf and North Beach and site of 1850s Meiggs' Wharf. Also called North Bay. Tonquin Shoal lay beneath the bay and Sewer Lake was its partly filled remnant. Named in 1870s for local polluted waters, "bilgewater" being the stale water collected in the holds (bilges) of ships that were constructed and repaired here. Beach curved to northwest and northeast from Chestnut and Powell. Behind the beach to the south was Laguna Briones.

BILLY GOAT HILL Upper north slope of Fairmount Hill, east of Diamond Heights, now a park. 1940s name for former resident who had a goat farm. "Billy" refers to the beard or "bill" of a male goat. See Bernal Heights, Dolores Heights, Potrero Hill.

BLACK HEAD ROCK Large low rock 100 yards northwest of Lands End and 100 yards west of Pyramid Rock. 19th-century name describes surface growth of black kelp.

BLACK HILLS Hilly ridge of McLaren Park and Bayview Heights. 19th-century name translated from the Spanish name Sierra Prictas de las Aguages, "Black or Dark Ridge of the Tides." Named perhaps for dark scrub vegetation or dark profile seen from the north. Also called the Southern Hills or Heights.

BLACK HOLE Housing project east of St. Mary's Park. Named in 1980s by local gang for its uncongenial setting on slope near Highway 280. Name refers to an imploding star from which nothing can escape.

BLACK POINT Headland and northern point of small peninsula between Gas House Cove and Aquatic Park Cove occupied by Fort Mason. 1775 Spanish name was Punta Medanos, "Sand Dune Point," for the extensive dunes to the west and south. Renamed Punta de San Jose, "Saint Joseph Point," in 1797 when Bateria San Jose was set up on the point. From mid-1850s to 1870s it was also called Black Point for the dark laurel thickets (*Umbellaria californica*) on the peninsula. Known as Black Point since 1870s, but Fort Mason is more commonly used.

BLACK ROCK Former rocky outcrop on western Pacific Heights ridge at present site of Raycliffe. Portions survive along Broderick. 20th-century name for dark eroded sandstone.

BLOSSOM ROCK Large and dangerous submerged rock two-thirds of the distance between Alcatraz and Yerba Buena Island, named in 1826 by English explorer Capt. Frederick W. Beechey for his ship HMS *Blossom*. Rock blown up 1870.

BLUE MOUNTAIN See Mount Davidson, Mount Sutro.

BONE ALLEY Today's Windsor on Telegraph Hill. 19th-century name, possibly for discarded bones.

BONITA CHANNEL Ocean channel at northwest entrance to Golden Gate between Point Bonita and Four Fathom Bank. South entrance of channel lies within San Francisco County. Named for adjacent point, named Punta Bonete in 1790s by Spanish for its resemblance in profile (from east or west) to a wide-brimmed clerical hat or "bonete." Altered by American usage to "bonita," Spanish for "pretty."

BONITA COVE Large northwest cove of Golden Gate whose shore is part of the border of San Francisco County. Named for the point. Also called Rialto Cove for a 19th-century salvaged shipwreck.

BRET HARTE Neighborhood south and southeast of Silver Terrace. Central portion was 1880s Bayview Homestead. Forms southern portion of Bayview district. Named for noted 19th-century Western writer. Bounded by Phelps, Williams, Van Dyke, San Francisco Bay, Bayview Heights, Highway 101. See Candlestick Heights, Double Rock.

BROOM POINT East end of racetrack (horses, then cars) called Speedway Meadow in Golden Gate Park. 19th-century

name may refer to stableboy's duties. South of Kennedy and Marx.

BUCKELEW'S POINT Former small point adjacent to Thompson's Cove and south of Clark's Point, near the north entrance of Yerba Buena Cove. Named for Benjamin R. Buckelew, watchmaker, whose shop stood near the point in the 1850s. Also called Watchman's Point ("watchman" = "watchmaker").

BUENA VISTA Heights or Hill and neighborhood in north-central San Francisco. Named in early 1870s to encourage development. Earlier name was South Hill. A park occupies the summit area, and the neighborhood lies on the eastern slope bounded by Haight, Divisadero, Castro, 15th, Roosevelt. Slopes east of Divisadero sometimes called Baja ("lower") Buena Vista.

BUNKER HILL Low sand ridge southeast of the Polo Field, Golden Gate Park. Possibly named for "Bill Bunker," one of the park's first buffalo. On "island" between King and Middle.

BUTCHERTOWN Former slaughterhouse district which has had three (or four) different locations. First, around Polk and Chestnut in the 1860s. Second and third, in the areas bounded by 6th, Townsend, Division, Brannan in the 1850s to 1890s and at Steamboat Point nearby to the east in the 1860s-1870s. Fourth, between Selby, Islais Creek Channel, San Francisco Bay, Evans from 1890s to 1960s. The Horn Pile, south of Army, was a well-known collection site for horns and hoofs. Area partly redeveloped as India Basin Industrial Park.

CAMARITAS, LAS Mexican farm east of Mission Dolores, south of Erie Creek and adjacent to Dolores Lagoon. Spanish name means "the cabins." Bounded by 16th, Folsom, 18th, Mission.

CAMEL ROCK Picturesque coastal rock, attached to cliffs northeast of Point Lobos. Named for profile similarity to a camel's head and hump.

CAMINO REAL, EL See El Camino Real.

CAMP AGNOS Homeless encampment at Civic Center Plaza was given this nickname in 1989 for Mayor Art Agnos. Another name was Tenement Square, a pun on Tiananmen Square, Beijing (Agnos said he didn't want another Tiananmen massacre).

CANDLESTICK COVE Large cove south of Bayview Heights and Candlestick Point Recreation Area and southeast of Visitacion Valley. Now half-filled, its present northern shore lies just within San Francisco County. Named for Candlestick Point.

CANDLESTICK HEIGHTS 1940s development north of Bayview Heights. Named for Candlestick Point. Bounded by Hollister, Candlestick Park, Bayview Heights, Third.

CANDLESTICK POINT Former bayshore point at southeast base of Bayview Heights, now located beneath Candlestick Stadium site. 1860s name refers to picturesque chert outcrop at point resembling a multibranched candlestick. Present point so named is a fill-created point northeast of the stadium near South Basin.

CANNON HILL Hill forming western summit of Pacific Heights ridge. Named in 1850s for cannon practice on northwest slope in Presidio and/or for symbolic cannon placed on summit (Pacific and Lyon), ca. 1876, by Capt. E. Keyes to mark the southeast corner of the Presidio.

CANTIL BLANCO Former prominent headland at southeast (inner) entrance to Golden Gate, removed in 1850s to make way for Fort Point. Site of 1794 Spanish battery (Castillo de San Joaquin) built on the Mesa del Castillo ("fort mesa"), the flat top of the bluff. The 1775 Spanish name means "white bluff" and refers to the pale green to white serpentine cliffs (and possibly bird droppings) of the former bluff. For names of actual point, see Fort Point.

CANUTALES, LAS Former extensive marshes extending westward from the shore of former Mission Bay, in particular the marshes northwest of the bay in the later South-of-Market district. 18th-century Spanish name refers to the abundant "horse-tail ferns."

CARVILLE Former outer Sunset district neighborhood using recycled cable cars as dwellings. Founded by A. B. Fitzgerald ca. 1900. Some cars are still in use today. Approximate boundaries were Lincoln, 47th, Kirkham, Great Highway. Another cable car village was set up after the 1906 fire and earthquake on the site of the Lavabeds at California and 5th Ave.

CASINO HILL AND CANAL Small hill west of the Conservatory in Golden Gate Park. Site of the 1874–1896 Casino resort and artificial canal/moat. North of Kennedy and west of Conservatory.

CASTRO District occupying Eureka Valley, northeast of Twin Peaks. Since the 1970s the center of San Francisco's gay community. 1890s promotional name Castro Village was derived from main street, named for the family of Mexican general Jose Castro. Popularly known since the 1970s as The Castro. Section along Market near Church, former Scandinavian neighborhood, is called the Silver Strip for its many gay bars and the nearby U.S. Mint (1980s name). Heart of district is bounded by Market, Noe, 20th, Diamond, 17th.

CASTRO HILL Western hill of ridge extending east from Twin Peaks between Noe and Eureka valleys. Hill adjacent to the east is Dolores Heights. Officially named in 1939 for principal cross street. Approximate boundaries: 19th, Noe, 24th, Douglass.

CASTRO STREET ADDITION 1900s tract on south slope of Fairmount Hill along southern segment of Castro. Approximate boundaries: Poppy, Castro, Chenery, extension north to Conrad.

CATHEDRAL HILL South shoulder of Holladay Heights, eastern Pacific Heights, and neighborhood. Named 1964 for future (1971) St. Mary's Roman Catholic Cathedral. Approximate boundaries: Post, Van Ness, Turk, Webster.

CAYUGA Neighborhood east of Merced Heights. Named in 1930s for principal street (an Iroquoian tribe). The earlier West End Map #1 tract (north half) and #2 (south half) of 1880s. Bounded by Onondaga, Mission, Sickles, Highway 280, line to Onondaga.

CEMETERIES, THE Area of north central San Francisco used as cemeteries from the 1860s to 1915. Includes Ignatian Heights, Lone Mountain, Anza Vista, Laurel Heights.

CENTRAL BASIN Bayside cove between the enlarged and filled Point San Quentin and Potrero Point. Named in 1880s. "Basin" usually refers to a harbor for commercial maritime use. Between Piers 64 and 68–70. (See China Basin, India Basin.)

CENTRAL PARK HOMESTEAD ca. 1884 tract in present Hunters Point district. Bounded by Evans, Keith, Oakdale, Third.

CHAIN OF LAKES Three lakes in western Golden Gate Park developed in 1890s from former willow swamps. Named North, Middle, and South lakes. .

CHICKEN POINT Hill south of the Conservatory in Golden Gate Park. Summit quarried away to form present site of Lily Pond. Named for chickens kept here by 1870s squatters (and still popular today with "campers"). Later called Favorite Point for its view of the Conservatory. South of Kennedy and west of Middle Drive East.

CHINA BASIN Artificial bayside basin between South Beach and Mission Bay districts and including northeast portion of Mission Creek Channel. Named for the China clippers of the Pacific Mail Steamship Line that docked here at Steamboat Point after the mid-1860s. Area jokingly called China Sink by 1980s bicycle messengers. Mission Creek Channel

portion called the Banana Belt for its use as a dock for the adjacent United Fruit Co. cannery in the 1930s and 1940s.

CHINA BEACH Beach in cliff-lined cove at north shore of Sea Cliff neighborhood, facing South Bay of the Golden Gate. Site of a Chinese fishing camp from the 1850s to early 1900s. Named James D. Phelan Beach in 1940s for former mayor and U.S. senator, but original name revived in 1980s.

CHINA CAMP Chinese fishing village at Rincon Point in the 1850s–1860s. Other camps were located at Hunters Point (Union Chinese Camp) and South Beach.

CHINATOWN Historic center of San Francisco's Chinese community, originally confined to lower east slope of Nob Hill. Began in 1850s on Sacramento (China St.) near Kearny, growing along Grant (Bush to Broadway), Stockton (Sacramento to Broadway), and adjacent connecting streets. Former non-Chinese names for Chinatown include Little China (1850s), Chinese Quarter, Little Canton. A Chinese name is Tangrebv (from "Ton Yen Fau" meaning "Port of the Tang or Chinese"). Boundary of commerical area is Green, Columbus, Kearny, California, Stockton, Clay, Powell. Residential Chinatown is bounded by Broadway, Mason, Columbus, Sacramento, Larkin (New Chinatown is the inner Richmond District).

CHINATOWN STREET NAMES Several Chinatown streets and alleys have received Chinese or Sinicized names. Most date from the early 1900s. Bak Wah Dian Gai (Beckett) = "plain-language John Street" for a local translator; Cum Cook Yen (Sullivan); Du Baan Gai (Dupont = Grant) = "street of the slatboard capital city"; Fah Yeun Guy (Brenham) = "flower street"; Fay Chie Hong (Duncan) = "fat boy alley"; Fo Sue Hong (St. Louis) = "fire alley"; Gow Louie Sun Hong (Ross); Gum Ohk Hong (Jason) = "golden chrysanthemum lane" (red light district); Mah Fong Hong (Washington below Stockton) = "livery stable"; Min Pow Hong (location unknown) = "bread alley"; On New Hong (off Ross) = "urinating alley"; Sun Louie Sun Hong (Spofford); Tong Yen Gai (Sacramento) = "China street"; Ten How Mui Gai (Waverly); Tuck Wo Gai (Washington) = "fish street"; Wa Sheng Dun Gai (Washington) = "way station to Chinese prosperity street."

CHRISTMAS TREE POINT North shoulder of Twin Peaks ridge, now viewpoint area. Named in 1927 for civic Christmas tree erected by the *San Francisco Examiner* on the site, visible from downtown.

CHUTCHUE Former Indian village west of Dolores Lagoon and/or near the west end of the Islais Creek estuary. Possibly the same as Suchui or Nuestra Señora de la Asumpcion ("Our Lady of the Assumption"), Ohlone Indian name may mean "gray tree squirrel" (possibly imitative of squirrel call).

CHUTES, THE Amusement park occupying four successive locations. First, at Haight and Cole (1895–1901); second, at Fulton and Tenth (1902–1908); third, at Fillmore and Turk (1910–1920); fourth, at Fulton and Great Highway (1921–1926). Chutes-at-the-Beach was succeeded by Playland-at-the-Beach.

CIRCUS LOT, THE Open sandlot in South-of-Market district used in 1920s for travelling circuses. At 7th and Mission.

CITY COLLEGE HILL Hill on ridge linking Merced Heights and Mount Davidson. Named ca. 1940 for new City College on site. Approximate boundaries: Judson, Highway 280, Ocean, Phelan.

CITY MAP TRACTS NO. 1, NO. 2, NO. 3, NO. 4 1880s tracts in and near Bernal Heights. No. 1 bounded by Powhattan, Highway 280, Bocana, Courtland. No. 2 bounded by Courtland, Highway 280, Crescent, Andover. No. 3 present Bernal Heights Park and south of Powhattan. No. 4 bounded by Oakdale, Loomis, Highway 280 (see Apparel City).

CIVIC CENTER Area of civic (plus later state and federal) buildings, in eastern Hayes Valley. Planned 1911. Outer boundaries are Golden Gate, Leavenworth, Market, Hayes, Franklin. Earlier, 1870s to 1906, City Hall complex bounded by McAllister, Market, Larkin. Official name: James Rolph, Jr. Civic Center.

CLAM ALLEY Alley near original shore of Yerba Buena Cove. Clementina between First and Second.

CLAREMONT COURT West Portal development of ca. 1923. Claremont between Ulloa and Dorchester.

CLARENDON HEIGHTS Hill and ridge linking Mount Sutro and Twin Peaks and local neighborhood. Named ca. 1890 for principal street. South end is site of Sutro Tower. Also called Sutro Crest (see Mount Sutro). Approximate boundaries are Clarendon, Twin Peaks, city reservoirs, La Avanzada. Early maps extend area down north slope as far as Grattan.

CLARK'S POINT Southeast point of early Telegraph Hill at north entrance to Yerba Buena Cove. Named for William C. Clark, who built the city's first pile wharf here in 1847. Mexican name was Punta del Embarcadero ("landing point") since water was deep enough for launches to land here. Site is Battery and Broadway. See Buckelew's Point.

CLIPPER COVE Bay cove between Treasure Island and Yerba Buena Island where "Flying Clipper" seaplanes docked during and after 1939 Fair when it was called Port of the Trade Winds. Named for 19th-century sailing ships that "clipped" or shortened time between ports.

COLE VALLEY Valley and neighborhood at southern edge of Haight-Ashbury district surrounding site of Laguna Seca. Named ca. 1916 for city appraiser R. Beverly Cole. Blocks surrounding Carl and Cole.

COLLEGE HILL Rise and neighborhood east of Fairmount Hill near St. Mary's Park, named for nearby St. Mary's Roman

Catholic College (founded 1862). Earlier name was George's Hill (possibly for local landowner). The former DeBoom tract named for 1860s developer Cornelius DeBoom. Bounded by College, Mission, Highway 280, Milton, San Jose.

COLLEGE HOMESTEAD ASSOCIATION TRACT Development on south slope of Islais Creek canyon. Named for nearby St. Mary's College. Bounded by Highway 280, line south to Colby, Silver, Mission.

COLUMBIA HEIGHTS Tract ca. 1906 south of San Miguel City, bounded by Summit to near Harold, line southeast between Lakeview and Mount Vernon, San Jose, line to Summit.

CONCERT VALLEY Graded interdune valley in east central Golden Gate Park, prepared as site of 1894 Midwinter Fair. Also called Music Concourse.

CONSERVATORY VALLEY Graded interdune valley in northeast Golden Gate Park. Between Conservatory (built 1879) and Kennedy.

COON HOLLOW Enclosed interdune valley northwest of Conservatory in Golden Gate Park. Includes western part of The Forest. Named for Mayor Henry P. Coon, an early supporter of the park (1860s).

CORNED BEEF AND CABBAGE ALLEY Former bayside South-of-Market alley used by ship chandlers for storage. Name recalls local Irish community. Near the south side of Howard between Steuart and Spear.

CORONA HEIGHTS Heavily quarried hill southeast of Buena Vista Heights. Named in the 1940s for crown-shaped chert outcrop at summit (Latin "corona" = "crown"). Earlier names Rock Hill, Rocky Hill, Big Rocky. The Flint tract of ca. 1884. Approximate boundaries: Roosevelt, 15th, Castro, States.

COUNTRY CLUB ACRES 1950s neighborhood north of Lake Merced (north). Boundaries are Skyline, Sloat, Sunset, Lake Merced.

COW HOLLOW Hollow and expanded neighborhood on north slope of Pacific Heights. Named in 1870s by local contractor George Walker for the many local dairy farms. Topographic boundaries are approximately Greenwich, Laguna, Vallejo, Divisadero. Present neighborhood extends further west to Lyon. 1850s name of area (particularly eastern portion) was Spring Valley for the many hillside springs. Eastern edge grades into Golden Gate Valley. Southern slopes also called Lower Pacific Heights or Upper Marina (see Gulliver's Hill).

CRABVILLE Former Danish American crab-fishing community at south end of Gas House Cove in 1880s–1890s. Site near Toledo and Majorca.

CRESCENT Neighborhood of 1920s in hillside valley south of Bernal Heights. Bounded by Eugenia and extension to Highway 101, Jarboe, Andover. North part of 1880s Holliday Tract. Named for principal street.

CRISSY FIELD BEACH Beach and dune area along northeast bay shore of Presidio. Named for former adjacent airfield, named by Maj. H. H. Arnold for Maj. Dana H. Crissy, killed 1919 in transcontinental air race. Spanish name was Arenas de Medanos Campos ("sand dune camps beach"). Located on Strawberry Island next to the Pozo de los Marineros estuary. (See Suds Side Road.)

CROCKER-AMAZON 1940s development and district on north slope of Mount San Bruno (north ridge) straddling San Francisco County line. Named for developer Crocker Land Co. and northern boundary, Amazon Ave. Bounded (in San Francisco) by Amazon, Crocker-Amazon Playground, Moscow, Geneva, Carter, San Francisco County line, Mission.

CRUSADER STREET Local pronunciation for Quesada St. in Hunters Point.

DEAD MAN'S CAVE Cave in chert outcrop on southwest slope of upper Glen Canyon. Supposedly used by cattle rustlers and Russian "smugglers" who were hung on nearby Gold Mine Hill, thus the name (see Devil's Cave).

DEAD MAN'S COVE Cove between Dead Man's Point and Eagles Point facing the Golden Gate. Named for point.

DEAD MAN'S POINT Steep cliffed point between Lands End and Eagles Point in Lincoln Park next to the Golden Gate. Named in 1950s by Coast Guard rescuers for frequent cliff-climbing accidents.

DE LAVEAGA DELL Narrow interdune valley south of Chicken Point in eastern Golden Gate Park. Named for landscaping donor Joseph V. De Laveaga in 1902. Later converted into Deer Glen for display of deer, but old name revived.

DELL, THE Former interdune valley among cemeteries west of Lone Mountain. A popular 19th-century picnic spot, site was near Parker and Anza.

DEVIL'S CAVE Shallow cave in chert outcrop on east slope of upper Glen Canyon. Fanciful name (see Dead Man's Cave).

DIAMOND HEIGHTS 1960s–1970s development and subsequent district on hilly ridge extending southeast from Twin Peaks. Principal hills (north to south) are Head Rock Hill, Gold Mine Hill (and Fairmount Hill, developed earlier). Promotional name derived from street crossing Gold Mine and Fairmount hills. District boundaries (excluding Fairmount Hill) are Portola, Diamond Heights Blvd., Glen Canyon Park.

DISCOUNT CITY Area of discount clothing stores in South-of-Market district in 1980s–1990s bounded by Howard, Second, Townsend, Third.

DOELGER CITY Central portion of Sunset district, developed beginning in 1928 by Henry Doelger. Also called Doelgerville. Bounded by Kirkham, 27th, Ortega, 39th.

DOGPATCH Residential/industrial area east of Potrero Hill. Named by local residents who noticed how dogs swarmed during fights (and a possible reference to cartoonist Al Capp's hillbilly village of 1940s). Former site of Irish Hill and later planned site of Eastshore Park tract. Bounded by 19th, Illinois, 23rd, Iowa.

DOLORES BEACH 1980s nickname for a section of Mission Dolores Park at 20th and Church named by local gay residents for its many sunbathers.

DOLORES CREEK Former creek which flowed down Eureka Valley and emptied into Dolores Lagoon at the Willows and the original water supply for Mission Dolores. The Arroyo de los Dolores (Spanish for "stream of sorrows") was so named in 1776 by explorer Anza because he discovered it on the feast day of Our Lady of Sorrows ("Nuestra Señora de los Dolores," Friday before Passion week). Also called Arroyo de la Mission ("mission creek"). Approximate route was 18th from Market to Valencia.

DOLORES HEIGHTS Eastern hill of ridge extending east from Twin Peaks toward the Mission district between Noe and Eureka valleys. (Adjacent western summit Castro Hill.) Probably named for Mission Dolores Park or adjacent street. Early name Battle Mountain recalls 1910s homeowner battles over street grading. Northeast slope was called Nanny Goat Hill for Jaeger goat farm (see Billy Goat Hill, Bernal Heights, Potrero Hill). Later names are Noe Hill (for crossing street) and Liberty Hill (for crossing streets Liberty and Hill). Approximate boundaries: 19th, Church, 24th, Noe.

DOLORES LAGOON The Spanish Laguna de los Dolores. Former large lagoon/lake west of Potrero Hill and east of Mission Dolores, fed by Erie and Dolores creeks (plus numerous springs), emptying via Mission Creek into Mission Bay. Lagoon extended south and southwest in two arms, the southwest arm ending at the Willows, entry point of Dolores Creek. Named for Dolores Creek in 1776. Full Spanish name was Laguna de Manantial (de Nuestra

Señora) de los Dolores ("spring-fed lake [of Our Lady] of sorrows"). Filled in the 19th century to become the southern extension of Mission Creek. Approximate boundaries were Alameda/Florida to 21st/ Potrero to 20th/Shotwell to 18th/Valencia to 18th/Shotwell to 15th/Folsom to start.

DOUBLE ROCK Pair of rocks in South Basin and housing development on small hill adjacent to west. Rocks (at extended intersection of Armstrong and Fitch) were visited by Humphrey the whale in 1990. Development dates from 1960s and is bounded by Cameron, Griffith, Fitzgerald.

DOWNTOWN Commercial and financial center of San Francisco as seen from outer districts. The term "down-town" dates from the 1920s. Approximate boundaries: Pacific, Embarcadero, Howard, Fourth, Mission, Fifth, Eddy, Taylor, Bush, Kearny.

DUBOCE TRIANGLE Neighborhood east of Buena Vista and Corona Heights. Named in 1960s by neighborhood association for park and street. Triangular boundary formed by Duboce, Market, Castro.

DUMP TOWN Two former sites used as city dumps and occupied by squatters. First site near former Mission Creek used 1870s to 1895, bounded by Berry, 7th, Hooper, DeHaro. Second site, also called Dumpville, was located on the partly filled Islais Creek estuary south of Potrero Hill in the early 1900s.

DUTCHMAN'S FLAT Former neighborhood in the area of Irish Hill, east of Potrero Hill. Named in 1870s for largely Dutch resident workers working at nearby steel mill.

EAGLES POINT Steep-faced point east of Dead Man's Cove in Lincoln Park adjacent to the Golden Gate. Named for eagles and hawks that ride rising air here to prepare for Golden Gate crossing during spring/fall migrations. (Eagles and hawks dislike flying over large stretches of water.)

EAST AND WEST CANTONMENTS 1890s camps, later permanent quarters, for Presidio soldiers. East Cantonment flanked Presidio Creek south of the parade ground (MacArthur) while West Cantonment was on the north slope of Cannon Hill (Simmonds).

EAST AND WEST WASHES Landslide-prone ravines in Lincoln Park near Lands End. East Wash is on the slope just west of Dead Man's Point. West Wash extends north from Fort Miley to slopes west of Lands End. Named by birdwatchers.

EDGEHILL HEIGHTS Prominent hill and neighborhood at center of Laguna Honda neighborhood between Golden Gate Heights and Mount Davidson. 1922 promotional name may refer to quarried cliff bordering Kensington. Also called Edgehill Mountain. Bordered by Idora, Laguna Honda, Ulloa, Kensington, Vasquez, Garcia.

EDGEWOOD Neighborhood on lower northeast slope of Mount Sutro. 20th-century name for location next to Sutro Forest. Bounded by line south of Parnassus, Willard, Sutro Forest (interior park belt and U.C. Medical Center).

EL CAMINO REAL Road linking the Spanish missions and presidios of California, created from Indian trails. Spanish name is literally "the royal road" but means simply "the highway." San Francisco segment approximately followed (south to north) San Jose to 22nd, diagonally to Dolores/Cumberland, Dolores to Mission Dolores (Mission to Presidio trail was northern extension).

ELK GLEN LAKE Artificial lake in south central Golden Gate Park. Named for the Roosevelt elk enclosure on the site 1890–1935. North of King and 25th.

ELKTON ca. 1910 development near today's Balboa Park. Name may be linked to Elk St., north on Gold Mine Hill.

EL POLIN SPRING Surviving spring that was the source of Presidio Creek and the early water supply of the Presidio. Spanish name means "wooden roller" used for moving cargo on ships, possibly a phallic reference, as the spring was known to the Indians for its powers of fertility. Also called Aguaita de la Concepcion ("Spring of the Conception [of the Virgin Mary]"). Multiple springs around park at south end of MacArthur.

EMBARCADERO, THE Waterfront area adjacent to Telegraph Hill and Downtown districts, created by filling bay behind the Seawall or Bulkhead from the 1860s to 1900s. Spanish name means "landing" or "quay" and originally referred to Clark's Point. Area also called the Waterfront or the "Front" by 1920s to 1950s teamsters. Also known as "City Front." Approximate boundaries are San Francisco Bay from Pier 39 to China Basin and filled areas extending to the west.

EMBARCADERO CENTER 1970s commercial/residential development north of Financial district. Bounded by Clay, Embarcadero, Sacramento, Battery.

ERIE CREEK Former small creek north of Mission Dolores, flowing into the north end of Dolores Lagoon. 19th-century name. Woodward's Gardens amusement park of 1860s–1870s stood near site of outlet. Approximate route was from Alert to Erie and Mission, east along Erie. Extended to 13th, 13th to Potrero.

EUREKA VALLEY Valley between Dolores Heights, Castro Hill, Mount Olympus, and Corona Heights. Probably named for the local Eureka Benevolent Society of the 1850s. (In Greek, "eureka" means "I have found it," a California gold-miners' motto.) The Castro district is located in the valley. Also called Mission Valley for nearby Mission Dolores. The west slopes are the Upper Market neighborhood. The heart of the valley is between 17th, Noe, 19th, Eureka. The Eureka Valley Homestead was between 18th, Castro, 20th, Douglass.

EXCELSIOR Homestead and district on western slope of McLaren Park ridge. Named 1869 possibly by association

president Charles C. Bode. (In Greek "excelsior" means "ever upward," implying progress and prosperity, a popular 19th-century motto.) Homestead and district bounded by Silver, Madison, west side of McLaren Park, Crocker-Amazon Playground, Amazon and extension, Alemany.

EXECUTIVE PARK 1980s business park south of Bayview Heights, bounded by Executive Park, Harney, Alana.

FAIRS The 1894 Midwinter Fair was held in and around Concert Valley in Golden Gate Park (see Heidelberg Hill). The 1915 Panama-Pacific International Exposition was held in the Harbor View/Marina district. The 1939 Golden Gate International Exposition was held on Treasure Island (see Gay Way, Clipper Cove).

FAIRMOUNT Tract, neighborhood, and southernmost hill of Diamond Heights ridge (but not part of the Diamond Heights development). Called Fairmount Heights in the 1860s, the promotional name probably derives from the fashionable Fairmount Park district of Philadelphia. Tract covered east and (envisioned) upper slopes of hill bounded by 30th, San Jose, Miguel, Bemis, line along Castro. Also called Upper Noe Valley (northeast slope), Lower Diamond Heights (upper part of hill), and North Glen Park (southern slopes). An early name for hill was Cannonball Mountain (possibly for its smooth contours). Castro Street Addition Tract was on lower south slope. Hill boundaries are Diamond and north extension to Laidley, line southeast to Randall, Chenery.

FAIRVIEW Development on southern and western slopes of Twin Peaks. Bounded by Marview, Twin Peaks Park, Burnett, Portola, Twin Peaks Blvd., Panorama.

FAIRY GATE Large chert outcrop on central stretch of Ishi's Trail, upper northeast slope of Mount Sutro. Named in 1880s by Adolph Sutro. North of Johnstone.

FARALLONES Small rocky islands in the

Pacific Ocean 28 miles west of San Francisco, part of San Francisco County.

FILLMORE Neighborhood in Western Addition. Named for principal street. Called "The Mo" or Motown by African American residents (comparing "more" or "mo" with "mo-town" or "motor-town," the largely black area of Detroit). Another name is The River (possibly for the busy main street). Approximate boundaries are Bush, Webster, Turk, Steiner, with commercial activity extending north on Fillmore to Jackson.

FILLMORE CENTER 1980s development in Western Addition bounded by Geary, Webster, Eddy, Steiner.

FINANCIAL DISTRICT The financial heart of San Francisco. Originally centered along Montgomery (Wall Street West) and lower California. Boundaries: Clay, Drumm, Main, Mission, Third, Kearny.

FISHERMAN'S ROCK Large rock on Seal Rocks Beach between the Cliff House and Point Lobos. Popular but dangerous fishing rock, linked to land by seawall (formerly rope bridge). 1890s name was Fishing Rock.

FISHERMAN'S WHARF Port and fish-processing center of the city's commercial fishing fleet. Has had three locations: in 1872 at foot of Union; in 1885–1900 at foot of Filbert; moved to present site east of Aquatic Park in 1900. Also called the Wharf. Central harbor between Hyde St. Pier and Pier 45 is Fisherman's Cove, and the alleys adjacent and leading off from it are called Fish Alley. Bounded by San Francisco Bay, Beach, Hyde, and north extension.

FOG BELT Informal name for outer Lake Merced, Parkside, Sunset, and Richmond districts. Frequently covered by ocean fog in summer.

FOREST, THE Grove of natural coast live oaks in northeast corner of Golden Gate Park in Coon Hollow and on Mount Lick. 19th-century name. North and east of Conservatory Dr. Another area so named is

north of the Golden Gate Park Golf Course (western part of park).

FOREST HILL Tract and district developed in 1910s on southeast slopes of Golden Gate Heights. 1912 promotional name of developers Newell and Murdock Co., a reference to the formerly forested hillside, part of Sutro Forest. Approximate boundaries: Ortega, Laguna Honda, Dewey, Taraval, line north on 12th Ave., 9th Ave.

FOREST KNOLLS 1960s development on upper south and west slopes of Mount Sutro adjacent to Sutro Forest. Approximate boundaries: Kirkham, 5th Ave., Mount Sutro Dr., Crestmont, Clarendon, Warren, 6th Ave.

FORT FUNSTON Former army reserve on bluff between Sand Dollar Beach and Lake Merced (south), now part of the Golden Gate National Recreation Area. Named 1917 for General Frederick N. Funston, commanding officer of Army's Dept. of California during 1906 earthquake and fire. Formerly the Laguna Merced Military Reservation.

FORT MASON Former army reserve on Black Point, now part of Golden Gate National Recreation Area. Named for Col. Richard Mason, fifth military governor of California. Bounded by San Francisco Bay, Van Ness, Bay, Laguna.

FORT MILEY Army reserve in south-central Lincoln Park, now part of Golden Gate National Recreation Area, part Veterans Administration Medical Center. Named 1900 for Col. John Miley, Spanish-American War hero. Original boundaries were line east from Vista Point, lines north from 40th and 48th avenues, Clement.

FORT POINT Northern point of (contiguous) San Francisco and the Presidio at the inner south entrance of the Golden Gate. Former site of Cantil Blanco, cut away for construction of surviving 1850s fort (Fort Point). Named ca. 1853 when fort was built. Earlier Spanish names were Punta de

San Jose (1770s and 1780s, name then transferred to Black Point) and Punta de Cantil Blanco. Early American names were Castle Point and Battery Point for the old Spanish battery on the site and Southeast Point (in relation to Golden Gate).

FORT POINT BEACH Beach stretching south from Fort Point to Baker Beach at the foot of the western cliffs of the Presidio. As a clothing-optional beach it is also called Bare Ass Beach. Fort Point Rock is the group of large rocks near shore at the north end. Helmet rock is the large cap-shaped rock off the south end.

FORT POINT SHOAL Submarine ledge stretching north into the Golden Gate from Fort Point. South pier of Golden Gate Bridge stands on shoal. Site of many shipwrecks. Also called Fort Point Ledge.

FORT WINFIELD SCOTT The northwest portion of the Presidio was so designated in 1905, deactivated 1948. Named for Civil War Union commander. (Official name of Fort Point since 1882.) Approximate boundaries: Lincoln, bluffs above Fort Point, Park, Lobos Creek.

FOUR FATHOM BANK Shallow northeast shoal of the San Francisco Bar submarine sandbank, west of the Golden Gate. Southeast edge of bank is within San Francisco County, southwest of Point Bonita. (Four fathoms is 24 feet.)

FRANCISCO HEIGHTS Neighborhood and development west of Lone Mountain. Former cemetery site. Named in 1935 by developers Coldwell, Cornwall, and Banker. Bounded by Geary, Parker, Turk, Arguello.

"FRISCO" Nonnative slang abbreviation for San Francisco, in use as early as 1851. Name may be a blending of several different homonyms: the British sailors' jargon for a port of refuge and ship repair, and/or the possibly related Spanish/Italian word for romp, gambol, or caper (perhaps a sailors' reference to the Barbary Coast), and of course, the name San Francisco. Use of "Frisco" is offensive to natives.

GARDEN TRACT 1870s development south of Bret Harte neighborhood. Part of later Reis-Paul Tract. Promotional name by Garden Valley Land Assoc. for area earlier called Garden Valley (small gardens and farms). Bounded by Paul, Third, Salinas, Highway 101.

GAS HOUSE COVE Cove between Sand Point on Strawberry Island and Black Point (Fort Mason) filled for the Panama Pacific Exposition and now the Marina district. Named for coal-gas manufacturing plants built near south end of cove beginning 1883 (coal barges docked in cove). Earlier names were Laguna Bay and Washerwoman's Bay (see Washerwoman's Lagoon) and West Bay all in the 1850s–1860s. Filled remnant of 1870s–1880s called Harbor Cove and Harbor View Basin.

GAY WAY Amusement zone at 1939 Golden Gate International Exposition on Treasure Island. North-central site.

GEARY CORRIDOR Redeveloped area flanking widened Geary Blvd. in Western Addition district. 1970s planners' name.

GENERAL ANCHORAGES #5, #6, #7, #8, #9 Post World War II name for designated ship anchorage zones in San Francisco Bay. #5 is south of Red Rock, #6 is east and north of Treasure Island, #7 is west of Treasure Island (temporary), #8 west of Alameda Island, and #9 east of southeast San Francisco. Anchorages #7 and #9 were Man-of-War Row, anchorage site of the 1908 Great White Fleet. A forbidden anchorage zone within anchorage #9 is for ships carrying explosives.

GERMAN TOWN Former neighborhood of German community in San Francisco in late 19th century. Centered in Polk Gulch. Approximate boundaries California, Larkin, Golden Gate, Gough.

GHOST ALLEY Former South-of-Market alley near Waterfront. 19th-century name of uncertain origin. Off south side of Howard between Spear and Steuart.

GILMAN BEACH Former bayside beach at South Basin, north of Bayview Heights. Used in the 1940s before the area was filled. Site was near Gilman and Fitch.

GLEN CANYON Canyon and ravine between Mount Davidson and Diamond Heights ridge occupied by the north branch of Islais Creek. Probably named for 1910 Glen Park development near its south entrance. Also called Glen Park Canyon. Northern ravine (now partially filled as a school site) was Frenchman's Valley. 19th-century name of canyon was Rock House Gulch or Ravine, for 1860s Rock Ranch at its entrance. Site of Dead Man's Cave and Devil's Cave.

GLEN PARK Tract and neighborhood at southeast base of Mount Davidson (southeast spur) at entrance to Glen Canyon (see Martha Hill). Promotional name of Crocker Estate Company in 1910 for nearby canyon, or "glen." Bounded by Bosworth, Diamond, Joost, line north to Malta.

GOLD COAST Name for a district of wealthy residents. In the 1850s to 1860s Rincon Hill was so called. More recently western Pacific Heights (Broadway from Divisadero to Lyon) has held the name.

GOLDEN CITY HOMESTEAD 19th-century development at south base of Potrero Hill. Approximate boundaries: 25th, San Francisco Bay, Islais Creek Channel, Napoleon, Highway 280.

GOLDEN GATE Major strait linking San Francisco Bay to the Pacific Ocean. Low water level along its north shore forms part of the boundary of San Francisco County. Named by explorer/soldier Col. John C. Fremont in 1848. He envisioned it as the entrance to a great future port city and named it "Chrysopylae," or "Golden Gate," in reference to the Graeco-Byzantine "Chrysoceras," or "Golden Horn," the harbor of Constantinople. Name was popularized worldwide by the 1849 California Gold Rush. Indian name was Yulupa, possibly meaning "sunset place." Spanish names were Entrada del Puerto ("port entrance"), Boca del Puerto ("port mouth"), and La Boca ("the mouth"). American mariners' name of 19th century was Hole in the Wall, a reference to the strait as a break through the coast ranges. The southern bay is South Bay, formerly South Bight (1870s) and Fatality Bay for its many shipwrecks. The narrow eastern neck where the bridge crosses is The Narrows. The 350-foot-deep central depression is called Deep Hole by fishermen.

GOLDEN GATE HEIGHTS A hilly ridge and district east of the Sunset District (included in the Sunset District by some). North peak is Grand View Hill, also called Mount Moria in the early 20th century for its dramatic setting. Neighborhood on lower slopes is Sunset Heights, another name for the ridge, and neighborhood boundaries are Kirkham, Funston, line to Noriega, 17th Ave. To north is Kirkham Heights between Kirkham, Funston, Aloha, Lomita, 17th Ave. Southern summit is Larsen Peak (topped by Sunset Heights Park) named for landowner/restaurateur Carl G. Larsen. Its south slope is Hawk Hill named by bird-watchers for migrating hawks that ride rising air currents there during the spring and fall migrations. Golden Gate Heights is a 1930s promotion name. Approximate boundaries are Lawton, Funston, Noriega, 11th Ave., Pacheco, 9th Ave. to Rivera, 15th Ave.

GOLDEN GATE NATIONAL RECREATION AREA Federally managed oceanside and bay shore parkland (1972) which includes Fort Funston, Ocean Beach, Lincoln Park, China Beach, Presidio Cliffs (and will include all of the Presidio by 1996), Crissy Field Beach, Marina waterfront, Black Point/Fort Mason, Aquatic Park, Alcatraz Island, as well as large parts of Marin County.

GOLDEN GATE PARK Major urban park in northwest San Francisco, developed largely from sand dunes beginning in 1870. Named for its proximity to the Golden Gate. Eastern extension called The Panhandle. Bounded by Fulton, Stanyan, Fell, Baker, Oak, Lincoln, and the Great Highway. See Great Sand Bank. Park lakes, meadows, and hills are individually listed.

GOLDEN GATE VALLEY A valley between Holladay Hill (now eastern Pacific Heights) and Russian Hill. Named for its view of the Golden Gate. Merged northwest into the former Spring Valley, now known as Cow Hollow.

GOLDEN GATEWAY Business and residential development between Jackson Square and Embarcadero Center. The development was named in 1962 by Perini Land Co., the developers, in partial reference to the preserved Produce Market gateway in Walton Park, which is on the site of the former Produce District. The area is bounded by Broadway, Embarcadero, Clay, and Battery streets.

GOLD MINE HILL Central hill of Diamond Heights ridge (southern hill of district). Probably named for mid–19th–century "gold strike" on hill (like that on Bernal Heights in 1876). Earlier name was Saddle Mountain for its summit-like shape. Approximate boundaries are Christopher Playground, Duncan, Diamond and Diamond extension, Chenery, Islais Creek/Glen Canyon.

GOOD CHILDREN STREET Late 19th-century name for today's Child St. on western slope of Telegraph Hill. Name origin is unclear.

GREAT SAND BANK The former extensive area of open sand dunes covering most of the Richmond, Sunset, and Parkside districts and Golden Gate Park. Other 19th-century names were Great Sand Waste, Great Sand Drift, Great Sand Dune and Great Desert. Site of later Seal Rock Rancho.

GREENWICH PARK 1880s development in western Pacific Heights. Named for street, with suggestions of London park. Bounded by Greenwich, Scott, Vallejo, Broderick.

GULF OF THE FARALLONES The wide Pacific Ocean bay, or bight, between the Farallones Islands, Point Reyes, and Point San Pedro. Includes offshore portion of San Francisco County (3-mile zone). Named Bahia de los Farallones (Spanish for "bay of the rocky islets") in 1777 (Font); earlier the Bahia de los Pinos (Spanish for "bay of pines") in 1542 (Cabrillo); and Bahia del Puerto de San Francisco in 1603 (Vizcaino). See Farallones.

GULLIVER'S HILL North slope of Holladay Heights. 19th-century name after local dairy man Captain Charles Gulliver.

HAIGHT-ASHBURY District between Golden Gate and Buena Vista parks. Named in 1920s for its principal intersection, but made famous by its late 1960s/early 1970s hippie culture. Also called The Haight. Inner boundaries are Oak, Central, Haight, Masonic, Frederick, Clayton, Grattan, Stanyan. Greater boundaries are Grove, Baker, 17th, Willard.

HAIGHT-FILLMORE Neighborhood south of Alamo Square. Named for principal intersection. Also called Lower Haight and Needle Alley for 1980s drug users. Bounded by Fell, Steiner, Waller, Webster.

HAMMOND VALLEY Shallow valley north of Children's Playground in Golden Gate Park. Named for Park Commissioner Major Richard P. Hammond around 1894.

HAPPY VALLEY Former interdune valley in South-of-Market area near Yerba Buena Cove. Named in 1849 by optimistic tent-dwelling pioneers. Approximate boundaries: Stevenson, First, Natoma, Second (see also Pleasant Valley, Spring Valley, St. Anne's Valley).

HARBOR VIEW Former name for southern Marina and northern Cow Hollow/Spring Valley districts next to Gas House Cove. Named for 1890 resort of Rudolph Hermann on Strawberry Island.

HARDING PARK Golf course on low plateau between north and south Lake Merced and Lake Merced Boulevard. Named in 1925 for President Warren Harding who died at the Palace Hotel on Market St. in 1923.

HARDING ROCK Submerged rock one mile northwest of Alcatraz Island, north of Shag Rocks. Earlier name Seal Rock. Origin of 20th-century name uncertain.

HAYES VALLEY Large interdune valley, former farm, 1850s tract, and neighborhood east of Alamo Square Hill and partly on site of James Rolph, Jr. Civic Center. Named in 1850s for Colonel Thomas Hayes, landowner and developer. Site of large underground stream flowing east into former marshes of Mission Bay. Original valley was between Golden Gate, Polk, Oak, Buchanan, but neighborhood extends to Fulton, Larkin, Market, Fell, Webster (sometimes extended west to Divisadero).

HEADS, THE 19th-century name for the headlands at the entrance of the Golden Gate. North Head was Point Bonita in Marin County; South Head was the Lincoln Park headland including Point Lobos, Lands End, and Dead Man's Point.

HEIDELBERG HILL Small hillock in northwest part of Strybing Arboretum in Golden Gate Park. Named for the site of the "Heidelberg Castle" in the 1894 Midwinter Fair's German Village.

HERMIT ROCK Large rock at the western edge of Lands End Beach west of Lands End. 1870s name refers to its prominence and isolation (see Seal Rocks).

HIPPIE HILL Low hill north of Children's Playground in Golden Gate Park. Named for being a popular hippie gathering spot in the late 1960s and early 1970s.

HOLLADAY HEIGHTS Eastern summit of Pacific Heights ridge, now crowned by Lafayette Park. South shoulder is Cathedral Hill. Named for house of landowner Samuel W. Holladay built on summit in 1867. 1850s promotional name was Plaza de Santiago (Spanish for St. James Square). Upper slopes bounded by Jackson, Franklin, Bush, Webster.

HOLLIDAY TRACT 1850s development south of Holly Park. Probably named for developer. Bounded by Crescent, Highway 280, St. Mary's Park (see Black Hole).

HOLLY PARK Originally Holly Oak Park Hill. Homestead, and neighborhood surrounding park southwest of Bernal Heights. Named in the 1860s for local scrub oaks (probably *Quercus agrifolia*) with hollylike leaves. Bounded by Courtland, Bennington and line south, Richland, Mission.

HORNER'S ADDITION First major planned development in San Francisco covering Noe Valley and Castro Hill/Dolores Heights (Horner's Corner). Development did not progress beyond planning stage. Named ca. 1860 for prospective developer Captain John M. Horner. Approximate boundaries: 20th, Dolores, 30th, Diamond.

HORSESHOE COVE OR HORSESHOE BAY Cove northeast of the inner entrance (The Narrows) of the Golden Gate, between Lime Point and Point Cavallo. Spanish name was Estero de Consuelo ("Consolation Cove"), given in 1775 by Ayala as he was able to repair his ship here after a near shipwreck on trying to enter the Golden Gate. Name "horseshoe" probably refers to its shape, although horses were once corralled on shore (thus the name Point Cavallo, Spanish for "horse point"). Early American name was Needles Cove (1826, Beechey) for the prominent Needles Rocks or The Needles near the western shore.

HOSPITAL CURVE Hazardous section of Highway 101 east of San Francisco General Hospital, on the western slope of Potrero Hill. Named in the 1960s by drivers.

HO' STO' Area at northwest corner of Tenderloin District frequented by prostitutes since 1960s. Name is abbreviation of "whore stroll." Also called Larkin Lane. Polk and Larkin between Pine and

O'Farrell.

HOTEL DISTRICT That portion of downtown San Francisco with many hotels west of the Shopping District. Western part of Union Square District. Approximate boundaries are Sutter, Powell, Eddy, and Taylor streets.

HUDSON-GARDEN TRACT An 1890s development south of Silver Terrace (see also Garden Tract). Approximate boundaries are Thorton, Vesta, William, Third, Carroll, Egbert, Phelps, and Highway 280.

HUNTERS POINT A point, peninsula, ridge, and district in southeast San Francisco. The original eastern point was near Fisher and Lockwood streets, and the present point is now a few yards east. It is the easternmost point in the City and County of San Francisco. The Spanish name for the point was Punta de Concha or "shell point." In 1833 it was called Point Alvisadera, perhaps combining the Spanish word "avistar," which means "to see at a distance," with "divisadero," which means a "place of a far view." The name evolved into Point Avisadero by the 1850s, but was also called South East Point. It was renamed in the 1860s for local landowners Robert E. and Philip Hunters, who attempted to develop South San Francisco on the peninsula. The name subsequently extended to include the peninsula and the surrounding areas, including the highest summit near Whitney Young Circle and Cashmere St. This high point was also called Stony Hill in the 1850s. The Harbor Shore housing project was built on the summit in the 1940s. The district was called "H.P." by local gang members in the 1980s (also see Potrero Hill). The approximate boundaries of the district are Mendell, Evans and Evans extension, San Francisco Bay, a line from South Basin to Palou, Griffith, Keith, and Newcomb. The district is often combined with the Bayview District to the west and south. Hunters Point was part of the Rancho Rincon de Salinas y Potrero Viejo.

HUNTERS POINT NAVAL SHIPYARD A naval shipyard and base which occupies the eastern one-third of the Hunters Point peninsula. It was purchased by the U.S. Navy in 1941, but became idle by the 1970s. Mariners Village housing is on the south slope of the hill at the west end of the base.

HUNTERS TRACT The original 1850s Hunters brothers' tract at Hunters Point, bounded by Quesada, San Francisco Bay, Underwood, and Ingalls.

IGNATIAN HEIGHTS The hill south of Lone Mountain that is occupied by the Catholic University of San Francisco, built in 1927. It is also called Saint Ignatius Heights, named for Saint Ignatius Loyola, the 16th-century founder of the Jesuit order which administers the university. The hill is the northeast extension of the Mount Lick ridge in adjacent Golden Gate Park. The approximate boundaries, including portions of the surrounding neighborhood, are Turk, Masonic, Grove, Stanyan, Fulton, and Willard. The campus was called the Bull Ring by female students at the adjacent Lone Mountain College before the 1964 merger with the University of San Francisco.

INDIA BASIN A partially filled cove between Hunters Point and Pier 96, named in the late 1860s for the freighters of the India Rice Mill Company which docked there. The filled portion of the area, also called India Basin, is bounded by Islais Creek Channel, San Francisco Bay, Evans, and Selby. (Also see Central Basin, China Basin.)

INDIA BASIN INDUSTRIAL PARK A 1974 light industrial development next to India Basin on the site of Butchertown, the only such development in a major American city. The park is bounded by Cargo Way, Jennings, Evans, and Third streets.

INGLESIDE A 1930s development on the north slope of eastern Merced

Heights, which is the eastern half of the earlier Lakeview Development. (Also see Ingleside Terrace.) The Ingleside District is bounded by Ocean Ave., Harold, Lakeview, and Ashton.

INGLESIDE HEIGHTS A development on the upper slopes of western Merced Heights, south of Ingleside Terrace. It includes portions of the former Lakeview and Oceanview developments. It is bounded by Garfield, Orizaba, Randolph, and Junipero Serra Boulevard.

INGLESIDE TERRACE A development north of western Merced Heights and west of the Ingleside area. Ingleside Terrace is a 1909 tract development of Urban Realty Co. and was developed in part on the side of the 1895–1905 Ingleside Racetrack. The area may have been named for an eastern racetrack by the developer. Urbano Drive follows the course of the original racetrack.

INTERNATIONAL SETTLEMENT The promotional name given to the former Barbary Coast district in 1939 to help improve the district's image. Remnants of the entrance gateway can be found at Pacific and Montgomery streets.

IRISH HILL The former ridge east of Potrero Hill (the Scotch Hill portion) extending to Potrero Point. A fragment of the hill remains at Illinois and 20th streets. It was named for Irish residents who worked at a nearby steel mill from the 1880s to about 1910. (Also see Dutchman's Flat.) The approximate boundaries are 19th, Michigan, 22nd, and Indiana streets.

IRISH TOWN While the South-of-Market area was predominantly Irish in the 19th century, newly arrived immigrants lived in the western corner in the area of Bradley and Colton streets. The name dates from around 1900.

ISHI'S CAVE AND TRAIL Ishi was the last survivor of the Yahi California Indian tribe and lived out his last years (1911–1916) at the University of California Medical College. He carved a trail along the upper northeast slope of Mount Sutro, north of Johnstone. A chert outcropping and a shallow cave along the trail are named for him.

ISLAIS COVE OR ISLAIS CREEK COVE A former cove between Potrero Hill and Hunters Point near the entrance to the estuary of Islais Creek. It was named after the creek, and later occupied in part by Butchertown.

ISLAIS CREEK Formerly a large creek that drained much of southern San Francisco. Islais Creek Channel, so named in the 1880s, is a modified estuary. The name comes from the Ohlone Indian word "is-lai," which refers to the holly-leaved cherry (*Prunus ilicifolia*). which grew nearby. The Spanish named it Estero Seco in 1775, which means "dry estuary." Later it was called Estero Angosto, "Narrow Estuary." By the 1850s it was called Du Vree's Creek after a local landowner. After partial filling and pollution it was called S--t Creek in the early 20th century. The estuarine section ended at Fanconia Landing at what is now McKinnon and Barneveld. The upper portion of the creek was called Arroyo de los Islais. The creek originally flowed from Glen Canyon and southern Alemany Boulevard tributaries into the canyon now occupied by Highway 280. It then wound east of Bernal Heights to enter San Francisco Bay near Army St. and Highway 280.

JACKSON SQUARE The historic district in the heart of the Barbary Coast. The area was saved from the 1906 fire, and was redeveloped and renamed in 1952. Technically speaking, there is no square as such in Jackson Square. The area is bounded by Pacific, Sansome, Washington, and Columbus Ave.

JAPANTOWN The commercial center for San Franciscans of Japanese ancestry. It was developed in 1970 on a part of the Western Addition once known as Little Osaka that had been settled by Japanese immigrants before World War II. Before the Japanese were interned the area was called Nihonmachi, "Japan-town." The approximate boundaries are Sutter, Octavia, Geary, and Fillmore. It also includes the adjacent residential areas to the north and east. A pre-1906 Japanese settlement was located at South Park.

JOHN F. SHELLEY LAKE An artificial lake on the summit ridge of John McLaren Park. Named in the 1970s for former labor leader and mayor John F. Shelley.

JOHN MUIR TRACT A 1970s development to the south and west of Lake Merced. It is named for the 19th-century California naturalist and conservationist. It is bounded by John Muir Drive, the San Francisco County line, and the Olympic Club golf course.

JORDAN PARK Developed in the 1910–1920 period in the eastern Richmond District. It was named by Urban Realty Co. developers for former landowner James Clark Jordan. The western portion was the site of Kelly's Pond. It is bounded by California, Parker, Geary, and Palm.

JUNIPER HOMESTEAD An 1880s tract around and including Lone Mountain. It is bounded by Geary, Masonic, Turk, and Parker.

KELLY'S COVE A small cove at the north end of Ocean Beach next to the Cliff House cliffs. Named in the 1970s in memory of a local surfer. This section of the beach was formerly named Cliff House Beach.

KENSINGTON An 1860s development in the Mission District near 21st and South Van Ness Ave.

KIRBY COVE A small cove on the north shore of the Golden Gate, east of Point Diablo. It was named for a local artillery battery that was constructed there. Battery Kirby was named in 1902 for Civil War hero Brig. Gen. Edmund Kirby.

KITE HILL There are two different sites which carry this name. One is the northwest

slope of Castro Hill, which is an undeveloped park at Yukon and 19th streets, and so named because of the constant high winds. This area was once called Solari Hill. The western summit of Merced Heights at Shields and Ramsell is also called Kite Hill.

LAGUNA BRIONES A former small lagoon in the North Beach area below Russian Hill. It was named for Mexican landowner Juan Briones. It was filled in the 1850s and was located in the area of Chestnut between Powell and Taylor streets.

LAGUNA DE LOS DOLORES See Dolores Lagoon.

LAGUNA DULCE A former freshwater pond near Yerba Buena Cove. It was, most likely, the site of an Ohlone Indian village. The lagoon, which was filled in the mid-1840s, was fed by a stream that originated at a pond located at Montgomery and Sacramento streets.

LAGUNA HONDA A lake that is now a reservoir in the canyon between Golden Gate Heights and Mount Sutro. It is fed by runoff from the surrounding San Miguel Hills. In Spanish, Laguna Honda means "deep lake." It was called Lake Honda from the 1860s to the 1890s when the Spring Valley Water Company used it as a freshwater storage facility. A portion of the lake in the area of 7th Ave. from Judah to Lawton was later drained. Laguna Honda is now a San Francisco Fire Department emergency water supply.

LAGUNA HONDA DISTRICT A development dating from the 1930s surrounding Edgehill Heights between Forest Hill and Miraloma Park. It was named for Laguna Honda Boulevard which traverses the development. It is bounded by Claremont, Dewey, Laguna Honda, Woodside, and Portola.

LAGUNA SECA A former seasonal pond in Cole Valley, northeast of Mount Sutro. The Spanish name means "dry lake," and it was located at Cole and Parnassus streets. It was filled in the 1880s.

LAKE BOWEN A former winter quagmire at Market St. and Grant Ave. It was named for a member of the Board of Supervisors. It was finally filled in the 1880s.

LAKE GENEVA A former pond along Islais Creek in the area bounded by Geneva, Alemany, Mt. Vernon, and Cayuga. The name was a humorous reference to the Swiss resort lake. The area was filled by the Southern Pacific Company before the 1906 earthquake.

LAKE MCCOPPIN See The Willows.

LAKE MERCED A pair of large lakes that serve as reservoirs for the San Francisco Water Department. The name originally had been applied to a pond about one mile south, but the name was transferred to the present lakes by Palou in 1775. The full Spanish name, Laguna de Nuestra Señora de la Merced, means "Lake of Our Lady of Mercy." The use of the Lake Merced name came into being in the 1850s, but the name Laguna de la Merced remained popular for decades. At various times, Lake Merced has had an outlet stream to the Pacific Ocean. This opening at Murray's Beach, along Ocean Beach, is generally opened and closed by earthquakes. The two units of the lake are North Lake and South Lake. Other names have been used for parts of the lake, including North Arm or La Laguna, and South Arm or Lake Merced.

LAKE MERCED DISTRICT Adjacent to Lake Merced and contains Country Club Acres, Lakeshore Park, Lakeside, Merced Manor, Parkmerced, and Stonestown neighborhoods. It also includes the Olympic Club, Harding, and San Francisco golf clubs, as well as Fort Funston, Fleishhacker Zoo, the National Guard Armory, and Stern Grove. The area is bounded by Sloat Blvd., 34th Ave., Pine Lake Park and Stern Grove, Junipero Serra, the San Francisco County line, and Ocean Beach.

LAKE MERCED HILL A small 1970s development on a low bluff east of the South Lake portion of Lake Merced. It is bounded by Brotherhood Way, the San Francisco Golf Club, the San Francisco County line, and Lake Merced.

LAKESHORE PARK A development of the 1940s and 50s north of Lake Merced's North Lake. Originally named Lake Shore Park by the Gellert Brothers who developed the area. It is bounded by Sloat, 19th Ave., Eucalyptus, Middlefield, and Gellert.

LAKESIDE A development begun in 1936 west of Merced Heights. The shopping district there is known as Lakeside Village. It is bounded by Ocean Ave., Junipero Serra Blvd., and 19th Ave.

LAKEVIEW TRACT A planned development that was begun in the 1890s on the north slopes of Merced Heights. It is now the site of Ingleside Terrace, Ingleside Heights, and the Ingleside neighborhood.

LAKMER A resort built upon the east shore of Lake Merced's South Lake around 1910. The name is a contraction of Lake Merced, and it was located at Brotherhood Way and Lake Merced Blvd.

LANDS END A prominent headlands bluff in Lincoln Park at the southwest entrance of the Golden Gate. It was named in 1827 as a general reference to the entire headlands. The name probably came from the famous southwest English headlands. The Spanish name for the bluff was Punta Angel de la Guarda "guardian angel point." The bluff was also known as Point Lobos from 1826 to the 1860s, when the present name was attached to the specific point. It is located north of Fort Miley and a northern extension of 44th Ave.

LANDS END BEACH The beach west of Lands End, also called Miles Rock Beach. It was the site of Hermit Rock, a 19th-century picnic spot. It is now a clothes-optional beach.

LASH LIGHTER BASIN An artificial basin created in 1972 at the north end of India Basin. It is used for cargo transfer from specially designed ships. LASH is an acronym for Lighter Aboard SHip. The LASH terminal is along the waterfront between Piers 96 and 98. Pier 98, incidentally, was the planned western anchorage for a proposed "Southern Crossing" bay bridge.

LATIN QUARTER Romaniticized early 20th-century name for the southern part of North Beach and southwest Telegraph Hill. It was named for the ethnic and Bohemian Left Bank student quarter in Paris. The approximate boundaries are Union, Kearny, and Columbus Ave.

LAUREL HEIGHTS OR LAUREL HILL A development dating from the 1940s and 1950s on the former site of Laurel Hill Cemetery.

LITTLE CHINA ca. 1850s. Upper part of Sacramento St., the entire length of Dupont St., and portions of other adjoining streets.

LOMA ALTA Name given Telegraph Hill by the early Spaniards.

MA DULCE (SWEET PLANT) Name given by early Spaniards to Strawberry Hill in Golden Gate Park.

MAN-OF-WAR ROW Anchorage off South Bay and Potrero shores, used by the Great White Fleet in 1908.

MARINA Bounded on the north by Marina Blvd., west by Lyon St., east by Laguna, south by Lombard. First named the Marina-Vanderbilt Tract after its former primary owner, Mrs. Virginia Vanderbilt.

MARTHA HILL Hill bounded by Baden St., Mangels, Burnside, Stillings, and Martha Ave.

McCOPPINS CANAL Roadbed along the center of Market St. from California to Third St. It was below grade, and many citizens narrowly escaped drowning in it during the rainy season.

MERCED HEIGHTS Located east to west at Summit and Thrift streets; Shields St. and Orizaba Ave.; and Ramsell St. near Shields.

MINT HILL The expression "Mint Hill" was coined in 1972 by neighbors who formed the Mint Hill Restorative Society. Mint stands for the U.S. Mint constructed in the 1930s, and also for the Spanish settlement of Yerba Buena, "good herb." This area has also been known as "North of Market" and "Lower Buena Vista."

MISSION CREEK From Harrison and 19th streets southeast to the Bay.

MISSION DISTRICT The district lying at the eastern base of Twin Peaks and adjacent to Old Mission Dolores.

MISSION VALLEY An opening into the Bay between Rincon Point and Potrero Point and extending back westward and then southward, with a minor fork to the northwest.

MOONEYSVILLE A settlement established by Con Mooney and Denis Kearney on the Ocean Beach below the Cliff House in 1883.

MOUNT DAVIDSON Highest of San Francisco's hills. Centered between Portola Drive, O'Shaughnessy Blvd., and Monterey Blvd.

MOUNT SUTRO Large forested hill immediately west of Sutro Tower, between Parnassus St., Stanyan St., Clarendon Ave., and 7th Ave.

MULTI-MEDIA GULCH Area of Second and Bryant streets near the Bay Bridge where many high-tech computer companies are headquartered. *PC World* magazine is published in Multi-Media Gulch.

NANNY GOAT HILL 18th to 19th St., between Church and Noe streets. So named by George M. Jaeger who lived in this area with his family and a number of goats.

NEW JERUSALEM San Bruno Ave. from Dwight St. to Silver Ave. Also called "The Flat."

NOB HILL Beginning at the northwest corner of Sutter and Kearny streets, north on Kearny to Pacific Ave., west on Pacific Ave. to Larkin St., south on Larkin St. to Sutter St., east on Sutter St. to point of beginning.

NOE VALLEY Clipper and Douglass to Dolores and over Dolores to 25th St. down to Mission, out Mission to San Jose, north on San Jose to Miguel, west on Miguel to Laidley St., over Laidley to 30th St. to Castro, over Castro to Valley, Valley to Diamond, and back to Clipper St.

NORTH BEACH So named because it follows the northern shore of San Francisco Bay. The district covers approximately 300 blocks extending from the Embarcadero to Van Ness Ave., and from Broadway to Fisherman's Wharf.

OJO DE FIGUEROA A prominent water well at Lyon Street, midway between Vallejo and Green streets.

OLD TOWN An eight-block area south of Market St., with the intersection at Kansas and Division streets as the focal point.

PACIFIC HEIGHTS California to Broadway, Fillmore to Arguello.

PARKMERCED 200 acres of apartments developed by Metropolitan Life Insurance Company in 1948. Located east of Lake Merced.

PARK PRESIDIO On Nov. 19, 1917, the supervisors passed ordinance No. 2309 changing the name of the Richmond District to Park Presidio District. The boundaries are Golden Gate Park on the south to the Presidio, Arguello Boulevard to Ocean Beach.

PARKSIDE Noriega on the north, 14th Ave. on the east, the Great Highway on the west, Sloat Blvd. on the south.

PETTICOAT LANE An area also known as Sydneytown during the 1850s, the haunt of thieves and cutthroats.

PICNIC BLOCK The block bounded by Pine, California, Pierce, and Scott, used as a picnic retreat during the 1860s.

PINE LAKE PARK Area bounded by Sloat Blvd. from 24th Ave. to 37th Ave. and Vicente on the north, developed by Parkside Realty Company in 1927.

PLAYLAND-AT-THE-BEACH A ten-acre amusement area, south of the Cliff House, containing rides, games of chance and skill, fun houses, shooting galleries, and eating places. The merry-go-round opened in 1916, the Big Dipper roller coaster in 1922, the Fun House in 1923. After George Whitney purchased the area in 1928, it was enlarged, remaining open until Sept. 4, 1972.

PLEASANT VALLEY Area east of Happy Valley, First to Third, Folsom to Brannan.

POINT ALVISADERA Name given to Hunters Point by Capt. Beechey in 1833. Name changed to Point Avisadero in 1884.

POINT LOBOS Westernmost point of San Francisco. "Lobos" is the Spanish word for "wolves," referring to seals or sea lions.

POINT MEDANOS Fort Mason area, later called Point San Jose.

POLK GULCH Name given to Polk Street business area, Geary to Broadway, during celebration of Bridge and Fair opening in the 1930s.

POTRERO HILL Hill east of the Mission District, south of Mission Bay. The former Potrero Nuevo.

POTREROS, THE Spanish word for "pasture." Under the pueblo system, a potrero was classed as land for the common use of the inhabitants of the pueblo. San Francisco had two potreros, one known as viejo (old), the other nuevo (new).

PRECITA VALLEY Originally a swamp flooded by Islais Creek. The Mexicans built a dam and from this dam came the name "Precita" (a little dam).

PRESIDIO Spanish word meaning garrison of fortified barracks. San Francisco's Presidio was founded in 1776. It fronts the Golden Gate with an area of 1,590 acres.

PRESIDIO HEIGHTS Portion of Pacific Heights which overlooks the Presidio.

PRESIDIO TERRACE Adjacent to Presidio on the north and west, Arguello on the east, Lake on the south. Access can be gained only from Arguello at Washington St. Developed by A. S. Baldwin, president of Baldwin & Howell, in 1905.

PRODUCE DISTRICT (OLD) Washington St., between Front, Drumm, and Davis, until relocated at Islais Creek in 1963.

PUNTA DE CONCHA Spanish name given to Hunters Point.

PUNTA SAN QUENTIN Easterly corner of Mission Bay.

RED SEA The pool of water bounded by Kentucky, Minnesota, 23rd, and 25th streets, condemned as a public nuisance in 1910.

REGAL PALE A small development project, covering 6.5 acres, built on the site of the Regal Pale Brewery at 20th and Treat streets.

REIS TRACT Tract bounded by Rutland, Visitacion, Wilde, and open space.

RICHMOND DISTRICT (PARK PRESIDIO) District lies just south of the Presidio and north of the Park, extending from Arguello on the east to the ocean on the west. Early maps designated the area as the "Great Sand Waste."

RINCON HILL The hill bounded by the Bay, Third, Folsom, and Fremont streets. Comprised 14 blocks of land, with an area of 86 acres.

RUSSIAN HILL Beginning at the northwest corner of Pacific and Grant avenues, north on Grant Ave. to Columbus Ave., northwest on Columbus Ave. to Bay St., west on Bay St. to Van Ness Ave., south on Van Ness Ave. to Pacific Ave., east on Pacific Ave. to point of beginning.

RUDESDALE SPRING Name given to a well in the vicinity of Pine and Sansome streets.

ST. ANNE'S VALLEY Where the Emporium stands today was a rift in the sandhills which was called St. Anne's Valley.

ST. FRANCIS WOOD 175 acres bounded by Portola Dr., Monterey Blvd., and Mount Davidson, purchased in May 1911 and developed by the Mason McDuffie Company.

SCOTCH HILL Now called Potrero Hill. In the 1880s known as "Scotch Hill" because of Scottish boat builders and iron workers living above the Union Iron Works.

SEA CLIFF Developed by the Allen Company with streets and terraces completed in April, 1924. Boundaries are those streets north of California from 28th Ave. to Lincoln Park and those north of Camino Del Mar from 25th Ave.

SEAL ROCKS Four prominent offshore rocks near Point Lobos and the Cliff House. Named for seal colonies but actually home to sea lions.

SEASHELL POINT Hunters Point now, but called Seashell Point by the Spanish explorers in 1775.

SEWER LAKE Located in the vicinity of Mason and Bay streets in the 1870s.

SHAG ROCK (BARREL ROCK) Until blown up April 30, 1900, located about three-eighth-mile from the mainland, southeast of Hunters Point.

SIGNAL HILL Name given to Telegraph Hill in the early 1850s after erection of a semaphore to announce the arrival of ships.

SILVER HUMMOCK Name given to what is now called Lone Mountain by Capt. Beechey in 1827.

SKID ROW Area bounded approximately by Mission, Harrison, 9th, and The Embarcadero.

SNOB HILL Nob Hill.

SOUTH BEACH Area southwest of Rincon Point, beach extended to Steamboat Point.

SOUTH OF MARKET Area south of Market from the Bay to the Mission, called earlier, "South of the Slot."

SOUTH OF THE SLOT After the cable car tracks were installed on Market St., the district south of Market was called "South of the Slot."

SOUTH PARK Area bounded by Second, Third, Bryant, and Brannan streets.

SPRING VALLEY Formerly, a small oasis at the foot of Nob Hill, a low place between Powell, Mason, Clay, and Broadway.

STEAMBOAT POINT Intersection of Third and Berry streets.

STONESTOWN 67-acre site off 19th Ave.,

between Eucalyptus Dr. and State University. Ground broken Nov. 4, 1948.

STRAWBERRY ISLAND Area in Harbor View which, when cut off from mainland by high tides, formed an island. Strawberries grew plentifully there.

SUDS SIDE ROAD The road in the Presidio, from the Life Saving Station to Fort Point, where the enlisted men's wives did laundry and the sudsy water flowed from the tubs to the beach.

SUNSET DISTRICT From Stanyan on the east, Sloat Blvd. on the south, Pacific Ocean on the west, and Golden Gate Park on the north.

SUNSHINE HILL Hill sloping to the north, along the east side of Potrero Ave. from 18th to 21st streets.

SUTRO HEIGHTS 21 acres located on the bluffs above the Cliff House, purchased in 1881 by Adolph Sutro.

SYDNEY GULCH Around the base of Telegraph Hill to the north, from Filbert and Montgomery streets to the Bay.

TAR FLAT Named from the tar that ran down Rincon Point from the old gas house, casting oil upon the bay waters. The boundaries were from 11th and Harrison over to Brannan St. and down to the waterfront.

TELEGRAPH HILL Beginning at the northwest corner of Broadway and Battery St., north on Battery St. to Filbert St., west on Filbert St. to Sansome St., north on Sansome St. to Chestnut St., west on Chestnut St. to Montgomery St., north on Montgomery to Francisco St., west on Francisco St. to Kearny St., north on Kearny St. to Bay, west on Bay St. to Stockton St., south on Stockton St. to Francisco St., west on Francisco St. to Powell St., south on Powell St. to Columbus Ave., southwest on Columbus Ave. to Broadway, east on Broadway to point of beginning.

THEATER DISTRICT The area bounded by Geary, California, Larkin, and Mason streets.

TONQUIN SHOAL Cadwalader Ringgold, in his 1852 charts of San Francisco Bay, defined the shoal as being "extensive." Lying off North Bay, it extends from and connects with Tonquin Point.

1930s interior view of Coit Tower. The interior of the tower is ringed with frescos and murals commissioned by the federal WPA Project, mirroring the "social realism" of the era. Fresco to the left is "California" by Maxine Albro depicting the abundance of California agriculture during the Depression. Many of the frescos were initially quite controversial.

TRANSVESTITE CENTER Area surrounding Mason and Turk streets.

TUCKERVILLE From Buchanan St. to Webster and from Washington St. to Pacific Ave. Area developed by J. W. Tucker, a jeweler.

UNIVERSITY MOUND Area north of McLaren Park bounded by Burrows, Wayland, Cambridge, and University.

UNIVERSITY TERRACE Comprises seven blocks fronting on Masonic, Golden Gate, Parker, and Turk streets. Developed by Coldwell, Cornwall, & Banker in 1936.

UPPER ASHBURY Bounded on the south side by 17th St., the west side by Stanyan St., the north side by Waller St., Buena Vista Ave. West, Java St., Piedmont St., and the east side by Ashbury St.

VISITACION VALLEY Visitacion Valley is roughly a V-shaped area, opening eastward to San Francisco Bay. It is walled on both sides by hills lying between Mansell St. and the San Mateo County line.

WARM WATER COVE Received its name from the constant splashing flow of water warmed after being used as a coolant by the PG&E power plant on Potrero Point, at the end of 24th St.

WASHERWOMAN'S LAGOON Large pond at Gough and Greenwich streets, used as laundry site in 1850's.

WESTERN ADDITION Its eastern boundary is the 125-foot-wide Van Ness Ave., westward to Lone Mountain, northward to the heights above the Marina, and southward almost to Market St.

THE WILLOWS Former willow marsh, later resort as west arm of Dolores Lagoon, 18th and Mission streets, and filled by Mayor McCoppin in 1881.

WINDMILL HILL Name given to Telegraph Hill in the 1840s after the construction of a coffee mill.

YERBA BUENA COVE A former shallow extending in a crescent between Clark's Point on the north to the Rincon on the south.

YERBA BUENA REDEVELOPMENT PROJECT A 25-acre site south of Market between Third and Fourth streets, from Market to Folsom.

YULUPA Indian word for Golden Gate, probably meaning "Sunset Place" ("place where the sun goes down").

MICHAEL D. LAMPEN

Turn-of-the-century view from Golden Gate Park shows the windmill on the left, the Cliff House in the center, and Sutro Conservatory to its right.

34 Police Department

Badge

Webster's Dictionary tells us that a star is a conventional figure having five or more points. Why then the seven-pointed star adorning the breasts of San Francisco's finest? The San Francisco Police, as far as can be ascertained, were the first to adopt the seven-pointed star, and the reason for adopting this celestial symbol involves quite a romantic prognosis. When the police force was organized in the 1850s, the commissioners appointed a committee to have designed a badge of authority, and the committee in turn left the selection to one of their members, who in his way, was a student of astronomy. He gave the matter considerable thought and finally concluded that no more fitting emblem could be found than his beloved star and he reasoned with symbolic conciseness. There should be seven points to the star and each should have a designation: Praising God, Glory, Honor, Virtue, Divinity, Prudence, Fortitude.

Police Journal,
April 1925

Police Department

In 1847, before San Francisco was chartered, the police force consisted of six men. By 1850 the force was increased to 12 men, hardly sufficient to control crime and the many riotous disturbances.

In June 1851, and again in 1856, a small band of citizens formed themselves into a Committee of Vigilance to arrest lawbreakers, try them, and pronounce and carry out sentences. Following the adjournment of the Vigilantes, the regular police force was again made responsible for enforcing the laws and keeping the peace.

After the Consolidation Act was passed in 1856, the responsibility for enforcing law and order rested with a Board of Police Commissioners. This board selected the members of the force, the Chief being chosen by popular vote, until 1878, when the position became appointive.

Marshals

(Title of City Marshal not used after 1856)
Malachi Fallon, *May 11, 1850*
Robert G. Crozier, *April 28, 1851*
David W. Thompson, *Jan. 1852*
Robert G. Crozier, *Nov. 2, 1852*
Brandt Seguine, *Sept. 14, 1853*
John W. McKenzie, *Oct. 2, 1854*
Hampton North, *July 1, 1855*
James McElroy, *July 6, 1856*

Max Fenner, the only police officer to die during the 1906 earthquake, was struck and killed by a falling wall on Mason St.

Police Chiefs

James F. Curtis, *Nov. 4, 1856*
Martin J. Burke, *Sept. 11, 1858*
Patrick Crowley, *Dec. 3, 1866*
Theodore G. Cockrill, *Dec. 1, 1873*
Henry H. Ellis, Dec. 6, *1875*
John Kirkpatrick, *Dec. 3, 1877*
Patrick Crowley, *Dec. 1, 1879*
Isaiah W. Lees, *April 7, 1897*
William P. Sullivan, Jr. , *Feb. 13, 1900*
George Wittmann, *Nov. 21, 1901*
Jeremiah F. Dinan, *April 5, 1905*
William J. Biggy, *Sept. 13, 1907*
Jesse B. Cook, *Dec. 25, 1908*
John B. Martin, *Jan. 28, 1910*
John Seymour, *Oct. 3, 1910*
David A. White, *June 15, 1911*
Daniel J. O'Brien, *Dec. 1, 1920*
Thomas P. Walsh, *Dec. 27–31, 1928*
William J. Quinn, *Jan. 1, 1929*
Charles W. Dullea, *Feb. 15, 1940*
Michael Riordan, *Oct. 9, 1947*
Michael Mitchell, *Jan. 13, 1948*
Michael Gaffey, *Jan. 2, 1951*
George Healy, *Nov. 15, 1955*
Francis J. Ahern, *Feb. 1, 1956*
Thomas J. Cahill, *Sept. 5, 1958*
Alfred J. Nelder, *Feb. 4, 1970*
Donald M. Scott, *Sept. 23, 1971*
Charles R. Gain, *Jan. 12, 1976*
Cornelius Murphy, *Jan. 8, 1980*
Frank Jordan, *Jan. 15, 1986*
Willis Casey, *Nov. 28, 1990*
Richard Hongisto, *Mar. 30, 1992*
Anthony Ribera, *Nov. 10, 1992*

Police Department History

In July 1847, San Francisco's population was 459. Colonel R. B. Mason, the military governor of California, wrote to Alcalde (Mayor) George Hyde that the town needed a police force. Because Colonel Mason expected a large number of whalers and a large increase in population by the arrival of immigrants, Mason said: "I therefore desire that you call a town meeting for election of six persons, who, with the alcalde, shall constitute the town authorities until the end of the year 1848." As a result, six councilmen, elected as "Police Regulators," became conservators of the peace within the limits of the town.

In addition to these "conservators," San Francisco had previously appointed S. Henry Smith and W. S. Thorpe as constables. On December 17, 1847, both constables were relieved of their duties; and Thomas Kittleman, who had migrated to California with Sam Brannan's group of Mormons the year before, was appointed in their place at a wage of $50 a month.

The discovery of gold, on January 24, 1848, proved disastrous to the small force of one constable and six conservators. Gold seekers from all over the world poured into San Francisco and the crime which came with them overwhelmed the seven officers. Looting, brawls, extortion, murder, and robbery were common, and criminals operated with bold and arrogant contempt of the law. Bands of hoodlums, amongst which were the notorious Sydney Ducks and the Hounds, terrorized the town. As crime grew, so did the resourcefulness of the criminals. On several occasions they set major fires to divert the police and firemen while criminals looted businesses and homes.

On July 15, 1849, under the authority of Alcalde Thaddeus M. Leavenworth, 230 volunteer policemen were deputized and put on patrol. The volunteer police worked quickly. The leaders of the Hounds were arrested and tried by "judges" and "district attorneys" who dispensed with legal technicalities to swiftly determine guilt or innocence. "Curbstone justice" was meted out swiftly and effectively.

The guilty were hanged or driven out of town, all with a great deal of public support. The actions of the volunteer police slowed crime and caused dissolution of both the Hounds and the Sydney Ducks. Subsequently, with the disbanding of the volunteer force, the Town Council increased the police force to twelve and appointed Malachi Fallon as Town Marshal on May 11, 1850. Fallon, born in Athlone, Ireland, in 1814, had formerly been keeper of New York's Tombs prison. (In 1852 Fallon moved to Oakland where he died, May 24, 1899.)

Within a year the City's population tripled. In the following year it again doubled; the miniscule force faced the impossible task of policing a crime-rampant city of 20,000 to 25,000 persons.

Gold brought an almost all male population to San Francisco. The City with its countless saloons, gambling dens, bawdy houses, and thugs worked industriously to separate the prosperous miners from their gold.

On June 9, 1851, local inhabitants formed the Vigilance Committee, an ad hoc group of citizens who took direct action to rid the City of its criminals. Again, lawless predators were swept into the nest of vigilantes who dispensed with the niceties of law. The accused were tried with an economical swiftness, and the guilty were punished without benefit of appeal.

Two months later, when the Vigilance Committee of 1851 disbanded, the Town Council reorganized the police force, with as much shortsightedness as it had before. A force of 50 patrolmen, two captains and two assistants, 54 in all, were appointed to police a city that had required several hundred men to "clean up." The newly reorganized force patrolled the City on foot from headquarters in the City Hall, located in the former Graham House on the northwest corner of Pacific and Kearny streets.

Three years later, businessmen organized a group of merchant police called "Special Police" to protect their businesses, and augment the regular police force.

The thirty-officer force allowed by the Consolidation Act of 1856 could not cope with the rising crime rate which once again plagued the City. The murders of U.S. Marshal William H. Richardson and

James King of William, publisher of the *San Francisco Daily Bulletin*, caused a determined citizenry to create the Vigilance citizenry to create the Vigilance Committee of 1856. This Committee, a formidable army of several thousand men, defied both City and State authorites and, with a vengeance, attacked the City's criminal element, disbanding only when all known criminals were either banished or hanged.

In 1863 the Consolidation Act of 1856 was amended by the State Legislature, and the police force was increased to 40. The Chief was elected by popular vote and a police commission was created. In November 1856 James F. Curtis, a "chief" of the Vigilance Committee of 1856, was elected Chief of Police.

By 1860 San Francisco had grown from a turbulent and "scofflaw" town to a more respectable city. Crime had not been abolished, but it had been appreciably lessened. Families were established, men were working at steady jobs, and the foundations for a thriving commercial community had been established. Among the arrests of that year were two for rape, two for keeping houses of ill fame, and 2,161 for drunkenness. Chief Martin John Burke, who had taken office in 1858, reported quite proudly that in almost every instance of known crime the perpetrators were arrested.

As the force grew in number, official equipment was designed for them: a star in 1852 and a uniform in 1856, consisting of a single-breasted dark blue frock coat with seven silver-colored buttons and a black velvet collar. This style uniform was worn until a gray one later replaced it in 1862.

Also in the 1860s the "wreath" police belt buckle became official. The "wreath" was used by the early Greeks to honor Athena, the Goddess of Wisdom and Art. Later the Romans used the wreath to symbolize power of valor. The wreath symbol continued to be used throughout history and remains primarily in the military context.

Chief Burke instituted professionalism in the Department. Officers were drilled in riot and emergency tactics, and the Department became the first in the nation to use photography in police work.

During his tenure, Chief Burke made an historic arrest. He took in custody Senator David C. Broderick and Supreme Court Justice David S. Terry as they prepared to engage in a pistol duel. However, the pair were swiftly released from jail, since they had committed no crime, although it was evident that criminal intent existed. The following day, September 13, 1859, at a spot just over the then county line, Terry shot and wounded Broderick. Broderick died three days later. Terry fled to Stockton but returned quickly to San Francisco. Due to a change in venue, he was tried in Marin County where a jury found him not guilty of Broderick's death.

In May 1864 the City contracted with Kennard & Co. of Boston to install the Department's first police telegraph system. By 1865 four stations were placed in operation. The stations were little more than sentry boxes from which an officer could report to Central Station periodically. Such stations, forerunners of the Department's present complex of district stations, were located at: Mission Dolores; the Chief's residence; 930 Clay Street; Harbor Station; and Central Office at City Hall.

In 1866, 35-year-old Patrick Crowley, a native of Albany, New York, was elected Chief. His 1868 report to the Board of Supervisors emphasized that "as soon as possible provisions be made in suitable localities for durable and substantial district police stations."

On March 23, 1872, the Consolidation Act of 1856 was again amended to increase the police force to 150 patrolmen.

Police Uniforms

During Chief Henry Hiram Ellis's term, the uniform, a single-breasted coat of dark gray cloth buttoned up to the neck with nine black buttons on the breast, a turn-down black velvet collar, the skirt of the same extending to the bend of the knee, with pants and vest of the same material and color, was changed in favor of the style then in use in New York City. It was a single-breasted "mission blue" frock coat, made to button up to the neck, with rolling collar. Nine buttons on the breast, two buttons on the hips, two buttons on the bottom of each pocket and three small buttons on the under seam of the cuffs; plain pantaloons, white shirt collar, black neckcloth, and vest with nine buttons placed at equal distances. However, the choice of color, "mission blue," was an unhappy one, because this color "ran" when the cloth was wet.

"Police Uniform.—The policemen have selected their uniform coats from the store of Messrs. Stobridge & Conner, corner of Commercial and Sansome streets. They are a blue beaver cloth, and the style is a common frock, single breasted, with a velvet collar. The cost of them was $18 each."—*Alta California*, March 3, 1856

In 1932 petitions were circulated among the officers requesting adoption of a more modern uniform from the Police Commission. The request was granted and shortly afterwards the uniformed police force was outfitted in short single-breasted coats of blue whipcord with turned down collars. A Sam Browne belt and pistol holster were authorized for wear on the outside of the uniform coat.

A few months before he retired as chief, Alfred J. Nelder, along with all members of the Department, were provided with new uniforms, more suitable to the times, using blue Eisenhower jackets to affect a "new look." The police were now provided free uniforms and equipment, all of which officers had to purchase previously at their own expense.

35 Presidential Visits

Presidential Visits to San Francisco
Rutherford B. Hayes, *Sept. 9, 1880*
Benjamin Harrison, *April 25, 1891*
William McKinley, *May 12, 1901*
Theodore Roosevelt, *May 14, 1903*
William Howard Taft, *Oct. 13, 1911*
Woodrow Wilson, *Sept. 17, 1919*
Warren Harding, *July 29, 1923**
Herbert Hoover, *Nov. 8, 1932*
Franklin D. Roosevelt, *July 14, 1938; Sept. 24, 1942*
Harry S. Truman, *June 25, 1945; June 13, 1948; Oct. 16, 1950; Sept. 3, 1951; Oct. 3, 1952*
Dwight D. Eisenhower, *Oct. 8, 1952; June 1, 1955; Aug. 21, 1956; Oct. 21, 1958; Oct. 20, 1960*
John F. Kennedy, *March 23, 1962*
Lyndon B. Johnson, *June 19, 1964; Oct. 11, 1964; June 25, 1965*
Richard M. Nixon, *July 23, 1969; Aug. 21, 1969; Sept. 4, 1972; Sept 27, 1972*
Gerald R. Ford, *April 4, 1975; Sept. 22, 1975; Oct. 30, 1975; March 26, 1976; Oct. 5 & 6, 1976*

Jimmy Carter, *May 4, 1979*
Ronald Reagan, *May 24, 1984*
George Bush, *Oct. 20, 1989; Feb. 7, 1990; March 1, 1990; Sept. 19, 1990; Oct. 28 & 29, 1990*
William J. Clinton, *Oct. 4, 1993*

Abraham Lincoln intended to visit California in 1868, at the end of his term. According to John W. Starr, Jr., in *Lincoln's Last Day*, the President wished to bring his children west for "a better chance for advancement in a prosperous state."

*Died in San Francisco at the Palace Hotel, August 2, 1923.

National Conventions Held in San Francisco
Democratic Convention
Civic Auditorium, June 28, 1920
Republican Convention
Cow Palace, August 20, 1956
Republican Convention
Cow Palace, June 19, 1964
Democratic Convention
Moscone Center, July 16, 1984

36 Saint Francis

Saint Francis—San Francisco's Name Saint

Few saints have undergone such a revival of popularity as Saint Francis. His appeal extends beyond Christianity, and has inspired several authors, composers, and filmmakers. Saint Francis's unpretentious idealism, his freedom from materialism, his delight in the natural world, and his deep love of God exert a powerful pull upon spiritual seekers.

Born Francesco Bernardone in 1181, Francis was the son of a wealthy cloth merchant in the Italian hill town of Assisi. Christened John, he was called Francis either because his father was in France on business at the time of the boy's birth, or because Francis as a young man enjoyed speaking French and singing French troubadour songs. The frivolous and carefree youth of the young Francis came to a sudden end when he became seriously ill after being captured in a war with nearby Perugia. The experience changed his life.

Literally obeying a vision of Christ, he began to rebuild a ruined local church.

Soon, he broke with his unsympathetic father and renounced his inheritance. Like Christ's disciples, he began a life of street preaching, eventually attracting several followers. Unlike other itinerant preachers of the day, the little group preached orthodox doctrine and obeyed church authorities. In 1210, Pope Innocent III authorized formation of the Order of Friars Minor. At first, the order rejected money, property, learning, and church promotion. In 1212, Saint Clare founded the female wing of the order.

Saint Francis next traveled to Egypt, and attempted to convert the Sultan, before making a pilgrimage to the Holy Land. Returning home, he found a greatly enlarged order burdened with administrative problems. He rewrote the Rule of the order, and then resigned its leadership. Saint Francis withdrew to the wilds of Monte La Verna where, in 1224, he received the stigmata—the wounds of the crucified Christ. After two more years of self-denial and teaching, he died at Assisi. He was canonized in 1228 and his feast day is October 4.

Beniamino Buffano's 18-foot black granite statue of St. Francis after it was installed on the steps of St. Francis of Assisi Church in North Beach.

Saint Francis's name was first used in California when Sebastian Rodriguez Cermeño gave it to Drake's Bay, north of San Francisco, in 1595. When the 1769 Portola expedition discovered the present San Francisco Bay, they saw it as the inner part of Cermeño's bay, Drake's Bay forming the north end of the Gulf of the Farallons which lies outside San Francisco Bay.

After founding Alta California's first Franciscan mission in 1769, Father Junipero Serra expressed his wish that a future mission be named for his order's founder. In 1776 the sixth mission—Mission San Francisco de Asis (Mission Dolores)—was founded near the shore of San Francisco Bay. In 1847, Alcalde Washington Bartlett changed the name of the nearby Mexican American trading post of Yerba Buena to San Francisco.

MICHAEL D. LAMPEN

The Canticle of Brother Sun

"The Canticle of Brother Sun," also called "The Canticle of the Sun" or "Canticle of Creatures," is thought to be the earliest example of northern Italian vernacular poetry. Similar in large part to Psalm 148, the work was probably composed in 1226, the year of St. Francis's death.

37 Schools

Children's Centers

Bessie Smith African American singer
Burnett Peter H. Burnett, governor of California
Campus Location: College campus
Excelsior District name
Florence Martin Educator
Geary John W. Geary, mayor of San Francisco
Harvey Milk Supervisor
John McLaren John McLaren, superintendent of Golden Gate Park
Las Americas Location: Latino neighborhood
Mission Franciscan mission and district name
Noriega Jose de la Guerra Noriega, early settler
Potrero Terrace District name
San Miguel District name
Sarah B. Cooper Philanthropist
Theresa Mahler School Administrator—Children's Center Division
Yerba Buena Prior name of San Francisco, "Good Herb" (Spanish)
Yoey Playgroup Named by children, (not translatable)

Elementary Schools

Alamo Texas Fort where 183 Americans defied Santa Ana in a revolt against the Mexican government
Alvarado Juan Bautista Alvarado, early Mexican governor
Andrew Jackson U.S. president
Anza Captain Juan Bautista de Anza, Spanish soldier and explorer
Argonne Forest in eastern France, site of World War I battle
Bessie Carmichael School principal
Bret Harte Author, editor
Bryant Edwin C. Bryant, American alcalde (mayor)
Buena Vista "Good view" (Spanish), not related to neighborhood of same name
Cabrillo Juan Rodriguez Cabrillo, Portuguese navigator
Candlestick Cove Location
Chinese Education Center Educational program for Chinese immigrants to the U.S.
Clarendon District name
Columbus Christopher Columbus, explorer
Commodore Sloat Commodore John D. Sloat, U.S.N.

Commodore Stockton Commodore Robert F. Stockton, military governor of California

Corbett School Pioneer family: John Corbett

Daniel Webster Statesman, orator, jurist

Diamond Heights District name

Dr. Charles R. Drew African American physician and pioneer in blood research

Dr. William L. Cobb African American principal and educational administrator, SFUSD

Douglass Steven Arnold Douglass, secretary of state, state of California

Edison Thomas Alva Edison, inventor

E. R. Taylor Edward Robeson Taylor, mayor of San Francisco

El Dorado Spanish word meaning "the gilded"

Fairmount District name

Filipino Education Center Program for immigrant students

Francis Scott Key Author of "The Star Spangled Banner"

Frank McCoppin Mayor of San Francisco

Frederic Burk Dr. Frederic Burk, first president of San Francisco State

Fremont General John C. Fremont, U.S.A., and U.S. senator

Garfield James Garfield, U.S. president

George Peabody Merchant, philanthropist, financier

George Washington Carver African American educator and botanist

Glen Park District name

Golden Gate Street name

Grattan Henry Grattan, lawyer, statesman, orator

Guadalupe Treaty of Guadalupe Hidalgo, treaty between U.S. and Mexico

Hancock John Hancock, American patriot

Hawthorne Nathaniel Hawthorne, American novelist

Hillcrest Location: top of Silver Ave. hill

Irving M. Scott President, Union Iron Works

Jean Parker Teacher, pioneer in progressive education

Jedediah Smith Pathfinder, mountain man

Jefferson Thomas Jefferson, U.S. president

John Muir Naturalist, author

John Swett Educator, superintendent of San Francisco schools

Jose Ortega Sgt. Jose Francisco de Ortega, member of Portola Expedition

Junipero Serra Franciscan father and founder of California missions

Kate Kennedy First female grammar school principal in San Francisco

Lafayette Marquis de Lafayette, general, patriot

Laguna Honda Location: near lake of same name

Lakeshore Location: near Lake Merced

Lawton General Henry W. Lawton, U.S. Army

Le Conte John and Joseph Le Conte, author, scientist, University of California professors

Leonard R. Flynn School principal

Longfellow Henry R. Longfellow, poet

Louise M. Lombard Educator

McKinley William McKinley, U.S. president

Madison James Madison, U.S. president

Mark Twain Author and humorist

Marshall James W. Marshall, discoverer of gold in California

Miraloma District name

Mission Education Center For Spanish-speaking newcomers

Monroe James Monroe, U.S. president

Pacific Heights District name

Parkside District name

Patrick Henry Orator, patriot

Paul Revere Revolutionary War hero

Phoebe Apperson Hearst Philanthropist, founder of PTA

Raphael Weill President, Board of

Official flag of the Italian School of San Francisco.

Education, department store owner
Redding Benjamin B. Redding, secretary of state, assemblyman
Robert Louis Stevenson Author
Rooftop Former location on top floor of Pacific Heights school building
Sanchez Jose de la Cruz Sanchez, commandante of Presidio

High Schools
Abraham Lincoln U.S. president
Alamo Park Texas fort where 183 Americans defied Santa Ana in a revolt against the Mexican government
Balboa Vasco Nunez de Balboa, explorer, first to sight Pacific Ocean
Bay Alternative school, originally located at Fort Mason
Phillip and Sala Burton U.S. congressman and congresswoman
Downtown Program Program: alternative school
Galileo Astronomer
George Washington U.S. president
J. Eugene McAteer State senator
John O'Connell Secretary of the San Francisco Labor Council, founder and President of the local Teamster's Union
Lowell James R. Lowell, poet, abolitionist
Mission Franciscan mission and district name
Raoul Wallenberg Swedish diplomat to Hungary during World War II, honorary citizen of the U.S.

San Francisco Community Programs
San Miguel District name
Sheridan General Phillip H. Sheridan, U.S. Army officer
Sherman General William T. Sherman, U.S. Army officer
Sir Francis Drake English navigator and admiral
Spring Valley District name
Starr King Thomas Starr King, Unitarian minister, orator
Sunnyside District name
Sunshine Curriculum: health school
Sutro Adolph Sutro, mayor of San Francisco
Treasure Island Location: Bay island and site of the 1939–40 Fair
Twin Peaks Location
Ulloa Francisco de Ulloa, navigator
Visitacion Valley District name
Washington Irving Writer, historian, humorist
West Portal District name
William de Avila School principal
Winfield Scott General Winfield Scott, U.S.A.
Yick Wo Name of Chinese laundry owner who took a civil rights case to the Supreme Court

38 Sister Cities

San Francisco has a special relationship with twelve other cities. Like the members of a family, the cities resemble each other in certain features. Geographically, most are sited close to the ocean, with natural harbors, or ringed by hills. Economically, the cities are dominant centers of commerce and their citizens have had experience of trade for many generations.

San Francisco's alliance with her sister cities brings many advantages: cultural exchange, business developments of mutual benefit, aid to the sister cities which are in Third World countries.

"The Sister City affiliation provides a living proof of the love and harmony of two municipalities...so far away from each other."

JOSEPH L. ALIOTO, MAYOR

SISTER CITY	SUPERVISORS RESOLUTION NUMBER	DATE
OSAKA, JAPAN	17773	APRIL 29, 1957
SYDNEY, AUSTRALIA	367-68	MAY 16, 1968
ASSISI, ITALY	366-69	MAY 19, 1969
TAIPEI, REPUBLIC OF CHINA	865-69	DEC. 15, 1969
HAIFA, ISRAEL	257-373	APRIL 9, 1973
SEOUL, KOREA	868-75	DEC. 15, 1975
SHANGHAI, CHINA*	509-79	JUNE 4, 1979
MANILA, PHILIPPINES	267-81	APRIL 6, 1981
CORK, IRELAND	123-84	FEB. 21, 1984
CARACAS, VENEZUELA	927-85	OCT. 21, 1985
ABIDJAN, IVORY COAST	280-86	APRIL 21, 1986
ESTELI, NICARAGUA	644-90	AUGUST 6, 1990

*Mayor Agnos briefly suspended sister city relationships with China shortly after the Tiananmen Square massacre.

39 Songs

City Song: "I Left My Heart in San Francisco"

On October 6, 1969, composers Douglass Cross and George Cory were ushered to the Board of Supervisors rostrum to be introduced after "I Left My Heart in San Francisco" was officially voted the City Song.

Mr. Cross told the supervisors and spectators, "This is a very proud moment for George Cory and me. If our song is a success, it is because it reflects in some small measure, perhaps, the history, the legend, the magic of this beautiful city that has fascinated the imagination of the world. I recall my favorite lines about San Francisco (not mine) by the distinguished San Francisco journalist, poet, and novelist of the early 1900s—Ambrose Bierce:

'Careful now.
'We're dealing here with a myth.
'This city is a point upon a map of fog;
'Lemuria in a city unknown.
'Like us,
'It doesn't quite exist.' "

City Song: "San Francisco"

The film *San Francisco*, starring Jeanette MacDonald, Clark Gable, and Spencer Tracy was released by MGM in 1936. This movie had the most extraordinary disaster sequences of San Francisco's 1906 earthquake and fire. The continuing popularity of the title song brought the citizens of the city to request the Board of Supervisors to make it the official city song. This was done on May 15, 1984.

San Francisco is probably the only city to have two official songs, one a ballad, "I Left My Heart in San Francisco," the other, "San Francisco," music by Bronislaw Kaper and Walter Jerman, lyrics by Gus Kahn.

"Holo Holo Kaa" Song

Possibly the most obscure San Francisco song is "Holo Holo Kaa" as performed by Hawaiian entertainer Hilo Hattie, who claimed in 1965 the song was written by her grandmother after a ride in a San Francisco taxicab.

The song "Holo Holo Kaa" was actually written by John Kamealoha, Johnny Almeida, and Johnny Noble—all well-known Hawaiian tunesmiths of the 1930s and 1940s. Noble also wrote "Hawaiian War Chant," "Sing Me a Song of Hawaii," and "When Hilo Hattie Does the Hilo Hop."

Songs About San Francisco

Alcatraz
Schroder, 1969
Music and lyrics: Malvina Reynolds

All the World Loves San Francisco
Florian Zettel, 1922
Music: Francis Flautino
Lyrics: Gertrude May

At That San Francisco Fair
T. B. Harms, 1915
Music: Dabney and Europe and Jerome Kern
Lyrics: Schuyler Greene

At the Panama-Pacific Fair
Hatch and Loveland, 1914
Music and lyrics: Laura Schick King

At the Panama-Pacific Fair Song
Charles N. Daniels, 1914
Music: Chas. N. Daniels
Lyrics: Sidney Carter

At the San Francisco's Fair Song
P. L. Eubank, 1915
Music: D. C. McGinnis
Lyrics: P. L. Eubank

Back to Market Street
Unknown
Music and lyrics: Virgil Moore

Back to the Barbary Coast
Cafe Frisco, 1966
Music: Roy Benowitz and Paul Green
Lyrics: John Everest and E. J. Mate

Back to Treasure Island
International Institute of Music and Arts, 1940
Music: Karl Stiska
Lyrics: G. E. Brey

Baghdad by the Bay
M. Anninos, F. Agnost, 1955
Music: Frank Agnost
Lyrics: Milton Anninos

Baghdad by the Bay
Conrad Susa, 1987
Music: Conrad Susa
Lyrics: Herb Caen

Ballad of Mr. Cooke
Remick, 1939
Music: John Milton Hagen
Lyrics: Bret Harte

Ballad of San Francisco Bay
D. N. Lehmer, 1937
Music and lyrics: Norman Lehmer

Beautiful San Francisco by the Sea
Michael Cryan, 1920
Music and lyrics: Michael Cryan

Belle of San Francisco
Clark Wise and Bro., 1894
Music: Jay H. Toler

Bells of Treasure Isle
Paramount, 1939
Music: Frank E. Churchill
Lyrics: Paul Francis Webster

Beside the Blue Lagoon
Melody Moderne, 1941
Music and lyrics: Estelle M. Davis

Big Town
Chappell, 1940
Music: Richard Rodgers
Lyrics: Lorenz Hart

Bridge Ahoy
Frank Cutler, 1936
Music and lyrics: Frank Cutler
About the San Francisco-Oakland Bay
Bridge

Cable Car
Kathryn Roy, 1982
Music and lyrics: Kathryn Roy

Cable Car Concerto
Leeds, 1951, 1956
Music and lyrics: Greig McRitchie and
Glen Hurlburt

Cable Car in San Francisco
Bregman, Vocco, and Conn
Music and lyrics: David Broekman

Cable Car on Powell Street
Carl Fischer, 1948
Music: Bethel Melvin

Cable Car Rag
Lee Green, 1979
Music: Lee Green
Lyrics: Virginia Haig Green

Cable Car Ride
David Rose
Music: Stephen McNeil
Lyrics: Libby McNeil

Cable Car Song
Wesley Webster, 1947
Music and lyrics: Bethel Melvin

Cable Car Song
Bregman, Vocco, and Conn
Music and lyrics: Greig McRitchie and
Glen Hurlburt

Cable Car Special
Grassroots, 1978
Music: Jack Bryson Bowden
Lyrics: Baron von Heisterkampf

Cafe Frisco
Cafe Frisco, 1966
Music: Roy Benowitz and Paul Green
Lyrics: John Everest and E. J. Mate

California's Path of Gold
California, 1916
Music and lyrics: Fenelon Foote Chevis

Carnival of the Golden State
Zenomauvais, 1897
Music: J. F. Lehritter

Chimes of Mission Dolores
S. Seiler, 1904
Music and lyrics: S. Seiler

Chinatown Ballad
Remick, 1939
Music: John Milton Haged
Lyrics: Wallace Irwin

Ching Chong
Lee S. Roberts, 1917
Music: Lee S. Roberts
Lyrics: J. Will Callahan

City that Knows How
Thos. H. Meek, 1923
Music and lyrics: Thos. H. Meek

Cocktails Atop of the Hyatt
Grassroots, 1981
Music and lyrics: Frank Levin

Come Swing with Me on the Golden Gate
Cy. W. Owens, 1915, 1939
Music and lyrics: Cy. W. Owens

Courtin' on a Cable Car
Harmony House, 1947
Music and lyrics: Sterlin Sherwin

*Crossing San Francisco Bay on the
Ferry Boat*
Alice Clyde Ellis, 1935
Music and lyrics: Alice Clyde Ellis

Dear Old 'Frisco
W. W. Brackett, 1905
Music and lyrics: W. W. Brackett

Dear Old San Francisco
Nordyke, 1953, 1955
Music and lyrics: Ed Morley

Dear Old South of Market Days
Chickering Ware Rooms, 1925
Music and lyrics: Lee S. Roberts

Destruction of San Francisco
A. W. Perry and Sons, 1906
Music: M. Thea Hays

Dinkly Little Cable Car
Oliver, 1947
Music and lyrics: Stephen McNeil and
Willie Chin

(Sittin' on) the Dock of the Bay
East, 1968
Music and lyrics: Steve Cropper and Otis
Redding

Down at Izzy Gomez
Remick, 1939
Music and lyrics: Sterling Sherwin

El Festival
Gregory, 1909
Music: Antonia Vallejo de Portola

*Every Night Is Saturday Night in San
Francisco*
Nomel, 1975
Music: Barnaby Conrad
Lyrics: Richard O. Kraemer

Fair Exposition Land
H. Nordman, 1914
Music and lyrics: M. Ernestine Nordman

Fair of the Golden West
H. Bennett, 1914
Music and lyrics: H. Bennett

Fireman March
New of Music, 1906
Music: Paul R. Godeska

Fireman's March
Matthias Gray, 1861
Music: Charles Schultz

Fisherman's Wharf
Denslow
Music and lyrics: Peggy Lee and Milton
Raskin

Fog over Frisco
David Rose
Music: Stephen McNeil
Lyrics: Libby McNeil

Foggy Night in San Francisco
O'Connor and Miller, 1954
Music and lyrics: Sidney Miller and
Herman Saunders

49ers Fight Song
Dexter, 1952, 1954, 1960, 1982
Music: Martin Judnigh
Lyrics: Tom Spinosa

Frisco
Jerome H. Remick, 1912
Music: Raymond Hubbell and Jean
Schwartz
Lyrics: Harry B. Smith

Frisco Bay
Virginia Dean Ware, 1938
Music and lyrics: Virginia Dean Ware

Frisco Dan
Jerome H. Remick, 1912
Music: Egbert Van Alstyne
Lyrics: Earle C. Jones

Frisco Flo
Mills, 1936
Music and lyrics: Benny David and J. Fred
Coots

Frisco Girl
Zeno Mauvais, 1896
Music and lyrics: Jas. H. Marshall and
Walter Wolff

Frisco Girls
Lee Johnson, 1904
Music and lyrics: Lee Johnson and Will
Carleton

Frisco Rag
M. Witmark and Sons, 1909, 1910
Music: Harry Armstrong
Lyrics: Bert Fitzgibbon, Billy Clark, Harry
Armstrong

Frisco You're a Bear
Wall-McClellan, 1911
Music and lyrics: Arthur Don and Jack
McClellan

From Frisco to the Cape
Chart, 1941
Music: Ernest Rofle
Foreign text: Martin Nilson
English lyrics: Walt Westley

Greetings from San Francisco
Co-operative, 1957
Music and lyrics: Lloyd Chase

Girl from Frisco
Cadillac, 1906
Music and lyrics: James Brockman

Glow of the Golden Gate
M. M. Foley, 1925
Music and lyrics: Mabel Mitchell Foley

Golden Gate
Edward Schuberth, 1877
Music: Louis Wallis

Golden Gate
C. H. Hammon
Music: Harding Tebbs
Lyrics: Sam Booth

Golden Gate
Irving Berlin, 1928
Music and lyrics: Al Jolson, Dave Dreyer,
Joseph Meyer, and Billy Rose

Golden Gate
Belwin, 1939
Music: Edwin Franko Goldman

Golden Gate
Peter Franch, 1970
Music and lyrics: Peter Franch

Golden Gate (Open for Me)
Leo Feist, 1919
Music and lyrics: Kendis and Brokman

Golden Gate Bridge
Consolidated, 1934
Music and lyrics: Irene B. Anderson

Golden Gate March
Florian Zettel
Music: Grancis Flautino

Golden Gate March
Channing Ellery, 1902
Music: Cavalier Emilio Rivela

Gotta Getta Goin' to the Golden Gate
Remick, 1939
Music and lyrics: Sterling Sherwin

Grand Old Frisco Fair
E. R. Cherryman, 1914
Music and lyrics: E. R. Cherryman

Grant Avenue
Williamson, 1958
Music: Richard Rodgers
Lyrics: Oscar Hammerstein II

Greetings from Sunny California
William Marsoun, 1914
Music and lyrics: William Marsoun

Grizzly Bear
Ted Snyder, 1910
Music: George Botsford
Lyrics: Irving Berlin

Hail to San Francisco State
San Francisco State College, 1941
Music and lyrics: Clarence Kaull

Happy Old San Francisco
Music and lyrics: George A. Cummings,
1917

He Took a Little Trip Across the Bay
Carroll Carrington, 1899
Music and lyrics: Carroll Carrington

Hello, Frisco!
M. Witmark and Sons, 1915
Music: Louis A. Hirsch
Lyrics: Gene Buck

Hello, San Francisco
Davis Rose
Music: Stephen McNeil
Lyrics: Libby McNeil

Hello San Francisco
Ed Devany and Bob Lesuine, 1984
Music: Bob Lesuine
Lyrics: Ed Devany

Hi There Frisco (San Francisco)
Open-Dor, 1970
Music: Harry Sukman
Lyrics: Joe Lubin

Hong Kong Blues
Larry Spier, 1939
Music and lyrics: Hoagy Carmichael

Hour at the Cliff
Dedicated to June Foster, Proprietor of the
Cliff House

Hum of the Hammer
Gabriel Heyerfeld, 1906
Music and lyrics: Migno Schocken

Hymn to the City
David Rose
Music: Stephen McNeil
Lyrics: Libby McNeil

I Always Feel Love in San Francisco
Joytone, 1982
Music and lyrics: Allen Joy

I Left My Heart in San Francisco
General, 1954
Music: George Cory
Lyrics: Douglass Cross

I Love You San Francisco
Oscar Brown, Jr.–Luiz Henrique, 1969
Music: Luiz Henrique
Lyrics: Oscar Brown, Jr.

I Want to Walk to San Francisco
Aberbach Group, 1970
Music: Gretchen Cryer
Lyrics: Nancy Ford

I Wonder What Has Become of Slim
Mills, 1935
Music: Will E. Dulmage and H. O'Reilly
Clint
Lyrics: Richard W. Pascoe

If the San Francisco Hills Could Only Talk
Robbins, 1958
Music and lyrics: Harry Harris

I'll Be There at the Fair in 'Thirty Nine'
Wallace Wakefield, 1936
Music and lyrics: Wallace Wakefield

I'll Be Waiting at the Golden Gate
M. Witmark and Sons, 1915
Music: Terry Sherman
Lyrics: Elmer Olson

I'm Always Drunk in San Francisco
Wolf Mills, 1962
Music and lyrics: Tommy Wolf

I'm Going Back to Frisco Town
Jerome H. Remick, 1915
Music and lyrics: William J. McKenna

I'm Going Back to San Francisco Town
Donald J. Garrison, 1914
Music and lyrics: Donald J. Garrison

*I'm in Love With the Gal in the
Goldfish Bowl*
Bimbo's 365 Club, 1949
Music and lyrics: Jack Marshall

I'm Off to California (in the Morning)
California Contented Club, 1938
Music and lyrics: Roll Grane

I'm San Francisco Bound
Harry Dudley, 1913
Music: Harry E. Dudley
Lyrics: Howard Patrick

In 1909
I. L. A. Brodersen, 1884
Music and lyrics: Charley Reed

In San Francisco the Fair Will Be Best
Southwest, 1910
Music: A. J. Bloom
Lyrics: Sam Harrison

It's Raining on San Francisco Bay
Music and lyrics: Chris Amburn and Allen
Joy, 1983

I've Been Kissed in San Francisco
Chas. K. Harris, 1909
Music: Jos. E. Howard and Harold Orlob
Lyrics: Will M. Hough and Frank R.
Adams

Jubilee Barcarolle
John Santarello, 1939
Music and lyrics: John Santarello

Just One San Francisco
Ludlow-MacDonald, 1907
Music: M. Ruth MacDonald
Lyrics: Lillian H. Shuey

Key of the Golden Gate
F. D. Piccirillo, 1894
Music: F. D. Piccirillo

Lady of the House
Dyke Davis, 1978
Music and lyrics: Dyke Davis, Myron
Crandall, Minco De Bruin, and William
Aaron

Leader of the Submarine Band
Stage Craft, 1911
Music: A. C. Southern
Lyrics: E. T. Southern

Let's Dump Dianne
Music: Anon
Lyrics: Baron von Heisterkampf

Let's Go to San Francisco
Peer International, 1967
Music and lyrics: Carter Lewis

Let's Go to San Francisco
Music and lyrics: Kenneth Alan "Jam"
Hawker and John Nichol Shakespeare

Lords of Frisco
Oh Boy, 1972
Music and lyrics: Dennis Hogan, Dave
Carlson and Barry Lewenthal

Louie Take Me to the Frisco Fair
Gallur and Lipton, 1912
Music: Damasus G. Gallur
Lyrics: Jack M. Lipton

Meet Me at the Golden Gate
Morrison, 1924
Music: Alice Nadine Morrison and
Clarence Oakdeane
Lyrics: Clinton Gordan Fogerty

Meet Me at the San Francisco Fair, 1915
San Francisco, 1914
Music and lyrics: Don J. Gono

Meet Me in Frisco
Seibel, 1915
Music and lyrics: Will A. Fentress

Midwinter Fair
Newspaper Article, 1893
Music and lyrics: Sam Booth

Mission Dolores
David Rose
Music: Stephen McNeil
Lyrics: Libby McNeil

Moonlight at the Cliff
S. Seiler, 1901
Music: S. Seiler

My Heart Goes Back to San Francisco
P. C. Lavey, 1911
Music and lyrics: "Jock" Colman

My Home Town
David Rose
Music: Stephen McNeil
Lyrics: Libby McNeil

My Portola Maid
Herzer, 1909
Music and lyrics: Wallie Herzer

My San Francisco
Sherman, Clay, 1921
Music: Walter Smith
Lyrics: R. E. Hausrath

My Theme Girl of Love
Remick, 1939
Music and lyrics: Sterling Sherwin
Never a White Christmas
Grassroots, 1979
Music: Frank Levin
Lyrics: Baron von Heisterkampf

1915 San Francisco
Floritine, 1914
Music and lyrics: S. and P. I. Jacoby

1915 the Time, San Francisco the Place
Jack Lipton, 1910
Music and lyrics: Jack Lipton

Nob Hill Waltz
Cafe Frisco, 1966
Music: Roy Benowitz and Paul Green
Lyrics: John Everest and E. J. Mate

Nob Hill Racquet
M. Gray, 1878
Music: R. L. Yanke

O'Farrell, Jones and Hyde
Kling, 1946
Music and lyrics: Jack Marshall

Oh San Francisco!
N. Gingold, 1975
Music: Norbert Gingold
Lyrics: Heddy Gingold

Old Chinatown
Carl Fischer, 1948
Music: Bethel Melvin

Old San Francisco Town
Williamson Wells Simons, 1985
Music and lyrics: Williamson Wells
Simons

On a Little Cable Car for Two
Remick, 1939
Music and lyrics: Sterling Sherwin

On San Francisco Bay
M. Witmark and Sons, 1906
Music: Gertrude Hoffman
Lyrics: Vincent Bryan

On San Francisco Bay
David Marconi, 1921
Music: Walter Smith
Lyrics: David Marconi

On San Francisco Bay
Fisk, 1923
Music and lyrics: Thomas H. Meek

On the Beach
Gray's Music
Music: Geo. T. Evans

On the Ferry Boat
Carl Fischer, 1948
Music: Bethel Melvin

One Hundred Days
Turner, 1972
Music: Dick Turner
Lyrics: B. Kay Turner

*Only Pal I Ever Had Came from
'Frisco Town*
Jerome H. Remick, 1911
Music: Charles N. Daniels
Lyrics: Earle C. Jones

Out San Francisco Way
M. Witmark and Sons, 1923
Music: Gertrude Hoffman
Lyrics: Vincent Bryan and Sam Marley

Palace Hotel (Waltz)
Henry Marsh, 1875
Music and lyrics: Henry Marsh

Palm Court
Sherman, Clay, and Co., 1918
Music: Herman Heller

Panama at Frisco, Calif.
Armstong, 1911
Music: Edward Armstrong

Panama Exposition
B. Quattrociocchie, 1918
Music: P. Frosini

Panama-Pacific Exposition
F. M. Pape, 1911
Music: F. M. Pape

Panama-Pacific Ray
Chas. K. Harris, 1911
Music: Mike Bernard
Lyrics: Willie Weston

Paris of the West
Twentieth Century, 1944
Music: Jimmy McHugh
Lyrics: Harold Adamson

Pier 39
Grassroots, 1979
Music: Frank Levin
Lyrics: Baron von Heisterkampf

Pleasure of His Company
Famous, 1961
Music: Alfred Newman
Lyrics: Sammy Cahn

Portola
Clark Wise, 1909
Music: Jose Sanco

Presidio
S. Seiler 1899
Music: S. Seiler

Queen of the Pacific
Nordyke, 1945
Music and lyrics: Paul Campiche

Rhapsody of Fisherman's Wharf
Leeds, 1951, 1956
Music and lyrics: Greig McRitchie and
Glen Hurlburt

Rose Room
Sherman, Clay, 1917, 1918
Music: Art Hickman
Lyrics: Harry Williams

San-Fran-Pan-American
Geo. W. Meyer, 1912
Music: George P. Corin

San Francisco
Success, 1906
Music and lyrics: John J. Burke

San Francisco
J. Gordon Temple, 1906
Music: James G. Dewey
Lyrics: J. Gordon Temple

San Francisco
Paul de Longpre, 1906
Music: Paul de Longpre

San Francisco
Broadway, 1914
Music: Geo. W. Meyer
Lyrics: Sam M. Lewis

San Francisco
Geo. A. Cummings, 1917
Music and lyrics: Geo. A. Cummings

San Francisco
Lawrence Wright Ltd, 1925
Music and lyrics: Harry Carlton and Harry Condor

San Francisco
Karen, 1929
Music and lyrics: Frederick A. Lockhart

San Francisco
John Lewis McDonald, 1932
Music and lyrics: John Lewis McDonald

San Francisco
Robbins, 1936
Music: Bronislaw Kaper and Walter Jurmann
Lyrics: Gus Kahn

San Francisco
Cafe Frisco, 1966
Music: Roy Benowitz and Paul Green
Lyrics: John Everest and E. J. Mate

San Francisco Banjo Band
Arch, 1961
Music: Dick Charles
Lyrics: Bob Goldstein

San Francisco Bay
Tebo, 1956
Music and lyrics: Bob Thiele, Jr.

San Francisco Bay Blues
Hollis, 1958, 1963
Music and lyrics: Jesse Fuller

San Francisco, Be Sure to Wear Some Flowers in Your Hair
Wingate, 1967, 1970
Music and lyrics: John Phillips

San Francisco Blues
Sherman, Clay, 1916
Music: Chris Smith

San Francisco Blues
Denslow
Music and lyrics: Peggy Lee and Milton Raskin

San Francisco Bound
Waterson, Berlin, and Snyder, 1913
Music and lyrics: Irving Berlin

San Francisco by the Golden Gate
Sands, 1947
Music: S. Hartman
Lyrics: S. Costa

San Francisco by the Sea
Neeley and Turner, 1923
Music: Aura Strother Turner
Lyrics: Florence Rhy Neeley

San Francisco Bye, Bye
Music and lyrics: Michael Reno
Recorded by Sharon McNight

San Francisco Cal., U.S.A.
Add, 1908
Music: A. G. Cummings
Lyrics: E. T. Southern

San Francisco Earthquake
Ernest Camp, 1906
Music: Ernest Camp
Lyrics: Mary F. Merrill

San Francisco Fair and Free
Robert A. Barker
Music and lyrics: Robert A. Barker

San Francisco Fallen
Alma A. Crowley, 1906
Music and lyrics: Alma A. Crowley

San Francisco Fog
Remick, 1939
Music: John Milton Hagen
Lyrics: Wallace Irwin

San Francisco Girls
Filigree, 1968
Music and lyrics: Scott Holtzman, Vivian
Holtzman, and Michael Knust

San Francisco Glide
Leo Feist, 1910
Music: Al. Piantadosi
Lyrics: Jos. McCarthy

San Francisco Is a College Town
Remick, 1939
Music and lyrics: Sterling Sherwin

San Francisco Is a Lonely Town
Shelby Singleton, 1969
Music and lyrics: Ben Peters

San Francisco Jazz (1984)
Music: Turk Murphy
Lyrics: Michael Hulett

San Francisco Long Ago
Dexter, 1984
Music and lyrics: Tom Spinosa, Stephen
McNeil, and Nick Therry

San Francisco Mabel Joy
Acuff-Rose, 1969
Music and lyrics: Mickey Newbury

San Francisco March
M. Gray, 1867
Music: Geo. Koppitz

San Francisco Memorial Song
Wm. E. Cornwell, 1906
Music and lyrics: Wm. E. Cornwell

San Francisco My Home
George James, 1972
Music and lyrics: George James

San Francisco Nights
Sea-Lark Enterprises, 1967
Music and lyrics: E. Burdon, V. Briggs, B.
Jenkins, G. Weider and D. McCulloch

San Francisco 1915
Sherman, Clay, 1914
Music: Eddie Hewell
Lyrics: Andy Graves

San Francisco-Oakland Bay Bridge March
Maurice, 1936
Music: Chars. W. Kramer

San Francisco of My Heart
Harms, 1922
Music: Victor Herbert
Lyrics: John Lyons Considine

San Francisco on a Sunny Day
Groene, 1969
Music and lyrics: George James

*San Francisco Open Your Golden Gate
For Me*
National, 1940
Music: Reginald Belcher
Lyrics: Kent Rhorer

San Francisco Our Beloved Arise! Arise!
Chartier and Greven, 1906
Music and lyrics: Joseph Greven

San Francisco Our Own
Wesley Webster, 1939
Music: Francisco Vallejo
Lyrics: Julia Schiffers

San Francisco-Panama 1915 March
Gallur, 1911
Music: Damasus G. Gallur

San Francisco Queen of Cities
Newland and Rucker, 1915
Music: Violet Wheeler-Rucker
Lyrics: Mrs. E. A. Newland

San Francisco Teardrops
Music and lyrics: Marty Robbins, 1973

San Francisco the Charmer
Dorothy Lecker, 1955
Music and lyrics: Dorothy Lecker

San Francisco the Gold Old Town
Sherman, Clay, 1928
Music: E. B. Robinson and C. H. White
Lyrics: C. H. White

San Francisco the Place for Me
Manfredi Chiaffarelli, 1915
Music: Manfredi Chiaffarelli
Lyrics: Jennie K. Merriam

San Francisco the World's Town
A. S. Graves, 1912
Music: Eddie Jewell
Lyrics: Andy Graves

San Francisco Tickle
Bert Keck, 1911
Music: Bert Keck

San Francisco Waltz
Oliver Ditson, 1850
Music: Anton Jantz

San Francisco Welcomes You
Chief Caupolican, 1945
Music and lyrics: Chief Caupolican

San Francisco (You're the Queen of the Golden West)
Louis Merik, 1925
Music and lyrics: Harry C. Sanxay

San Francisco You're the Town for Me
Ryland, 1947
Music and lyrics: Richard Lancaster

San Francisco, You've Got Me
Can't Stop Music, 1977
Music and lyrics: J. Morali, H. Belolo, P. Whiteheard, and P. Hurtt

Save the Cable Cars
Save Me Too, 1982
Music and lyrics: Earl Steven
Recorded by Earl Steven

Souvenir De Carnival Portola
Walter J. Brunt, 1909
Music: R. J. Harrison

State Victory Song
San Francisco State College, 1941
Music: Mildred Roof
Lyrics: Dorothy Williamson

Stricken City
American Advance Music, 1906
Music: F. Fanciulli
Lyrics: Ella Wheeler Wilcox

Strolling Down Maiden Lane
Golden Harp, 1960
Music and lyrics: Paul Brock Killeen

Sutro March
Frank Kuba, 1895
Music: Frank Kuba

Sweet Mooneyville
J. L. A. Brodersen, 1884
Music and lyrics: Charley Reed

Sweetheart that I Lost in Dear Old Frisco
Pacific, 1906
Music: Ealter Potter
Lyrics: Helen Osborne

Swinging on the Golden Gate
Music and lyrics: Mel Torme

Take Me Back to San Francisco
Belland, 1914
Music: Frank A. Taber
Lyrics: J. F. Belland

Taraval Street Rag
Grassroots, 1985
Music: Frank Levin

Tassels on Her Boots
Mattius Gray, date and
publisher unknown

Telygraft Hill
Remick, 1939
Music: John Milton Hagen
Lyrics: Wallace Irwin

Texas Tommy Swing
Harris and Brown, 1911
Music: Sid Brown
Lyrics: Val Harris

Thank God for San Francisco
Grassroots, 1982
Music: Frank Levin
Lyrics: Baron von Heisterkampf and Frank
Levin

Thanks for Taking the Muni
Grassroots, 1978
Music: Jack Bryson Bowden
Lyrics: Baron von Heisterkampf

That Miner, That 49er
Music and lyrics: Don Pierazzi

There's a Silver Moon on the Golden Gate
Irving Berlin, 1936
Music and lyrics: Charles Tobias, Bob
Rothberg, and Joseph Meyer

Three Cold Days in San Francisco
Skywitch, 1985
Music and lyrics: John Wallowitch

Ticky Tacky
Music and lyrics: Malvina Reynolds

Tivoli March
J. D. Robertson, 1881
Music: George Loesch

Took My Wife to the Frisco Fair
Luciel Wilkie, 1915
Music and lyrics: Luciel Wilkie

Tough Sledding Tonight
Grassroots, 1981
Music: Frank Levin
Lyrics: Baron von Heisterkampf

Treasure Island
Rex, 1938
Music: George Rex
Lyrics: Don Rodricks

Treasure Island
20th Century, 1939
Music: Samuel Kaylin

Treasure Island
Charles Beck, 1939
Music: Charles Beck

Treasure Island March
Golden Gate, 1939
Music: Ray Meany and Bernie Kaal

Treasure Island March
National Institute of Music and Arts, 1939
Music: Karl Stiska
Lyrics: E. F. Copenhafer

Treasure Island, Pride of the Golden West
W. Vernon Huey, 1939
Music and lyrics: W. Vernon Huey

Treasure Island Souvenir
Fred Whitfield, 1939
Music and lyrics: Morrie Morrison

True Sons of '49
Pioneer, 1906
Music: Louis Meyer
Lyrics: Arthur Price

Two Bridges That Bridged Two Hearts
Remick, 1939
Music and lyrics: Sterling Sherwin

University of San Francisco Victory Song
Sherman, Clay & Co., 1930, 1931
Music and lyrics: Bud Smith

Viva L'italiane
Remick, 1939
Music: adapted
Lyrics: Sterling Sherwin

Waitin' for the Cable Car at the Cable Car Turnaround Rag
Save Me Too, 1982
Music and lyrics: Earl Steven

Waterfront Sketches
Weston S. Wilson, 1921
Music: Maud Fulton

We Met in Dear Old Frisco, We Were Sweethearts in Chicago, Now We'll Wed in New York
Carl Laemmle, 1911
Music: Alfred Solmna
Lyrics: Jeff T. Branen

We'll Start for San Francisco in the Morning
J. E. Hamilton, 1915
Music and lyrics: John Edward Hamilton

Welcome to Treasure Isle
Pauline Schaackey, 1939
Music and lyrics: Pauline Schaackey

We're the 49ers
Gratitude Sky, 1984
Music and lyrics: Narada Michael Walden and Jeffrey Cohen

When the Golden Gate was Silver
Famous Music, 1934
Music: Ralph Rainger
Lyrics: Leo Robin

When You Call It Frisco, Smile
David Rose
Music: Stephen McNeil
Lyrics: Libby McNeil

Wonderful San Francisco
Mary H. Fleshman, 1982
Music and lyrics: Mary H. Fleshman, 1962

You'll Remember San Francisco
Wesley Webster, 1956
Music and lyrics: Helen L. Wright

Zone
San Francisco Publishers, 1915
Music and lyrics: Don J. A. Gono

BOB GRIMES

40 Spanish/Mexican Era

Castillo de San Joaquin and Its Cannon

Castillo de San Joaquin was a fortified battery built by the Spanish in 1793-94. The brick-reinforced adobe battery stood atop Punta del Cantil Blanco ("White Cliff Point"), the impressive serpentine bluff later cut away to make room for Fort Point. The battery had 14 gun ports. Six surviving bronze cannon, all cast in Lima, Peru, are on display in various parts of the Presidio.

San Martin
("Saint Martin"), cast 1684; Fort Point parade yard

Santo Domingo
("Saint Dominic"), cast 1628; Presidio Army Museum entry (Funston Avenue)

San Francisco
("Saint Francis"), cast 1679; Main Parade Ground (flagpole)

La Virgen de Barbaneda
("The Virgin [Mary] of Barbaneda), cast 1693; Main Parade Ground (flagpole)

Poder
("Power, Authority") Presidio Officers' Club entry (Moraga Ave.)

San Pedro
("Saint Peter") Presidio Officers' Club entry (Moraga Ave.)

Jose Cubas cast San Martin, San Francisco, La Virgen, and Poder over a twenty-year period. Earlier, Alexo Texeda cast Santo Domingo. Antonio de Rivera cast San Pedro. All but Poder and San Pedro bear the arms of the then-ruling Viceroy of Peru.

The two 18th-century cannon at the Lombard Street gate of the Presidio were captured during the Spanish-American War. They were cast in Seville in 1783 and bear the arms of King Charles III.

City of St. Francis

Vizcaino in 1542 discovered "the fine harbor of Monterey." Two centuries later Russia extended her settlements down the Alaska coast. Jose del Galvez in Mexico sounded the alarm. Carlos III was a king who did not temporize, and he proceeded to colonize California.

By sea Fages came with his Catalan Volunteers. Portola, Serra, and Crespi

marched up the Peninsula to found San Diego. Hero of this difficult trek was Sergeant Francisco Ortega. As chief scout he traveled three times over the entire distance. Each morning he went ahead, selected the next campsite, returned to Portola's bivouac and guided him to the next.

From San Diego, Portola continued up the coast; Ortega as before covered each league three times. At Monterey they recognized Vizcaino's landmarks—the great oak by the water's edge, the Point of Pines, Carmel Bay and River. But where was the great harbor? To make sure he had made no mistake, Portola continued up the coast, and on November 1 from Sweeney Ridge looked down upon the Bay of San Francisco. Next year Monterey was founded and became the capital of Spanish California.

To occupy and make secure the really great harbor, Juan Bautista de Anza, with consummate skill and infinite care, in 1775 led a colony overland from Mexico to Monterey. Sites were now chosen for a settlement on San Francisco Bay. Father Palou set up a cross at Point Lobos. Ayala sailed in the *San Carlos* and, on August 5, 1775, drifted with the tide through the Golden Gate. Ten days later he anchored behind Angel Island. The following year Anza and Font chose a site for a presidio at the Golden Gate and for a mission at Arroyo de los Dolores.

On June 17, 1776, Moraga set out from Monterey with the colony for San Francisco, by way of Salinas and Santa Clara valleys. On June 27 the pioneers halted at the site called Dolores. The little bowery erected there was San Francisco's first building. In August the construction of the Presidio was begun, and on September 17 it was dedicated. The mission chapel was blessed on October 3, and on the 8th the dedication ceremonies were held.

Thus, just after July 4, 1776, when a new nation was born on the Atlantic Coast, the city of San Francisco was begun beside the Harbor of Harbors on the Pacific Coast.

DR. HERBERT E. BOLTON
University of California
Written for the South of Market
Boy's Founders' Day Program,
June 29, 1948, at the Palace Hotel

Colonial Records of San Francisco
MAY 13, 1789

Whenever there may arrive at the port of San Francisco a ship named the *Columbia*, said to belong to General Washington, of the American States, commanded by John Rendric, which sailed from Boston in September, 1787, bound on a voyage of discovery to the Russian establishments on the northern coast of this peninsula, you will cause the said vessel to be examined with caution and delicacy, using for this purpose a small boat, which you have in your possession, and taking the same measures with every other suspicious foreign vessel, giving me prompt notice of the same.

May God preserve your life many years.

PEDRO FAGES
Santa Barbara, May 13th, 1789.
To Josef Arguello.

First Election in San Francisco

The first election in the Districto de San Francisco was held at the Presidio on December 7, 1834.

There was no City or County of San Francisco, not even a Town of San Francisco—nor would there be until January 1847 when Alcalde Bartlett changed the name of the Town of Yerba Buena to the Town of San Francisco.

The Town of San Francisco only went west to about Taylor Street, and southwest to about Tenth Street, leaving outside practically all of the earlier District of San Francisco, including the original Presidio of San Francisco.

Romantic 1930s' view of the Mission Dolores by famed San Francisco photographer Gabriel Moulin.

Mexican Governors of California
Luis Antonio Arguello, *1822–1825*
Jose Maria de Eschendia, *1825–1831*
Manuel Victoria, *1831–1832*
Pio Pico, *1832 (for 20 days)*
Jose Figueroa, *1833–1835*
Jose Castro, *1835–1836*
Nicholas Gutiérrez, *1836*
Mariano Chico, *1836*
Juan Bautista Alvarado, *1836–1842*
Manuel Micheltorena, *1842–1845*
Pio Pico, *1845–1846*
Jose Maria Flores, *1846–1847*

MICHAEL D. LAMPEN

Mexican Ranchos of San Francisco
MEASUREMENTS:
1 vara = 33 inches or 2.75 feet
1 square vara = 7.56 square feet
5760 square varas = 1 acre
5000 varas = 1 league or 2.60 square miles
25 million square varas = 1 square league
which is equal to 6.78 square miles, or
4340 acres.

When the Mission Dolores was formally secularized in 1834, local grazing and farming lands covered about half the area of the future San Francisco and included the central, southern, and southeastern parts of the city. During the 1830s and '40s, this land was divided into ranchos and suertes—the Spanish word for farms.

The major ranchos were:

RANCHO LAGUNA DE LA MERCED—Lake Merced Ranch—comprised 0.51 square-leagues (2219 acres) granted on September 23, 1835, to Jose Galindo by Governor Castro. It was then sold on May 12, 1837, to Francisco de Haro. The site of the farmhouse was near Westlake Park in Daly City.

RANCHO RINCON DE LAS SALINAS Y POTRERO VIEJO covered 1.03 square leagues or about 4446 acres, and was granted to Jose Cornelio de Bernal by Governor Pico. The name was translated as Saltmarsh Meadow and old Pasture Ranch. Potrero Viejo was Bernal Heights. The ranch was enlarged in 1852 to include the upper Islais Creek drainage near San Jose Avenue. The farmhouse was located near Mission and Army streets.

RANCHO CAÑADA DE GUADALUPE VISITACION Y RODEO VIEJO—Guadalupe Canyon, Visitation and Old Corral Ranch—that covered 1.26 square leagues, or 5473 acres. It was granted to Jacob P. Leese by Governor Alvarado on July 31, 1841.

RANCHO POTRERO DE SAN FRANCISCO—SAINT FRANCIS PASTURE RANCH was 0.26 square leagues, or 1112 acres, and was granted to Ramon and Francisco de Haro by Gov. Micheltorena on April 30, 1844. This ranch covered most of the area of the Inner Mission.

RANCHO SAN MIGUEL—SAINT MICHAEL RANCH covered 1.03 square leagues, or 4443 acres, and was granted to José de Jesus Noe on December 23, 1845, by Governor Pio Pico. The farmhouse stood near Douglass and Alvarado streets. This rancho covered much of the Outer Mission District, the Excelsior and Twin Peaks areas, and extended as far north as Junipero Serra Boulevard.

What was then left of the Mission Dolores lands were sold off as farms.

Mission Dolores Priors and Resident Priests of Mission Dolores
This list is limited to Franciscan friars who served at Mission Dolores for three or more years. Another 23 friars served for less than three years. Mission Dolores was founded in 1776, secularized in 1834, and returned to the Church by Presidential Proclamation, 1857.

Francisco Palou, *1776–1785*
Pedro Benito Cambon, *1776–1779, 1782–1791*
Thomas de la Peña, *1777–1781, 1783–1786, 1788–1793*
Vincente de Santa Maria, *1777–1782*
Miguel Giribet, *1775–1787*
Fermin de Lasuen, *1786–1791, 1796*

Diego Garcia, *1787–1790*
Faustino de Sola, *1787–1790*
Antonio Danti, *1790 1796*
Martin de Landaeta, *1791–1798,*
1800–1806
Diego de Noboa, *1791–1793*
Manuel Fernandez, *1794–1796*
Jose de la Cruz Espi, *1797–1799*
Ramon Abella, *1796–1819*
Luis Gil y Taboada, *1800–1806,*
1819–1820
Juan Sainz de Lucio, *1806–1816*
Buenaventura Fortuny, *1810–1819*
Vicente de Sarria, *1814, 1806, 1818, 1816*
Vicente Oliva, *1815–1818*
Jose Altimira, *1820–1823*
Thomas Estenega, *1821–1833*
Lorenzo Quijas, *1833–1840 1841–1843*
        REVEREND FEPHYRIM ENGELHARDT

Mission Dolores Surveys— The American Period

The University of California library system holds some of the most important Mission-era documents. Many early maps of the period are housed at the University of California's Bancroft Library at Berkeley. This is a guide to the maps held at the Bancroft Library.

1. Sketch of a lot 400 varas square, Mission Dolores. Surveyed for Dn. Francisco Guerrero by Milo Hoadley, Deputy County Surveyor. December 24th, 1850. Scale ca. 1:1,342. UC Berkeley Bancroft Land Case Map D-284

2. Mission Dolores surveyed by G. Black, C.E., October 1854. Scale 1:1,584. 2 chains to an inch. UC Berkeley Bancroft Land Case Map D-916R UC Berkeley Map Room G4361.G465 svar .L3D-916R:Case D

3. Plat of the tract of land in Mission Dolores, finally confirmed to C. S. de Bernal et al. Surveyed under instructions

from the U.S. Surveyor General by Wm. I. Lewis, Deputy Surveyor. March 1861. Scale 1:1,584. 2 chains to 1 inch. UC Berkeley Bancroft Land Case Map D-373

4. Two hundred varas square in Mission Dolores: Surveyed with the exception of the Bernal Lot as per diagram by W. P. Humphreys, Surveyor. October 1861. Scale 1:1,584. 2 chains to an inch. UC Berkeley Bancroft Land Case Map E-375

5. Plat of two 50 vara lots in Mission Dolores, finally confirmed to the heirs of Francisco de Haro. Surveyed under instructions from the U.S. Surveyor General by H. B. Edwards, Deputy Surveyor. April 1862. Scale 1:792. 1 chain to 1 inch. UC Berkeley Bancroft Land Case Map D-377

Pioneer Families of Yerba Buena

Here are the names of the first twelve settlers of Yerba Buena, their dates of settlement, and their families. Because of frontier conditions at Yerba Buena, many husbands settled their families in Monterey, the Mexican capital of Alta California. A known exception is Jacob Leese, whose daughter, Rosalia, was the first non-native child born in Yerba Buena (1838).

William A. Richardson (1835), wife Maria Antonia Martinez, daughter Mariana.

Jacob P. Leese (1836), wife Rosalia Vallejo, children Rosalia (b. 1838), Jacob (b. 1839).

Juan C. Fuller (1837), wife Concepcion Avila, children Concepcion, Santiago, 3 others.

Francisco Caceres (1838), wife Anastasia Boronda, children Anastasia, Francisco, Carmen, Guadalupe, Julian, Rafaela, Cino, Helena, Teresa.

Nathan Spear (1838), wife half-Hawaiian.

A. B. Thompson (1838), wife a member of the Carrillo family.

John Perry (1838), family in Nicaragua.

John C. Davis (1839), nephew of Spear, married a Yount daughter in 1844.

William S. Hinckley (1839), first wife left 1837, remarried 1848.

Victor Prudhon (1839), wife Teodocia Bojoroques.

J. B. R. Cooper (1840), wife Encarnacion Vallejo, children Anna Maria, Juan Bautista, Henry B., Francisco, Amelia, George H., William R., five others.

John J. Vioget (1840), wife a member of the Benavides family.

San Francisco Ranchos

RANCHO: CAMARITAS
300 varas located at The Willows
Granted by: Juan B. Alvarado
Granted to: Jose de Jesus Noe
Date: Jan. 21, 1840

RANCHO: CAÑADA DE GUADALUPE
Visitacion y Rodeo Viejo, 2 square leagues
Granted by: Juan B. Alvarado
Granted to: Jacob P. Leese
Date: July 31, 1841

RANCHO: LAGUNA DE LA MERCED
1½ leagues.
Granted by: Jose Castro
Granted to: Jose Antonio
                 Galindo
Date: Sept. 27, 1835

RANCHO: OJO DE AGUA DE FIGUEROA
100 varas at Lyon and Vallejo streets.
Granted by: Jose Sanchez
Granted to: Apolinario Miranda
Date: Nov. 16, 1833

RANCHO: PARAJE DEL ARROYO
½ league near the Presidio
Granted by: Pio Pico
Granted to: Henry D. Fitch
Date: July 24, 1846

Spanish Cattle and Horse Brands of San Francisco

The **Presidio** brand was a number 4 with an open top. A small capital A was attached to the top left stroke of the 4 with the left stroke of the A superimposed on the left stroke of the 4. The A probably stood for ayuniaento or company. The 4 referred to the Presidio as the fourth such establishment in Alta California.

The **Mission Dolores** brand was a capital F which referred to the Mission's true name "Mision San Francisco de Asís."

The longhorn cattle horses and sheep of the Mission had a V-shaped section cut out of one ear which left the ear with a distinctive "swallowtail" appearance.

El Camino Real

El Camino Real was originally an Indian trail. It translates as The Highway, or literally The Royal Road. The San Francisco portion ran close to the present route of San Jose Avenue northeast to 22nd Street, then northwest to the intersection of Dolores and Cumberland streets. It then went north on Dolores St. to the Mission.

Trails of Northern San Francisco

The **Mission Dolores–Presidio Trail** wound across scrub-covered hills and dunes where grizzly bears were sometimes encountered. It passed along the west side of Alamo Square hill and then climbed to the "portezuelo," or "pass," at McAllister and Divisidero streets. It continued along the east slope of Buena Vista Heights and then across Presidio Heights. The trail then wound down to El Polin Spring where the horses could be watered. From the spring it was a short descent and quick climb that ended at the Presidio.

The **Presidio–Yerba Buena Trail** ran east through the open grassland of Cow Hollow and Golden Gate Valley, then up to Pacific and Jones streets between Russian and Nob hills. It meandered down to the little trading post on Yerba Buena Cove near Portsmouth Square.

The **Yerba Buena–Mission Trail** ran southwest, entirely through scrub-covered sand dunes and occasional grassy swales. The route was very difficult for horses because it wound through 10- to 30-foot dunes directly into the winds. Market Street to Kearny and then to the cove was the approximate route.

Spanish Governors of California 1767–1822
Don Gaspar de Portola, *1767–1771*
Felipe de Barri, *1771–1774*
Felipe de Neve, *1774–1782*
Pedro Fages, *1782–1790*
Jose Antonio Romeu, *1790–1792*
Jose Joaquin de Arrillaga, *1792–1794*
Diego de Borica, *1794–1800*
Jose Joaquin de Arrillaga, *1800–1814*
Jose Dario Arguello, *1814–1815*
Pablo Vicente Sola, *1815–1822*

Presidents of Mexico during Mexican Rule of California 1822–1851
Augustin de Iturbide, *1822–1823*
Guadalupe Victoria, *1824–1828*
Vicente Guerrero, *1828–1829*
Anastasio Bustamante, *1829–1832*
Antonio Lopez de Santa Ana, *1833*
Gomez Farias, *1833–1834*
Antonio Lopez de Santa Ana, *1834–1836*
Anastasio Bustamante, *1836–1841*
Antonio Lopez de Santa Ana, *1841–1844*
Jose Joaquin Herrera, *1844–1846*
Mariano Paredes, *1846–1851*

41 Sports

Baseball

San Francisco's first organized baseball game was played at 16th and Harrison streets in the Mission.

This game was followed by others played at sandlots throughout the city until proper diamonds were established in the following parks:

25th and Folsom Streets, opened November 26, 1868.

Central Park, 8th and Market streets, opened 1885.

Haight Street Grounds, Stanyan Street across from Golden Gate Park, opened April 3, 1887.

Recreation Park, 8th and Harrison streets, opened Oct. 3, 1887.

Ewing Field, Masonic Ave., opened May 16, 1914.

Seals Stadium, 16th and Bryant streets, opened April 7, 1931.

Football

Early San Francisco football teams regularly played against the University of California football varsity team at locations throughout this city. The first Stanford-California game was held in San Francisco at the Haight Street Grounds on March 19, 1892. These highly publicized games were played in San Francisco until 1904 when California Field opened in Berkeley.

Football Fields

Recreation Park, 8th and Harrison streets

Haight Street Grounds, Stanyan Street across from Golden Gate Park

Central Park, 8th and Market streets

16th and Folsom Street Grounds

Richmond Field, 6th Avenue and Lake Street

Golden Gate Park

Ewing Field, Masonic Avenue

Kezar Stadium, Golden Gate Park

Candlestick Park, Exit from Highway 101

Welcoming ticker-tape parade along Montgomery Street for the new San Francisco Giants.

Golf Courses

Public Courses

Golden Gate Park (9 holes), opened April 4, 1951.

Harding Park (18 holes), opened July 18, 1925. (Named for President Warren G. Harding who died in San Francisco.)

Lincoln Park (18 holes), opened as a 6-hole course in 1909 and enlarged to 18 holes in 1913.

McLaren Park (9 holes), opened Sept. 1961.

Sharp Park (18 holes), opened in San Mateo County in 1932.

Private Courses

The Olympic Club's two 18-hole courses were constructed in 1923, the "Lake Course" and the "Ocean Course."

Presidio Golf Club established June 28, 1905.

San Francisco Golf Club established in 1895 as a 9-hole course laid out in the Presidio of San Francisco. Moved in 1905 to Junipero Serra Blvd., south of Ocean Ave.

Racetracks

Racetracks were operating early in the 1850s and continued to do so until the last track closed in 1905. The first racing ovals appeared in the Mission District, followed by those in the Outside Lands, and still later by the Ingleside Track.

Bay District Between First and Fifth avenues, Anza and Fulton streets. Opened November 12, 1873. Closed May 27, 1896.

Bayview Between 24th and 28th streets and Ingalls and Railroad avenues. Opened Sept. 3, 1864.

Half Mile Between 24th and 28th avenues and Point Lobos Avenue and Clement Street.

Ingleside Between Ocean Avenue and Junipero Serra Boulevard. Opened Nov. 28, 1895. Closed Dec. 31, 1905.

Ocean View — Between Ocean Avenue and Sloat Boulevard, and 26th and 34th avenues. Opened May 23, 1865.

Pioneer Between Mission and Bryant streets, and 24th and Army streets.

The Willows (Union Track) Between 19th and 23rd streets, and Mission and Harrison streets.

Swimming Pools

Balboa (indoor) Opened June 15, 1958. San Jose Ave. and Havelock Street

Coffman (indoor) Opened November 15, 1958. Visitacion Ave. and Hahn Street

Garfield (indoor) Opened December 2, 1957. 26th and Harrison streets

Hamilton (indoor) Opened October 16, 1955. Geary Blvd. and Steiner Street

King (indoor) Opened August 3, 1968. 3rd and Carroll streets

Larsen (indoor) Opened November 15, 1958. 19th Ave. and Wawona

Mission (outdoor) Opened June 18, 1916, 19th and Angelica streets

North Beach (indoor) Opened December 5, 1956. Mason and Lombard streets (remodeled)

Rossi (indoor) Opened September 22, 1957. Arguello Blvd. and Anza Street

Baths Almost Forgotten

Crystal Baths Powell and Bay streets. Opened 1886. Closed 1906.

Crystal Palace Salt Water Baths 775 Lombard Street. Opened 1924. Closed January 8, 1956.

Fleishhacker Pool End of Sloat Boulevard. The city's largest outdoor pool which contained 6,500,000 gallons of warmed salt water. Pool measured 1,000 feet long by 150 feet wide. It opened April 23, 1925, and closed July 1, 1971.

Harbor View Hot Salt Water Baths Northwest corner Baker and Jefferson streets. Opened 1890. Closed 1912.

Lick Baths 10th Street near Howard Street. Opened November 1890. Closed November 30, 1919.

Lurline Baths Northwest corner Larkin and Bush steets. Opened 1894. Closed 1936. Building still in use for offices.

Palace Baths Filbert near Powell Street. Opened 1887. Closed 1906.

Sutro Baths Point Lobos Avenue. Opened March 14, 1896. Closed September 1, 1952.

Yachting

Since the 1850s, the American period, the 450 square miles of water in San Francisco Bay have lured weekend sailors to race in sport on a variety of sailing craft.

The participants very early organized themselves into informal sailing clubs, followed by these more permanent organizations.

Yacht Clubs

Pioneer Yacht Club
Organized September 9, 1852

San Francisco Yacht Club
Organized July 16, 1869

Pacific Yacht Club
Organized June 1878

Corinthian Yacht Club
Organized March 16, 1886

St. Francis Yacht Club
Organized May 13, 1927

Golden Gate Yacht Club
Organized 1939

Bayview Boat Club
Organized 1976

Sailing

Lake Merced Sport Center adjacent to Harding Park Golf Course on Skyline Blvd.

42 Streets

49 Mile Scenic Drive

The famous "49 Mile Scenic Drive" was dedicated Wednesday September 14, 1938, by a young flyer named Douglas Corrigan. Corrigan became famous that year when aviation officials refused him permission to fly to Europe in his private plane. He filed a flight plan for Los Angeles, but flew instead to Ireland. He became immediately known as "Wrong Way" Corrigan.

He was accompanied on the dedicatory "49 Mile Scenic Drive" ride by William Hughson, President of the Downtown Association, who sponsored the scenic drive.

World War II closed the route. It reopened in 1947 as a much longer drive, covering more of the eastern section of the city.

Gas Lamps

Exit San Francisco's gas lamps! Their yellow beams replaced by the brilliance of modern electric street lights, the old lighting fixtures take their place in memory's storehouse along with horse cars, Woodward's Gardens, the steam trains that used to run to the Cliff House, and other relics of old San Francisco. This doesn't mean they're on the scrap heap, however, for the latest types have been sent to Philadelphia, to see service there until that city switches completely to electricity.

Last of the gas lamps to go were fourteen along Hyde Street, between Sutter and McAllister—a section that was "out in the country" when San Francisco got its first gas lights back in 1854.

What an event that was! Gas lamps seemed perfection after three or fours years of oil lamps in the district bounded by Battery, Jackson, Kearny and California streets, and no street lights at all before then. How enthusiastically the change from oil to gas was received was recorded by one of the historians of the day. In 1856, when the number of new lights had grown to 515, he wrote in Colville's Directory: "The clear light furnished by the San Francisco Gas Company, from three miles of pipe and hundreds of burners, illuminates the streets and the hearts of the people."

San Francisco started out with 47 gas street lamps in '54. The number grew to

Elmer Johnson of the San Francisco Junior Chamber of Commerce readied San Francisco street signs for shipment to Alaska. The signs were requested by homesick San Franciscans on duty there to block further Japanese advances.

379

3,249 in 1880 and to 5,462 at the time of the 1906 fire, which cut the total to 2,229.

POLICE AND PEACE OFFICERS' JOURNAL
May 1931

Great Highway

Completion of the Great Highway was celebrated Sunday June 9, 1929, by a monster celebration. More than 50,000 people massed at the end of Lincoln Way for the festivities, with music provided by a band of 1,014 musicians.

Fronting Golden Gate Park, it is the widest stretch of pavement anywhere in the U.S. and runs a distance of approximately 3,000 feet.

San Francisco Toll Roads

In the early years, San Francisco lacked funding to build and improve roads leading out of the city, then confined largely to the present downtown area. Seven-year franchises were granted to various private road builders over the protests of many prominent citizens. Thus, for a time, most roads leading out of the city were toll roads with gateways and toll booths. Tolls were set at 75 cents for a two-horse vehicle, 50 cents for a horse and rider, and 5 cents each for a herd of sheep, hogs, etc. Some of the more prominent toll roads were:

Mission Road

This 2.5-mile plank road across the sand dunes linked San Francisco and Mission Dolores. The toll house was at Third and Stevenson. Road built 1851. The parallel Folsom Road was built in 1853.

Ocean Road

Following the route of today's Corbett, Portola, and Ocean avenues, this 4.5-mile road wound over the central hills linking the Mission district to the Lake Merced district. Toll houses were at Market Street and Corbett Ave., and 42nd Ave. at Sloat Blvd. Road built ca. 1866.

Point Lobos Road

A three-mile macadamized road through the sand dunes along the present route of Geary Boulevard, this road linked San Francisco to the Cliff House and adjacent Ocean Beach. The toll house was at 6th Ave. and Geary Blvd. Road built 1864.

San Bruno Road

Following the later route of Bayshore Boulevard, this 1861 road skirted the Islais Creek marsh and various coves. The toll house was at Courtland Ave. and Bayshore Blvd.

Fulton Road

A three-mile macadamized road along the future route of Fulton Street, this 1861 road was the first to Ocean Beach. The toll house was at Broderick and Fulton streets.

MICHAEL D. LAMPEN

Street Signs

First street signs

Ordinance No. 468 issued on November 17, 1853, provided for the making and affixing of street signs at various intersections. After 1883 the street names were painted on the glass of the street lamps.

New Street Sign Tried Out Here

Samples of a new form of street sign, described as larger and more legible than those now in use, have been installed on Golden Gate Avenue at its intersections with Hyde, Leavenworth, and Larkin streets, the Department of Public Works announced today.

The new signs are in black letters 4 inches high on a white background 33 inches long and 7 inches wide, and contain, besides the name of the street, the number of the block beginning at the intersection, as an aid in finding addresses.

Present signs are in 3 inch white lettering on blue backgrounds 22 by 5 1/2 inches, and bear no block numbers.

CALL-BULLETIN
November 2, 1946

Streets

Total mileage
850 miles

Oldest
Grant Avenue. Formerly Calle de la Fundacion and later Dupont Street. Known as Dupont Gai to the Chinese community.

Longest
Mission Street, 7.29 miles long.

Widest
Sloat Blvd., 135 feet.

Narrowest
De Forest Way, four and a half feet, between Beaver and Flint above Castro.

Crookedest
Lombard Street, eight turns in one block from Hyde to Leavenworth. 259 stairs, south side; 250 stairs, north side. Vermont Street, five full turns and two half-turns from McKinley to 22nd Street.

Shortest
Charlestown Place, off north side of Harrison, east of 2nd Street, 141.69 feet.

First numbered
No. 1 Montgomery was the first house number known to have been used in San Francisco following Jasper O'Farrell's survey in 1845.

Smallest property
501 Corbett Ave.

Alleys
Public right-of-way with a width of 30 feet or less. Total number in San Francisco, 345.

First paved
Kearny between Clay and Washington was the first street paved, in 1854.

Names
Final approval of all names (except highways) comes from the Board of Supervisors. In practice, developers supply the names for the subdivisions with which they are concerned. When the city opens new streets, names are supplied by the Board of Public Works.

Widths
The streets of San Francisco are not of uniform width. Zoeth Eldredge in his history, *The Beginnings of San Francisco*, states: "In the Vioget survey of 1839 the streets were, as has been stated, very narrow. Vioget ran no east line for Montgomery street and consequently that street, being completed later, was the widest in the village and was made sixty-two and a half feet wide. Kearny street was made forty-five feet, five inches wide, and Dupont Street, forty-four feet, this irregularity being probably due to want of knowledge in regard to the lines and when buildings were erected the street lines were made, in a degree, to conform. Kearny street was afterwards widened to seventy-five feet between Market street and Broadway, and Dupont to seventy-four feet from Market street to Bush. Vioget laid out five streets running east and west, viz: Pacific, Jackson, Washington, Clay, and Sacramento. These streets were forty-nine feet, one and a half inches wide. The Vioget survey was extended some time before the American occupation to include Stockton and Powell streets on the west, Broadway and Vallejo on the north, and California, Pine, and Bush on the south. Stockton and Powell were made sixty-six feet nine inches wide, Broadway, eighty-two and a half feet, California, eighty-five feet, and the others sixty-eight

feet, nine inches, which became the regulation width for the Main streets of the Fifty vara and the Western addition surveys; the exceptions being, in addition to California street and Broadway, Van Ness avenue one hundred and twenty-five feet, and Divisadero street, eighty-two and a half feet wide. The five westerly streets of the Vioget survey extend with their narrow width to Larkin street, the limit of the Fifty vara survey, and from Larkin street they were widened to sixty-eight feet, nine inches, by taking from the lots on either side. Market street is one hundred and twenty feet wide, and the main streets of the Hundred vara survey are eighty-two and a half feet wide. In the Mission the main streets are eighty-two and a half feet, except Dolores, which is one hundred and twenty; Tenth, Eleventh, Twelfth, Thirteenth, and Sixteenth streets, which are eighty feet wide and the streets from Fourteenth to Twenty-sixth inclusive (excepting Sixteenth street) which are sixty-four feet wide."

Origin of Street Names

(All are known as "street," unless otherwise designated.)

ACEVEDO AVE.
Luis Joaquin Alvarez de Acevedo
ALEMANY BLVD.
Archbishop Joseph S. Alemany
ALVARADO
Juan B. Alvarado
ANNIE
Annie Russ
ANZA
Capt. Juan Bautista Anza
ARBALLO DR.
Señora Feliciana Arballo
ARELLANO AVE.
Manuel Ramirez Arellano
ARGUELLO BLVD.
Jose Dario Arguello
ARMSTRONG AVE.
Gen. Samuel Strong Armstrong

ARTHUR AVE.
Chester A. Arthur
ASHBURY
Munroe Ashbury
BAKER
Col. E. D. Baker
BALBOA
Vasco Nunez de Balboa
BANCROFT AVE.
George Bancroft
BARNARD AVE.
Major J. C. Barnard
BARTLETT
Lt. Washington A. Bartlett
BARTOL
Abraham Bartol
BATTERY
Named for early city fortification, originally called Fort Montgomery.
BEALE
Lt. Edward E. Beale, U.S.N.
BERNAL BLVD.
Juan Francisco Bernal
BERRY
Richard W. Berry
BLUXOME
Isaac Bluxome, Jr.
BRANNAN
Samuel Brannan
BRENHAM PLACE
Charles J. Brenham
BRET HARTE TERRACE
Bret Harte
BROADWAY
Named after a street in New York City.
BRODERICK
David Colbert Broderick
BROTHERHOOD WAY
A highway jointly owned by the Roman Catholic Archbishop of San Francisco, Congregation Judea, The Seventh Church of Christ of San Francisco, the Richmond Masonic Temple, and the Greek Orthodox Church.
BRYANT
Edwin Bryant

BUCARELI DR.
Lt. Gen. Baylio Fray Don Antonio Maria Bucareli y Ursua

BUCHANAN
John C. Buchanan

BURKE AVE.
General John Burke

BURNETT AVE.
Peter H. Burnett

BUSH
Dr. J. P. Bush

CABRILLO
Juan Rodriguez Cabrillo

CALIFORNIA
State of California

CAMBON DR.
Fray Pedro Cambon

CAMERON WAY
Donaldina Cameron

CARDENAS AVE.
Señora Juana Cardenas

CARROLL AVE.
Charles Carroll

CASTELO AVE.
Gertrudis Castelo

CASTRO
Joaquin Isidro de Castro

CHESLEY
George W. Chesley

CHUMASERO
Dr. Maria Angela Chumasero

CLARK
William S. Clark

CLAY
Henry Clay

CLAYTON
Charles Clayton

CLEARY COURT
Alfred J. Cleary

CLEMENT
Roswell P. Clement

CLEVELAND
Charles T. Cleveland

COLE
R. Beverly Cole

COLEMAN
William T. Coleman

COLIN P. KELLY ST.
WWII air hero

COLTON
C. O. Colton

COLUMBUS AVE.
Christopher Columbus

COLUSA PLACE
Indian tribe

CRESPI DR.
Fray Juan Crespi

CUSTER AVE.
Gen. George A. Custer

DAVIDSON AVE.
Prof. George Davidson

DAVIS
William Heath Davis

DE BOOM
Cornelius De Boom

DE HARO
Francisco De Haro

DIAZ AVE.
Fray Juan Diaz

DIVISADERO
Received its name on account of its position, the summit of a high hill. The name comes from the Spanish verb "divisar," to descry at a distance. Street name was changed from "Divisidero" to "Divisadero" in 1906.

DOLORES
Named for the Mission Dolores.

DONAHUE
Peter Donahue

DONNER AVE.
George and Jacob Donner

DOW PLACE
William H. Dow

DOYLE DR.
Frank Pierce Doyle

DRUMM
Lt. Richard C. Drumm

DUBOCE AVE.
Col. Victor D. Duboce

DUPONT
Capt. Samuel F. DuPont (now Grant Ave.)

EARL
John O. Earl

ECKER
George O. Ecker
EDDY
William M. Eddy
EGBERT
Col. Egbert
ELLIS
Alfred J. Ellis
EMBARCADERO
Spanish name for place of embarkation
ESSEX
U.S. Warship Essex
EVANS AVE.
Adm. Robley D. Evans
FAIR AVE.
James G. Fair
FAIRFAX AVE.
Thomas Fairfax
FALLON PLACE
Thomas Fallon
FANNING WAY
Charles Fanning
FEDERAL
Probably named for the U.S. Bonded
Warehouse established in its vicinity.
FELL
William Fell
FILLMORE
President Millard Fillmore
FITCH
George K. Fitch
FITZGERALD AVE.
Edward Fitzgerald
FLOOD AVE.
James C. Flood
FOLSOM
Capt. Joseph L. Folsom
FONT BLVD.
Fray Pedro Font
FRANKLIN
May have been named for pioneer merchant
Selim Franklin or Benjamin Franklin.
FREELON
Judge T. W. Freelon
FREMONT
Lt. Col. John C. Fremont

FUENTE AVE.
Pedro Perez de Fuente
FUNSTON AVE.
Brigadier-General Frederick Funston
GALINDO AVE.
Jose Galindo
GALVEZ AVE.
Jose de Galvez
GARCES DR.
Fray Francisco Garces
GEARY
John W. Geary
GERKE ALLEY
Henry Gerke
GILBERT
Lt. Edward Gilbert
GILMAN AVE.
Daniel C. Gilman
GOLDEN GATE AVE.
Golden Gate Park
GONZALEZ DR.
Joseph Manuel Gonzalez
GORDON
George C. Gordon
GOUGH
Charles H. Gough
GRANT AVE.
Gen. U. S. Grant
GREEN
Talbot H. Green
GREENWICH
A New York street
GRIFFITH
Millen Griffith
GRIJALVA DR.
Sgt. Juan Pablo Grijalva
GUERRERO
Francisco Guerrero
HAIGHT
Henry Haight
HALLECK
Capt. Henry W. Halleck, U.S.A.
HARE
Elias C. Hare
HARLAN PLACE
George C. Harlan

HARNEY WAY
Charles L. Harney
HARRISON
Edward H. Harrison
HAWES
Horace Hawes
HAYES
Col. Thomas Hayes
HEARST AVE.
Sen. George Hearst
HERMANN
Sigismund Hermann
HERON
James Heron
HIGUERA AVE.
Ygnasio Anastasio Higuera
HINCKLEY
William Sturgis Hinckley
HOLLAND COURT
Nathaniel Holland
HOLLISTER AVE.
Sgt. Stanley Hollister
HOTALING PLACE
Anson P. Hotaling
HOWARD
William Davis Howard
HUDSON AVE.
Henry Hudson
HUNT
Henry Brown Hunt
HUNTINGTON DR.
Collis P. Huntington
HYDE
George Hyde
INGALLS
Gen. Rufus Ingalls
INGERSON AVE.
Dr. H. H. Ingerson
INNES AVE.
George Innes
IRVING
Washington Irving
JACKSON PLACE
Andrew Jackson
JENNINGS
Thomas Jennings

JERROLD AVE.
Douglas W. Jerrold
JESSIE
Jessie Russ
JOHN MUIR DR.
John Muir
JONES
Dr. Elbert P. Jones
JOSEPHA AVE.
Señora Petronila Josepha
JUDAH
Theodore D. Judah
JUNIPERO SERRA BLVD.
Fray Junipero Serra
KEARNY
Stephen Watts Kearny
KEITH
William Keith
KEY AVE.
Francis Scott Key
KING
Thomas Starr King
KIRKHAM
Gen. Ralph W. Kirkham
KIRKWOOD AVE.
Samuel J. Kirkwood
KRAMER PLACE
Jacob Kramer
LAGUNA
Named for pond in area known as
Washerwoman's Lagoon
LANE
Dr. L. C. Lane
LAPHAM WAY
Mayor Roger Lapham
LA PLAYA
Spanish word for "beach"
LARKIN
Thomas O. Larkin
LA SALLE AVE.
Robert Cavalier, Sieur de la Salle
LAWTON
Gen. Henry W. Lawton
LEAVENWORTH
Thaddeus M. Leavenworth

LE CONTE AVE.
Prof. Joseph Le Conte

LEE AVE.
Lt. Curtis Lee

LEESE
Jacob Primer Leese

LEIDESDORFF
William A. Leidesdorff

LICK PLACE
James Lick

LINCOLN WAY
Abraham Lincoln

LOMBARD
A New York street

LYON
Nathaniel Lyon

MCALLISTER
Hall McAllister

MAIN
Charles Main

MARKET
Probably named after Market Street,
Philadelphia.

MASON
Col. Richard B. Mason

MCKINNON AVE.
Father William McKinnon

MCLAREN AVE.
John McLaren

MEADE AVE.
Gen. George C. Meade

MENDELL
George H. Mendell

MISSION
First street from the city to Mission Dolores

MONTGOMERY
John B. Montgomery

MORAGA
Lt. Jose Joaquin Moraga

MORRIS
George R. Morris

MOSS
J. Mora Moss

NATOMA
Indian tribe inhabiting banks of Sacramento
and Feather rivers.

NELSON
General William Nelson

NEWCOMB AVE.
Simon Newcomb

NEWHALL
Henry M. Newhall

NOE
Jose de Jesus Noe

NORIEGA
Jose de la Guerra y Noriega

OCTAVIA
Octavia Gough

O'FARRELL
Jasper O'Farrell

OPERA ALLEY
Adjoins old Opera House off Mission Street
near Third.

ORA WAY
Mrs. Elmer (Ora) Robinson

ORTEGA
Jose Francisco de Ortega

O'SHAUGHNESSY BLVD.
Michael M. O'Shaughnessy

OTIS
James Otis

PACHECO
Juan Salvio Pacheco

PAGE
Robert C. Page

PALOU AVE.
Fray Francisco Palou

PERALTA AVE.
Gabriel Peralta

PERRY
Dr. Alexander Perry

PETER YORKE WAY
Father Peter Yorke

PHELAN AVE.
James Phelan

PHELPS
Timothy Phelps

PICO AVE.
Pio Pico

PIERCE
President Franklin Pierce

PINE
Isaac B. Pine

PINTO AVE.
Pablo Pinto

PIOCHE
Francis Pioche

POLK
President James K. Polk

PORTOLA DR.
Gaspar de Portola

POST
Gabriel Post

POTRERO AVE.
Spanish word for "pastureland"

POWELL
Dr. William J. Powell

QUESADA AVE.
Gonzalo Ximinez de Quesada

QUINT
Leander Quint

QUINTARA
A Spanish family

RALSTON
William C. Ralston

RAUSCH
Joseph N. Rausch

REVERE AVE.
Paul Revere

RICHARDSON AVE.
William A. Richardson

RINGGOLD
Lt. Cadwalader Ringgold

RIVAS AVE.
Señora Gertrudis Rivas

RIVERA
Capt. Fernando Rivera y Moncada

ROBINSON
Elmer Robinson

ROSSI AVE.
Angelo J. Rossi

RUSS
Russ family

SACRAMENTO
Named after the city

SAMPSON
Adm. William T. Sampson

SANCHEZ
Jose Antonio Sanchez

SANDOVAL
Christoval Sandoval

SANSOME
A Philadelphia street

SANTIAGO
Spanish battle cry

SCOTT
Gen. Winfield Scott

SERRANO DR.
Dona Ana Regina Serrano

SHAFTER AVE.
Gen. William R. Shafter

SHARON
William Sharon

SHELLEY DR.
John F. Shelley

SHRADER
A. J. Shrader

SLOAT BLVD.
Commodore John D. Sloat

SPEAR
Nathan Spear

STANFORD
Leland Stanford

STANLEY
Lee Stanley

STANYAN
C. A. Stanyan

STEINER
L. Steiner

STEUART
William M. Steuart

STEVENSON
Col. Jonathan Drake Stevenson

STOCKTON
Commodore Robert F. Stockton

SUTRO HEIGHTS AVE.
Adolph Sutro

SUTTER
John A. Sutter

TAPIA DR.
Felipe Santiago Tapia

TARAVAL
Named for an Indian guide on the Anza expedition.

TAYLOR
President Zachary Taylor
THOMAS AVE.
Gen. George H. Thomas
TIFFANY AVE.
Robert J. Tiffany
TOLAND
Dr. H. H. Toland
TOVAR
Don Pedro de Tovar
TOWNSEND
Dr. John Townsend
TREAT AVE.
George Treat
TURK
Frank Turk
ULLOA
Francisco de Ulloa
UNDERWOOD AVE.
Gen. Franklin Underwood
UPTON
Mathew C. Upton
VALENCIA
Jose Manuel Valencia
VALLEJO
Gen. Mariano Guadalupe Vallejo
VAN DYKE AVE.
Walter Van Dyke
VAN NESS AVE.
James Van Ness
VARELA AVE.
Casimiro Varela
VICENTE
Spanish name
VIDAL DR.
Don Mariano Vidal
WALLACE AVE.
William T. Wallace
WALLER
R. H. Waller
WASHINGTON
Pres. George Washington
WAWONA
Indian name
WEBSTER
Daniel Webster

WELSH
Charles Welsh
WHIPPLE AVE.
Major Gen. Emile W. Whipple
YORBA
Antonio Yorba

Street Name Changes

Before 1909, San Francisco had three sets of numbered streets and two sets of streets designated by letters of the alphabet. Two sets of the numbered streets were called "avenues" and one had the suffix "south"; one set of lettered streets were treated similarly. To remedy this condition the mayor appointed a commission to recommend such changes as might be considered necessary. The Board of Supervisors in December 1909 adopted Ordinances Nos. 988, 989, and 1029 which changed the names of the following streets:

A

A St. to Anza St.
A St. South to Alvord St.
Ada Alley to Amity Alley
Adele Alley to Ade Alley
Aileen Ave. to Aileen St.
Albert Alley to Alert Alley
Albion Ave. to Albion St.
Alder Alley to Ames St.
Aldine Street to Golden Gate Ave.
Alemany St. to Abbey St.
Allen St. (that portion thereof from Union St. to angle north of Union St.) to Eastman St.
Alma Ave. to Alma St.
Alta Alley to Acme Alley
Amazon St. to Amazon Ave.
Andover Ave. to Andover St.
Ankeny Pl. to Anson Pl.
Anna Ln. to Glasgow St.
Arlington Ave. to Ashton Ave.
Army St. North to Andrew St.
Ash Ave. to Ash St.
Ashbury St. (that portion thereof extending from junction of Clayton St. to Corbett Ave.) to Clayton St.

Austin Ave. to Austin St.

B

B St. to Balboa St.

B St. South to Boalt St.

Bacon Pl. to Quincy St.

Bagley Pl. to Savings Union Pl.

Baker Ave. to Barton St.

Barry St. to Campbell Ave.

Bartlett Alley to Beckett St.

Bay View Pl. to Black Pl.

Belcher Ct. to Boynton Ct.

Bellevue Ave. to Burnham St.

Belmont Ave. (that portion thereof extending from junction of Willard St. to Woodland Ave.) to Willard St.

Benton St. (from Octavia St. to Laguna St., between Francisco and Bay sts.) to Bennett St.

Berkshire St. to Bosworth St.

Berry Pl. to Harlan Pl.

Bessie Ave. to Bessie St.

Beta St. to Rutland St.

Birch Ave. to Birch St.

Bird Ave. to Bird St.

Blanche Alley to Blanche St.

Bond Alley to Brant Alley

Bourbin Pl. to Bourbin St.

Dourbon St. to Bristol St.

Bowie Ave. to Kissling St.

Brannan Pl. to Butte Pl.

Broadway St. to Broadway

Browns Alley to Breen Pl.

Bruce Pl. to Brush Pl.

Bryant Ct. (off Bryant St., between Sterling St. and Rincon Pl.) to Bradley Ct.

Bryant Terrace to Brice Terrace

Buena Vista St. to Bonview St.

Burnside St. to Bishop St.

Burnett Pl. to Treasury Pl.

Butler Ave. to Butler St.

Byington Ave. to Byington St.

C

C St. to Cabrillo St.

C St. South to Coleman St.

Caledonia Alley to Caledonia St.

California Ave. to Coleridge St.

California St. South to Cornwall St.

Cannon or Condon St. (between York St. and Holladay Ave.) to Hampshire St.

Caroline Pl. to Carmine Pl.

Carson Ave. to Carson St.

Cedar Ave. to Cedar St.

Cedar St. to Ceylon St.

Central Ct. to Conway Ct.

Central Pl. to St. Anne St.

Charles Pl. to Charlestown Pl.

Church Alley to Cameron Alley

Church Ave. to Churchill St.

Church Ln. to Chula Ln.

Clara Ave. to Ord St.

Clara Ln. to Claude Ln.

Clarence Ct. to Canning Ct.

Clary St. to Clara St.

Clay Ave. to Collier St.

Cliff Ave. to Point Lobos Ave.

Clinton Ave. south of Glen Ave. to Chilton Ave.

Clinton Ave. between Surrey St. and Glen Ave. to Lippard Ave.

Clover Alley to Clover St.

College St. to Colby St.

Colton Ct. to Chase Ct.

Colton Pl. to Colusa Pl.

Concord Ave. to Concord St.

Corbet Pl. to Corbin Pl.

Cotta St. to Lamartine St.

Cottage Pl. to Colin Pl.

Cumberland Pl. to Cunningham Pl.

Cypress Alley to Cypress St.

D

D St. South to Donahue St.

Dearborn Pl. to Dearborn St.

Delaware Ave. to Delano Ave.

De Long Ave. to Delmar St.

Devisadero St. to Divisadero St.

Diamond Alley to Dixie Alley

Division St. (that portion thereof from Florida St. to Eighteenth St.) to Treat Ave., its continuation

Dore Alley to Doric Alley

E

E St. South to Earl St.

Eagle St. (that portion thereof extending from Douglass St. to point 206 feet westerly) to Nineteenth St.

Eagle St. (that portion thereof extending from easterly junction of Short and Eagle sts. northeasterly) to Yukon St.

East Ave. to Highland Ave.

East Arbor St. to Orchard St.

East Lake Ave. to Winnipeg Ave.

East Park St. to Park St.

East St. North and East St. South to the Embarcadero

Eddy St. West to Edward St.

Edgar Pl. to Edgardo Pl.

Eighteenth Ave. South to Revere Ave.

Eighteenth St. (that portion thereof extending from point east of Lower Terr. to Clayton St.) to Deming St.

Eighteenth St. (that portion thereof extending from point east of Stanyan St. to Stanyan St.) to Estee St.

Eighth Ave. South to Hudson Ave.

Eleventh Ave. South to Kirkwood Ave.

Elizabeth Pl. to Eliza Pl.

Ellery St. to Rincon St.

Elliot Park to Endicott Park

Elliot Ln. to Elton Ln.

Elm Ave. to Elm St.

Esmond St. to Concord St.

Eugenie St. to Emerson St.

Eureka Alley to Drummond Alley

Ewing Pl. to Hemlock St.

F

F St. South to Fitch St.

Falcon Pl. to Fallon Pl.

Farren Ave. to Farren St.

Farrollones St. to Farallones St.

Fay St. to Sawyer St.

Fern Ave. to Fern St.

Fifth Ave. South to Evans Ave.

Fifteenth Ave. South to Oakdale Ave.

Filbert Pl. to Genoa Pl.

Fillmore Pl. to Calumet Pl.

First Ave. to Arguello Blvd.

First Ave. South to Arthur Ave.

Fitch Alley to Fenton Alley

Flint Alley to Cowell Pl.

Florence Ave. to Florentine St.

Folsom Pl. to Richardson Pl.

Folsom Ave. to Rodgers St.

Fortieth Ave. South to Pulaski Ave.

Forty-first Ave. South to Quebec Ave.

Forty-second Ave. South to Richter Ave.

Forty-third Ave. South to Sampson Ave.

Forty-fourth Ave. South to Tovar Ave.

Forty-fifth Ave. South to Ugarte Ave.

Forty-ninth Ave. to La Playa

Fourteenth Ave. South to Newcomb Ave.

Fourth Ave. South to Davidson Ave.

Franconia Ave. to Franconia St.

Fremont Alley to Frisbie Alley

Fremont Ct. to Freeman Ct.

Front Ave. to Contra Costa Ave.

Fulton Ave. to Brompton Ave.

G

G St. South to Griffith St.

Garden Ave. to Garden St.

Garfield Ave. to Lucky St.

Gavin Pl. to Grover Pl.

Geneva St. to Lucerne St.

Germania Ave. to Germania St.

Glen Ave. (from Diamond and Chenery sts. to Elk St.) to Chenery St.

Gold Alley to Golding Alley

Good Children St. to Child St.

Grand St. to Grace St.

Grant Pl. to Grote Pl.

Grant St. to Buell St.

Green Pl. to Windsor Pl.

Groveland Ave. to Groveland St.

H

H St. to Lincoln Way

H St. South to Hawes St.

Hamilton Ave. to Hamerton Ave.

Hamlin St. (from Mansell St. to Arieta Ave.) to Cambridge St.

Hanna St. to Hanover St.

Hardy St. to Harlow St.

Harkness Ave. to Harkness St.

Harrison Ave. to Hallam St.

Harry Pl. to Harris Pl.

Heath St. to Holladay Ave.

Hermann St. (that portion thereof extending from West Mission St. to Market St.)

to McCoppin St.
Hickory Ave. to Hickory St.
Hodge Ave. (from Greenwich Street to
Lombard Street, between Steiner and
Pierce sts.) to Holden St.
Hoff Ave. to Hoff St.
Hoffman St. to Homans St.
Holly Park Ave. to Holly Park Circle
Holly St. to Leese St.
Horace Alley to Horace St.
Howard Ct. to Holland Ct.

I

I St. to Irving St.
I St. South to Ingalls St.
India Ave. to Peru Ave.
Ivy Ave. to Ivy St.

J

J St. to Judah St.
J St. South to Jennings St.
Jackson Alley to James Alley
Jackson Ct. to Jason Ct.
Japan St. to Colin P. Kelly St.
Jefferson Ave. to Jarboe Ave.
Jones Alley to Jessop Pl.

K

K St. to Kirkham St.
K St. South to Keith St.

L

L St. to Lawton St.
L St. South to Lane St.
Lafayette Pl. to Varennes St.
Laura Pl. to Petrarch Pl.
Laurel Ave. to Larch St.
Laurel Pl. to Lansing St.
Laussat Ave. to Laussat St.
Lee St. to Hilton St.
Lewis Pl. to Cosmo Pl.
Lexington Ave. to Lexington St.
Lick Alley to Elim Alley
Lilac Alley to Lilac St.
Lily Ave. to Lily St.
Linadil Ave. to Niagara Ave.
Lincoln Ave. to Burnett Ave.
Lincoln Pl. to Hastings Pl.
Lincoln St. to Macondray St.
Linden Ave. to Linden St.
Locust Ave. to Redwood St.

Lombard Alley to Tuscany Alley
Lyon Terr. to Leona Terr.

M

M St. to Moraga St.
M St. South to Mendell St.
Madison Ave. to Merlin St.
Magnolia Ave. to Magnolia St.
Maple Ct. to Rosemont Pl.
Margaret Pl. to Margrave Pl.
Mariposa Terrace to Berwick Pl.
Market St. (that portion thereof extending
from point 796 feet east of Thirty-ninth
Ave., now forming a portion of Sloat
Blvd.) to Sloat Blvd.
Marshall St. to Maynard St.
Mary Ln. to Mark Ln.
Medwey Alley to Severn St.
Merced Ave. (Hillcrest Tract) to San
Mateo Ave.
Mersey Alley to Mersey St.
Michigan Pl. to Chatterton Pl.
Midway St. (South from Stillings Ave.) to
Nordhoff St.
Miles Pl. to Miller Pl.
Milliken St. to San Bruno Ave.
Milton Ave. to Marston Ave.
Mint Ave. to Mint St.
Montgomery Ave. to Columbus Ave.
Montgomery Ct. to Verdi Pl.
Morris Ave. to Morris St.
Morse Pl. to Cyrus Pl.
Moss Alley to Mono St.
Moulton Ave. to Moulton St.
Moulton Pl. to Montague Pl.
Myrtle Ave. to Myrtle St.

N

N St. to Noriega St.
N St. South to Newhall St.
Nebraska Ave. to Nebraska St.
Nevada Ave. to Nevada St.
New Anthony St. to Anthony St.
New Grove Ave. to Newburg St.
Nineteenth Ave. South to Shafter Ave.
Ninth Ave. South to Innes Ave.
Nome Ave. to Danvers St.
Norma St. to Altamont St.
North Ave. to Bocana St.

Norton Pl. to Darrell Pl.

O

O St. to Ortega St.
Oak Grove Ave. to Oak Grove St.
Ocean Terr. to Sunset Terr.
Ohio Pl. to Osgood Pl.
Old Hickory St. to Ogden Ave.
Olive Ave. to Olive St.
Olive Ct. to Charlton Ct.
Orient Alley to Orient St.

P

P St. to Pacheco St.
P St. South to Phelps St.
Pacific Alley to Pelton Pl.
Palmer St. (that portion thereof between Harper and Randall Sts.) to Randall St.
Palmer St. (that portion thereof extending from Randall St. to Chenery St.) to Whitney St.
Park Ct. to Prior Ct.
Park Ln. North to Taber Pl.
Park Ln. South to Varney Pl.
Park Way to Payson St.
Parker Alley to Parkhurst Alley
Parkside Ave. to Parsons St.
Paul St. to Saul St.
Pearl Alley to Morgan Alley
Perry Ave. to Reynolds St.
Ploche Alley to Pagoda Pl.
Pixley Ave. to Pixley St.
Point Lobos Ave. to Geary St.
Poplar Alley to Poplar St.
Porter Ave. to Ellington Ave.
Powell Ave. to Powers Ave.
Powhattan St. to Powhattan Ave.
Presidio St. to Miley St.
Prospect Pl. to Joice St.

Q

Q St. to Quintara St.
Q St. South to Quint St.
Quince Alley to Quane St.

R

R St. to Rivera St.
R St. South to Rankin St.
Railway Ave. to Railway St.
Randall Pl. to Southard Pl.
Reed Pl. to Reno Pl.

Riley St. to Pleasant St.
Rincon Ct. to Elkhart St.
Rincon Pl. to Rincon St.
Rivoli Ave. to Rivoli St.
Rose Ave. to Rose St.
Rose Alley to Aldrich Alley
Rose Lyon Ave. to Primrose St.
Rutledge Ave. to Rutledge St.

S

S St. to Santiago St.
S St. South to Selby St.
Salina Pl. to Sabin Pl.
San Carlos Ave. (from Sycamore Ave. to Twenty-first St.) to San Carlos St.
San Carlos Ave. (Hillcrest Tract) to Santa Cruz Ave.
Scott Ave. to Scotia Ave.
Scott Pl. to Wayne Pl.
Second Ave. South to Burke St.
Serpentine Pl. (that portion thereof extending southwesterly from the easterly end of Lower Terr. to Saturn St.) to Lower Terr.
Serpentine Pl. (that portion thereof extending westerly from Saturn St. to Lower Terr.) to Saturn St.
Serpentine Rd. to Locksley Ave.
Seventeenth Ave. South to Quesada Ave.
Seventh Ave. South to Galvez Ave.
Seymour Ave. to Seymour St.
Sherman Ave. to Lawrence Ave.
Short Alley to Yukon St.
Short St. (that portion thereof extending south from junction of Eagle and Short sts. to Short Alley) to Yukon St.
Silver Alley to Argent Alley
Silver St. to Stillman St.
Sixteenth St. (from point east of Juno St. to Ashbury St.) to Clifford St.
Sixteenth Ave. South to Palou Ave.
Sixth Ave. South to Fairfax Ave.
South Ave. to Murray St.
South St. to Daggett St.
South Broderick St. to Buena Vista Terr.
Spreckels Ave. to Staples Ave.
St. Charles Pl. to Nottingham Pl.
St. Mary's Pl. to St. Anne St.

Stable Alley to Sparrow St.
Stanton St. (that portion thereof extend-
ing west and northwest from Douglass
St.) to Corwin St.
Stanley Ct. to Stetson Ct.
Stanley Pl. to Sterling St.
Stanyan Ave. to Kenyon Ave.
Stockton Pl. to Campton Pl.
Stout's Alley to Ross Alley
Surman St. to Severance St.
Sutter Pl. to Belknap Pl.
Sycamore Ave. to Sycamore St.

T

T St. to Taraval St.
T St. South to Toland St.
Tacoma Ave. to Tacoma St.
Taylor Terr. to Aladdin Terr.
Tehama Pl. to Tenny Pl.
Telegraph Pl. (that portion thereof from
Greenwich St. to angle north of
Greenwich St.) to Child St.
Tenth Ave. South to Jerrold Ave.
Thirteenth Ave. South to McKinnon Ave.
Third Ave. South to Custer Ave.
Thirtieth Ave. South to Fitzgerald Ave.
Thirty-first Ave. South to Gilman Ave.
Thirty-second Ave. South to Hollister Ave.
Thirty-third Ave. South to Ingerson Ave.
Thirty-fourth Ave. South to Jamestown Ave.
Thirty-fifth Ave. South to Key Ave.
Thirty-sixth Ave. South to Le Conte Ave.
Thirty-seventh Ave. South to Meade Ave.
Thirty-eighth Ave. South to Nelson Ave.
Thirty-ninth Ave. South to Olney Ave.
Thornton St. to Beverly St.
Tiffany Pl. to Everett Pl.
Tilden St. (from Castro St. to Fifteenth
St.) to Beaver St.
Tilden St. (from Fifteenth St. to Park Hill
Ave.) to Fifteenth St.
Treat Ave. (between Thirteenth Street and
Fourteenth Street) to Trainor St.
Tremont Ave. to Downey St.
Trent Alley to Mersey St.
Tustin Ave. (that portion thereof from end
of Congo St. to first angle north of
Stillings Ave.) to Congo St.

Twelfth Ave. South to LaSalle Ave.
Twentieth St. (from Burnett Ave. to point
west of Stanyan St.) to Palo Alto Ave.
Twentieth Ave. South to Thomas Ave.
Twenty-first Ave. South to Underwood Ave.
Twenty-second Ave. South to Van Dyke Ave.
Twenty-third Ave. South to Wallace Ave.
Twenty-fifth Ave. South to Armstrong Ave.
Twenty-sixth Ave. South to Bancroft Ave.
Twenty-seventh Ave. South to Carroll Ave.
Twenty-eighth Ave. South to Donner Ave.
Twenty-ninth Ave. South to Egbert Ave.

U

U St. to Ulloa St.
U St. South to Upton St.
Unadilla Ave. to Niagara Ave.
Union Ave. to Tompkins Ave.
Union Pl. to Jasper Pl.
Union Square Ave. to Manila St.
Uranus St. to Lower Terr.

V

V St. to Vicente St.
Vallejo Alley to Tracy Pl.
Vernon Pl. to Warner Pl.
View Ave. to Grand View Ave.
View Rd. (from intersection of Grand
View Ave. and Acme St. north to Stanton
St.) to Blair St.
Vincent St. to Garibaldi St.
Virginia Ct. to Vinton Ct.
Virginia Pl. to Cordelia St.
Virginia St. to Oklahoma St.
Vulcan Ln. to Emery Ln.

W

W St. to Wawona St.
Wall Pl. to Coolidge Pl.
Walnut Ave. to Hemlock St.
Washington Ave. to Washburn St.
Washington Pl. to Wentworth St.
Webb St. to Spring St.
Webster Pl. to Bromley Pl.
West Ave. to Appleton Ave.
West Clay St. to Drake St.
West Diamond Street to Berkeley St.
West El Dorado St. to Barstow St.
West End Alley to Eastman St.
West Lake Ave. to Otsego Ave.

West Mission St. to Otis St.
West Park St. to Park St.
White Pl. to Victor St.
Wieland Ave. to Judson Ave.
Wilde Ave. to Wilde St.
Wildey Ave. to Wilmot St.
William St. to Shannon St.
Willow Ave. to Willow St.
Winfield Ave. to Winfield St.
Winslow St. to Franconia St.
Worden Ave. to Whipple Ave.
Woodwards Ave. to Woodwards St.

Wyoming Ave. to Winnipeg Ave.
X
  X St. to Yorba St.
Y
  Yerba Buena St. to Cushman St.
Z
  Zoe Pl. to Zeno Pl.

STEEPEST STREETS

HILL	GRADE
1 FILBERT BETWEEN LEAVENWORTH AND HYDE	31.5 %
2 22ND STREET BETWEEN CHURCH AND VICKSBURG	31.5 %
3 JONES BETWEEN UNION AND FILBERT	29 %
4 DUBOCE BETWEEN BUENA VISTA AND ALPINE	27.9 %
5 JONES BETWEEN GREEN AND UNION	26 %
6 WEBSTER BETWEEN VALLEJO AND BROADWAY	26 %
7 DUBOCE BETWEEN ALPINE AND DIVISADERO	25 %
8 JONES BETWEEN PINE AND CALIFORNIA	24.8 %
9 FILLMORE BETWEEN VALLEJO AND BROADWAY	24 %

SOURCE: PUBLIC WORKS DEPT. BUREAU OF ENGINEERING

Right: Lombard Street, "The Crookedest Street in the World." The constant flow of traffic drives residents nearly frantic, and they often call for the street to be closed to cars. A study was commissioned to determine if the street should be closed. The proposal was rejected.

43 Transportation

Bay Area Rapid Transit

BART's function is to move people rapidly from place to place. This is done by a 75-mile rail complex which follows the region's natural transportation corridors along existing highway and railroad rights-of-way and through an underwater tube. There are 34 stations on the line, 17 in Alameda County, 8 in San Francisco, 8 in Contra Costa County, and 1 in Daly City, San Mateo County. Three transfer points are available, all in Oakland.

BART was financed by a $792-million bond issue approved by the voters on November 6, 1962, and $180 million in Bay Bridge tolls to pay for the Transbay Tube. Additional money has been granted by the U.S. Department of Housing and Urban Development (HUD).

BART was first governed by a 12-member board of directors appointed by the County Board of Supervisors and City Mayors. Today nine directors are elected by the voters.

Tracks

Track: welded rail 1,517 ft. in length

Track gauge: wide gauge 5 ft. 6 in.

Ties: prestressed concrete weighing 525 pounds each

Power: electric third rail carrying 1,000 volts D.C.

Cost: approximately $32 million

Designers: Parsons Brinckerhoff-Tudor-Bechtel

First track laid: February 19, 1965 (Contra Costa County)

Transbay Tube

Length: Largest underwater rapid transit tube in the world. 3.6 miles in tube (19,113 feet); 6 miles overall including approaches.

Construction: 57 binocular-shaped sections of tubular steel and reinforced concrete, each about 350 feet long by 48 feet wide by 24 feet high. Constructed by Bethlehem Steel Company.

Above left: The Modern Ferry building constructed on the site of its predecessor in 1896. Goat Island—now Yerba Buena—is in the background. Lower left: Motormen and conductors pose alongside a funeral car run by the Market St. Railway. The coffin was carried in the lead streetcar and the mourners followed in a long streetcar procession out to Colma.

Depth: Deepest point is 130 feet below the Bay surface.

Starting date: First scoopful of mud raised from Bay for tube construction April 15, 1966.

Completion date: Last tube connected April 3, 1969.

Contractors: Transbay Contractors (4 contracting firms)

Cost: $89.9 million

Openings: Public walk in tube Nov. 9, 1969 with some 20,000 participating. First train through tube June 9, 1972 taking 1 hour, 15 minutes. First three-car train with more than 50 BART officials, news reporters, and technicians aboard traveled between the Seventh Street Station in Oakland and the Montgomery Street Station in San Francisco in six minutes, 55 seconds. Opening day through tube Monday, Sept. 16, 1974.

Cars
Length: 72 feet
Width: 10 1/2 feet
Height: 10 1/2 feet
Ceiling Height: 6 feet 9 inches
Weight: 56,000 pounds
Seating capacity: 72 people
Average Speed: 80 mph
Cost of 250 cars: $66.7 million
Manufacturer: Rohr Corporation, Chula Vista, California

Cable Cars

Andrew Smith Hallidie developed his system of cable roads now in use in this city in 1873. The first trial run of his dummy* was down the Clay Street hill between Jones and Kearny, a distance of 2,880 feet on August 2, 1873, at 4 a.m. Later the same day, the dummy with a car attached made another round trip, this time with a large crowd in attendance. There were many changes and alterations made to the system before complete success crowned Mr.

CABLE CAR SPECIFICATIONS

	SINGLE-END CARS	DOUBLE-END CARS
Weight	12,180 pounds	11,500 pounds
Seating capacity	30	34
Length over bumpers	27 feet	30 feet 5 inches
Length over closed section	12 feet	10 feet 7 inches
Length over open section	15 feet	9 feet
Width over steps	7 feet 10 inches	8 feet
Truck centers	11 feet 8 inches	19 feet
Height	10 feet 3 inches	10 feet 3 inches
Size and type of wheel	22 inches, cast steel	
Track gauge:	3 feet 6 inches	
Cable speed:	840 feet per minute or 9 mph	

Hallidie's endeavors and public recognition was forthcoming.

In 1881 at the San Francisco Industrial Exhibition the Honorable W. W. Morrow stated, ". . . what a revolution it [the cable car] has made in the mode of transporting passengers in this city! The hills have fallen down before it, and they are now even more accessible, and certainly more desirable for residence than the level portions of the city."

The cable cars were made a National Historic Landmark on October 1, 1964.

*Dummy: a small locomotive having condensing engines, consequently having no noise of escaping steam. The name was promptly given to the first "platform" or operator's car of the Clay Street cable road, 1873, because it too was noiseless—though not, of course, a locomotive.

Steepest grades
59 Powell-Mason Line, Powell between Bush and Pine: 17.5%
60 Powell-Hyde Line, Hyde between Bay and Francisco: 21.3%
61 California Line between Grant and Stockton: 18.2%

Cable Turntables
(Single-end cars require a turntable at each end)
1. Powell-Market
2. Bay-Taylor
3. Beach-Hyde
4. Washington-Mason carhouse

San Francisco International Airport

Early sites proposed for San Francisco's Airport were located at Millbrae, South San Francisco, Beresford, Lomita Park, San Mateo Point, San Bruno, Bay Farm Island, the Marina, and Redwood City. The site approved by the Board of Supervisors through Ordinance No. 7428 was the 150 acres owned by the Mills Estate, located in San Mateo County above the Bay tidelands. The adjoining 1,000 acres of submerged land that could be later reclaimed were an important factor in deciding the airport's location.

The new San Francisco Municipal Airport (called Mills Field) was dedicated May 7, 1927, and operation began June 7 of that year.

The March 15, 1929 supplement to the third edition of *Airplane Landing Fields of the Pacific West* describes the San Francisco Airport as: "Three Runways - (1) 5700' x 200', (2) 1800' x 200', (3) Emergency runway across highway 1200' x 250'. Surface on all runways excellent. Completely equipped administration building and hospital. Restaurant. Mechanical service. Weather Bureau representative located here for survey of meteorological and aerological conditions on San Francisco peninsula. Gasoline and oil supplied by Standard Oil Company at airport."

In 1930 the city began a 10-year purchase program of the then-existing 1,112 acres of airport land. By June 9, 1937 the name of the airport had been officially changed from Mills Field to San Francisco Airport.

Today's airport comprises approximately 2,400 acres with control of 2,800 acres of Bay tidelands. Since 1970 the airport has been controlled by a five-member Airports Commission. Previously the Public Utilities Commission had been responsible for its development, given this duty by the 1932 charter.

A new Master Plan initiated after voter approval of a $98-million airport development bond issue in November 1967 has allowed for terminal, runway, and garage expansion.

Street Railroads
In 1860 the Market Street Railroad Company was formed and consisted of five

cable lines: Valencia, Castro, Haight, Hayes, McAllister—and one horse line—5th Street, Market to Townsend.

In the consolidation of 1893 the following companies were taken over: Omnibus Railroad Company, North Beach and Mission Company, Central Railroad Company, and the Ferries and Cliff House Company.

The first electric line in San Francisco was the San Francisco and San Mateo Railroad Company, built by Behrend Joost in 1891. It ran from Steuart and Market streets to the county line, via Steuart, Harrison, Fourteenth, Guerrero, and San Jose Avenue. It was purchased by the "Baltimore Syndicate" in 1896 and later formed the nucleus for the United Railroads, which on March 18, 1902, began operating all lines in the city, with the exceptions of the Presidio & Ferries line, California Street cable line, and the Geary Street line.

The City Charter adopted in 1900 declared ultimate municipal ownership for all public utilities, but it was not until December 1909 that a $2,000,000 bond issue was passed.

The Municipal Street Railway was inaugurated December 28, 1912. Mayor Rolph spoke to the crowd, saying: "It is in reality 'the people's road,' built by the people and with the people's money. The first cable road in the country was built in San Francisco, and now the first municipal railway of the country is built in San Francisco. Our operation of this road will be closely watched by the whole country. It must prove a success. We must run it by proper methods. When we have it built from the Ferry to the Ocean, it will be the best single route in the city, and we must extend it wherever possible, until it becomes a great municipal system."

The merger of the Market Street Railway Company with the Municipal Railway occurred on September 29, 1944.

Transportation Definitions

Heavy Rail Heavy rail, also called rail rapid transit or metro, carries city passengers in trains over an exclusive right-of-way, such as a subway, and elevated line, or a grade-separated right-of-way near ground level. Heavy-rail systems have differing degrees of automatic train controls, and they use high-level station platforms, which allow passengers to enter or leave the trains without having to use steps, shortening train waiting times and speeding service. BART, the New York City subway, and the Paris Metro are examples of this kind of operation. Muni Metro, although it uses high-level station platforms and some automatic controls in its subway and tunnel operations, is essentially a light-rail system, not a metro system.

Horsecars Horsecars in the U.S. were generally of two types: a 2-horse car carrying 20 passengers with a conductor and driver, and a smaller 1-horse car carrying 14 passengers and a driver.

Light Rail "Light rail" is a term first used in the 1970s, in part to sell the system as something more than a reintroduction of "Toonerville Trolley" service. It provides a medium-capacity service, between a bus line's lower capacity to carry passengers per hour and the higher capacity (and higher construction costs) of heavy rail. Light rail can be more flexible in its operations than heavy rail, with trains or single cars operating over a variety of rights-of-way including grade-separated, mid-street median or shared with street traffic. Operations are mostly manually controlled, and modern cars have movable steps, allowing passengers to use either high-level station platforms, low-level platforms (such as islands in the middle of the street), or the street surface. While heavy rail must use high-level station platforms, light rail can maintain efficient service wih different types of passenger stops, and with more frequent ones.

For some, the term "light rail" is used only for operations on reserved rights-of-way, while "streetcar" is used for operations shared with street traffic. For others, light rail had its beginnings either with the introduction of the PCC cars in 1936, or going even further back, with the first horsecar service in New York City in 1832.

Omnibus The omnibus was an enlarged version of a stagecoach, seating about 18, and hauled by 2- or 4-horse teams. An omnibus ride could be a rough one, on the often poorly paved or unpaved streets of their era of operation.

Horsedrawn streetcar on Market Street before the Great Earthquake and Fire. The earthquake and fire swept away this form of transportation which was replaced by an electrified, overhead system to propel new streetcars. The California Masonic Temple is in the background at the intersection of Post, Market, and Montgomery. A Wells Fargo Bank occupies the site today.

44 Vital Statistics

San Francisco's Antipode

The farthest point on Earth from San Francisco (a point located at 37°45' S Latitude, 56°34' E Longitude) is in the southern Indian Ocean approximately 2,120 miles east of Capetown, South Africa, and 1,160 miles south of Reunion Island. The ocean depth at this point is approximately 15,100 feet. The sea floor here is moving SSW at about 1/2 inch per year due to sea-floor spreading. The ocean floor at the antipodal point comprises the southeastern foothills of the Southwest Indian Ocean Ridge (source of the sea-floor spreading) in the Crozet Basin. The closest land to the antipodal point is Île de l'Est, easternmost of the sub-Antarctic Crozet Islands, approximately 600 miles SSW of the point.

MICHAEL D. LAMPEN

Land and Water Areas of San Francisco

Because of changes brought about in recent years by tideland reclamation, we have computed the land and water areas within the City and County of San Francisco as they existed on February 1, 1960.

The areas were planimetered from, and in some cases computed from dimensions scaled from, the 1956 edition of the United States Geological Survey Map of the area, excluding piers, supplemented by Bureau of Engineering Plans SSP 8006, 8007, and 8008, all three of which are dated February 1960, and entitled "Shoreline Outlets Survey." The latter plans, which are on file in the office of the City Engineer, delineate the shoreline of reclaimed tidelands in the Hunters Point-Candlestick Park vicinity, the additional areas of which were added to the mainland areas computed from the U.S.G.S. map.

It should be noted that the figure shown as the area of the "Bay Waters" is exclusive of the island land areas therein, and that the area for Treasure Island does not include the area of its connection to Yerba Buena Island. This connection is included in the Yerba Buena Island area. For the purpose of these computations and in the absence of knowledge to the contrary, the south boundary of Treasure Island is assumed to continue to a right angle intersection with its west boundary.

First seal of San Francisco, adopted in 1852.

The computed areas are as follows:

Mainland (U.S.G.S. Map, 1956 Edition): 45.185 square miles
Reclaimed Tidelands: 0.266 square miles
Treasure Island: 0.635 square miles
Yerba Buena Island: 0.242 square miles
Alcatraz Island: 0.034 square miles
Angel Island (Portion): 0.014 square miles
Red Rock Island (Portion): 0.004 square miles
Bay Waters (Less Island Areas): 54.460 square miles
Ocean Waters: 28.407 square miles
Total Mainland Areas: 45.451 square miles
Total Island Areas: 0.929 square miles
Total Water Areas: 82.867 square miles
GRAND TOTAL: 129.247 square miles

REUBEN H. OWENS
Director of Public Works
Department of Public Works,
December 15, 1960

Latitude and Longitude

San Francisco is located at the same latitude as several natural and historic sites. American locations at the same latitude include scenic Yosemite Valley, California; Great Sand Dunes National Monument in Colorado; famed Dodge City and Wichita, Kansas; the "St. Francois" Mts. in Missouri; and the southern boundary of Fort Knox in Kentucky. Sao Miguel, largest of the Azore Islands, in the Atlantic Ocean, is at the same latitude.

European sites at San Francisco's latitude include historic Jaen in southern Spain; Marsalla (of sweet wine fame); Mount Etna (tallest Mediterranean volcano) in Sicily, Italy; as well as ancient Mycenae and Samos Island (home of Pythagoras) in Greece. Olympia, site of the Original Olympic Games is only six miles south of San Francisco's (south city border) latitude. Denizli, Burdur, and Isparta (known for its attar of roses) are three of several Turkish towns at San Francisco's latitude. Further east are Lake Urmia in Iran, and the southern part of the Caspian Sea.

In western China, the latitude three times crosses the fabled Silk Road travelled by Marco Polo. The latitude then crosses western (rammed earth) sections of the Great Wall four times before crossing the great Yellow River three times.

Uijongbu, ten miles north of Seoul, South Korea, lies on San Francisco's latitude, and Niigate, Japan is eight miles south. The town of Soma, Japan, faces San Francisco across the Pacific Ocean at the same latitude.

San Francisco's longitude is shared by Seattle and Bellingham, Washington, and the western arms of Great Bear Lake, Canada. If projected around to the other side of the globe, the equivalent longitude passes through the southern Ural Mountains of Russia, and the island of Mauritius in the Indian Ocean.

MICHAEL D. LAMPEN

45 Vital Statistics, Population

San Francisco's Ethnic Neighborhoods

San Francisco has always been a city of ethnic and racial diversity, a fact that has certainly contributed much to the city's unique variety and charm. Many ethnic groups settled in particular neighborhoods as the city grew after the Gold Rush. Shifting population patterns have brought many changes; some neighborhoods have changed ethnic makeup two or three times as old groups moved or dispersed, and new groups arrived.

The Irish community settled in North Beach and the South-of-Market areas before moving into the Mission District after the Great Earthquake and Fire, and into the Richmond District in the 1920s. Italians settled in North Beach and the Telegraph Hill area in the 1880s, then spread into the Excelsior and Marina districts after 1906. The Chinese community, originally confined to Chinatown, spread across Nob Hill after 1940, and then to North Beach and the Richmond District in the 1970s. The Chinese population continues to grow in the Sunset and other outer districts. Hunters Point, south Potrero Hill and the Western Addition became African-American neighborhoods during the 1940s and soon after moved into the Ingleside–Merced Heights districts. A still-growing Hispanic community, largely from Central America, settled in the Mission District after 1940, and a small Mexican district in North Beach disappeared.

Germans settled northwest and north of the Civic Center in the 1870s, Dutch workers lived north of Potrero Hill during the same decade. Japanese settled at South Park after the Great Earthquake and Fire, then in what became known as Japantown on the south slope of eastern Pacific Heights. Many returned there after release from relocation camps during World War II.

Jews settled in the Western Addition after 1906 and later moved to the Richmond District.

Filipinos lived on the northeast edge of Chinatown in the area of Kearny Street before moving to Japantown after the Japanese were forcibly evacuated by the U.S. Government. They also moved to the South-of-Market area.

The Russian community was centered in the Western Addition and on Potrero Hill in the 1920s, and later moved to the Richmond District. Greeks lived in the South-of-Market District around 5th and Folsom streets in the 1920s, and there was a thriving Greek business community in the

POPULATION OF SAN FRANCISCO BY ETHNIC GROUPS

ETHNIC GROUP	1990	1980	1970	1960	1950
TOTAL	723,959	667,700	715,674	740,316	775,357
WHITE	337,118	450,000	511,186	604,403	693,888
NONWHITE	217,700	204,488	135,193	81,469	
AFRICAN AMERICAN	76,343	99,000	96,078	74,383	43,502
CHINESE	205,686*	63,200	58,696	36,445	24,813
FILIPINO	29,100*	24,694	12,327	INC. IN OTHER	
JAPANESE	10,800*	11,705	9,464	5,579	
AMERICAN INDIAN	2,635	3,200	2,900	1,068	331
OTHER NONWHITE	1,460	12,400	10,415	2,226	7,244
HISPANIC ORIGIN	100,717				

PERCENT DISTRIBUTION

	1990	1980	1970	1960	1950
TOTAL	100.0	100.0	100.0	100.0	100.0
WHITE	46.6	67.4	71.4	81.6	89.5
NONWHITE	32.6	28.6	18.4	10.5	
AFRICAN AMERICAN	10.5	14.8	13.4	10.1	5.6
CHINESE	28.4 *	9.5	8.2	4.9	3.2
FILIPINO	4.4 *	3.5	1.7		
JAPANESE	1.6*	1.6	1.3	0.7	
AMERICAN INDIAN	0.4	2.5	0.4	0.1	
OTHER NONWHITE	0.2	1.9	1.5	0.3	0.9
HISPANIC ORIGIN	13.9				

Asian and Pacific Islanders combined

Tenderloin around Mason and Ellis as late as the 1960s. Scandinavians, as well as some Germans, settled in the Duboce Triangle district in the 1920s.

Maltese settled in the Bayview in the 1940s, followed by the Samoans.

A large Southeast Asian community has grown in the western Tenderloin since the 1980s.

MICHAEL D. LAMPEN

Ethnic Patterns in San Francisco

The highly diverse ethnic mix that comprises the population of San Francisco is the result of several overlapping waves of immigration. The original Indian population was replaced by a Hispanic population by the early 19th century, which was in turn displaced by a middle and northern European population by the late 19th century. The African-American population increased after World War II, followed by a second Hispanic influx, still in progress. The Asian population has grown slowly since the 19th century, with a major and still active increase in the last quarter century. Currently, the European and African-American populations are slowly decreasing. The current (1990) population of San Francisco is 46.6% white, 28.4% Asian, 13.9% Hispanic, 10.5% African-American and 0.6% other.

Metropolitan Population

The San Francisco Bay Area (Metropolitan Statistical Area) of San Francisco/Oakland/San Jose is the fifth-largest metropolitan area in the United States with a population of 6,253,331 people (1990 census). (The order is New York, Los Angeles, Chicago, Washington/Baltimore, San Francisco/Oakland/San Jose.) San Francisco alone ranks as the 14th-largest city in the nation, with 723,959 people (1990 census). (The order is New York, Los Angeles, Chicago, Houston, Philadelphia, San Diego, Detroit, Dallas, Phoenix, San Antonio, San Jose, Indianapolis, Baltimore, San Francisco.)

Mother Tongue

About 41.9 percent of San Francisco's population spoke a language other than English in their homes when they were children, according to a U.S. Census report.

MOTHER TONGUE	NUMBER	PERCENT
TOTAL POPULATION	715,674	100.0
ENGLISH ONLY	387,587	54.2
FRENCH	13,219	1.8
GERMAN	26,283	3.7
HUNGARIAN	1,343	0.2
ITALIAN	30,232	4.2
POLISH	2,986	0.4
RUSSIAN	8,549	1.2
SPANISH	64,395	9.0
SWEDISH	3,797	0.5
YIDDISH	5,917	0.8
ALL OTHER	123,074	17.2
NOT REPORTED	48,291	6.7

SUNDAY EXAMINER AND CHRONICLE, *October 29, 1972*

Population

DEC. 31, 1798

Presidio de San Francisco	*260**
Mission de San Francisco	*625**
	*2***
Total	*833*

* Indians
** Spanish or other caste
(First census of California taken by order of the King of Spain)

1800

Presidial-Pueblo of San Francisco	*223*
Mission de San Francisco (Indian)	*644*

1815

Presidial-Pueblo of San Francisco	*373*
Mission de San Francisco (Indian)	*1,115*

1830

Presidial-Pueblo of San Francisco	*131*
Mission de San Francisco (Indian)	*219*

(Dwinelle, John W., Colonial History of the City of San Francisco)

1846

"On the 7th of July, A.D., 1846, the then pueblo, now city of San Francisco, was a town of the population of about one thousand inhabitants, and on the 3rd of March, A.D., 1851, the population thereof amounted to about thirty thousand persons, and that on the said 7th of July, and on said third of March, the said pueblo or city, under and by virtue of the grant aforesaid, and under and by virtue of the laws, usages and customs of the government of Mexico and California, all and singular the premises aforesaid, were part and parcel of the land and premises of said pueblo or city."

(Documents, depositions, and brief of law points raised thereon on behalf of the United States, in case No. 280, before the U.S. Board of Land Commissioners. The City of San Francisco vs. the United States. San Francisco: Commercial Power Press, 1854.)

1847

"San Francisco, last August, contained 459 souls, of whom 375 were whites, four-fifths of these being under 40 years of age. Some idea of the composition of the white population may be gathered from the following statement as to the nationality of the larger portion: English, 22; German, 27; Irish, 14; Scotch, 14; born in the United States, 228; Californians, 89."

(St. Louis Reville, Feb. 12, 1848.)

"In 1847, we find her with a population of less than 400, with no commerce, no wealth, no power, and without a name, save as a small trading post and mission station."

(Rincon de las Salinas, Part of the Bernal Rancho, Fronting on the Bay, and Immediately South of the City of San Francisco, California. New York: Latimer, Bros. & Seymour, 1857.)

1848

"A school census recently completed in the town indicates the population as follows: 575 Males; 177 Females; 60 Children, totaling 812 white population."

(California Star, March 18, 1848)

1850

"The first directory, of Sept. 1850, contained 2,500 names, and the votes cast in Oct. reached 3,440. Hittell assumes not over 8,000 in Nov. 1949, on the strength of the vote then cast of 2,056, while allowing about 25,000 in another place for Dec. The Annals of San Francisco insists upon at least 20,000 probably nearer 25,000."

(Bancroft, Hubert Howe. History of California. Vol. VI)

1852	34,776*
1860	56,802**
1870	149,473**
1880	233,959**
1890	298,997**
1900	342,782**
1906	175,000***
1907	EST. 300,000
1910	416,912**
1920	506,676**
1930	634,394**
1940	634,536**
1950	775,357**
1960	740,855**
1970	715,674**
1972	685,600****
1978	658,700****
1980	678,974**
1982	692,000
1983	705,400****
1985	719,200**
1986	711,800
1987	744,600

(S.F. Chronicle, February 5, 1991)

1990	711,407**
1991	726,700

(S.F. Chronicle, May 8, 1991)

1993	723,959**
1993	739,600

(S.F. CHRONICLE, February 8, 1994)

San Francisco added 9,800 residents to reach 739,600. Most of the city's gain was from immigration, as births outnumbered deaths by only 1,129.

* State Census
** U.S. Census
*** After the 1906 earthquake and fire; estimate by General Adolphus Greely, U.S.A.
****Calif. State Department of Finance

San Francisco is unique in its multiracial and ethnic mix with more Asian, American Indian, and other nonwhite residents than African-American population. Ethnic group estimates for 1975 follow the trends experienced during the decade 1960 to 1970 with a decrease of 61,186 or 12.0% in the white population, and an increase of 13,212 or 6.5% in the nonwhite groups in 1975 over 1970. African Americans gained nearly 1.5% while Chinese showed a numerical increase of 4,504, Filipinos 4,406, and Other nonwhites 1,985.

SAN FRANCISCO
DEPARTMENT OF PUBLIC HEALTH,
October 18, 1976

Population Comparisons by Ethnic Group

San Francisco is the second most ethnically diverse city in the United States, exceeded only by Queens, New York. San Francisco's ethnic distribution is remarkably similar to world distribution.

Note: Hispanics can be of any race. White Hispanics are listed below as Hispanic.

	SF	CAL.	U.S.	WORLD
WHITE	46.6	57.3	75.1	43.0
ASIAN	28.4	9.5	2.8	35.2
HISPANIC	13.9	25.8	9.0	8.2
BLACK	10.5	7.4	12.1	13.0
OTHER	0.6	1.0	1.0	0.4

Sources: See San Francisco's Ethnic Population map plus information derived from 1990 U.S. Census in *World Almanac* (Pharos Books, NY). World population distribution extrapolated from population figures in *World Almanac*, 1992.

MICHAEL D. LAMPEN

History and Vital Statistics

Highest point: Mount Davidson, 938 ft.
Lowest point: Sea level
Land Area: 49.2 square miles (City Engineer, 1988) 31,360 acres of land (based on 49 square miles)

"The waters of the Pacific Ocean rise 0.1 foot per year. Thus the land area of the city of San Francisco has been reduced 1.25 feet around its water periphery from 1864 as far as it applies to this phenomena."

SCHLOWITZ, A. L., SHORE AND SEA
BOUNDARIES, U.S. COAST AND
GEODETIC SURVEY,
1964

Lowest point of San Francisco County is the floor of the Golden Gate 3,200 feet west-southwest of midspan of the Golden Gate Bridge: 351 feet below sea level.

SAN FRANCISCO ENTRANCE—NAUTICAL
CHART 18649, NOAA, 1979

San Francisco City and County

Total area: 129 square miles
Water Area: 82.38 square miles
Geographical Center (land only): Between Alvarado and 23rd streets on the east side of Grandview Ave. (Latitude N. 37°45' 10", Longitude W. 122°26' 27")
Geographical Center (City and County land and water area combined): Southwest corner of Fulton and Baker streets. (Latitude N. 37°46' 33", Longitude W. 122°26' 24")
Outside Lands: 1,706.61 outside acres consist of 492.09 at Camp Mather in Tuolumne County; 454.72 in Sharp Park Golf Course in San Mateo County; and the other 760 acres in Kern, Fresno, and Monterey counties as assets of a trust fund.

46 Water

San Francisco Water
Hetch Hetchy

Hetch Hetchy takes its name from a small flat mountain valley north of Yosemite. The Central Miwok Indians referred to the area as "Hatchatchie," meaning plant or grass bearing edible seeds, which grew in the valley.

The expense of building the Hetch Hetchy system was met entirely by the City of San Francisco without State or Federal assistance. It was therefore built as economically as possible, at an approximate cost of $100 million from the initial drawing of the plans by City Engineer C. E. Grunsky and Marsden Manson, to the first flowing of water into the city in 1934.

San Francisco's water flows west by gravity from the Hetch Hetchy Project in Tuolumne County, 149 miles to the terminal reservoir, Crystal Springs. Construction of this water system followed passage of the Raker Act in 1913, granting necessary permission for use of a portion of Yosemite National Park. The Raker Act did not consti-

tute a free gift as there were many conditions and requirements to be met before San Francisco could draw water from the Tuolumne River.

Eighty-nine men lost their lives during the course of construction and 12 days before the completion of the project, chief engineer Michael Maurice O'Shaughnessy died of a heart attack. The O'Shaughnessy Dam in Yosemite is named in his honor.

The mountain water supply system includes three impounding reservoirs: Hetch Hetchy on the Tuolumne River, Lloyd on the Cherry River, and Lake Eleanor on Eleanor Creek. Water stored in lakes Lloyd and Eleanor is utilized to generate power at Dion R. Holm Powerhouse and to meet the downstream irrigation priorities. Hetch Hetchy Reservoir is drawn upon mainly for San Francisco's domestic and suburban water supply. In the course of its journey the water generates electric power at Robert C. Kirkwood and Moccasin powerhouses. This source supplies over three-quarters of the total consumption in the city's water service area.

City Reservoirs
CAPACITY IN MILLIONS OF GALLONS

BALBOA	150.0
COLLEGE HILL	14.1
FRANCISCO	2.5
(EMERGENCY SUPPLY ONLY)	
HUNTERS POINT	1.1
LAKE MERCED	2,565.0
(EMERGENCY SUPPLY ONLY)	
LOMBARD	3.3
MCLAREN PARK TANKS	8.0
MERCED MANOR	9.5
POTRERO	1.0
STANFORD HEIGHTS	12.9
SUMMIT	14.0
SUNSET	174.8
SUTRO	31.4
UNIVERSITY MOUND	140.9
WILDE AVENUE	0.5

San Francisco Water Chemical Analyses
Sierra-Calaveras Sample
PARTS PER MILLION

TOTAL SOLIDS	82.0
CALCIUM (CA)	8.0
MAGNESIUM (MG)	1.0
SODIUM (NA)	3.0
IRON (FE)	0.2
SILICA (SiO_2)	0.6
SULFATES (SO_4)	24.0
CHLORIDES (CL)	21.3
CARBONATES (CO_3)	0.0
BICARBONATES (HCO_3)	18.0
ALKALINITY	
(METHYL ORANGE AS $CaCO_3$)	15.0
TOTAL HARDNESS AS $CaCO_3$	24.0
COLIFORM PER 100 MILLITERS	
OF SAMPLE	LESS THAN 2.0
NITRATES (NO_3)	LESS THAN 0.1

San Mateo County Watershed Sample
PARTS PER MILLION

TOTAL SOLIDS	78.0
CALCIUM (CA)	12.0
MAGNESIUM (MG)	1.9
SODIUM (NA)	4.0
IRON (FE)	LESS THAN 0.1
SILICA (SiO_2)	0.4
SULFATES (SO_4)	3.3
CHLORIDES (CL)	16.0
NITRATES (NO_3)	LESS THAN 0.1
CARBONATES (CO_3)	LESS THAN 0.1
BICARBONATES (HCO_3)	37.0
ALKALINITY	
(METHYL ORANGE AS $CaCO_3$)	30.0
TOTAL HARDNESS AS $CaCO_3$	38.0
COLIFORM PER 100 MILLITERS	
OF SAMPLE	2.0

(Both samples were taken when ideal weather conditions prevailed.)

Spring Valley Water Company

San Francisco has paid the Spring Valley Water Company $40,021,540 for its properties and a dream of more than sixty years is at last a reality. The people of this city now own their own water system, as they already own a great source of water in the Sierras and an aqueduct that is crawling through hills and across valleys to San Francisco.

Far back before the American came to California the people of Yerba Buena drew their waters from springs and streams. There was a sweet spring where the Presidio reservation now stands; it was called El Polin and Spaniards and Indians alike said that he who drank a rich draught from El Polin would have many children and would live to see them prosper.

When the gold diggers came the water company was a donkey owned by Juan Miguel Aguirre, who brought water from El Polin, from Mountain Lake, and from a spring on Washington near Montgomery. His profits were $30 a day.

The city grew, various water companies were organized, and finally the Spring Valley Water Company was capitalized for $60,000 with a first outlay of less than $100 that eventually grew into great properties of more than 100,000 acres of land. The greatest dam the United States had ever seen was built and old time resorts were submerged beneath the great Crystal Springs Lake.

But the people complained unendingly because they did not own their own water source. Mayor William Alvord said in 1873:

"I cannot abstain from expressing my conviction that an element as vital as the air we breathe, and as free furnished by the Creator should not be confined as a merchantable commodity in the hands of a few individuals."

Three years later the supervisors offered the Spring Valley owners $11,000,000 for their property and they were refused. Four years later a bill was introduced into the Legislature authorizing San Francisco to buy the company for $15,000,000. The price was far too much, the people said no, the bill was never passed, the Spring Valley was not purchased.

It grew as the city grew, but it could not grow fast enough. The city went into the mountains, developed Hetch Hetchy and a bountiful water supply, and now buys the water company's lakes and holdings and water mains for $40,000,000. James D. Phelan, while Mayor, made the first fight for that mountain water.

The quiet music of El Polin has grown into a mighty roar. The people of San Francisco, after two generations, have come into their own at last and the vision of the fathers is realized in their grandchildren.

CALL-BULLETIN,
February 28, 1930,
Editorial page

Water, Water, Everywhere

San Francisco Water Department serves 2.2 million people in San Francisco, San Mateo, and parts of Santa Clara and Alameda counties with water from the Tuolumne River in Yosemite National Park.

East Bay Municipal Utility District serves 1.1 million people in Alameda and Contra Costa counties with water from the Mokelumne River in the central Sierra Nevada.

Marin Municipal Water District serves 167,000 people in central and southern Marin County with water from the Mount Tamalpais watershed.

47 Weather

History of the Weather Service in San Francisco

Weather conditions have been observed in San Francisco since 1847 when the first observations were made at the Presidio of San Francisco. However, the Presidio records were taken only intermittently. It was not until the summer of 1849, when the population of San Francisco increased significantly because of the Gold Rush, that the consecutive rainfall record began. Official consecutive temperature records have been kept from 1871 until present. Measurements of wind, pressure, humidity, and sunshine were taken for approximately 102 years, also beginning in 1871, but were discontinued in 1973 when the Weather Bureau Office moved to San Francisco Airport.

Rainfall has been measured by a number of individuals and governmental agencies since 1849, and more importantly, at a number of different locations.

The continuous San Francisco rainfall record extends back to August 14, 1849 when Thomas Tennent, a maker of nautical

and mathematical instruments, began taking daily measurements shortly after his arrival in San Francisco. Tennent was born a Quaker in Philadelphia in 1822, and apprenticed as an instrument maker. Early in 1849 he made the 95-day journey to California from the east coast via the Panama Route, walking the final 110 miles from Monterey. While waiting for his instruments to arrive from the East, Thomas Tennent served as a surveyor and also as a miner.

When he finally set up his shop, making nautical instruments for the many ships stopping at San Francisco during the Gold Rush, he installed a rain gauge on the roof. This location was on the northeast corner of Union and Dupont (now Grant), and was the first of six locations at which Tennent would take observations between August 14, 1849 and February 1, 1871. These sites were all confined to a relatively small area in the vicinity of Nob Hill and Telegraph Hill. He supplied his meteorological data, along with sunrise, sunset, moon, and tide tables, to the local newspapers. His meteorological data were eventually published in *Tennent's Nautical Almanac* beginning in 1868 and continuing until 1890.

Tennent became a prominent San Franciscan and served three terms as a member of the Board of Supervisors. During his tenure as a surveyor he designed the street layout for all of San Francisco west of Larkin Street, and the house numbering system which is still in use.

Several other individuals also took weather observations during the Gold Rush. Dr. William O. Ayres took complete weather observations from 1856 until 1868; however, nearly thirty months of data during that period are either missing or were never taken.

Another prominent early San Franciscan, Dr. Henry Gibbons, took observations of rainfall and temperatures from 1850 until at least 1880. Like Tennent he sold his data to the newspapers as a Meteorological Table. Gibbons was one of the founders of California Academy of Sciences, a president of the California State Medical Society, and a professor at the Medical College of the Pacific.

Prof. Alexander McAdie, in charge of the San Francisco office of the Weather Bureau at the turn of the century, also noted that records of rainfall and temperature were taken by Dr. T. M. Logan and Mr. John Pettee. This is the only reference in the literature to these individuals.

On March 1, 1871, the U.S. government took over as the official weather observer for San Francisco when the Army Signal Service began to take the observations. The Signal Service accepted the rainfall data from Thomas Tennent as the "official" early record. This was because of Tennent's expertise as an instrument maker and the fact that he recorded rainfall to the nearest one-hundredth of an inch, while Gibbons measured only to the nearest one-tenth inch. Because of the extreme variability of temperatures, the early temperature records of Tennent, Ayres, and Gibbons were not incorporated into the official record. Consequently, the official San Francisco temperature records do not begin until 1871.

From that time to present, the U.S. government has taken weather observations in San Francisco, first as the Signal Service, and then the United States Weather Bureau (later renamed the National Weather Service). Since 1871, the observation site was moved another six times, but has remained in the northeastern quadrant of the city.

The ninth observation site, at the Mills Building, was destroyed by the fire that followed the earthquake of April 18, 1906, and observations were taken at a private residence about 2 miles to the west until October 1, 1906. There is a discrepancy in the records as to whether observations were taken between April 18 and May 1, 1906. However, records complied by Prof. McAdie indicate rainfall for San Francisco on several dates during that period. This corresponds to data available at several other nearby sites during the same period.

In 1936, the observation site was moved to the roof of the Federal Office Building on Fulton Street, where it remained until 1983. The 47 years at this locale was the longest at any site. In April 1973, the Climatology Office in the Federal Building was closed. Readings from that site, and subsequently Mission Dolores, were transmitted by telephone line to the National Weather Service Office at San Francisco International Airport.

Observers discovered that there was a "minor malfunction" in the rain gauge at the Federal Office Building from January 1973 to April 1982. The Federal Office Building readings were found to be only about 70 percent of actual amounts (by comparison to data from surrounding sites). The record was corrected by substituting data from KGO Television (then at 277 Golden Gate Ave.), which was only 2 blocks away, and has been accepted by the National Climatic

Data Center.

The most recent San Francisco rainfall site is at Mission Dolores, 1.3 miles south of the Federal Office Building, where it was moved in April 18, 1983. This site is the southernmost of the 13 locations, yet it remains within a 1.5-mile-radius circle that encompasses all of the aforementioned sites.

The rain gauge that Thomas Tennent used was a six-inch square container which funneled into a two-inch square receiver, and was capable of holding 4 inches of precipitation. With the establishment of the Signal Service observations in 1871, all observations have been made using a "standard" eight-inch circular gauge.

Geography and the Weather

San Francisco is in an area of "exceedingly diversified topography" that is favorable to numerous microclimates. Winds are channeled over and around the City of San Francisco by the terrain, resulting in pronounced differences in the weather across relatively short distances.

The development of the extremely varied California landscape is a consequence of the interaction between the North American and Pacific tectonic plates. The most prominent features, and most important in their effect upon the state's climate, are the Sierra Nevada and Coast ranges, between which lies the Great Valley. All three, generally oriented from northwest to southeast, are parallel to the motion of the North American plate.

San Francisco, which is described by approximately a seven-mile by seven-mile square, sits at the northern end of a peninsula, straddling the Coast Range just south of where it is broken by the Golden Gate. The melting of the ice sheets that covered the North American continent during the Pleistocene era caused the sea level to rise and flood the structural depression which is now San Francisco Bay. Outflow from the Sacramento and San Joaquin rivers, fed by the drainages from the surrounding Sierra

Nevada and Coast Range, maintains the breach as the only major outlet to the Pacific. San Francisco's steep topography is the boundary between the Pacific Ocean on the west, San Francisco Bay to the east and the Golden Gate to the north. The highest terrain is toward the south, where the elevations rise to more than 900 feet, with Mount Davidson's peak of 938 feet the tallest, followed closely by Mount Sutro at 918 feet and both North (903 ft. 8 in.) and South (910 ft. 5 in.) Twin Peaks. In addition to the primary north-northwest to south-southeast ridgeline, a number of significant hills dominate the San Francisco horizon, as spurs off of the main axis. The city's steepness is shown by the fact that the 60 meter elevation contour is generally within one mile of sea level.

Because of the small area that San Francisco covers there are no significant natural drainage basins within the city limits. Those which may have existed historically have long since been constrained to underground culverts and the storm drain system.

Climate

The sharp topography and maritime surroundings of San Francisco couple with the unique California climate to produce a number of extremely varied microclimates within its 49 square miles. California's location in the middle latitudes and on the west coast of the North American continent places it in the relatively rare Mediterranean-type climate. The only other regions of the earth sharing this climate type are the southwestern tip of Africa, the west coast of Chile, the west coast of Australia, and of course, the region surrounding the Mediterranean Sea. This climate type is generally characterized by moist mild winters and dry summers.

San Francisco's climate is further modified by the location of the City on the northern end of a peninsula, surrounded on three sides by the relatively cool waters of the Pacific Ocean and San Francisco Bay. In addition to the normal cool temperatures of the mid-latitude Pacific Ocean, the water temperatures are modified by the upwelling of cold water along the California coast. This phenomenon is caused by the persistence of the Pacific High and the northwest winds that are constrained by the Coast Range to blow parallel to the coastline.

The effects of these winds, the Coriolis Force and resultant subsurface Ekman Spiral, causes a net transport of surface waters away from the shore. Consequently, as the surface waters drift away from the coast, they are replaced by the upwelling of colder waters from below.

Summertime in San Francisco is characterized by cool marine air and persistent coastal stratus and fog, with average maximum temperatures between 60 and 70° F, and minima between 50 and 55° F. The mornings will typically find the entire city overcast followed by clearing on the warmer bay side, but only partial clearing on the cooler ocean side. The summertime temperature gradient across the city is generally from northwest to southeast, with the warmer readings farthest from the coast and in the wind sheltered valleys east of the Coast Range bisector. These differences are enhanced further by a strong afternoon and evening sea breeze that is a result of the temperature (and consequently pressure) difference between the Pacific Ocean and the interior valleys of California. These westerly winds are channeled through the Golden Gate and lesser breaks in the high terrain of the Coast Range, reaching a maximum during the afternoon with speeds between 20 and 30 miles per hour.

Rainfall from May through September is relatively rare, with an aggregate of less than an inch, or only about 5 percent of the yearly average total of approximately 21.5 inches. Off-season rains which do occur are usually the result of weak early or late season occluded fronts, or surges of subtropical moisture from the south that result in brief showers or thundershowers spreading into the area. Considerable moisture is due to drizzle when the marine layer deepens sufficiently. This is seldom enough to measure (i.e., less than .01 inch) on any given day, except along the immediate coast.

Winter temperatures in San Francisco are quite temperate, with highs between 55 and 60° F and lows in the 45 to 50° F range. The main source region of wintertime fog in San Francisco is the Great Valley. Radiation fog is formed in the moist regions of the Sacramento River Delta and is advected through Suisun and San Pablo bays and into San Francisco Bay on cool easterly drainage winds. This type of fog is less common than that of summer, but is typically much denser and has a greater impact upon transportation systems due to greatly reduced visibilities.

Over 80 percent of San Francisco's seasonal rain falls between November and March, occurring over about 10 days per month. Winter rains on the California coast are primarily due to occluded fronts on a trajectory from the west-northwest, and an occasional cold front from the Gulf of Alaska. These systems are driven southward during the winter as the Pacific High drifts south and westerlies and polar jetstream dip south of 40° N latitude. Winter thunderstorms occur on the average only twice per season in cold, unstable, post-frontal airmasses.

There is also considerable areal variation of annual precipitation amounts. This is primarily due to the orographic effects resulting from uplift of the airflow from the Pacific striking the Coast Range.

Snow is extremely rare in San Francisco, with only 10 documented instances of measurable snow at the official observing site in the past 143 seasons. Snow has fallen on a number of other occasions, but usually only in trace amounts or at the higher elevations. In addition, some of these occurrences are not true snow events but rather the result of either small hail or ice pellets.

Spring and fall are transition periods for San Francisco. These seasons usually produce the most cloud-free days between the overcast days of summertime stratus and the rain-laden clouds of winter. San Francisco's hottest days are typically during the spring and fall when high pressure builds into the Pacific Northwest and Great Basin, and dry offshore winds replace the Pacific sea breeze. The three hottest days on record in San Francisco occurred in September and October.

The occurrence of rainfall during the early spring and fall is infrequent, with only about 5 days per month on the average. While most storms during these periods produce light precipitation, the occasional coupling of polar and subtropical airmasses can produce heavy rainfall events. For example, the "Columbus Day Storm" (October 11, 1962 through October 13,

1962) dropped over five inches of rain on San Francisco.

The diversity of San Francisco's microclimates, in general, and its rainfall patterns, in particular, must be considered when utilizing the data from a single site. In a relatively flat region, without the influences of the ocean and topography, there is little discernible change in annual rainfall averages with distance. However, within a distance of only a few miles in San Francisco there can be as much as a 20 percent difference in average annual.

E. Jan Null
Lead Forecaster
National Weather Service, San Francisco

City of San Francisco Rain Gauges

The San Francisco Department of Public Works also maintains 25 rain gauges throughout San Francisco. The gauges are part of the San Francisco Hydrologic and Hydraulic Data Acquisition and Recording

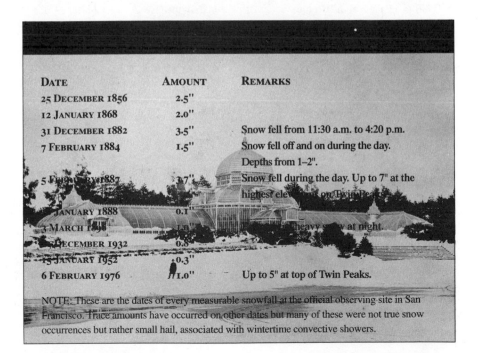

Date	Amount	Remarks
25 December 1856	2.5"	
12 January 1868	2.0"	
31 December 1882	3.5"	Snow fell from 11:30 a.m. to 4:20 p.m.
7 February 1884	1.5"	Snow fell off and on during the day. Depths from 1–2".
5 February 1887	3.7"	Snow fell during the day. Up to 7" at the highest elevations on Twin Peaks.
January 1888	0.1"	
3 March 1896	1.0"	heavy snow at night.
December 1932	0.8"	
15 January 1952	0.3"	
6 February 1976	1.0"	Up to 5" at top of Twin Peaks.

NOTE: These are the dates of every measurable snowfall at the official observing site in San Francisco. Trace amounts have occurred on other dates but many of these were not true snow occurrences but rather small hail, associated with wintertime convective showers.

system developed to provide data about water flows for the sewer and storm drainage system. Installation of the gauges began in 1976 and they are located at:
- Livingston and Marine, Presidio of San Francisco
- The Ferry Building
- Bay and Kearny sts.
- The San Francisco Maritime Museum, foot of Polk St.
- Corbett Ave. and Romain St.
- Twin Peaks Blvd. and Corbett Ave.
- 18th and Church sts.
- 3rd St. at 4th St.
- Scott and California sts.
- Lobos St. and Plymouth Ave.
- Prague at Cordova sts.
- Candlestick Park
- Olmstead at Bowdoin sts.
- City College North Gymnasium
- 30th and Laidley sts.
- Starr King School Cafeteria
- 7th Ave. and Cabrillo St.
- 30th Ave. and Anza St.
- California Palace of the Legion of Honor
- Baker Beach
- Eucalyptus Dr. at Sylvan St.
- Marne Ave. and Portola Dr.
- 34th Ave. and Quintara St.
- Lurline St. and Funston Ave.
- Clean Water Project Main Building in the Sunset District

There have been 13 sites where official weather recordings have been taken:
- NE corner Union and Dupont (now Grant Ave.) from August 14, 1849 to July 1, 1851.
- Stockton and California from July 2, 1851, to July 1862.
- Powell between Pacific and Broadway from July 1, 1862, to Summer 1863.
- Sacramento between Taylor and Jones from Summer 1863 to July 1864.

- Leavenworth between Pine and California from July 1864 to July 1866.
- Battery St. between Washington and Jackson from July 1866 to February 1, 1871.
- Merchants' Exchange Building at Sacramento and Leidesdorff from February 2, 1871, to August 3, 1890.
- Phelan Building at Market and O'Farrell from September 4, 1890, to October 31, 1892.
- Mills Building at 220 Montgomery St. from November 1, 1892, to April 18, 1906.
- Alexander McAdie residence at 3018 Clay St. from May 1, 1906, to October 1, 1906.
- Merchants' Exchange Building at 465 California St., from October 1, 1906, to April 12, 1936.
- Federal Office Building at 50 Fulton Street from April 13, 1936, to April 18, 1983.
- Because of a malfunctioning rain guage, data for the period of October 1, 1973, through March 10, 1982, has been corrected using rainfall data from the then nearby KGO-TV at 277 Golden Gate Ave., approximately 500 feet north of the Federal Office Building.
- Mission Dolores at 16th and Dolores from April 18, 1983, to present.

Official Weather Records at the Mission Dolores

The official temperature and rainfall records for the City of San Francisco are recorded at the Mission Dolores. The National Weather Service temperature and rain gauge are atop the garage on 16th Street at Landers, directly behind the basilica.

The 30-year, average seasonal rainfall total recorded here at the Mission is 20.52 inches.

The normal monthly rainfall recorded in inches at the Mission's rain gauge:

JANUARY	4.25	(108MM)
FEBRUARY	3.11	(79MM)
MARCH	3.21	(82MM)
APRIL	1.32	(34MM)
MAY	0.25	(6.5MM)
JUNE	0.15	(4MM)
JULY	0.04	(1MM)
AUGUST	0.07	(2MM)
SEPTEMBER	0.27	(7MM)
OCTOBER	1.30	(33MM)
NOVEMBER	3.32	(84MM)
DECEMBER	3.23	(82MM)

The **highest temperature** officially recorded at the Mission Dolores was 103° F. (39° C.) on July 2, 1988.

The **coldest temperature** recorded in San Francisco: 27° F. (-3° C.) on December 11, 1932.

Weather data from the Mission Dolores are automatically transmitted by telephone circuit at ten minutes before every hour to the National Weather Service Office at San Francisco International Airport.

Rainfall Records

The **average yearly rainfall** in San Francisco, based upon readings between 1849 and 1993, is 19.33 inches.

The **wettest year on record** for San Francisco was the winter of 1861–62 with 49.27 inches of rain.

The **driest winter on record** was 1975–1976 with a rainfall total of 7.95 inches.

The **most rain to fall in a 24-hour period** was 6.16 inches on April 4–5, 1982.

Index